Standard Arabic

An elementary – intermediate course

This book presents a comprehensive foundation course for beginning students of written and spoken Modern Standard Arabic (MSA), providing an essential grounding for successful communication with speakers of the many colloquial varieties. This long-established and successful text has been completely revised with the needs of English-speaking learners especially in mind, and will prove invaluable to students and teachers alike.

- step-by-step guide to understanding written and spoken texts
- develops conversational ability as well as reading and writing skills
- Arabic–English Glossary containing 2600 entries
- fresh texts and dialogues containing up-to-date data on the Middle East and North Africa
- includes Arab folklore, customs, proverbs, and short essays on contemporary topics
- grammatical terms also given in Arabic, enabling students to attend language courses in Arab countries
- provides a wide variety of exercises and drills to reinforce grammar points, vocabulary learning and communicative strategies
- includes a key to the exercises
- accompanying cassettes also available

Eckehard Schulz is Professor of Arabic Studies at the Oriental Institute, University of Leipzig. He is an experienced teacher and interpreter of Arabic and the author of several textbooks in the field.

D0161883

STANDARD ARABIC

اللغة العربية

AN ELEMENTARY - INTERMEDIATE COURSE

دورة أساسية ومتوسطة

ECKEHARD SCHULZ
GÜNTHER KRAHL
WOLFGANG REUSCHEL

Revised English Edition by
ECKEHARD SCHULZ
University of Leipzig

Editorial Consultants

James Dickins (University of Durham)
Janet C. E. Watson (University of Durham)
Alan S. Kaye (California State University at Fullerton)

CAMBRIDGE
UNIVERSITY PRESS

PUBLISHED BY THE PRESS SYNDICATE OF THE UNIVERSITY OF CAMBRIDGE
The Pitt Building, Trumpington Street, Cambridge, United Kingdom

CAMBRIDGE UNIVERSITY PRESS
The Edinburgh Building, Cambridge CB2 2RU, UK
40 West 20th Street, New York, NY 10011–4211, USA
10 Stamford Road, Oakleigh, VIC 3166, Australia
Ruiz de Alarcón 13, 28014 Madrid, Spain
Dock House, The Waterfront, Cape Town 8001, South Africa

http://www.cambridge.org

First published in English by Cambridge University Press 2000

Printed in the United Kingdom at the University Press, Cambridge

Typeface Monotype Times   [AU]

A catalogue record for this book is available from the British Library

ISBN 0 521 77313 X hardback
ISBN 0 521 77465 9 paperback
ISBN 0 521 78739 4 cassette set

CONTENTS

INTRODUCTION

This book is based on the well-tried *Lehrbuch des modernen Arabisch* by Günther Krahl, Wolfgang Reuschel and Eckehard Schulz and has been conceived as a comprehensive course for beginners, in which particular attention is given to a speaking-focused training. It presents the basic grammar, vocabulary and phraseology of written and spoken Modern Standard Arabic (MSA).

The book centers on imparting the grammatical and lexical basics to enable the learner step by step to understand written and spoken texts, to hold a conversation with an Arabic speaker independently and, moreover, to translate and write Arabic texts. A variety of highly different texts (reports, commentaries, interviews, dialogues, letters etc.) together with appropriate exercises have been included in the book in addition to the description of the grammar to achieve these objectives. Quite naturally, style and vocabulary of the texts in the first lessons are influenced to a greater extent by the grammar in the respective lesson. If the knowledgeable user is of the opinion that it would have been better to use a different word or construction in some passages, then he may know that it was of importance to me for didactic reasons not to keep anticipating morphological and syntactic structures to be treated later.

When conceiving the texts, particular attention was paid to impart and to consolidate those patterns which occur over and over again in spoken and written MSA and to provide the learner with a guide to master different communicative situations and strategies. The book also contains more or less timeless news and exercises to practice listening comprehension and to introduce the style of the news in newspapers and in radio and television to the students.

The grammar comprises all substantial phenomena of MSA which are necessary for a good command of Arabic as a spoken and written language. The teacher might miss some important grammatical topics but he/she should always have in mind that this book is a book for beginners which covers all grammatical and syntactic phenomena necessary for a correct and active command of Arabic, but it can not be exhaustive. The basic grammatical terms are also given in Arabic to enable the student to use the Arabic terminology needed when attending language courses in the Arab countries.

The book aims at imparting MSA because it is well-known that it is impossible to cope with the numerous Arabic dialects without these foundations. Nevertheless, the dialogues are partially adapted to colloquial usage as far as sentence structures and vocabulary are concerned. There are also exercises and notes focusing on the dialects to give the students those patterns which are the outcome of the widespread diglossia in Arabic, i.e. the coexistence of MSA and dialects and their use according to the communicative needs and circumstances.

This tightrope walk is, of course, not an easy undertaking but I wanted to build bridges for the students where the exclusive use of MSA would be longwinded and not appropriate to the situation. The endings in the dialogues are written according to the rules of MSA to prevent the students from complete confusion, although (spoken) reality is different. In this field, the teacher must always decide whether to tolerate the omission of the endings or not.

Our experience is not to ask the students to read all the endings of the dialogues but to follow the Arabic language of the educated (لغة المثقفين) to enable the students to speak Arabic as soon as possible. In all the other texts and exercises, special attention must be paid to the correct use of the rules of MSA.

The imparting and permanent repetition of stereotype phrases (greetings, wishes, forms of address, introduction, apologizing etc.), proverbs and sayings as well as historical facts and cultural traditions (religion, Arabic and Islamic history) and the appropriate terminology do not only aim at illustrating the grammar of the respective lesson but also at achieving a growing knowledge about this region of the world.

The exercises are subdivided into lexical exercises, grammar exercises and conversation drills as well as into a final exercise to arrive at a better structure of the process of teaching, even though a strict separation of these fields is impossible. The repetition exercises systematically deal with topics discussed two or three lessons before to help the students not to forget basic structures. Some grammar exercises are repeated as lexical exercises with new vocabulary because it is assumed that the grammar dealt with long before is now consolidated.

From my own experience, I can tell the student that Arabic with all its peculiarities in morphology, syntax and pronunciation really can be learned as spoken and written language. You will be able to learn the basics of grammar and the vocabulary of this book with diligence, a little bit of talent and the help of your teachers and might soon realize when meeting Arabs that you are a most welcome partner because of your good command of Arabic. Even educated Arabs encounter sometimes considerable difficulties in using their own language according to the rules which are valid and nearly unchanged since the revelation of the Koran approximately 1300 years ago.

This book will be accompanied by cassettes with all the texts as well as a key to the exercises to help the student work through the book independently.

I wish to express my deep gratitude to Janet C.E. Watson, James Dickins and Alan S. Kaye, the editorial consultants for Cambridge University Press, who contributed to this book as editorial consultants and generously provided valuable observations and excellent advice.

I am deeply grateful to Monem Jumaili who gave the texts, which were almost completely conceived and written by myself, their final shape. I am indebted to Birgit Bouraima, who rendered valuable assistance to the English translation, and to Christfried Naumann who took responsibilty for the subject index and provided greatly appreciated advice.

I wish to express my sincere gratitude to Avihai Shivtiel thanks to whose initiative this English edition can now be presented to the public and to all those who have contributed to this undertaking.

I hope and wish that this book - like its German predecessor - will find its way to the students. I readily accept comments, suggestions and critical remarks and hope to incorporate them in future editions.

Leipzig 2000   ECKEHARD SCHULZ

NOTES FOR THE USER

This revised textbook has been conceived as an elementary course for beginners, in which particular attention is given to a speaking-focused training.

The lessons consist of the following parts: **Grammar (G)**, **Vocabulary (V)**, **Text 1** and **Text 2** (except in Lesson 1) and **Exercises**, which are subdivided into lexical exercises (**L**), grammar exercises (**G**) and conversation drills (**C**) from Lesson 4 onwards as well as into a **Final exercise** in each lesson (from Lesson 2 onwards).

I permit myself to offer the following hints regarding the use of this book to teaching staff and students, which should be understood as a suggestion:

Seven to eight class hours are planned for each lesson with at least the same number of hours needed for the students' preparation and further study of the subject matter. One should see to it that there is enough time (e.g. the weekend) after the introduction of the new grammar subject and lexical items and that exercises which were to be prepared by pre-set homework only follow after this period, so that the students can have sufficient time to internalize the new subject matter and to learn the new vocabulary.

The subject matter should be presented in the following order:

- Introduction to grammar (1 class hour)
- Phonetics/calligraphy (1 class hour, only in the 1st semester)
- Lexical exercises (1 class hour)
- Grammar exercises (1 class hour)
- Text interpretation (1 class hour)
- Conversation (1 class hour in the 1st semester, 2 class hours in the 2nd semester)
- Final exercise (1 class hour)

Phonetics and calligraphy

This lecture, which is intended for the 1st semester, centers on imparting the correct pronunciation and the Arabic script. Reading the texts aloud is of particular importance; while one student does so, the other students note the mistakes and analyze and evaluate them afterwards together with the teacher. Suitable grammar and lexical exercises and particularly the texts marked by No. 1 should serve as a basis for the writing exercises. We have been quite successful here in Leipzig using dictations in which certain groups of Arabic sounds are systematically practiced. The students learn step by step to write by hearing and distinguishing sounds like

ع / ء، ظ / ض، ض / د، ذ / د، ز / س، س / ص / ص، ت / ط

which sound very similar at first.

Grammar and grammar exercises

The discussion of every new lesson should begin with the introduction of the new grammatical subject(s). The teacher should take the passages marked by **A** (= annotation) into consideration from the beginning, even if they, in most cases, only comprise elucidations or comments for the purpose of explaining the grammatical rules more accurately, and although they only refer to colloquial or dialectal usage in some places.

Only part of the vocabulary contained in the respective lesson is used in the grammar exercises in order not to overload the students with the requirement of mastering too many new lexical items in addition to their having to cope with new grammatical phenomena. Most grammar exercises are transformation exercises, but there are also fill-in, linking and sentence completion exercises. The objective here is to obtain the best learning results, while excluding the use and influence of the mother tongue.

Lexical exercises and text interpretation

The aim of these exercises is for the teacher to elucidate the new lexical items, to impart them in collocations, if possible, and to clarify paradigmatic relations in the vocabulary step by step. The translations given in the glossaries of the lessons only provide the meaning referred to in the respective text in order not to overstrain the learner. Additional translations we confined to a minimum. On this basis the texts are to be translated orally and/or in writing by the students, and possible variants of the translation are to be discussed. It is also possible to read and discuss the texts marked No. 2, which are always drafted as dialogues, within the conversation.

The glossaries are arranged alphabetically by root, listing the new words from the texts of the respective lesson. The exercises only occasionally contain words which do not appear in the texts. Words used for the purpose of explaining new grammar, which were not derived from the texts have not been included in the glossaries. Additional vocabulary imparted in some lexical exercises and conversation drills (specific terms, proverbs and idioms) has not been included in the glossaries either.

Conversation

The pre-set conversation drills are to be understood as suggestions; the teacher should vary them in accordance with the interests and requests of the learners. Role-play, which has been demanded time and time again, is of particular importance for the success of these exercises; here the teacher may recede more and more into the background with the increasing progress of the learners. The teacher must apply judgement as to whether he should interfere immediately and correct every mistake the students make, or if he should refrain from constantly interrupting the flow of speech and only correct the mistakes later in the interest of breaking down natural inhibitions. The seating arrangement usually found in school should be avoided particularly in the conversation lessons, so that the atmosphere can become relaxed. Only 1 class hour of conversation drills per lesson should be planned in the first semester because the students still need more development in the fundamentals at this stage. From the scond semester onwards, two class hours are to be allocated to conversation drills, and therefore the calligraphy and phonetics exercises should be reduced.

Final exercise

The final exercise at the end of each lesson is aimed at checking whether the students have internalized the grammar and lexical items and is intended to lay the foundations for translation into the foreign language. Review of subject matter which was taught in previous lessons is a methodical principle of these exercises.

The final exercises can be worked through in class, and they can form the basis for holding a written test after each lesson.

I readily accept criticism of the textbook's being "organized on school lines" by these kinds of checks if they help students consolidate their knowledge of the subject-matter and make them work steadily with the book. The teacher can also decide which revision exercises need to be worked through in a particularly intensive way in the following lessons or whether some can be omitted, depending on the results achieved in the Final Exercise.

Glossary

The Arabic-English glossary comprises roughly 2600 entries; unlike the glossaries in the lessons, it has been computerized in alphabetical order, and the items are only partly vocalized. This system has been chosen in order to make the book easier for the beginner to use, even if a whole series of important paradigmatic relations in the Arabic vocabulary become concealed by this approach.

Tables

Tables containing the essential Arabic verbal and nominal forms as completely vocalized items can be found in the appendix in addition to tables containing the cardinal and ordinal numerals.

Key

The key to the exercises gives the solutions in all those cases where only one solution is possible as well as the translations asked for based on the vocabulary and the texts of this book. Some of the translations should be understood as suggestions and not as the only possibility. The student should never resort to the key before trying to find the answer in the respective lesson(s).

Subject index

The subject index, which is subdivided into two indexes, comprises all essential English and Arabic morphological-syntactic and linguistic terms which are used in the textbook. Its purpose is to facilitate finding the relevant passages for the student. The page numbers of the pages which focus on the topics concerned are indicated in bold type.

ABBREVIATIONS

A	annotation	lit.	literal
a., acc.	accusative case	loc.	local
adv.	adverb	m., masc.	masculine
Alger.	Algerian	n.	nominative case
appr.	approximately	of so.	of someone
C	conversation	off.	official
cf.	compare	osf.	oneself
coll.	collective noun	pass.	passive
colloq.	colloquial	p.	person
conj.	conjunction	perf.	perfect
def.	definite	pl., plur.	plural
dimin.	diminutive	poss.	possibly
Ex	exercise	part.	participle
e.g.	for example	prep.	preposition
Eg.	Egyptian	R_1	1st radical
Elat.	Elative	R_2	2nd radical
Engl.	English	R_3	3rd radical
etc.	et cetera	rel. pr.	relative pronoun
f., fem.	feminine	Russ.	Russian
fig.	figurative sense	s.	see
foll.	following	s.a.	see also
Fr.	French	so.	someone
G	grammar exercise	so.'s.	someone's
g.	genitive case	sg., sing.	singular
gen.	genitive	sth.	something
geogr.	geographical	Syr.	Syrian
Glo.	glossary	temp.	temporal
Gr.	grammar of the lesson	th.s.	the same
gram.	grammar	thmsv.	themselves
imp.	imperative	to sb.	to somebody
indef.	indefinite	trans.	transitive
interj.	interjection	V	vocabulary
intrans.	intransitive	Yem.	Yemeni
Ital.	Italian	ث	*muthannan* = dual
itsf.	itself	ج	*jam^c* = plural
L	lexical exercises	م	*mu'annath* = feminine

1. The Alphabet (أَلحُرُوف الأَبْجِدِيَّة)

Arabic has 29 characters (حرْف ج حُرُوف): 26 consonants (حُرُوف ساكِنة) and 3 vowels (حُرُوف عِلَّة). Two of the three, however, occur both as vowels and consonants.

1.1. The characters and their pronunciation

The following consonants have more or less similar equivalents in English and therefore should not present any difficulties.

'	ء	Hamza	like *['a]* in *arm*, like *['i]* in *inn*, like *['oo]* in *ooze* (initial occlusive element, *glottal stop*)
b	ب	Bā'	like *[b]* in *big*
t	ت	Tā'	like *[t]* in *tea*
th	ث	Thā'	like *[th]* in *three*
j	ج	Jīm	like *[g]* in *gentle*
kh	خ	Khā'	like *[ch]* in Scottish English, *loch*
d	د	Dāl	like *[d]* in *door*
dh	ذ	Dhāl	like *[th]* in *the*
r	ر	Rā'	like *[r]* in Scottish English, *room*
z	ز	Zāy	like *[z]* in *zero*
s	س	Sīn	like *[s]* in *sun*
sh	ش	Shīn	like *s]* in *sure*
f	ف	Fā'	like *[f]* in *fog*
k	ك	Kāf	like *[k]* in *key*
l	ل	Lām	like *[l]* in *long, live* or *luck*
m	م	Mīm	like *[m]* in *monkey*
n	ن	Nūn	like *[n]* in *noon*
h	ه	Hā'	like *[h]* in *hot*
w	و	Wāw	like *[w]* in *wall*
y	ي	Yā'	like *[y]* in *year*

Arabic has the following long vowels:

ā	ا	Alif	like *[a]* in *far*
ī	ي	Yā'	like *[ee]* in *deer*
ū	و	Wāw	like *[oo]* in *school*

✋**A1** The short vowels *a (hut, pat), i (lift)* and *u (look)* as well as the diphthongs *ay (write)* and *aw* (like in *how*, but short) are also the same as in English. Cf. Gr 1.2.2.

The following letters are typical Arabic consonants which do not have equivalents in English and can only be learned by regular practicing with native speakers:

ḥ	ح	*Ḥāʾ*	like *[h]* articulated with friction
ᶜ	ع	*ᶜAyn*	like *[a]* articulated in the pharynx with friction
gh	غ	*Ghayn*	like the Parisian *[r]* in renaissance
ṣ	ص	*Ṣād*	like *[s]* articulated with emphasis
ḍ	ض	*Ḍād*	like *[d]* articulated with emphasis
ṭ	ط	*Ṭāʾ*	like *[t]* articulated with emphasis
ẓ	ظ	*Ẓāʾ*	like voiced *[th]* articulated with emphasis
q	ق	*Qāf*	like *[k]* articulated with emphasis

The last five of these consonants are the so-called emphatic consonants. They normally affect the pronunciation of adjacent consonants, vowels and diphthongs. Their correct pronunciation and the modifications in the adjacent sounds need special practicing.

✋**A2** The order of the Arabic consonants according to the place where they are articulated:

bilabial:	*b, m, w*
labiodental:	*f*
interdental:	*dh, th*
dental:	*d, t, ḍ, ṭ*
prepalatal:	*n, l, r, z, ẓ, s, ṣ, sh, j, y*
postpalatal:	*k*
velar:	*gh, q, kh*
pharyngal:	*ᶜ, ḥ*
laryngal:	*ʾ, h*

1.2. Writing

1.2.1. Arabic is written from right to left. The letters differ in size, but there are no capitals. Each of them has a basic form, but modifications in their shapes occur according to their positions in words.

A number of letters share the same shape and are only distinguished by diacritic dots:

Examples: ن *Nūn,* ت *Tāʾ,* ث *Thāʾ,* ب *Bāʾ,* ي *Yāʾ*

The letters و ا د ذ ر ز are only connected with the respective preceding letter, whereas all the others are connected with both sides. The shapes of Arabic letters are generally similar both in script and printed form. However, a few differences occur (see Lesson 3).

This book plans for the student to learn how to read and write the Arabic characters at the same time. For that reason we suggest beginning the writing exercises with the characters in their printed shape and to proceed step by step to script. In this way the prototypes of the Arabic characters impress themselves on the student's mind both when being read and written. Introducing script already in Lesson 1 might result in severe confusion. Nevertheless the way the characters are actually used in script must be taken into account at as early a time as possible, i.e. as soon as the student has a fairly good command of the Arabic characters. This can be achieved by the students reading print type and writing script from that time onwards.

The peculiarities of script are put together in the form of tables at the end of Lesson 3. These tables include a number of words previously introduced to the student which are contrasted with each other in print type and script as examples.

It is recommended that the teacher uses Arabic script from Lesson 4 onwards when he/she writes examples on the blackboard, and to practice it with the students as well.

1.2.2. Auxiliary Signs (ألحركات)

Since Arabic expresses only long vowels by special characters, a system of auxiliary signs was developed to distinguish whether or not a consonant is followed by a short vowel. But normally these signs do not appear in printed or written texts, since the reader who is acquainted with the morphology of Arabic will be able to read the words correctly without such signs.

The auxiliary signs are mainly used in the Koran, poetry and children's books. Texts which contain such signs are called vocalized texts, whereas those which do not have them are referred to as unvocalized.

In this book these signs are only used when they are essential for proper reading. The signs may be divided into two main groups:

1. Short vowels (for which Arabic has no characters)

Fatḥa = a short oblique stroke (´) written on top of the letter

بَ *ba,* فَ *fa,* وَ *wa*

denoting that the consonant is followed by a short *a*.

(*Fatḥa* followed by *Alif* = long *ā*: مَا *mā*)

Kasra = a short oblique stroke (ˎ) written below the consonant

بِ *bi,* لِ *li,* مِ *mi*

denoting that the consonant is followed by a short *i*.

(*Kasra* followed by *Yā'* = long *ī*: كَبِير *kabīr*)

Ḍamma = a sign similar in shape to a small *Wāw* (´) written on top of the letter

مُدُن *mudun,* كُم *kum,* هُم *hum*

denoting that the consonant is followed by a short *u*.

(*Ḍamma* followed by *Wāw* = long *ū*: نُون *Nūn*)

2. Other signs

Sukūn   = a small circle (˚) on top of the letter

تَحْتَ *taḥta,* نَحْنُ *naḥnu,* مِنْ *min*

denoting that the consonant is not followed by any vowel.

Shadda = a small *Sīn* (ّ) written on top of the letter denoting that the consonant is doubled, which is pronounced in a somewhat prolonged way then. *Fatḥa* and *Ḍamma* are written on top of *Shadda*, whereas *Kasra* may be placed either below *Shadda* or below the doubled letter:

شُبَّاك *shubbāk,* مُعَلِّم / مُعَلِّم *muʿallim,* تَقَدُّم *taqaddum*

Madda = a sign on top of *Alif* (آ) denoting a long *'ā*.

الآن *al-āna,* القُرْآن *al-qurʾān*

Diphthongs:

Fatḥa followed by a و with *Sukūn* denotes the diphthong *aw*, whereas *Fatḥa* followed by a ي with *Sukūn* denotes the diphthong *ay*:

لَوْح *lawḥ,* فَوْقَ *fawqa,* بَيْت *bayt,* كَيْفَ *kayfa*

1.2.3. *Hamza* ء and *Tā' marbūṭa* ة

Hamza, which has the shape of a small *ʿAyn*, normally needs a character to "carry" it. The characters which carry *Hamza* are أ (*Alif*), ؤ (*Wāw*) and ئ (*Yā'*), and they are referred to as chairs of *Hamza*. At the beginning of a word the chair of *Hamza* is always *Alif*:

أَنْتَ *'anta,* أُمّ *'umm,* إِنْ *'in*

(see the rules for writing *Hamza* in Lesson 24.)

The *Tā' marbūṭa* ة is a special form of the *Tā'*. It only occurs when final, and denotes feminines. It is pronounced as a short *a* when the word occurs isolated. However, if the word is the 1st term of a genitive construction, it turns to *t* (cf. Lesson 6).

1.2.4. *Allāh* (God) is mostly written in the form of الله (in calligraphy: ﷲ).

The *Shadda* above the *Lām* shows that the *Lām* is doubled here; the small *Alif* above the *Shadda* means that a long *ā* has to be pronounced after it.

This small *Alif* is also put in the word *raḥmān* (the Merciful) and others, i.e. a long *ā* has to be pronounced after it here as well. Thus the following image is produced in a calligraphy, representing the text "In the name of God, the Merciful, the Compassionate":

بِسْمِ اللهِ الرَّحْمَنِ الرَّحِيمِ

Such writings designed artistically are only readable with some experience and are predominantly in use in editions of the Koran as well as in mosques.

Here are some more uncommented examples, which you can decipher together with the teacher:

1.2.5. The alphabet in its traditional order

name of the letter	transliteration	isolated position	final position	medial position	initial position
Alif	ā	ا	ـا	ـا	ا
Bā'	b	ب	ـب	ـبـ	بـ
Tā'	t	ت	ـت	ـتـ	تـ
Thā'	th	ث	ـث	ـثـ	ثـ
Jīm	j	ج	ـج	ـجـ	جـ
Ḥā'	ḥ	ح	ـح	ـحـ	حـ
Khā'	kh	خ	ـخ	ـخـ	خـ
Dāl	d	د	ـد	ـد	د
Dhāl	dh	ذ	ـذ	ـذ	ذ
Rā'	r	ر	ـر	ـر	ر
Zāy	z	ز	ـز	ـز	ز
Sīn	s	س	ـس	ـسـ	سـ
Shīn	sh	ش	ـش	ـشـ	شـ
Ṣād	ṣ	ص	ـص	ـصـ	صـ
Ḍād	ḍ	ض	ـض	ـضـ	ضـ
Ṭā'	ṭ	ط	ـط	ـطـ	طـ
Ẓā'	ẓ	ظ	ـظ	ـظـ	ظـ
ʿAyn	ʿ	ع	ـع	ـعـ	عـ
Ghayn	gh	غ	ـغ	ـغـ	غـ
Fā'	f	ف	ـف	ـفـ	فـ
Qāf	q	ق	ـق	ـقـ	قـ
Kāf	k	ك	ـك	ـكـ	كـ
Lām	l	ل	ـل	ـلـ	لـ
Mīm	m	م	ـم	ـمـ	مـ
Nūn	n	ن	ـن	ـنـ	نـ
Hā'	h	ه	ـه	ـهـ	هـ
Wāw	w, ū	و	ـو	ـو	و
Yā'	y, ī	ي	ـي	ـيـ	يـ

&A3 1. The first letter of the alphabet is actually *Hamza*, but since *Alif* is the chair of *Hamza* in most cases, it appears in its place as the first letter. In the grammar part of this book *Alif* is written as أ when *Hamza* is vocalized with *Fatḥa*, if it is not a *Hamzat al-waṣl* (cf. Lesson 2, p. 38).

2. The transliteration system in this book ignores *Hamza* in the initial position. That is to say, أَنْتَ أُمّ , or إنْ are transliterated as *umm, anta* and *in*, and not as *'umm, 'anta* and *'in*.

3. *Yā'* (ى) without diacritical dots in the final position is always preceded by *Fatḥa* and is pronounced as the long vowel *ā.:* إلى *ilā,* على *°alā,* متى *matā*.

Final *Yā'* (ي) with diacritical dots is usually preceded by *Kasra:* في *fī,* كتابي *kitābī*.

However, many texts do not seem to be consistent in regard to the use of diacritical dots with ي when it occurs in the final position.

Exercises

In the exercises of Lessons 1, 2 and 3 (which will take about 3 weeks) the basics of the Arabic pronunciation and writing are taught. The principle is *hearing - speaking - reading - writing*.

Since it takes a certain time - according to our experience - until the student is acquainted with reading and writing the Arabic script, we begin with exercises for hearing and speaking, which are based on a vocabulary of about 80 words denoting things and persons in the room.

Using the direct method, we start speaking straight away, although the student does not know yet how the words which are used are written. At the same time the student memorizes the correct stress of the words without being required to know the rules.

Since the first exercises are to be read at home by the students after having been discussed in the lessons, we have added the transliteration of the words despite some doubts which exist from the methodical point of view.

The arrangement of the exercises in the form of three columns enables the student to check his way of reading at home with the aid of the transliteration. Nevertheless, we advise the student from the beginning to uncover only the Arabic column.

The texts of the exercises of Lessons 1, 2 and 3 may be used as writing exercises later on. First, however, the student has to do the writing exercises of Lesson 1 (Ex8), which are composed according to the principle of similarity of the letters, and are to give him/her a feeling for a certain technique of writing.

All words used in the exercises of Lesson 1 can be found in the vocabulary of Lesson 2.

Ex1 The teacher should read the following words aloud, and the student should repeat them after him/her. The teacher will correct the reading and comment on the pronunciation when necessary, and will make sure that the students understand the meanings by pointing to the things he/she refers to. The students are also advised to test their knowledge by covering the transliteration one time and the English equivalents another, and finally both the transliteration and the English equivalents.

as-salāmu ᶜalaykum	Peace be with / upon you *(one of the numerous Arabic forms of greeting)*	اَلسَّلامُ عَلَيْكُمْ
ana	I *(the ā at the end of* أنا *is pronounced as a short a)*	أَنَا
anta	you *(m.)*	أَنْتَ
anti	you *(f.)*	أَنْتِ
wa	and *(it precedes the following word without a gap between them)*	و
ana wa-anta	I and you	أَنَا وأَنْتَ
ana wa-anti	I and you *(f.)*	أَنَا وأَنْتِ
anta wa-ana	you and I	أَنْتَ وأَنَا
anti wa-ana	you *(f.)* and I	أَنْتِ وأَنَا
anta wa-anti	you and you *(f.)*	أَنْتَ وأَنْتِ
anti wa-anta	you *(f.)* and you	أَنْتِ وأَنْتَ
huwa	he	هُوَ
hiya	she	هِيَ
huwa wa-hiya	he and she	هُوَ وهِيَ
hiya wa-huwa	she and he	هِيَ وهُوَ
ana wa-anta wa-huwa	I and you and he	أَنَا وأَنْتَ وهُوَ
ana wa-anti wa-hiya	I and you *(f.)* and she	أَنَا وأَنْتِ وهِيَ

Ex2 See instructions for Ex1!

ana muᶜallim.	I am a teacher.	أَنَا مُعَلِّم.
ana muᶜallima.	I am a teacher (f.).	أَنَا مُعَلِّمة.
anta ṭālib.	You are a student.	أَنْتَ طَالِب.
anti ṭāliba.	You are a student (f.).	أَنْتِ طَالِبَة.
huwa ṭālib.	He is a student.	هُوَ طَالِب.
hiya ṭāliba.	She is a student (f.).	هِيَ طَالِبَة.
ana muᶜallim wa-anta ṭālib.	I am a teacher, and you are a student.	أَنَا مُعَلِّم وَأَنْتَ طَالِب.
ana muᶜallim wa-anti ṭāliba.	I am a teacher, and you (f.) are a student (f.).	أَنَا مُعَلِّم وَأَنْتِ طَالِبَة.
huwa ṭālib wa-ana muᶜallim.	He is a student, and I am a teacher.	هُوَ طَالِب وَأَنَا مُعَلِّم.
hiya ṭāliba wa-ana muᶜallim.	She is a student (f.), and I am a teacher.	هِيَ طَالِبَة وَأَنَا مُعَلِّم.
hiya ṭāliba wa-huwa ṭālib.	She is a student (f.), and he is a student.	هِيَ طَالِبَة وهُوَ طَالِب.

Ex3 See instructions for Ex1!

hunā	here	هُنَا
hunāka	there	هُنَاكَ
hunā wa-hunāka	here and there	هُنَا وهُنَاكَ
ana hunā wa-anta hunāka.	I am here, and you are there.	أَنَا هُنَا وأَنْتَ هُنَاكَ.
ana hunā wa-anti hunāka.	I am here, and you (f.) are there.	أَنَا هُنَا وأَنْتِ هُنَاكَ.
huwa hunā wa-hiya hunāka.	He is here, and she is there.	هُوَ هُنَا وهِيَ هُنَاكَ.
anta hunā wa-huwa hunāka.	You are here, and he is there.	أَنْتَ هُنَا وهُوَ هُنَاكَ.
hunā waraq.	Here is paper.	هُنَا وَرَق.

hunā qalam.	Here is a pen.	هُنَا قَلَم.
hunā kurrāsa.	Here is a notebook.	هُنَا كُرَّاسَة.
hunā kitāb.	Here is a book.	هُنَا كِتَاب.
hunā shanṭa.	Here is a bag.	هُنَا شَنْطَة.
hunā waraq wa-hunāka qalam.	Here is paper, and there is a pen.	هُنَا وَرَق وهُنَاكَ قَلَم.
hunā kurrāsa wa-hunāka kitāb.	Here is a notebook, and there is a book.	هُنَا كُرَّاسَة وهُنَاكَ كِتَاب.
hunā kitāb wa-hunāka shanṭa.	Here is a book, and there is a bag.	هُنَا كِتَاب وهُنَاكَ شَنْطَة.
hunā ṭāwila.	Here is a table.	هُنَا طَاوِلَة.
hunā kursī.	Here is a chair.	هُنَا كُرْسِيّ.
hunā khizāna.	Here is a cupboard.	هُنَا خِزَانَة.
hunā miṣbāḥ.	Here is a lamp.	هُنَا مِصْبَاح.
hunā lawḥ.	Here is a blackboard.	هُنَا لَوْح.
hunā ṭāwila wa-hunāka kursī.	Here is a table, and there is a chair.	هُنَا طَاوِلَة وَهُنَاكَ كُرْسِيّ.
hunā khizāna wa-hunāka miṣbāḥ.	Here is a cupboard, and there is a lamp.	هُنَا خِزَانَة وهُنَاكَ مِصْبَاح.
hunā khizāna wa-hunāka lawḥ.	Here is a cupboard, and there is a blackboard.	هُنَا خِزَانَة وهُنَاكَ لَوْح.
hunā bāb.	Here is a door.	هُنَا بَاب.
hunā shubbāk.	Here is a window.	هُنَا شُبَّاك.
hunā jidār.	Here is a wall.	هُنَا جِدَار.
hunā bāb wa-hunāka shubbāk.	Here is a door, and there is a window.	هُنَا بَاب وهُنَاكَ شُبَّاك.
hunā jidār wa-hunāka bāb.	Here is a wall, and there is a door.	هُنَا جِدَار وهُنَاكَ بَاب.

Ex4 The teacher puts the following questions to the students:

What is here?	مَا هُنَا ؟
What is there?	مَا هُنَاكَ؟
Who is here?	مَنْ هُنَا ؟
Who is there?	مَنْ هُنَاكَ؟

and points at an object or a person while doing so. The student should answer accordingly by using the phrase هُنَا ... or هُنَاكَ ... and adds the word that is asked for.

Teacher:	What is here?	مَا هُنَا؟
Student:	Here is a door.	هُنَا بَاب.
Teacher:	Who is here?	مَنْ هُنَا؟
Student:	Here is a teacher.	هُنَا مُعَلِّم.
Teacher:	What is here, and what is there?	مَا هُنَا وَمَا هُنَاكَ؟
Student:	Here is a door, and there is a table.	هُنَا بَاب وَهُنَاكَ طَاوِلَة.
Teacher:	Who is here, and who is there?	مَنْ هُنَا وَمَنْ هُنَاكَ؟
Student:	Here is a student, and there is a student (f).	هُنَا طَالِب وَهُنَاكَ طَالِبَة.

The following words can be used:

بَاب، خِزَانَة، كُرْسِي، طَاوِلَة، كُرَّاسَة، كِتَاب، وَرَق، شَنْطَة، قَلَم، لَـوْح، جِدَار، شُبَّاك، مِصْبَاح، طَالِبَة، طَالِب، مُعَلِّم، مُعَلِّمَة

Ex5 The teacher should ask the students to read the words and sentences of Ex1 - 4 again, covering the columns on the left and in the middle.

Ex6 (Homework) Repeat Ex5!

Ex7 The teacher prepares Ex8 by explaining the different letters according to the order given in Ex8. The teacher explains how to do Ex8, which is to be done as homework, and lays special emphasis on those letters which cannot be linked to the following letter.

Ex8 (Homework) The following exercise is planned to develop the students' writing skills; it should not impart new vocabulary items to them. The examples given for each group of letters should be considered as an orientation for proper writing. It is very important that the teacher gives general hints with respect to writing in order to avoid the students using incorrect forms of writing.

ا أ إ آ ا ، بـ ـبـ ـب ب ، تـ ـتـ ـت ت
ثـ ـثـ ـث ث ، نـ ـنـ ـن ن ، يـ ـيـ ـي ي
بت بن بي

Connect the following letters which are written in their isolated form:

1) أ+ب   2) أ+ب+ا   3) أ+ن+ا   4) أ+ن+ت   5) ي+ا   6) ب+ي

7) أ+ي   8) أ+ن   9) ب+ي+ت   10) ب+ي+ن   11) ا+ب+ن

12) ب+ن+ت   13) ب+ا+ب   14) ت+ي+ن   15) ب+ي+ن+ا

16) ب+ي+ت+ي   17) ث+ا+ب+ت   18) ب+ث

جـ ـجـ ـج ج ، حـ ـحـ ـح ح ، خـ ـخـ ـخ خ

Connect the following letters which are written in their isolated form:

1) أ+خ   2) أ+خ+ا   3) ن+ح+ن   4) ت+ح+ت   5) ح+ج   6) ح+ا+ج

7) ج+ي+ب   8) ج+ب+ن   9) ح+ب   10) ب+خ   11) ح+ي+ن

12) ح+ب+ي+ب   13) ح+ب+ي+ب+ي   14) أ+ح+ب

15) ن+ح+ب   16) ت+ا+ج   17) أ+ح+ت+ا+ج   18) ن+ح+ت+ا+ج

دـ ـد ، ذـ ـذ ، رـ ـر ، زـ ـز ، وـ ـو ، ير يد خذ بو

Connect the following letters which are written in their isolated form:

1) د+ب+ر   2) د+ا+ر   3) ت+د+ب+ي+ر   4) د+ج+ا+ج

5) د+ح+ر+ج   6) أ+د+ر+ي   7) ت+د+ر+ي+ب

8) ي+د+ر+ي   9) ذ+ب+ذ+ب   10) ر+ب   11) ر+ي+ح

12) ر+و+ح   13) ت+ر+ت+ي+ب   14) ج+د+د

15) ج+د+ي+د   16) ب+ي+ت   17) ب+ا+ب

18) أ+ب+و+ا+ب   19) ح+ب+ر   20) خ+ذ   21) أ+و

22) ز+ج+ا+ج   23) ي+د   24) ي+ر+ي   25) أ+ر+ى

26) ر+أ+ي   27) د+و+ن   28) أ+ب+و

سـ ـسـ ـس س ، شـ ـشـ ـش ش، سا سيـ

صـ ـصـ ـص ص ، ضـ ـضـ ـض ض

طـ ـطـ ـط ط ، ظـ ـظـ ـظ ظ، بط طن ضر

Connect the following letters which are written in their isolated form:

4) ض+ا+د   3) ص+ا+د   2) ش+ي+ن   1) س+ي+ن

8) ص+ح+ا+ح   7) ص+ح+ي +ح   6) د+ر+و+س   5) د+ر+س

11) ش+خ+ص   10) س+ب+ب   9) ص+ب+ا+ح

14) ش+ر+ب   13) أ+س+ب+ا+ب   12) س+ب+ح

17) ت+ش+د+ي +د   16) ش+ر+ح   15) ش+ر+ط+ي

20) إ+ج+ا+ص   19) ض+ر+ب   18) ص+د+ر

23) ط+ب+ي+ب   22) ط+ر+ب   21) إ+ص+د+ا+ر

26) ض+د   25) أ+ر+ض   24) أ+ظ+ن

عـ ـعـ ـع ع ، غـ ـغـ ـغ غ ، فـ ـفـ ـف ف

قـ ـقـ ـق ق ، كـ ـكـ ـك ك ، لـ ـلـ ـل ل

لا ـلا عيـ يه فل فك كا حق

Connect the following letters which are written in their isolated form:

5) ف+و+ق   4) ف+ي   3) غ+د+ا   2) غ+ي+ن   1) ع+ي+ن

9) ا+ل+آ+ن   8) ك+ر+س+ي   7) ك+ي+ف   6) ص+د+ي+ق

13) ك+ل   12) ر+ج+ل   11) و+ر+ق   10) ط+ا+ل+ب

17) أ+و+ر+ا+ق   16) ر+ج+ا+ل   15) ح+ق+و+ق   14) ح+ق

20) ن+ظ+ي+ف   19) ص+غ+ي+ر   18) ك+ب+ي+ر

23) أ+ع+ط+ي   22) ط+و+ا+ل   21) ط+و+ي+ل

26) ص+ب+ا+ح   25) ح+ا+ل   24) ي+ح+ك+ي

29) ع+ف+و+ا   28) ش+ك+ر+ا   27) ا+ل+خ+ي+ر

مـ ـمـ ـم م ، هـ ـهـ ـه ة ، ـة ة

لم مجـ مما يها فيه طة ، لها

Connect the following letters which are written in their isolated form:

1) ا+ن+ت+م   2) ن+ع+م   3) ه+ذ+ا   4) ه+ذ+ه   5) ه+ل

6) م+ن   7) م+إ+ذ+ا   8) م+ع   9) ج+م+ي+ع   10) ه+ن+ا

11) ه+ن+ا+ك   12) م+ع+ل+م   13) م+ع+ل+م+و+ن

14) ط+ا+و+ل+ة   15) خ+ز+ا+ن+ة   16) م+ص+ب+ا+ح

17) غ+ر+ف+ة   18) ق+ل+م   19) م+د+ي+ن+ة   20) ا+س+م

21) ف+ت+ا+ة   22) ه+ا+ت   23) ش+ن+ط+ة   24) ق+د+ي+م

25) ت+ر+ج+م   26) ا+س+م+ع   27) م+ر+ح+ب+ا

28) ا+ل+س+ل+ا+م   29) م+ر+ة   30) م+ه+م   31) م+ه+م+ة

32) م+ا+ه+م

See also the writing exercises at the beginning of the key!

1. The Article (أَدَاة التَّعْرِيف)

1.1. The definite article "the" is أَلْ in Arabic. It remains unchanged for any noun, adjective, participle or numeral regardless of gender, case and number. أَلْ is connected with the following noun, forming a phonetical unit with it. There is no indefinite article in Arabic.

the house	أَلْبَيْت	al-bayt	house	بَيْت	bayt
the notebook	أَلْكُرَّاسة	al-kurrāsa	notebook	كُرَّاسة	kurrāsa

A noun which is preceded by the article أَلْ is called a definite noun.

☞**A1** Although proper names are definite as such and therefore do not need the definite article, many Arab names contain the article.

لُبْنَان "Lebanon", مُحَمَّد "Muḥammad", دِمَشْق "Damascus"

But: عَبْد الله "Abdullāh", أَلْأُرْدُنّ "Jordan", أَلقَاهِرة "Cairo"

Other possibilities of defining a noun will be taught later.

1.2. If the noun preceded by the article begins with one of the following consonants

ت ، ث ، د ، ذ ، ر ، ز ، س ، ش ، ص ، ض ، ط ، ظ ، ل ، ن

the ل of the article is assimilated, and therefore not pronounced, and the respective above-mentioned consonant is doubled, i.e. it takes the *Shadda*:

	assimilated			not assimilated	
the friend	أَلصَّدِيق	aṣ-ṣadīq	the house	أَلْبَيْت	al-bayt
the man	أَلرَّجُل	ar-rajul	the room	أَلْغُرْفة	al-ghurfa
the sun	أَلشَّمْس	ash-shams	the moon	أَلْقَمَر	al-qamar

☞**A2** The letters the ل of the article is assimilated to are called حُرُوف شَمْسية "sun letters", the others are called حُرُوف قَمَرية "moon letters".

1.3. The *Hamza* of the article أ is only pronounced as a glottal stop when the respective word preceded by the article introduces a sentence or an independent part of a sentence. Otherwise *Hamza* is replaced by *Waṣla* ٱ, which denotes that the ا is no longer pronounced as a glottal stop.

A *Hamza* that is pronounced is called *Hamzat al-qaṭ*ᶜ. A *Hamza* that is not pronounced is called *Hamzat al-waṣl* or simply *Waṣla*.

He is the teacher.	هُوَ ٱلْمُعَلِّم	the teacher	ٱلْمُعَلِّم
pronounced:	*huwal-muᶜallim*		*al-muᶜallim*
with the friend	مَعَ ٱلصَّدِيق	the friend	ٱلصَّدِيق
pronounced:	*maᶜaṣ-ṣadīq*		*aṣ-ṣadīq*
Where is the sun?	أَيْنَ ٱلشَّمْس؟	the sun	ٱلشَّمْس
pronounced:	*aynash-shams*		*ash-shams*

1.3.1. All final vowels followed by the article أل of the next word are pronounced as short vowels in order to allow smooth linkage between the words:

fī + al-bayt > fil-bayt فِي ٱلْبَيْت > فِي + أَلْبَيْت (in the house)

ᶜalā + aṭ-ṭāwila > ᶜalaṭ-ṭāwila عَلَى ٱلطَّاوِلة > عَلَى + أَلْطَّاوِلة (on the table)

1.3.2. If a word ends with *Sukūn* which is followed by the article أل of the next word, the final *Sukūn* usually turns to *Kasra*, which fulfills the function of an auxiliary vowel:

خُذِ ٱلْكِتَاب > خُذْ "Take the book!"

The preposition مِنْ , however, takes *Fatḥa* as an auxiliary vowel:

مِنَ ٱلْبَيْت "from/out of the house"

Some pronouns and verbal suffixes which contain the vowel *u* take *Ḍamma* as their auxiliary vowel.

✋**A3** *Waṣla* is not printed in the following Arabic texts of this book; instead, *Alif* ا without *Waṣla* takes its place.

2. Gender (ٱلْجِنْس)

There are two genders in Arabic: masculine (مُذَكَّر) and feminine (مُؤَنَّث). Words ending with ة *-a (Tā' marbūṭa)* are nearly always feminine, whereas words which do not end with *Tā' marbūṭa* are mostly masculine.

✋**A4** *Tā' marbūṭa* is normally not pronounced as *t*, but as a short *a* when the word occurs isolated or at the end of a clause or a sentence (see also Lesson 4, Gr. 3. and Lesson 6, Gr. 2.2.1.1.).

✋**A5** A number of words denoting feminines do not end with *Tā' marbūṭa*:

a) words for persons which are feminine by nature: أُمّ mother, أُخْت sister, بِنْت daughter

b) the names of most countries and of all cities

c) designations of parts of the body which exist in pairs: يَد hand, عَيْن eye, أُذْن ear

d) Some words are always used as feminines: أَرْض land, شَمْس sun

e) Some words are used as either masculine or feminine: سِكِّين knife, سُوق market, سَمَاء sky
Feminine nouns which are not easily identifiable as such are marked in this book by a (م) placed behind them when mentioned for the first time.

3. The Equational Sentence (أَلْجُمْلة الإِسْمِيَّة)

The simple equational sentence in Arabic language consists of two parts: the subject (أَلْمُبْتَدَأ) and the predicate (أَلْخَبَر).

It denotes a general present tense or an action taking place regularly and has no copula (i.e. derivatives of the verb *to be*).

3.1. Its subject may be a noun (اِسْم), a personal pronoun (ضَمِير) or a demonstrative pronoun (اِسْم إِشَارة). Its predicate may be an adjective (صِفة), a noun, an adverb (ظَرْف) or a prepositional phrase. (All these parts of speech can be found in the basic vocabulary.)

The following structures occur frequently:

Sentence structure 1 = The subject is a definite noun (اِسْم مُعَرَّف) or a pronoun and appears at the beginning of the sentence.

a1) Noun	- adjective
The house is big.	أَلْبَيْت كَبِير.

a2) Noun	- (indef.) noun
The man is a teacher.	أَلرَّجُل مُعَلِّم.

a3) Noun	- adverb
The teacher is here.	أَلْمُعَلِّم هُنَا.

	- prepositional phrase
The teacher is in the room.	أَلْمُعَلِّم في الْغُرْفَة.

b1) Personal pronoun	- adjective
He/(it) is big.	هُوَ كَبِير.

b2) Personal pronoun	- (indef.) noun
He is a teacher.	هُوَ مُعَلِّم.

	- (def.) noun
He is the teacher.	هُوَ الْمُعَلِّم.

b3) Personal pronoun   - adverb

He is here.	هُوَ هُنَا.

- prepositional phrase

He is in the room.	هُوَ فِي الْغُرْفَة.

c1) Demonstrative pronoun   - adjective

This (one) is big.	هَذَا كَبِير.

c2) Demonstrative pronoun   - (indef.) noun

This (one) is a teacher.	هَذَا مُعَلِّم.

c3) Demonstrative pronoun   - adverb

This (one) is here.	هَذَا هُنَا.

- prepositional phrase

This (one) is in the room.	هَذَا فِي الْغُرْفَة.

☞**A6** A demonstrative followed by a definite noun may be ambiguous:

هَذَا الْمُعَلِّم may be translated as: This teacher / This is the teacher.

However, if ambiguity is to be avoided, the personal pronoun must be inserted:

This is the teacher.	هَذَا هُوَ الْمُعَلِّم.
This is the teacher *(f.)*.	هَذِهِ هِيَ الْمُعَلِّمَة.

The demonstrative pronouns هَذَا and هَذِهِ have a small ا above the ه when the words are fully vocalized, which is to denote the long vowel *ā* : *hādhā, hādhihī*. However, in modern texts this ا does not appear in the typeface.

Sentence structure 2 = The subject is an indefinite noun (مُنكَّر) and therefore appears at the end of the sentence.

Adverb   - noun

Here is a teacher.	هُنَا مُعَلِّم.

Prepositional phrase   - noun

In the room there is a teacher. (There is a teacher in the room.)	فِي الْغُرْفَة مُعَلِّم.

3.2. In the 'yes/no' question the word order of the declarative sentence is retained, but the sentence begins with the interrogative particle هَل , or rarely أ.

| Is he here? | أَ هُوَ هُنَا؟ هَلْ هُوَ هُنَا؟ |
| Is this big? | أَ هَذَا كَبِير؟ هَلْ هَذَا كَبِير؟ |

In case of alternative questions the alternative particle أَمْ must be used:

| Is this big or small? | هَلْ هَذَا كَبِير أَمْ صَغِير؟ |

The interrogatives ما for "what" and مَنْ for "who" act as subjects in *wh*-questions:

What is this?	مَا هَذَا / هَذِهِ؟
Who is this?	مَنْ هَذَا / هَذِهِ؟
What is here / there?	مَا هُنَا / هُنَاكَ؟
Who is here / there?	مَنْ هُنَا / هُنَاكَ؟

The interrogative pronoun must be followed by a personal pronoun if the predicate is a noun or an adjective.

| Who is a/(the) teacher? | مَنْ هُوَ (ال) مُعَلِّم؟ |

☞A7 In sentences which are introduced by a verb normally the interrogative مَاذَا is used instead of ما.

3.3. Agreement in gender
3.3.1. There is agreement in gender between the subject and the adjectival predicate.

	feminine subject = feminine form of the adjectival predicate		masculine subject = masculine form of the adjectival predicate
a1)	أَلْخِزَانَة كَبِيرَة.	The cupboard/ the house is big.	أَلْبَيْت كَبِير.
b1)	هِيَ كَبِيرَة.	It is big.	هُوَ كَبِير.
c1)	هَذِهِ كَبِيرَة.	This one is big.	هَذَا كَبِير.

3.3.2. Agreement in gender also exists between a pronominal subject and a nominal predicate:

| He is a teacher. | هُوَ مُعَلِّم. |
| She is a teacher. | هِيَ مُعَلِّمة. |

3.3.3. The question whether هذا، هذه، هو or هي should be chosen as a predicate in a *wh*-question introduced by ما or مـن is determined by the gender of the persons or objects referred to:

What is this?	مَا هَذَا؟
Who is this?	مَنْ هَذَا؟
Who is he?	مَنْ هُوَ؟

when a masculine is asked about,

What is this?	مَا هَذِهِ؟
Who is this?	مَنْ هَذِهِ؟
Who is she?	مَنْ هِيَ؟

when a feminine is asked about.

That is why the personal pronoun which has to be inserted into the *wh*-question must be هو when the predicate of the latter is masculine, and هي when its predicate is feminine:

What is the name?/ What is his/her name?	مَا هُوَ الإِسْمُ؟
What is the sun?	ما هِيَ الشَّمْسُ؟
Who is a/(the) teacher?	مَنْ هُوَ (الـ)مُعَلِّمُ؟
Who is a/(the) teacher?	مَنْ هِيَ (الـ)مُعَلِّمَةُ؟

✎**A8** Agreement in gender is also to be observed between the verb which introduces a sentence and the following noun: The masculine form يُوجَدُ and the feminine form تُوجَدُ may be used for indicating existence, i.e. "there is":

The teacher is in the room.	يُوجَدُ الْمُعَلِّمُ فِي الْغُرْفَةِ.
The cupboard is in the room.	تُوجَدُ الْخِزَانَةُ فِي الْغُرْفَةِ.
Here is a teacher.	يُوجَدُ هُنَا مُعَلِّمٌ.
Here is a cupboard.	تُوجَدُ هُنَا خِزَانَة.

In interrogative sentences introduced by ماذا the masculine form يُوجَدُ is used:

What is in the room?	ماذا يُوجَدُ فِي الْغُرْفَةِ؟

Glossaries are provided in each lesson from here forward. They contain all the words not yet known from the preceding lessons which occur in the texts, the exercises and some encountered in the grammar. Polysemous words are mostly only given their respective current meaning at issue in the text. The vocabulary items are listed alphabetically by root, i.e. R₁ is invariably regarded as the first letter relevant in the order (cf. Lesson 4 about this). In the interest of clearness *Fatḥa* has only been inserted partially.

Identifying the root of every word may present a difficulty to the student at the beginning. With increasing practice, however, she/he will quickly acquire the skill of finding every word in the glossary she/he looks for. This skill is nevertheless required so that the student will be able to use HANS WEHR's DICTIONARY OF MODERN WRITTEN ARABIC edited by J. Milton Cowan, which is most frequently used and which is arranged according to the root-system.

Here, another general hint is given, which will facilitate the student's ability to find many words. م (*Mīm*) as the first letter of a word is rarely R₁, but is mostly a prefix (مُ ، مِ ، مَـ). The word مَخْزَن is not entered under *Mīm* in the glossary nor in the dictionary, but under *Khā'*, the word مِصْباح under *Ṣād*, and the word مُعَلَّم under *ʿAyn*.

V (Including the vocabulary of Lesson 1 and 2)

father	أب ج آباء	Welcome!	أهْلاً وسهْلاً
Take (it)! *(m./f.)*	خذ ! / خُذِي !	now	الآن
brother	أخ ج إخوة	also, too	أيْضاً
sister	أُخْت ج أخوات	where	أيْنَ
earth	أرْض (م) ج أراضٍ	Paris	باريس
Allah, God	اللهُ	not bad	لا بأسَ (بهِ/ بها)
by God	واللهِ	door	باب ج أبْواب
(prep.) to	إلى	house	بَيْت ج بُيُوت
mother	أُمّ ج أُمَّهات	*(prep.)* under	تحْتَ
(prep.) in front of *(loc.)*	أمامَ	down, downwards	إلى تحْتُ
I	أنا	good, "okay"	تمام
you *(m.)*	أنْتَ	new	جدِيد ج جُدُد
you *(f.)*	أنْتِ	wall	جدار ج جُدْران
you *(2ⁿᵈ p.pl.m.)*	أنتُمْ	sitting	جلُوس
you *(2ⁿᵈ p.pl.f.)*	أنتنَّ	beautiful	جمِيل ج ـون
Miss	آنِسة ج ات	apparatus, device	جهاز ج أجْهِزة
fig: Hello!	أهْلاً بكَ / بكِ	tv-set	~ تلفزيون

video-recorder	~ فيديو	friend	صدِيق ج أصْدِقاءُ
good	جَيِّد ج ون	friend (f.)	صدِيقة ج ــات
garden	حدِيقة ج حدائِقُ	small, short	صغِير ج صِغار
letter, character	حرْف ج حُرُوف	table	طاولة ج ــات
bathroom	حمّام ج ــات	doctor	طبِيب ج أطِبّاءُ
Thank God!	الحمْدُ للهِ	doctor (f.)	طبِيبة ج ات
situation	حال ج أحْوال	kitchen	مطْبخ ج مطابخُ
cupboard	خِزانة ج ات، خزائِنُ	student	طالِب ج طُلّاب/ طلبة
good	خيْر	student (f.)	طالِبة ج ــات
I am fine.	أنا بخيْر	long, tall	طوِيل ج طِوال
I do not know.	لا أدْري.	good	طيِّب ج ون
radio	رادِيو ج رادِيوهات	pardon (and response after	عفْواً (شكراً)
man	رجُلٍ ج رِجال	teacher	مُعلِّم ج ـون
fig: Hello!	مرْحبا	teacher (f.)	مُعلِّمة ج ــات
bed	سرِير ج أسِرَّة	(prep.) on; upon	علَى
ceiling	سقَف ج سُقُوف	(prep.) at	عِنْدَ
peace	سلام	I have	عِنْدِي
Peace be with/upon you!	السلامُ عليْكُم	you have (m./f.)	عِنْدَكَ / عِنْدَكِ
So long!	مع السلامة	family	عائِلة ج ــات
name; noun	اِسم	room	غُرْفة ج غُرف
Mr.	سيِّد ج سادة	girl	فتاة ج فتيات
Mrs.	سيِّدة ج ات	Fāṭima	فاطِمة
window	شبّاك ج شبابِيكُ	(prep.) up, over, on top of	فوْقَ
Thank you!	شُكْراً	(adv.) above	فوْقُ
the sun	الشَّمْس (م)	up(wards)	إلى فوقُ
bag	شنْطة ج شُنط، ـات	(prep.) in	في
health	صِحَّة	old	قدِيم ج قُدماءُ
morning	صباح	progress	تقدُّم
Good Morning!	صباح الخير	short, small	قصِير ج قِصار
(answer)	صباح النور	pencil	قلم ج أقلام
lamp	مِصْباح ج مصابِيحُ	moon	قمر

Cairo	القاهِرة	who	مَنْ
big	كَبير ج كِبار	(prep.) from, out of	مِنْ
book	كِتاب ج كُتُب	we	نَحْنُ
notebook	كُرّاسة ج ـات، كَراريسُ	clean	نَظيف ج نُظَفاءُ
chair	كُرْسِيّ ج كَراسيّ	yes	نَعَمْ
telephone call	مُكالمة تلفونِيَّة	sleeping	نَوْم
how	كَيْفَ	Hello!	هالو
How are you? (m.)	كَيْفَ حالُكَ /	this	هذا
~ (f.)	كَيْفَ حالُكِ؟	this (f.)	هذِهِ
(prep.) for	لِ	Give!	هات
for me	لِيَ	interrogative particle	هَل
no, not	لا	they (3rd p.pl.m.)	هُمْ
So long!	إلى اللِقاء	they (3rd p.pl.f.)	هُنَّ
table; blackboard	لَوْح ج أَلْواح	here	هُنا
what	ما	there	هُناكَ
what (followed by a verb)	ماذا	he	هُوَ
when	متَى	she	هِيَ
city, town	مَدينة ج مُدُن	and	وَ
Maryam	مَرْيَم	there is	يُوجَدُ / تُوجَدُ
evening	مَساء	paper (coll.)	وَرَق ج أَوْراق
Good evening!	مَساء الخير	dirty	وَسِخ
(answer)	مَساء النُّور	Japanese	يابانِيّ
(prep.) with	مَعَ		

البيت

Text 1

البيت كبير وجميـل. توجـد في البيـت غرفـة للجلـوس وغرفـة للنـوم وغرفـة للأخت وغرفـة لي ومطبـخ وحمـام وأمـام البيت حديقـة جميلـة. الأب معلِّم والأم طبيبة والأخت طالبة وأنا طالب أيضاً. عنـدي غرفـة كبيـرة وفي الغرفـة طاولة وكرسي وسرير وخزانة وراديو قديم وجهاز فيديو يابـاني وجهـاز تلفزيون جديد ومصباح قديم وشبّاك كبير.

Text 2   مكالمة تلفونية

محمّد: هالو، من هناك؟

مريم: هنا مريم.

محمّد: مرحباً. هنا محمّد. صباح الخير. كيف حالك؟

مريم: صباح النور. أنا بخير الحمد لله.

محمّد: أين أنت الآن؟

مريم: أنا الآن في باريس. كيف الحال؟

محمّد: أنا بخير. كيف الصحة؟

مريم: شكراً، لا بأس. وكيف حال العائلة؟

محمّد: العائلة بخير، شكراً. وكيف الأب؟

مريم: هو الآن في القاهرة وهو بخير الحمد لله.

محمّد: كيف فاطمة؟

مريم: هي بخير، الحمد لله.

محمّد: أين فاطمة؟

مريم: هي في البيت مع طالبة.

محمّد: كيف باريس؟

مريم: والله باريس مدينة جميلة وكبيرة. أين صالح؟

محمّد: لا أدري أين هو.

مريم: طيّب، مع السلامة وإلى اللقاء.

محمّد: مع السلامة.

Exercises:

Ex1 (Homework) Identify and write all the nouns seen in Text 1 and add in brackets the appropriate personal pronoun!

Ex2 The teacher reads the nouns:

بيت، جدار، غرفة، جلوس، نوم، مطبخ، حمام، حديقة، طاولة، كرسي، سرير، خزانـة، راديو، فيديو، جهاز، تلفزيون، مصباح، شباك، قلم، شنطة، لوح، ورق، سقف، أرض

explains the writing and ask the students to speak the words loudly.

Ex3 The teacher repeats the words quoted in Ex2. The students repeat them and add the definite article (أل).

Ex4 The teacher reads the words of Ex2 with the definite article. The students repeat them and add the preposition مع to them.

Ex5 Same exercise with the preposition في.

Ex6 Same exercise with the preposition على.

Ex7 Same exercise with the preposition أمام.

Ex8 Same exercise with the preposition عند.

Ex9 Same exercise with the preposition إلى.

Ex10 Same exercise with the preposition فوق/تحت.

Ex11 Same exercise with the preposition لـ.

Ex12 Add the appropriate preposition(s)!

أنا ... البيت. القلم ... الشَّنطة. الحديقـة ... البيت. فاطمـة ... الصَّديـق. أحمـد ... المطبخ. الورق ... الشَّنطة. الطَّاولة ... الغرفـة. الرَّاديـو ... الخزانـة. محمَّـد ... الأم. الطَّالـب ... المعلِّم. الكراسة ... الشَّنطة. أحمد ... بـاريس. الأب ... القـاهرة. اللوح ... الجدار. الكرسي ... الطَّاولة. الورق ... الطَّاولة.

Ex13 The teacher reads the following words:

معلِّم، طالب، الأب، الصَّديق، رجل، السَّيد...

and the students form equational sentences by adding the personal pronouns هو, أنا and أنت.

☞ معلِّم   >   هو معلِّم.   صديق   >   أنت الصَّديق.
☞ طالب   >   أنا طالب.   السَّيد   >   هو السَّيد.

Ex14 The same as Ex13 with the words

طبيبة، معلِّمة، طالبة، المعلِّمة الطَّالبة، صديقة، الفتاة، الآنسة، السَّيدة...

and the personal pronouns هي and أنتِ.

Ex15 The teacher reads the words:

الشُّبَّاك، المصباح، اللوح، البيت، الرَّجل، القلم، الطَّالـب، الكتـاب، الرَّاديـو، السَّـرير، الأب، النَّوم، الجلوس، المعلِّم، الطَّالب، الكرسي، الصَّباح

and the students form equational sentences with the following adjectives:

كبير، صغير، جميل

☞   الشُّبَّاك كبير.   >   الشُّبَّاك

Ex16 The same as Ex15 with the words:

الغرفة، الشَّنطة، الطَّاولة، الكرَّاسة، الخزانة، الطَّالبة، الفتاة، المدينة، القاهرة، الأم، الكرَّاسة، الحديقة.

Ex17 The teacher explains the meaning of the following adjectives

جديد/قديم ، طويل/قصير ، نظيف/وسخ

and the students form equational sentences using the words mentioned in Ex15 and 16:

☞   الطَّاولة جديدة والكرسي قديم.
☞   الطَّالب طويل والطَّالبة صغيرة.
☞   الغرفة نظيفة واللوح وسخ.

Ex18 The teacher reads the following equational sentences:

الكتاب جديد. البيت قديم. الخزانة كبيرة. الشُّبَّاك صغير. الطَّالبة جميلة. الغرفة نظيفة. الأرض وسخة. المعلِّم طويل. الطَّالب صغير. القلم قصير. الخزانة جديدة. اللوح نظيف. الغرفة وسخة. المصباح صغير. الشَّنطة قديمة. الطَّاولة كبيرة. البيت جميل. الرَّجل صغير.

and the students should repeat the sentence and than replace the subject by هو or هي.

Ex19 The students form questions using أيـنَ "where" and the words given in Ex15 and 16 and answer the questions.

Ex20 Answer the following questions!

ماذا يوجد في الغرفة (في البيت، في الخزانة، في الشَّنطة)؟
ماذا يوجد على الطَّاولة (على الجدار، على الخزانة، على السَّرير، على الكرسي)؟

Ex21 The teacher points at certain objects in the room and asks the question:

ما هذا؟ ما هذه؟

The answers should be a complete sentence!

Ex22 The teacher asks:

هل هذا شبَّاك (لوح، كرسي، ...)؟

the students answer with نَعَم "yes":

نعم، هذا ... / نعم، هذه ...

or with لا "no":

لا، هذا ... / لا، هذه ...

Ex23 Answer the following questions with نعـم or لا and the first personal pronoun singular as a subject:

هل أنتَ طالب (معلِّم، المعلِّم، رجل، السَّيِّد ...، كبير، صغير، جديد، طويل)؟

هل أنتِ طالبة (معلِّمة، المعلِّمة، فتاة، الآنسة ...، كبيرة، صغيرة، جديدة، طويلة)؟

Ex24 The teacher explains the usage of عِنْدي "I have/possess" and عِنْدَكَ/عِنْدَكِ "you have/possess" and asks:

☞   هل عِنْدَكَ/عِنْدَكِ كرسي (راديو، شنطة، قلم، بيت، خزانة، كرَّاسة، غرفة، فيديو ...)؟
The students answer:

☞   نعم، عندي ...

Ex25 The teacher asks:

هل عندكَ/ عندكِ بيت كبير (غرفة جديدة، قلم طويل، شنطة نظيفة ...) ؟
The students answer with "no" and the antonym of the adjective:

☞   لا، عندي بيت صغير.

Ex26 The teacher asks:

☞   مَن عندكَ/ عندكِ؟

The students answer as follows:

☞   عندي الأخت. عندي المعلم. عندي ...

Ex27 The teacher asks the student to give him/her or offers him/her something and the student should thank:

هاتِ الـ...	teacher:
خذِ الـ ...	student:
شكراً	teacher:
عفواً	student:

Ex28 The teacher explains the forms of greeting and practices them with the students based on Text 2.

صباح الخير / النور	أهلاً وسهلاً
مع السَّلامة	أهلاً بكَ/بكِ
السَّلام عليكم	كيفَ حَالَكَ / حَالُكِ؟
وعليكم السَّلام	كيف الصِّحَّة؟
إلى اللقاء	كيف الـ...؟
مَرْحَباً	الحَمْدُ لله
مساء الخير / النور	أنا بخير
	أنا تمام

Ex29 The teacher asks:

☞ أين البيت (الغرفة، الشَّنطة، الطاولة، الكرسي، المعلّم، الطالب ...) ؟

The students answer as follows:

☞ لا أدْرِي أين البيت. لا أدري أين ال ...

Ex30 Translate into Arabic! (written homework)!

I am big. He is a student. The bag is new. The room is big. The mother is a doctor. She is a student. I have a Japanese video-recorder. You *(m.)* have a big garden. You *(f.)* have a nice bag. Ahmed is a student. The table is old. The lamp is new. He is in the kitchen. The window is clean. The blackboard is dirty. The father is a teacher.

Ex31 All students answer the question:

مَا اسمُكَ؟ مَا اسمُكِ؟

Final Exercise:

1. Connect the following letters!

6. ص+ب+ا+ح	1. ا+ن+ا
7. ا+ل+خ+ي+ر	2. ط+ا+ل+ب
8. ك+ي+ف	3. ا+م+ر+ي+ك+ي
9. ح+ا+ل+ك	4. ا+ل+س+ل+ا+م
10. ا+ل+ح+م+د ل+ل+ه	5. ع+ل+ي+ك+م

2. Read and translate the words in 1.!

3. Translate into Arabic!

The table is big. The bag is old. The student is new. The blackboard is dirty. You *(f.)* have a bag. You *(m.)* have a house. He is in the kitchen. The father is a teacher. The mother is a doctor. The window is old. I am a student. There is a garden in front of the house. I have a bed, a lamp and a radio. The lamp is old.

4. Replace the subject by the appropriate personal pronoun!

الطَّاولة كبـيرة. البيـت جميـل. المصبـاح صغير. القلـم قصيـر. الطّالبـة جميلـة. الأرض وسخة. الشَّنطة قديمة. الحديقة أمام البيت. الخزانة جديدة.

5. Form equational sentences with the following words and the adjectives كبير and صغير.

جدار، سرير، سقف، حرف، جهاز، مصبـاح، صديـق، حمـام، طاولـة، ورق، كتـاب، كرّاسة، كرسي، مدينة، لوح، غرفة، قمر، شمس، شبّاك، باب، بيت

6. Answer the following sentences with "no" and the antonym of the adjective in question!

هل عندك بيت جديد؟

هل عندك قلم قصير؟

هل عندك غرفة كبيرة؟

هل عندك لوح نظيف؟

7. Add the appropriate preposition!

الكتاب ... الطَّاولة. المعلِّم ... الغرفة. هو ... البيت ... الصَّديق.

8. Write the following words in transliteration!

الطَّالِب، الخزانة، المُعلِّم، الله، الشَّمس، الحمد لله، مع السَّلامة، الصَّديق

Lesson 3	الدرس الثالث

1. Number (أَلْعَدَد)

Arabic has three numbers as far as nouns, pronouns and verbs are concerned :
singular (أَلْمُفْرد), dual (أَلْمُثْنَى) and plural (أَلجمْع).

This lesson will concentrate on the plural of the nouns and personal pronouns.

1.1. The personal pronoun

sg.		pl.	
he	هُوَ	they (m.)	هُمْ
she	هِيَ	they (f.)	هَنَّ
you (m.)	أَنْتَ	you (m.)	أَنْتُمْ
you (f.)	أَنْتِ	you (f.)	أَنْتُنَّ
I	أَنَا	we	نَحْنُ

📖A1 The auxiliary vowel for هُمْ and أَنْتُمْ is *Ḍamma -u* (cf. Lesson 2, Gr 1.3.2.).
As to the order of the personal pronouns above see Lesson 5, Gr 1.3.

1.2. The noun and the adjective

The Arabic noun has two types of plurals: the external and the internal, i.e. the sound plural (أَلجمْع السَّالِم) and the broken plural (جمْع التَّكْسِير). The external or sound plural is formed by suffixes being added.

The internal or broken plural is formed by the structure of the vowels of the singular form being altered and/or by prefixes, infixes or suffixes being added to the singular form.

1.2.1. The sound plural has two forms:

The suffix وْنَ – (-ūna) for the masculine (جمْع مُذكَّر سالِم) and the suffix ات – (-āt) for the feminine plural (جمْع مُؤَنَّث سالِم) are added to the singular masculine form.

pl.		
m.	diligent teachers *muᶜallimūna mujtahidūna*	مُعَلِّمُونَ مُجْتَهِدُونَ
f.	diligent teachers (f.) *muᶜallimāt mujtahidāt*	مُعَلِّمات مُجْتَهِدات

sg.		
m.	a diligent teacher *muᶜallim mujtahid*	مُعَلِّم مُجْتَهِد
f.	a diligent teacher *(f.)* *muᶜallima mujtahida*	مُعَلِّمَة مُجْتَهِدَة

1.2.2. The broken plural has many patterns, of which we mention فِعَال *fiᶜāl* and أَفْعَال *afᶜāl* here (see also Lesson 4).

sg.		pl.	
rajul	رَجُل	*rijāl*	رِجَال
ṭawīl	طَوِيل	*ṭiwāl*	طِوَال
qalam	قَلَم	*aqlām*	أَقْلَام

🎧**A2** Since there are no specific rules regarding the plural forms, the student must learn each plural together with the singular. This book provides you with the most common plural forms of the nouns and of the adjectives. In the glossaries of this book the singular and the plural form are separated by the letter ج for جَمْع (= plural). If several plurals are present they are divided by a comma. A ج in front of a word will indicate when only the plural form of this word is used.

2. The Adjective (ألصِّفَة)

2.1. The form: each adjective has a masculine and a feminine singular form:

m.	كَبِير	طَوِيل	كَثِير	مُجْتَهِد
f.	كَبِيرَة	طَوِيلَة	كَثِيرَة	مُجْتَهِدة

as well as a masculine sound or broken and a feminine plural form:

m.	كِبَار	طِوَال	كَثِيرُونَ	مُجْتَهِدُونَ
f.	كَبِيرَات	طَوِيلَات	كَثِيرَات	مُجْتَهِدات

Determining which form has to be used depends on the word which the adjective belongs to.

2.2. The function: the adjective has two functions, an attributive and a predicative one (as to the latter cf. Lesson 2, Gr 3.1.).
predicative

The house is big.	ألْبَيْتُ كَبِيرٌ.
The room is new.	ألْغُرْفَةُ جَدِيدَةٌ.

attributive

the big house	أَلْبَيْتُ الكَبِيرُ
the new room	أَلْغُرْفَةُ الجَدِيدَةُ
a big house	بَيْتٌ كَبِيرٌ
a new room	غُرْفَةٌ جَدِيدَةٌ

☞**A3** The final *Ḍamma* in البيتُ (*al-baytu*), الغرفةُ (*al-ghurfatu*), الكبيرُ (*al-kabīru*) and الجديدةُ (*al-jadīdatu)* and the ٌ (*Tanwīn*) will be explained in detail in Lesson 4, Gr 3.

2.3. There is agreement in number and gender between the noun and the adjective in their singular forms (cf. Lesson 2, Gr 3.3.1.-3.3.2.):

in number

The house is big.	singular	أَلْبَيْتُ كَبِيرٌ.
the big house	singular	أَلْبَيْتُ الْكَبِيرُ

in gender

The house is big.	m.	أَلْبَيْتُ كَبِيرٌ.
the big house	m.	أَلْبَيْتُ الْكَبِيرُ
The room is new.	f.	أَلْغُرْفَةُ جَدِيدَةٌ.
the new room	f.	أَلْغُرْفَةُ الْجَدِيدَةُ

If the adjective has an attributive function, there is also **agreement in state** (i.e. definite or no article)

the big house	definite	أَلْبَيْتُ الْكَبِيرُ
the new room	definite	أَلْغُرْفَةُ الجَدِيدَةُ
a big house	indefinite	بَيْتٌ كَبِيرٌ
a new room	indefinite	غُرْفَةٌ جَدِيدَةٌ

and **in case** (see Lesson 4, Gr 3.1., 3.2.).

2.4. If the noun and the adjective are in the plural, the agreement between them depends on whether the noun denotes a person or not. If it denotes a person, agreement in number and gender applies; if the adjective is used in an attributive function, there is also agreement in state and case.

predicative:

The teachers are diligent.	أَلْمُعَلِّمُونَ مُجْتَهِدُونَ.
The teachers (f.) are diligent.	أَلْمُعَلِّمَاتُ مُجْتَهِدَاتٌ.
The men are tall.	أَلرِّجَالُ طِوَالٌ.

attributive:

the diligent teachers	أَلْمُعَلِّمُونَ الْمُجْتَهِدُونَ
the diligent teachers (f.)	أَلْمُعَلِّمَاتُ الْمُجْتَهِدَاتُ
the tall men	أَلرِّجَالُ الطِّوَالُ
tall men	رِجَالٌ طِوَالٌ

If the noun denotes a non-person, the adjective takes the feminine singular form both when fulfilling an attributive and when fulfilling a predicative function.

Strictly speaking, there is only agreement when the adjective is used as an attribute, i.e. agreement in state and case. Nevertheless we also refer to it as agreement in gender and number, because the **plural of words denoting non-persons is treated as a feminine singular.**

predicative:

The tables are big.	أَلطَّاوِلَاتُ كَبِيرَةٌ.
The pens are new.	أَلْأَقْلَامُ جَدِيدَةٌ.

attributive:

the big tables	أَلطَّاوِلَاتُ الْكَبِيرَةُ
the new pens	أَلْأَقْلَامُ الْجَدِيدَةُ

2.5. If the adjective is used as a predicate, the subject can be replaced by the personal pronoun.

هُوَ كَبِيرٌ.	أَلْبَيْتُ كَبِيرٌ.
هِيَ كَبِيرَةٌ.	أَلْغُرْفَةُ كَبِيرَةٌ.
هُمْ مُجْتَهِدُونَ.	أَلْمُعَلِّمُونَ مُجْتَهِدُونَ.

هُنَّ مُجْتَهِدَاتٌ.	أَلْمُعَلِّمَاتُ مُجْتَهِدَاتٌ.
هِيَ كَبِيرَةٌ.	أَلطَّاوِلاَتُ كَبِيرَةٌ.
هِيَ جَدِيدَةٌ.	أَلأَقْلاَمُ جَدِيدَةٌ.

In the last two examples above هِيَ must be used because أقْلام and طَاوِلاَت are regarded as feminine singulars as they denote non-persons.

V

meal, dish	أكْلة ج أكْلات	marmelade	مُربّىً
emirate	إمارة ج إمارات	butter	زُبْدة
Daddy	بابا	Saudi Arabia	السعودِية
bus	باص ج ـات	sugar	سُكّر
refrigerator	برّادة ج ات	Sudan	السُّودان
(prep.) after (temp.)	بعْدَ	Syria	سُوريا
country	بلد ج بلاد / بُلْدان	market	سُوقَ (م) ج أسْواق
eggs (coll.)	بَيْض (الواحدة بيضة)	car	سيّارة ج ـات
Translate.	تُرْجِمْ / تَرْجِمِي	tea	شاي
Tunisia, Tunis	تونِسُ	drinks	ج مشْروبات
cheese	جُبْنة	street	شارِع ج شوارِعُ
Algeria	الجزائرُ	right, correct	صحيح
university	جامِعة ج ـات	airport	مطار ج ـات
diligent	مُجْتَهِد ج ون	air-plane	طائِرة ج ـات
station	محطّة ج ـات	Iraq	العِراق
shop	محلّ ج ـات	honey	عسل
milk	حليب	juice	عصير
bread	خُبْزٌ	capital city	عاصِمة ج عواصِمُ
bakery	مخْبِز ج مخابِزُ	great	عظيم ج عُظماءُ
shop	مخْزِن ج مخازِنُ	Oman	عُمانُ
vegetables	ج خضْراوات	Repeat.	أعِدْ ! / أعِيدِي!
school	مدْرسة ج مدارسُ	lunch	غداء
shop	دُكّان ج دكاكينُ	Maghreb, Morocco	المغْرِب
I go to ...	أذْهبُ إلى	mistake, wrong	غلط ج أغْلاط

breakfast	فُطُور	Kuwait	الكُوَيْت
fruits	فاكِهة ج فواكِهُ	clothes	ج ملابِسُ
train	قِطار ج ات	Libya	لِيبيا
few, little	قليل ج ـون	for example	مثَلاً
coffee	قهْوة	Egypt	مِصرُ
library, bookshop	مكْتبة ج ات	Yemen	اليَمَن
many	كثير ج ـون، كِثار	day	يَوْم ج أيّام
computer	كُمْبْيُوتَر ج ات	today	اليَوْمَ

Text 1

في المدينة

المدينة كبيرة وجميلة. توجـد فـي المدينـة بيـوت صغيرة قليلـة وبيـوت كبيـرة كثيـرة. الشوارع نظيفة وطويلة وفي الشوارع سيّارات كثيرة وتوجـد فـي المدينـة محطّـة وفـي المحطّـة قطارات وأمـام المحطّـة باصـات ومخـازن ومحـلّات كثيـرة مثـلاً للسيّـارات وللملابس وللكمبيوتر ومخابز ودكاكين للخضراوات وللمشروبات ومكتبات.
وفي المدينة مطار كبير وجديد وفي المطار طائرات مـن بلـدان كثيـرة مثـلاً مـن مصـر وسوريا واليمن والسعودية والعراق وتونس والجزائر والمغرب وليبيا والسـودان وعمـان والإمارات والكويت. أنا من هذه المدينة وأنا طالب في الجامعة.

Text 2

في البيت

محمّد: صباح الخير.

الأم: صباح النور.

محمّد: كيف حالكِ؟

الأم: بخير الحمد لله. وكيف حالكَ؟

محمّد: والله، أنا بخير. أين بابا؟

الأم: هو في المدينة.

محمّد: أين فاطمة؟

الأم: هي في المدرسة.

محمّد: أين الفطور؟

الأم: ألفطور في المطبخ.

محمّد: ما هو الفطور اليوم؟

الأم: على الطاولة قهوة وشاي وفي البرّادة جبنة وبيض وعسل ومربّى وعصير وخبز وفواكه وزبدة.

محمّد: أين السُّكَّر والحليب؟

الأم: السُّكَّر هنا والحليب في البرّادة.

محمّد: شكراً. هل أنتِ اليوم في البيت؟

الأم: نعم، في الصباح أنا في البيت وبعد الغداء أذْهَبُ إلى السوق. وأنت؟

محمّد: أنا في الجامعة إلى المساء.

الأم: مع السلامة.

محمّد: مع السلامة.

Exercises:

Ex1 The teacher explains the plurals in Lesson 2 and 3 and reads the following nouns (singular and plural) out loud and the students repeat them:

رجل – رجال	معلّمة – معلّمات
صديقة – صديقات	الطاولة – الطاولات
المعلّم – المعلّمون	الرجل – الرجال
القلم – الأقلام	شنطة – شنطات
الصديقة – الصديقات	طالبة – طالبات
قلم – أقلام	طاولة – طاولات
السيِّدة – السيِّدات	الطالبة – الطالبات
الشنطة – الشنطات	الآنسة – الآنسات
مدرسة – مدارسُ	فاكهة – فواكهُ
برّادة – برّادات	أكلة – أكلات

بيت – بيوت	سوق – أسواق
يوم – أيّام	جامعة – جامعات
شارع – شوارع	مدينة – مدن
محطّة – محطّات	سيّارة – سيّارات
باص – باصات	قطار – قطارات
كتاب – كتب	مخزن – مخازن
طائرة – طائرات	مطار – مطارات
الشارع – الشوارع	بلد – بلدان

This exercise should be repeated several times until the students memorize the plurals.

Ex2 The teacher quotes the singular of the words in Ex1 and the student gives the plural.

Ex3 The teacher reads the plural and the student gives the singular.

Ex4 The teacher reads the following adjectives (singular and plural) and the student repeats them.

قصير – قِصار	كثير – كثيرون	كبير – كِبار
مجتهد – مجتهدون	طويل – طوال	جميل – جميلون
جديد – جدد	قليل – قليلون	صغير – صغار
جيد – جيدون	عظيم – عُظماء	قديم – قُدماء
		نظيف – نظفاء/نظاف

Ex5 The teacher reads the plural of the adjectives in Ex4 and the student gives the singular.

Ex6 The teacher reads the singular of the adjectives in Ex4 and the student gives the plural.

Ex7 The teacher reads a noun from Ex1-4 in the singular or in the plural and an adjective in the masculine singular. The student forms an equational sentence.

الشنطة صغيرة.	<	☞ شنطة – صغير
الطالبات جميلات.	<	☞ طالبات – جميل

Ex8 The teacher reads an equational sentence from Ex.7 consisting of a definite noun (sg. and pl.) and an adjective. The student replaces the noun with a personal pronoun.

☞ الرجل مجتهد.   <   هو مجتهد.

☞ الأقلام جديدة.   <   هي جديدة.

Ex9 The student answers the following questions with نعم or لا:

هل أنتَ كبير (صغير، جميل، مجتهد، طويل، معلم، طالب)؟

هل أنتِ كبيرة (صغيرة، جميلة، مجتهدة، طويلة، طالبة، معلِّمة)؟

هل أنتم كبار (صغار، مجتهدون، طوال، كثيرون، قليلون)؟

هل أنتنّ كبيرات (صغيرات، مجتهدات، كثيرات، صديقات، طالبات)؟

هل أنتَ صغير؟   <   نعم، أنا صغير.

هل أنتِ معلِّمة؟   <   لا، أنا طالبة.

هل أنتم كثيرون؟   <   لا، نحن قليلون.

هل أنتنّ طالبات؟   <   نعم، نحن طالبات.

Ex10 The teacher points at objects in the room and asks the following questions, and the student should use a noun and an adjective in their reply.

ما هذا، ما هذه؟ or ماذا يوجد هناك؟

☞ يوجد هناك شبّاك كبير.

☞ يوجد هناك كرسي صغير.

☞ هذا كتاب جديد.

☞ هذه خزانة قديمة.

Ex11 The students form equational sentences according to structure 2 (see Lesson 2, Gr 3.1.) by starting the sentence with the following words

هنا	هناك	في الشنطة
في الغرفة	في الخزانة	على السقف
على الطاولة	على الجدار	في البيت

and complete it with a noun and an appropriate adjective.

☞ هنا كتاب جديد.

☞ في الشنطة أقلام كثيرة.

☞ على السقف مصباح كبير.

The teacher repeats the sentence and the student repeats it again.

It is recommended to the teacher to comment on the sentences formed by the students with صحيح "right", عظيم "great" and غلط/خطأ "wrong", "mistake". He asks the students to repeat the sentence with أعيدي بر, أعِد and to translate it with ترجمي بر ترجم.

Ex12 Read
a) all nouns, adjectives and pronouns of the basic vocabulary of Lessons 2 and 3 and pay particular attention to the plurals.
b) the examples in Arabic given in G 2.2. - 2.5.

Ex13 Copy the examples in Ex.9. The teacher should write the words on the blackboard.

Ex14 (Homework) Write the following adjectives

صغير، كبير، جميل، جديد

as a definite attribute to the following nouns:

بيت، شنطة، شنطات، قلم، أقلام، كُرسي، طاولـة، طاولات، غُرفـة، طالبـة، طالبـات،

صديقة، صديقات

☞   بيت + جديد   >   البيت الجديد

☞   طاولات + كبير   >   الطاولات الكبيرة

Ex15 (Homework) Repeat Ex.11 in writing composing at least 12 sentences.

Ex16 (Homework) Repeat Ex. 7 and 8.

Ex17 The teacher explains the usage of the following greetings and forms of address and the student should practice them orally and in writing.

Ex18 (Homework) Answer the following questions in writing.

ما هي العاصمـة السـورية (اللبنانيـة، العراقيـة، المصريـة، اليمنيـة، السـعودية، التونسـية، الجزائرية، المغربية، الليبية، السودانية، العمانية، الكويتية)؟

Ex19 Add an appropriate adjective to all the nouns in the vocabulary of this Lesson. Form first the indefinite and then the definite form.

☞   أكلة   >   أكلة جيدة

☞   الأكلة   >   الأكلة الجيدة

Ex20 The same as Ex.18 but with the plural of nouns.

Ex21 Replace the adjectives in Text 1 by their opposite.

Ex22 Translate into English.

البيت جديد. توجد هناك باصات كثيرة. أنا في المكتبة الصغيرة. المحطّة في المدينة. المدن كبيرة. الطالبات المجتهدات في الجامعة. هناك خضراوات وفواكه. أذهب إلى السوق. هنا في المطار طائرات كثيرة. الزبدة والعسل والحليب والعصير والجبنة والبيض في البرّادة. القهوة والشاي والسكر على الطاولة.   هناك طائرات من الإمارات وتونس والجزائر والسعودية والسودان والعراق وعمان والمغرب والكويت وليبيا وسوريا ومصر واليمن.

Ex23 (Homework) Memorize the plurals of the nouns in Lesson 2 and 3. The teacher should ask the students to prepare for **oral** and **written tests**.

Final Exercise

1. Write the following characters to form words.

5. ه+و ف+ي ا+ل+ب+ر+ا+د+ة.   1. ك+ي+ف ح+ا+ل+ك؟

6. أ+ي+ن ا+ل+م+ش+ر+و+ب+ا+ت؟   2. ب+خ+ي+ر.

7. ه+ي ع+ل+ى ا+ل+ط+ا+و+ل+ة.   3. و+ك+ي+ف ح+ا+ل+ك؟

8. م+ع ا+ل+س+ل+ا+م+ة   4. أ+ي+ن ا+ل+ف+ط+و+ر؟

2. Read and translate the words in 1.

3. Form the plural of the following nouns and add an appropriate adjective.

رجل، صديقة، معلّم، قلم، سيِّدة، سيِّد، شنطة، مدرسة، برّادة، آنِسة، شارِع، قِطار، محطّة، باص، كِتاب، طائِرة، مطار، يوم، بيت، طاولة، سوق، مدِينة، سيّارة، مخزن، دُكّان، بلد، جامِعة، طالِب، طالبة، كُرّاسة، أكلة، كُرْسي

4. Form the masculine plural of the following adjectives and add an appropriate noun.

كبير، جميل، صغير، قديم، نظيف، كثير، طويل، قصير، مجتهد، جديد، جيِّد، قليل، عظيم

5. Translate into Arabic.
The students are new. The teachers (*f.*) are beautiful. There are many men. The bags are new. The new drinks are in the refrigerator. The big airplanes are from Kuwait. The new clothes are from Tunisia.

6. Write the Arabic equivalents of
Hello. / Good morning. / Good evening. / How are you? / Good bye.
and the appropriate answer.

7. Write the following words in transcription.

بابا، إمارة، طائِرة، الجُبنـة، الجزائِر، محطّة، محـلّ، دُكّـان، سيّارة، سُـكّر، مُجتهـد، خضْراوات، عُظماءُ، عسل، شوارِعُ، مدارِسُ

8.   Form a sentence with each Arabic personal pronoun using a personal pronoun, an indefinte noun and an appropriate adjective.

9. Translate into Arabic.
a big table - The tables are big.
a small house - The houses are small.
a diligent student *(f.)* - The student *(f.)* is diligent.
a big man - The men are big.
an old bag - The bags are old.

Peculiarities of Arabic Script
Examples

Printed type (Naskh)	Script (Ruqᶜa)
بيت	بيت
جدار	جدار
خزانة	خزانة
سقف	سقف
شباك	شباك
مصباح	مصباح
طاولة	طاولة
غرفة	غرفة
كتاب	كتاب
كرسي	كرسي
ورق	ورق
مجتهد	مجتهد
في	في
مع	مع
من	من
نعم	نعم
لا	لا
السلام عليكم	السلام عليكم
كل	كل
كان	كان
ممتاز	ممتاز

Alphabet in printing *(Naskh)*

initial position	medial position	final position	isolated position
ا	ـا	ـا	ا
بـ	ـبـ	ـب	ب
تـ	ـتـ	ـت	ت
ثـ	ـثـ	ـث	ث
جـ	ـجـ	ـج	ج
حـ	ـحـ	ـح	ح
خـ	ـخـ	ـخ	خ
دـ	ـد	ـد	د
ذـ	ـذ	ـذ	ذ
رـ	ـر	ـر	ر
زـ	ـز	ـز	ز
سـ	ـسـ	ـس	س
شـ	ـشـ	ـش	ش
صـ	ـصـ	ـص	ص
ضـ	ـضـ	ـض	ض
طـ	ـطـ	ـط	ط
ظـ	ـظـ	ـظ	ظ
عـ	ـعـ	ـع	ع
غـ	ـغـ	ـغ	غ
فـ	ـفـ	ـف	ف
قـ	ـقـ	ـق	ق
كـ	ـكـ	ـك	ك
لـ	ـلـ	ـل	ل
مـ	ـمـ	ـم	م
نـ	ـنـ	ـن	ن
هـ	ـهـ	ـه	ه
وـ	ـو	ـو	و
يـ	ـيـ	ـي	ي

Alphabet in script *(Ruqᶜa)*

initial position	medial position	final position	isolated position
١	ـا	ـا	١
بـ	ـبـ	ـب	ب
تـ	ـتـ	ـت	ت
ثـ	ـثـ	ـث	ث
جـ	ـجـ	ـج	ج
حـ	ـحـ	ـح	ح
خـ	ـخـ	ـخ	خ
د	ـد	ـد	د
ذ	ـذ	ـذ	ذ
ر	ـر	ـر	ر
ز	ـز	ـز	ز
سـ	ـسـ	ـس	س
شـ	ـشـ	ـش	ش
صـ	ـصـ	ـص	ص
ضـ	ـضـ	ـض	ض
طـ	ـطـ	ـط	ط
ظـ	ـظـ	ـظ	ظ
عـ	ـعـ	ـع	ع
غـ	ـغـ	ـغ	غ
فـ	ـفـ	ـف	ف
قـ	ـقـ	ـق	ق
كـ	ـكـ	ـك	ك
لـ	ـلـ	ـل	ل
مـ	ـمـ	ـم	م
نـ	ـنـ	ـن	ن
هـ	ـهـ	ـه	ه
و	ـو	ـو	و
يـ	ـيـ	ـي	ي

1. Radical, Root, Pattern

1.1. Most Arabic words can be reduced to a root, which, as a rule, consists of three consonants. They are called *Radicals*. We refer to them as R_1, R_2 and R_3.

This triliteral root expresses a certain conceptual content. Thus, e.g. the meaning "to write" is inherent in the root K-T-B (ك – ت –ب), the meaning "to go" in the root DH - H - B (ذ – ه – ب), and the meaning "to drink" in the root SH - R - B (ش – ر – ب).

This conceptual content is specified by short and long vowels between the consonants and by prefixes and suffixes regarding the part of speech (verb, noun, adjective) as well as regarding the grammatical category (tense, mood, number, case, etc.).

One can say by way of simplification that the root consonants (*Radicals*) fulfill a semantic function and the vowels a grammatical function in the Arabic word. Examples:

KaTaBa	(كَتَبَ)	=	he wrote / has written
KāTiB	(كَاتِب)	=	writing; writer, author
KiTāB	(كِتَاب)	=	book
KuTuB	(كُتُب)	=	books
maKTūB	(مَكْتُوب)	=	written; letter
maKTaBa	(مَكْتَبَة)	=	library, bookshop

1.2. The Arab grammarians use patterns, which they represent by ف for R_1 (1ˢᵗ *Radical*), ع for R_2 (2ⁿᵈ *Radical*) and ل for R_3 (3ʳᵈ *Radical*) in order to describe the numerous word forms systematically.

Fā', *°Ain* and *Lām* fulfill the function of variable quantities in the patterns, for which theoretically any consonant can be substituted.

فَعَلَ	*fa°ala*	is the pattern used for the perfect (3ʳᵈ p.sg.m.):	كَتَبَ، ذَهَبَ
فَاعِل	*fā°il*	is the pattern used for the active participle:	كَاتِب
فَعِيل	*fa°īl*	is a typical pattern of the adjective:	كَبِير، صَغِير

فِعَال	fiʿāl	is a typical pattern of the broken plural:	كِبَار
أَفْعَال	afʿāl	is a typical pattern of the broken plural:	أَقْلام

A reliable knowledge of the patterns occurring most frequently is useful for obtaining a good command of the language.

2. The Broken Plural (جَمْع التَّكْسِير)

2.1. The majority of nouns has the broken plural. There are hardly any rules according to which the appropriate plural form can be derived with certainty from the singular form. Therefore, the student has to learn (at least) two word forms for every noun, namely singular and plural form.

✋**A1** Regularities in the forms of the plural only occur in some groups of verbal nouns which have the sound plural. Appropriate hints are given in the respective lessons.

2.2. There are numerous forms of the broken plural. The ones which occur most frequently are the following: فُعُول، أَفْعَال، فِعَال

The following words have the pattern فِعَال :

كبير ج كِبَار، صغير ج صِغَار، قصير ج قِصَار، طويل ج طِوَال، صحيح ج صِحَاح

The following words have the pattern أَفْعَال :

قلم ج أَقْلام، ورق ج أَوْرَاق، لوح ج أَلْوَاح، باب ج أَبْوَاب

The following words have the pattern فُعُول :

بيت ج بُيُوت، سقف ج سُقُوف

✋**A2** Other patterns of the broken plural are the following:

فُعُل، فُعَل، فُعَّال، أَفْعِلَة، أَفْعُل، فَوَاعِلُ، فَعَالِلُ، فَعَالِيلُ، أَفْعِلَاءُ، فُعَلَاءُ، فَعَائِلُ

As regards final Ḍamma, see Lesson 7, Gr 3.

3. Declension and Nunation

3.1. Three cases are characterized in Arabic by means of the three short vowels: -u = nominative (حالة الرَفْع), -i = genitive (الجرّ / الإضافة), -a = accusative (حالة النَصْب). The signs Ḍamma, Kasra and Fatḥa represent themselves in vocalized texts.

n.	the new teacher	أَلْمُعَلِّمُ الجَدِيدُ	al-muʿallimu l-jadīdu
g.	of the new teacher	أَلْمُعَلِّمِ الجَدِيدِ	al-muʿallimi l-jadīdi
a.	the new teacher	أَلْمُعَلِّمَ الجَدِيدَ	al-muʿallima l-jadīda

n.	the new teacher (f.)	أَلْمُعَلِّمَةُ الْجَدِيدَةُ	al-muʿallimatu l-jadīdatu
g.	of the new teacher (f.)	أَلْمُعَلِّمَةِ الْجَدِيدَةِ	al-muʿallimati l-jadīdati
a.	the new teacher (f.)	أَلْمُعَلِّمَةَ الْجَدِيدَةَ	al-muʿallimata l-jadīdata

3.2. An *-n* (*Nūn*) is pronounced after the case endings *-u, -i, -a* as a characteristic of indefiniteness. This process is called *Nunation* (تَنْوِين). Consequently, the endings *-un, -in, -an* are formed. *Nunation* is expressed in vocalized texts by the doubling of the respective sign that represents the vowel:

  ُ or ٌ = *-un*,   ٍ = *-in*,   ً = *-an*

  Indefinite nouns in the accusative case which do not end with ة (*Tāʾ marbūṭa*) terminate in *Alif*, which, however, does not express a sound quality.

n.	a new teacher	مُعَلِّمٌ جَدِيدٌ	muʿallimun jadīdun
g.	of a new teacher	مُعَلِّمٍ جَدِيدٍ	muʿallimin jadīdin
a.	a new teacher	مُعَلِّماً جَدِيداً	muʿalliman jadīdan
n.	a new teacher (f.)	مُعَلِّمَةٌ جَدِيدَةٌ	muʿallimatun jadīdatun
g.	of a new teacher (f.)	مُعَلِّمَةٍ جَدِيدَةٍ	muʿallimatin jadīdatin
a.	a new teacher (f.)	مُعَلِّمَةً جَدِيدَةً	muʿallimatan jadīdatan

✋**A3** Certain Arabic words have only two case endings because of their word structure, some even only one.

✋**A4** A considerable number of words, among them many broken plurals, do not terminate in a nunation, even in case of being indefinite, e.g. قُدَمَاءُ، أَصْدِقَاءُ، شَبَابِيكُ ; cf. about this subject: Lesson 7, Gr 3.

3.3. The declensional endings of the sound plural of masc. words are: ـُونَ *-ūna* = nominative and ـِينَ *-īna* = genitive and accusative, of feminine words: ـَاتٌ *-ātu(n)* = nominative and ـَاتٍ *-āti(n)* = genitive and accusative.

	definite	indefinite	
n.	أَلْمُعَلِّمُونَ	مُعَلِّمُونَ	(al-)muʿallimūna
g.	أَلْمُعَلِّمِينَ	مُعَلِّمِينَ	(al-)muʿallimīna
a.	أَلْمُعَلِّمِينَ	مُعَلِّمِينَ	(al-)muʿallimīna

n.		مُعَلِّمَاتٌ	mu^callimātun
g.		مُعَلِّمَاتٍ	mu^callimātin
a.		مُعَلِّمَاتٍ	mu^callimātin
n.	ألمُعَلِّمَاتُ		(al-)mu^callimātu
g.	ألمُعَلِّمَاتِ		(al-)mu^callimāti
a.	ألمُعَلِّمَاتِ		(al-)mu^callimāti

3.4. The broken plural has the same declensional endings as the singular.

pl.			sg.	
indefinite				
n.	أقْلاَمٌ	aqlāmun	قَلَمٌ	qalamun
g.	أقْلاَمٍ	aqlāmin	قَلَمٍ	qalamin
a.	أقْلاَماً	aqlāman	قَلَماً	qalaman
definite				
n.	ألأقْلاَمُ	al-aqlāmu	ألْقَلَمُ	al-qalamu
g.	ألأقْلاَمِ	al-aqlāmi	ألْقَلَمِ	al-qalami
a.	ألأقْلاَمَ	al-aqlāma	ألْقَلَمَ	al-qalama

3.5. The functions of the cases:
- nominative = case of the subject,
- genitive = case required by prepositions and case of the attributive adjunct,
- accusative = case of the direct object and of adverbs.

3.6. Arabic texts are generally not vocalized, as has already been noted in Lesson 1. Nor are the case endings indicated by signs expressing vowels for the same reason. There is no universally valid rule for the pronunciation of these endings, i.e. whether they are pronounced or not. Whereas they can be fully heard in recitations, they are mostly omitted in colloquial language.

We recommend that the teacher and the student adapt their pronunciation of Arabic to the one used on the radio and to pronounce the case endings (and the other inflections containing a short vowel), except in the last word before a pause and at the end of a contextual unit (sentence, clause) for the period of training. The syntactical connections become clearer by the case endings being pronounced.

هَذَا بَيْتٌ، هَذِهِ غُرْفَةٌ، هَذَا بَيْتٌ كَبِيرٌ، هَذِهِ غُرْفَةٌ جَمِيلَةٌ، هُنَاكَ مُعَلِّمُونَ، هُنَاكَ الْمُعَلِّمُونَ الْجُدُدُ.

4. Stress

4.1. Only the last three syllables of a word can be stressed. If the *Nunation* is pronounced, it is included in the count.

4.2. The last syllable that contains a long vowel is stressed:

ki-*tāb*   ki-*tā*-bun
ja-*dīd*   ja-*dī*-dun
ma-*khā*-zin   ma-*khā*-zi-nu

however, the vocalic final sound of the word is never stressed:

hu-nā
kur-sī *(but:* kur-*sī*-yun*)*

4.3. If the last three syllables do not contain a long vowel, the second to last syllable is stressed if it is a closed syllable (sequence of sounds: consonant - short vowel - consonant):

mu-ᶜ*al*-lim
mu-*tar*-jim,

and the same applies if the word consists of only two syllables:

an-ta
ra-jul

Otherwise the third to last syllable is stressed, regardless of its structure:

mu-ᶜ*al*-li-ma
muj-ta-hi-dun

4.4. The demand accepted in modern Arabic language that the stress may not advance beyond the last syllable but two requires the stress to be shifted if the number of syllables changes, because the nunation is pronounced or suffixes are added.

ṭā-*li*-ba   ṭā-*li*-ba-tun
mu-ᶜ*al*-li-ma   mu-ᶜal-*li*-ma-tun
ku-tu-bun   ku-*tu*-bu-nā *(our books)*
mu-ᶜ*al*-li-mun   mu-ᶜal-*li*-mu-nā *(our teacher)*
ṭā-*li*-ba   ṭā-*li*-ba-tun
                    ṭā-li-*ba*-tu-nā *(our student (f.))*
mu-ᶜ*al*-li-ma   mu-ᶜal-*li*-ma-tun
                    mu-ᶜal-li-*ma*-tu-nā *(our teacher (f.))*

In general, the students do not find it difficult to stress the Arabic words in the correct way. They have sufficient opportunity to impress the stress upon their memories by hearing and reading the texts and by means of the numerous exercises. This is why we refrained from putting stress marks in this textbook.

5. Prepositions (حُرُوف الجرّ)

All prepositions are construed with the genitive.

يُوجَدُ عَلَى الطَّاوِلَةِ كِتَاب. تُوجَدُ فِي الْبَيْتِ غُرَفٌ كَثِيرَة. ذَهَبَ مِنَ الْبَيْتِ إِلَى الْمَحَطَّة.

بِ "with / by means of" and لِ "for" are written together with the following word. Additionally, the *Alif* of the article is omitted after لِ: بِالْقَلَمِ ، لِلرَّجُلِ .

☞A5 As is the case in many other languages, the prepositions frequently serve to express the case governed by the verb in Arabic as well. They form an inseparable unit together with the verb in such cases and need to be learned together with it. Thus, e.g. قامَ means "to get up", قامَ بِ means "to carry out, to undertake" and قامَ عَلَى "to rise against sb. or sth.".

V

German	ألْماني ج ألْمان	you (f.) bought	اِشْتَرَيْتِ
or	أمْ	clever	شاطِر ج شُطّار
that is	أيْ	medicine (as science)	طِبٌّ
(prep.) with, by means of; in	بِ	road, street	طريق ج طُرُق
appr.: Congratulations!	مُبارك !	number	عدَد ج أعْداد
~ (colloq.)	مبْرُوك !	some, a number of	عدَدٌ مِن
answer: God bless you.	الله يُبارك فِيكَ	Arab, Arabic, Arabian	عربي ج عرب
very	جِدًّا	that means	يعْني
leather	جِلْد / جِلْدِي	I understood	فَهِمْتُ
ink	حِبْر	you (m.) understood	فَهِمْتَ
modern, new	حديث ج حِداث	you (f.) understood	فَهِمْتِ
bus-stop	محطّةُ الباصاتِ	dictionary	قامُوس ج قواميسُ
lesson, class hour	درْس ج دُرُوس	about, nearly	تقْريباً
study, courses, classes	دِراسة ج ـات	I wrote	كَتَبْتُ
I went	ذَهَبْتُ	you (m.) wrote	كَتَبْتَ
you (m.) went	ذَهَبْتَ	you (f.) wrote	كَتَبْتِ
you (f.) went	ذَهَبْتِ	writing	كِتابة ج ـات
I saw	رأيْتُ	writer, secretary	كاتِب ج كُتّاب
you (m.) saw	رأيْتَ	written; pl. letters	مكْتُوب ج مكاتِيبُ
you (f.) saw	رأيْتِ	faculty	كلّية ج ـات
convenient	مُريح	eraser	مِمْحاة
novel	رواية ج ـات	left (side)	يسار
ruler	مِسْطرة ج مساطِرُ	to the left	إلى اليسار
tree	شجرة ج أشْجار	right (side)	يمِين
I bought	اِشْتَرَيْتُ	to the right	إلى اليمين
you (m.) bought	اِشْتَرَيْتَ		

☝A6 The *Alif* in اِشْتَرَيْت is a *Hamzat al-waṣl* and is rendered in the vocabulary with اِ . *Hamzat al-waṣl* in the interior of a sentence is to be found in the article (See Lesson 2 Gr 1.3.), in the imperatives (see Lesson 8 Gr 2.) and in the verbs and infinitives of the Forms VII, VIII, IX and X (see Lesson 18 and 22).

Text 1

في السُّوق

ذَهَبْتُ مِنَ الْبَيْتِ إِلَى الْمَدِينَةِ بِالسيَّارَةِ الْجَدِيدَةِ وَرَأَيْتُ فِي الطَّرِيقِ إِلَى الْمَدِينَةِ سيَّارَاتٍ وَبَاصَاتٍ كَثِيرَة. وَفِي الْمَدِينَةِ ذَهَبْتُ إِلَى مَكْتَبَةٍ وَاشْتَرَيْتُ مِنَ الْمَكْتَبَةِ كُتُباً أَيْ قَامُوساً عَرَبِيًّا ـ إِنْكْلِيزِيًّا وَقَامُوساً إِنْكْلِيزِيًّا ـ عَرَبِيًّا وَرِوَايَةً وَوَرَقاً لِلْكِتَابَةِ وَأَقْلَاماً وَحِبْراً وَمِمْحَاةً وَمِسْطَرَةً وَكَرَارِيسَ وَشَنْطَةً جِلْدِيَّةً لِلدِّرَاسَةِ. أَنَا طَالِبٌ فِي كُلِّيَّةِ الطِّبّ. هَذِهِ الْكُلِّيَّةُ هِيَ كُلِّيَّةٌ كَبِيرَةٌ وَحَدِيثَة.

Text 2

أين الطريق إلى ...؟

أحمد: أهلاً وسهلاً. كيف حالك؟

مريم: بخير الحمد لله وأنت؟ كيف حالك؟

أحمد: تمام وكيف العائلة؟

مريم: العائلة بخير.

أحمد: وكيف البيت الجديد؟

مريم: البيت الجديد جميل ومريح جدّاً.

أحمد: مبروك!

مريم: الله يبارك فيك.

أحمد: أين الطريق إلى محطّة الباصات؟

مريم: من هنا إلى هذا البيت الكبير ومن هناك إلى اليمين ومن شارع القاهرة إلى اليسار وعند المحلّ الكبير إلى اليمين وهناك تحت الأشجار الكبيرة محطّة الباصات. هل فهمت؟

أحمد: نعم، فهمت تقريباً. يعني من هنا إلى هذا البيت الكبير ومـن هنـاك إلى اليمـين
ومـن شارع القاهرة إلى اليسار وعند المحـلّ الكبير إلى اليمـين وهنـاك تحـت
الأشجار الكبيرة محطّة الباصات.

مريم: هذا صحيح، أنت فهمت، والله أنت شاطر.

أحمد: شكراً، مع السلامة.

مريم: مع السلامة وإلى اللقاء.

Exercises:

L1 Add an appropriate adjective to the nouns in Text 1 which do not have an attribute.

L2 What is the root of the following nouns?

معلّم، طالب، صديق، خزانة، مصبـاح، شبّاك، جـدار، غرفـة، لـوح، كتـاب، كرّاسـة،
ورق، سيّارة، قطار، مخزن، مدينة

L3 The teacher reads the following nouns. The student repeats them and adds the plural:

طاولـة، معلّمـة، شبّـاك، بـاب، كرّاسـة، كتـاب، رجـل، معلّـم، طـالب، قلـم، كرسـي،
مصباح، مخزن، سيّارة، قطار، فتاة

L4 Add a subject in the plural to the sentence توجد في المدينة... "There are .... in the city." Use all appropriate nouns that you know.

L5 Insert the correct prepositions in the following sentences. Choose the prepositions from the list below.

ب، من، إلى، مع، أمام، على، عند، في
ذهبت ... الصديق ... هناك.
رأيت الأصدقاء .../... المحطّة.
اشتريت الكراريس ... المخزن.
هل ذهبت ... المحطّة ... البيت؟
هل ذهبت ... هناك ... السيّارة أم ... القطار؟
ماذا يوجد ... الطاولة؟
ماذا يوجد .../... الخزانة؟
هل توجد ... البيت سيّارات كثيرة؟

L6 (Homework) Form a sentence with each preposition given in L5. Prepare the sentences in writing for the next lesson.

G1 Replace in Text 2 - where possible - the subject of the sentences by the respective personal pronoun of the 3rd person.

G2 (Written homework) Transform the subject which is given in the singular in the following sentences into the plural. Pay attention to the correct form of the adjective.

☜ هناك بيت جميل.   >   هناك بيوت جميلة.

هناك مدينة جميلة.

في البيت غرفة كبيرة.

الجدار نظيف.

اللوح كبير.

الصديق في الغرفة.

في الغرفة باب.

على الطاولة شنطة.

الدرس جديد.

هناك مخزن جديد.

في المدينة محطّة.

في المحطّة قطار.

هنا فتاة جميلة.

G3 The student reads his homework (G2). The teacher checks the spelling and pronunciation.

G4 Add an appropriate adjective to the subject of the sentences of G3.

☜ توجد في المدينة بيوت.   >   توجد في المدينة بيوت قديمة.

G5 Same as G4 starting with توجد في الغرفة "There are ... in the room."

G6 Add an appropriate adjective to the subject of the sentences of G5.

G7 Same as G4 starting with توجد على الطاولة "There are ... on the table."

G8 Add an appropriate adjective to the subject of the sentences of G7 as an attribute.

G9 Answer the question ماذا رأيت أمام البيت؟ "What did you see in front of the house?" with رأيت أمام البيت + undefined object in the plural. Use the plural of words like

فتاة، معلّم، سيّارة، رجل، طالب.

G10 Add an appropriate adjective to the object of the sentences in G9 as an attribute.

G11 Same as G9. The question is ‏ماذا اشتريت من الدكّان/ المحلّ؟‏ "What did you buy in the shop?"

G12 Expand the sentences formed in G11 with ‏عدداً من‏ ... "some, a number of ", in accusative.

اِشتريت من المخزن عدداً من الأقلام.

G13 Add an appropriate adjective to the object of the sentences formed in G11 and G12.   In the sentences of G12 you have to add an adjective to the noun ‏عدد‏ and to the object in the plural.

اِشتريت من المخزن كرّاسات كثيرة.

اِشتريت من المخزن عدداً كبيراً من الأقلام الجميلة.

G14 (Written Homework) Define the object in the singular or the plural in the following sentences by adding the article.

رأيتُ بيوتاً قديمة.

هل رأيتَ فتاة جميلة؟

هل رأيتَ معلّمين جدداً؟

هلِ اشتريتَ كتباً كثيرة؟

اِشتريتُ أقلاماً جديدة.

اِشتريتُ سيّارة قديمة.

رأيتُ في الطريق بيوتاً كثيرة.

اِشتريتُ قاموساً وورقاً وأقلاماً وحبراً.

رأيتُ في الشنطة الجلدية كتاباً وممحاة ومسطرة.

هلِ اشتريت مشروبات وجبنة ومربّى وعسلاً؟

هل رأيت كمبيوترات كثيرة في الدكّان؟

هل كتبْتَ روايات؟

هل كتبْتَ قاموساً؟

C1 (Homework) Read Text 2 several times until you are able to run a similar conversation without using a written text. The students should work in groups with role-play when preparing the dialogue which will also be asked for in all forthcoming lessons.

C2 (Homework) Write a short essay about shopping and read your paper in the next class hour.

C3 Describe the way from the main station or from your flat to the university. Use the patterns given in Text 2. The teacher checks the pronunciation and the correctness of grammar and vocabulary.

Final Exercise:

1. Replace the *Radicals* in the following words by ف / ع / ل and insert the respective vowels.

درس، بيت، شمس، قمر، ورق، قطار، كتـاب، جهـاز، صبـاح، سلام، حبـر، مصـر، شجرة، كاتب، طالب، طالبة، فاطمة، عائلة، شنطة، غرفة، سيّارة، كبير، صغير، وسـخ، طبيب، صديق، مطبخ، مكتب، لوح، مدينة، شبّاك، دكّان

2. What is the root of the following words?

مكتبة، دراسة، مسطرة، مكتوب، شاطر، طريق، محطّة، كبير، أشجار، كراريس

3. Insert the appropriate preposition.

ذهبت ... المحطّة ...البـاص. توجـد ... الغرفـة كراسـي كثيرة. كتبـت ... الـورق الجديد. الشنطة ... الطاولة. أحمد ... المعلّم. ذهبت ... المكتبـة. رأيت ... البـرّادة مشروبات كثيرة. المحطّة ... الأشجار. ذهبـت ... شـارع القاهرة ... اليسار و ... المحلّ الكبير ... اليمين. إشتريت ... المكتبة كتباً. ذهبت ... البيـت ... المدينـة ... السيّارة. ذهبت ... اليسار ... اليمين و ... هناك ... المحطّة.

4. Translate into Arabic.
I saw a new train. I bought new books and pencils. I saw cheese, butter, bread, marmelade, milk and vegetables in the refrigerator. I bought a dictionary, ink and an eraser. I went to the city. The bus-stop is under the big trees. There are a few small and many big houses in the city. There are planes from Egypt, Yemen, Syria, Tunisia, Iraq, Algeria, Libya and the Emirates in the airport.

5. Translate the following words and groups of words into Arabic and add the proper form of the adjective جديد and include the correct vowels on the endings.
house, in houses, trains, with the teacher, the woman teachers, men, on the papers, chairs, with the drinks, in front of the shops, by car, in the universities, in front of the station, in the libraries, with the female students, the friends, busses, street, in the airplanes, to the tree, in the novel, in the beds, on the apparatuses

6. Write the words you know which have the following pattern structure:

فاعِل، مَفْعَلَة، فِعَال، فعْل، فِعَالة، فِعْل

Arabic Ligatures:

Arabic has developed numerous ligatures. We didn't use these ligatures in the previous lessons in order to avoid additional problems for the students when reading and writing. Starting with Lesson 5 we will use those ligatures provided by computer programs and to be found in printed texts.

Common ligatures:

بم لم لما محمد ممل مجد مختار بحر نخر تجر يحر الهموم أحمد اختي

بم لم لما محمد ممل بجد مختار بحر نخر تجر يحر الهموم أحمد اختي

Lesson 4 Text 1 (without ligatures)   في السوق

ذهبتُ من البيت إلى المدينة بالسيّارة الجديدة ورأيت في الطريق إلى المدينـة سيّارات وباصات كثيرة. وفي المدينة ذهبت إلى مكتبة واشتريت مـن المكتبـة كتبـاً أي قاموساً عربياً ـ ألمانياً وقاموساً ألمانياً ــ عربياً ورواية وورقاً للكتابـة وأقلامـاً وحبراً وممحـاة ومسطرة وكراريسَ وشنطة جلدية للدراسة. أنا طالب في كلّية الطب. هذه الكلّية هـي كلّية كبيرة وحديثة.

Lesson 4 Text 1 (with ligatures)   في السوق

ذهبتُ مـن البيـت إلى المدينـة بالسيّارة الجديـدة ورأيـت في الطريـق إلى المدينـة سيّارات وباصات كثيرة. وفي المدينة ذهبت إلى مكتبة واشتريت من المكتبة كتباً أي قاموساً عربيـاً ـ ألمانياً وقاموساً ألمانياً ـ عربياً وروايـة وورقـاً للكتابة وأقلامـاً وحـبراً وممحـاة ومسطرة وكراريسَ وشنطة جلدية للدراسة. أنا طالب في كلّية الطب. هذه الكلّية هي كلّية كبـيرة وحديثة.

1. The Perfect Tense (أَلْمَاضِي)

1.1. The perfect tense is one of the two simple forms of the verb in Arabic and basically narrative in function. In most cases it denotes a completed event or action.

✍A1 The perfect form can also be used to express actions that (will) take place in the present and future, like e.g. in conditional sentences and optative clauses, in maledictions a.o. This is connected with the fact that the perfect tense is actually neutral as to tense and merely states the verbal action.

The Arabic perfect tense corresponds to both the English past tense and present perfect:

كَتَبَ   He wrote. He has written.

ذَهَبَ   He went. He has gone.

The proper translation will depend on the context.

✍A2 As in the English language, the infinitive of the verb is entered in dictionaries. The Arabic dictionary entry form, however, is the 3rd p. sg. m. of the perfect tense.

In English thus it is: to write, in Arabic: كَتَبَ He wrote./He has written.

The vocabulary in this textbook is given according to the common practice in both languages. Example: كتب "to write" (instead of the exact equivalent "he wrote/ has written").

1.2. The vowel *a* (*Fatḥa*) invariably follows R$_1$ and R$_3$ in the perfect tense.

R$_2$ is mostly followed by *a* (*Fatḥa*): كَتَبَ to write   ذَهَبَ to go   فَعَلَ to do

often by *i* (*Kasra*):   شَرِبَ to drink   سَمِعَ to hear

✍A3 Verbs in which *u* (*Ḍamma*) follows R$_2$ are relatively rare. They are always intransitives, occur only in literary language and are equivalent to groups of verbs consisting of an adjective + auxiliary verb (e. g. حَسُنَ "sth. was [or became] good, nice", كَبُرَ "sth. became big" a. o.).

1.3. Conjugation (تَصْرِيف الأَفْعال)

The order of persons in the conjugational paradigm is 3rd person - 2nd person - 1st person. This complies with Arab tradition and the practice pursued in nearly all Arabic textbooks. The persons are expressed by means of suffixes. In the following paradigm the independent pronoun has been added in parentheses in order to achieve a clear arrangement and to be able to do without information otherwise necessary about person, gender and number.

(هو) فَعَلَ		(هم) فَعَلُوا
(هي) فَعَلَتْ		(هنَّ) فَعَلْنَ
(أنتَ) فَعَلْتَ	perfect tense	(أنتم) فَعَلْتُم
(أنتِ) فَعَلْتِ	(Form I)	(أنتنَّ) فَعَلْتُنَّ
(أنا) فَعَلْتُ		(نحن) فَعَلْنَا

The 3ʳᵈ p. pl. m., i.e. the form فعلوا, is also used to express the impersonal "one". The *Alif* in فعلوا is not pronounced. It is omitted in writing if suffixes are added.

✍A 4 The auxiliary vowel in the form فَعَلْتُم is *u*, in فَعَلْتْ it is *i*; cf. Lesson 2, Gr 1.3.2.

2. The verbal sentence (أَلْجُمْلَة الفِعْلِيَّة)

2.1. The Arabic verbal sentence either consists of only a verb (فِعْل)

He drank / has drunk.	شَرِبَ.
He arrived / has arrived.	وَصَلَ.

(the subject being included in the verb; the independent pronoun may be added for the purpose of emphasis),

or of a **verb + subsequent subject** (ألفاعِل)

The man has drunk.	شَرِبَ الرَّجُلُ.
The friend has arrived.	وَصَلَ الصَّدِيقُ.

or of a **verb (+ subject) + object**

He (the man) has drunk wine.	شَرِبَ (الرَّجُلُ) النَّبِيذَ.
He (the man) has asked about that.	سَأَلَ (الرَّجُلُ) عَنْ ذَلِكَ.

These sentences can be extended by prepositional phrases and subordinate clauses.

2.2. The normal word order in the verbal sentence is verb - subject - object. This word order does not change in the verbal interrogative sentence either. The verb immediately follows the interrogative هَلْ, the interrogative pronoun or interrogative adverb.

شَرِبَ الرَّجُلُ النَّبِيذَ. ⇦ هَلْ شَرِبَ الرَّجُلُ النَّبِيذَ؟

The word order verb - object - subject in the declarative and interrogative sentence is used when the subject is the part of the sentence which is to be emphasized.

Has Muḥammad done that?	هَلْ فَعَلَ ذَلِكَ مُحَمَّدٌ؟
Yes, Muḥammad has done that.	نَعَمْ ، فَعَلَ ذَلِكَ مُحَمَّدٌ.

✎A5 Here the word order depends on the sentence accent. The part of the sentence which is emphasized is usually placed at the end, but it can be placed at the beginning of the sentence as well.

The word order subject - verb - (object) is possible as well in the declarative sentence. The sentence in anteposition is mostly preceded by a conjunction or particle. Here we only mention the conjunction أَنَّ "that" for the moment, which introduces objective clauses (cf. below, Gr 2.4.).

2.3. The following rules of agreement apply to the verbal sentence:

2.3.1. If the verb precedes the subject, there is always agreement in gender, but not in number between them. The sentence is invariably introduced by a singular form of the verb. In this connection, the 3rd p. sg. m. form precedes a masculine singular noun or a plural noun that denotes male persons, the 3rd p. sg. f. form precedes all feminine singular nouns and all other types of plural.

subject: m. sg.		ذَهَبَ الرَّجُلُ إِلَى هُنَاكَ.
pl.		ذَهَبَ الرِّجَالُ إِلَى هُنَاكَ.
f. sg.		ذَهَبَتِ الْفَتَاةُ إِلَى هُنَاكَ.
pl.		ذَهَبَتِ الْفَتَيَاتُ إِلَى هُنَاكَ.
like f. sg.		وَصَلَتِ الرَّسَائِلُ إِلَى هُنَاكَ. *(pl. of non-human beings)*

✎A6 The masculine form is also used with some verbs which are construed impersonally or passively - in spite of occurring together with a feminine subject. Moreover, it can be used if the (feminine) subject does not immediately follow the verb.

2.3.2. If the verb follows the subject, there is agreement in gender as well as in number between them.

subject: m. sg.		سَمِعْتُ أَنَّ الرَّجُلَ ذَهَبَ إِلَى هُنَاكَ.
pl.		سَمِعْتُ أَنَّ الرِّجَالَ ذَهَبُوا إِلَى هُنَاكَ.

f. sg.	سَمِعْتُ أَنَّ الْفَتَاةَ ذَهَبَتْ إِلَى هُنَاكَ.
pl.	سَمِعْتُ أَنَّ الْفَتَيَاتِ ذَهَبْنَ إِلَى هُنَاكَ.
like f. sg.	*(pl. of non-human beings)* سَمِعْتُ أَنَّ الرَّسَائِلَ وَصَلَتْ إِلَى هُنَاكَ.
	(I have heard that ...) (as to the construction with أَنَّ cf. 2.4.)

The student is reminded once more of the following rule: **The plural of words which denote non-human beings is regarded as feminine singular.**

2.4. The objective clause

We have got to know the normal word order of the verbal sentence in the sections 2.1. and 2.2. The object in the shape of a noun can also be replaced by a clause. Such a so-called objective clause is often introduced by the conjunction أَنَّ (حرف الربْط / العطف) "that", after which the noun is in the accusative:

The friend has written that Muhammad has arrived in Berlin.	كَتَبَ الصَّدِيقُ أَنَّ مُحَمَّداً وَصَلَ إِلَى برلين.
I have heard that the delegation arrived yesterday.	سَمِعْتُ أَنَّ الْوَفْدَ وَصَلَ أَمْسِ.

The word order invariably is

subject - verb - (object)

in the objective clause itself which is introduced by أَنَّ . Consequently, a verb **never** occurs immediately after أَنَّ .

		subordinate clause			main clause	
برلين.	إِلَى	وَصَلَ	مُحَمَّداً	أَنَّ	الصَّدِيقُ	كَتَبَ
		verb	subject			
		objective clause			subject	verb
أَمْسِ.		وَصَلَ	الْوفدَ	أَنَّ	ـتُ	سَمِعْـ
		verb	subject			
		objective clause			(subject +)	verb

✍A7 As a matter of course, the function of an objective clause can also be fulfilled by an equational sentence. The normal word order does not change. The subject follows أَنَّ in the accusative, as is the case in the verbal sentence. The predicate remains in the nominative:

"I have heard that Muhammad is ill."   سمعت أَنَّ محمَّداً مريضٌ.

3. The *Nisba* ending (أَلنِّسْبَة)

3.1. The so-called *Nisba* ending is ـيّ *f.* ـيَّة (in transcription -ī, *f.* -iyya, with Nunation -iyyun or -iyyatun); it is added to nouns and various verbal nouns (مَصْـدَر), but rarely to numbers, prepositions and pronouns, and forms (relative) adjectives and nouns.

The *Nisba* ending is the most productive word forming suffix in Arabic, and it is comparable to the English suffixes -al, -en a.o. which form adjectives and to the suffixes -ian, -ese which form nouns. The endings ة and ـيَا are omitted when the *Nisba* is added.

Lebanese; a Lebanese	لُبْنَانُ > لُبْنَانِيّ	Lebanon
political; politician	سِيَاسَة > سِيَاسِيّ	policy
Syrian; a Syrian	سُورِيَا > سُورِيّ	Syria
gold(en)	ذهب > ذهبِيّ	gold

☞**A8** Details about certain changes of sounds which occur when the *Nisba* is added especially to words which terminate in rather rare endings can be seen from a more voluminous grammar (e.g. the "Grammar of the Arabic Language" by W. Wright).

A noun followed by an adjective with the *Nisba* is often equivalent in English to constructions of the type noun + noun:

| school-book, textbook | كِتَاب + مَدْرَسَة > كِتَابٌ مَدْرَسِيٌّ |
| trade relations | عَلاَقَات + تِجَارة > عَلاَقَاتٌ تِجَارِيَّةٌ |

3.2. The rules of agreement given in Lessons 2 and 3 for the equational sentence (subject - adjectival predicate) and for the attributive construction (noun - adjectival attributive adjunct) also apply to the relative adjective.

3.3. Nouns terminating in a *Nisba* ending which denote persons and relative adjectives which are related as an attributive adjunct to nouns denoting persons mostly have the sound plural:

لُبْنَانِيّ / لُبْنَانِيُّون، لُبْنَانِيَّة / لُبْنَانِيَّات، طُلاَّب لُبْنَانِيُّون، طَالِبَات لُبْنَانِيَّات

☞**A9** Some *Nisba* nouns or relative adjectives have a (collective) endingless plural:

عَرَبِيّ / عَرَب Arab (adj.), Arab(s) / طُلاَّب عَرَب Arab students .

They have to be learned as vocabulary items just in the same way as some descriptions of occupations need to be learned which terminate in the plural ending ة , or other *Nisba* nouns which have a broken plural, e.g. صَيْدَلِي pl. صَيَادِلَة "pharmacist", تُرْكِيّ pl. أَتْراك "Turkish; Turk".

V

other (m./ f.)	آخَرُ / أُخْرَى	dance hall	مرْقص ج مراقِصُ
Spain	إسْبانيا	center	مرْكز ج مراكِزُ
to eat	أكل	Russia	رُوسيا
Germany	ألْمانيا	to ask (about)	سأل ه (عن)
yesterday	أمْسِ	I asked him.	سألتُهُ
that (+ accusative)	أنَّ	to travel	سافر
family, relatives	أهْلٍ ج أهالٍ	Regards to (Aḥmad).	سلِّمْ على (أحمد)!
Portugal	البُرْتغال	Give my regards to so...	سلِّمْ لي على
program	بِرْنامج ج برامِجُ	~ (fem.)	سلِّمي لي على
Great Britain	بريطانيا	to hear so., sth.	سمِع ه ، هـ
after that	بعد ذلكَ	politics	سِياسة
Belgium	بلْجيكا	political, politician	سِياسي ج ـون
Poland	بُولَنْدا	Susan	سُوسَن
(prep.) among, between	بَيْنَ	Sweden	السويد
trade	تِجارة / تِجاري	Switzerland	سْوِيسْرا
trader	تاجِر ج تُجَّار	to drink sth.	شرب هـ
Turkish	تُرْكِي ج أتْراك	eastern, oriental	شرْقِي
tired, exhausted, colloq. ill	تَعْبان	firm, enterprise, company	شركة ج ـات
meeting	اِجْتِماع ج ـات	month	شهْر ج شُهُور، أشْهُر
republic	جُمْهُورية ج ـات	thing, matter	شَيْء ج أشْياءُ
talk; also: tradition of the actions and sayings of the prophet and his companions	حديث ج أحادِيثُ	appr.: May you be well tomorrow. (parting word at night)	تصْبِح على خير!
news	خبر ج أخْبار	~ (fem.)	تصْبِحِين على خير
to exit, to leave	خَرَج من	(answer) The same to you.	وأنتَ من أهْلِهِ
Denmark	الدَّنْمارك	pharmacist	صيْدلِيٌّ ج صيادِلة
disco	دِيسْكُو	meal	طعام ج أطْعِمة
that (dem. pr.)	ذلِك	restaurant	مطْعم ج مطاعِمُ
to go (to)	ذهب (إلى)	to know so., sth.	عرف ه ، هـ
letter	رسالة ج رسائِلُ	to hold (conference); to make a contract	عقد هـ
to dance	رقص	relation	علاقة ج ـات

sites	ج معالِمُ	I was	كُنْتُ
to work	عمِل	you (m./f.) were	كُنْتَ / كُنْتِ
work	عمل ج أعْمال	he/she was	كان / كانتْ
(prep.) about, over	عنْ	Lebanon	لُبْنانُ
France	فرنسا	tasty	لذيذ
to do sth.	فعل هـ	Hungary	المجر
idea	فِكْرة ج أفْكار	once again	مرّةً أخْرَى
hotel	فنْدُق ج فنادِقُ	ill, ill person	مريض ج مرْضَى
Finland	فنْلندا	wine	نبيذ
(prep.) before (temp.)	قبْلَ	Norway	النُّرويج
reception	إسْتِقْبال ج ـات	Austria	النمْسا
to read sth.	قرأ هـ	Holland	هُوْلندا
economic	اقْتِصادِي	to arrive (at, in)	وصل (إلى)
I told him.	قُلْتُ لهُ	to put sth.	وضع هـ
you (m./f.) said	قُلْتَ / قُلْتِ	home country	وطن ج أوْطان
he/she said	قال / قالتْ	delegation	وفد ج وُفود
to write sth.	كتب هـ		

Text 1

الاستقبال

وصل أحمد أمس إلى لندن. ذهبت إلى المطار وقلت لـه : أهـلاً وسهلاً في بريطانيا! مـن المطار ذهبنا إلى الفندق وفي الطريق إلى الفندق سألته: كيف حالك وكيف العائلة وكيف محمّد والأصدقاء؟

قال: أنا بخير والعائلة ومحمّد والأصدقاء أيضاً والحمد لله.

وبعد ذلك سألته عـنِ العمـل وقـال: العمـل جيّد الآن. سافرت قبـل شـهر إلى النمسـا وسويسرا وهولندا وفرنسا وعقدتُ هناك اجتماعات مع تجّار من هذه البلدان وسمعت أنّ العلاقات الاقتصادية والتجارية جيّدة بين هذه البلدان والبلدان العربية وكتبت من هنـاك رسائلَ كثيرة إلى شركات في الوطن العربي وإلى الأهل أيضاً.

وبعد الحديث عن العمل ذهبنا إلى المطعم وأكلنا طعاماً شرقياً وقـال أحمـد: الطعـام لذيـذ جدًّا. وبعد الأكل شربنا الشاي.

Text 2   في المدينة

أحمد:	هالو! مساء الخير.

أحمد: هالو! مساء الخير.

مريم: مساء النور. أنت هنا؟

أحمد: نعم ، ذهبت إلى المحطّة. كيف حالك؟

مريم: أنا بخير، الحمد لله وكيف حالك؟

أحمد: شكراً بخير. أين كنتِ أمس؟

مريم: أمس كنتُ في الجامعة وأنت؟ أين كنتَ أمس؟ سمعتُ أنّ سوزن وصلت إلى الفندق. هل هذا صحيح؟

أحمد: نعم ، هذا صحيح. هي الآن في الفندق.

مريم: وماذا فعلتَ أمس؟

أحمد: والله، كُنْتُ أمس مع سوزن في الفندق وفي المساء خرجنا من الفندق وذهبنا إلى مرقص ورقصنا إلى الصباح في ديسكو صغير.

مريم: واليوم؟ ما هو البرنامج ؟ ديسكو مرّة أخرى؟

أحمد: لا، اليوم سألتُ في الفندق عن معالم هذه المدينة والآن أنا في الطريـق إلى المدينـة. هناك أشياء جميلة كثيرة.

مريم: وسوزن؟

أحمد: والله، هي في السرير. هي تعبانة.

مريم: هذه أيضاً فكرة جيّدة. أنا ذهبت إلى مركز المدينة أمس. هـو جميـل وكبيـر جـدّاً وأنا تعبانة إلى اليوم. مع السلامة، وسلّم لي على سوزن.

أحمد: مع السلامة وسلّمي على صالح وتصبحين على خير.

مريم: وأنت من أهله. مع السلامة.

Exercises:

L1 Put the correct form of وصل in front of the nouns.

... المعلم. ... المعلّمون. ... الطلاّب. ... الفتاة.
... الفتيات. ... الوفود. ... الرجال. ... المعلّمات.
... الوفد. ... الصديق. ... الأصدقاء. ... محمّد.

L2 Put the verb in L1 after the nouns. Remember to apply the rules of agreement.

L3 Complete the sentences by adding the verb ذهب.

...الصديق إلى البيت. ... الأصدقاء إلى الفندق. ... الفتيات إلى الأصدقاء. ... الفتاة إلى الصديقة. ... الطالب إلى المعلّم. ... الطلاّب إلى الغرفة. ... السياسيون إلى الاجتماع. ... الرجال إلى المحطّة. ... الطالبات إلى المخزن. ... أحمد إلى المطار.

L4 Put the proper form of وضع in the following sentences without reading the nouns and pronouns in brackets.

(الطالب) ... الكتاب في الخزانة. (المعلّمة) ... القلم على الطاولة. (أنا) ... المصباح على الكرسي. (أنت) ... المصباح على الأرض. (نحن) ... الخزانة في الغرفة. (هي) ... الكتب في الشنطة.

L5 Answer the following questions.

هل ذهبت إلى الصديق؟ هل ذهبت إلى هناك مع الصديقة؟ إلى أين وصل الوفد العراقي؟ إلى أين وصلت الوفود العربية؟ إلى أين ذهب الوفد العراقي؟ إلى أين ذهبت مع الوفد العراقي؟ أين وضعت الكتب؟ هل سمعتم الخبر؟ لمن كتبت الرسالة؟ مع من شربت النبيذ؟ من أين اشتريت المصباح؟ من عقد الاجتماع؟ هل فعلن ذلك؟ أين رأيتم الأصدقاء؟ من عرف ذلك؟ مع من ذهبتم إلى هناك؟ هل قرأت الأخبار؟ من فعل ذلك؟ إلى أين ذهبوا؟ إلى أين سافروا؟ ماذا رأيتم هناك؟ ماذا اشتريت من المخزن؟ ماذا قلت للأصدقاء العرب؟

L6 (Homework) Put the vowel endings in the sentences given in L7.

L7 Ask about the subject, the object or the prepositional phrase of the following sentences by using the the following interrogatives: من، لِمن، مع من، ماذا، أين، إلى أين، مِن أين.

Change the 1st person of the verbs into the 2nd person.

☞   فعل ذلك محمد.   <   من فعل ذلك؟

☞   قرأت الكتب.   <   ماذا قرأت؟

☞   اشتريت ذلك من المخزن.   <من أين اشتريت ذلك؟

كتب الرسالة صديق عربي. كتبت للصديق رسالة. كتبت رسالة للصديق. قرأت كتاباً جديداً. وصل الوفد إلى المطار. اشتريت القلم من المخزن. اشتريت من المخزن قلماً جديداً. ذهب الوفد إلى الفندق. عقدت الوفود العربية اجتماعاً. عقدت الوفود اجتماعات كثيرة. ذهبوا إلى الفندق. وضعت الكتاب على الطاولة. وضعنا الكتب في الخزانة. شربنا النبيذ مع الأصدقاء. سمعت أخباراً جديدة. فعل ذلك صديق. رأينا فتيات جميلات. يوجد المصباح على السقف. توجد الكراسي والطاولة على الأرض. يوجد اللوح على الجدار. وصلت الوفود من البلدان العربية.

L8 Add the *Nisba* to the second noun.

☞   بلدان – عرب   <   بلدان عربية

علاقـات – تجـارة، كتاب – مدرسـة، اِجتمـاع – سياسـة، كتـب – عـرب، علاقـات – سياسـة، طالب – العراق، طلاب – الجزائر، معلمون – لبنان، عرب – أرض، جمهوريـة – عـرب، حروف – شمس، حروف – قمر

G1 The teacher quotes personal pronouns and the students add the proper perfect form of the following verbs:

شرب / قرأ / وصل / ذهب / سمع / كتب / فعل / سأل / عمل / أكل / عقد/ وضع

G2 The verbal sentences given in the 1ˢᵗ person are to be changed into interrogative sentences in the 2ⁿᵈ person.

☞   فعلتُ ذلك   >   هل فعلتَ ذلكَ؟

كتبت الرسالة. كتبت رسائل. كتبت الخبر. سمعت الأخبـار. سمعـت أن الوفد العراقي وصل إلى برلين. عرفت الرجل. عرفت الفتاة. عرفت أن الطالب ذهب إلى هناك. عرفت أن الطلاب ذهبوا إلى البيت. قرأت الخبر. قرأت الأخبار. قـرأت أن الوفـد (السـوري، العراقي، الجزائري، السـعودي، الكويتـي، المصـري) وصـل إلى برلين. قـرأت الرسالة. قرأت الرسائل. وصلت إلى هناك. وصلّت إلى برلين .ذهبت إلى الفندق. ذهبت إلى هنـاك. ذهبت إلى الصديق. ذهبت إلى المعلِّم. رأيت الفتيات. اشتَريت السـيّارة. سافرت بالقطار. شربت الشاي. سألت المعلِّم. أكلت الخبز. شربت القهوة. سألت الأم. عـملت في البيت. عملت في المخزن. عقدت اجتماعاً.

🔊**A11** Since سافر "to travel" - although differing in structure from فعل، كتب، ذهب and the other verbs known   until now - is conjugated in the perfect tense in the same way as the verbs mentioned, we use this verb in the exercises as well as اشتريت، رأيت etc. which you learned as vocabulary items.

G3 Same as G2, but starting with the 1ˢᵗ person plural.

☞   كتبنا الرسالة   >   هل كتبتم الرسالة؟

G4 Same as G3 but starting with the 3ʳᵈ person singular masculine which has to be kept in the interrogative sentence.

☞   كتب الرسالة.   >   هل كتب الرسالة؟

(The sentences with اشتريت رأيت and must be omitted in G 4; 5; 6.)

G5 Same exercise, but starting with the 3ʳᵈ person singular feminine.

G6 Same exercise, but starting with the 3ʳᵈ person plural masculine.

G7 Transform the following sentences into objective clauses introduced by أنَّ.

الغرفة جميلة. البيت قديم. المعلِّم طويل. وصلت الوفـود أمـس. وصـل الوفـد إلى المطـار. عقدت الوفود اجتماعـاً. سـافر الأصدقـاء إلى برلين. العلاقـات التجارية جيّـدة. ذهـب الأصدقاء العرب إلى هناك. وصلت الصديقة إلى المحطّة. وصلت وفود كثيرة.

Start the sentence with one of the following main clauses according to the objective clause you wish to form:

هل عرفتُ؟ قرأنا، هل سمعتم؟ سمعتُ

☞   سمعت أن البيت جميل.   >   البيت جميل.

Do not forget that the word order changes after أنّ in verbal sentences.

C1 What are the names of the capitals of the following countries?

النمسـا، هولنـدا، بريطانيـا، فرنسـا، بولنـدا، روسـيا، المجـر، فنلنـدا، الدنمـارك، الـنرويج، السويد، بلجيكا، إسبانيا، البرتغال

Answer as follows:

عاصمةُ النمسا هي. ...

C2 Write your name and your address in Arabic.

C3 Prepare a dialogue according to Text 2 for the next class hour (greetings, questions about past activities, good-bye).

Final Exercise:

1. Fill in the gaps with the correct form of وصل.

... الصديقة. ... الوفود. ... الرجال. ... أحمد إلى المطعم. ... المعلّمون. ... البرنامج. ... الطالبات إلى المرقص. ... السياسي إلى سويسرا.

2. Fill in the gaps with the correct form of شرب.

سمعت أنّ الرجال ... العصير. كتب أحمد أنّ الطالبات ... الشاي. ... الأصدقاء القهـوة مع السكّر. عرفت أنّ المعلّمـات ... العصير في الفندق. سمعـت أنّ مريـم ... كوكـا في الصباح. سمعت أنّ الطلاّب ... المشروبات. كتب أحمد أنّ محمّداً ... القهوة مع العصير.

3. Transform the second noun into a *Nisba*-adjective to get an attributive construction.

جمهورية – عرب، حروف – شمس، طالب – جزائر، اِجتماع – سياسة، معلّمـون – لبنان، كتب – العراق، أرض – عرب، كتاب – مدرسة، علاقات – سياسة

4. Transform the verbal sentences with the verb in the 1st person singular into interrogative sentences with the verb in the 3rd person plural masculine and translate the answers.

عملت في المخزن. وصلت إلى الفندق. وضعت الكتاب تحت الشنطة. سمعت خبراً جيّداً. سألت عن الطريق. عملت في الشركة الفرنسية. رقصت في المرقص. سألت عـن معـالم المدينة. كتبت رسالة طويلة. أكلت في المطعم طعاماً شرقياً. سمعت أنّ فاطمة تعبانة. وضعت الجبنة على الطاولة.

5. Translate into Arabic.

Good evening. How are you? I am fine. How are you? I am fine, thank you. Where were you yesterday? I was in the university in the faculty of medicine with Aḥmad. What did you do there? I read books and drank tea in the restaurant. What did you do in the evening? In the evening, I was in a disco with Aḥmad. What did Aḥmad do in France? He wrote many letters and held meetings with French companies.

6. Write a list of words in the plural having the pattern structure أَفْعال and فواعِل.

7. Write the following terms in Arabic: equational sentence, verbal sentence, perfect tense, number, singular, plural, masculine and feminine.

1. The Genitive Construction (*Iḍāfa*) (أَلْمُضاف والْمُضاف إِلَيْهِ)

A noun cannot only be defined more closely by an attributive adjective, but also by a subsequent noun in the genitive. The relation of both nouns to each other is that of a governing noun (nomen regens) to an attributive adjunct (nomen rectum) in the function of the 1st term (أَلْمُضاف) and the 2nd term (الْمُضاف إِلَيْهِ) of an *Iḍāfa* (a genitive construction).

1.1. The governing word is in the so-called **construct state**; it does not take the article or nunation.

the house of a man	بَيْتُ رَجُلٍ
the house of the man	بَيْتُ الرَّجُلِ

If the word in the construct state terminates in ة, the *Tā' marbūṭa* changes

into -*tu* in the nominative	شَنْطَةُ الْمُعَلِّمَةِ	*Pronounce: shanṭatu l-muᶜallimati*
into -*ti* in the genitive	شَنْطَةِ الْمُعَلِّمَةِ	*Pronounce: shanṭati l-muᶜallimati*
into -*ta* in the accusative	شَنْطَةَ الْمُعَلِّمَةِ	*Pronounce: shanṭata l-muᶜallimati*

By no means does the genitive construction only characterize possession, as in the example بَيْتُ رَجُلٍ, it also characterizes membership or close association:

the member of an Arab delegation	عُضْوُ وَفْدٍ عَرَبِيٍّ

and a characteristic feature or a quality:

the symbol of a deep friendship	رَمْزُ صَدَاقَةٍ عَمِيقَةٍ

A1 Inquiring about ownership is also expressed in the form of a genitive construction.
"Whose house is this?"   بَيْتُ مَنْ هَذَا؟

As there are almost no compound words in Arabic, the genitive construction, along with other syntagms, is also used to create word combinations with a stable lexical content, which are roughly comparable to compounds in English.

the students' hostel	بَيْتُ الطَّلَبَةِ

In this connection, the translation of the indefinite بَيْتُ طَلَبَةٍ is not "the house of students", but "a students' hostel".

A2 Word combinations like "a house of the man", "a member of the Arab delegation" etc. are expressed by means of prepositions.
Particularly the preposition مِنْ (sometimes لِ) is suitable for this purpose:

a house of the man	بَيْتٌ مِنْ بُيُوتِ الرَّجُلِ
lit.: a house out of the houses of the man	
a member of the Arab delegation	عُضْوٌ مِنْ أَعْضَاءِ الْوَفْدِ الْعَرَبِيِّ
lit.: a member out of the members of the Arab delegation	

1.2. All terms except the last in a genitive construction consisting of several terms (genitive chain) are in the construct state.

the appropriateness of the policy of the government of the country	صِحَّةُ سِيَاسَةِ حُكُومَةِ الْبَلَدِ

1.2.1. Not more than one noun should constitute the 1st term of a genitive construction - in good style. Whereas we say in English e.g. "the head and the members of the delegation", i.e. two nouns followed by a genitive, we only take one noun as governing noun in Arabic, put the other one behind the genitive construction and relate it with the 2nd term of the latter by the appropriate affixed pronoun (cf. below, Gr 2.):

lit.: the head of the delegation and its members	رَئِيسُ الْوَفْدِ وَأَعْضَاؤُهُ

1.2.2. The following rules regarding definiteness apply to the genitive construction:

a) If the 2nd term of the *Iḍāfa* is definite, the 1st term, which is in the construct state, is also regarded as definite. Consequently, an adjectival attributive adjunct ascribed to the 1st term has to be construed with the article.

However, as the terms of the genitive construction must not be separated (with one exception - cf. lesson 7, Gr 2.5.), the attributive adjunct must either follow the whole genitive construction:

the beautiful house of the man	بَيْتُ الرَّجُلِ الْجَمِيلُ

or else it follows the 1st term, so that a possible confusion with "the house of the handsome man" can be avoided, and the 2nd term of the genitive construction which has been dissolved by now is added by means of لِ:

$$\text{أَلْبَيْتُ الْجَمِيلُ لِلرَّجُلِ}$$

This type of construction is rather frequent in modern Arabic.

b) If the 2nd term of the *Iḍāfa* is indefinite, the 1st term in the construct state is regarded as indefinite:

a students' hostel	بَيْتُ طَلَبَةٍ

An adjectival attributive adjunct ascribed to the 1ˢᵗ term of *Idafa*, i.e. to بيت, follows indefinite:

a new students' hostel	بَيْتُ طَلَبَةٍ جَدِيدٌ

The sound masculine plural drops the نِ if it functions as the 1ˢᵗ term of *Idafa*.

the teachers of the student	مُعَلِّمُو الطَّالِبِ
with the teachers of the student	مَعَ مُعَلِّمِي الطَّالِبِ

2. Affixed Pronouns (أَلضَّمَائِرُ المُتَّصِلَة)

There are affixed pronouns in addition to the so-called independent pronouns in Arabic.

2.1. They are:

pl.		sg.
هُمْ -	3ʳᵈ p. m.	ـهُ -
هُنَّ -	3ʳᵈ p. f.	ـهَا -
ـكُمْ	2ⁿᵈ p. m.	ـكَ
ـكُنَّ	2ⁿᵈ p. f.	ـكِ
نَا -	1ˢᵗ p.	ـي —
		(at the end of the verb نِي)

👉A3 The auxiliary vowel after هُمْ and كُمْ is -*u*.

2.2. The affixed pronouns can be added to
• nouns,
• prepositions,
• various particles and conjunctions (a. o. أَنَّ "that") and
• verbs.

2.2.1. When combined with nouns, the affixed pronouns are equivalent to the possessive pronouns in English.

The noun is to the affixed pronoun what the 1ˢᵗ term of a definite genitive construction is to its 2ⁿᵈ term. The noun is the governing word and is in the construct state, i.e. it does not take an article or the nunation.

pl.		sg.	
their (m.) house	بَيْتُهُمْ	his house	بَيْتُهُ
their (f.) house	بَيْتُهُنَّ	her house	بَيْتُهَا
your (m.) house	بَيْتُكُمْ	your (m.) house	بَيْتُكَ

your (f.) house	بَيْتُكُنَّ	your (f.) house	بَيْتُكِ
our house	بَيْتُنَا	my house	بَيْتِي

An adjective added as an attributive adjunct must take the article:

your new house	بَيْتُكُمُ الْجَدِيدُ

2.2.1.1. Peculiarities of pronunciation and spelling:

The affixed pronoun of the 1st p. sg. assimilates every short vowel that immediately precedes it.

my book	كِتَابِي
in my book	فِي كِتَابِي
Have you seen my book?	هَلْ رَأَيْتَ كِتَابِي؟

If the vowel -i or -ī (also -ay), usually found as an ending of the genitive case, precedes the affixed pronoun, the -u of the suffixes of the 3rd person changes into -i:

هِنَّ > هُنَّ   هِمْ > هُمْ   هِ > هُ

in his house	فِي بَيْتِهِ
in their (pl. m.) house	فِي بَيْتِهِمْ
in their (pl. f.) house	فِي بَيْتِهِنَّ

The -u or -i following the suffix ه has to be pronounced as a long vowel: *baytuhū / fī baytihī*. The final ة changes into ت if affixed pronouns are added.

a woman teacher	مُعَلِّمَةٌ
my (woman) teacher	مُعَلِّمَتِي
your (woman) teacher etc.	مُعَلِّمَتُكَ

The sound masculine plural does not only drop the ن when it functions as the 1st term of an *Iḍāfa*, but also if affixed pronouns are added.

your teachers	مُعَلِّمُوكَ
at / with their teachers	عِنْدَ مُعَلِّمِيهِمْ
I have seen your teachers.	رَأَيْتُ مُعَلِّمِيكُمْ

The affixed pronoun of the 1st p. sg. changes into ي after the long vowels *ā*, *ī* and *ay*.

with my teachers	(مُعَلِّمِي] نَ [+ يَ) مَعَ مُعَلِّمِيَّ

☞A4 Remember: "My teachers" is مُعَلِّمِيَّ, and not مُعَلِّمُوِيَ.

☞A5 أَب "father" and أَخ "brother" have special forms when followed by another noun in an *Iḍāfa* or by a pronoun suffix: nominative: his father / his brother = أَبُوهُ / أَخُوهُ, genitive: his father / his brother = أَبِيهِ / أَخِيهِ and accusative: his father / his brother = أَبَاهُ / أَخَاهُ.

2.2.2. When combined with prepositions, the affixed pronouns are equivalent to the objective of the personal pronouns in English with the personal pronoun functioning as a prepositional complement.

with him ; of / from among them ; with us	مَعَهُ ، مِنْهُمْ ، عِنْدَنَا

The English word "to have" is rendered by means of the prepositions مَعَ، لِ، عِنْدَ + affixed pronoun. The preposition عند "at /with" is the one most frequently used:

Do you have many books?	هَلْ عِنْدَكَ كُتُبٌ كَثِيرَةٌ؟

☞A6 The preposition لَدَى is sometimes used in the same sense as عِنْدَ. It is an upgraded or more formal version of عِنْدَ.

The preposition لِ "for", which mainly serves to emphasize ownership, and the preposition مَعَ "with", which is used to express that somebody has something with him at the moment, are employed for this purpose as well.

2.2.2.1. Peculiarities of pronunciation and spelling:
لِ takes on the form لَ , when it precedes suffixes: لَكَ ، لَهَا ، لَهُ etc., except for the suffix of the 1st p. sg.: لِي .
The ن in مِنْ is doubled if the suffix of the 1st p. sg. is added: مِنِّي .
إِلَى and عَلَى take on the forms -إِلَيْ and -عَلَيْ , when construed with suffixes:

pl.		sg.	
عَلَيْهِمْ	إِلَيْهِمْ	عَلَيْهِ	إِلَيْهِ
عَلَيْهِنَّ	إِلَيْهِنَّ	عَلَيْهَا	إِلَيْهَا
عَلَيْكُمْ	إِلَيْكُمْ	عَلَيْكَ	إِلَيْكَ
عَلَيْكُنَّ	إِلَيْكُنَّ	عَلَيْكِ	إِلَيْكِ
عَلَيْنَا	إِلَيْنَا	عَلَيَّ	إِلَيَّ

This rule applies to the preposition لَدَى as well.

2.2.3. If added to a verb, the affixed pronouns fulfill the function of a direct object.

I have bought the book.	.اِشْتَرَيْتُ الكِتَابَ
I have bought it.	.اِشْتَرَيْتُهُ
You have written the letters.	.كَتَبْتُمُ الرَّسَائِلَ
You have written them. (الرسائل is regarded as f. sg., this is why the verb is construed with ها)	.كَتَبْتُمُوهَا
Take the pencil.	.خُذِ الْقَلَمَ
Take it.	.خُذْهُ
Have they drunk the juice?	هَلْ شَرِبُوا العَصِيرَ؟
Yes, they have drunk it.	.نَعَمْ شَرِبُوهُ
Did you attend the event? = Were you present at the event?	هَلْ حَضَرْتَ الْحَفْلَةَ؟
Yes, I attended it (= yes, I was there).	.نَعَمْ حَضَرْتُهَا

2.2.3.1. Peculiarities of pronunciation and spelling:

The 3rd p. pl. m. of the perfect form drops the *Alif* if an affixed pronoun is added: شَرِبُوهُ . *Wāw* is inserted in front of the affixed pronoun in the 2nd p. pl. m.: كَتَبْتُمُوهَا.

3. Definiteness (Summary)

A noun is definite if it is construed with

• **the article:**	أَلْبَيْتُ
• **a subsequent genitive:**	بَيْتُ الرَّجُلِ
• **an affixed pronoun:**	بَيْتُهُ

4. The adverb (أَلظَّرْف)

There is no specific form for the adverb in Arabic. Adverbial relations are expressed by the accusative or by prepositional phrases. The adverbial of time (ظَرْف الزمان), takes on the accusative case.

in the morning	صَبَاحاً	⇐ morning	صَبَاح
(at) noon, midday	ظُهْراً	⇐ midday	ظُهْر
in the evening	مَسَاءً	⇐ evening	مَسَاء
in the morning of this day = this morning	صَبَاحَ الْيَوْمِ		
in the evening of this day = this evening	مَسَاءَ الْيَوْمِ		

A prepositional phrase construed with فِي can take the place of the accusative in some cases: صَبَاحاً = فِي الصَّبَاحِ. In general, however, the adverbs are lexicalized. The student cannot form them on his own, but has to learn them as vocabulary items. Lesson 22 addresses adverbial constructions more extensively.

V

professor, master	أُسْتاذ ج أَساتِذة	*fig.*: May I help you?	أية خدمة؟
thousand	أَلْف ج آلاف	to go out	خرج (يَخْرُجُ) من
America	أمْريكا	sincere	خالِص / مُخلِص
first (m./f.)	أوَّل م أُولَى	diplomatic, diplomat	دِبْلوماسِيّ ج ـون
which (m./f.)	أيٌّ م أيَّة	class, step, level	درجة ج ـات
How much is ... ?	بكمِ (الـ...)؟	teacher, lecturer	مُدرِّس ج ـون
give so. so.'s regards	بلِّغ هـ ل (imp.)	dollar	دُولار ج ات
second (m./f.)	ثـان م ثانية	ticket, card	تذْكِرة ج تذاكِرُ
the second (m./f.)	الثانِي م الثانية	president, leader, chairman, manager	رئيس ج رُؤَساءُ
foreigner, foreign	أجْنبِي ج أجانِبُ		
answer, reply	جواب ج أجْوِبة	escort, companion, attendant	مُرافِق ج ـون
to attend sth.	حضر هـ	symbol, sign	رمْز ج رُمُوز
You (elaborated style of address)	حَضْرة / حضْرتُكَ / حضْرتُكُمْ	I want ... (sth.)	أُريدُ ... (هـ)
lecturer, reader, professor	مُحاضِر ج ـون	wonderful, excellent, marvelous	رائِع
celebration, party, fête	حفْلة ج ـات	week	أسْبُوع ج أسابيعُ
government	حُكُومة ج ـات	theatre, stage	مسْرح ج مسارِحُ
greeting	تحِيَّة ج ـات	(stage) play	مسْرحِية ج ـات
appr.: Best greetings ... (standard opening of a letter)	تحِيَّة طيبة وبعد ...	price	سِعْر ج أسْعار
service	خِدْمة ج ـات	journey, trip	سفر ج أسْفار
		to be on a journey, traveling,	مُسافِر ج ـون

traveler		office; desk	مَكْتَب ج مَكاتِبُ
touristic	سِياحِيّ	travel agency	مَكْتَب السفر
niveau, level	مُسْتَوًى ج ات	chemistry	كِيمياء
to thank so. for	شكر هـ على	(prep.) at (loc. a. temp.)	لدىَ
to see; to look at	شاهد هـ	language	لُغة ج ـات
difficult	صعْب ج صِعاب	enjoyable, excellent	مُمْتِع
midday, noon	ظُهْر	subject	مادَّة ج موادُّ
dear, beloved	عزيز ج أعِزّاءُ	yesterday evening	مساءَ الأمْس
my dear	عزيزي	king, monarch	مَلِك ج مُلُوك
my dear (f.)	عزيزتي	waiting for	اِنْتِظار
member	عُضْو ج أعْضاء	like this, this way, thus	هكذا
world, universe	عالَم ج عوالِمُ	there is / are	هُناك
international	عالَمِيّ	civil/public servant, officer,	مُوظَّف ج ـون
deep	عميق	employee, pl. staff	
title; also: address	عُنْوان ج عناوينُ	time, period of time	وقْت ج أوْقات
physics	فِيزياء		
strong, mighty, powerful	قَوِيّ ج أقْوِياءُ		

Text 1

رسالة إلى محمّد

عزيزي محمّد

تحية طيّبة وبعد...

كيف حالك؟ وصلتني رسالتك قبل أسبوع وقرأت فيها أنّك ذهبت إلى المسرح. أنا ذهبت مساء الأمس أيضاً إلى المسرح هنا في لندن. المسرح في مركز المدينة. شاهدت مسرحية لشيكسبير ، عنوانها ((الملك لير)). هذه المسرحية طويلة جدّاً ومتعة. رأيت في المسرح الكثير من الأجانب وبينهم سياسيون ودبلوماسيون وعرفت كثيرين منهم. وحضرت بعد المسرحية حفلة جميلة ورائعة مع أصدقائي في بيت الطلبة.

كيف فاطمة ومريم وأحمد؟ وكيف الدراسة؟ هل فهمت الدروس في الطبّ؟ دراستي إلى الآن جيّدة والمدرِّسون والمحاضرون والأساتذة على مستوى جيّد جدّاً وحضرت إلى الآن دروساً كثيرة في الطبّ والكيمياء والفيزياء وهي موادّ صعبة. كيف الدروس عندكم في الجامعة؟ هل المستوى جيّد؟

أنا في انتظار جوابك. بلّغ تحياتي لفاطمة وأحمد ومريم وسلّم لي كثيراً عليهم.

صديقك المخلص

بيتر

في مكتب السفر

Text 2

الموظّفة: أهلاً وسهلاً، أية خدمة؟

بيتر: نعم، أنا أريد تذكرة الى أمريكا.

الموظّفة: متى؟

بيتر: اليوم.

الموظّفة: في أي وقت؟

بيتر: الآن أو في المساء.

الموظّفة: إلى أية مدينة؟

بيتر: إلى وشنطن.

الموظّفة: درجة أولى أو ثانية أي سياحية؟

بيتر: درجة أولى.

الموظّفة: هناك طائرة في المساء.

بيتر: جيّد جدّاً. بكم التذكرة؟

الموظّفة: بألف دولار.

بيتر: هذا كثير جدّاً.

الموظّفة: نعم، الأسعار هكذا. حضرتك من أين؟

بيتر: أنا أمريكي.

الموظّفة: لغتك العربية جيّدة جدّاً، أين درستها؟

بيتر: درستها في الجامعة في أمريكا.

الموظّفة: هل سافرت إلى بلدان عربية أخرى؟

بيتر: نعم سافرت إلى تونس والجزائر والمغرب والكويت والسعودية وسوريا.

الموظّفة: يعني، أنت مسافر إلى بلدان كثيرة؟

بيتر: نعم، هذا صحيح، أنا موظّف في شركة عالمية.

الموظّفة: شكراً، مع السلامة.

بيتر: مع السلامة.

Exercises:

L1 Every student answers the question ‏ما اسْمُكَ / اسْمُكِ؟‏ as well as the the
following questions: ‏ما اسْمُها / ما اسْمُهُ / ما اسم هذا / هذه؟‏

L2 A student forms interrogative sentences with the following words

‏بيت، غرفة، شنطة، رسالة، كتاب، كتب، قلم، كرّاسة، كراريس، سيّارة‏

according to the structure ‏بيــت مـن هـذا؟‏ "Whose house is it?" Another student
answers as follows:

‏هذا بيتي /   هذا بيت المعلّم /   هذا بيت صديقي‏

a.o. The predicate should be an *Iḍāfa* or a noun defined by a suffix.

L3 A student asks questions as follows:

‏هل هذا بيتك؟ هل هذه غرفتك؟‏

Another student answers with "Yes":

‏نعم، هذا بيتي. نعم، هذه غرفتي.‏

or with "No":

‏لا، هذا بيت صديقي. لا، هذه غرفة صديقتي.‏

Take the words for the questions from the glossary of this lesson.

L4 Add the adjective ‏جديد‏ (‏جُدُد، جديدة‏) to the following nouns defined by a
suffix as an attribute.

‏☞   بيتي   <   بيتي الجديد‏

‏غرفتك، معلّمكم، أصدقاؤنا، كتبنا، سيّارته، بسيّارته، في فندقنا، أمام مسرحنا، صديقتي،‏

‏مرافقكم، في مطارهم، سياستهم، مدرستك، جامعتها، مخزنه‏

L5 Answer the questions with one of the following adverbs denoting a certain
time.

‏اليوم، أمس، في الصباح، في المساء‏
‏صباحاً، ظهراً، مساءً‏
‏صباح اليوم، صباح الأمس‏
‏ظهر اليوم، ظهر الأمس‏
‏مساء اليوم، مساء الأمس‏

‏متى سافر صديقكم إلى لندن (دمشق، بيروت، بغداد، الجزائر)؟‏

‏متى ذهبت إلى الجامعة (المسرح، المحطة، بيتك، بيته، هناك)؟‏

متى عقد الوفد اجتماعه؟

متى شربت الشاي مع أصدقائك (مع أصدقائك العرب، مع أصدقائك الأجانب)؟

متى كتبتم رسالتكم؟

متى اشتريت الكتب (الكتاب، الشنطة، الكراريس، السيّارة)؟

متى رأيت الأصدقاء (الوفد، أعضاء الوفد، مرافقكم)؟

متى حضرتم الحفلة؟

متى سمعت الخبر؟

متى عرفت ذلك؟

متى فعلوا ذلك؟

متى سافروا إلى سوريا (العراق، مصر، تونس، ...)؟

L6 What is the root of the following words?

مكتب / مسرح / مدرسة / مركز / مرقص / مكتبة / مطعم / محطّة / مطبـخ / مطـار / مخزن / مُعلّم / مُوظّف / مُدرّس / مُحاضِر / مُرافِق / مِصباح / مِمْحاة / مِسْطرة / طالِب / تاجِر / كاتِب

G1 Form genitive constructions with the following words.

1st term	2nd term (defined)
باب، أبواب، جدار، جدران، شبابيك، غرف	1. بيت
أبواب، جدار، جدران، شبابيك، سقف، أرض	2. غرفة
كتاب، كتب، غرفة، بيت، سيّارة، شنطة	3. صديق
كتب، بيت، غرفة، سيّارة، شنطة، قلم	4. محمّد
أقلام، بيوت، سيّارة، رسائل، كتب	5. صديقة
مسرح، مسارح، جامعة، شوارع، مخازن، محطّة	6. مدينة
مدارس، محطّات، معالم، جامعات، مخازن	7. عاصمة
عضو، أعضاء، مرافق، مرافقون، رئيس، سيّارة	8. وفد

G2 Form genitive constructions with the words given in G1 1.-7. in which the 2nd term is not defined by the article but by an affixed pronoun.

☞   شبابيك غرفتي، مسرح مدينتنا

G3 Transform the genitive constructions of G2, 1. and 2. into the accusative by forming a verbal sentence starting with رأيتُ.

☞   رأيت باب البيت، رأيت أبواب الغرفة.

G4 Replace the noun after the prepositions ل، على، إلى by the respective affixed pronoun.

ذهب إليه.	<	☞ ذهب إلى الصديق.
وصل الوفد إلى المطار.		سافر إلى العاصمة.
قلت للأصدقاء: مع السلامة.		توجد الكتب على الطاولة.
ذهبوا إلى أصدقائهم.		كتب للصديق رسالة.
يوجد اللوح على الجدار.		كتبت للصديقة رسالة.
ذهبنا إلى المسرح.		قلت للمعلّم: صباح الخير.
سلّم على الأصدقاء!		وصلت القطارات إلى المحطّة.

G5 Convert the following collocations into the genitive by preceding them with the preposition في or مع.

في بيته الجديد   >   ☞ بيته الجديد

مسرحنا الجميل، جامعتنا القديمة، سيّارته الجديدة، صديقتي الجديدة، أصدقاؤك العرب، وفدهم التجاري، حكومتنا القديمة، صديقاتهن السوريات، جامعاتكم الجديدة، مطارنا الكبير، كرّاسته الصغيرة، مرافقهم الألماني، وفودنا الأجنبية، اجتماعاتكم الطويلة

C1 (Written homework) Write a letter to an Arab friend based on Text 1 in which you inform him about the reception of mutual friend in your city.

C2 Prepare a conversation based on Text 2 about the topic "Travel Agency" (greeting, destination: country, city, time).

Final Exercise:

1. Transform the following words into genitive constructions.

	1st term	2nd term
أعضاء، مرافق، رئيس، سيّارة، إجتماع، سياسيون، غرف		الوفد
مسارح، شوارع، جامعة، دكاكين، مدارس، فندق، محطّات		مدينة
شنطات، كتب، إجتماعات، رسائل، معلّمون، مرقص، مطعم		المعلّمون
موظّفون، مرضى، عمل، وفود، سياسيون، أطبّاء، مكاتب		الحكومة
غرف، جدران، أبواب، شبابيك، حديقة، بلكون		بيته

2. Translate into Arabic.

the old address of my girlfriend, the old office of the new president, one of the offices of the civil/public servant, one of the kings of the Arab World, one of the beautiful houses of the city, the leader and the members of the Arab delegation, the teacher's new bag/ the new bag of the teacher, one of the new theatres of the capital, the numerous sights of Syria, the staff and the managers of the travel agencies, the numerous enterprises of the royal family, a member of the delegation, the offices of the employees of the travel agency, the car of an Arab student, the theatre and the houses of the city, the lecturers and the students of the university of the capital, the sincere greetings of the friend, the new plays of the theatre of the city

3. Replace the prepositional object of the following sentences by the respective affixed pronoun.

ذهبوا إلى المحطّة. كتبوا أسماءهم على الكراريس. رأيته على الخزانة. وضعت الأوراق على

الطاولات. سافرنا إلى الأصدقاء. سلّم على فاطمة ومريم وصباح ! وصلوا إلى العاصمـة.

كتبنا حروفاً عربية على اللوح. شكرتهم على التذاكر. وصلنا إلى مطعم المحاضرين.

4. Translate the following letter into Arabic.

Dear Mary

How are you? How is Fāṭima?

I have a lot of work to do. The courses are difficult and I attended a lot of lectures. Up until now, I have attended lectures in medicine, physics and chemistry. The lecturers and the professors of the university are at a good level. What about the courses in your university?

Did you travel to Muḥammad? I wrote him a letter. His reply arrived yesterday. He wrote that he went to the theatre in Cairo and that he saw the Egyptian president and a lot of politicians and diplomats there.

I am waiting for your reply. Give my regards to Fāṭima.

Your friend

Peter

1. The Imperfect Tense (أَلْمُضَارِع)

1.1. The imperfect tense is the second of the two simple verb forms in Arabic in addition to the perfect tense (Lesson 5). It almost always indicates an action or state taking place in the present (أَلْحَاضِر) or future tense (أَلْمُسْتَقْبَل) and may express a habitual, progressive, future or stative meaning.

☞**A1** The imperfect tense can sometimes be employed to express actions having taken place in the past, as is the case in some subordinate clauses. This is connected with the fact that the imperfect tense is actually neutral as to tense and merely describes the verbal action in its course.

1.2. It is characteristic of the imperfect tense that R_1 is vowelless and that R_2 is followed by a so-called **imperfect stem vowel**, which can be a (*Fatḥa*) as well as i (*Kasra*) or u (*Ḍamma*). The vowel u or a suffix follows R_3. The persons are expressed by prefixes.

1.3. The conjugation: imperfect/indicative

pl.	sg.
(هم) يَفْعَلُونَ	(هو) يَفْعَلُ
(هنَّ) يَفْعَلْنَ	(هي) تَفْعَلُ
(أنتم) تَفْعَلُونَ	(أنتَ) تَفْعَلُ
(أنتنَّ) تَفْعَلْنَ	(أنتِ) تَفْعَلِينَ
(نحن) نَفْعَلُ	(أنا) أَفْعَلُ

The imperfect stem vowel in the verbs treated up to now

فَعَلَ	to do		يَفْعَلُ
ذَهَبَ	to go		يَذْهَبُ
سَأَلَ	to ask	is a,	يَسْأَلُ
قَرَأَ	to read	therefore	يَقْرَأُ
			(2nd p. sg. f.) تَقْرَئِينَ
			(3rd/2nd p. pl. m.) يَقْرَؤُونَ / تَقْرَؤُونَ

likewise in

شَرِبَ	to drink	يَشْرَبُ
سَمِعَ	to hear	يَسْمَعُ

It is *u* in

كَتَبَ	to write	يَكْتُبُ

and *i* in

عَرَفَ	to know	يَعْرِفُ
عَقَدَ	to hold	يَعْقِدُ

✍**A2** Verbs with و as R₁ drop this و in the imperfect tense:
يَضَعُ > وَضَعَ، يَصِلُ > وَصَلَ . Cf. Lesson 11 regarding this subject.

✍**A3** The imperfect tense of all verbs will be placed in brackets after the perfect tense in the vocabulary list of each lesson. It is strongly recommended to the student to learn both forms, as there are no rules according to which the imperfect stem vowel could be derived. Verbs in which R₂ is followed by *i* in the perfect tense have the imperfect stem vowel *a* with very few exceptions.

1.4. The particle سَوْفَ or its abridged form سَـ (as a prefix) can be placed in front of the imperfect tense, so that its future aspect is emphasized:

He will definitely write to you. / He is sure to write to you.	سَوْفَ يَكْتُبُ لَكَ ، سَيَكْتُبُ لكَ.

1.5. The particle قَدْ + **imperfect tense** meaning "**perhaps**" also denotes a future action or event as a possibility:

Perhaps, he will write.	قَدْ يَكْتُبُ.

2. Demonstrative Pronouns (أَسْمَاءُ الإِشَارَة)

2.1. The demonstrative pronoun that indicates what is near with respect to place or time is:

	pl.	sg.
this, these	هؤُلاءِ	هَذَا m. هَذِهِ f.

The demonstrative pronoun that indicates what is farther or more distant with respect to place or time is:

	pl.	sg.
that, those	أُولَئِكَ	m. ذَلِكَ f. تِلْكَ

☞A4 The first syllable in هَذا، هَذِه، هؤُلاء and ذلك , the second in أُولَئك , contains the long vowel *ā*, which is not expressed by *Alif*, as is otherwise usual. However, the initial *u* in أُولَئك is short.

2.2. The demonstrative pronoun is placed in front of the noun which is defined by the article:

this man	هَذَا الرَّجُلُ
that man	ذَلِكَ الرَّجُلُ
this girl	هَذِهِ الْفَتَاةُ
that girl	تِلْكَ الْفَتَاةُ
these men	هَؤُلاءِ الرِّجَالُ
those men	أُولَئِكَ الرِّجَالُ
these girls	هَؤُلاءِ الْفَتَيَاتُ
those girls	أُولَئِكَ الفَتَيَاتُ

☞A5 Note that the fem. sing. form of the demonstrative pronoun precedes the plural forms of words which denote non-human beings: تلك البيوت، هذه الغرف .

2.3. The demonstrative pronoun follows the noun which is defined by an affixed pronoun:

this friend of mine	صَدِيقِي هَذَا
these books of his	كُتُبُهُ هَذِهِ
these friends of ours	أَصْدِقَاؤُنَا هَؤُلاءِ

2.4. If the demonstrative pronoun refers to the 1st term of an *Iḍāfa*, it follows the genitive construction as well:

this book of the teacher	كِتَابُ الْمُعَلِّمِ هَذَا
those friends of my teacher	أَصْدِقَاءُ مُعَلِّمِي أُولَئِكَ

2.5. If it refers to the 2nd term of the *Iḍāfa*, it precedes it, i.e. its position is between the 1st and the 2nd term:

the book of this student	كِتَابُ هَذَا الطَّالِبِ
the friend of that girl	صَدِيقُ تِلْكَ الْفَتَاةِ

✍A6 However, it follows the 2nd term of the genitive construction if the latter is a noun which is defined by an affixed pronoun:

the book of this friend of mine	كِتَابُ صَدِيقِي هَذَا

It is consequently possible that a construction of this kind may be ambiguous, as the demonstrative pronoun may refer to the 1st term (this book of my friend) as well as to the 2nd term of the *Iḍāfa* (if both terms of the latter have the same gender). (Cf. above 2.3.)

2.6. The demonstrative pronouns do not only fulfill a deictic function, as described in 2.2. - 2.5., but they are also used as nouns. They can fulfill the function of the subject in an equational sentence, and of the subject or the object in a verbal sentence:

This is a teacher.	هَذَا مُعَلِّمٌ.
These have drunk the wine.	شَرِبَ هَؤُلاءِ النَّبِيذَ.
That (is what) Muḥammad has done.	فَعَلَ ذَلِكَ مُحَمَّدٌ.

Agreement in gender and number between subject and predicate has to be observed here in the equational sentence; if the predicate is defined by the article, one should insert the independent pronoun as well (cf. Lesson 2, A7):

feminine predicate	masculine predicate
هَذِهِ مُعَلِّمَةٌ.	هَذَا مُعَلِّمٌ.
هَذِهِ كَبِيرَةٌ.	هَذَا كَبِيرٌ.
هَذِهِ هِيَ الْمُعَلِّمَةُ.	هَذَا هُوَ الْمُعَلِّمُ.
هَذِهِ هِيَ الْكُتُبُ.	
هَؤُلاءِ هُنَّ الْمُعَلِّمَاتُ.	هَؤُلاءِ هُمُ الْمُعَلِّمُونَ.

Combinations including ذلِكَ occur quite often in the lexical area: لِذلِكَ
"therefore", مَعَ ذلِكَ "yet", قَبْلَ ذلِكَ "before that", بَعْدَ ذلِكَ "after that",
"nevertheless" a. o.

3. Diptotes (أَلْمَمْنُوع مِنَ الصَّرْف)

3.1. We have got to know the declension of nouns in Lesson 4 which have
nunation and three cases, when indefinite. They are called triptotes. Nouns which
do not have the nunation and which only have two cases, when indefinite, are
called diptotes. We compare triptotes and diptotes with each other in the
following table:

	diptotes/triptotes (definite)	diptotes (indefinite)	triptotes
n.	أَلْخَزَائِنُ الْبَيْضَاءُ	خَزَائِنُ بَيْضَاءُ	رَجُلٌ كَبِيرٌ
g.	أَلْخَزَائِنِ الْبَيْضَاءِ	خَزَائِنَ بَيْضَاءَ	رَجُلٍ كَبِيرٍ
a.	أَلْخَزَائِنَ الْبَيْضَاءَ	خَزَائِنَ بَيْضَاءَ	رَجُلاً كَبِيراً

Accordingly, the characteristic of diptotes consists in the fact that the final
Nūn is missing and that the genitive and accusative endings are the same if the
diptotes are not defined by the article or otherwise.

✍A7 Particularly the plural forms of words containing several consonants (*fawāᶜil, faᶜālil, faᶜālīl,
fuᶜalā' a. o.*) and adjectives of the form *afᶜal*, fem. *faᶜlā'* (many adjectives of colour have this
structure; cf. the glossary of this lesson and Lesson 25) are diptotes. Diptotes are indicated by a final
Ḍamma in the glossaries contained in the lessons and at the end of the book: أَصدقاءُ ، أبيضُ .

3.2. All place names which end in a consonant and do not have the definite article
(except those ending in ات -*āt*) are also diptotes (لبنانُ، مصرُ، بغداد).

3.3. Diptotes which are defined by the article, an affixed pronoun or a subsequent
genitive consequently change into triptotes by this process:

فِي الْخَزَائِنِ الْبَيْضَاءِ / فِي رَسَائِلِهَا / مَعَ أَصْدِقَاءِ الطَّالِبِ

V

✍A8 Some words are marked with *(coll.)* as collective nouns which will be dealt with in detail in Lesson 20.

to take sth.	أَخذ (يأخُذ) هـ	food, dish, meal	مأكُولات ج
and so on, *abbr:* إلخ	إلى آخِرِه	European	أورُبِّيّ
certainly, surely, definitely	بِالتَّأكِيدِ	ice cream	أيْس كريم
eat sth.	أكل (يأكُلُ) هـ	aubergine, eggplant	باذِنجان *(coll.)*

oranges	بُرْتُقال (.coll)	cucumber	خِيار (.coll)
onions	بصل (.coll)	chicken	دجاج (.coll)
watermelons	بَطّيخ / بطّيخ (.coll)	to enter sth.	دخل (يدْخُلُ) هـ
potatoes	بطاطِسُ	to study sth.	درس (يدرُسُ) هـ
cattle	بقر (.coll)	flour	دقيق
green-grocer	بقّال ج ــون	without, under	دُونَ / بدون
balcony	بَلْكُون	that, those	ذلِك م تِلْكَ ج أولِئكَ
beer	بيرة	to go (to)	ذهب (يذْهَبُ) (إلى)
white	أَبْيَضُ م بَيْضاءُ	to come back to	رجع (يرْجِعُ) إلى
among them	(مِن) بَيْنَهُمْ / بينَهَا	looking up, consulting, review	مُراجعة
apples	تفّاح (.coll)	rice	رُزّ
following	تـال (التالِي)	bottle	زُجاجة ج ــات
after that	ثُمَّ	plant sth.	زرع (يزْرَعُ) هـ
garlic	ثُوم (.coll)	olive	زيْتُون (.coll)
waiter (Fr. garçon)	جرْسُون ج ــات	to ask sb. about sth.	سأل (يسْأَلُ) ه عن
waitress	جرْسونة ج ــات	question	سُؤال ج أسْئِلة
to sit, to be seated on	جلس (يجْلِسُ) على	to live in	سكن (يسْكُنُ) في
nuts	جوْز (.coll)	knife	سِكّين ج سكاكينُ (.m. and f)
hungry	جوْعانُ م جوْعَى ج جِياع	salad	سلطة / سلاطة
pilgrim	حاجّ ج حُجَّاج، حجيج	fish	سمك ج أسْماك (.coll)
hot (also food), spicy	حارّ	year	سنة ج سنوات، سِنون
dessert; sweets	حلْوَى ج حلاوَى	black	أسْودُ م سوْداءُ
red	أحْمرُ م حمْراءُ	haggling about	مُساومة ج ــات في، على
life	حياة	soup	شُورْبة / شُرْبة
sometimes	أحْيانًا	buying, purchase	شِراء
mutton, lamb	خرُوف ج خِرْفان	apartment, suite	شِقّة ج شِقق
(especially) for	خاصّ بِـ	form, way, manner	شكْل ج أشْكال
green	أخْضرُ م خضْراءُ	in the following way	بالشكل التالي
vinegar	خلّ	fork	شوْكة ج ــات
different	مُخْتلِف	expression, term	مُصْطلح ج ــات
plum, peach	خوْخ (.coll)	necessary for	ضَرُوري لِـ

dinner	طعام العشاء	menu	قائِمة الطعام
weather	طقْس	as, like, furthermore	كما
to order sth.	طلب (يطْلُبُ) هـ، أنْ	glass	كأس (م) ج كُؤُوس
to ask for sth., to demand	طلب مِنه أنْ	alcohol	كُحُول
tomato(es)	طَماطِمُ	too, also	كذلِك
ᶜAbd ar-Razzāq	عبد الرزَّاق	meat	لحْم ج لُحُوم
lentils	عدس (coll.)	necessary (for)	لازم (ل)
mineral	معْدِنيّ	friendly, nice	لطيف ج لُطفاءُ
Iraqi	عِراقيّ	spoon	مِلْعقة ج ملاعِقُ
thirsty	عطْشانُ م عطْشَى ج عِطاش	almonds	لوْز (coll.)
to know sth., that	علِم (يعْلَمُ) هـ، أنَّ	colour	لوْن ج ألْوان
to work	عمِل (يعْمَلُ)	day and night	ليَل نهارَ
grapes	عِنب (coll.)	lemons	لَيْمُون (coll.)
normal	عاديّ	period of time	مُدَّة ج مُدد
open, opened	مفتوح	time	مرَّة ج ات
radish	فجْل (coll.)	for the first time	لِلْمَرة الأُولىَ
mushroom	فطْر (coll.)	apricots	مِشْمِش (coll.)
please	تفضَّلْ م تفضَّلِي	salt	مِلْح
please (as request)	مِن فضْلِكَ (م) مِن فضْلِكِ	forbidden, prohibited	ممْنُوع
pepper	فِلْفِل	bananas	موْز (coll.)
cup	فِنجان ج فناجينُ	water	ماء ج مِياه
to understand sth.	فهِم (يفْهَمُ) هـ	as far as ... is concerned	بالنِسْبةِ ل
beans	فول	to look at	نظر (ينْظُرُ) إلى
hors d'oeuvre	مُقبِّلات ج	the people	الناس
to read sth.	قرأ (يقْرأُ) هـ	this, these	هذا م هذِهِ ج هؤُلاء
close to, nearby	قريب مِن	I hope you will enjoy it. (the food)	هنيئًا مريئًا!
café	مقهىً ج مقاهٍ	(answer)	هنَّأك ا لله!
hall	قاعة ج ـات	meal, dish	وجْبة ج وجَبات
list	قائِمة ج ـات، قوائِمُ		

Text 1   عند البقّال

أدرس اللغة العربية لمدّة سنة في جامعة القاهرة وأسكن في بيت قريب من الجامعة. أجلـس أحياناً مع أصدقائي في بلكون شقّتي وننظر إلى النـاس والسيّارات والمحـلّات في الشـارع. توجد في هذا الشارع محلّات كثيرة ومن بينها بقّال قريب من بيـتي وذلك المحـلّ مفتوح تقريباً ليلَ نهار.

واليوم أذهب للمرّة الأولى إلى هذا البقّال لشراء الأشياء الضرورية للحيـاة اليوميـة مثـل المأكولات والمشروبات وأشياء أخرى كثيرة. سأطلب منه ما كتبته على ورقـة بالشـكل التالي:

مشروبات: عصير برتقال، ماء معدني

مأكولات: دقيق، عدس، زبدة، جبنة، ملح، فلفل أسود، رزّ

لحوم: لحم خروف، دجاج، سمك، لحم بقر

فواكه: تفّاح، موز، عنب، زيتون، ليمون، بطّيخ، خوخ، مشمش

خضراوات: باذنجان، بصل، ثوم، خيار، بطاطس، طماطم، فول

علمت من أصدقائي العرب أنّ البقّال الحاجّ عبد الرزّاق رجل لطيف وشاطر في المساومة وأنه سيسألني بالتأكيد: أية خدمة، يا سيّدي؟ وكذلك: هل تفهم اللغة العربية؟ ومن أيـن أنت؟ وأسئلة أخرى. وبعد ذلك سأدخل مقهىً من مقاهي الشارع وأشرب هناك فنجاناً من الشاي، ثم أرجـع إلى البيـت وآخـذ قاموسي لمراجعـة المصطلحـات العربيـة الخاصّـة بالمأكولات والمشروبات.

Text 2   في المطعم

الجرسونة: أهلاً وسهلاً، مساء الخير، أية خدمة؟

بيتر: مساء النور، هات قائمة الطعام من فضلك، أنا جوعان، أقرأ ما عندك من أكلات.

الجرسونة: تفضّل، هنا القائمة! عندنا مأكولات شرقية مختلفة وأيضاً مأكولات أوربية.

بيتر: هل عندكم بيرة؟ أنا عطشان.

الجرسونة: لا، والله، الكحول ممنوع في بلدنا.

بيتر: وماذا أشرب؟

الجرسونة: عندنا عصير وماء معدني وبيبسي وبيرة بدون كحول.

بيتر: أشرب بيرة بدون كحول وما هذه الأكلات؟

الجرسونة: هي أكلات شرقية أي عربية وبينها أكلات حارّة جدّاً.

بيتر: هات هذه الوجبة مع الرزّ ولحم الدجاج والخضـراوات والسـلاطة. هـل هـذه الأكلة حارّة؟

الجرسونة: لا، هي عادية وكيف بالنسبة للمقبّلات والشوربة؟

بيت: لا آكل شوربة في هذا الطقـس الحـارّ. المقبّلات فكرة جيّـدة. مـا هـي هـذه المقبّلات؟

الجرسونة: عندنا مقبّلات كثيرة جدّاً مثلاً لحوم مختلفة وسمك وفطر وزيتـون وخضـروات وفواكه ولوز وجوز وباذنجان وفجل وفول إلى آخره.

بيتر: أنا آخذ هذه المقبّلات أي لحم البقر والسمك والفطر.

الجرسونة: وبعد الأكل شاي أو قهوة؟

بيتر: قهوة، من فضلك.

الجرسونة: مع السكّر؟

بيتر: لا، بدون سكّر.

الجرسونة: وكيف بالنسبة للحلوى بعد الأكل أو الأيس كريم؟

بيتر: أيس كريم فكرة جيدة.

الجرسونة: تفضّل، هنا البيرة والأكل. هنيئاً مريئاً.

بيتر: هنّأك الله وهات من فضلك ملعقة وشوكة وسكّين.

Exercises:

L1 Define the following nouns by means of the article and put the appropriate demonstrative pronoun (هذا، هذه، هؤلاء) in front of it.

☞   بيت   >   هذا البيت   بيوت   >   هذه البيوت

☞   رجال   >   هؤلاء الرجال

غرفة، غرف، فواكه، طلّاب، بلد، بلدان، كتاب، طالبات، علاقات، يـوم، مسـاء، مسـرح، سيّارة، سيّـارات، مشـروبات، مـأكولات، لغـة، لـون، ألـوان، لـون، فتيات، فتـاة، أصدقاء، صديق، أرض، خضروات، شوكة، سكّين، ملعقة، كأس، فنجان

L2 The same as L1 preceded by ذلك، تلك، أولئك.

L3 The following exercise gives you a couple of examples of the *Iḍāfa*. Put the appropriate form of هذا in the way that it refers to
a) the 2nd term of the *Iḍāfa* and
b) the 1st term of the *Iḍāfa*.

☞   كتاب الصديق   >   كتاب هذا الصديق / كتاب الصديق هذا

☞   كتاب صديقي   >   كتاب صديقي هذا

لون السيّارة، بيوت الطلّاب، أصدقاء الفتاة، عاصمة البلد، جامعة المدينة، غـرف البيـت، معلّم صديقي، طلاب جامعتنا، معلّمو المدرسة، علاقات البلد، أعضاء الوفد، فواكه البلد

L4 The same examples as in L3, but with ذلك / تلك or أولئك.

L5 Form equational sentences by means of the following nouns and collocations using the demonstratives هذا / هذه or هؤلاء as subject and the defined noun as predicate.

☞   بيّت   >   هذا هو البيت.   غرفة   >   هذه هي الغرفة.

معلّم، طلّاب سوريون، طالبات جديدات، صديق، أصدقاء عرب، رجـل، فتـاة، جميلـة، رسالة، كتاب جديـد، شـنطة، كأس، غرفـة كبيـرة، عاصمـة، مدينـة، مطعـم، مسـرح، جامعة، قائمة، قاعة.

L6 (Homework) Put the nouns and adjectives in brackets into the proper case and vocalize the endings.

اشتريت (أقلام سوداء، ورق جديد، كرسي أحمر، فنجان عربية، فنجان أخضـر، فواكـه، خضراوات).

رأيت (رجال، معلّمونا، الطلّاب العراقيون، أصدقاء عرب، مدن كثيرة).

ذهب إلى (أصدقاء عرب، أصدقاؤنا هؤلاء، مطاعم كثيرة، معلّمتنا).

كتبت (رسالة، رسائل كثيرة، كتاب).

دخلت (بيتكم، القاعة الحمراء، مطعم جميل، مسرح المدينة).

وضعت الكتب في (الشنطة السوداء، خزائن بيضاء).

شربت (نبيذ أحمر، نبيذ أبيض، كأس من النبيذ، كأس من النبيذ الأبيض).

درست (اللغة العربية، لغات كثيرة، الحياة في البلدان العربية).

عرفت (المعلّمون العرب، المسافرون، طلاّب منهم).

L7 (Repetition) Ask about the subject, object or the prepositional phrase using the proper interrogative. Transform the verb from the 1st p. into the 2nd p.
Use the following interrogatives:

من، لِمن، مع من، ماذا، أين، إلى أين، مِن أين.

☞   فعل ذلك محمّد.   >   من فعل ذلك؟

☞   قرأت الكتب.   >   ماذا قرأت؟

☞   اشتريت ذلك من المخزن.   >   من أين اشتريت ذلك؟

ذهبوا إلى الفندق. وضعت الكتاب على الطاولة. وضعنا الكتب في الخزانة. شـربنا النبيـذ مع الأصدقاء. سمعت أخباراً جديدة. فعـل ذلك صديق. رأينا فتيـات جميـلات. يوجـد المصباح على السقف. توجد الكراسي والطاولة على الأرض. يوجد اللوح على الجـدار. وصلت الوفود من البلدان العربية. كتب الرسالة صديق عربي. كتبـت للصديـق رسالة. كتبت رسالة للصديق. قرأت كتاباً جديداً. وصل الوفـد إلى المطار. اشـتريت القلم مـن المخزن. اشتريت من المخزن قلماً جديداً. ذهب الوفد إلى الفندق. عقدت الوفود العربيـة اجتماعاً. عقدت الوفود اجتماعات كثيرة.

G1 Transform the following sentences from the perfect tense (3rd p. sg. m.) irto the imperfect tense (3rd p. sg. m.).

☞   كتب رسالة.   >   يكتب رسالة.

خرج من الغرفة. ذهب إلى المطعم. دخل القاعة. أخذ قائمة الطعام.

شرب القهوة (الشاي، البيرة، الماء، النبيذ).

أكل اللحم (الرزّ، الخضراوات، الفواكه).

كتب رسالة. قرأها. وضعها في الخزانة.

G2 Replace the perfect tense given in G1 by the imperfect tense 1st p. sg. and after that by the 1st p. pl.

☞   كتب رسالة.   >   أكتب رسالة. ٰ نكتب رسالة.

G3 Transform the sentences of G1 into questions using the imperfect tense 2nd p. sg. and pl. m..

هل تكتب رسالة؟ هل تكتبون رسالة؟   >   كتب رسالة.   ☞

G4 Answer the sentences formed in G3 with نعم or لا. Use the imperfect tense of the 1st p. sg. or pl..

نعم، أكتب رسالة.   >   هل تكتب رسالة؟   ☞

نعم، نكتب رسائل.   >   هل تكتبون رسائل؟   ☞

لا، أشرب البيرة.   >   هل تشرب القهوة؟   ☞

G5 Transform the following sentences from the perfect tense into the imperfect tense and vice versa.

يصل الوفد العراقي اليوم. تصل الوفود العربية ظهر اليوم. يجلسون في القاعة الكبيرة. أشرب فنجاناً من القهوة. هل تأكل اللحم والخضراوات؟ يطلب لحم الدجاج. أكلوا طعاماً شرقياً. نشرب الشاي بعد الأكل. يجلسون في مطعم من مطاعم المدينة. هل تعرف هؤلاء الأصدقاء؟ نعم، أعرفهم. هل تفهمون ذلك الرجل؟ هل فهمتني؟ هل تفهمونني؟ عقدوا اجتماعاً. كتبن رسائل كثيرة. أسمع ذلك. وضع كتبه في الشنطة. قرأنا تلك الكتب. فعل ذلك أصدقاؤنا الألمان. ندرس اللغة العربية.

G6 The teacher quotes the verbs given in the perfect tense in different persons and the student gives the respective imperfect tense.

ذهب، درس، كتب، شرب، فعل، سمع، وصل، وضع، سأل، قرأ، حضر، عقد، عرف، خرج، رجع، زرع، أكل، عمل، طلب، علم، دخل

G7 Vice versa.

G8 (Repetition) The simple verbal sentences in the 1st p. sg. are to be transformed into interrogative sentences with the verb in the 2nd p. sg. m.

هل فعلتَ ذلك؟   >   فعلتُ ذلك   ☞

قرأت الخبر. قرأت الأخبار. قرأت أن الوفد (السوري، العراقي، الجزائري، السعودي، الكويتي، المصري) وصل إلى برلين. قرأت الرسالة. قرأت الرسائل. وصلت إلى هناك. وصلت إلى برلين. ذهبت إلى هناك. ذهبت إلى الفندق. ذهبت إلى الصديق. ذهبت إلى المعلّم. رأيت الفتيات. اشتريت السيّارة. سافرت بالقطار. شربت الشاي. سألت المعلّم. أكلت الخبز. شربت القهوة. سألت الأم. عملت في البيت. عملت في المخزن. عقدت اجتماعاً. كتبت الرسالة. كتبت رسائل. سمعت الخبر. سمعت الأخبار.

سمعت أن الوفد العراقي وصل إلى برلين. عرفت الرجل. عرفت الفتاة. عرفت أن الطالب ذهب إلى هناك. عرفت أن الطلّاب ذهبوا إلى البيت.

C1 Answer the questions.

ماذا تشرب (تشربين) صباحاً / في الصباح (ظهـراً / في الظهـر، مسـاءً / في المسـاء، قبـل الطعام، بعد الطعام)؟

ماذا تأكل (تأكلين) صباحاً/ في الصباح (ظهراً / في الظهر، مساءً / في المساء)؟

C2 Prepare a paper to say what you are going to do tomorrow. Use the particle سوف or the prefix سـ.

سأخرج من البيت صباحاً. سأذهب إلى ...، سأعمل في...

C3 (Homework) Write down what you are going to buy for the weekend or a party. Consult the dictionary and ask your teacher about regional or dialectal variations for certain foods.

C4 Prepare a dialogue based on Text 2 about having dinner in a restaurant.

Final exercise:

1. Add the appropriate demonstrative pronoun for what is nearer with respect to place or time.

...الطقس، ... المعلِّمون، ... الطالبات، ... الشوكات، ... المدرسة، ... المقبّلات، ... السنة، ... السـادة، ... الكراريس، ... السيّدات، ... الرسـائل، ... الزجاجـة، ... الأعضاء، ... المكتب

2. Add the appropriate demonstrative pronoun for what is farther or more distant with respect to place or time.

3. Translate into Arabic.
this friend, this book of my friend, that bag of the woman teacher, the new house of that civil/public servant, the drinks of that restaurant, these vegetables of the green-grocer, this bottle of the friend, these notebooks of his, these friends of ours, those restaurants of the city
This is the teacher. This is a school. Those drank the juice. This is the waitress.

4. Transform the verb into the imperfect tense.

وصل الوفد العراقي اليوم. وصلت الطـائرات إلى القـاهرة. درسـنا اللغـة العربيـة. عرفت الكثير من الدبلوماسيين. قرأت كتباً جديدة. حضرن حفلة طويلة. طلبتِ مشـروبات. أكلتم أطعمة شرقية. عملتنّ في المطعم. رجعتُ إلى البيت. دخلت المحلّ. عقدوا اجتماعاً. فهِمتُ الدرس. أكلتم لحماً وبيضاً.

5. Write the following weekend shopping list in Arabic.

Eggs, butter, cheese, milk, bread, marmelade, sugar, juice, honey, fruits, vegetables, apples, eggplants, oranges, watermelon, potatoes, beer, garlic, nuts, vinegar, plums, cucumber, flour, rice, olives, fish, tomatoes, lentils, grapes, radish, mushroom, pepper, salt, beans, almonds, apricots, bananas, lemons

6. Translate into Arabic.

I will study Arabic for a year at Cairo University. He will live in the students' hostel. She will write a letter. They will drink tea. No, I drink beer. Will you drink alcohol? No, we will drink juice. I am hungry and thirsty. Do you have starters? Yes, we have a lot of starters. Is the meal hot? No, it is normal. Hot food is good with hot weather. Have you got mineral water? Please give me a knife, fork and spoon.

1. Subjunctive (أَلْمُضَارِع الْمَنْصُوب) and Jussive (أَلْمُضَارِع الْمَجْزُوم)

The imperfect tense consists of several moods.

The indicative (cf. Lesson 7) generally serves to express an action (an event, also a state). The same applies to the subjunctive and the jussive, which, however, never occur alone, but are only used after certain conjunctions and particles.

1.1. The conjugation

Jussive	Subjunctive	Indicative
يَفْعَلْ	يَفْعَلَ	(هُوَ) يَفْعَلُ
تَفْعَلْ	تَفْعَلَ	(هِيَ) تَفْعَلُ
تَفْعَلْ	تَفْعَلَ	(أَنْتَ) تَفْعَلُ
تَفْعَلِي	تَفْعَلِي	(أَنْتِ) تَفْعَلِينَ
أَفْعَلْ	أَفْعَلَ	(أَنا) أَفْعَلُ
يَفْعَلُوا	يَفْعَلُوا	(هُمْ) يَفْعَلُونَ
يَفْعَلْنَ	يَفْعَلْنَ	(هُنَّ) يَفْعَلْنَ
تَفْعَلُوا	تَفْعَلُوا	(أَنْتُمْ) تَفْعَلُونَ
تَفْعَلْنَ	تَفْعَلْنَ	(أَنْتُنَّ) تَفْعَلْنَ
نَفْعَلْ	نَفْعَلَ	(نَحْنُ) نَفْعَلُ

☞A1 Only the imperfect tense has the subjunctive and the jussive. The perfect tense has only one mood, the indicative.

The subjunctive and the jussive differ from the indicative by an *a* (subjunctive) replacing the short vowel *u* after R$_3$ or by R$_3$ being vowelless (jussive) and by the suffixes *-īna* and *-ūna* being abridged. In the last-mentioned case an *Alif*, which is not pronounced, is added in spelling to the long vowel *-ū*, which has become final now - like in the 3rd p. pl .m. of the perfect form.

1.2. The usage

1.2.1. The subjunctive occurs only after certain conjunctions in subordinate clauses:

أَنْ "that"

I ask you to do that (*lit.:* ... that you do that).	.أَطْلُبُ مِنْكَ أَنْ تَفْعَلَ ذَلِكَ
(fem.) I ask you to do that.	.أَطْلُبُ مِنْكِ أَنْ تَفْعَلِي ذَلِكَ
(pl.) I ask you to do that (*lit.:* ... that you do that).	.أَطْلُبُ مِنْكُم أَنْ تَفْعَلُوا ذَلِكَ

أَنْ لا, contracted أَلَّا "that ... not"

I ask you not to do that. (*lit.:* ... that you do not do that)	.أَطْلُبُ أَنْ لا / أَلَّا تَفْعَلَ ذَلِكَ

لِ ، كَيْ and لِكَيْ "in order that", حَتَّى "so that, until"

He asked the friend in order that he would know the way.	.سَأَلَ الصَّدِيقَ لِيَعْرِفَ / لِكَيْ/كَيْ يَعْرِفَ الطَّرِيقَ
He asks, in order to get the answer. (lit.: so that/until he knows the answer)	.يَسْأَلُ حَتَّى يَعْرِفَ الْجَوَابَ

The negatives are كَيْلا or لِكَيْلا , or لِئَلَّا .

The negation لَنْ, which negates verbs in the future tense, also takes the subjunctive (cf. 3.3.).

♪A2 أَنْ is the conjunction which occurs most frequently among the ones mentioned above. The following applies regarding the differentiation between أَنْ and أَنَّ, which also means "that":
Verbs which state something introduce the objective clause by means of أَنَّ (the subject in the shape of an accusative noun or of an affixed pronoun is positioned after the verb followed by a verb in the perfect or imperfect tense).

Verbs which express a hope, fear, wish or demand introduce the objective clause by means of أَنْ (+ following subjunctive). Only بَعْدَ أَنْ "after" and مُنْذُ أَنْ "since" take the perfect tense.
See in detail Lesson 20, Gr 3.

1.2.2. The negative particles لَمْ and لا, and furthermore لِ , take the jussive.

Actions having taken place in the past are negated by means of لَمْ "not" (cf. below, 3.2.); the negative imperative is formed by لا "not" + jussive (cf. below, 3.1.).

The indirect command (hortative) is expressed by the preposition لِ + jussive.

Let's go.	.لِنَذْهَبْ
He shall do that.	.لِيَفْعَلْ ذَلِكَ

2. The Imperative (الأَمْر)

Forming and conjugation: the 2^(nd) p. sg. and pl. of the jussive is the form to start from. The prefix *ta-* is omitted, and the double consonant, which has now been formed, is resolved by a prosthetic vowel.

The prosthetic vowel is represented in writing by an *Alif* with *Hamza* (**in the interior of the sentence** *Hamzat al-waṣl*!). The vowel is *i-* in verbs of which the imperfect stem vowel is *a* or *i*:

(أنتَ)	إفْعَلْ	إعْرفْ
(أنتِ)	إفْعَلِي	إعْرِفِي
(أنتم)	إفْعَلوا	إعْرَفوا
(أنتنَّ)	إفْعَلْنَ	إعْرِفْنَ

It is *u-* in verbs of which the imperfect stem vowel is *u*:

(أنتَ)	أُدْخُلْ
(أنتِ)	أُدْخُلِي
(أنتم)	أُدْخُلوا
(أنتنَّ)	أُدْخُلْنَ

A3 The imperative of the verbs R₁ = و and of some verbs R₁ = أ is formed without a prosthetic vowel: خُذْ "Take!", كُلوا "Eat!" (Cf. Lessons 11 and 24). Negative imperative see 3.1.

A4 Another mood of the imperfect tense is the so-called energetic mood to express emphasis. It is formed   by adding the suffix ـنَّ or ـنْ to the imperative or jussive. However, it is extremely rare in modern Arabic.

3. Negation

We have already   become acquainted with three types of negation with لا , لَمْ and لَنْ. Now a summary follows about the application of all types of negation in use.

3.1. **لا + imperfect tense** = negation of actions taking place in present and future tenses:

He does not do that / he will not do that.	لا يَفْعَلُ ذَلِكَ.

A5 If a verb form having a particle of future tense is to be negated by لا, it is only possible to construe it with سوف: سوف لا يفعل ذلك "He will (definitely) not do that", but not with the abridged form سـ (consequently it would be **wrong** to say: لا سيفعل).

لا + jussive = negative imperative:

Do not do that!	لا تَفْعَلْ ذَلِكَ! لا تَفْعَلِي ذَلِكَ!
Do (pl.) not do that!	لا تَفْعَلوا ذَلِكَ! لا تَفْعَلْنَ ذَلِكَ!

لا **+ indefinite noun in the accusative without nunation** = general negation "there is no ...":

There is no god but God, Muḥammad is the Messenger of God (the Muslim creed).	لا إِلاهَ إِلا اللهُ مُحَمَّدٌ رَسُولُ اللهِ.

👉**A6** لا is largely lexicalized in this particular function: لا مَفَرَّ مِنْهُ "there is no escape from it" = "unavoidable"; لا بُدَّ (مِن) "there is no way out" = "it is necessary", لا شَكَّ فِي أَنْ "there is no doubt that ..." = "without doubt" a.o.

👉**A7** لا also resumes a negation already expressed by another negative particle if no new verb is mentioned: لَمْ يَشْرَبِ البِيرَةَ وَلا النَّبِيذَ "He has not drunk the beer and not the wine." The double negation is equivalent to "neither - nor" in English.

3.2. لَمْ **+ jussive** = negation of actions having taken place in the past:

He has not done that.	لَمْ يَفْعَلْ ذَلِكَ.
He has not drunk the wine.	لَمْ يَشْرَبِ النَّبِيذَ.

👉**A8** The auxiliary vowel *i-*, instead of *Sukūn*, precedes *Hamzat al-waṣl*. (Cf. Lesson 2, Gr 1.3.2.) لَمْ in connection with the post-positive word بَعْدُ produces the meaning "not yet":

He has not done that yet.	لَمْ يَفْعَلْ ذَلِكَ بَعْدُ.

3.3. لَنْ **+ subjunctive** = (strong) negation of actions taking place in the future tense:

He will not (or is not to) do that.	لَنْ يَفْعَلَ ذَلِكَ.

👉**A9** The construction with سَوْفَ لا **+ imperfect form** is possible as well for the purpose of the certainty of negation in the future tense:

He will (definitely) not write /(I am sure) he will not write.	سَوْفَ لا يَكْتُبُ.

3.4. مَا **+ perfect tense** = negation of actions having taken place in the past:

He has not done that.	مَا فَعَلَ ذَلِكَ.

👉**A10** مَا + perfect form is widespread in the dialects. However, in modern literary language, لم + jussive is almost exclusively used. But there are several lexicalized expressions with مَا, both of verbal and of nominal construction, like e.g. مَا زَالَ (يَشْرَبُ) "he has not ceased (drinking)" = "(he) still (drinks)", مَا أَنْ ... حَتَّى "scarcely had he ... when ...; no sooner had he ... than" a. o. مَا is the particle in general use for negating the perfect as well as the imperfect form in colloquial language.

3.5. لَيْسَ

لَيْسَ is the negated copula and means "not to be". It is regarded as being in the present tense, though it is conjugated analogously to the perfect tense.

Conjugation:

sg.   هو لَيْسَ ، هي لَيْسَتْ ، أَنْتَ لَسْتَ ، أَنْتِ لَسْتِ ، أَنا لَسْتُ

pl.   هُم لَيْسُوا ، هُنَّ لَسْنَ ، أَنْتُم لَسْتُمْ ، أَنْتُنَّ لَسْتُنَّ ، نَحْنُ لَسْنَا

He is not, you are not ... etc.

The affirmative equational sentence, which does not have a copula (cf. Lesson 2, Gr 3), is negated by لَيْسَ . The predicate complement is in the accusative after لَيْسَ :

The house is not big.	لَيْسَ البَيْتُ كبيراً.
I am not a student.	لَسْتُ طالباً.
They are not diligent men.	لَيْسُوا رجالاً مُجتهِدِينَ.
There is no teacher in the room. (lit.: (There) is not in the room a teacher.)	لَيْسَ في الغُرْفَةِ مُعَلِّمٌ.

3.6. "neither ... nor"

The Arabic equivalent for "neither ... nor" is always indicated by the negation. If there are several verbs, each verb is negated by means of لن / لا / لم :

I have neither read nor written.	لَمْ أَقْرَأْ ولَمْ أَكْتُبْ.
Neither do I read nor write.	لا أَقْرَأُ ولا أَكْتُبُ.
I will neither read nor write.	لَنْ أَقْرَأَ ولَنْ أَكْتُبَ.

If there are several nouns, the first clause is negated by لم / لا / لن as well, followed by ولا / أو / وليس:

I wrote neither books nor letters.	لَمْ أَكْتُبْ كُتُباً ولا / أو / وليْس رسائِلَ.
I write neither books nor letters.	لا أَكْتُبُ كُتُباً ولا / أو / وليْس رسائِلَ.
I will write neither books nor letters.	لَنْ أَكْتُبَ كُتُباً ولا / أو / وليْس رسائِلَ.

If the predicates are to be negated, ليس ... ولا is used here:

He is neither handsome nor large / big / tall.	لَيْسَ جَميلاً ولا كَبيراً.

V

literature	أدب ج آداب	to get, to obtain sth.	حصل (يَحْصُلُ) على
original	أصْلِيّ	governorate, county	مُحافظة ج ــات
frame(work)	إطار ج أُطُر	ceremony	اِحْتِفال ج ــات
many thanks, thanks a lot	ألْف شُكر	law, right	حقّ ج حُقُوق
conference	مُؤْتمر ج ات	You are right.	أنت على حقّ.
to hope that	أمل (يأْمُلُ) أنْ	Khartoum	الخَرْطُوم
secretary	أمِين ج أُمناءُ	defense	دِفـاع
General Secretary	أمِين عامّ ج أُمناءُ عامُّون	democratic	دِيمُقراطِيّ
God willing; I (we) hope so	إنْ شاءَ ا لله	under the leadership of (+ gen.)	بِرئاسةِ
particle introducing an equational sentence	إنَّ	synonym	مُتَرادِف ج ــات
qualification	تأْهِيل	prophet, envoy, messenger	رسُول ج رُسُل
discuss sth.	بحث (يبْحَثُ) ـه	the messenger of God	رسُولُ ا لله
to search for, to look for	بحث عن	to wish sth., that	رغِب (يرغَبُ) في، (في) أنْ
exchange	تبادُل ج ــات	shelf	رفّ ج رُفُوف
to make efforts	بذل (يبْذُلُ) جُهُوداً	Russian	رُوسِيّ ج روس
simple, easy	بسِيط ج بُسطاءُ	farm	مزْرعة ج مزارعُ
(the day) after tomorrow	بعْدَ غدٍ	visit	زيارة ج ات
saleslady, ~clerk	بائِعة ج ــات	corner	زاوية ج زوايا
cultural	ثقافِيّ	responsible for	مسْؤُول ج ــون عن/لـ
newspaper	جريدة ج جرائدُ	early, in the past, previously	سابقاً
Algiers	(مدِينة) الجزائِر	way, path	سبِيل ج سُبُل
his royal highness	جلالة المَلِكِ	allow so. to do sth.	سمِح (يسْمَحُ) له بـ، ـه
effort	جهْد ج جُهُود	explain sth.	شرح (يشْرَحُ) ـه
award, prize	جائِزة ج جوائِزُ	project	مشْرُوع ج مشاريعُ
Nobel prize	جائِزة نوبل	Do us the honor!	شَرِّفْنا
tour	جوْلة ج ــات	the Middle East	الشرْق الأوْسطُ
field, area, sphere, sector	مجال ج ــات	common, joint, mutual	مُشترك
so that, in order to	حتّى	socialist, Socialist	اِشْتراكِيّ ج ــون
negotiations, talks	ج مُحادثات	famous	مشْهُور ج ون، مشاهِيرُ
(political) party	حِزْب ج أحْزاب	chancellor	مُستْشار ج ون

not to be sth.	لَيْسَ	factory, plant	مَصْنع ج مصانِعُ
Christian	مسيحيّ ج ـون	naturally (adv.)	طبْعاً
possibility	إمْكانِية ج ـات	Tripoli	طرابُلُس (م)
(conj.) since	مُنْذُ / منذ أنْ	Ṭaha Ḥusain	طه حسين
occasion, opportunity	مُناسبة ج ـات	dictionary; lexicon	مُعْجم ج معاجمُ
on the occasion of	بمُناسبةِ	military; soldier	عسْكريّ ج ـون، عساكِرُ
Najīb Maḥfūẓ	نَجيب محفوظ	education	تعْليم
advise so. to do sth, to recommend doing sth.	نصح (يَنْصَحُ) ه بِ	higher education	التعْليم العالي
counterpart	نظير ج نُظراءُ	plant, laboratory	مَعْمل ج معامِلُ
discussion	مُناقشة ج ـات	worker, employee	عامِل ج عُمَّال
to aim at sth.	هدف (يَهْدُفُ) إلى	Amman	عمَّان (م)
engineer	مُهنْدِس ج ـون	cooperation	تعاوُن
existing, available	موْجُود	holiday	عِيد ج أعْياد
minister	وزير ج وُزراءُ	to meet so.	قابل (يُقابِلُ) ه
ministry	وزارة ج ات	coming from	قادِماً من
widening, extension, enlargement	تَوْسِيع	department	قِسْم ج أقْسام
wide	واسِع	economy	اقْتِصاد
clear, obvious	واضِح	valuable	قيِّم
national	وطنِيّ	speech	كِلمة ج ـات
signing, signature	توْقيع	in order to	كَيْ / لِكَيْ
news agency	وَكالةُ أنْباء ج ـات	moment	لَحْظة ج لَحَظات
		not (+ jussive)	لَمْ

Text 1

أخبار عالمية

وكالات الأنباء

لندن: وصل وفد اقتصادي سوري إلى لندن قادماً من النمسا وسيقابل الوفد وزير الاقتصاد ووزير الصحة.

القاهرة: قابل وزير العمل المصري نظيره الإنكليزي في الوزارة بعد جولة في مصانع العاصمة ومعاملها ومزارع المحافظات لمناقشة برنامج التعاون في مجال تأهيل العمال والمهندسين المصريين.

موسكو: وصل وفد أمريكي إلى موسكو وقابل الرئيس الروسي وعـدداً مـن المسـؤولين الروس وطلب من الحكومة الروسية دراسة مشروع التعاون الاقتصادي.

طرابلس: قابل وزير الدفاع نظيره الفرنسي وبحث معـه سـبل توسيع التعاون السياسي والعسكري. وتهدف الزيارة إلى توقيع برنامج مشترك.

دمشق: وصل وزير التعليم العالي البريطاني وهو عضـو في حزب العمـال إلى دمشـق في إطار جولة في الشرق الأوسط وقابل نظيره السوري لمناقشة سبل التعاون في مجال التعلـيم الجامعي.

عمّان: قابل جلالة الملك الوفد الألماني برئاسة المستشار الألماني وبحث معه سـبل التعاون السياسي والاقتصادي والعسكري والثقافي.

الجزائر: حضر الوفد الفرنسي الاحتفالات بمناسبة العيد الوطني. وقـال رئيس الوفد الفرنسي في كلمته القصيرة: إن فرنسا سـوف تبـذل جهـوداً واسـعة لتوسيع التبـادل التجاري مع الجزائر.

باريس: قابل الأمين العام للحزب الوطني السوداني الأمين العام للأمم المتحدة بعـد مؤتمر باريس العالمي.

في المكتبة

Text 2

البائعة: أهلاً وسهلاً ، مساء الخير ، أية خدمة؟

بيتر: مساء النور ، اِسمحي لي أن أسألك عن رف القواميس؟

البائعة: المعاجم هناك في تلك الزاوية.

بيتر: أه ، شكراً وهل عندك معجم للمترادفات العربية؟

البائعة: طبعاً، عندنا معاجم مختلفة، حديثة وقديمة وهي هناك.

بيتر: آخذ هذا الكتاب.

البائعة: إسمح لي أن أنصحك بذلك المعجم، هو جديد وقيّم.

بيتر: شكراً، سآخذه. أين قسم الروايات؟ أبحـث عـن رواية لطه حسين أو لنجيب محفوظ.

البائعة: خذ رواية لنجيب محفوظ! هو كاتب رائع ومشهور وحصل علـى جـائزة نوبـل للآداب.

بيتر: أنا أعرف ذلك و لم أحصل على رواياته في بريطانيا.

البائعة: أنت لست عربياً؟ لغتك العربية واضحة وجيّدة جدّاً.

بيتر: لا، أنا لست عربياً، أنا من بريطانيا.

البائعة: لماذا تقرأ هذه الكتب بالعربية وليس بالإنكليزية؟

بيتر: قرأت الروايات سابقاً بالإنكليزية والآن بعد أن درست اللغة العربية أرغب في أن أقرأ هذه الروايات بلغتها الأصلية.

البائعة: هذا ليس بسيطاً. هل تفهم ما تقرأ؟

بيتر: لم أفهم كلمات كثيرة ولكن منذ أن اشتريت قواميس جيّدة بدأت أفهم أشياء كثيرة.

البائعة: لا بدّ أن تقرأ الروايات بلغتها الأصلية.

بيتر: أنت على حقّ. آمل أن أحصل على هذه الكتب بالعربية ولن أرجع إلى بريطانيا بدونها.

البائعة: هذه الكتب موجودة عندنا.

بيتر: عظيم. آخذ هذه الروايات وهذه الجرائد أيضاً.

البائعة: لحظة من فضلك، تفضّل.

بيتر: ألف شكر، مع السلامة.

البائعة: مع ألف سلامة، شرّفنا مرة أخرى.

Exercises:

L1 (Homework) Complete the following sentences:

أرغــب في أن ...، هــل ترغـب في أن ...؟ يرغبــون في أن ...، ترغب في أن ...، هـل ترغبون في أن ...؟ رغب الطالب في أن ...، رغبت الفتاة في أن ...، هـل رغبتَ في أن ...؟ هل رغبتم في أن ...؟ رغبوا في أن ...، رغبنا في أن ...

Use the following verbs, nouns and phrases.

☞   أرغب في أن أذهب إلى البيت.

☞   هل ترغب في أن تشرب فنجاناً من القهوة؟

☞   رغب الطالب في أن يصل صديقه غدا.

L2 (Homework) Practice the verb طلب by filling in the blanks:

طلب منّي أن ...، طلبت منه أن ...، طلبت منهم أن ...، طلبوا منّا أن ...، طلبنا منهم أن ...، يطلب منك أن ...، هل تطلب منّي أن ...؟ نطلب منكم أن ...، هـل تطلبون منّا أن ...؟

L3 (Homework) Practice the verb أمل by filling in the blanks:

يأمل صديقنا أن ....، تأمل صديقتي أن ....، نـأمل أن ....، آمـل أن ....، هـل تأملين أن ...؟ يأملون أن ....، هل تأملون أن ...؟ أمل صديقه أن ....، أملـت الفتـاة أن ....، هـل أملتم أن ...؟ أملنا أن....،

L4 The teacher asks the students to read some sentences from their homework (L1-L3). A second student repeats the sentence and a third translates it. Request the students to discuss whether the sentences were formed correctly or not.

L5 Say it in Arabic:
Do not do this! I didn't do this. Why didn't you do this? They did not arrive yet. They will not come tomorrow. Take the book! Put it on the table! Don't leave the room! You don't know him. You don't know us. He asked me not to go there.

L6 (Homework) Form 5 sentences using the following phrases:

بعد غد، مساء الغد، ظهر الغد، صباح الغد، غداً.

L7 The teacher asks questions using متى, the students answer them as follows:

☞   متى ستذهب إلى المسرح؟   >   سأذهب إلى المسرح مساء الغد.
☞   متى سألتني عن الكتاب؟   >   سألتك عن الكتاب صباح اليوم.

L8 (Repetition) Add (جُدُد، جديدة) جديد or another appropriate adjective to the following nouns which are defined by an affixed pronoun.

☞   بيتي   >   بيتي الجديد

غرفتك، معلمكم، أصدقاؤنا، كتبنا، سيّارته، بسيارته، في فندقنا، أمام مسرحنا، صديقتي، مرافقكم، في مطارهم، سياستهم، مدرستك، جامعتها، مخزنه

G1 Negate the following sentences by means of لم.

☞   فعلت ذلك.   >   لم أفعلْ ذلك.

عرفتُ ذلك. عرفنا ذلك. عرفوا ذلك. عرفَت ذلك. عمل هناك. عملتُ هناك. عملَت في ذلك المصنع. عملوا في تلك المدينة. عملنا هناك. عملوا بأجهزة حديثة. أخذوا ذلـك. أخذ الكتاب. أخذنا الجرائد. أخذن ذلك. أخذتم ذلك. فعل ذلك. فعلنا ذلك. فعلتِ ذلك. ذهبَت إلى هناك. ذهبتِ إلى المكتبة. ذهبـوا إلى القاعة. شربت النبيـذ. شربوا القهوة. شربنا البيرة. أكلنا اللحم. أكلوا في المطعم. أكلتـم هناك. خرجت مـن البيت. خرج من المعهد. خرجن من المطعم. دخل بيـت صديقـه. دخلنا المطعم. دخلتِ ذلك البيت. وصل الوفد أمس. وصلت الوفود مسـاء أمـس. وصلـوا صبـاح اليوم. فهمتُ. فهمتم. فهم. فهمَت. فهمنا. درس هناك طلاّب أجانب. شرح لهم عمل المكتبة. رجعـوا إلى البيت. طلبنا منه ذلك. طلبوا منّي ذلك. طلبتُ منكم ذلك. رغبوا في أن يكتبوا لهـا. رغبتُ في أن يدخل بيت.

G2 Negate the following sentences by means of لم, لا or لن.

☞   أشرب البيرة.   >   لا أشرب البيرة.
☞   سأذهب إلى المعهد.   >   لن أذهب إلى المعهد.

☞ فهمت ذلك.   >   لم أفهم ذلك.

أعرف ذلك. أخذ الكتاب. فعلوا ذلك. دخلت ذلك المعهد. قرأنا كتباً كثيرة. يدرسون اللغة العربية. نعرف ذلك. سيعقدون اجتماعاً. سيعمل في برلين. ستكتبون لهم. وضعت الكتب في الخزانة. نرغب في أن نذهب إلى هناك. طلب منّي أن أذهب إلى هناك. خرجت من البيت صباحاً. سمعنا هذا الخبر. نفهم ذلك. يأكلون فواكه كثيرة. سيذهبون إلى المعهد. ذهبَت إلى صديقتها. عمل بالأجهزة الحديثة. ينظرون إلى الكتب.

G3 Negate the following equational sentences by means of ليس.

☞ الطالب مجتهد.   >   ليس الطالب مجتهدًا.

☞ الغرفة جميلة.   >   ليست الغرفة جميلة.

البيت كبير. البيوت جميلة. المعلمون في الغرفة. هؤلاء الرجال طيّبون. هؤلاء الرجال معلّمون. تلك الفتاة معلمة. أولئك الفتيات طالبات. هذه الكرّاسة جديدة. سيّارتي يابانية. لونها أبيض. عندي كتب كثيرة. في الغرفة طلاّب. هناك أجهزة حديثة. في المعهد طلبة أجانب.

Pay attention to the fact that in the last four examples the noun or phrase following the prepositional phrase is not the predicate, but the subject of the sentence. It is the type of sentence dealt with in Lesson 2, Gr 3.1., sentence structure 2.

G4 Negate the following imperatives.

إشرب! إشربوا الشاي! إذهب إلى هناك! إذهبن إلى هناك! أدخل ذلك البيت! أدخلي ذلك المخزن! إفعلوا ذلك! إفعل ذلك! أخرج! أخرجوا! خذ الجهاز! خذوا ذلك! إسمعي! إسمعوا! إقرأ هذا الكتاب! إقرؤوا هذه الكتب! أكتب لي! أكتبن لنا! ضعوا ذلك في الشنطة!

G5 Transform the negated imperatives into positive commands.

لا تفعلي ذلك! لا تفعلوا ذلك! لاتكتبوا لهم! لا تأخذ ذلك الجهاز! لا تدخل ذلك المطعم! لا تذهبوا إلى هناك! لا تشربي النبيذ! لا تخرج من هنا! لا تقرؤوا تلك الرسالة! لا تضع ذلك في الخزانة!

G6 (Repetition) Form genitive constructions out of the following words.

	1st term	2nd term (defined)
1. محمّد		كتب، بيت، غرفة، سيّارة، شنطة، قلم
2. صديقة		أقلام، بيوت، سيّارة، رسائل، كتب
3. مدينة		مسرح، مسارح، جامعة، شوارع، مخازن، محطّة
4. عاصمة		مدارس، محطّات، معالم، جامعات، مخازن

5. بيت	باب، أبواب، جدار، جدران، شبابيك، غرف
6. غرفة	أبواب، جدار، جدران، شبابيك، سقف، أرض
7. صديق	كتاب، كتب، غرفة، بيت، سيّارة، شنطة
8. وفد	عضو، أعضاء، مرافق، مرافقون، رئيس، سيّارة

C1 The teacher explains the colloquial usage of "I want/would like to have ...", like نِبْغِي (*Iraqi*), أريد (*Syrian, Palestinian*), بِدّي (*Egyptian*), عـاوز/عـايز (*Maghrib*) including their pronunciation and the omitting of the final endings in the colloquial language. Their usage should be practiced without pronouncing the endings.

I would like to have a beer / a book / a white bag / a new car / fork and spoon / a dictionary / a big room / chicken with rice / tea / coffee / ice cream ...

☙ أنا عايز، عايزة / بدي / أريد / نبغي ماء.

C2 The teacher explains the question "Do you want/Would you like to ... ?" using the colloquial forms given above and practices them without pronouncing the endings.

☙ (هل) أنت عايز / أنتِ عايزة كتاب(اً)؟

☙ (هل) بِدَّك / بِدِك شاي؟

☙ (هل) تَريد كوكا؟

C3 The teacher explains the colloquial usage of "I don't want ..." and asks the question ?... (هل) أنتَ عايز/أنتِ عايزة using the phrases from C2.

☙ أنا مُش / مِش عايز / عايزة كتاب(اً).

☙ ما بدّي كتاب.

☙ لا / ما أريد كتاب(اً).

☙ لا / ما نبغي كتاب(ا).

C4 Put a colloquial variant of "to want" in the places possible in Text 2 (orally). Pay attention not to mix different variants with the same speaker.

C5 Prepare a dialogue about the same topic based on Text 2.

C6 Discuss the meaning of the following sayings and proverbs with لا together with your teacher.

لا تُؤَجِّلْ (postpone) عمل اليوم إلى غد!

لا تبِعْ دجاجة بُكرة (tomorrow) ببيضة (egg) اليوم.

لا تَخَفْ (to be afraid of) مِن الدولة (state) وخَفْ من كِلابها (dogs).

لا تشرَبْ من كُوز (jug) أكبر (bigger) من رأسك (head) .

لا دينَ (religion) إلا (except) دين الدم (blood) .

لا سلامَ (here: shake hands) على الطعام.

Final Exercise:

1. Negate the following sentences by means of لم .

طلبنا منه ذلك. رغب في أن يكتب رسالة. فهمتُ. أخذنا الجرائد. شربوا القهوة.
وصلت الوفود أمس. أكلنا اللحم. شربن العصير. خرج من المعهد. رجعتِ من الفندق
إلى المعهد. عملوا في تلك المدينة. بذلوا جهوداً كبيرة. أمل أن يكتب له. بحثتم عن
الكتب في رفوف كثيرة. وصل أمناء عامّون لأحزاب كثيرة. فعلن ذلك. كتبتِ الرسالة.
شكرته على الجرائد الجديدة. فهمنا الدرس. رغب في أن يشرب العصير وأن يأكل
اللحم.

2. Translate into Arabic.
You didn't write this letter. The Egyptian delegation didn't arrive in London. He
didn't take the newspaper. They didn't know the Arabic dictionaries. You (f.)
didn't write novels. I didn't advise you (sg. f.) to take these books. I didn't want
you (pl. m.) to learn Arabic. We didn't drink beer.

3. Negate the following sentences by means of لن, لا or لم .

ينظرون إلى الكتب. ستعملين بالأجهزة الحديثة. نفهم ذلك. سيأكلون لحم الدجاج.
خرجتُ من البيت صباحاً. أعرف ذلك. دخلت ذلك الفندق. يدرسن اللغة العربية.
نرغب في أن نكتب رسائل كثيرة. وضعت الكتب في الخزانة. ذهبت
مع صديقته. طلبتم أن نذهب معكم. تجلسنَ في المقهى. خرجتِ من المعهد. عرفنا أين
يسكن أحمد.

4. Negate the following sentences by means of ليس .

هو معلّم. هي جديدة. نحن طلّاب. أنتَ بائع. أنتم مجتهدون. هنّ في المعهد. أنتِ
مرافقة. هم رجال طيّبون. عندي كتب كثيرة. أنا طالب. في المعهد طلبة أجانب. هناك
جرائد عربية. الأكل حارّ. العصير في البرّادة. هو شاطر.

5. Translate into Arabic.
He is not big. I don't have a lot of dictionaries. She is not in London. You are not
diligent. The students (f.) are not tall. You are not a teacher (f.). We are not
clever. The wine is not in the refrigerator. They are not in the university. You are
not right.

6. Negate the following imperatives.

إشرب العصير ! كل اللحم ! خذ الكتاب ! أخرجي من الغرفة ! إسمعي ! إسمحوا لي أن
أكتب ! أكتب الرسالة ! إذهبن إلى هناك ! إفعلي ذلك ! أدخل ! إسمح لي أن أخرج !
إبحث عنه ! أدرسوا العربية ! أطلب قهوة!

7. Translate into Arabic.
The discussions are not long. He wrote on the occasion of the national holiday.
The minister didn't get the Nobel prize. The newspaper didn't write about
military cooperation. The president and the government of the country don't
make efforts to widen trade. The German minister arrived in Damascus in the

framework of a tour in the Middle East. The Russian president met his American counterpart. I didn't know many answers.

8. Fill in the blanks and vocalize the patterns.

Jussive	Subjunctive	Imperfect	Perfect
		تَكْتُبِينَ	
يَذْهَبْ			
	تَدْرُسُوا		
		يَطْلُبُون	
			خَرَجْتِ

1. The Dual (أَلْمُثَنَّى)

The Arabic language has a third number in addition to the singular and the plural: the dual. It is used when two things or persons are denoted. The dual is formed by means of suffixes the characteristic morpheme of which is the long vowel *ā*, which is expanded by *n* in some cases.

1.1. The dual of the noun

Suffix: ـَانِ in the nominative, ـَيْنِ in the genitive and accusative:

	pl.		sg.	
n.	أَلْمُعَلِّمُونَ	مُعَلِّمُونَ	أَلْمُعَلِّمُ	مُعَلِّمٌ
g.	أَلْمُعَلِّمِينَ	مُعَلِّمِينَ	أَلْمُعَلِّمِ	مُعَلِّمٍ
a.	أَلْمُعَلِّمِينَ	مُعَلِّمِينَ	أَلْمُعَلِّمَ	مُعَلِّماً
dual				
n.			أَلْمُعَلِّمَان	مُعَلِّمَان
g.			أَلْمُعَلِّمَيْن	مُعَلِّمَيْن
a.			أَلْمُعَلِّمَيْن	مُعَلِّمَيْن

☝A1 The genitive and the accusative of the dual cannot be distinguished from the same cases of the sound masculine plural in the unvocalized typeface.

	pl.		sg.	
n.	أَلْمَعَلِّمَاتُ	مُعَلِّمَاتٌ	أَلْمُعَلِّمَةُ	مُعَلِّمَةٌ
g.	أَلْمُعَلِّمَاتِ	مُعَلِّمَاتٍ	أَلْمُعَلِّمَةِ	مُعَلِّمَةٍ
a.	أَلْمُعَلِّمَاتِ	مُعَلِّمَاتٍ	أَلْمُعَلِّمَةَ	مُعَلِّمَةً
dual				
n.			أَلْمُعَلِّمَتَان	مُعَلِّمَتَان
g.			أَلْمُعَلِّمَتَيْن	مُعَلِّمَتَيْن
a.			أَلْمُعَلِّمَتَيْن	مُعَلِّمَتَيْن

The ending ن is dropped if the dual is in the construct state, e.g. if it functions as the 1ˢᵗ term of an *Iḍāfa* or if an affixed pronoun has been added. The same applies to the sound plural.

the two companions of the delegation	مُرَافِقَا الْوَفْدِ
with the two companions of the delegation	مَعَ مُرَافِقَي الْوَفْدِ
her two escorts	مُرَافِقَاهَا
with her two escorts	مَعَ مُرَافِقَيْهَا

A2 The affixed pronoun of the 1ˢᵗ p. sg., if added to a dual form, is يَ : my two friends صديقايَ; (cf. lesson 6, Gr 2.2.1.1.).

There is agreement in case, state, gender and number between a noun in the dual and an adjectival attributive adjunct:

مُعَلِّمَتَان جَدِيدَتَان   مُعَلِّمَان جَدِيدَان

أَلْمُعَلِّمَتَان الْجَدِيدَتَان   أَلْمُعَلِّمَان الْجَدِيدَان

رَأَيْتُ الْمُعَلِّمَتَيْن الْجَدِيدَتَيْن   عِنْدَ الْمُعَلِّمَيْن الْجَدِيدَيْن

Two attributive adjuncts in the singular can also be employed instead of one attributive adjunct in the dual. In this case each of them belongs to only one of the two concepts embodied in the dual form of the noun respectively:

the two teachers, the old one and the new one = the old and the new teacher	أَلْمُعَلِّمَان الْقَدِيمُ والْجَدِيدُ
The Syrian and the Iraqi government	أَلْحُكُومَتَان السُّورِيَّةُ والْعِرَاقِيَّةُ

1.2. The dual of the pronoun

Both the independent and the affixed pronouns have dual forms in the 3ʳᵈ and 2ⁿᵈ p. The suffix is *-ā*.

affixed pronouns		independent pronouns	
them both; both their	ـهُمَا -	both of them	هُمَا
both of you/you both; both your	ـكُمَا -	both of you	أَنْتُمَا

The demonstrative هَذَا has the same dual suffix that the noun has:

	f.	m.
n.	هَاتَان	هَذَان
g. / a.	هَاتَيْن	هَذَيْن

✋A3 In the feminine dual form of the demonstrative the long vowel *ā* in the first syllable is also expressed in the typeface.

1.3. The verbal dual forms

Perfect tense: The suffix -*ā* is added to the 3rd p. sg. m. and f. and to the 2nd p. pl. m.
Imperfect tense: The suffix -*āni* is added to the 3rd p. sg. m. and f. and to the 2nd p. sg. m.:

	imperfect tense	perfect tense	
3rd p. m.	يَفْعَلَانِ	فَعَلَا	(هما)
3rd p. f.	تَفْعَلَانِ	فَعَلَتَا	(هما)
2nd p.	تَفْعَلَانِ	فَعَلْتُمَا	(أنتما)

✋A4 The ending ن is omitted in the subjunctive and in the jussive.

   Imperative: The dual suffix *ā* is added to the masculine imperative of the singular: أُكْتُبَا ، إِفْعَلَا (appendix: Table 9).

✋A5 There is no verbal dual form in any modern Arabic dialect, but some dialects have the nominal dual. Adjectives, however, are not attested in the dual in any known colloquial. This is why we, in the interest of actual usage, refrained from employing the dual forms in Text 2 of this lesson in the passages in which, according to the rules of Modern Standard Arabic, a dual form would have to be employed.

2. The Numerals 1 and 2
2.1. The Arabic words for the cardinal numerals 1 and 2 are adjectives and agree as such with the principal noun in case, state, gender and number:

2.2. They are:

	2		1	
	f.	m.	f.	m.
n.	إِثْنَتَانِ	إِثْنَانِ	وَاحِدَةٌ	وَاحِدٌ
g.	إِثْنَتَيْنِ	إِثْنَيْنِ	وَاحِدَةٍ	وَاحِدٍ
a.	إِثْنَتَيْنِ	إِثْنَيْنِ	وَاحِدَةً	وَاحِداً

✋A6 The initial *Hamza* of إِثْنَانِ is a *Hamzat al-waṣl*: مَعَ اثْنَيْنِ مِنْهُم.

   وَاحِدَةٌ / وَاحِدٌ are not employed as an indefinite article (the latter is exclusively expressed by the indefiniteness of the noun: nunation, no article; cf. Lesson 4, Gr 3.2.), but are strictly used as a numeral: كِتابٌ وَاحِدٌ one book.

   إِثْنَتَانِ / إِثْنَانِ rarely occur as an attributive adjunct (they are at most, added to the noun as an emphasis), as duality is already expressed by the dual form of the latter.

2.3. The ordinal numerals of 1 and 2 are adjectives as well and are subject to the above-mentioned rules of agreement. They are (if the numerals are definite):

	2.		1.	
	f.	m.	f.	m.
n.	أَلثَّانِيَةُ	أَلثَّانِي	أَلأُولَى	أَلأَوَّلُ
g.	أَلثَّانِيَةِ	أَلثَّانِي	أَلأُولَى	أَلأَوَّلِ
a.	أَلثَّانِيَةَ	أَلثَّانِيَ	أَلأُولَى	أَلأَوَّلَ

The numeral adverbs "first(ly)" and "secondly" are expressed by the indefinite accusative of the ordinal numeral: أَوَّلاً ، ثانِياً.

3. كَمْ "how much/many"

3.1. To ask about the quantity of people or things, كَمْ is used. The construction is as follows:

a) كَمْ + indefinite noun in the accusative singular:

how many books	كَمْ كِتَاباً
how many men	كَمْ رَجُلاً
how many times = how often	كَمْ مَرَّةً

b) كَمْ + مِنْ + definite noun in the genitive plural:

how many books, how many of the books	كم مِنَ الْكُتُبِ
how many men, how many of the men	كم مِنَ الرِّجَالِ

Uncountable nouns or single concepts (usually designated in the singular) are treated as follows:

how much time, how long	كم مِنَ الْوَقْتِ
how much meat	كم مِنَ اللَّحْمِ
how much money	كم مِنَ النُّقُودِ

3.2. The predicate follows the indefinite noun:

How many books have you bought?	كم كِتَاباً اشْتَرَيْتَ؟
How many books do you have?	كم كِتَاباً عِنْدَكَ؟

The same word order applies to interrogative sentences which are introduced by كَمْ + مِنْ + definite noun. However, the predicate is set directly after كَمْ in some cases:

How many books do you have?	كَمْ لَكَ / عِنْدَكَ مِنَ الْكُتُبِ؟

3.3. كَمْ can be combined with various prepositions. The following noun is either in the accusative according to the given rule, or in the genitive, in subordination to the preposition:

for how much, by how much	بِكَمْ
For how many pounds did you buy that?	بكم لِيرَةً / لِيرَةٍ اشْتَرَيْتَ ذَلِكَ؟
with how much/many	مَعَ كَمْ
With how many students did you study there?	مع كم طَالِباً / طَالِبٍ دَرَسْتَ هُنَاكَ؟
for how long	مُنْذُ كَمْ
For how many years have you been studying there?	منذ كم سَنَةً / سَنَةٍ تَدْرُسُ هُنَاكَ؟

3.4. كَمْ also occurs as a (predicative) term of an equational sentence. The noun - the subject of the sentence - which follows كم is not in the accusative here, but in the nominative:

How (much) is your age? = How old are you?	كَمْ عُمْرُكَ؟
How (much) is its price? = How much does it cost?	كَمْ سِعْرُهُ؟
How (much) is its height? = How high is it?	كَمِ ارْتِفَاعُهُ؟
How (much) is the hour? = What time is it?	كَمِ السَّاعَةُ؟

An inversion of the word order is also usual in the last example: أَلسَّاعَةَ كَمْ؟.

It is possible that هُوَ or هِيَ comes between كم and the subject, especially if the latter is a noun which is defined by the article:

How much is the rent?	كم هِيَ الأُجْرَةُ؟
How (much) is the distance between ... and ...? = How far is it from ... to ...?	كم هِيَ الْمَسَافَةُ بَيْنَ ... و...

☞A7 ما can be used in the same meaning instead of the predicative كم:

ما هي المسافة؟ ما هو السعر؟

The Names of the Months:

	Syrian/Iraqi كانُونُ الثّاني	*Egyptian* يَنايِرُ
January		
February	شُباطُ	فِبْرايِرُ
March	آذارُ	مارِسُ
April	نِيسانُ	أبْرِيلُ
May	آيّارُ	مايُو
June	حَزيرانُ ، حُزَيْرانُ	يُونِيو
July	تَمُّوزُ	يُولْيو
August	آبُ	أغُسْطُسُ
September	أيْلُولُ	سِبْتَمْبَرُ
October	تِشْرِينُ الأوَّلُ	أُكْتوبَرُ
November	تِشْرِينُ الثّاني	نُوفَمْبَرُ
December	كانُونُ الأوَّلُ	دِيسَمْبَرُ

A8 All names of months are diptotes. They are regarded as proper names and are definite without having an article.

The Names of the Twelve Months of the Islamic Calendar:

number of days	name of the month	number of the month	number of days	name of the month	number of the month
(30)	رجبٌ	7th	(30)	مُحَرَّمٌ	1st
(29)	شعْبانُ	8th	(29)	صَفَرٌ	2nd
(30)	رمضانُ	9th	(30)	ربيع الأوَّل	3rd
(29)	شوَّالٌ	10th	(29)	ربيع الثّاني	4th
(30)	ذُو القَعْدِةِ	11th	(30)	جُمادَى الأُولَى	5th
(29)	ذُو الحِجَّةِ	12th	(29)	جُمادَى الآخِرة	6th

The last month of the year, which consists of 30 days in leap years, is the month of the pilgrimage to Mecca. (See also the summary in the appendix.)

The days of the week in Arabic are as follows:

الجُمْعَةِ	الخَميس	الأرْبِعاء	الثُّلاثَاء	الاثْنَيْن	الأحَدِ	السَّبْتِ	يوم
Friday	Thursday	Wednesday	Tuesday	Monday	Sunday	Saturday	

V

(interrogative particle)	أ
..., isn't it?	أ ليس كذلك؟
antiquities	ج آثار
ethnologic, anthropological	إثْنولوجيّ
history; date	تاريخ /تأْريخ ج تواريخ
Spanish, Spaniard	إسْبانيّ ج ـون
Asian	آسْيويّ ج ـون
African	إفْريقي ج ـون، أفارقة
As far as (Aḥmad) is concerned ...	أمّا (أحمد) فـ(هو) ...
form, questionnaire (mostly written استمارة)	اسْتِئْمارة ج ـات
English	إنْكْليزي ج إنْكْليز
cold	برْد / بارد
tip (colloq.)	بقْشِيش
porter, doorman	بوّاب ج ـون
to belong to so.	تبع (يتْبَعُ) ه / لِ
belonging to	تابِع لِ
thirty	ثلاثونَ
snow, ice	ثلْج ج ثُلوج
mountain	جبل ج جِبال
to collect sth.	جمع (يَجْمَعُ) هـ
side	جانِب ج جوانِبُ
beside	إلى جانب
passport	جواز (السفر)
to order sth., to book sth.	حجز (يَحْجُزُ) هـ
heat, temperature	حرارة
civilization, culture	حضارة ج ـات
suitcase	حقيبة ج حقائبُ
to carry sth.	حمل (يحْمِل) هـ
servant (f.)	خادِمة ج ـات
autumn, fall	خريف
specialization	تخصّص ج ات
especially	خاصّة
low	مُنْخفِض
state	دوْلة ج دُول
religion	دِين ج أدْيان
spring	ربيع
education	ترْبية
reference book	مرْجع ج مراجِعُ
cheap, reasonable (price)	رخيص
number	رقْم ج أرْقام
mathematics	الرِّياضيّات
agriculture	زراعة
wife	زوْجة ج ـات
to fall (down)	سقط (يسْقُطُ)
thick, heavy	سميك
sky	سماء (م)
winter	شِتاء
person	شخْص ج أشْخاص
oriental studies	اسْتِشْراق
to feel sth.	شعر (يشْعُرُ) بِ
to be cold, to freeze	شعر بالبرد
Thank you very much.	شُكْراً جزيلاً!
north	شمال
source (for information)	مصْدر ج مصادِرُ
summer	صيْف
Chinese	صينيّ ج ـون
to comprise	ضمّ (يضُمُّ) هـ
in addition to	إضافة إلى
floor	طابق ج طوابِقُ
dissertation	أطْرُوحة ج ـات

moderate, temperate	مُعْتدِل	hat, cap	قُبَّعة ج ـات
twenty	عِشْرُونَ	coming	قادِم
coat	مِعْطف ج معاطِفُ	village	قَرْية ج قُرىً
science, studies	عِلْم ج عُـلُوم	glove	قُفاز ج قفافيزُ
scientific	عِلْميّ	how much / many	كَمْ
sociology	عِلْم الإجْتِماع	for how much / many	بِكَمْ
biology	عِلْم الأحْياء	air condition	مُكَيِّف هواء ج ـات
information	ج مَعْلُومات	to dress sth.	لبِس (يلْبَسُ) هـ
institute	مَعْهد ج معاهِدُ	German mark	مارك ج ـات
a medical doctor's office	عِيادة ج ـات	to stay	مكث (يمْكُثُ)
to leave sth.	غادر (يُغادِرُ) هـ	minibar	مينيبار
expensive	غال	Indian	هِنْدِي ج هُنُود
branch	فَرْع ج فُرُوع	to have to, must	وجب (يجِبُ) (عليه) أنْ
French	فِرنْسيّ ج ـون	I was born	وُلِدْتُ
section, paragraph; season	فصْل ج فُصُول	birth(day)	مِيلاد
peasant, farmer	فلّاح ج ـون	daily	يَوْمِياً

Text 1

جامعتي

جامعتي حديثة وكبيرة ويدرس فيها طلّاب من أمريكا والكثير من الطلّاب الأجانب ومن بينهم طلّاب عرب. وأعرف الكثير من هؤلاء الطلّاب العرب. أنا طالب في كلّية الطبّ. كلّيتي هذه كبيرة جدّاً.

وتضم الجامعة من الفروع العلمية كلّيات الفيزياء والكيمياء والزراعة وعلم الأحياء والرياضيات. أما من الفروع الأدبية فتتبعها كلّية اللغات، أي اللغة الانكليزية والفرنسية والإسبانية والروسية واللغات الأوربية الأخرى واللغات الافريقية والآسيوية، إضافة إلى كلّيات التربية والحقوق والاقتصاد وعلم الاجتماع.

وتدرس صديقتي في معهد الدراسات الشرقية التابع للجامعة وتخصّصها هو الدراسات العربية أي تاريخ العرب وحضارتهم وآدابهم قديماً وحديثاً. وتوجد إلى جانب ذلك المعهد معاهد أخرى للدراسات الإفريقية والهندية والصينية والتركية والاثنولوجية ومعهد تاريخ الأديان ومعهد علم الآثار المصرية.

سوف أعمل بعد الدراسة طبيباً في هذه المدينة في عيادة أمّي. أما صديقتي فستسافر إلى مصر لمدّة سنة في السنة الدراسية القادمة وستجمع هناك المراجع والمصادر اللازمة لكتابة أطروحتها.

Text 2

في الفندق

الخادمة: مساء الخير، تفضّلوا، أدخلوا، أهلاً وسهلاً، أية خدمة؟

بيتر: مساء النور. أنا أرغب في أن أحجز غرفة لشخصين.

الخادمة: غرفة أم شقّة؟

بيتر: شقّة.

الخادمة: عندنا شقق كبيرة وهي غالية وكذلك شقق صغيرة رخيصة.

بيتر: بكم الشقّة الصغيرة؟

الخادمة: الشقّة الصغيرة بدون مكيّف بعشرين دولاراً.

بيتر: وبمكيّف هواء؟ الطقس حار جدّاً والمكيّف لازم.

الخادمة: بمكيّف بثلاثين دولاراً. ولكن الطقس ليس حارّاً ونحن نشعر بالبرد الآن، نحن الآن في فصل الشتاء والحرارة الآن معتدلة. أنت لا تعرف الحرارة هنا في الربيع والصيف والخريف.

بيتر: أنا أعرف ذلك. وعندنا في شمال أوربا يسقط الثلج يومياً وخاصة في الجبال ونحن نلبس معاطف سميكة وقبّعات وقفافيز. أنا آخذ الشقّة الصغيرة بالمكيّف. هل في الغرف مينيبار؟

الخادمة: لا، يجب عليكم أن تطلبوا المشروبات من خدمات الغرف.

بيتر: أنا أفهم، مَن يحمل المشروبات إلى الغرف يأمل أن يحصل على بقشيش، أ ليس كذلك؟

الخادمة: أنت على حقّ، الأجور منخفضة والبقشيش خبز الخادم. أكتب من فضلك اسماءكم وعنوانكم وتاريخ الميلاد ورقم الجواز على هذه الاستمارة.

بيتر: بالعربية أو بالإنكليزية؟

الخادمة: بالأنكليزية، من فضلك. متى تغادرون؟

بيتر: نغادر بعد أسبوع.

الخادمة: سيحمل البوّاب حقائبكم إلى الشقّة.

بيتر: شكراً جزيلاً، أين المطاعم؟

الخادمة: المطعم الكبير في الطابق الأول ومطعم الفطور في الطابق الثاني.

بيتر: شكراً وتصبحين على خير.

الخادمة: وأنت من أهله وشكراً.

Exercises:

L1 Identify the nouns in the Vocabularies of Lesson 8 and 9. Form the indefinite and the definite dual and transform one of the two into the genitive by means of an appropriate preposition.

معهد – معهدان – المعهدان – في المعهدين ☜

مكتبة – مكتبتان – المكتبتان – في المكتبتين ☜

L2 Answer the following questions using the dual or واحد / واحدة.

كم ساعة عملت هناك؟ > عملت هناك ساعة واحدة. ☜

أو: عملت هناك ساعتين. ☜

كم ساعة	عملت في البيت (في المكتبة، في المعهد)؟
	شرحت له العمل (عمله، هذه الأعمال، الدرس)؟
	جلست في المطعم (في القاعة، هناك، عندهم)؟
كم يوماً	عملت في المصنع (في بيتك، في المكتبة، في المعهد)؟
	مكثت في تلك المدينة (في ذلك البلد، في العاصمة، في المقهى)؟
	سكنت في الفندق (في بيته، في بيت الطلبة، هناك)؟
كم أسبوعاً	درست هذه اللغة (في هذا المعهد)؟
	سكنت في الفندق (عندهم، عند أصدقائك)؟
	عملت في المصنع (في المكتبة، في المخزن)؟
كم شهراً	عملت في ذلك المصنع (هناك، معه هناك، في بيتهم)؟
	سكنت في تلك الغرفة (تلك المدينة، ذلك البيت)؟
	مكثت في ذلك البلد (في تلك المدينة، في عاصمتنا)؟
كم سنةً	درست اللغة العربية (اللغة الألمانية، هذه اللغة)؟
	عملت هناك (في تلك المدينة، في ذلك المصنع)؟
	مكثت في تورونتو (في برلين، في القاهرة، في العاصمة)؟
كم كأساً	من العصير (النبيذ، الماء) شربت؟
كم فنجاناً	من القهوة (الشاي) شربت؟
كم كتاباً	(قلماً، كرّاسة، جهازاً، محّاةً) أخذت / طلبت؟
كم شهراً	(سنةً) درست في تلك الجامعة؟
بكم	(دولار) اشتريت هذا القلم ذلك الكتاب، (تلك الكرّاسة، ذلك الجهاز)؟
مع كم	من الأصدقاء ذهبت إلى هناك (إلى المحطّة، إلى المطعم)؟

كم عندك _____ من البيوت (السيّارات، الكتب العربية، الصديقات)؟

منذ كم شهر (سنة، ساعة، أسبوع، يوم) تعمل هنا؟

L3 Same as L2 but the question in the 2nd p. pl., answer in the 1st p. pl.

L4 Same as L2 but using the corresponding verb in the imperfect tense.

L5 Same as L3 but using the corresponding verb in the imperfect tense of the 2nd p. pl. in the question and the 1st p. pl. in the answer.

L6 Answer the following questions.

ما هي أسماء فصول السنة في أوربا؟

ما هي أسماء شهور الربيع في أوربا؟

ما هي أسماء شهور الصيف في أوربا؟

ما هي أسماء شهور الخريف في أوربا؟

ما هي أسماء شهور الشتاء في أوربا؟

L7 (Repetition) A number of genitive constructions are quoted in the following exercise. Put the respective form of هذا in such a way that it a) refers to the 2nd term and b) to the 1st term of the *Iḍāfa*.

☞ كتاب الصديق   >   كتاب هذا الصديق / كتاب الصديق هذا

☞ كتاب صديقي   >   كتاب صديقي هذا

لون السيّارة، بيوت الطلّاب، أصدقاء الفتاة، عاصمة البلد، جامعة المدينة، غرف البيت، معلّم صديقي، طلّاب جامعتنا، معلّمو المدرسة، علاقات البلد، أعضاء الوفد، فواكه البلد.

L8 Pratice the usage of يجب (عليّ، عليك، عليه، عليها and so on) أنْ based on the following material:

أكتب رسالة / أسافر إلى برلين / تحجز شقّتين / تطلبون مشروبات وأكلاً / تحمل الحقيبتين إلى فوق / تدرسين اللغة العربية / يعملون في الخارج / أعمل في عيادة أمّي / تسافرين إلى مصر لمدّة شهرين / تجمعون المراجع والمصادر اللازمة / تسمح له بالدخول / تفهم ما تقرأ / نرجع إلى المدينة / نأخذ زجاجتين / تشرب العصير / نأكل السمك

G1 Replace the object / the noun of the prepositional phrase by the affixed pronoun.

☞ رأيت الرجلين.   >   رأيتهما.

☞ ذهبنا إلى المكتبة.   >   ذهبنا إليها.

قرأت (قرأنا، هل قرأتم) الكتابين.

قرأت (لم أقرأ، لم نقرأ) هذه الكتب.

رأيت (رأينا، هل رأيتم) الفتيات.

مكثت (مكثتْ، مكث) في تلك المدينة.

شربت (شربا، شربتا) كأسين من العصير.

ذهبت (ذهبنا، ذهبوا) إلى هناك مع الصديقين.

ذهبت (ذهبن) إلى هناك مع الصديقتين.

ذهبت (ذهبوا، ذهب) إلى هناك مع الأصدقاء.

درست (درسنا، درس) لغتين.

درست (درسوا، هل درست) لغات كثيرة.

وضعت (وضعتْ) القلمين في الشنطة.

أخذت (أخذنا، أخذوا) الجهازين.

كتبت (كتبتْ، كتبن) رسالتين.

خرجت (خرجنا، خرجوا) من البيت.

سمعت (سمعنا، هل سمعتم) هذا الخبر.

عملت (عملوا، هل عملت) في تلك المصانع.

أكلت (أكلنا، أكلوا) اللحم (الخبز، الفواكه، الجبنة).

رجعت (رجعنا، هل رجعتم) إلى الفندق.

شكرت (شكرنا، شكروا) المدير.

نظرت (نظر، هل نظرت) إلى هاتين الفتاتين.

G2 Put the proper demonstrative in front of the following nouns.

☞   الرجل   >   هذا الرجل

☞   مع الرجال   >   مع هؤلاء الرجال

☞   مع الرجلين   >   مع هذين الرجلين

الدولة، البُلْدان، البَلَدان، الجهازان، الأرض، اللغة، الاجتماع، المدرستان، المشروبات، الأيام، الخزانتان، في الرسالتين، المسرح، المحطّات، الوفود، الشهران، الأسبوعان، المعهـد، الدول، في الغرفتين، الزجاجات، بالسيّارتين، المعطفان، مع الأصدقاء، الطالبان، الأسئلة، الأعمال، القرية، الجبلان، الملابس، العمّال، الفلاّحون.

G3 Transform the perfect to imperfect tense and vice versa in the following sentences.

☞   هل كتبتما رسالة   >   هل تكتبان رسالة؟

يذهبان إلى المكتبة.   ... إلى المكتبة.

عقدتا اجتماعاً   ... اجتماعاً

متى يخرجان من البيت؟   متى ... من البيت؟

لماذا ... ذلك؟ أو: لماذا ... ذلك؟	لماذا تفعلان ذلك؟
أين ...؟	أين يعملان؟
ماذا ...؟	ماذا شربتما؟
ماذا.. ؟ أو: ماذا ...؟	ماذا تدرسان؟

G4 (Homework) Put the dual in those passages in Text 2 where the context allows it. (However, pay attention to Gr 1.3., A 5 in this lesson.)

G5 (Repetition) Transform the perfect into the imperfect tense and vice versa.

أكلوا طعاماً شرقياً. نشرب الشاي بعد الأكل. يجلسون في مطعم من مطاعم المدينة. هــل تعرف هؤلاء الأصدقاء؟ نعم، أعرفهـم. هـل تفهمـون ذلك الرجـل؟ هـل فهمتـني؟ هـل تفهمونني؟ عقدوا اجتماعاً. كتبن رسائل كثيرة. أسمع ذلك. وضع كتبه في الشنطة. قرأنـا تلك الكتب. فعل ذلك أصدقاؤنا الألمان. ندرس اللغة العربية. يصل الوفد العراقي اليـوم. تصل الوفود العربية ظهر اليوم. يجلسون في القاعة الكبيرة. أشرب فنجاناً من القهوة. هـل تأكل اللحم والخضراوات؟ يطلب لحم الدجاج.

G6 (Repetition) The teacher quotes the following verbs in different persons in the perfect or imperfect tense and the student adds the verb in the other tense.

ذهب، درس، كتب، شرب، فعل، سمع، وصل، وضع، سأل، قرأ، حضر، عقـد، عـرف، خرج، رجع، زرع، أكل، عمل، طلب، علم، جمع

C1 Every student answers the question about the month of his birthday.

وُلِدْتُ في شهر...   متى وُلِدْتَّ / وُلِدْتِّ؟

C2 Have a conversation about your arrival and the check-in at a hotel based on Text 2.

C3 Create a telephone conversation from your room in a hotel asking the servant to bring drinks / breakfast / lunch / dinner to your room. The teacher plays the role of the room service.

C4 Complain by phone to the reception desk of the hotel about the malfunction of your tv, air conditioner, a telephone call abroad and so on. The teacher plays the role of the hotel receptionist.

Final Exercise

1. Answer the following questions using the dual.

كم شهراً عملت في ذلك المصنع؟
كم يوماً سكنت في الفندق؟
كم ساعة جلست في الغرفة؟
كم كأساً من البيرة شربت؟

بكم اشتريت ذلك الجهاز؟

مع كم من الأصدقاء ذهبت إلى المسرح؟

كم عندك من السيّارات؟

منذ كم سنة تدرس العربية؟

2. Transform into genitive constructions.

1st term	2nd term
أطروحات، هذه الجوازات، هاتان الغرفتان	المعلّمون
مسارح، فندقان، موظّفون، محطّات، شوارع	هذه المدينة
صديقتان، هذه الكتب، ذلك التخصص	صديقه

3. Translate into Arabic.

I have to write two letters. He has to work abroad. She must eat the fish. You *(f.)* must book two rooms. We must carry the two suitcases to the rooms. They have to wear coats, hats and gloves. You *(pl.)* must ask the second teacher.

4. Transform the perfect into the imperfect tense and vice versa.

ماذا تدرسان؟ ماذا شربتما؟ أين يسكنان؟ سألتما الثاني. لبستما المعطف الثاني. شعرتما بالبرد في غرفتكما. تدرسان في الفصلين الربيعي والخريفي. أين وضعتما الجوازين؟ يجمعان المصادر والمراجع.

5. Translate into Arabic.

The faculties of the university are the faculties of physics, chemistry, biology, mathematics, the faculty of languages as well as the faculty of education, the faculty of law and the two faculties of economics and agriculture. I am studying at the Institute for Arabic Studies. My institute is small and old. Apart from this institute there are institutes for African, Egyptian, Indian, Chinese and Turkish studies and an institute for the history of religions in the framework of oriental studies.

1. Cardinal Numerals (أَلأَعْداد الأَصْلِيّة)

The Arabic numerals are written in the following way:

10	9	8	7	6	5	4	3	2	1	0
١٠	٩	٨	٧	٦	٥	٤	٣	٢	١	٠

✍ **A1** The numerals for 2 and 3 differ in writing from the printed signs given above, namely ٢ for 2 and ٣ for 3. Compound numbers which are expressed by numerals are written from the left to the right as in English: 1994 ١٩٩٤.

1.1. The numerals are:

٠	صِفر	ṣifr
١	واحد	wāḥid
٢	إِثنان	ithnān
٣	ثلاثة	thalātha
٤	أَربعة	arbaᶜa
٥	خمسة	khamsa
٦	ستَّة	sitta
٧	سبعة	sabᶜa
٨	ثمانية	thamāniya
٩	تسعة	tisᶜa
١٠	عشرة	ᶜashara

According to grammatical rules the numerals 3 - 10 are regarded as diptotes in abstract counting. Consequently the correct pronunciation would be *wāḥidun, ithnāni, thalāthatu, arbaᶜatu, khamsatu,* etc. In general, however, the endings are dropped in oral usage. Accordingly we pronounce: *wāḥid, ithnān, thalātha, arbaᶜa,* etc.

1.2. The numerals 1 and 2 are adjectives. They were treated in Lesson 9. By contrast 3 -10 are nouns. Each numeral from 1-10 has a masculine and a feminine form. The numerals are used in abstract counting as shown, i.e. 1 and 2 in their masculine, 3 -10 in their feminine forms.

1.3. The rule of so-called polarity applies to 3 -10 in connection with a noun as the counted item, i.e., a masculine word is preceded by the feminine form of the numeral, a feminine word by the masculine form of the numeral. The numeral and the noun are the 1st and the 2nd term of a genitive construction. The noun is indefinite and takes the genitive plural.

in connection with a feminine noun		in connection with a masculine noun
ثلاثُ فتياتٍ	٣	ثلاثةُ رجالٍ / مُعلِّمينَ
أَرْبعُ فتياتٍ	٤	أَرْبعةُ رجالٍ / مُعلِّمينَ
خَمْسُ فتياتٍ	٥	خَمسةُ رجالٍ / مُعلِّمينَ
سِتُّ فتياتٍ	٦	سِتّةُ رجالٍ / مُعلِّمينَ
سَبْعُ فتياتٍ	٧	سبعةُ رجالٍ / مُعلِّمينَ
ثماني فتياتٍ	٨	ثمانيةُ رجالٍ / مُعلِّمينَ
تِسْعُ فتياتٍ	٩	تِسْعةُ رجالٍ / مُعلِّمينَ
عَشْرُ فتياتٍ	١٠	عَشَرَةُ رجالٍ / مُعلِّمينَ

This rule about polarity also applies when the noun does not immediately follow the numeral or is not mentioned at all.

three men	ثلاثةُ رجالٍ
three of the men	ثلاثةٌ من الرِّجالِ
three of them	ثلاثةٌ مِنْهُم
I have seen three.	رأيتُ ثلاثةً

1.4. The numerals 11-19 are indeclinable (مَمْنوع من الصرْف) with one exception, namely the numeral 12. There is agreement in gender, not polarity in gender, between the numeral *m.* عَشَرَ , *f.* عَشْرَةَ which denotes ten and the following noun. The noun takes the **accusative singular**.

in connection with a feminine noun		in connection with a masculine noun
إِحْدَى عَشْرَةَ فتاةً	١١	أحد عَشَرَ رجُلاً
إِثْنَا عَشْرَةَ فتاةً	١٢	إِثْنا عَشَرَ رجُلاً
ثلاثَ عَشْرَةَ فتاةً	١٣	ثلاثةَ عَشَرَ رجُلاً
أَرْبعَ عَشْرَةَ فتاةً	١٤	أَرْبعةَ عَشَرَ رجُلاً
خَمْسَ عَشْرَةَ فتاةً	١٥	خَمسةَ عَشَرَ رجُلاً

سِتَّ عَشْرَةَ فتاةً	١٦	سِتَّةَ عَشَرَ رجُلاً
سبْعَ عَشْرَةَ فتاةً	١٧	سبْعةَ عَشَرَ رجُلاً
ثمانيَ عَشْرَةَ فتاةً	١٨	ثمانية عَشَرَ رجُلاً
تِسْعَ عَشْرَةَ فتاةً	١٩	تِسعةَ عَشَرَ رجُلاً

A2 The rule of polarity in gender which applies to the numerals 3-10 also applies to the numerals 13-19 in so far as the masculine numeral denoting the unit is connected with the feminine numeral denoting ten and, vice versa, the feminine numeral denoting the unit with the masculine numeral denoting ten. Accordingly polarity in gender exists within the two terms of these compound numerals. On the other hand, there is agreement in the numerals 11 and 12: a masculine numeral denoting the unit is connected with a masculine numeral denoting ten, and a feminine numeral denoting the unit with a feminine numeral denoting ten.

A3 The dual inflection already treated occurs in the genitive and accusative of the numeral 12:

I went there with twelve girls.	ذهبْتُ إلى هُناك مع اثْنتيْ عَشْرَةَ فتاةً.
I saw twelve men there.	رأيْتُ هُناك اثْنيْ عَشَرَ رجُلاً.

A4 The numeral 10 is masc. عَشْر, fem. عَشَرَة, whereas it is عَشَر and عَشْرَة when it functions as a component of the compound numerals 11-19.

1.5. The numerals 20 - 99 are followed by the noun in the accusative singular as well. The numerals 20, 30, 40 up to 90 which denote tens have the form of the sound masculine plural (n. ـُونَ , g., a. ـِينَ). The units compounded with them follow the rules stated under 1.3. and 1.4., i.e. there is agreement in gender between the numerals 1 and 2 which denote units and the counted item, polarity in gender between the numerals 3-9 which denote units and the counted item. The word order is different from modern English; units come before tens.

in connection with a feminine noun		in connection with a masculine noun
عِشْرُونَ فتاةً	٢٠	عِشْرُونَ رجُلاً
إحْدَى وعِشْرُونَ فتاةً	٢١	واحِدٌ / أحدٌ وعِشْرُونَ رجُلاً
إثْنتان وعِشْرُونَ فتاةً	٢٢	إثْنان وعِشْرُونَ رجُلاً
ثلاثٌ وعِشْرُونَ فتاةً	٢٣	ثلاثةٌ وعِشْرُونَ رجُلاً
ثلاثُونَ فتاةً	٣٠	ثلاثُونَ رجُلاً
إحْدَى وثلاثُونَ فتاةً	٣١	واحِدٌ / أحدٌ وثلاثُونَ رجُلاً
إثْنتان وثلاثُونَ فتاةً	٣٢	إثْنان وثلاثُونَ رجُلاً
ثلاثٌ وثلاثُونَ فتاةً	٣٣	ثلاثةٌ وثلاثُونَ رجُلاً

أَرْبَعُونَ فَتاةً	٤٠	أَرْبَعُونَ رَجُلاً
خَمْسُونَ فَتاةً	٥٠	خَمْسُونَ رَجُلاً
سِتُّونَ فَتاةً	٦٠	سِتُّونَ رَجُلاً
سَبْعُونَ فَتاةً	٧٠	سَبْعُونَ رَجُلاً
ثَمانُونَ فَتاةً	٨٠	ثَمانُونَ رَجُلاً
تِسْعُونَ فَتاةً	٩٠	تِسْعُونَ رَجُلاً

1.6. The whole hundreds (i.e. 100, 200, 300 ...), the numerals thousand, million, billion when functioning as the 1st term of a genitive construction are construed with the following noun in the genitive singular. The numerals 300, 400,... 900, each of which is constructed out of the respective units and the word for hundred, مِائة or مِئة (pronounced mi'a[tun]), as a genitive construction, are written together. Since the rule about polarity of the units applies here as well, these take the masculine form when preceding مِائة, and the feminine form when preceding مِلْيار، مَلـْيُون، أَلْف. The plural of the three last-named words is مِلْيارات، مِلايين، آلاف. The plural of مِائة is مِئات, which, however, is only used in the meaning of "hundreds".

مِائة is in the singular when the numerals 300 - 900 are formed, although the numerals 3 - 9 are otherwise construed with the plural:

١٠٠٠	أَلْفُ رَجُلٍ		١٠٠	مِائةُ رَجُلٍ	
٢٠٠٠	أَلْفا رَجُلٍ		٢٠٠	مِائتا رَجُلٍ	
٣٠٠٠	ثلاثةُ آلافٍ رَجُلٍ		٣٠٠	ثَلاثُمِائةِ رَجُلٍ	
١٠٠٠٠٠٠	مَلْيُونُ رَجُلٍ		٤٠٠	أَرْبَعُمِائةِ رَجُلٍ	
			٩٠٠	تِسْعُمِائةِ رَجُلٍ	

1.7. The order in compound numerals is thousand + hundred + unit + ten, which are connected by a copulative و respectively. If the units 3 - 9 or the numeral 10 are there, polarity in gender is to be observed.

١٠٣	مِائةٌ وثَلاثةُ رِجالٍ
١١٢	مِائةٌ واثْنتا عَشْرَةَ فتاةً
٢٠٠	مِائتا مارْكٍ
٢١٠	مِائتانِ وعَشْرَةُ أشْخاصٍ
٣٠٠	ثلاثُمِائةِ مَلِيمٍ
٤٨٦	أَرْبَعُمِائةٍ وسِتٌّ وثَمانُونَ لَيرةً

أَلْفٌ وسَبْعُمائةٍ وتِسْعةٌ وخَمْسُونَ عاماً	١٧٥٩
أَلْفا سنةٍ	٢٠٠٠
ثمانيةُ آلافٍ دِينارٍ	٨٠٠٠
أَحَدَ عَشَرَ أَلْفَ جُنيهٍ	١١٠٠٠
مِائَتا أَلْفٍ	٢٠٠٠٠٠
ثلاثُمائةٍ وخَمْسةٌ وعِشْرُونَ أَلْفاً	٣٢٥٠٠٠

☞A5 With regard to the numerals 101, 102, 1001, 1002, the abstract count differs somewhat from the construction numeral + noun as the counted item:

مِائَةٌ وواحِدٌ	but:	مِائَةُ دِينارٍ ودِينارٍ
مِائَةٌ واثْنانِ	but:	مِائَةُ دِينارٍ ودِيناران
أَلْفٌ وواحِدٌ	but:	أَلْفُ لَيْلةٍ ولَيْلةٌ
أَلْفٌ واثْنان	but:	أَلْفُ لَيْلةٍ ولَيْلتانِ

1.8. The numerals are in the **genitive**:

after prepositions   مع ثلاثةِ رجالٍ

after nouns   صاحِبُ ثلاثةِ بيوتٍ

after the numerals 3 - 10   ثلاثةُ آلافٍ

and the hundreds   مِائةُ أَلْفٍ

and in the **accusative**:

after verbs (as the object)   رأَيتُ ثلاثةَ رجالٍ

after إنَّ **and** أنَّ   أعْرِفُ أَنَّ ثلاثةَ رجالٍ ...

after the numerals 11 - 99   واحِدٌ وعِشْرُونَ أَلْفاً

☞A6 The declension of the numeral 8 is: n. and g. ثمانٍ, a. ثمانياً and when definite الثماني or الثمانيَ. Cf. also Table 37 in the Appendix.

1.9. The years are in the genitive, namely after the words سنة and عام "year". Polarity in gender, which applies to the numerals 3 - 10, and agreement in gender, which applies to the numerals 1 and 2 are to be observed again with regard to them.

in the year 1990   في سنةِ أَلْفٍ وتِسْعِمائةٍ وتِسْعِينَ

in the year 1991   في سنةِ أَلْفٍ وتِسْعِمائةٍ وإحْدَى وتِسْعين

in the year 1991	في عام ألفٍ وتِسْعِمائةٍ وواحِدٍ وتِسْعِين
in the year 1992	في سنةِ ألفٍ وتِسْعِمائةٍ واِثْنَتَيْنِ وتِسْعِين
in the year 1992	في عام ألفٍ وتِسْعِمائةٍ واِثْنَيْنِ وتِسْعِين
in the year 1993	في سنةِ ألفٍ وتِسْعِمائةٍ وثلاثٍ وتِسْعِين
in the year 1993	في عام ألفٍ وتِسْعِمائةٍ وثلاثةٍ وتِسْعِين

☝A7 The numerals are also read from the right to the left: في عام ثلاثة وتسعين وتسعمائة وألف .

☝A8 The states of the Maghrib mostly use the same numerals used in Europe and America; and their use is not restricted to dates. Newspapers from the East are also beginning to use the numerals of Europe and America in the last few years.

1.10. If the word combination consisting of a numeral and a noun is to be definite (3 men > the 3 men), the numeral follows the noun, as is also the case with the numerals 1 and 2. The noun takes the plural then in any case. The rule about polarity is not affected by this.

أَلرِّجالُ الثلاثةُ، أَلفتياتُ الثلاثُ، أَلأشخاصُ الثلاثةَ عَشَرَ، أَلمُدُنُ المائةُ ، أَلكُتُبُ الألفُ

☝A9 The construction which consists of a numeral defined by the article + a noun without an article is also frequently found: أَلثلاثة عشر شخصاً، أَلثلاثة رجال .

The numerals are not included in the vocabulary list of this lesson. They are located in the detailed list in the Appendix.

V

to come after, to succeed so.	تبِع (يتْبَعُ) ه	last	أخير
pilgrimage	حجّ ج ـات، حِجَج	eventually, finally	أخيراً
according to	حسب	so, therefore, then	إذن
calculation, account, bill	حِساب ج ـات	basis, foundation	أساس ج أُسُس
here: place, square	محلّ ج ـات	basically	أساسيّ
present, current, contemporary	حالِي	Sunnites	أهْل السُنّة
nearly, approximately, about	حوالَىْ	to begin, to start	بدأ (يبْدَأُ)
to succeed to so.	خلف (يخْلُفُ) ه	beginning	بداية
caliph	خليفة ج خُلفاءُ	blessed	مُبارك
the Rightly Guided Caliphs	الخلفاء الراشدون	to amount to	بلغ (يبْلُغُ) هـ
administration	إدارة ج ات	son	اِبْن ج أبْناء، بَنُون
dinar (*currency*)	دِينار ج دنانِيرُ	died (*pass.*)	ت. > تُوُفِّيَ

school of law	مذهَب ج مذاهِبُ
I beg your pardon.	أرْجُو الإعْتِذار.
May God be pleased with him.	رضِيَ اللهُ عنه
pillar	رُكْن ج أرْكان
you want (m.)	تُرِيدُ أنْ
Zakāt	زكاة
Zakāt at the end of Ramaḍān	زكاة الفِطْر
plus	زائد
registration	تسْجِيل ج ـات
staircase, steps	سُلّم ج سلالِمُ
Peace be upon him.	عليهِ السلام
Muslim	مُسْلِم ج ـون
Islam	الإسْلام
Islamic	إسْلامِيّ
the Sunna	السُّنّة
equals	يُساوِي
the act of testimony	الشهادة (ب)
honest, upright (epithet of the 1st Caliph)	الصّدِّيق
lift	مِصْعد ج مصاعِدُ
God bless him and grant him salvation! (often used in the shortened form صلعم)	صلّى الله عليه وسلّم
prayer	صلاة ج صلوات
morning prayer	صلاة الفجْر / الصُبْح
midday prayer	صلاة الظُّهر
afternoon prayer	صلاة العصْر
evening prayer	صلاة المغْرِب
night prayer	صلاة العِشاء
fasting	صوْم
equals	يُعادِلُ
pardon	عفْوًا
relying on	إعتماد (على)

building	عِمارة ج ات
year	عام ج أعْوام
majority	غالِبِيّة ج ـات
before	مِن قَبْلُ
estimation	تقْدِير ج ات
divided by	(مقْسُوم) على
calendar	تقْوِيم
stay	إقامة ج ـات
I told you.	قُلْتُ لَكَ/ لَكِ
They told me. / I was told.	قالُوا لِي
venerable (epithet of Mecca)	المُكَرَّمة
tongue; language	لِسان ج ألْسُن، ألْسِنة
faculty of languages	كلّيّة الألسُن
cf. ميلادي	م
why	لِماذا
including, inclusive of	بِما في ذلك
percent	بالمائة
Medina	المَدِينة المُنوَّرة
Mecca	مكّةُ المُكَرَّمة
one can (+ verbal noun)	يُمْكِنُ الـ...
prophet, messenger	نبِيّ ج ـون، أنْبِياء
minus	ناقِص
end	نِهاية
shining, enlightened (epithet of Medina)	المُنوَّرة
to emigrate	هاجر (يُهاجِر)
the Hijra	الهِجْرة
of the Hijra	هِجْرِيّ
engineering	هنْدسة
(the) finding	إيْجاد
corresponding	مُوافِق
AD; abbr: م	مِيلادِيّ
Yathrib (Medina)	يثرِبُ

الإسلام والمسلمون   **Text 1**

سيبلغ عدد المسلمين في العالم حسب التقديرات الجديدة حوالى مليار مسلم بعـد سنوات
قليلة وغالبيتهم من أهل السنّة أي ٩٠ بالمائة تقريــاً. وتوجـد في الدين الإسلامـي أربعـة
مذاهب أساسية وهي: مذهب أبي حَنِيفَةَ النُّعْمَانِ بْنِ ثَابِتٍ (ت. ٧٦٧ م) ومذهب مَالِكِ
ابْـنِ أَنَسٍ (ت.٧٩٥ م) ومذهـب مُحمَّدِ بْـنِ إِدْرِيسَ الشَّافِعِي (ت.٨٢٠ م) ومذهـب
أَحْمَدَ بْنِ حَنْبَلٍ (ت.٨٥٥ م).

وأركان الإسلام الخمسة هي الشهادة بأنّه ﴿لا إِلاهَ إِلاّ ا اللهُ محمّدٌ رسُولُ ا اللهِ﴾ ، والصلاة
خمس مرّات في اليوم، أي صلاة الفجر والظهـر والعصر والمغرب والعشـاء، والصوم في
شهر رمضانَ المباركِ والزكاة بما في ذلك زكاة الفطر في نهاية شهر رمضان وأخيراً الحـجّ
إلى مكّةَ المكرّمة.

ونبيّ الإسلام هو مُحمّدُ بْنِ عبْدِ ا الله بْنِ عبْدِ المُطَّلِبِ بْـنِ هَاشِمٍ، صلَّى ا الله عليه وسلَّم
(ت.٦٣٢ م) وهو من بَني هَاشِمٍ من قُرَيْشٍ في مكّة. وخلفـه الخلفاء الراشِدون الأربعـة
وهم أبُو بكرٍ الصِّدِّيقُ (٦٣٢ – ٦٣٤م) وعُمر بْـنُ الخَطَّابِ (٦٣٤ – ٦٤٤م) وعُثْمَانُ
ابْنُ عَفَّان (٦٤٤ – ٦٥٦م) وعليُّ بْنُ أبي طَالِبٍ (٦٥٦ – ٦٦١م)، رضي ا الله عنهم.

وهاجر مُحمّد، صلَّى ا الله عليه وسلَّم، في سنة ٦٢٢ من مكّةَ إلى يَثْرِبَ (المدينة المنوّرة)
وهذه السنة هي بداية التقويم الهجري على أساس الســنة القمريـة أي ٣٥٤ يومـاً وأسمـاء
الأشهر الإسلامية هي:

مُحـرّم وصفـر وربيـع الأول وربيـع الثاني وجُمـادَى الأولى وجُمـادَى الآخِرةُ ورجـب
وشعْبانُ ورمضانُ وشَوّال وذُو القعْدةِ وذو الحِجّة.

ولإيجاد التاريخ الميلادي يمكن الاعتماد على الحساب التالي: السنة الهجرية الحالية ناقص
السنة الهجرية مقسومة على ٣٣ زائد ٦٢٢ (م = هـ – $\frac{هـ}{٣٣}$ + ٦٢٢).

والسنة الهجرية الحالية هي ١٤٢١ الموافقة ٢٠٠٠ م.

🖎**A10** Ibn is only written with *Alif* (اِبن) at the beginning of a sentence or a new line or if اِبن is the
first part of a name, e.g. اِبن سينا، اِبن خلدون، a.o.; otherwise the spelling is بن :
محمّد بن عبد ا الله بن عبد المطلّب، عليّ بن أبي طالب

Text 2

عند التسجيل

الموظّفة: صباح الخير، أية خدمة؟

بيتر: صباح النور، نعم، قالوا لي إنّ التسجيل هنا.

الموظّفة: هذا صحيح، هل عندك الأوراق اللازمة؟

بيتر: نعم، الأوراق معي.

الموظّفة: إذن نبدأ. ما اسمك؟

بيتر: بيتر ميلر.

الموظّفة: في أية سنة ولدتَّ؟

بيتر: ولدتُ في سنة ١٩٧٦.

الموظّفة: العنوان؟

بيتر: لندن، شارع باركلين، رقم ١٥٢، بريطانيا.

الموظّفة: رقم الجواز؟

بيتر: .١٩٨٧٦٥٤

الموظّفة: محلّ الإقامة هنا؟

بيتر: شارع الرشيد، رقم العمارة ١٨٧، رقم الطابق ١٢.

الموظّفة: منذ متى أنت هنا؟

بيتر: وصلت قبل شهر.

الموظّفة: في أي فرع من فروع الهندسة تريد أن تدرس؟

بيتر: هذه إدارة تسجيل كلّية الألسن، أ ليس كذلك؟

الموظّفة: لا، والله، أنت هنا في قسم تسجيل كلّية الهندسة، كلّية الألسن في الطابق الثاني. لماذا لم تسأل من قبل؟

بيتر: عفواً، أنت لم تسأليني وأنا لم أعرف أنّني وصلت إلى قسم تسجيل كلّيات الهندسة. أرجو الاعتذار. أين كلّية الألسن؟

الموظّفة: أنا قلت لك في الطابق الثاني، أي من هنا إلى اليمين إلى المصعد أو إلى السلم، إلى الغرفة رقم ٢٢٢.

بيتر: شكراً، مع السلامة.

الموظّفة: مع السلامة.

Exercises:

L1 Form sentences according to the following pattern using the names of currencies you know.

اشتريت هذا الـ... / هذه الـ... بـ ...

اشتريت هذا الكتاب بثلاثة دولارات.

اشتريت هذا المصباح بثلاث عشرة ليرة.

L2 (Homework) Form equational sentences using currencies and time definitions according to the following patterns.

A month consists of 30 or 31 days.

الشهر ٣٠ أو ٣١ يوماً.

February consists of 28 or 29 days.

شهر شباط ٢٨ أو ٢٩ يوماً.

A pound is 100 cents.

الجنيه ١٠٠ قرش.

L3 Answer the following questions.

كم مرةً كنتَ (كنتِ، كنتـم) في المكتبة (في المعهد، عند أصدقائنـا، في بيته، في ذلك المطعم)؟

كم كأساً من العصير (النبيذ) شربتَ (شربتِ، شربتم)؟

كم كتاباً (قلماً، كراسة، جهازاً، بيتاً، لوحاً) اشتريت (أخذتِ، طلبتم)؟

كم من الكراسي (المصابيح، الشبابيك، الأبواب، الجدران) توجـد في غرفتـكَ (في غرفتكِ، في بيتكم)؟

منذ كم أسبوعاً (شهر، سنة) تدرس في جامعتنا؟

كم عندك من الكتب (الأقلام، الشنطات، الأصدقاء، المعلمين)؟

كم عمرك؟

كم سعر ذلك الكتاب (الشنطة، الجهاز، السيّارة، الكمبيوتر)؟

L4 (Repetition) Negate the following sentences by means of ليس.

الطالب مجتهد.   <   ليس الطالب مجتهداً.

الغرفة جميلة.   <   ليست الغرفة جميلة.

عندي كتب كثيرة. في الغرفة طلاب. هناك أجهزة حديثة. في المعهد طلبة أجانب. البيت كبير. البيوت جميلة. المعلّمون في الغرفة. هؤلاء الرجال طيِّبون. هؤلاء الرجـال معلّمـون. تلك الفتاة معلّمة. أولئك الفتيات طالبات. هذه الكرّاسة زرقـاء. سيّارتي بيضـاء. لونهـا أبيض.

Pay attention to the fact that the noun or phrase following the prepositional phrase in the first four examples is not the predicate, but the subject of the sentence. It is the type of sentence dealt with in   Lesson 2, G 3.1., sentence structure 2.

G1 Combine the nouns and numerals.

ليرة، دينار	٢٣	١٣	٣
ساعة، شهر	٣٤	١٤	٤
كيلومتر، سنة	٤٥	١٥	٥
مليم، قرش	٥٦	١٦	٦
متر، يوم	٦٧	١٧	٧
سنتيمتر، كتاب	٧٨	١٨	٨
يوم، سنة	٨٩	١٩	٩
دقيقة، أسبوع	٣٠	٢٠	١٠
جنيه، يوم	٤٠	٢١	١١
فلس، شخص	٥٠	٢٢	١٢
موظف، سنة	٨٠	٧٠	٦٠
ليرة، جنيه	١٠١	١٠٠	٩٠
متر، دولار	٤٠٠	٣٠٠	٢٠٠
شخص، كيلومتر	١٠٠٠٠	٢٠٠٠	١٠٠٠

G2 (Written homework) Add the definite article to the following collocations.

☞ ثلاثة رجال   <   الرجال الثلاثة

☞ عشرون يوماً   <   الأيّام العشرون

عشرة طلّاب – خمس علب – ثلاثة معلّمين – ثمانية زبائن – إثنا عشر كتاباً – أحد عشر بيتاً – سبع فتيات – تسعة شبابيك – عشرون يوماً – ثلاثة عشر أسبوعاً – سبعة عشر دولاراً – أربع ساعات – أربع وعشرون ساعة – ثلاثون يوماً – ستة وستون شخصاً – أحد وسبعون كيلومتراً – مئة رجل – ست عشرة دقيقة – عشرة موظّفين – مائتا شخص.

G3 (Repetition) Negate the following sentences by means of لم.

☞ فعلت ذلك.   <   لم أفعلْ ذلك.

خرجت من البيت. خرج من المعهد. خرجـن مـن المطعـم. دخل بيت صديقـه. دخلنا المطعم. دخلتِ ذلك البيت. وصل الوفد أمس. وصلت الوفود مساء أمس. وصلوا صباح اليوم. فهمتُ. فهمتم. فهم. فهمَت. فهمنا. درس هناك طلاب أجانب. شرح لهم عمـل المكتبة. رجعوا إلى البيت. طلبنا منه ذلك. طلبوا منّي ذلك. طلبتُ منكم ذلك. رغبوا في أن يكتبوا لها. رغبتُ في أن يدخل بيتي. عرفتُ ذلك. عرفنا ذلك. عرفوا ذلك. عرفت ذلك. عمل هناك. عملتُ هناك. عملت في ذلك المصنع. عملـوا في تلك المدينـة. عملنا

هناك. عملوا بأجهزة حديثة. أخذوا ذلك. أخذ الكتاب. أخذنـا الجرائد. أخـذن ذلـك. أخذتم ذلك. فعل ذلك. فعلنا ذلك. فعلتِ ذلك. ذهبَـت إلى هنـاك. ذهبـتِ إلى المكتبـة. ذهبوا إلى القاعة. شربت النبيـذ. شـربوا القهـوة. شـربنا البيرة. أكلنـا اللحـم. أكلـوا في المطعم. أكلتم هناك.

G4 (Repetition) Negate the following sentences by means of لا, لن or ما / لم.

☞ أشرب البيرة.   <   لا أشرب البيرة.

☞ سأذهب إلى المعهد.   <   لن أذهب إلى المعهد.

☞ فهمت ذلك.   <   لم أفهم ذلك.

طلب منّي أن أذهب إلى هناك. خرجت من البيت صباحاً. سمعنا هذا الخبر. نفهـم ذلـك. يأكلون فواكه كثيرة. سيذهبون إلى المعهد. ذهبَت إلى صديقتها. عمل بالأجهزة الحديثة. ينظرون إلى الكتب. أعرف ذلك. أخذ الكتاب. فعلوا ذلك. دخلت ذلـك المعهد. قرأنـا كتباً كثيرة. يدرسون اللغة العربية. نعرف ذلك. سيعقدون اجتماعـاً. سيعمـل في برلـين. ستكتبون لهم. وضعت الكتب في الخزانة. نرغب في أن نذهب إلى هناك.

C1 The teacher asks the students to count in Arabic.

C2 The teacher quotes English numbers and the students give their Arabic equivalent.

C3 The teacher quotes Arabic numbers and the students give their English equivalent. The speed of speaking should be gradually increased.

C4 The teacher quotes nouns with numerals first in English and then in Arabic and the students give the respective equivalent.

C5 The teacher asks the students to do calculations as follows:

٤ زائد ٤ يساوي كم؟   >   ٤ زائد ٤ يساوي ٨.

٢٠ ناقص ١ يساوي كم؟ > ٢٠ ناقص ١ يساوي ١٩.

٣٠ على ٦ يساوي كم؟ > ٣٠ على ٦ يساوي ٥.

٥ في ٥ يساوي كم؟   >   ٥ في ٥ يساوي ٢٥.

C6 Prepare a dialogue based on Text 2 about the registration in a faculty/ university. Use as many numerals as possible.

C7 Prepare notes for a "lecture" based on Text 1 about the most important dates of the history of Islam.

Final Exercise:

1. Combine the following nouns and numerals.

٥	ركن	١٠	مسلم	١١	جواز	
٤	مذهب	٥	صلاة	١٧	طابق	
١٢	شهر	٢٣	عمارة	٢١	مصدر	
٢	دين	٦٢٢	سنة	٢	قبّعة	
١٢	معلّم	٤٥٦	دولار	٣٢	أسبوع	

2. Translate into Arabic.

after the Four Rightly Guided Caliphs, the Five Pillars of Islam, the four Islamic schools of law, the twelve Islamic months, with the three wives, in front of the seven mountains, the two dissertations, the thirteen chairs, in the eleven universities, in the month Rabīᶜ ath-thānī, in the second year

3. Negate the following sentences by means of لا, لم, لن or ليس.

أنا مسلم. هاجر محمّد في عام ٦٣٣. سيبلغ عدد المسلمين حـوالى مليـون مسـلم. عرفنـا المذاهب الأربعة. غالبيتهم من أهل السنّة. بدأ التاريخ الإسلامي في عام ٦٢١. سألنا عـن أبي حنيفة وأحمد بن حنبل. هو قرشي. تبعه هارون الرشيد. درستم الهندسـة. سـتخرجن من المطعم. فهمت العربي. خرج في شهر آب.

4. Write out in words:

١٠٠١ ، ١٩١٨ ، ٧٥٠ ، ١٩٤٥ ، ٢٠٠٥ ، ١٢٥٨ ، ٦٢٢ ، ١٩٩١

5. Translate into Arabic. (Numerals have to be written out in words.)

I was in Baghdad three times. They went to the theatre with five friends. The registration is on the second floor. He lives in the 2ⁿᵈ room. He entered the 3ʳᵈ building. I have 4 brothers. Two million pilgrims travelled to Mecca this year. I was born in 1414 AH. *Muḥammad b. ᶜAbdallāh b. ᶜAbd al-Muṭṭalib b. Hāshim*, peace be upon him, is the messenger of Islam. The four Rightly Guided Caliphs are *Abū Bakr aṣ-Ṣiddīq, ᶜUmar b. al-Khaṭṭāb, ᶜUthmān b. ᶜAffān* and *ᶜAlī b. Abī Ṭālib*, may God be pleased with them.

6. Write the following Arabic words in transliteration.

زكاة، هـجرة، حجّ، السُنّة، خليفة، صلاة الفجر، صوم، رمضان، حاجّ، دين

7. Write the names of the months used in Iraq and Syria.

1. The Perfect Tense of Verbs with و and ى (أَلأَفْعالُ الْمُعْتَلّة)

Up to now, in dealing with the perfect and the imperfect tense, we have only encountered the so-called strong verbs (أَلأَفْعال الصحيحة), i.e. verbs in which R_1, R_2 and R_3 are full consonants. There are certain peculiarities in the conjugation of the so-called defective or weak verbs. The verbs in which the "weak" consonants و (*Wāw*), ى (*Yā'*) or ء (*Hamza*) occur as R_1, R_2 or R_3 are to be understood by this.

The perfect tense of these verbs with و or ى is treated on the basis of model verbs in this lesson, the conjugational paradigms of which are to be applied analogously to verbs of the same structure.

☝A1 The weak verbs are often designated by Latin terms in the grammar or textbooks of Arabic:

R_1 = و or ى = verba primae (radicalis) و et ى
R_2 = و or ى = verba mediae (radicalis) و et ى
R_3 = و or ى = verba tertiae (radicalis) و et ى

1.1. The perfect tense of verbs with R_1 = و or ى is formed in the same way as that of the strong verbs.

model verb وَصَلَ "to arrive":

(هو) وَصَلَ
(هي) وَصَلَتْ
(هم) وَصَلُوا

etc. (Cf. Appendix tables 1 and 15)

1.2. R_1 has the long vowel *ā* in the perfect tense in verbs in which R_2 = و or ى if a vowel follows R_3.

Examples with the model verbs:

و = R_2 (فَعَلَ = قَوَمَ >) "to get up" قَامَ I

(هو) قَامَ   (هي) قَامَتْ   (هم) قَامُوا

ى = R_2 (فَعَلَ = بَيَعَ >) "to sell" بَاعَ II

(هو) بَاعَ   (هي) بَاعَتْ   (هم) بَاعُوا

و = R_2 (فَعِلَ = خَوِفَ>) "to fear" خَافَ III

(هو) خَافَ   (هي) خَافَتْ   (هم) خَافُوا

☝A2 Consequently, in these forms it is not clear from the outward appearance whether it is a verb R_2 = و or a verb R_2 = ى. The dictionary supplies information about this. It is also possible to discern which group the respective verb belongs to from the imperfect tense (see Lesson 12, Gr 1.2.).

R$_1$ has the short vowel *u* or *i* in the perfect tense in verbs with R$_2$ = و or ى if R$_3$ is vowelless. With this the following conjugational paradigm is produced for these verbs:

III	II	I	
خَافَ	بَاعَ	قَامَ	(هو)
خَافَتْ	بَاعَتْ	قَامَتْ	(هي)
خِفْتَ	بِعْتَ	قُمْتَ	(أنتَ)
خِفْتِ	بِعْتِ	قُمْتِ	(أنتِ)
خِفْتُ	بِعْتُ	قُمْتُ	(أنا)
خَافُوا	بَاعُوا	قَامُوا	(هم)
خِفْنَ	بِعْنَ	قُمْنَ	(هنَّ)
خِفْتُمْ	بِعْتُمْ	قُمْتُمْ	(أنتم)
خِفْتنَّ	بِعْتنَّ	قُمْتنَّ	(أنتنَّ)
خِفْنا	بِعْنا	قُمْنا	(نحن)

Accordingly, the verbs which belong to group I have the short vowel *u*, the verbs which belong to groups II and III have the short vowel *i* (Appendix: tables 1, 18, 20, 22).

☞ **A3** The same rules apply to the dual forms. Since they are relatively rare in occurrence, they are not expressly mentioned here nor in the following lessons. They are listed in full in the tables of the Appendix.

1.3. Verbs with R$_3$ = و or ى

R$_3$ is omitted in the 3rd p. sg. f. (groups I and II).

Examples with the model verbs:

I دَعَا "to invite" (فَعَلَ = دَعَوَ) R$_3$ = و   (هي) دَعَتْ   (هو) دَعَا

II مَشَى "to walk" (فَعَلَ = مَشَيَ) R$_3$ = ى   (هي) مَشَتْ   (هو) مَشَى

III لَقِيَ "to meet" (فَعِلَ =) R$_3$ = ى   (هي) لَقِيَتْ   (هو) لَقِيَ

☞ **A4** ى which represents R$_3$ has the phonetic value *ā* when identified in the verbs of group II (model verb مشى). We have already got to know ى = *ā*, called *Alif maqṣūra* in Arabic terminology, in such words as أَلْمَقْهى and أَلْمُسْتوى. This final long vowel *ā* (ى) in some words also becomes visible in writing as *Alif* (ا) if an affixed pronoun is added to these words: مَقْهَاهُ "his café", تَرَاني "you see me" (Appendix: table 37).

All other forms are characterized by a diphthong after R_2 in verbs belonging to groups I and II, and by a long vowel after R_2 in verbs of group III. This produces the following paradigm:

III	II	I	
لَقِيَ	مَشَى	دَعَا	(هو)
لَقِيَتْ	مَشَتْ	دَعَتْ	(هي)
لَقِيتَ	مَشَيْتَ	دَعَوْتَ	(أنتَ)
لَقِيتِ	مَشَيْتِ	دَعَوْتِ	(أنتِ)
لَقِيتُ	مَشَيْتُ	دَعَوْتُ	(أنا)
لَقُوا	مَشَوْا	دَعَوْا	(هم)
لَقِينَ	مَشَيْنَ	دَعَوْنَ	(هنَّ)
لَقِيتُمْ	مَشَيْتُمْ	دَعَوْتُمْ	(أنتم)
لَقِيتُنَّ	مَشَيْتُنَّ	دَعَوْتُنَّ	(أنتنَّ)
لَقِينا	مَشَيْنا	دَعَوْنا	(نحن)

(Appendix: tables 1, 23, 24, 25)

2. Word Order: إِنَّ and the Subject of the Sentence

The normal word order in the sentence is verb - subject. If the subject is to be emphasized in the main clause, it is placed in front of the verb, and the particle إِنَّ is set in front of the subject. The word order consequently is:

إِنَّ + subject + verb + (object)

A5 Likewise, first the subject, then the verb comes after the conjunction لكِنَّ "but". Moreover, this word order occurs without employing the particle إِنَّ if the main clause is introduced by a conjunction (وَ، فَ).

The word order subject - verb - without a particle in anteposition - is especially common in headlines in newspapers.

The particle إِنَّ causes the subject to be in the accusative.

(They have told us:) The Arab delegation visited the city of Berlin yesterday.	(قالُوا لَنَا) إنَّ الوفْدَ العربيَّ زَارَ مدِينةَ برلين أمْسِ.

The particle إِنَّ is used after the verb قَالَ "to tell, to say" to introduce direct speech. Since "to tell, to say" is mostly followed by indirect speech in English, the illustrative sentence is best translated by: "They have told us that the Arab delegation ..."

👆A6 When reading unvocalized texts, the student must observe in the beginning that he does not read the إنَّ after قَالَ as أنَّ ("that") under the influence of his mother tongue.

A personal pronoun instead of a noun can follow إنَّ; its affixed form is used, which is also the case after أنَّ :

sg. إنَّه ، إنَّها ، إنَّكَ ، إنَّكِ ، إنَّنِي / إنِّي

pl. إنَّهم ، إنَّهنَّ ، إنَّكم ، إنَّكنَّ ، إنَّنا / إنَّا

👆A7 The particle لَعَلَّ ("perhaps, maybe") is a sister of إنَّ. It may introduce an equational sentence, with the subject in the accusative and the predicate in the nominative. The subject of لَعَلَّ may also be a pronoun. لَعَلَّ can also introduce a verbal sentence and must therefore receive a pronoun suffix agreeing with the verb that would otherwise follow immediately after it.

Perhaps the student will write the book.	لَعَلَّ الطَّالِبَ يَكْتُبُ الكِتَابَ.
Perhaps there are teachers in the university.	لَعَلَّ في الجامِعَةِ مُعَلِّمِينَ.
Perhaps he does not write the letter.	لَعَلَّهُ لا يَكْتُبُ الرِّسالَةَ.

V

The imperfect tense of the so-called weak verbs is given here as well as the imperfect of the strong verbs, although they will only be dealt with in detail in the next lesson.

for; in order to	مِن أَجْلِ	meeting, session	جَلسة ج ـات
crisis	أزْمة ج أزَمات	council	مَجْلِس ج مَجالِسُ
founding	تأسِيس	Security Council	مجلس الأمن
to be sure (that)	مُتأكِّد (من)	neighboring	مُجاوِر
nation, people	أمَّة ج أُمم	fixed	مُحدَّد
the United Nations	الأمم المتَّحِدة	to happen	حدث (يَحْدُثُ)
thing, matter	أمْر ج أُمُور	war	حرْب م ج حُرُوب
security	أمْن	improving	تحسِين
parliamentary, parliamentarian	برْلَمانِيّ	improvement	تحسُّن
proof, evidence for	بُرْهان ج براهِينُ على	presence	حُضُور
to build, to erect, to set up sth.	بنى (يبْنِي) هـ	dear guests	ج حضرات الضيُّوف
building, construction	بناء	power, control, rule	حُكْم
to sell sth.	باع (يبِيعُ) هـ	regulation, rule, provision	حُكْم ج أحْكام
to let/to leave sth. for so.,	ترك (يتْرُكُ) هـ لِ	court	مَحْكمة ج محاكِمُ

solution	حلّ ج حُلُول	making so. take part (in)	إشْراك (في)
situation, state, condition	حالة ج ـات	doubt (about)	شكّ ج شُكُوك (في)
the exterior, foreign, abroad	الخارج	undoubtedly, without doubt	بلا شكَّ
quarrel, argument (في ،على)	خِلاف ج ـات	creation, formation	تشْكِيل ج ـات
to be afraid of so., sth.	خاف (يخافُ) من ه، هـ	problem	مُشْكِلة ج مشاكِلُ
the interior, inland	الداخِل	consulting	تشاوُر
to invite, to call (up)on so. to do sth.	دعا (يدْعُو) (ل، إلى)	journalist	صُحُفيّ ج ـون
invitation, call	دعْوة ج دعوات	friendly, be friends with	صديق
religious	دِينيّ	declaration	تصْريح ج ـات
memory	ذِكْرَى م ج ذِكْريات	authority, power(s)	صلاحِيَة ج ـات
anniversary of the foundation	ذكرى تأسيس	industry	صِناعة ج ـات
opinion (of, about, on sth., so.) (في)	رأي	extra, extraordinary	طارىءٌ
salary	راتِب ج رواتِبُ	development	تطوُّر ج ات
to ask so. to do sth.	رجا (يرْجُو) ه أنْ	opposition	مُعارضة ج ـات
I greet / welcome you	أُرَحِّبُ بكم	carrying out, holding (a meeting)	عقْد
reaction	ردّ فِعْلٍ ج رُدُود فعل	general, public	عامّ
bribery	رشْوة	to work towards	عمل على
to refuse, reject, turn down sth.	رفض (يرْفُضُ) هـ	to return (to)	عاد (يعُودُ) (إلى)
to visit so., sth.	زار (يزُورُ) ه، هـ	return	عَوْدة
rising, going up (beyond)	زائِد (عن)	re-,	إعادة
question, case	مسْألة ج مسائِلُ	to live, to experience, to see ه	عاش (يعيشُ)
reason, cause	سبب ج أسْباب	victory over; overcoming, surmounting	تغلُّب على
speed	سُرْعة	(coordinating conjunction)	فْ
fast	سريع	period	فتْرة ج ات
peaceful	سِلْميّ	scandal	فضِيحة ج فضائِحُ
In the name of God the Merciful	بسْمِ اللهِ الرحْمٰن الرحِيم	law	قانون ج قوانِينُ
		interview	مُقابلة صُحُفية ج ـات
contribution (to) (في)	مُساهمة ج ـات	future	مُسْتقْبل
His Excellency (الرئيس)	سِيادةُ	(particle cf. Lesson 13, p.163)	قدْ
to move (to)	سار (يسيرُ) إلى	able to, capable, qualified	قادِر على
ghost	شبَح ج أشْباح	clear-cut	قاطِع

to steer, to drive sth. (to)	قاد (يقُودُ) هـ (إلى)
to say sth., that	قال (يقُولُ) هـ، إنَّ
to get up, to rise	قام (يقومُ)
to carry out, to realize	قام بـ
to conceal, to hide	كتم (يكتُمُ) هـ
catastrophe	كارثة ج كوارثُ
sufficient	كافٍ
was (with predicate complement)	كان (يكونُ)
therefore, that's why	لذا
(particle of confirmation)	لَقدْ
committee	لجنة ج لِجان
urgent	مُلِحّ
to meet so.	لقِي (يلْقَى) ه
representative	مُمثِّل ج ـون
alike, similar	مُماثِل
carrying on, performing, exerting	مُمارسة
to run, to walk, to go	مشَى (يمْشِي)
past	ماضٍ
to grant, to give so. sth.	منح (يمْنَحُ) ه هـ
result	نتيجة ج نتائجُ
to be successful (in)	نجح (ينْجَحُ) (في)

success	نجاح ج ـات
(prep.) to (direction)	نحْو
election	انتِخاب ج ـات
relating to	بِالنّسْبة لِ
victorious, triumphant	مُنْتصِر
checking, inspection	النظَر في
system, regime	نِظام ج نُظُم، أنْظِمة
(him)self	نفس ج أنفُس
to sleep, to fall asleep	نام (ينام)
task	مُهمَّة ج ـات
board, body	هيئة ج ـات
tension	توتر ج ات
positive	إيجابيّ
to find sth.	وجد (يجد) هـ
situation	وضع ج أوْضاع
citizen	مُواطِن ج ـون
to stand in front of	وقف (يقِفُ) أمام
post, point	موْقِف ج مواقِفُ (من)
representative, agent	وكيل ج وُكلاءُ
(Under) Secretary of State, Permanent Secretary	وكيل الدولة

Text 1

كلمة الرئيس

بسم الله الرحمن الرحيم

حضرات السيدات والسادة

إسمحوا لي أولاً أنْ أُرَحِّبَ بكم وأن أشكركم على حضوركم احتفالَنا بالعيد الوطني. لقد عاش بلدنا كما تعرفون في السنوات الماضية حالةً مـن التوتُّرات السياسـية والاجتماعـية وقد عملنا الكثير من أجل التغلُّب على هذه الحالة. ونجحنا في حلّ الكثير من المشـاكل الاجتماعية كما أنّ الأوضاع العامَّة في الداخل والخارج سارت نحو التحسُّن وخرجنا مـن هذه الأزمة الطويلة منتصرين.

وكما قلت في كلمتي اليوم في الصباح فإنّ الحرب قادت البلد إلى كارثة كبيرة وإنّنا وقفنا أمام مشاكل كثيرة. لذا دعونا أصدقاءنا للتشاور كما أنّني زرت البلدان المجاورة ودعوتها للتعاون معنا في سبيل تحسين العلاقات وكانت ردود الفعل إيجابية ووضعنا حلولاً سلمية لخلافاتنا.

لقد قمت أيضاً بزيارة لهيئة الأمم المتّحدة ومجلس الأمن. وحضرت جلسة طارئة للأمم المتّحدة وأنتم تعرفون نتائج هذه الجلسة التاريخية.

إنّ احتفالنا اليوم هو برهان قاطع على صحة سياستنا ونجاحها والآن وبعد أن نجحنا في بناء النظام الديمقراطي وبعد أن خفنا من عودة شبح الحرب مرّة أخرى إلى البلد نقف أمام مهمّة بناء البلد في مجالي الصناعة والزراعة. إنّني متأكد من أنّا سنخرج من مشاكلنا ومن أزمتنا منتصرين.

إسمحوا لي أن أشكركم مرّة أخرى على حضوركم احتفالنا بالعيد الوطني.

Text 2   مقابلة صحفية

الصحفية: سيادة الرئيس، اسمحوا لي أن أسألكم عن موقفكم من التطوُّرات الجارية في البلد؟

الرئيس: كما قلت في تصريحي الرسمي قبل يومين فالحكومة تعمل على إيجاد حلول سريعة لمشاكل المواطنين ولدينا الوقت الكافي.

الصحفية: وكيف حدثت هذه المشاكل وما هي أسبابها؟

الرئيس: إنّ أسباب هذه المشاكل كثيرة وهي اقتصادية واجتماعية وثقافية ودينية.

الصحفية: ما هو رأيكم في إعادة تشكيل مجلس الوزراء وهل صحيح أنّكم ترغبون في إشراك المعارضة في الحكومة؟

الرئيس: لا، أنا أرفض هذه الفكرة. إن المعارضة ليست قادرة على المساهمة في حلّ المشاكل الملحّة والانتخابات الأخيرة منحتنا صلاحيات ممارسة الحكم في البلد للسنوات الأربع القادمة.

الصحفية: وكيف الأمر بالنسبة للفضائح الأخيرة يعني فضائح رشوة الوزراء ووكلاء الدولة والرواتب الزائدة عن الرواتب المحددة في أحكام قانون رواتب موظّفي الدولة؟

الرئيس: إنّنا نترك النظر في حلّ هذه المسائل للّجان البرلمانية وللمحـاكم. و لم أسمـع مـن

المعارضة في هذه المسألة أشياء جديـدة وعلمنـا أنّ المعارضة في فتـرة حكمهـا

كتمت مشاكل مماثلة وفضيحتنا أيضاً فضيحتهم!

الصحفية: أشكركم على هذه المعلومات القيّمة واسمحوا لي بسؤال أخير.

الرئيس: تفضّلي!

الصحفية: هل سوف تسافرون إلى أمريكا في الأسبـوع القـادم لحضـور اجتماعـات هيئـة

الأمم المتّحدة؟

الرئيس: إن شاء ا لله.

الصحفية: شكراً جزيلاً.

Exercises:

L1 Insert the appropriate preposition(s).

إسمحوا ... أن أشكركم ... الرسالة. عاش البلد حالة ... التوتُّر السياسي والاجتمـاعي

... السنوات الماضية. نشعر ...أن الأوضـاع العامّـة ... الداخـل والخـارج خرجـت ...

الأزمة الطويلة. ...إمكاننا أن ننظـر ... المسـتقبل السـلمي. قلـت ... كلمتـي اليـوم ...

الصبـاح إن الحرب قادت البلد ... كارثـة. وقفنـا ... مشـاكل كبيـرة. دعونـا أصدقاءنـا

...التشاور ...نا. سـارت الأمـور ... التحسُّـن بسرعة. دعوتهـم ... العمـل ...نا ...

تحسين العلاقات. لقيت رد فعل إيجابياً ... هذه البلدان. قام الرئيس ...زيارة هيئـة الأمـم

المتحدة وأمينها العام. دعا الأمين العام ...الأمم المتحدة ...انعقاد (عقـد) جلسة طارئـة.

إن احتفالنا هو برهان قاطع ... نجـاح سياستنا ... السـنوات الماضيـة. خفنـا ... عـودة

الحرب مرّة ثانية ... البلد. نقف ... مهمة بناء البلد ...بجالي الصناعة والزراعة. أنا متأكّد

... أننا سنخرج ... مشاكلنا و... أزمتنا. أسافر ... أمريكا ... الأسـبوع القـادم. عـاد

... الخارج. هو قادر ... كتابة هذه الرسالة.

L2 Insert an appropriate verb.

... لي أن ... عن موقفكم من التطوُّرات الجارية في البلد. ... في تصريحي الرسمي قبـل

يومين إنّ الحكومـة ... على إيجاد حلـول سريعة لمشـاكل المواطنين. كيف ... هـذه

المشاكل وما هي أسبابها؟ هل صحيح أنّكم ... في إشراك المعارضة في الحكومة؟ أنـا ...

هذه الفكرة. إن المعارضة ...قادرة علـى المسـاهمة في حلّ المشـاكل الملحّـة. الانتخابات

الأخيرة ... الصلاحيات لممارسة الحكم في البلد للسنوات الأربع القادمة. إنّنـا ... النظـر

في حلّ هذه المسائل للجان البرلمانية وللمحاكم. لم ... من المعارضة في هذه المسألة أشيـاء

جديدة. ... المعارضة في فترة حكمها مشاكل مماثلـة. ... علـى هـذه المعلومـات القيّمـة.

... لي بسؤال أخير. ... إلى أمريكا في الأسبوع القـادم لحضـور اجتماعـات هيئة الأمـم المتّحدة.

L3 Transform the meaning of the following sentences into the opposite by means of an antonym or negation.

قام الرئيس. سافر محمّد. وصل الوفد. الجهاز جديد. دخل المطعم. باع السيّارة. فهمت السؤال. علمتُ منهم أنّه رجل لطيف. هم مجتهدون. يعرف أشياء كثيرة. عرف السـؤال الأخير.

L4 Form genitive constructions with the following words.

1st term

رؤسـاء / سياسـة / فضـائح / رواتـب / مـترجمون (translator/interpreter)/ نتـائج / مرافقون / وزراء

2nd term

بلـدان، وفـود، حكومـة، الخارجيـة (the exterior)، صناعـة، زراعـة، وزيـر، رئيـس، حكومات، الداخلية (the interior)، الأمم المتحدة، جلسة، حرب، معارضة

L5 Same as L4; but add an appropriate adjective to the 1st term.

☞   رواتب – وزراء < رواتب الوزراء الجديدة

L6 (Homework) Form 10 sentences with numerals and Arabic equivalents for "to have".

☞   عندي / عنده خمسة كتب. لي / له عشرة أقلام. للبيت بابان.

☞   معي / معه سيّارتان.

G1 The following exercises are mainly to practice the change of persons in the perfect tense. A sentence is given, and the student has to repeat it and then to transform it as shown in the following example:

☞   given sentence: عاد محمّد إلى الفندق.

☞   repetition: عاد محمّد إلى الفندق.

☞   completion: وعُدتُ أنا إلى البيت.

If a clause or a part of a sentence is to be completed by another word or phrase, or if an additional word should be used in the completion, this addition is put in brackets after the given sentence.

Thus the example given would be written as follows:

☞   عاد محمّد إلى الفندق (إلى البيت)

The affixed pronouns of the 3rd p. have to be changed into the 1st p. if necessary.

☞   عاد محمّد إلى فندقه ... وعُدْتّ أنا إلى بيتي

In the first place the change of the 3rd p. sg. m. or f. into the 1st p. sg. is practiced.

(معهم)	زار الرجال المركز الجديد للعاصمة.
(كسلان) (lazy)	قال صديقي إنّني مجتهد.
	باع الرجل سيّارته.
(أن يكتب لي)	رجا الطالب الجزائري أن أكتب له.
(معهم)	مشى الأصدقاء إلى المقهى.
	وعد (to promise) المرافق أصدقاءه بزيارة الجامعة.
(على الطاولة)	وضع محمّد المعطف في الخزانة.
(مرافقي الوفود)	دعت الحكومة الوفود الأجنبية إلى الحفلة.
(أمام المخزن)	لقي المعلّم أصدقائي في المخزن.
	قاد المرافق السيّارة بسرعة.
	خافت المعلّمة من السفر بالطائرة.
(تشرين الأول)	كان صديقي هناك في شهر أيلول.
(بالسيّارة)	سافر بالقطار.
(ظهراً)	قام من النوم صباحاً.
(معه)	عاد صديقي من برلين.
(قليلاً)	نامت كثيراً.
(زجاجتي عصير)	وضعت صديقتي كؤوساً على الطاولة.
(مدينة تورونتو)	وعد الطالب صديقته بزيارة العاصمة.
(معها)	رجت الفتاة أن تذهب إلى المسرح.
(أيضاً)	زار الوفد جامعتنا.
(كأسين)	قال محمّد إنّني شربت كأساً واحدة فقط (only).
(صباحاً)	سار إلى المكتبة مساءً.
	باع صديقي بيته
(في هذه الغرفة)	نام مرافق الوفد في تلك الغرفة.
(أيضاً)	مشى الرجال إلى قاعة الاجتماع.
(أحمد)	دعا صديقي العربي محمّداً إلى الحفلة.
(brown/brunette) (سمراء)	لقي صديقي فتاة شقراء (blond).
(في مصر)	خاف أعضاء الوفد من الطقس الحارّ هناك.
(في تونس)	كان أحمد في القاهرة.
(خوخاً)	وضعت صديقتي على الطاولة تفّاحاً.

(في الخزانة)	وضع الطالب الكتاب في الشنطة.
	دعا صديقته إلى الحفلة.
(إلى المعهد)	مشت الطالبات إلى المخزن.
	باع الطالب كتبه.
(قليلاً)	قالت الطالبة إنّني أكلت كثيراً.
	عادت إلى بيتها.
(الأوربية)	زار صديقي عدداً من البلدان العربية.
(معهم)	قام أصدقائي بنزهة (walk, stroll) جميلة.
(اليوم)	عاد الوفد أمس.
(معها)	زارت الفتاة مدينة برلين.
(صباح اليوم)	وصلت صديقتي مساء الأمس.
(أيضاً)	سارت إلى البيت.
(فيها)	عادت الطائرة من دمشق.

G2 Same as G1. Practice changing from the 3rd p. sg. m. or f. to the 1st p. pl..
Example:

given sentence:	عاد محمد إلى الفندق.
repetition:	عاد محمد إلى الفندق.
completion:	وعُدنا نحن إلى البيت.

G3 Transform the sentences in G1 into interrogative sentences starting with هل
لماذا or متى, in the 2nd p. sg. f. Of course, the noun-subject must be omitted in this
case. Affixed pronouns of the 3rd p. have to be changed into the 2nd p. when
required.

☞   زار الرجال المركز الجديد للعاصمة.

☞   متى / هل / لماذا زُرْتِ المركز الجديد للعاصمة.

C1 (Listening comprehension) The teacher reads the following news in Arabic.
The students render the basic contents in English.

صنعاء: وصل وزير التعليم العالي الإيطالي وهو عضو في الحزب الاشـتراكي الديمقراطي
إلى صنعاء في إطار جولة في الشرق الأوسط وقابل نظيره اليمني لمناقشة سبل التعاون بـين
البلدين في مجال التعليم الجامعي.

عمان: قابل جلالة الملك الوفد الألماني برئاسة المستشار الألماني وبحث معه سـبل التعـاون
السياسي والاقتصادي والعسكري والثقافي.

الجزائر: حضر الوفد الفرنسي الاحتفالات بمناسبة العيد الوطني. وقال رئيس الوفد الفرنسي في كلمته القصيرة: إن فرنسا سوف تعمل على توسيع التعاون السياسي والاقتصادي والتبادل التجاري مع الجزائر.

الخرطوم: قابل الأمين العام للحزب الوطني السوداني الأمين العام لحزب العمال البريطاني بعد مؤتمر باريس العالمي.

لندن: وصل وفد اقتصادي كويتي إلى لندن قادماً من النمسا وسيقابل الوفد وزيري الاقتصاد والصحة.

تونس: قابل الوفد الإنكليزي برئاسة وزير العمل وزير العمل التونسي في الوزارة بعد جولة في مصانع العاصمة ومعاملها ومزارع المحافظات لمناقشة برنامج التعاون في مجال تأهيل العمّال والمهندسين التونسيين.

موسكو: وصل وفد مغربي إلى موسكو وقابل الرئيس الروسي وعدداً من المسؤولين الروس وطلب من الحكومة الروسية دراسة مشروع التعاون الاقتصادي.

C2 (Homework) Prepare an interview with the leader of an Arab delegation based on Text 2. Ask about the reason and the results of the visit, with whom he met, possibilities of cooperation in industry, agriculture, trade, research and education, where he will go to after this visit etc. Record your interview with a cassette recorder and play it in the next class hour.

Final Exercise:

1. Transform the verbs into the 1st p. sg. (perfect tense).

زار الأمم المتّحدة. دعاه إلى المطعم. عاد إلى البرلمان. عاش في مصر. قاد السيّارة. مشى إلى وكيل الدولة. قال إنّه قام بزيارة المعاهد. قام بجولة في الشرق الأوسط. وقف أمام المحطّة. وجد القلم تحت السرير. بنى عمارات جميلة. قام بإعادة بناء بيتي. خاف من عودة الحرب. باع سيّارتي. نام في فندق قديم. كان في باريس. لقي صديقتي في المدينة.

2. Transform the verbs in G1 into the 3rd p. pl. and vocalize the ending of the verbs R$_3$ = و or ى.

3. Translate into Arabic.
Allow me to welcome you and to thank you for your return. We found a peaceful solution for those urgent problems. The reactions were positive. Her clothes were a scandal. We visited six countries. The men said that the minister was afraid of the opposition. These four neighbouring countries called for an extraordinary session of the United Nations. We went back to the parliament. The military

government concealed the results of the elections and the success of the democratic parties. This permanent secretary met with the members of the committee. The situation at home and abroad (in the interior and in the exterior) moved in the direction of the improvement of these relations. We came out of this crisis victoriously. The Security Council of the United Nations called for a peaceful solution.

4. Put the appropriate verb in the perfect tense.

... في تصريحي إنّ الحكومة ... على إيجاد الحلّ. ... لي بسؤال. ...نا الانتخابات الصلاحيات الكافية. ... أمام مشاكل مماثلة. هو ... قادراً على كتابة هذه الرسالة. كيف ... تلك المشاكل؟ متى ... بزيارة صديقتك؟

5. Translate into English. Give more than one variant where possible.

رئيس حكومة أجنبية، شنطات المعلِّمة الصغيرة الأربع هذه، بيت الطالب الشاطر هذا، عودة هذا الرئيس إلى الحكم، رئيس محكمة، أسباب الأزمة هذه

6. Add the appropriate preposition.

خفنا ... عودة الحرب. نقف ... مهمّة بناء البلد. نشعر ... التحسُّن. قاد البلد ... كارثة. خرجنا ... هذه الأزمة. عملنا ... تحسين الوضع. عاش ... الخارج. شكرته ... الجهاز.

1. The Imperfect Tense of Verbs with و or ى

1.1. The imperfect tense of verbs with R_1 = و is formed with R_1 being omitted.

Examples with the model verb وَصَلَ "to arrive":

(وصل has the imperfect vowel *i*)

يَصِلُونَ	(هم)	يَصِلُ	(هو)
يَصِلْنَ	(هنَّ)	تَصِلُ	(هي)
تَصِلُونَ	(أنتم)	تَصِلِينَ	(أنتِ)
تَصِلْنَ	(أنتنَّ)	تَصِلُ	(أنتَ)
نَصِلُ	(نحن)	أَصِلُ	أنا

☝**A1** Verbs with R_1 = ى are very rare and occur nearly exclusively in the so-called derived forms (cf. Lesson 14, Gr 1.). Their imperfect tense is formed in the same way as it is with the strong verbs, i.e. R_1 is not omitted. (Appendix: Tables 2, 17)

1.2. Verbs with R_2 = و or ى have the long vowel $\bar{u}$ in the imperfect tense if they belong to group I, and the long vowel $\bar{\imath}$ if they belong to group II. Verbs belonging to group III have the long vowel $\bar{a}$, when a vowel follows R_3.

Examples with the model verbs:

I قَامَ "to get up" (قَوَمَ = فَعَلَ >) R_2 = و

(هو) يَقُومُ   (هي) تَقُومُ   (نحن) نَقُومُ

II بَاعَ "to sell" (بَيَعَ = فَعَلَ >) R_2= ى

(هو) يَبِيعُ   (هي) تَبِيعُ   (نحن) نَبِيعُ

III خَافَ "to fear" (خَوِفَ = فَعِلَ >) R_2 = و

(هو) يَخَافُ   (هي) تَخَافُ   (نحن) نَخَافُ

☝**A2** Verbs with R_2 = ى, e.g. نَالَ (<نَيِلَ) يَنَالُ "to obtain", have the same forms as well.

R_1 has the short vowel *u* in the imperfect tense of verbs with R_2 = و or ى if they belong to group I, the short vowel *i* if they belong to group II, and the short vowel *a* if they belong to group III, when R_3 is vowelless.

Examples with the model verbs (Appendix: Tables 2, 18, 20, 22):

III	II	I	
يَخَفْنَ	يَبِعْنَ	يَقُمْنَ	(هنَّ)
تَخَفْنَ	تَبِعْنَ	تَقُمْنَ	(أنتنَّ)

Thus the following conjugational paradigms ensue:

III	II	I	
يَخَافُ	يَبِيعُ	يَقُومُ	(هو)
تَخَافُ	تَبِيعُ	تَقُومُ	(هي)
تَخَافُ	تَبِيعُ	تَقُومُ	(أنتَ)
تَخَافِينَ	تَبِيعِينَ	تَقُومِينَ	(أنتِ)
أَخَافُ	أَبِيعُ	أَقُومُ	(أنا)
يَخَافُونَ	يَبِيعُونَ	يَقُومُونَ	(هم)
يَخَفْنَ	يَبِعْنَ	يَقُمْنَ	(هنَّ)
تَخَافُونَ	تَبِيعُونَ	تَقُومُونَ	(أنتم)
تَخَفْنَ	تَبِعْنَ	تَقُمْنَ	(أنتنَّ)
نَخَافُ	نَبِيعُ	نَقُومُ	(نحن)

1.3. R_2 has the long vowel $\bar{u}$ in verbs with R_3 = و or ى if they belong to group I, the long vowel $\bar{\imath}$ if they are verbs of group II and the long vowel $\bar{a}$ (*Alif maqṣūra*) if they belong to group III.

Examples with the model verbs:

I دَعَا "to invite" (فَعَلَ = دَعَوَ>) R_3 = و

(هو) يَدْعُو   (هي) تَدْعُو   (نحن) نَدْعُو

II مَشَى "to walk" (فَعَلَ = مَشَيَ >) R_3 = ى

(هو) يَمْشِي   (هي) تَمْشِي   (نحن) نَمْشِي

III لَقِيَ "to meet" (= فَعِلَ) R_3 = ى

(هو) يَلْقَى   (هي) تَلْقَى   (نحن) نَلْقَى

☞A3 Occasionally, we find verbs in group II, model verb مشى, which are inflected in the imperfect tense like the verbs in group III, model verb لقِي, e.g. سَعَى "to endeavor, to strive" يَسْعَى، تَسْعَى etc. Cf. also below, Gr 4., the conjugation of رَأَى.

The forms which have a suffix are characterized by a long vowel following R_2 if the respective verb belongs to the groups I and II, and by a diphthong following R_2 in the verbs which belong to group III.

III	II	I	
تَلْقَيْنَ	تَمْشِينَ	تَدْعِينَ	(أنتِ)
تَلْقَوْنَ	تَمْشُونَ	تَدْعُونَ	(أنتم)

Thus the following conjugational paradigms ensue:

III	II	I	
يَلْقَى	يَمْشِي	يَدْعُو	(هو)
تَلْقَى	تَمْشِي	تَدْعُو	(هي)
تَلْقَى	تَمْشِي	تَدْعُو	(أنتَ)
تَلْقَيْنَ	تَمْشِينَ	تَدْعِينَ	(أنتِ)
أَلْقَى	أَمْشِي	أَدْعُو	(أنا)
يَلْقَوْنَ	يَمْشُونَ	يَدْعُونَ	(هم)
يَلْقَيْنَ	يَمْشِينَ	يَدْعُونَ	(هنَّ)
تَلْقَوْنَ	تَمْشُونَ	تَدْعُونَ	(أنتم)
تَلْقَيْنَ	تَمْشِينَ	تَدْعُونَ	(أنتنَّ)
نَلْقَى	نَمْشِي	نَدْعُو	(نحن)

(Appendix: Tables 2, 23, 24, 25)

2. Subjunctive and Jussive of Verbs with و or ى

2.1. The subjunctive and the jussive of the defective verbs are formed according to the same principles which apply to their formation regarding the strong verbs (see Lesson 8, Gr1.). Tables 3 and 4 in the Appendix provide a complete survey.

2.2. We only show some peculiarities here:

2.2.1. Subjunctive of the verbs R_3 = و or ى

يَدْعُوَ   يَمْشِيَ   يَلْقَى   etc.

2.2.2. Jussive of the verbs R_2 = و or ى

يَقُمْ   يَبِعْ   يَخَفْ   etc.

2.2.3. Jussive of the verbs R_3 = و or ى

يَدْعُ   يَمْشِ   يَلْقَ   etc.

2.3. In such jussive forms as mentioned under 2.2.2. and 2.2.3., it is not clear from the outward appearance in unvocalized texts, which root the respective form is based on. The typeface does not provide us with any information whether the last consonant is R₂ (يَقُمْ > قام) or R₃ (يدْعُ > دعا).

3. The Imperative of the Verbs with و or ى

The imperative is formed according to the same principles which apply to its formation regarding the strong verbs. The jussive is the form the imperative is derived from (see Lesson 8, Gr 2.). Table 9 in the Appendix provides a complete survey.

4. The Verbs جَاءَ , أَتَى and رَأَى

Some of the verbs which are most frequently used in Arabic are doubly defective, i.e. two of their three radicals are ى, و or ء. As the peculiarities of the verbs which contain a *Hamza* are nearly exclusively of an orthographic nature, there are hardly any difficulties regarding the conjugation of جَاءَ "to come", أَتَى "to come" and رَأَى "to see":

جَاءَ is conjugated like the model verb بَاعَ ,

أَتَى is conjugated like the model verb مَشَى ,

رَأَى is conjugated in the perfect tense like the model verb مَشَى , in the imperfect tense - with the *Hamza* being omitted - like the model verb لَقِيَ :

رأى		أتى		جاء		
imperfect	perfect	imperfect	perfect	imperfect	perfect	
يَرَى	رَأَى	يَأْتِي	أَتَى	يَجِيءُ	جَاءَ	(هو)
تَرَى	رَأَتْ	تَأْتِي	أَتَتْ	تَجِيءُ	جَاءَتْ	(هي)
تَرَى	رَأَيْتَ	تَأْتِي	أَتَيْتَ	تَجِيءُ	جِئْتَ	(أنتَ)
تَرَيْنَ	رَأَيْتِ	تَأْتِينَ	أَتَيْتِ	تَجِيئِينَ	جِئْتِ	(أنتِ)
أَرَى	رَأَيْتُ	آتِي	أَتَيْتُ	أَجِيءُ	جِئْتُ	(أنا)
يَرَوْنَ	رَأَوْا	يَأْتُونَ	أَتَوْا	يَجِيئُونَ	جَاؤُوا	(هم)
يَرَيْنَ	رَأَيْنَ	يَأْتِينَ	أَتَيْنَ	يَجِئْنَ	جِئْنَ	(هنَّ)
تَرَوْنَ	رَأَيْتُمْ	تَأْتُونَ	أَتَيْتُمْ	تَجِيئُونَ	جِئْتُمْ	(أنتم)
تَرَيْنَ	رَأَيْتُنَّ	تَأْتِينَ	أَتَيْتُنَّ	تَجِئْنَ	جِئْتُنَّ	(أنتنَّ)
نَرَى	رَأَيْنَا	نَأْتِي	أَتَيْنَا	نَجِيءُ	جِئْنَا	(نحن)

شَاف, which is conjugated like قامَ , is mostly used in place of رأى in colloquial language.

🖐A4 As to the spelling of the *Hamza* (chairs of the *Hamza*) cf. Lesson 24 and Table 36 in the Appendix.

As to verbs with R₁ = و and R₃ = ى, the conjugational peculiarities of both types of verbs are to be taken into account. Cf. the verb وَفَى , imperfect tense يَفِي , in Text 2 of this lesson.

V

to come (to)	أتى (يأْتِي) (إلى)	director	مُدِير ج مُدراءُ
(with verbal sentence) since, because	إذ	to see so., sth.	رأى (يرَى) ه، هـ
Emir	أمِير ج أُمراءُ	athlete, sportsman,	رياضِيّ
human	إنسانِيّ	Riyadh	الرِّياض
automatic	آلِيّ	here: rate of exchange	سِعْر
to stay, to remain	بقِيَ (يبْقَى)	highness	سُمُوّ
sum, amount	مبْلغ ج مبالِغُ	condition	شرْط ج شُرُوط
technical	تقْنِيّ	provided that	بشرْط
it is worth mentioning that ...	من الجدِيرِ بِالذِّكْر أنَّ	to take part in	شارك (يُشارِكُ) في
pound	جُنيْه ج ـات	to be a witness of	شهِد (يشْهَدُ) على
neighbor	جار ج جِيران	colloq.: see	شاف (يشُوفُ)
to come (to)	جاء (يجِيءُ) (إلى)	will	مشِيئة
event	حدث ج أحْداث	with the will of God	بمشِيئةِ ا لله
computer, calculator	حاسِب ج ـات	hall	صَالة ج ـات
much better than	أحْسنُ بكثِير من	owner	صاحِب ج أصْحاب
demand, need	حاجة ج ـات	His Royal Highness	صاحب السمو الملكيّ
to need sth., so., to require	بحاجةٍ إلى	to change sth.	صرف (يصْرِفُ)
discount, reduction	تخْفِيض ج ـات	exchange officer	صرَّاف ج ـون
during, in the course of	خِلالَ	bank	مصْرِف ج مصارِفُ
doctor	دُكْتور ج دكاتِرة	huge, giant	ضخْم
house	دار (م) ج دُور	child	طِفْل ج أطفال
publishing house	دار نشْر	fair, exhibition	معْرِض ج معارِضُ
international	دَوْلِيّ / دُوَلِيّ	knowledge	معْرِفة ج معارِفُ

reasonable, sensible	مَعْقُول	elite, selection, choice	نُخْبة ج نُخَب
(mass) media; communication	إعْلام	*here:* chosen responsibles	
Come here! Let's go! *(m./f.)*	تَعالَ / تَعالِي!	house	مَنْزِلِيّ
in addition to	عِلاوةً على	rate, exchange rate	نِسْبة ج نِسَب
His Excellency (the minister)	مَعالِي (الوزير)	forget so., sth.	نَسِيَ (يَنْسَى) ه، هـ
currency	عُمْلة ج ـات	women	نِساء، نِسْوة، نِسْوان
opening	افْتِتاح ج ـات	publishing	نَشْر
thinking, thought, ideology	فِكْر ج أفْكار	publisher	ناشِر ج ـون
proposal	مُقْتَرح ج ـات	fan, lover; amateur	هاوٍ ج هُواة
piaster	قِرْش ج قُرُوش	to promise so. sth.	وعَدَ (يَعِدُ) ه ب
sector	قِطاع ج ـات	promise	وَعْد ج وُعُود
meeting point	مُلْتَقىً ج ـات	appointment, date	مِيعاد ج مَواعيدُ
campus	مدينة جامِعيّة	to keep *(a promise)*	وفَى (يَفِي) بِ
possible	مُمْكِن	to lie *(geogr.)*; to fall	وقَع (يقَعُ)
royal	مَلِكِيّ	place, spot, ground	مَوْقِع ج مَواقِعُ
monarchy, kingdom	مَمْلكة ج مَمالِكُ		

معرض الرياض الدولي للكتاب

Text 1

تشهد الجامعة مساء يوم غد الثلاثاء حدثاً ثقافياً ضخماً ومناسبة علمية كبيرة إذ يقوم صاحب السمو الملكي الأمير ... بحضور معالي مدير الجامعة الأستاذ الدكتور ... بافتتاح معرض الرياض الدولي للكتاب العلمي. ويشارك في هذا المعرض ٥٠٠ ناشر من داخل المملكة وخارجها، وذلك بالصالة الرياضية في المدينة الجامعية.

ويحضر الافتتاح بمشيئة الله عدد من كبار المسؤولين ورجال الفكر والأدب والثقافة والإعلام وسيكون في استقبالهم عند وصولهم إلى الجامعة وموقع المعرض معالي مدير الجامعة ونخبة من كبار المسؤولين بالجامعة.

وخلال الأيّام العشرة القادمة ستكون الجامعة ملتقىً لآلاف من هواة الثقافة وطلبة العلم والمعرفة ليقوموا بجولة في دور النشر المختلفة وليروا مئات الآلاف من الكتب وتقريباً ٥٠ ألف عنوان في قطاعات المعرفة الإنسانية والاجتماعية والعلوم التقنية وكتب الثقافة

الإسلامية والأدب العربي علاوة على كتب الأطفال والاقتصاد المنزلي والحاسب الآلي.
وستصل نسبة التخفيض إلى ١٥ ٪ من السعر الأصلي.
ومن الجدير بالذكر أن المعرض سيفتح أبوابه لمدّة يومين للنساء فقط وهما الخميس
والاثنين.

عند الصرّاف   **Text 2**

الصرّاف: مساء الخير، أدخلي، تفضّلي.

ماري: مساء النور، أنا بحاجة إلى دنانير.

الصرّاف: عندك أية عملة؟

ماري: عندي دولارات وفرنكات وجنيهات إنكليزية. كم سعر الدولار عندك؟

الصرّاف: ٤٠٠ دينار لمائة دولار.

ماري: هذا قليل جدّاً، جارك على اليمين قال إنّ سعر الدولار عنده هو أربعة دنانير
وخمسة قروش.

الصرّاف: يمكن، لا أعرف، ولكن أسعاري أحسن بكثير من أسعار المصرف وممكن أنْ
أعمل لك سعراً جيِّداً بشرط واحد.

ماري: ما هو الشرط؟

الصرّاف: الشرط هو أنّك تصرفين مبلغاً كبيراً.

ماري: أي كم دولاراً وكم السعر؟

الصرّاف: ٥٠٠ دولار والسعر سيكون أربعة دنانير وعشرة قروش للدولار الواحد.

ماري: هذا المقترح معقول، سأمشي إلى جيرانك وسأرى أسعارهم.

الصرّاف: لماذا؟ سعري جيِّد. تعالي!

ماري: سأعود إليك بعد معرفة أسعار جيرانك.

الصرّاف: إن شاء الله.

ماري: سأفي بوعدي أو كما يقول العرب: من وعد وفى. إلى اللقاء.

Exercises:

L1 Form sentences with the imperfect tense of the verb (وقع) يقعُ and the words for north (شمال), south (جنوب), east (شرْق) and west (غرْب). Use the following nouns and the names of countries you know as subject

جامعة، مخازن، مطعم، مقهى، مدينة، بلد، بلدان، فندق، محطة

☞   تقع المحطة في جنوب مدينتنا.

☞   يقع المغرب في شمال إفريقيا.

L2 Form sentences using different imperatives of the following verbs:

a) وضع b) قام c) زار d) عاد e) مشى f) بقي

Use the given phrases or other prepositional phrases and time markers.

Chose from the following imperatives, nouns, affixed pronouns and prepositional phrases.

على الطاولة	الكؤوس، الفناجين الزجاجة، التفاح، الكتب، الخبز، الفواكه، الطعام	ضع، ضعي
الآن، بسرعة	من النوم	قم، قومي، قوموا
غدا، في شهر...	ـني، العاصمة هذا البلد، تلك البلدان ضواحي (surroundings) المدينة، ذلك البرْج (tower)، ذلك المطعم، ذلك المقهى، صديقنا، المسرح	زر، زوري زوروا، زرن
إلى هنا، إلى هناك، إليّ، إلينا، غدا، بعد ساعة	إلى البيت، إلى الفندق،	عد، عودي
إلى المعهد، إليه، إلى هناك		إمش، إمشي، إمشوا
هنا، هناك، في البيت، في الفندق، عندنا حتى الغد		إبق، إبقوا

L3 Add the definite article where possible.

سيكون في ..استقبالهم عنـد ..وصولهم للجامعة و..موقـع ..معرض ..جامعـة و..نخبة من ..كبار ..مسؤولين بـ..جامعة. ستكون ..جامعـة ملتقـىً لآلاف مـن هـواة ..ثقافة و..طلبـة ..علم و..معرفـة. يقـوم بـ..جولـة في ..دور ..نشر ..مختلفـة ويرى ..مئات ..آلاف من ..كتب وتقريباً ٥٠.. ألف ..عنوان في ..قطاعات ..معرفة ..إنسانية

و..اجتماعية و..علوم ..تقنية و..كتب ..ثقافة ..إسلامية و..أدب ..عربي عـلاوةً علــى كتب ..أطفال و..اقتصاد ..منزلي و..حاسب ..آلي. ستصل ..نسبة ..تخفيض إلى ١٥ ٪ من ..سعر ..أصلي.

من ..جدير ب..ذكر أن ..معرض سيفتح ..أبوابه لمدة يومين للنساء فقط وهما ..خميس و..اثنين. تشهد ..جامعة ..مساء ..يوم ..غد ..ثلاثاء ..حدثاً ..ثقافياً ..ضخمــاً و..مناسبة ..علمية ..كبيرة. يقوم ..صاحب ..سمو ..ملكي ..أمير سلمان بن عبد العزيز ب..حضور معالي ..مدير ..جامعة ..أستاذ ..دكتور أحمد بن محمد الوهّاب ب..افتتــاح ..معرض ..رياض ..دولي للكتاب ..علمي. يشارك في هذا ..معرض ٥٠٠ ..ناشـر مـن ..داخل ..مملكة وخارجها. يحضـر ..افتتـاح بمشيئة الله عـدد مـن ..كبـار ..مسؤولين و..رجال ..فكر و..أدب و..ثقافة و..إعلام.

L4 The teacher explains the colloquial usage of شاف (يشُوفُ) "to see" and asks the students to replace رأى in the following sentences with شاف, and then to negate them by means of لا or ما.

رأيتُ المعلّم. رأيته. رأتهم في المطعم. نراها في المعهد. رأوا الرئيس في المحكمـة. نراه في البرلمان. رأيتم الكتب عنده. ترين هذه الشنطة. ترون الأقلام. أراه بعد يومين.

G1 Transform the following sentences (without taking into account the words in brackets) into the imperfect tense of the 3rd p. sg. m. or f.

☞   عاد محمّد إلى الفندق.   <   يعود محمّد إلى الفندق.

وفى محمّد بوعده.

نسي الطالب الكلمات الجديدة.

أتى الوفد مساء اليوم.   (مساء الغد)

جاء أحمد حسب الموعد.

رأى أحمد صديقه أمام مخزن السيارات.   (في مخزن السيّارات)

رجا محمّد أصدقاءه أن يحضروا إليه.

زار الرجال ذلك الجبل.   (معهم)

قال صديقي إنّني مجتهد.   (كسلان)

باع الرجل سيّارته.

مشى الأصدقاء إلى المقهى.

وعد أحمد أصدقاءه بألف دولار.

وضع الطالب المعطف في الخزانة.   (على الطاولة)

لقي المعلم أصدقائي في المخزن.   (أمام المخزن)

قاد المرافقِ السيّارة بسرعة.   (أيضاً)

خافت المعلمة من السفر بالطائرة.

سافر صديقي بالقطار.   (بالسيّارة)

قام محمّد من النوم.	(ظهراً، صباحاً)
عاد صديقي من برلين.	(معه)
وفت صديقتي بوعدها.	
نسيت الطالبة مواعيدها.	
وضع الطالب الكتاب تحت الشنطة.	
أتى أعضاء الوفد صباحاً.	(مساء)
رأى عمر في المخزن كتباً جديدة.	
رجت هيفاء أصدقاءها أن يذهبوا معها.	
نامت الطالبات كثيرا.	(قليلاً)
وضعت صديقتي على الطاولة كؤوساً.	(زجاجتي عصير)
وعد الطالب صديقه بزيارة العاصمة.	(مدينة دبلين)
رجت الفتاة أن تذهب إلى المسرح.	(معها)
زار الوفد جامعتنا.	(أيضا)
قال محمّد إنّني شربت كأساً واحدة.	(كأسين)
باع صديقي بيته.	
مشى الرجال إلى قاعة الاجتماع.	(أيضاً)
لقي صديقي فتاة شقراء (blond).	(سمراء)
وضع الطالب الكتاب في الشنطة.	(في الخزانة)
دعا الطالب صديقته إلى الحفلة.	
مشت الطالبات إلى المخزن.	(إلى المعهد)
باع الطالب كتبه.	
قال صديقنا العربي إنّني أكلت قليلاً.	(كثيراً)
عادت الفتيات إلى بيتهن.	
زار صديقي عدداً من البلدان العربية.	(الأوربية)
قام أصدقائي بنزهة جميلة.	(معهم)
عاد الوفد اليوم.	(أيضا)
زارت الوفود مدينة لندن.	(معها)
وفى المعلمون بوعودهم.	
جاء المرافق إلى قاعة الطعام.	
جاءت صديقتي إليّ.	(إليها)
رأى محمّد هناك رجالاً كثيرين.	(قليلين)
وصل الأصدقاء مساء اليوم.	(صباح اليوم)
عادت الطائرة من القاهرة.	(فيها)
وصل الوفد إلى الكويت بالطائرة.	(بالسيّارة)
عاد الأصدقاء صباحا.	(مساء)
وصلت الوفود إلى هنا.	(معها)

(أيضاً)

(بيتاً جميلاً)

قام رئيس الوفد.

بنى العمّال مباني رائعة.

G2 (Written homework) Same as G1. Write down only the transformed sentences in the imperfect tense.

G3 The teacher uses the sentences from G1 but quotes the imperfect instead of the perfect tense. The student repeats the sentence and then transforms it into the 1st p. sg. using the words and phrases in brackets:

given sentence:	يعود محمّد إلى الفندق.
repetition:	يعود محمّد إلى الفندق.
completion:	وأعود أنا إلى البيت.
given sentence:	يعود محمّد إلى بيته.
repetition:	يعود محمّد إلى بيته.
completion:	وأعود أنا إلى بيتي.

G4 Same as G3. Practice the transformation of the 3rd p. sg. m. or f. into the 1st p. pl.

given sentence:	يعود محمّد إلى بيته.
repetition:	يعود محمّد إلى بيته.
completion:	ونعود نحن إلى بيتنا.

G5 The teacher quotes the 1st p. sg. or pl. based on the sentences from G1. The students transform them into interrogative sentences introduced by هل، متى or أين. The affixed pronouns of the 1st p. are to be changed into the 2nd p.

teacher:	أعود إلى البيت.
student:	متى تعود إلى البيت؟
teacher:	أراهم أمام المخزن.
student:	أين تراهم؟
teacher:	أفي بوعدي.
student:	هل تفي بوعدك؟

G6 (Homework) Form 20 sentences based on G1 introduced by an interrogative. The verb should be in the imperfect tense.

C1 The teacher quotes amounts of money in different currencies which are to be converted to $ or £.

teacher:	كم تساوي ١٠٠ دولار؟
student:	١٠٠ دولار تساوي تقريباً ١٧٠ ماركاً.

١٠٠ فرانك فرنسي، ٢٠٠ جنيه استرليني، ١٠٠٠ ليرة إيطالية، ٣٠٠٠ دولار، ٥٠٠٠ روبل، ٤٠٠ فرانك سويسري، ١٠٠٠٠ زلوتي بولندي، ١٠٠٠ ريال يمني، ٢٠٠٠ دينار كويتي، ١٠٠ ليرة لبنانية، ٦٠٠٠ جنيه مصري ...

C2 Prepare a conversation with a bank clerk and use the following nouns and phrases for this purpose.

payment form	إِستمارة الصرف
bank	بنْك ج بُنُوك
periodic payment order	حوالة دائمة
deposit form	إِستمارة الدفع
fee	رسْم ج رُسُوم
money/ to withdraw money	نقْد ج نُقُود / سحب مبْلغاً
current account, cheque account	حِساب جارٍ
account / to open an account	حِساب ج ـات / فتح حساباً
credit	قرْض ج قُرُوض
installment	قِسْط ج أقْساط
cheque, check / to cash a cheque	شيك ج ـات / صرف شيكاً
traveller's cheque, ~ check	شِيكات السفر
to pay by cheque	دفع بالشيك
cheque-book, checkbook	دفْتر الشيكات
savings book	دفتر التوْفير
savings depot	مبْلغ التوفير
to save	وفّر (يُوَفّرُ)
to transfer / transfer, remittance	حَوّل (يُحَوّلُ) / حوالة ج ـات
interest / interest rate	فائِدة ج فوائِدُ / نِسْبة الفوائد

Final Exercise:

1. Transform the following sentences into the imperfect tense.

وفى بوعده. نسيَت الحاسب. جاء بعد صاحب السمو الملكي. رأيتُ الإنكليـز. رجوتُه أن يصرف الدولارات. زاروا الجيران. قلتم إنّكم نخبة الجامعة. باعت الحكومة المصرـف. مشينا إلى الافتتاح. وعد بكتابة رسالة طويلة. لقي الجواب. قاد سيّارته بسرعة. خفنا من مدير المعهد. سارت الأمور نحو التحسّن. قمنا بجولة في الشرق الأوسط. أتى بعد هـذا

الحدث الثقافي. نام ١٠ ساعاتٍ. وصل بعد ٦ أيّامٍ. عادت من جولتها. دعونا الأصدقـاء
إلى الحفلة. بنوا بيوتاً جميلة. عاش في أوربا. نمتُ في الفندق.

2. Translate into Arabic.

The reception was attended by the President of the University and high officials.
The university will be a meeting point for many book-lovers. He will make a
round of the book fair. About 50,000 books were sold at the fair. The opening
ceremony was carried out by H.E. the Minister of Culture. I forgot the names of
the publishing houses. I sold children's books, books about housekeeping,
technical sciences, Islamic culture and Arabic literature. He kept his promise.
They came two hours after the appointment. I saw him on the campus. He
promised 5 dinars.

3. Translate into English.

ضع الكؤوس على الطاولة ! قومي من النـوم ! زوروا المعـرض ! عـودي إلى البيـت قبـل
الظهر ! إمش بسرعة ! لا تخف من الوزير ! لا تنم في الدرس ! قولي من أنت ! قـل أيـن
كنت ! كل اللحم ! أدخل ! إمش إلى الجامعة ! هات الدنانير!

4. Replace the noun-object or the noun in the prepositional phrase by the
appropriate affixed pronoun.

دعوت الرجلين إلى الحفلة. إشتريت الكتب. أخاف مـن المديـر. نرجـع إلى المدينـة. أرى
الطالبات. أنسى الدرس. مشيت إلى الجامعة بسرعة. شكرت المدير على الدعوة.

5. Translate into Arabic.

I have to reserve two rooms. We must buy drinks. They must keep their promises.
You *(f.)* must invite your mother. You must come tomorrow. He must forget a lot
of events. She must come back.

6. Fill in the blanks.

Jussive	Subjunctive	Imperfect	Perfect
			قالوا
			مشتْ
			لقيتُ
			رجوتم
			نسيتِ
			وَفى
			خِفْتِ

1. The Use of كَانَ

The verb كَانَ (imperfect tense يَكُونُ) is a temporal auxiliary verb, which localizes the action (state, event) in a certain tense.

1.1. كَانَ in the equational sentence

كَانَ is the copula in the equational sentence and as such is comparable to the English auxiliary verb "to be".

The nominal predicate (خَبَر كَانَ) is in the accusative after كَانَ. The perfect tense of كَانَ localizes the predicate of the equational sentence in the past tense.

| The student was diligent. | كَانَ الطَّالِبُ مُجْتَهِداً. |
| Muḥammad was our teacher. | كَانَ مُحَمَّدٌ مُعَلِّمَنَا. |

كان is negated by لَمْ + jussive, accordingly لَمْ يَكُنْ:

| The student was not diligent. | لَمْ يَكُنِ الطَّالِبُ مُجْتَهِداً. |

The imperfect tense of كَانَ localizes the predicate of the equational sentence in the present and future tense.

| The student is diligent. | يَكُونُ الطَّالِبُ مُجْتَهِداً. |
| Muḥammad is the headmaster/ will be the headmaster. | يَكُونُ مُحَمَّدٌ مُدِيرَ الْمَدْرَسَةِ. |

كَانَ is rare in the imperfect, i.e. يَكُونُ = "is", and then merely serves to emphasize the predicate. In general, affirmative equational sentences which are regarded as being in the present tense do not have a copula (cf. Lesson 2, Gr 3.).

☝A1 However, the use of كَانَ is obligatory when the conjunction أَنْ "that" is employed, which is required to be followed by a verb in the subjunctive:

| I am afraid that Aḥmad has a new illness. (*lit.*: ... is stricken with/attacked by a new illness.) | أَخَافُ أَنْ يَكُونَ أَحْمَدُ مُصَاباً بِمَرَضٍ جَدِيدٍ. |

لا يَكُونُ is negated by لا + imperfect tense, accordingly لا يَكُونُ:

| Aḥmad is not /will not be the headmaster. | لا يَكُونُ أَحْمَدُ مُدِيرَ الْمَدْرَسَةِ. |

كَانَ is also rare in the negated imperfect, i.e. لا يَكُونُ = "is not". In general the present equational sentence it is negated by لَيْسَ (cf. Lesson 8, Gr 3.5.).

1.2. كَانَ in the verbal sentence

As is the case in the equational sentence, كَانَ also serves to temporalize the predicate in the verbal sentence.

كَانَ + perfect tense (فَعَلَ) and كَانَ + imperfect tense (يَفْعَلُ) are compound forms, which are comparable to certain compound tenses in English.

The following forms are compounded with كَانَ:

(1) كَانَ قَدْ فَعَلَ   he had done
= Past perfect as an expression of anteriority or of a completed action in the past which took place prior to another action also in the past

(2) كَانَ يَفْعَلُ   he did, he used to do
= Imperfect as an expression of a constant, repeated or customary action which took place in the past

(3) يَكُونُ قَدْ فَعَلَ   he will have done
= Future perfect as an expression of an action which is to be expected with certainty to happen in the future

Accordingly, five forms are available to describe the temporal relations: the two simple forms فَعَلَ "he has done", "he did" and يَفْعَلُ "he does", "he will do" and the three compound forms which have just been mentioned.

كَانَ / يَكُونُ is to be understood in these as a temporal determinator, whereas فَعَلَ and يَفْعَلُ have their original value which is neutral with regard to tense.

فَعَلَ and يَفْعَلُ are most frequently used. كَانَ يَفْعَلُ is often found both in oral and written usage as well. يَكُونُ قَدْ فَعَلَ and كَانَ قَدْ فَعَلَ are less common.

✍A2 There are difficulties when translating into Arabic, especially regarding the differentiation between the forms كَانَ يَفْعَلُ and فَعَلَ. There are no binding rules which specify that it is obligatory to use فَعَلَ in one case and كَانَ يَفْعَلُ in the other. It occurs fairly often that both forms are used as stylistic variants, so we can assume that they are interchangeable. The form كان يَفْعَلُ should be employed if a routine or repeated action from the past is to be described; it can often be translated by "he used to ... ".

قَدْ is a particle which precedes the verb. If قَدْ precedes the perfect tense (كَانَ قَدْ فَعَلَ، قَدْ فَعَلَ), it shows the definite execution of the action in the past or the execution of the action to be expected with certainty in the future (يَكُونُ قَدْ فَعَلَ).

If قَدْ precedes the imperfect tense (قَدْ يَفْعَلُ), it indicates a possibility that the verbal action is taking place or will take place. (See about the negation of these verb forms in Lesson 26, Gr 1.1.1.7. and 1.1.1.8.)

👉**A3** Verbs with similar functions are referred to in Arabic as أَخَوَاتُ كَانَ *"sisters of kāna"*. The most important verbs of this type are:

meaning	
not (to be)	لَيْسَ
still, yet	لَمْ يَزَلْ / كان لا يَزَالُ / لا يَزَالُ / ما زَالَ
to continue to do sth., to go on doing sth.	ظَلَّ / يَظَلُّ
to remain, to continue to be	بَقِيَ / يَبْقَى
to become	أَصْبَحَ / يُصْبِحُ ، صارَ / يصيرُ
to do sth. no more or no longer	لَمْ يَعُدْ
to be almost, almost, (with negation) scarcely; no sooner ...	كادَ / يَكادُ

2. كُلّ and جَمِيع

كُلّ and جَمِيعٌ are nouns, which are employed in the sense of the English indefinite pronouns "every(one)/everybody", "all", "whole". They are always in the construct state in these cases. They are either followed by a definite or an indefinite noun or by an affixed pronoun.

2.1. كُلّ and جَمِيعٌ + noun
2.1.1. كُلّ + indefinite noun in the singular = "every":

every student	كُلُّ طَالِبٍ
every day	كُلُّ يَوْمٍ

2.1.2. كُلّ + مِنْ + definite noun in the singular or plural often serve to introduce enumerations like

the rector as well as the teachers and the students	كُلٌّ مِنَ المُدِيرِ والمُعَلِّمِينَ والطَّلَبَةِ
Syria as well as Iraq and Libya	كُلٌّ من سُورِيَا والعِرَاقِ ولِيبِيَا

and should be translated by "both ... and .../... as well as ...".

2.1.3. كُلّ + definite noun in the singular = "whole":

the whole family	كُلُّ العائِلَةِ

2.1.4. كُلّ + definite noun in the plural = "all":

all books	كُلُّ الكُتُبِ

2.1.5. جَمِيع + definite noun in the plural = "all":

all students	جَمِيعُ الطُّلابِ

2.2. كُلّ and جَمِيع + affixed pronoun

2.2.1. كُلّ (seldom جَمِيع) in the meaning of "whole" and "all" is predominantly used as an apposition when it occurs in this construction. The affixed pronoun agrees with the preceding noun in gender and number:

the whole family	ألعائِلَةُ كُلُّها
I have seen all friends.	رَأَيْتُ الأَصْدِقاءَ كُلَّهُمْ.

Like every apposition, كُلّ and جَمِيع are in the same case in this context as the antecedent is.

2.2.2. كُلّ and جَمِيع also occur without an antecedent, when connected with the affixed pronoun:

all of them	كُلُّهُمْ
all of us	كُلُّنا
all (of it)	كُلُّهُ

A4 Additionally, remember أَلْجَمِيعُ = "all (people)" and جَمِيعاً = "all of them", "altogether" which is post-positive as an apposition.

A5 كافّة in the meaning of "all" is used less frequently; it is either in anteposition, or postpositive, taking the accusative:

all students	كافّةُ الطُّلابِ/ الطّالِباتِ، أَلطُّلابُ/ أَلطّالِباتُ كافّةً

A6 The noun كُلّ must not be mixed with كِلا (gen. and acc. كِلَيْ) fem. كِلْتا (gen. and acc. كِلْتَيْ) "both". كِلا / كِلْتا are always followed by a dual noun in the genitive or by a dual pronoun suffix. If كِلا / كِلْتا receive the pronoun suffix they must be inflected for case:

They both went to ...	ذَهَبَ كِلاهُما إلى ...
We know both of them.	نَعْرِفُ كِلَيْهِما / كِلْتَيْهِما

Used before nouns, كِلا / كِلْتا are not declined:

I know both students.	أَعْرِفُ كِلا الطّالِبَيْنِ / كِلْتا الطّالِبَتَيْنِ.

3. نَفْس

The noun نَفْسٌ (pl. نُفُوس، أَنفُس) is employed in the sense of the English words of identification "the same, himself/herself/itself" and "the same" - in addition to its being used in its original meaning "soul". It is always in the construct state. It is either followed by a definite noun or by an affixed pronoun.

3.1. نَفْس + noun

on the same day	فِي نَفْسِ الْيَوْمِ
I bought the same book.	إِشْتَرَيْتُ نَفْسَ الْكِتَابِ.

3.2. نَفْس + affixed pronoun

3.2.1. The appositional construction in which نَفْس + affixed pronoun follow the noun has the same meaning as 3.1.:

on the same day	فِي الْيَوْمِ نَفْسِهِ
I bought the same book.	إِشْتَرَيْتُ الكِتَابَ نَفْسَهُ.

3.2.2. نَفْس + affixed pronoun also occur without a preceding noun. The English pronouns "he (you, I - ...) himself/yourself/myself" are expressed by this construction in connection with the preposition بِ:

he himself, she herself	بِنَفْسِهِ، بِنَفْسِهَا	(هو، هي)
you yourself	بِنَفْسِكَ، بِنَفْسِكِ	(أَنتَ، أَنتِ)
I myself	بِنَفْسِي	(أنا)
they themselves	بِأَنْفُسِهِمْ، بِأَنْفُسِهِنَّ	(هم، هنَّ)
you yourselves	بِأَنْفُسِكُمْ، بِأَنْفُسِكُنَّ	(أنتم، أنتنَّ)
we ourselves	بِأَنْفُسِنَا	(نحن)

I have done that by myself.   فَعَلْتُ ذَلِكَ بِنَفْسِي.

🕮A7 نفس + affixed pronoun are also employed as a reflexive pronoun (oneself/himself/herself/ itself, yourself, myself etc.) in Arabic: Help yourself!   أُخْدُمْ نَفْسَكَ بِنَفْسِكَ.

4. أَحَد / إِحْدَى and عِدَّة ، بَعْض

The nouns أَحَدٌ / إِحْدَى and بَعْضٌ , عِدَّةٌ are used in the sense of various English indefinite pronouns:

بَعْضٌ means "some", عِدَّةٌ "several" and أَحَدٌ / إِحْدَى "one".

بَعْض and أَحَد / إِحْدَى are followed by a definite noun or an affixed pronoun; عدّة is followed by an indefinite noun.

4.1. بَعْض + definite noun in the plural = "some (of)":

some of the teachers	بَعْضُ المُعَلِّمِينَ
with some friends, with some of the friends	مع بَعْضِ الأَصْدِقاءِ
with some of them	مع بَعْضِهِمْ

👉A8 The reciprocal بعضُهُمْ البعضَ means "each other" and is mostly used with a prepositional object, more rarely with a direct object.

4.2. عِدَّة + indefinite noun in the plural = "several":

several teachers	عِدَّةُ مُعَلِّمِينَ
after several days	بَعْدَ عِدَّةِ أَيَّامٍ

4.3. أَحَد , f. إِحْدَى + definite noun in the plural = "one":

one of the teachers	أَحَدُ المُعَلِّمِينَ
one of them	أَحَدُهُمْ
one of the woman teachers	إِحْدَى المُعَلِّماتِ
in one of the rooms	في إِحْدَى الغُرَفِ

5. أَيّ

The interrogative pronoun أَيٌّ, f. أَيَّةٌ means "what/which". It is always in the construct state as the 1st term of a genitive construction.

5.1. أَيّ + indefinite noun = "what/which":

in which month?	في أَيِّ شَهْرٍ؟

which city?	أَيَّةُ مَدينةٍ؟
Which city did you visit?	أَيَّةَ مَدينةٍ زُرْتَ؟
which delegations?	أَيَّةُ وُفودٍ؟

The following construction with أَيّ is possible as well:

5.2. أَيّ+مِنْ + definite noun in the plural:

which one of the friends?/ which one of them?	أَيٌّ مِن الأصْدِقاءِ؟ / أَيٌّ مِنْهُم؟

☞A9 The interrogative pronoun أَيّ must not be confused with the indeclinable particle أيْ , which has the meaning "i.e.".

V

ear	أُذْن (م) ج آذان	in any case, anyhow	على أيٍّ حال
pain	ألم ج آلام	cheek	خدّ ج خُدُود
man	إنسان	*here*: stool	خُرُوج
nose	أنْف ج أُنوف	dangerous	خطِير
belly, stomach	بطْن ج بُطُون	*fig.*: Everything okay, God willing?	خيراً إن شاء الله؟
some	بعْض		
urine	بوْل	blood	دم ج دِماء
forehead	جبِين ج جُبُن	medicine	دواء ج أدْوية
forehead	جبهة ج ـات	arm	ذِراع (م) ج أذْرُع
body	جسْم ج أجْسام	chin	ذقن ج أذْقان، ذقُون
all	جَميع	beard	ذقْن ج ذُقُون
holiday	إجازة ج ات	penis	ذكر ج ذُكُور
sick leave	إجازة مرضية	lungs	رئة ج ـات
tablet, pill	حبّة ج حُبُوب	head	رأْس ج رُؤُوس
eyebrow	حاجب ج حواجِبُ	main	رئيسيّ
truth; fact	حقِيقَة ج حقائقُ	leg, foot	رجْل (م) ج أرْجُل
analysis	تحْليل ج تحاليلُ	knee	رُكْبة ج ـات
fever	حُمَّى (م)	neck	رقبة ج ـات
pelvis	حوْض ج أحْواض	arm	ساعِد ج سواعِدُ

tooth	سِنّ (م) ج أسْنان	examination	فحْص ج فُحُوص
hour, watch	ساعة ج ـات	vagina	فرْج ج فُرُوج
thigh	ساق (م) ج سِيقان	spoiled; bad	فاسِد
violent, fierce, heavy, furious	شدِيد	jaw	فكّ
hair	شعْر (coll.)	upper ~	الفكُّ الأعْلَى
lip	شفة ج شِفاه	lower ~	الفكُّ الأسْفل
hospital	مُسْتشْفى ج ـات	mouth	فم ج أفْواه
finger; toe	إصْبع ج أصابِعُ	use	فائِدة ج فوائِدُ
chest	صدْر ج صُدُور	foot, leg	قدم (م) ج أقْدام
headache	صُداع	heart	قلْب ج قُلُوب
photo	صُورة ج صُوَر	I vomited.	تقيَّأتُ
(prep.) against	ضِدّ	shoulder (blade)	كتِف (م) ج أكْتاف
guest	ضيْف ج ضُيُوف	all	كافّة
limbs	طرف ج أطْراف	all	كُلّ
Live long!	طال عُمرُك !	place	مكان ج أماكِنُ، أمْكِنة
several	عِدَّة	illness	مرض ج أمْراض
offer sth. to so.	عرض (يعْرِضُ) على هـ	nurse	مُمرِّضة
upper arm (also m.)	عضُد (م) ج أعْضاد	stomach	معِدة ج مِعد
organ, part of the body	عُضْو ج أعْضاء	self; soul	نفس (م) ج نُفُوس، أنْفُس
canned (meat)	(لحْم) مُعلَّب	important	مُهِمّ
medical treatment	عِلاج	more important	أهَمّ
not necessary	غيْر ضَرُورِيّ	occurring (in)	وارِد (في)
spine	عمُود فِقرِيّ	to prescribe sth. for so.	وصف (يصِفُ) له هـ
throat, neck	عُنق ج أعْناق	to come after	ولِيَ (يَلِي)
eye	عيْن (م) ج عُيُون	in what follows	فيما يلي
open sth.	فتح (يفْـتَحُ) هـ	hand	يد (م) ج أيدٍ
examine	فحص (يفْـحَصُ)		

جسم الإنسان   **Text 1**

فيما يلي نعرض على حضراتكم صورة لجسم الإنسان مع بعض أعضائه وأطرافه الرئيسية وتجدون أسماءها العربية في قائمة المصطلحات الواردة تحت الصورة. ضعوا الأرقام الواردة في القائمة في المكان الصحيح!

٥) العين	٤) الأذن	٣) الشعر	٢) الجبهة	١) الرأس
١٠) اللسان	٩) الشفة	٨) الفم	٧) الأنف	٦) الحاجب
١٤) الأسنان	١٣) الخد	١٢) الذقن	١١) الفكّ الأعلى / الأسفل	
١٨) الذراع	١٧) العنق	١٦) الكتف	١٥) العمود الفقرى	
٢٣) الصدر	٢٢) الإصبع	٢١) اليد	٢٠) الساعد	١٩) العضد
٢٨) الذكر	٢٧) الحوض	٢٦) البطن	٢٥) الرئة	٢٤) القلب
٣٢) القدم	٣١) الركبة	٣٠) الساق	٢٩) الفرج	

Text 2   عند الطبيب

صباح: صباح الخير يا دكتور.

الطبيب: صباح النور، أهلاً وسهلاً ومرحباً، خيراً إن شاء ا لله؟

صباح: في الحقيقة، يا دكتور، أنا مريضة، عندي صداع شديد وآلام في المعدة وفي جسمي كلّه وفي جميع الأطراف.

الطبيب: منذ متى وهل عندك حمّى؟

صباح: كنت أشعر بهذه الآلام لمدّة يومين وليس عندي حمى ولكنّني لم أنم كثيراً وتقيّأت عدة مرّات.

الطبيب: ماذا أكلت؟

صباح: أكلت شيئاً من اللحوم المعلّبة.

الطبيب: قد تكون هذه اللحوم فاسدة.

صباح: لا أعرف، قد تكون، ولكن أخي كان قد أكل من نفس اللحوم فلم يشعر بأية آلام.

الطبيب: هل أخذت بعض الحبوب أو الأدوية؟

صباح: أخذت عدّة حبوب من الأسبيرين ولكن بدون فائدة.

الطبيب: على أية حال يجب تحليل الدم. قد نرى فيه شيئاً.

صباح: هل المرض خطير والعلاج صعب وهل يجب عليّ أن أدخل المستشفى؟

الطبيب: هذا غير ضروري، أنت تبقين عندنا في العيادة بعض الوقت وستقوم الممرضة بفحص الدم والبول والخروج هنا وسأصف لك بعض الأدوية ضد الألم.

صباح: هل يجب عليّ أن أعود مرّة أخرى؟

الطبيب: نعم، تعالي يوم الأربعاء القادم، على أيّ حال كتبت لك إجازة مرضية لمدّة ثلاثة آيّام.

صباح: ولكن عندي مواعيد مهمّة كثيرة، يا دكتور.

الطبيب: لا تنسَي أنّ صحتك أهمّ من المواعيد.

صباح: طال عمرك يا دكتور، مع السلامة.

الطبيب: مع السلامة.

Exercises:

L1 The teacher points to parts of the body using a poster or a picture on the blackboard and the students give the Arabic equivalent.

L2 (Written homework) Form 10 sentences with the Arabic words denoting time preceded by كل. (ساعة، يوم، صباح، مساء، سنة)

☞ أشرب كل صباح فنجاناً من القهوة.

☞ أمشي كل أسبوع إلى مكتبة مدينتنا.

L3 Form sentences with نفس and the following nouns:

فندق، سنة، شهر، أسبوع، يوم، كتاب، مستشفى، طبيب، بلد، مدينة

Written homework: appositional construction
oral performance: genitive construction

written: كنت في المستشفى نفسه

oral: كنت في نفس المستشفى

L4 Add the Arabic equivalent for "he / she, ... himself / herself".

☞ كتب الرسالة. > كتب الرسالة بنفسه.

كتبت الرسالة.

كتبوا الرسائل.

هل قدت السيّارة؟

فعلت ذلك.

هل فعلت ذلك؟

هل فعلتم ذلك؟

إفعل ذلك!

إفعلي ذلك!

إفعلوا ذلك!

L5 Form sentences of the type كان + adverb or adverbial phrase + عدّة. Use the following time markers after عدّة:

مرّات، سنوات، شهور، أسابيع، أيّام!

☞ كنت هناك عدّة مرّات.

☞ كنت في قرية صديقي عدّة أيّام.

L6 Form sentences with the verbs كتب، كان، قرأ، اشترى، أخذ، دعا، شرب in which عدّة and one of the nouns in the plural become the object of the sentence.

nouns: رسالة، كتاب، جريدة، صديق، كأس، فنجان، يوم، أسبوع.

☞ قرأت عدّة كتب عربية.

☞ كان عدّة أيّام في السعودية.

L7 Form sentences in which one of the following nouns مُعلّم، صديق، عضو،
فتـاة، مرافـق، وفـد، طبيـب، ممرِّضـة، طـالب، مدير، رئيـس is the subject preceded by بعض is the
subject of the sentence.

Use the following verbs: حضر، جاء، أتى، سكن، عاد، عمل، رجع

☞   حضر بعض الأصدقاء الحفلة مساء الأمس.

☞   جاء بعض الأصدقاء العرب إليَّ.

L8 Transform the following sentences into questions introduced by

من أي/ أية، في أي/ أية، إلى أي/ أية

☞   أنا من بلد أوربي. <   من أي بلد أنت؟

☞   اشتريت كتاباً عربياً. <   أي كتاب اشتريت؟

أنا من بلد عربي.

ولدت في شهر نيسان.

سافرت إلى مدينة بغداد.

درست في جامعة دمشق.

كنت أسكن في فندق "هيلتون".

كان عندنا وفد لبناني.

دخل أحمد المستشفى.

حضرت الحفلة وفود كثيرة.

G1 Transform the following sentences into the past tense.

☞   الطالب مجتهد. >   كان الطالب مجتهداً.

الطلاب مجتهدون.

الطقس بارد.

الفتاة جميلة.

مرافق الوفد طالب.

الطبيب جديد.

الأطباء جدد.

الأكل جيد.

الغرفة مريحة.

الأدوية أجنبية.

الممرِّضة جميلة.

المستشفى حديث.

أحمد مريض.

حالته حسنة (good).

الباص قديم.

الأدوية غالية.

G2 Replace the past tense in the following examples by كان يفعل.
Add one of the following time markers:

كلّ يوم	لمدّة أسبوع
كلّ يوم بعد الظهر	لمدّة أسبوعين
كلّ أسبوع	لمدّة شهر
كلّ شهر	لمدّة شهرين
كلّ سنة	لمدّة سنة
كلّ مساء	لمدّة سنتين

☞   عمل الرجل في المصنع.   >   كان الرجل يعمل في المصنع لمدّة شهر.

سكن صديقي في مدينة تورونتو.

مشى الطالب إلى المعهد.

عمل أخي في المدرسة.

زارت المعلمة مكتبة المدينة.

نام المريض ساعة واحدة.

كتب صديقي رسالة.

مشى أحمد في شوارع المدينة.

درس عمر الطب في جامعة برلين.

زارنا صديقنا العربي.

دعانا المرافق إلى بيته.

شربت كأساً من العصير.

G3 Same as G2, but with the subject in the plural.

☞   عمل الرجال في المصنع.   >   كان الرجال يعملون في المصنع كلّ يوم.

G4 Transform the subject/object into the plural preceded by كلّ "all".

☞   وصل الوفد أمس.   >   وصلت كلّ الوفود أمس.

Pay attention to the fact that agreement in gender between the verb and subject is not based on the masculine كلّ but on the 2nd term of the genitive construction.

وصل الصديق أمس الأول (before yesterday).

وصل صديقي أمس الأول.

بقي الطالب في المعهد.

سافرت الفتاة إلى مدينة لندن.

دعونا معلمنا إلى الحفلة.

يعمل الطبيب هناك.

بعت الكتاب.

رأيت المرافق.

قرأت الكتاب.

زرت المدينة.

فتحت الشبّاك (to open).

G5 Same as G4. كل is to be replaced by جميع in those sentences in which a person is the subject or object.

G6 (Written homework) Use كل in the sentences of G4 in its appositional position.

☞   وصل الوفد أمس.   >   وصلت الوفود كلها أمس.

G7 (Repetition) Combine the following numerals, nouns and adjectives.

جديد	رجل	٥
قديم	بيت	١٢
ألماني	مارك	٥٠
مشترك	مشروع	١١٣
عربي	وفد	٧
دراسي	كتاب	٢
مجتهد	طالبة	٢٢
حديث	عمارة	٩
أجنبي	دولة	٤١
أمريكي	دولار	١١١٢
مصري	مسلم	مليون

C1 (Homework) Use the dictionary to write a list of common diseases. The list is to be discussed and completed in the next class hour.

C2 The teacher asks about pains in different parts of the body:

☞   هل عندكَ / عندكِ آلام (في المعدة / في الصدر ...)؟

The student answers with "Yes" or "No":

☞   نعم، عندي آلام في المعدة.

☞   لا، ليست عندي آلام في المعدة، عندي آلام في رجليّ.

C3 Create a form in Arabic to be used to obtain a medical history as follows:

last name, first name:
age:
weight:
sex:
childhood diseases:
operations:
etc.
Use the dictionary, your list of common diseases, and the following words and phrases:

blood pressure	ضغْط الدم
to take so.'s blood pressure	قاس (يقيس) ضغط الدم
blood sugar level	نِسْبة السُكَّر في الدم
diagnosis	تشْخِيص
electroencephalogram	تخْطِيط القلب
electrocardiogram	تخْطِيط الدِماغ
weight	وزْن
childhood diseases	أمْراض الطُفُولة
operation	عملية جراحية
plaster, band-aid	بلاسْتر
prophylaxis	وقاية من
pulse / to take so.'s pulse	نبْض / جسّ (يجُسّ) نبْضَهُ
menstruation	عادة شهرية
to X-ray	فحص بالأشِعّة
X-ray picture	صُورة شُعاعية

Final Exercise:
1. Transform the following sentences into the past tense.

صديقه طبيب. أذناه كبيرتان. أنفه طويل. في دمه كحول. الحبوب مُرّة. هو مريض. في فمه أسنان قليلة. الألم شـديد. العلاج صعـب. قلبـه كبـير. سـاقاه طويلتـان. المستشفى جديد. الممرِّضات جميلات. الغرفة مريحة. الباص قديم. مرافق الوفد طالب. اللحم فاسد. عيناها جميلتان.

2. Translate into English.

كان قد أكل كلّ اللحم. كان الطبيب يعمل في نفس المدينة. قد يأتي إلى الحفلة. كانت المعلّمة تذهب إلى نفس المقهى كلّ يوم لمدّة أسبوعين. قـد يعـرف الحـلّ، قـد لا يعـرف. كان قد شرب العصير كلّه قبل وصول الضيوف. يكون قد خرج من عيادته.

3. Translate into Arabic.

He has got the same illness. Her brother ate the same canned meat. All students came. They sold the same book. They sold the book themselves. The whole family was at the doctor's. You wrote this yourself. Do it yourselves! He took some pills himself. One of the sick persons had already gone several days ago. He asked some of them about the treatment. One of the nurses was very pretty.

4. Put the numbers into the picture according to the given list.

١) الرأس   ٢) الجبهة   ٣) الشعر   ٤) الأذن   ٥) العين   ٦) الحاجب

٧) الأنف   ٨) الفم   ٩) الشفة   ١٠) اللسان   ١١) الفكّ الأعلى / الأسفل

١٢) الذقن   ١٣) الخد   ١٤) الأسنان   ١٥) العنق   ١٦) الكتف

١٧) العمود الفقرى   ١٨) الذراع   ١٩) العضد   ٢٠) الساعد   ٢١) اليد

٢٢) الإصبع   ٢٣) الصدر   ٢٤) القلب   ٢٥) الرئة   ٢٦) البطن

1. The Forms of the Verb (أَوْزان الأَفْعال) : II, III and IV

1.1. The base form of the Arabic verb (فَعَلَ / يَفْعَلُ), as we have got to know it up to now, can be extended by gemination of consonants, prolongation of vowels, prefixation or infixation, or a combination of two of the possibilities that have been given. The extensions of the base form, like the base form itself, are called Forms.

There are 15 Forms, only 10 of which, however, are in common use. They are referred to by Roman numerals in European grammar books and dictionaries: base Form = Form I, derived Forms = Form II, III, ... X. Theoretically all Forms can be formed out of every verb. Practically speaking, however, a verb rarely occurs in more than 4 or 5 Forms, and in fact it often occurs only in its basic Form or a derived Form.

☞**A1** Originally changes with regard to meaning correspond to the formal extensions of the base form as well. Thus e.g., an intensifying, causative and denominative meaning is stated for Form II, a reflexive meaning for Form VII. As, however, every individual verb is lexically fixed and the original "value of the Form" is often not identifiable any more, we refrain from stating the basic meanings of the individual Forms at the moment. Cf. the summary in Lesson 19 with respect to this subject.

1.2. Form II
Characteristic: doubling of R_2

Perfect tense:	فَعَّلَ
Imperfect tense:	يُفَعِّلُ
Imperative:	فَعِّلْ

☞**A2** The quadriliteral verb has the same vocalization of the imperfect form.

Pattern:	فَعْلَلَ ، يُفَعْلِلُ
Example: "to translate"	تَرْجَمَ ، يُتَرْجِمُ

Table 35 in the Appendix supplies information about all forms of the quadriliteral verb.

1.3. Form III
Characteristic: prolongation of the vowel that follows R_1

Perfect tense:	فَاعَلَ
Imperfect tense:	يُفَاعِلُ
Imperative:	فَاعِلْ

1.4. Form IV

Characteristic: prefix *a-* أَ, vowellessness of R$_1$

Perfect tense:	أَفْعَلَ
Imperfect tense:	يُفْعِلُ
Imperative:	أَفْعِلْ

✍ **A3** The prefixed *Hamza* of Form IV is a *Hamzat al-qaṭᶜ*.

1.5. Forms II, III, IV have the same succession of vowels in the imperfect forms: *u - (a/ā/-) - i*. We group them together for that reason.

Here is the summary once more:

	imperative	imperfect tense	perfect tense
Form II	فَعِّلْ	يُفَعِّلُ	فَعَّلَ
Form III	فَاعِلْ	يُفَاعِلُ	فَاعَلَ
Form IV	أَفْعِلْ	يُفْعِلُ	أَفْعَلَ

(Appendix: Tables 5, 6, 9, 14)

✍ **A4** The imperfect tense of Forms II and IV are neither distinguishable from each other nor from the basic Form without auxiliary signs.

2. The Attributive Relative Clause (أَلصِّلة والصِّفة)

Not only a word or a group of words, but also a whole clause can be added to a noun as an attributive adjunct. The relative clause is the form of the attributive clause that occurs most frequently.

2.1. There are two types of attributive relative clauses:
a) relative clauses which are employed as attributive adjuncts related to definite nouns (صِلة).
b) relative clauses which are employed as attributive adjuncts related to indefinite nouns (صِفة).

2.2. If the relative clause is the modifier of a definite noun, it is preceded by a relative pronoun.

✍ **A5** There is the same agreement in state between a noun and an attributive clause as there is between a noun and an adjectival attributive adjunct. If the antecedent is definite, the adjective is defined by the article أَل, the relative attributive clause by the so-called relative pronoun. The term relative pronoun is therefore not quite correct, because it expresses, above all, the definiteness of the attributive clause in addition to characterizing gender and number. The relative pronoun does not, however, indicate the syntactic function (of the modified antecedent) in the relative clause.

2.2.1. The relative pronouns (أَلْأَسْمَاء المَوْصُولة) are:

أَلَّذِي	after a masc. noun in the singular
أَلَّتِي	after a fem. noun in the singular and after plurals which denote non-persons
أَلَّذِينَ	after a masc. noun in the plural which denotes persons
أَللَّاتِي، أَللَّوَاتِي	after a fem. noun in the plural which denotes persons
أَللَّذان	after a masc. dual
أَللَّتان	after a fem. dual

👉**A6** Whereas the four first-mentioned forms are neutral as to case, the two dual forms are inflected. When following a noun in the genitive or accusative, they are اللَّتَيْنِ / اللَّذَيْنِ.

👉**A7** Note the different spelling:

with one ل: الَّذي / الَّتي / اللَّواتي ; with two ل: اللَّاتي / اللَّذان / اللَّتان.

👉**A8** The article ال is the first component of the relative pronoun, therefore the initial *Hamza* of الَّذي، الَّتي etc. is *Hamzat al-waṣl*.

2.2.2. الَّذِي، الَّتِي etc. are equivalent to the English relative pronouns "who, which, that" in the nominative. The noun which is modified by the relative clause is the subject of this clause at the same time.

the student who came from Iraq	أَلطَّالِبُ الَّذِي جَاءَ مِنَ الْعِرَاق
the student (f.) who came from Iraq	أَلطَّالِبَةُ الَّتِي جَاءَتْ مِنَ الْعِرَاق
the students who came from Iraq	أَلطُّلَّابُ الَّذِينَ جَاؤُوا مِنَ الْعِرَاق
the students (f.) who came from Iraq	أَلطَّالِبَاتُ اللَّاتِي جِئْنَ مِنَ الْعِرَاق
the two students who came from Iraq	أَلطَّالِبَان اللَّذَان جَاءَا مِنَ الْعِرَاق
the two students (f.) who came from Iraq	أَلطَّالِبَتَان اللَّتَان جَاءَتَا مِنَ الْعِرَاق

A literal translation of the Arabic examples makes the difference in word order in the Arabic and in the English relative clause clear to us. In Arabic: normal word order of the verbal sentence, accordingly "the student who he has come", in English: inverted word order, consequently "the student who has come".

2.2.3. الَّذِي , الَّتِي etc. are also employed in sentences when the subject is not identical with the antecedent. In English, the relative pronoun is in the genitive or objective (as an indirect or direct object or the complement of a preposition) in these cases.

In Arabic the affixed pronoun in the relative clause makes the connection with the antecedent.

the friend whom I have met	أَلصَّدِيقُ الَّذِي قَابَلْتُهُ
the (girl)friend whom I have met	أَلصَّدِيقَةُ الَّتِي قَابَلْتُهَا
the friends whom I have met	أَلأَصْدِقَاءُ الَّذِينَ قَابَلْتُهُمْ
the two friends whom I have met	أَلصَّدِيقَان اللَّذَان قَابَلْتُهُمَا
the friend (to) whom I have written a letter	أَلصَّدِيقُ الَّذِي كَتَبْتُ لَهُ رِسَالَةً
the (girl)friend (to) whom I have written a letter	أَلصَّدِيقَةُ الَّتِي كَتَبْتُ لَهَا رِسَالَةً
the friends (to) whom I have written a letter	أَلأَصْدِقَاءُ الَّذِينَ كَتَبْتُ لَهُم رِسَالَةً
the (girl)friends (to) whom I have written a letter	أَلصَّدِيقَاتُ اللاَّتِي كَتَبْتُ لَهُنَّ رِسَالَةً
the friend whose doctor I have met	أَلصَّدِيقُ الَّذِي قَابَلْتُ طَبِيبَهُ
the (girl)friend whose doctor I have met	أَلصَّدِيقَةُ الَّتِي قَابَلْتُ طَبِيبَهَا
the friends whose doctor I have met	أَلأَصْدِقَاءُ الَّذِينَ قَابَلْتُ طَبِيبَهُمْ
the two (girl)friends whose doctor I have met	أَلصَّدِيقتَان اللَّتَان قَابَلْتُ طَبِيبَهُمَا
the friend with whom I have been to the theatre	أَلصَّدِيقُ الَّذِي كُنْتُ مَعَهُ فِي الْمَسْرَح
the friends with whom I have been	أَلأَصْدِقَاءُ الَّذِينَ كُنْتُ عِنْدَهُمْ
with the two friends from whom I have received the books	عِنْدَ الصَّدِيقَيْن اللَّذَين أَخَذْتُ الْكُتُبَ مِنْهُمَا
the (girl)friend at whose house I was	أَلصَّدِيقَةُ الَّتِي كُنْتُ فِي بَيْتِها

A9 Of course forms which are defined in a different way than by the article could also be employed in place of الصديقة, الأصدقاء, الصديق etc. which were chosen as an example, e.g.:

صديقُ محمَّد، صديقي a.o.

2.3. If the relative clause is the modifier of an indefinite noun (صِفة), **no** relative pronoun is used.

☞A10 There is agreement in state here, as well. The antecedent is indefinite, consequently the attributive clause does not get a sign of definition either.

Word order and the affixed pronoun are just as they are in the syndetic relative clause:

I have read a piece of news in the newspaper al-Ahrām, in which it says: ...	... قَرَأْتُ فِي جَرِيدَةِ الأَهْرَام خَبَراً جَاءَ فِيهِ
I have met a friend today who came from London yesterday.	قَابَلْتُ الْيَوْمَ صَدِيقاً وَصَلَ أَمْسِ مِن لندن.
There are delegations in the hotel who came from the Arab countries.	فِي الْفُنْدُق وُفُودٌ وَصَلَتْ مِنَ الْبُلْدَانِ الْعَرَبِيَّة.
a present which I have sent to my friend	هَدِيَّةٌ أَرْسَلْتُهَا إلى صَدِيقِي

V

Jordanian	أُرْدُنِّيّ	(Minister of) Foreign Affairs	(وزير) الخَارِجِيّة
enterprise, firm	مُؤَسَّسة ج ـات	(Minister of) the Interior	(وزير) الدَاخِلِيّة
Israel	إسْرائيل	to mention so., sth. to so.	ذكر (يَذْكُرُ) ه، هـ
rel. pr.	الّذي م الّتي ج الّذين م اللاّتي واللّواتي	to lead, to head so., sth.	رأَسَ (يَرْأَسُ) ه، هـ
	ث اللّذان م اللّتان	to connect between	ربط (يَرْبُطُ) بين
security, protection	أمان	to go back to	رجع إلى
with the protection of God	في أمان الله	II رحَّب (يُرحِّبُ) بِ to welcome, to greet so.	
to seem (as if)	بدا (يَبْدُو) (وكأَنَّ)	trip, journey	رِحْلة ج ـات
ticket, card	بِطاقة ج ـات	IV أرْسَل (يُرْسِلُ) ه هـ إلى / ل to send so., sth. to so.	
big, considerable	بالِغ		
building	بناء ج أَبْنِية	high	رفيع
to translate sth. from ... to	تَرْجم (يُتَرْجِمُ) هـ من ... إلى	III رافق (يُرافِقُ) ه to accompany so.	
pupil, student	تِلْميذ ج تلاميذُ	satisfaction	إرْتِياح
bilateral	ثُنائِيّ	IV أسْفَر (يُسْفِرُ) عن to produce sth.	
II حدَّث (يُحَدِّثُ) ه هـ/ ب to say sth. to so.		II سلَّم (يُسَلِّمُ) ه هـ / ل / إلى to hand over, to bring sth. to so.	
IV أحْضَر (يُحْضِرُ) إلى to bring sth. along to		I hope you feel better soon.	سلامتُكَ/سلامتُكِ
probably	مُحْتَمل	diarrhea	إسْهال
at any rate	على كُل حال	drink	شراب ج أشْرِبة
to inform so. of sth.	IV أخْبَر (يُخْبِرُ) ه ب	III شارك (يُشاركُ) في to take part in	
final	خِتامِيّ	people	شَعْب ج شُعُوب

brother (having the same father and mother)	شَقِيق ج أَشِقَّاءُ	resolution	قرار ج ـات
health, hygienic	صِحّيّ	drop	قَطْرة ج قَطَرات
newspaper	صَحِيفة ج صُحُف	piece	قِطْعة ج قِطَع
edited, published (by)	صادِر (مِن، عن)	top, summit	قِمّة ج قِمم
Ṣanʿāʾ (Sanaa)	صَنعاءُ	cholera	كوليرا
pharmacy	صَيْدَلِيّة ج ـات	bitter	مُرّ
exactly	بالضَّبْط	IV to be able to	أَمْكَن (يُمكِنُ) ٥، أَنْ
II to express sth.	عَبَّر (يُعبِّرُ) عن	he/she is able to ...	يُمْكِنُهُ / يُمْكِنُها أَنْ ...
many, numerous	عَدِيد	outstanding	مُتَميِّز
IV to give so. sth.	أَعْطَى (يُعطِي) ٥ هـ	IV to accomplish, to carry out	أَنْجَز (يُنْجِزُ) هـ
he must	عَلَيْهِ أَنْ	region, district	مِنْطقة ج مناطِقُ
IV to please so., that	أَفْرح (يُفرِحُ) ٥، أَنْ	according to	نَقْلاً عن
film	فِلْم ج أَفْلام	present	هَدِية ج هدايا
at once, instantly, immediately	فوراً	duty, task	واجب ج ـات
II to introduce so., sth. to so.	قَدَّم (يُقدِّمُ) ٥، هـ إلى / لـ	prescription	وصْفة ج وصَفات
to present, to submit sth. (to so.)	قَدَّم (له) هـ	III to continue sth.	واصل (يُواصِلُ) هـ
		death	وفاة ج وفيات

Text 1

أخبار عالمية

صنعاء – ذكرت الصحف اليمنية الصادرة أمس نقلاً عن مسؤولين في وزارة الصحّة أنّ أمراض الإسهال والكوليرا في عدد مـن محافظات اليمن أسفرت عـن وفاة العديد مـن المواطنين في هذه المحافظات وقالت المصادر إنّ هذا الوضع يرجع إلى أسباب صحّية.

القاهرة – يصل إلى القاهرة يوم الاثنيـن القـادم وزير خارجية إسرائيل في زيارة عمل قصيرة وسيبحث خلالها مع كلّ من وزير الخارجية ووزير الدفـاع تطوّرات الوضع في المنطقة. ويبدو أنّه سيقدّم مشروعاً جديداً لحلّ الأزمة.

القاهرة – قال الرئيس المصري في كلمته في الجلسة الختامية للقمّة الإفريقيـة : إسمحـوا لي أن أعبّر عن ارتياحي البالغ بقرارات القمّة الأساسية ويفرحـني جـدّاً أنّكم أنجـزتم أعمـالاً عظيمة في هذه الأيّام القليلة.

وشارك في أعمال القمّة الـتي أسفرت عـن نتائج مهمّة ٣٢ رئيـس دولـة و٥ رؤسـاء حكومات و١٤ رئيس وفد.

الرياض – يواصل الوفد الأمريكي الـذي يرأسـه وزير الخارجيـة اليـوم زيارتـه للمملكـة بجولة في بعض المؤسّسات والمشاريع الاقتصادية. ومن الجدير بالذكر أنّ رئيس الوفد الأمريكي سيقابل نظيره السعودي لمناقشة سبل التعاون الثنائي.

بغداد – وصل إلى بغداد وزير التعليم العالي الأردنّي ورحّب بـه عنـد وصولـه إلى المطـار نظيره العراقي وقال الوزير في تصريح صحفي إنّ العلاقات المتميِّزة بين البلدين الشقيقين في مجال التعليم العالي هي برهان قاطع على مستوى التعاون الرفيع الذي يربط بين شعبينا ودولتينا. ومن الجدير بالذكر أن الوزير الأردنّي سلّم الرئيس العراقي رسالة شخصية مـن جلالة الملك.

Text 2   في الصيدلية

صباح: مساء الخير.

الصيدلي: مساء النور، أهلاً وسهلاً.

صباح: لقد كنت اليوم عند الطبيـب ووصـف لي هـذه الوصفـة وأرسلني إليـك، هـل عندك هذه الأدوية؟

الصيدلي: هات الوصفة، من فضلك.

صباح: تفضّل.

الصيدلي: لقد وصف لك الطبيب قطرات للمعدة وحبوب ضدّ الصداع، هـل عنـدك ألم في المعدة؟

صباح: بالضبط، عندي آلام شديدة، كما أني تقيّأت عدّة مرّات.

الصيدلي: هل أخبرك الطبيب بسبب هذه الآلام؟

صباح: حدّثني الطبيب إنّ السبب قد يرجع إلى اللحم المعلّب الفاسد الذي أكلتـه قبـل يومين.

الصيدلي: هذا محتمل جدّاً، على كلّ حال، هذه الأدوية جيّدة جدّاً وستشـعرين بتحسُّن سريع.

صباح: وكيف آخذ هذه الأدوية؟

الصيدلي: خذي من هذه الحبوب ثلاث مـرّات في اليـوم حبّتين بعـد الأكـل ومـن هـذه
القطرات عشرين قطرة في الصباح بعد الفطور وقبل النوم.

صباح: هل هذه القطرات مرّة؟

الصيدلي: إنها مرّة قليلاً وعليك أن تأخذيها مع قطعة من السكّر.

صباح: سكّر عادي أم خاصّ؟

الصيدلي: لا، سكّر عادي.

صباح: شكراً جزيلاً ، في الأمان.

الصيدلي: عفواً، سلامتك وفي أمان ا لله.

Exercises:

L1 Transform the following sentences into imperatives (2nd p. sg. m./f. and 2nd p. pl. m.) using the verbs: ترجم، أَنجز، قدّم، سافر، رحّب، سلّم

☞   ... ذلك الكتاب!   >   ترجم ذلك الكتاب!
☞   >   ترجمي ذلك الكتاب!
☞   >   ترجموا ذلك الكتاب!

... إلى نيو يورك يوم الأربعاء!

... بالوزير!

... بهم الآن!

... الأعمال حتى يوم الاثنين!

... الكلمات إلى اللغة العربية!

...ـنا إلى الأصدقاء!

... لها كرّاسة جديدة!

... بالضيوف في المطار!

... هذه الكلمة!

... لهم مشروعاً جديداً!

... له تلك الرسالة شخصياً!

... إلى هناك بالقطار!

... هذا العمل اليوم!

L2 (Homework) Insert the proper form of the verbs قابل، أَنجز، أرسل، حدّث، سافر.

☞   هل يمكنك أن ... عملك حتى يوم الأربعاء؟   >

☞ هل يمكنك أن تنجز عملك حتى يوم الأربعاء؟

هل يمكنك أن ... غداً إلى هناك؟

متى أمكنكم أن ... ـه عن الرحلة؟

أمكنني أن ... ـهم في الفندق.

أمكنها أن ... ـنا في الحفلة.

يمكننا أن ... إليكم هذه الأشياء.

أمكنه أن ... معنا إلى لندن.

لماذا لم يمكنكم أن ... واجباتكم؟

أين يمكنني أن ... ـك؟

L3 Insert the relative pronoun.

الوفد ... يسافر إلى لندن

الوفود ... وصلت إلى المطار

الأصدقاء ... يزوروننا غداً

المرافق ... رافقنا

الطالبان ... يدرسان اللغة العربية

مع الطالبتين ... تدرسان في معهد هيردر

الفتاة ... حضرت الحفلة

الفتيات ... حضرن الحفلة

التلاميذ ... ينجزون واجبات كثيرة

عند صديقي ... قدّم لي كأساً من الماء

أخي ... أرسل إليّ رسالة

L4 Insert the relative pronoun and the affixed pronoun in the following clauses.

الرسائل ... كتبتـ.. لها

الأخبار ... سمعنا.. أمس

القلم ... اشتريتـ.. من ذلك المخزن

السياسيون ... قابلتـ.. يوم الخميس

الوفد التجاري ... رافقتـ.. لمدة ثلاثة أسابيع

في الرسالة ... أرسلتـ.. إلى عائلتي

الواجبات ... أنجزـ.. بسرعة

الهدية ... قدّمتـ .. لي صديقتي

الضيوف ... قدّمـ .. صديقنا إلينا

الفلم ... نشاهد ... يوم الجمعة

العائلة ... أعرف ...

الضيوف ... نرحّب بـ ...

هنا المكتبة ... أذهب إليـ ... كل يوم

السيّارة الجديدة ... أسافر بـ ... إلى لندن غداً

الجامعة ... قابلت صديقتي أمامـ ...

هذا الشخص ... حدّثتني صديقتي عنـ ...

في البَلَدين ... سمعنا عنـ ... كثيراً

الخزانة ... وضعت الكتب فيـ ...

أين المخزن ... اشتريت الهدايا منـ ...

المدن ... كنتم فيـ ... مدّة طويلة

القاعة ... كنّا فيـ ...

L5 Try to find out the English equivalents of the following proverbs and sayings with الذي :

الذي بيته من زجاج ما يراجم (to throw stones at) الناس.

الذي في الجبل (mountain) يقول: يا ليتني (I wished I would be) في الـوادي (valley) والذي في الوادي يقول: يا ليتني في الجبل.

الذي ليس له عقل (brain)، عقله الشيطان (devil).

الذي ما ينظر في العواقب (consequences) ما له الدهر (time, eternity) صاحب.

الذي يدخل فيما لا يُخصّه (what is not his business) يندَم (regret).

G1 Transform the perfect into the imperfect tense.

☞ قدّم أحمد صديقه إلينا.   >   يقدّم أحمد صديقه إلينا.

قدّمنا إليكم أصدقاءنا – متى قدّموه إليك؟ – قدّم أحمد نفسه – قدّمت له هذه الهدية – هل قدّمتم لهم بعض الشراب؟

رحّب بنا مدير المعهد – رحّبنا بضيوفنا الأجانب – رحّب الرئيس بأعضاء الوفد الفرنسي.

إلى أين سافرت الوفود؟ – سافرتْ إلى لندن بالقطار – سافرنا إلى هناك بالطائرة – هل سافر السياسيون اليوم؟

هل شاهدتّ ذلك الفلم؟ – نعم شاهدتُه مساء اليـوم – نعم شـاهدناه اليـوم – شـاهدوا اليوم الأبنية الحديثة.

ترجم الطالب الكلمات الجديدة إلى اللغة الإنكليزية – ترجمتُها إلى اللغة العربية – ترجمت المعلمة الرسالة من اللغة الفرنسية إلى اللغة الإنكليزية.

هل حدّثكم صديقكم عن رحلته؟ – حدّثناه عن دراستنا في مصر – حدّثتنا هيفاء عن الحياة في بلادها.

سلّم أحمد عدنان الكتاب – سلّمناكم المبلغ اليوم – سلّمتُ الأشياء فوراً.

أفرحنا ذلك – أفرحني ذلك – هل أفرحتكم الهدايا؟

رافقت الوفد طالبة ألمانية – رافقتُ صديقي إلى المحطّة – رافقني إلى المسرح صديق إنكليزي.

من قابلت هناك؟ – قابلت هناك صديقاً جزائرياً – قابلنا اليوم عدداً من الضيوف الأجانب.

هل أمكنك أن تسافر إلى هناك؟ – أمكنني أن أفعل ذلك – أمكننا أن ننجز واجباتنا فوراً.

متى أنجزتم واجباتكم؟ – هل أنجزت عملك بنفسك؟ – أنجزوا العمل بعد ثلاث ساعات.

أرسل الطالب رسالة إلى عائلته – هل أرسلت هدية إلى صديقك؟ – متى أرسلت البطاقة إلى أصدقائك؟

لماذا أحضرت جميع الطلاب إلى هنا؟ – لماذا أحضرتم معكم أربعة كتب فقط؟– أعرف أنهما أحضرا معهما نقوداً كثيرة.

G2 (Homework) Insert the given verb in the proper tense.

☞   (قدّم) > (أنا) ... إليه صديقي اليوم   >   قدّمت إليه صديقي اليوم.
☞   >   أقدّم إليه صديقي اليوم.

آ) قدّم   ... الطالب هدية لصديقه.

(هم) ... إلينا أصدقاءهم.

متى ... (أنتم) إليّ ذلك الرجل؟

ب) حدّث متى ... ـهم (أنتم) عن واجباتهم؟

هل ... ـها المعلّم؟

لماذا ... ـك الموظف؟

ج) رحّب هل ... بهم الرئيس؟

من ... بالوفد المصري؟

متى ... (هم) بالضيوف؟

د) سافر   إلى أين ... الوفد؟

هل ... (أنتم) بالسيّارة أم بالقطار؟

(هم) ... يوم الأحد؟

ه) شاهد   هل ... (أنتَ) تلك البطاقات؟

(هنَّ) ... كل الأفلام.

متى ... (أنتِ) أولئك الأشخاص؟

و) أمكن   هل ... ـك أن تفعل ذلك؟

متى ... ـكم أن تذهبوا إلى هناك؟

أين ... ـكم أن تقابلوهم؟

ز) أنجز   (نحن) ... عملنا بعد ساعتين.

... الوفد واجبه بعد أسبوع.

... التلاميذ هذا العمل بسرعة.

ح) أرسل   إلى من ... (أنتَ) هذه الرسالة؟

... الحكومة أدوية إلى مصر.

(نحن) ... ـها إلى المعهد.

A11 If Arabic letters are used for numbering as in G2 أ - ح then an order different from the alphabet is to be observed. This order can be memorized by means of the following mnemonic sentence:

أَبْجَدْ هَوَّزْ حُطِّي كلمُنْ سعْفصْ قرشتْ ثخذْ ضظغْ

G3 Answer the following questions by means of بعدُ ... لم ، لا، "No, ... not yet".

هل أنجزت واجباتك؟   >   لا، لم أنجز واجباتي بعد.

هل واصلت الجولة؟

هل أرسلتم لهم رسالة؟

هل أنجزتم عملكم؟

هل أمكنكم أن تفعلوا ذلك؟

هل قابلتها؟

هل شاهدتِ ذلك الفلم؟

هل سافرت إلى القاهرة؟

هل رحّبتم بصديقنا؟

هل حدّثتموهم عن الدراسة؟

هل قدّمت الصديق إليهم؟

هل ترجمت الكلمات؟

G4 (Repetition) Transform the following sentences into the imperfect tense of the 3rd p. sg. m. or f. .

عاد محمّد إلى الفندق.   >   يعود محمّد إلى الفندق.

عاد صديقي من لندن.

وفت صديقتي بوعدها.

نسيت الطالبة مواعيدها.

وضع الطالب الكتاب تحت الشنطة.

أتى أعضاء الوفد صباحاً.

رأى عمر في المخزن كتباً جديدة.

رجت هيفاء أصدقاءها أن يذهبوا معها.

نامت الطالبات كثيراً.

وضعت صديقتي على الطاولة كؤوساً.

وعد الطالب صديقه بزيارة العاصمة.

رجت الفتاة أن تذهب إلى المسرح.

زار الوفد جامعتنا.

قال محمد إنّني شربت كأساً واحدة.

باع صديقي بيته.

مشى الرجال إلى قاعة الاجتماع.

لقي صديقي فتاة شقراء.

وضع الطالب الكتاب في الشنطة.

دعا الطالب صديقته إلى الحفلة.

مشت الطالبات إلى المخزن.

باع الطالب كتبه.

قال صديقنا العربي إنّني أكلت قليلاً.

عادت الفتيات إلى بيتهن.

زار صديقي عدداً من البلدان العربية.

قام أصدقائي بنزهة جميلة.

عاد الوفد اليوم.

زارت الوفود مدينة لندن.

وفى المعلِّمون بوعدهم.

جاء المرافق إلى قاعة الطعام.

جاءت صديقتي إليَّ.

رأى محمّد هناك رجالاً كثيرين.

وصل الأصدقاء مساء اليوم.

عادت الطائرة من القاهرة.

وصل الوفد إلى لندن بالطائرة.

عاد الأصدقاء صباحاً.

وصلت الوفود إلى هنا.

قام رئيس الوفد.

بنى العمّال مباني رائعة.

وفى محمّد بوعده.

نسي الطالب الكلمات الجديدة.

أتى الوفد مساء اليوم.

جاء أحمد حسب الموعد.

رأى أحمد صديقه أمام مخزن السيّارات.

رجا محمّد أصدقاءه أن يحضروا إليه.

زار الرجال ذلك الجبل.

قال صديقي إنّني مجتهد.

باع الرجل سيّارته.

مشى الأصدقاء إلى المقهى.

وعد أحمد أصدقاءه بألف دولار.

وضع الطالب المعطف في الخزانة.

لقي المعلّم أصدقائي في المخزن.

قاد المرافق السيّارة بسرعة.

خافت المعلّمة من السفر بالطائرة.

سار صديقي بالقطار.

قام محمّد من النوم.

C1 (Listening comprehension) The teacher reads the following news. The students summarize and repeat it in English.

القاهرة – قال الرئيس المصري في الكلمة الافتتاحية في الجلسة الأولى للقمّة الإفريقية :

إسمحوا لي أن أعبّر عن ارتياحي البالغ بعقد القمّة الإفريقية في مصر العربية ويفرحني جـدّاً أنّكم أتيتم إلى هنا لكي تنجزوا أعمالاً عظيمة في هذه الأيّام القليلة.

ويشارك في أعمال القمة ٣٣ رئيس دولة و٨ رؤساء حكومات و ١١ رئيس وفـد وأيضـاً ممثّلون عن الأمم المتحدة.

الرياض – يواصل الوفد الفرنسي الذي يرأسه وزير خارجية فرنسا اليوم زيارته للمملكة بجولة في بعض المؤسّسات الاقتصادية والمشاريع الزراعية. ومن الجدير بالذكر أنّ رئيس الوفد الفرنسي سيقابل نظيره السعودي لمناقشة سبل التعاون الثنائي في المجالين الزراعي والعسكري.

بغداد – وصل إلى بغداد وزير الدفاع الأردني ورحّب به عند وصوله إلى المطار نظيره العراقي وقال الوزير في تصريح صحفي إن العلاقات المتميِّزة بين البلدين الشقيقين في مجال الدفاع هي برهان قاطع على مستوى التعاون الرفيع الذي يربط بين شعبينا ودولتينا. ومن الجدير بالذكر أنّ الوزير الأردني سلّم رسالة شخصية من جلالة الملك.

صنعاء – ذكرت الصحف اليمنية الصادرة أمس نقلاً عن مسؤول في وزارة الصحّة أنّ أمراض الإسهال والكوليرا في عدد من محافظات اليمن أسفرت عن وفاة العديد من المواطنين في هذه المحافظات وقالت المصادر أيضاً إنّ هذا الوضع قد يرجع إلى أسباب صحّية.

القاهرة – يصل إلى القاهرة يوم الجمعة القادم وزير خارجية سوريا في زيارة عمل قصيرة سيبحث خلالها مع كلٍّ من وزير الخارجية ووزير الدفاع تطوُّرات الوضع في المنطقة. ويبدو أنّه سيقدّم مشروعاً جديداً لتوسيع التعاون الثنائي في المجال العسكري.

C2 The teacher varies the news in C1 (names, functions, numbers); the students give the contents in Arabic. Such exercises should be continued using recordings from tv, video and radio.

C3 Prepare a conversation that takes place in a pharmacy based on Text 2. Use your list of common diseases (Lesson 13) and ask for medicine to treat headache, diarrhea, fever, etc. and their prices.

Final exercise:
1. Transform into the imperfect tense.

قدّمنا إليكم ضيوفنا. رحّبوا بالرئيس. سافرن إلى باريس. شاهدنا هذه المسرحية. ترجمت الكلمة الطويلة. سلّم الكتاب. رافقتها إلى البيت. قابلتم الوفود. أنجزنا العمل. أرسلت رسائل كثيرة. أمكنه أنْ يسافر إلى مصر. أخبرهم بنتائج الانتخابات. أسفرت الجولة عن حلول سريعة. شاركوا في المؤتمر. عبّرتم عن ارتياحكم. أعطيته كتاباً. أفرحتني هذه الأخبار. أسفرت الأزمة الطويلة عن مشاكل كبيرة. واصلنا المناقشة. حدّثنا عن التطوُّرات في الداخل. أرسلناه إلى الطبيب.

2. Translate into Arabic.

The minister who arrived yesterday was ill. The ministry of health in which I was yesterday has sent many doctors to the governorates. I read news which reported that cholera caused the death of many citizens. The foreign minister, who came from Israel, continued his tour in Syria. He submitted a project in which he welcomes the new solutions. The speech, in which he expressed his satisfaction, was not very long. He said in his negotiations with the ministers of health and of defense that he will continue his work. The German chancellor, who expressed his satisfaction about the good relations, informed the president that he will present new evidence. The two delegations, which were headed by ministers of education and the minister of economy, continued the negotiations after two hours. He sent a letter in which he submitted new evidence. The teachers *(f.)*, whom the ministry sent to the governorates, came back to the capital. He discussed the new situation in the region with some African presidents after the final session of the African summit.

3. Negate the following sentences.

أرسلتُ لهم عدّة رسائل. أنجزتم عملكم. قابلتُ الوزير. شاهدوا المسرحية. رحّبنا بالوفد. حدّثتُه عن زيارة الطبيب. واصل الكلمة. أفرحته بعض هـــذه الحلـول. أسـفر القـرار عـن بعض النتائج الجيّدة. كان في غرفته. كانت بعض الطالبات جميـلات. هـو وزيـر. واصـل الكلمة ! قوموا بزيارة هذا البلد ! عودي إلى البيت قبل الظهر ! كل اللحم الفاسد!

4. Translate into Arabic (write out the numerals).

5	drops	2	books
7	pharmacies	18	students
12	hospitals	33	years
21	tablets	102	chairs
100	prescriptions	in the year 1412 AH	
1000	guests	in the year 622 AD	
5000	sick people	in the year 1999 AD	

Lesson 15

الدرس الخامس عشر

1. Forms II, III, IV of the Verbs with و or ى

The derived forms of the verbs R_1, R_2, R_3 with و or ى have the same characteristics as the derived forms of the strong verbs. Apparent peculiarities only arise out of the fact that و or ى appear as consonants in some forms and as vowels in others. The latter are contracted in some jussive and imperative forms, and therefore do not appear in the typeface any more, as we have already got to know with regard to Form I of these so-called defective verbs.

وصـل، قـام، بـاع and لقي are employed as model verbs in the derived forms as well. They serve the purpose of representing the respective pattern, without actually being really in use in each individual form. Thus e.g., قام only occurs in Forms I - IV and X, but not in Forms V - IX.

1.1. Forms II, III, IV of verbs R_1 = و or ى are formed like those of the strong verbs. The verbs R_1 = ى are not listed separately.

1.1.1. Form II
Characteristic: doubling of R_2

Perfect tense:	وَصَّلَ
Imperfect tense:	يُوَصِّلُ
Imperative:	وَصِّلْ

1.1.2. Form III
Characteristic: prolongation of the vowel that follows R_1

Perfect tense:	وَاصَلَ
Imperfect tense:	يُوَاصِلُ
Imperative:	وَاصِلْ

1.1.3. Form IV
Characteristic: prefix *a-* أَ, vowellessness of R_1

Perfect tense:	أَوْصَلَ
Imperfect tense:	يُوصِلُ
Imperative:	أَوْصِلْ

☞**A1** It is not possible to differentiate the imperfect tense of Forms II and IV without auxiliary signs. (See Appendix: Tables 5, 6, 9, 16, 17.)

1.2. Forms II and III of verbs R_2 = و or ى are formed like those of the strong verbs, because و and ى are regarded as full consonants here. R_1 is not vowelless in Form IV. The verbs R_2 = و or ى have the same forms as in Form IV. Therefore we give only one model verb here.

1.2.1. Form II
Characteristic: doubling of R_2

Perfect tense:	بَيَّعَ	(pronounced: qawwama)	قَوَّمَ
Imperfect tense:	يُبَيِّعُ	(pronounced: yuqawwimu)	يُقَوِّمُ
Imperative:	بَيِّعْ	(pronounced: qawwim)	قَوِّمْ

1.2.2. Form III
Characteristic: prolongation of the vowel that follows R

Perfect tense:	بَايَعَ	قَاوَمَ
Imperfect tense:	يُبَايِعُ	يُقَاوِمُ
Imperative:	بَايِعْ	قَاوِمْ

1.2.3. Form IV
Characteristic: prefix *a-* أ

Perfect tense:	أَقَامَ
2nd p. sg. m.	أَقَمْتَ
Imperfect tense indicative:	يُقِيمُ
Imperfect tense jussive:	يُقِمْ
Imperative:	أَقِمْ

☞**A2** Most imperfect tenses of Form II (R_2 = ى) and IV (R_2 = و or ى) cannot be differentiated without auxiliary signs. The same is the case regarding Form I and II of the verbs R_2 = و. (See Appendix: Tables 5, 6, 9, 19, 21.)

1.3. The derived forms of verbs R_3 = و or ى are the same, therefore we give only one model verb for the individual forms. ·

1.3.1. Form II

Characteristic: doubling of R_2

Perfect tense:	لَقَّى
Imperfect tense indicative:	يُلَقِّي
Imperfect tense jussive:	يُلَقِّ
Imperative:	لَقِّ

1.3.2. Form III

Characteristic: prolongation of the vowel that follows R_1

Perfect tense:	لاَقَى
Imperfect tense indicative:	يُلاَقِي
Imperfect tense jussive:	يُلاَقِ
Imperative:	لاَقِ

1.3.3. Form IV

Characteristic: prefix *a-* أ, vowellessness of R_1

Perfect tense:		أَلْقَى
Imperfect tense indicative:		يُلْقِي
Imperfect tense jussive:		يُلْقِ
Imperative:		أَلْقِ

Forms II, III and IV of the verbs R_3 = و or ى are conjugated like Form I of the model verb مشى.

✍A3 The imperfect tense of Forms II and IV can neither be differentiated from each other nor from Form I (R_3 = ى, in some forms also R_3 = و) without auxiliary signs. (Appendix: Tables 5, 6, 9, 26)

2. The Nominal Relative Clause

2.1. We have become familiar with the type of relative clause that is employed as an attributive adjunct related to a noun in Lesson 14, which we refer to as the attributive relative clause. In addition to this, there is another type of relative clause known as the nominal relative clause which is also utilized in the English language. It is introduced here by the determinative relative pronoun "who, which":

honor to whom honor is due (to the one honor is due to),

or, when related to indefinite quantities, by the generalizing relative pronoun "who" or "what":

Who (everyone who) visits us will be welcome.

What (that which) he did was not right.

A conditional sense is frequently discernable in this context:

He who seeks shall find. (If someone seeks, he shall find.)

Idleness rusts the mind. (If someone is idle, his mind will rust.)

2.2. These relative clauses are introduced in Arabic by the determinative relative pronoun:

اَلَّذِي pl. اَلَّذِين (related to persons, seldom to non-persons)   he ... who / the one ... who; they ... who / the ones ... who; that ... which / the one ... which;

by the generalizing relative pronoun:

مَن (related to persons) (he) who / who(ever); someone who;

and the generalizing relative pronoun:

مَا (related to non-persons) what; that ... which / the one ... which; something.

2.3. Such sentences can fulfill the syntactic function of:

a) a subject

What happened to me yesterday will not happen to me again.	مَا حَدَثَ لِي أَمْس لَن يَحْدُثَ لِي مَرَّةً ثَانِيَةً.
The one who delivered the speech is my friend.	اَلَّذِي أَلْقَى الكَلِمَةَ صَدِيقِي.

b) an object

We know who is holding the negotiations.	نَعْرِفُ مَنْ يُجْرِي المُحَادَثَاتِ.

c) a predicate or

This is (that which)/what happened to me.	هَذَا مَا حَدَثَ لِي.

d) the 2ⁿᵈ term of a genitive construction or

He told us all he knew.	حَكَى لَنَا كُلَّ مَا عَرَفَ.

e) be construed in subordination to a preposition.

He has told us about the things he has seen there (lit.: about that which)	حَكَى لَنَا عَمَّا شَاهَدَ هُنَاكَ.
The price of it is 10 pounds including postage (lit.: with that which is in that of).	سِعْرُهَا عَشْرُ لِيرَاتٍ بِمَا فِي ذَلِكَ أُجْرَةُ البَرِيد.

2.4. A construction in which مَنْ and مَا are modified by a post-positive مِنْ + noun is typical for Arabic.

We know (that which)/what is in them (in their souls) of doubts = we know which doubts they entertain.	نَعْرِفُ مَا فِي أَنْفُسِهِم مِن شُكُوكٍ.
You came with the ones who (were) with you of the men = you came with the men who were with you.	جِئْتَ بِمَنْ عِنْدَكَ مِنَ الرِّجَالِ.
that which they have of apparatuses = the apparatuses they have.	مَا عِنْدَهُم مِنْ أَجْهِزَةٍ

Nominal relative clauses of this kind are preferred to the corresponding attributive relative clauses in many cases.

attributive:	نَعْرِفُ الشُّكُوكَ الَّتِي تُوجَدُ فِي أَنْفُسِهِمْ.
nominal:	نَعْرِفُ مَا فِي أَنْفُسِهِم مِن شُكُوكٍ.
attributive:	جِئْتَ بِالرِّجَال الَّذِينَ (كَانُوا) عِنْدَكَ.
nominal:	جِئْتَ بِمَنْ عِنْدَكَ مِنَ الرِّجَالِ.
attributive:	أَلأَجْهِزَةُ الَّتِي (تُوجَدُ) عِنْدَهُمْ
nominal:	مَا عِنْدَهُم مِنْ أَجْهِزَةٍ

2.5. Furthermore, مَنْ / مَا + affixed pronoun + مِنْ belong to the nominal relative clause constructions:

there are some among them who ...	مِنْهُمْ مَنْ ...
there is something among them which ...	مِنْهَا مَا ...

2.6. مَا and مَنْ are contracted with some prepositions:

$$(\text{مِنْ} + \text{ما}) > \text{مِمَّا}, \quad (\text{فِي} + \text{ما}) > \text{فِيما}$$
$$(\text{عَنْ} + \text{ما}) > \text{عَمَّا}, \quad (\text{مِنْ} + \text{مَنْ}) > \text{مِمَّنْ}$$

2.7. Some phraseology in the form of nominal relative clauses:

including (*lit.*: with that which is in it)	بِمَا فِي ذَلِكَ
after approximately one year (*lit.*: after the passing of what approximates one year)	بَعْدَ مُرُورِ مَا يُقَارِبُ عَاماً وَاحِداً

it is worth mentioning (*lit.*: of that which is worth mentioning that ...)	مِمَّا هُوَ جَدِيرٌ بِالذِّكْرِ أَنَّ		
it must be mentioned (*lit.*: of that the remarking of which is necessary)	مِمَّا يَجِبُ مُلاَحَظَتُهُ أَنَّ		
as for/to..., with regard to, as regards ..., as far as ... is concerned	فِيمَا يَخُصُّ		

V

to lead to	II أَدَّى (يُؤَدِّي) إلى	care, caution	حِذْر/ حَذَر
Australia	إستراليا	careful, cautious	حَذِر
inch	إِنْش ج ـات	injection	حُقْنة ج حُقَن
to support so., sth.	II أَيَّد (يُؤَيِّدُ) ٥، هـ	reserve	اِحْتِياطِيّ ج ـات
well, spring, fountain	بِئر (م) ج آبار	to prevent sth.	حال (يَحُولُ) دون هـ
Bedouins	بَدو	snake	حَيَّة ج ـات
nomadic Bedouins	بَدو رُحَّل	creature, living being	حَيَوان ج ـات
battery	بَطّارية ج ـات	to store sth.	II خَزَّن (يُخَزِّنُ) هـ
blanket	بَطّانِية ج ـات	fertility	خِصْب
remaining	مُتبق	line	خطّ ج خُطُوط
rifle, gun	بُنْدُقية ج بنادِقُ	equator	خط الإسْتِواء
to make clear, to explain sth.	II بَيَّن (يُبَيِّنُ) هـ	danger	خطَر ج أخْطار
snake	ثُعْبان ج ثعابينُ	to facilitate, to ease sth.	II خفَّف (يُخفِّفُ) من
with the exception of	باسْتِثْناء	light	خَفِيف
to carry out, to hold sth.	IV أَجْرى (يُجْرِي) هـ	to prepare, to provide sth.	II دبَّر (يُدبِّرُ) هـ
part	جُزْء ج أجْزاء	degree centigrade	درجة مِئوية
dry	جافّ	warm	دافِئ
journal	مَجَلّة ج ـات	raising, rise, increase	رفْع
freezing (*intrans.*)	تَجمُّد	high	مُرْتفِع
below zero	دون درجة التجمُّد	height, altitude, level	اِرْتِفاع ج ـات
wireless, mobile phone	جِهاز لا سِلْكِيّ	sand	رمْل ج رمال
to answer so. or sth.	IV أَجاب (يُجيبُ) على	wind	ريـح (م) ج ريـاح
pocket	جَيْب ج جُيُوب	to want sth.	IV أراد (يُريدُ) هـ، أنْ
(*prep.*) until	حتى	to wish sth.	رام (يرُومُ) هـ
to speak, to talk about	حكى (يَحْكِي) عن	according to the wishes	على ما يُرامُ

to supply so. with sth.	II زوّد (يُزوِّدُ) ه ب هـ
provisions	زاد ج أزواد
to go beyond, to exceed	زاد (يزيدُ) عن
to precede so., sth.	سبق (يسبقُ) ه، هـ
secret	سِرّ ج أسرَار
very soon	سُرعانَ ما
fall (rain)	سُقُوط
poison	سمّ ج سُمُوم
poisonous	سامّ
driver	سائق ج ـون
flood	سَيل ج سُيُول
vast, spacious	شاسِع
desert	صحْراءُ ج صِحار ، صحارَى
Sahara	الصحراء الكُبرَى
rock	صخر ج صُخور (coll.)
to hit so., sth.	IV أصاب (يُصِيبُ) هـ، ه
Somalia	الصُومال
pressure	ضغْط ج ضُغُوط
to loose sth.	II ضيّع (يُضيِّعُ) هـ
at all	على الإطلاق
to develop sth.	II طَوّر (يُطَوِّرُ) هـ
energy, potential	طاقة ج ـات
(prep.) during	طِيلةَ
average; rate	مُعدَّل ج ـات
storm	عاصِفة ج عواصِفُ
damage	عُطْل
to give so. sth.	IV أعْطَى (يُعْطِي) ه/ ل ، هـ
scorpion	عقْرب ج عقارِبُ
God knows everything.	الله أعْلَمُ
to announce, to declare sth.	IV أعْلن (يُعْلِنُ) هـ

spider	عنْكبُوت ج عناكِبُ
to suffer from sth.	III عانى (يُعانِي) من
dust	غُبار ج أغْبِرة
strange	غريب ج غُرباءُ
Gobi	الغُوبي
to trickle away (in)	غار (يغورُ) (في)
to change, to alter, to vary sth.	II غيّر (يُغيِّرُ) هـ
to think (of)	II فكّر (يُفكِّرُ) (في)
flooding	فَيَضان ج ـات
fate, destiny	قدَر ج أقْدار
in the vicinity of	بِالقُرْبِ من
highest	قُصْوَى
problem, case	قضية ج قضايا
satellite, artificial moon	قمَر صِناعِيّ
to hold, to organize sth.	IV أقام (يُقِيمُ) هـ
power, strength	قُوَّة ج ات، قوى
dune	كثِيب ج كُثْبان
ball, globe	كرة ج ات
complete, whole, entire	كامِل
to be about to do sth. almost (with negation "scarcely, hardly")	كاد (يكادُ) (يفْعلُ) (أنْ)
Kenya	كينيا
to cancel, to call off sth.	IV ألْغَى (يُلْغِي) هـ
to throw sth.	IV ألْقَى (يُلْقِي) هـ
to make a speech	ألقى كلمة
hundred	مِئوي
permanently	بِاسْتِمْرار
to go by, to pass	مضَى (يمْضِي)
rain	مطر ج أمْطار
full of	مليء ب
Mongolia	مُنْغُوليا

wavy	مَوْجِيّ	to finish sth.	IV أَنْهَى (يُنْهِي) هـ
characteristic	مِيزة	climate	مُناخ
plant	نبات ج ـات	to sink, to go down	هبط (يهبُطُ)
to result (from)	نجم (ينجُمُ) (عن)	raining	هُطُول المطر
star	نَجْم ج نُجُوم	India	الهِند
engraved	منحُوت	air	هواء ج أهْوية، أهْواء
rareness, scarcity	نُدْرة / نَدْرة	heaviness	وَطْأة
rare, scarce	نادِر	oasis	واحة ج ـات
copy	نُسْخة ج نُسخ	wadi	وادٍ ج أوْدية، وِدْيان
half	نِصْف ج أنصاف	to bring so., sth. to	IV أوْصل (يُوصِلُ) ه،، هـ إلى
middle, half	مُنْتصف	to explain sth.	IV أوْضح (يُوضِحُ) هـ
growing	نُمُو		
day	نهار ج أنْهُر		

مناخ الصحراء   Text 1

إن ميزة المناخ في الصحارى هي نُدرة المطر ممّا يحول دون خصب أراضيها ونمـو النباتـات والأشجار فيها. ومعدّل هطول الأمطـار في المنـاطق الصحراوية يكـاد لا يزيد عـن ١٠ إنشـات في العـام الواحـد. وقـد تمضي أحيانـاً سنوات عديـدة دون سقوط المطر علـى الإطلاق.

وتقع الصحارى الحارّة في مناطق الضغط المرتفع وهي الصحراء الكبرى والصحراء العربية وأجزاء كبيرة من العراق وإيران وشمالي غرب الهند وكاليفورنيا وذلك في نصف الكرة الشمالي، أما نصف الكرة الجنوبي فيضمّ جنوب إفريقيا (كالاهاري) وأجزاء كبيرة مـن إسـتراليا إضافة إلى منطقة صحراوية شاسعة في شمالي كينيا والصومـال بـالقرب مـن خط الاستواء. أما الصحراء المتبقيّة فهي الغوبي في منغوليا، وهـي شـديدة الحرارة في الصيـف وباردة جدّاً في الشتاء.

ونجد في هذه المناطق الصحراوية الشمس الحارّة طيلة العـام باستثناء فصل الشتاء، وقـد تبلغ درجة الحرارة القصوى ٦٠ درجة مئوية في منتصف النهار ولكنّها تهبـط بسـرعة في الليل. أما في الشتاء فقد تهبط درجة الحـرارة في الليل إلى دون درجة التجمُّد. ويكون الهواء جافّاً جدّاً باستمرار ممّا يخفِّف الحرارة.

أما هطول الأمطار فيكون نادراً جدّاً وقد تحدث عواصف شديدة ممّا يؤدّي إلى سيول في الوديان وقد تنجم عنها فيضانات. وسرعان ما تغور المياه في داخل الأرض التي تخزنها وتزود بها الآبار والواحات. وتعمل الرياح هنا على رفع الغبار والرمال إلى ارتفاعات عالية بشكل كثبان موجية وتعطي للصخور أشكالاً منحوتة رائعة وغريبة.

الرحلة إلى الصحراء   **Text 2**

ماري: صباح الخير، كيف حالك؟

أحمد: صباح النور، بخير الحمد لله، كيف حالك؟

ماري: كلّ شيء على ما يرام. هل يمكن أن نقوم اليوم برحلتنا إلى الصحراء؟

أحمد: طبعاً، دبّرت كلّ شيء لكي لا نعاني من مشاكل، أي سيّارة لاندروفر وسائقاً شاطراً والزاد والشراب لسبعة أيّام.

ماري: هل نبقى أسبوعاً كاملاً في الصحراء؟

أحمد: لا، كما قلنا نبقى هناك ثلاثة أيّام، ولكن من يقوم برحلة إلى الصحراء يجب أن يكون معه احتياطي لأنّ الصحراء، كما تعرفين، مليئة بالأسرار والأخطار. يمكن أن نضيّع الطريق أو أن يحدث عطل في السيّارة أو عاصفة أو سيل إلخ.

ماري: إن شاء الله لا تحدث كل هذه الكوارث في رحلة واحدة.

أحمد: الله أعلم، ولكن لا تخافي ! معنا أيضا جهاز لا سلكي.

ماري: هل بطّاريات الجهاز جديدة؟

أحمد: الجهاز يأخذ طاقته من بطارية السيّارة ويعمل عن طريق الأقمار الصناعية.

ماري: وماذا يجب أن آخذ معي من الملابس والأشياء الأخرى؟

أحمد: ملابس خفيفة للنهار ودافئة لليل وبطّانية نوم لأنّنا سوف ننام تحت نجوم سماء الصحراء.

ماري: وكيف الأمر بالنسبة للعقارب والثعابين والحيات والعناكب السامّة والحيوانات الخطيرة الأخرى؟

أحمد: لا تخافي! أوّلاً معي بندقية وثانياً هذه الحيوانات تنام أيضاً في الليل. وإضافة إلى ذلك عندي صيدلية جيب وفيها أيضاً الحقن والحبوب اللازمة ضدّ سموم هذه الحيوانات.

ماري: أنت حذر جدّاً، فكرت في كلّ شيء. وإن شاء الله تعرف كيف تصيب العقارب والعناكب بالبندقية.

أحمد: يقول البدو الرحل : سبق الحذر القدر.

Exercises:

L1 Try to find English equivalents for the following (partly colloquial) proverbs and sayings preceded by مَن.

من أبوه الدولة، من يشتكي (to complain about) به؟

من أحبّ الجمل أحبّ جمّاله (camel herdsman).

من احتاج للصوف (wool) جزّ (to shear) الكلب.

من أدخلته بيدك أخرجك برجله.

من استمع (to listen to) شور (advice) النساء كان من عديدهن (their equals).

من أكل بالاثنتين اختنق (to suffocate).

من أمه في الدار عاد قرصه (bread) حار.

من باع بارك (to give one's blessing).

من بدع (to do something for the first time, to begin) ختم (to finish).

من تكلّم (to speak) بلغة قومه ما لحن (to make mistakes).

من جدّ وجد.

من أحبّ نفسه فارق (to separate) أصحابه.

من خاف العصفور (sparrow) ما زرع.

من خان (to cheat) لك خان عليك.

من دقّ (to knock) الباب لقي الجواب.

L2 Identify the Form (I, II, III or IV) of the following verbs

أعطى / ألغى / أراد / طوّر / ألقى / أنهى / بيّن / أعلن / أوضح / أجاب / أيّد / أجرى / واصل / غيّر

and insert them in the given phrases.

الموعد مع المدير

أن يمشي إلى المدينة

صديقه بطّانية

الوضع في البلد

نتائج الانتخابات

المؤتمر بكلمة ختامية

أهداف الحكومة

على الأسئلة الصعبة

سياسة البلدان العربية

كلمة بمناسبة العيد الوطني

محادثات مع الوفود العربية

لنا ميزة مناخ الصحراء

برنامج الزيارة

الرحلة بعد يومين

L3 (Homework) Insert the appropriate relative pronoun.

لا أعرف ... حدث.

لا أعرف كلّ ... حضروا الحفلة.

إحك لي ... قابلت من الأشخاص!

نرحّب ب... جاؤوا إلينا من الخارج.

حكى لنا ... سمع من أخبار.

هل تعرف ... عندهم من قضايا؟

كتب لي عن ... يدرس من اللغات.

أعرف كلّ ... زار معهدنا أمس.

رحّبنا ب ... عندكم من الضيوف.

ألغوا كلّ ... في برنامجهم من مواعيد.

G1 Transform the following sentences into the imperfect tense. Replace أمس
with اليوم.

☞   أجرى رئيس الوفد العربي محادثات في لندن.

☞   يجري رئيس الوفد العربي محادثات في لندن.

أقام وزير الخارجية حفلة استقبال.

ألقى رئيس الجمهورية كلمة قصيرة.

رحّب مدير المعهد بضيوفه.

رحّبنا مساء الأمس بضيوفنا.

رحّب وزير الخارجية برئيس الوفد العربي.

أيّدت ألمانيا سياسة البلدان العربية.

أيّدت فرنسا سياسة العرب.

أجاب رئيس الوفد العربي بكلمة قصيرة.

أجابت الطالبة على سؤال المعلم.

أوضح رئيس الوفد موقفه.

أنهى الوفد السوري زيارته لبلدنا أمس.

أنهينا سفرنا أمس.

بيّن لي معلّمي الدرس الجديد.

بيّن لنا من هو صديقنا.

وقفنا إلى جانب البلدان العربية.

أعلن رئيس الجمهورية أنّنا سنطوّر بلادنا.

طوّرنا بلادنا.

أراد محمّد أن يسافر إلى باريس.

أردتُ أن أدرس اللغة العربية.

أرادت صديقتي أن تشرب كأساً من النبيذ.

غيّر الوفد العربي برنامجه.

ألغيت سفري.

أعطاني أحمد كتابه.

هل أعطيته كرّاستك؟

أرسلت كلّ البطاقات إلى الخارج.

واصل الطالب دراساته.

واصلت الطالبة دراساتها في الجامعة.

واصل الوفد السوري سفره.

واصل الوفد محادثاته مع المسؤولين.

أوصلنا المرافق إلى مدير المصنع.

أوصلته إلى مدير المعهد.

G2 (Homework) Repeat G1 and write down the sentences in the imperfect tense.

G3 Transform the following sentences into the perfect tense. Replace غـدا with أمس.

☞   يجري المدير محادثات مع الوفد التجاري. <

☞   أجرى المدير محادثات مع الوفد التجاري.

نرحّب غداً بالضيوف العرب.

أرحّب بصديقتي أمام المسرح.

نجيب على أسئلة معلمينا.

نؤيّد هذه السياسة.

يوضح الوزير القضايا التجارية.

ينهي الوفد سفره غداً.

أنهي هذا العمل غداً.

نقف إلى جانب البلدان العربية.

يبيّن وزير الخارجية للطلاب سياسة تلك البلدان.

تطوّر حكومة الجزائر علاقاتها السياسية مع ألمانيا.

يريد أحمد أن يشاهد الفلم الجديد.

أريد أن أشرب كأساً من البيرة.

تريد صديقتي أن تشرب فنجاناً من القهوة.

نريد أن نسافر إلى مدينة لندن.

يريد أخي أن يرسل رسالة إلى عائلته.

يلغي الوزير سفره.

يواصل الوفد محادثاته مع المسؤولين.

يواصل وزير الخارجية سفره.

G4 Give the imperative of the following verbs according to the instructions in brackets.

أجب على السؤال!	<	☞ أجاب – على السؤال
أجيبي على السؤال!	<	☞
أجيبوا على السؤال!	<	☞
(sg. + pl. m.)	- بالضيوف	رحّب
(pl. m.)	- هذه السياسة	أيّد
(sg. + pl. m.)	- على الأسئلة	أجاب
(sg. + pl. m.)	- هذه القضية	أوضح لي
(pl. m.)	- بلادكم بكل قواكم	طوّر
(sg. + pl. m.)	- البرنامج	غيّر
(sg. + pl. m.)	- زجاجة من العصير	أعطى + ني
	- كأساً من الماء	
	- فنجاناً من القهوة	
	- كأساً من البيرة	
	- فنجاناً من الشاي	
	- بعض البطاقات	
	- العدد الجديد من المجلّة	
	- نسخة واحدة	
	- الكتاب	
	- النقود	
	- هذا	
(sg. m.)	- دراستك	واصل

(sg. + pl. m.)	- العمل حتى صباح اليوم	أنهى
	- العمل حتى صباح الغد	
	- الواجب حتى مساء اليوم	
	- الكتابة حتى مساء الغد	
	- المشروع بعد ساعة	
	- الاستقبال بعد ساعتين	
(sg. + pl. m.)	- إلى هناك	أوصل + نا

G5 Replace the perfect tense with

لم + jussive or

لم + jussive + بعدُ "not yet" or

لم + jussive + فقط "not only".

☞ أجرى الوفد المصري محادثات في لندن.

☞ لم يجر الوفد المصري محادثات في لندن بعد.

☞ لم يجر الوفد المصري محادثات في لندن فقط.

أجاب الطالب على السؤال.

أنهى الوفد السوري زيارته لبلدنا.

أنهيت عملي.

أراد محمّد أن يسافر بالسيارة.

أرادت الفتاة أن تشرب كأساً من العصير.

لماذا غيّر الوفد برنامجه؟

لماذا ألغوا الزيارة؟

أعطاني كتاباً واحداً.

لماذا أعطيتني نقوداً؟

أرسلت كلّ البطاقات إلى الخارج.

أنهيت هذا العمل أمس.

أراد أحمد أن يشاهد الفلم القديم.

أردتُ أن أشرب كأساً واحدة.

أراد أخي أن يرسل رسالة إليهم.

واصل الطالب دراساته.

واصل الوفد المحادثات مع المسؤولين.

C1 (Homework) Write a list of things you need for a journey to prepare C2. The list is to be discussed and completed together with your teacher.

C2 Prepare a dialogue about the preparations for a trip (to the desert, historical or archeological site, etc.) based on Text 2.

Final Exercise:

1. Transform the verbs into the text to the imperfect tense.

أقام وزير الخارجية حفلة استقبال. ألقى الرئيس كلمة. أوضحت المعلّمة الـدرس الجديـد. أردنا أن نقوم برحلة إلى الصحراء. أصاب الهدف بالبندقية. أعلن الرئيس افتتـاح المؤتمـر. أنهوا الرحلة في الشتاء. أيّدت الحكومة كلّ القرارات. أجبتم علـى كـلّ الأسئلة. يخفّـف الهواء الجافّ من وطأة الحرارة. أدّت الكوارث إلى وفاة الكثير من المواطنين. عـانى البلـد من عواصف شديدة. غيّر أحمد برنامج الرحلة. أعطيته الحبوب والأدوية الأخرى. أصابوا العقارب والعناكب بالبندقيـة. خـافت مـن الحيوانـات الخطيـرة. بقينـا في الصحراء لمـدّة أسبوع. ضيّعنا الطريق. فكّرتم في حلول جديدة. ألغت الوزارة كلّ البرامج.

2. Negate the sentences of 1. by means of لم + jussive.

3. Translate into Arabic.
He hasn't come yet. She hasn't canceled the trip yet. He hasn't given me a book yet. The haven't finished the meeting yet. We haven't carried out negotiations yet. They won't hold a reception. He will not shoot the scorpion with the gun.

4. Insert the proper relative pronoun.

ألغوا كلّ ... في البرنامج من مواعيد. لا أعرف كلّ ... زاروا المعهد في هـذا اليـوم. قـل لي ... رأيت في الصحراء. لم يقل ... حدث في أيّام الرحلة. ... أصاب الهدف صديقي.

5. Translate the following letter into Arabic.
Dear Muḥammad
How are you and your family? I was in the desert with some friends. The trip was very nice. It was very hot during the day and very cold at night. I saw a flood and many creatures of the desert, i.e. poisonous scorpions, snakes, spiders and other dangerous animals, the names of which I don't know. We have been sleeping under the stars of the desert sky for three days. Next week we'll go to the mountains.
As far as my studies are concerned, everything is as could be hoped for, including the lectures in medicine.
I'll see you next month, God willing.

Your friend Peter

1. Ordinal Numbers (أَلْأَعْدَاد التَّرْتِيبِيَّة)

1.1. The ordinal numbers from 1-10 are:

	f.	m.
1st	أُولَى	أَوَّلُ
2nd	ثَانِيَة	ثَانٍ
3rd	ثَالِثَة	ثَالِث
4th	رَابِعَة	رَابِع
5th	خَامِسَة	خَامِس
6th	سَادِسَة	سَادِس
7th	سَابِعَة	سَابِع
8th	ثَامِنَة	ثَامِن
9th	تَاسِعة	تَاسِع
10th	عَاشِرة	عَاشِر

The ordinal numbers 2-10 are adjectives of the pattern فاعِل *fāʿil*, which have been formed out of the corresponding cardinal numbers.

A1☞ ثانٍ, definite أَلثَّانِي, is declined like ثمانٍ, definite أَلثمانِي; cf. Lesson 10, A 6, and Table 37.

1.2. The ordinal numbers from 11-19 are:

	f.	m.
11th	حَادِيَةَ عَشْرَةَ	حَادِيَ عَشَرَ
12th	ثَانِيَةَ عَشْرَةَ	ثَانِيَ عَشَرَ
13th	ثَالِثَةَ عَشْرَةَ	ثَالِثَ عَشَرَ
14th	رَابِعَةَ عَشْرَةَ	رَابِعَ عَشَرَ

15th	خَامِسَةَ عَشْرَةَ	خَامِسَ عَشَرَ
16th	سَادِسَةَ عَشْرَةَ	سَادِسَ عَشَرَ
17th	سَابِعَةَ عَشْرَةَ	سَابِعَ عَشَرَ
18th	ثَامِنَةَ عَشْرَةَ	ثَامِنَ عَشَرَ
19th	تَاسِعَةَ عَشْرَةَ	تَاسِعَ عَشَرَ

The numbers 11th - 19th are not inflectional.

1.3. The Arabic ordinal numbers are treated like adjectives with regard to syntax. Accordingly they follow the noun, and there is agreement in case, state, gender and number between them and the noun. Unlike the case of the cardinal numbers, there is is no polarity in gender in the ordinal numbers.

in connection with a feminine noun		in connection with a masculine noun	
the 1st year	أَلسَّنَةُ الأُولَى	the 1st day	أَلْيَوْمُ الأَوَّلُ
		1st Tishrīn (October)	تِشْرِينُ الأَوَّلُ
		2nd Kānūn (January)	كَانُونُ الثَّانِي
the 2nd year	أَلسَّنَةُ الثَّانِيَةُ	the 2nd day	أَلْيَوْمُ الثَّانِي
the 3rd year	أَلسَّنَةُ الثَّالِثَةُ	the 3rd day	أَلْيَوْمُ الثَّالِثُ
the 10th year	أَلسَّنَةُ الْعَاشِرَةُ	the 10th day	أَلْيَوْمُ الْعَاشِرُ
the 11th year	أَلسَّنَةُ الْحَادِيَةَ عَشْرَةَ	the 11th day	أَلْيَوْمُ الْحَادِيَ عَشَرَ
the 12th year	أَلسَّنَةُ الثَّانِيَةَ عَشْرَةَ	the 12th day	أَلْيَوْمُ الثَّانِيَ عَشَرَ
the 19th year	أَلسَّنَةُ التَّاسِعَةَ عَشْرَةَ	the 19th day	أَلْيَوْمُ التَّاسِعَ عَشَرَ

A2 The ordinal numbers for 1st, i.e. أَوَّل or أُولَى , are frequently connected with the following noun in the form of a genitive construction and are neutral as to gender in this case:

i.e. for the 1st time لأَوَّلِ مَرَّةٍ

The ordinal numbers from 2-10 also occasionally precede the noun just as أَوَّل does.

1.4. The ordinal numbers of the tens (20th, 30th, . . . 90th), hundreds, thousands etc. are expressed by means of the cardinal numbers.

in connection with a feminine noun		in connection with a masculine noun	
the 20th year	أَلسَّنَةُ الْعِشْرُونَ	the 20th day	أَلْيَوْمُ الْعِشْرُونَ
the 100th year	أَلسَّنَةُ الْمِائِةُ	the 100th day	أَلْيَوْمُ الْمِائَةُ
the 1000th year	أَلسَّنَةُ الْأَلْفُ	the 1000th day	أَلْيَوْمُ الْأَلْفُ

but: the 20 days   أَلْأَيَّامُ الْعِشْرُونَ

the 1000 years   أَلسَّنَوَاتُ الْأَلْفُ

1.5. The ordinal numbers over 20 in which units occur as well, consist of ordinals (units) and cardinal numbers (tens).

Take note of the numeral 1 in ordinal numbers like 21st, 31st etc. in this context.

in connection with a masculine noun	
the 21st day	أَلْيَوْمُ الْحَادِي وَالْعِشْرُونَ
the 22nd day	أَلْيَوْمُ الثَّانِي وَالْعِشْرُونَ
the 31st day	أَلْيَوْمُ الْحَادِي وَالثَّلَاثُونَ
the 38th day	أَلْيَوْمُ الثَّامِنُ وَالثَّلَاثُونَ
in connection with a feminine noun	
the 21st year	أَلسَّنَةُ الْحَادِيَةُ وَالْعِشْرُونَ
the 22nd year	أَلسَّنَةُ الثَّانِيَةُ وَالْعِشْرُونَ
the 31st year	أَلسَّنَةُ الحَادِيَةُ وَالثَّلَاثُونَ
the 38th year	أَلسَّنَةُ الثَّامِنَةُ وَالثَّلَاثُونَ

A3 Ordinal numbers over 100 naturally occur rarely. They are either paraphrased or expressed in terms of the preposition بَعْدَ "after": the 101st day   أَلْيَوْمُ الْأَوَّلُ بعد المائة.

1.6. Dates

1.6.1. Dates are expressed by means of the ordinal numbers:

on May 1st   في الْيَوْمِ الْأَوَّلِ مِنْ شَهْرِ مايو

(*lit.*: on the 1st day of the month of May)

In general a shortened form is chosen that does not contain the words شهر and يوم:

في الْأَوَّلِ مِنْ آيَّار

👆A4 An even shorter form usually appears in the text instead, the numeral being employed:

في ٢٠ تَمُّوز ، في ١ أَيّار

The month can be represented by the corresponding numeral as well, so that the Arabic date does
not differ from the form used in America and Europe: 1/5/1990   في ١٩٩٠/٥/١
In the region of the Maghrib the form 01/05/1990 is also typical.

1.6.2. To find out the date, we ask the following question:

What is today's (tomorrow's) date? The answer is e.g.:	ما هو تاريخُ الْيَوْمِ (الْغَدِ) ؟
Today (tomorrow) is May 1st.	أَلْيَوْمَ (غَداً) الأوّلُ مِن أيّارٍ.

1.7. The time
1.7.1. The ordinal numbers are also used with regard to the time. They serve the
purpose of stating the full hours:

at 2 o'clock	في السَّاعَةِ الثانِيَةِ
at 5 o'clock	في السَّاعَةِ الخامِسَةِ
at 10 o'clock	في السَّاعَةِ العاشِرةِ
at 11 o'clock	في السَّاعَةِ الحادِيَةَ عَشْرَةَ

Only 1 o'clock is expressed by the cardinal numeral: في السَّاعَةِ الواحِدةِ.

👆A5 There are some more differentiations in Arabic besides 1.00 p.m., 2.00 p.m. ... 12.00 p.m. with
regard to indicating the time. The words مَساءً، ظُهْراً، بعدَالظُّهْر، قَبْلَ الظُّهْر، صَبَاحاً are added in
the following way: مَساءً، بعد الظُّهْر، ظُهْراً، قَبْلَ الظُّهْر، صَبَاحاً.

at 1.00 a.m.	في السَّاعةِ الْواحِدةِ صَبَاحاً
at 9.00 a.m.	في السَّاعةِ التّاسِعَةِ صَبَاحاً
at 10.00 a.m.	في السَّاعةِ الْعاشِرةِ قَبْلَ الظُّهْر
at 11.00 a.m.	في السَّاعةِ الْحادِيةَ عَشْرةَ قَبْلَ الظُّهْر
at 12.00 a.m.	في السَّاعةِ الثانِيةَ عَشْرةَ ظُهْراً
at 1.00 p.m.	في السَّاعةِ الْواحِدةِ بَعْدَ الظُّهْر
at 5.00 p.m.	في السَّاعةِ الخامِسةِ بَعْدَ الظُّهْر
at 6.00 p.m.	في السَّاعةِ السَّادِسةِ مَساءً
at 12.00 p.m.	في السَّاعةِ الثّانِيةَ عَشْرةَ مَساءً

أَلسَّاعة is often omitted, and في التّاسِعَةِ صَبَاحاً / مَساءً is spoken. The use of the corresponding
cardinal number is widespread in colloquial language as well.

1.7.2. The corresponding words for ¹/₄ (رُبْع), ¹/₃ (ثُلْث) and ¹/₂ (نِصْف) are used in indications of time containing 15, 20 and 30 minutes (cf. below, Gr 3.1.). They are added by means of the conjunctions و or إلّا. The noun is in the accusative after إلّا.

at 2.30	في السَّاعَةِ الثَّانِيَةِ والنِّصْفِ
at 3.15	في السَّاعَةِ الثَّالِثَةِ والرُّبْعِ
at 4.20	في السَّاعَةِ الرَّابِعَةِ والثُّلْثِ
at 4.45 (a quarter to 5)	في السَّاعَةِ الخَامِسَةِ إلّا الرُّبْعَ
at 5.40 (a third to 6)	في السَّاعَةِ السَّادِسَةِ إلّا الثُّلْثَ

1.7.3. Time by minutes is indicated in the same way by means of و or إلّا with the corresponding cardinal numeral and the Arabic word for minute (دَقِيقة) being added.

at 1.05	في السَّاعَةِ الْوَاحِدَةِ وخَمْس دَقَائِقَ
at 7.12	في السَّاعَةِ السَّابِعَةِ واثنَتَي عَشْرَةَ دقِيقَةً
at 8.25	في السَّاعَةِ الثَّامِنَةِ وخَمْس وعِشْرِينَ دَقِيقَةً
at 8.35 (25 min. to 9)	في السَّاعَةِ التَّاسِعَةِ إلّا خَمْساً وعِشْرِينَ دَقِيقَةً
at 9.42 (18 min. to 10)	في السَّاعَةِ الْعاشِرَةِ إلّا ثَمانِيَ عَشْرَةَ دَقِيقَةً
at 10.55 (5 min. to 11)	في السَّاعَةِ الْحادِيَةَ عَشْرَةَ إلّا خَمْسَ دَقَائِقَ

👆**A6** The indication of time "... minutes to half past ..." or "... past half past ..." is possible in Arabic, namely up to 9 minutes to or past the half hour:

five minutes to half past five   في السَّاعَةِ الخَامِسَةِ والنِّصْفِ إلّا خَمْس دَقَائِقَ
nine minutes past half past six   في السَّاعَةِ السَّادِسَةِ والنِّصْفِ وتِسْع دَقَائِقَ

1.7.4. The time is asked for by ألسَّاعَةُ كَمِ (الآن)؟ or by كم السَّاعَةُ؟

= What time is it (now)?
The answer is:

It is 1.15 now.	ألسَّاعَةُ (الآن) الْواحِدَةُ والرُّبْعُ.
It is 12.30 now.	ألسَّاعَةُ (الآن) الثَّانِيَةَ عَشْرَةَ والنِّصْفُ.
It is 3.50 now. (10 min. to 4)	ألسَّاعَةُ (الآن) الرَّابِعَةُ إلّا عَشْرَ دَقَائِقَ.

2. Numeral Adverbs

The (adverbial) indefinite accusative forms of the ordinal numbers are used as numeral adverbs up to 10:

sixth(ly), in (the) sixth place	سَادِساً	first(ly), in the first place	أَوَّلاً
seventh(ly), in (the) seventh ~	سَابِعاً	second(ly), in the second ~	ثَانِياً
eighth(ly), in (the) eighth ~	ثَامِناً	third(ly), in the third ~	ثَالِثاً
ninth(ly), in the ninth ~	تَاسِعاً	fourth(ly), in the fourth ~	رَابِعاً
tenth(ly), in the tenth ~	عَاشِراً	fifth(ly), in the fifth ~	خَامِساً

3. Fractional Numbers

3.1. The fractional numbers $^1/_3$, $^1/_4$, $^1/_5$ ... $^1/_{10}$ are formed out of the corresponding cardinal number according to the pattern فُعْل pl. أَفْعال:

$^2/_3$	ثُلْثَان	$^1/_3$	ثُلْث / أَثْلاث
$^3/_4$	ثَلاَثَةُ أَرْبَاع	$^1/_4$	رُبْع / أَرْباع
$^2/_5$	خُمْسَان	$^1/_5$	خُمْس / أَخْماس
$^4/_5$	أَرْبَعَةُ أَخْمَاس	$^1/_6$	سُدْس / أَسْداس
$^5/_6$	خَمْسَةُ أَسْدَاس	$^1/_7$	سُبْع / أَسْباع

etc.

Only the fractional number $^1/_2$: نِصْف is not derived from the cardinal numeral.

3.2. Fractions, in which the denominators are greater than 10, are paraphrased by means of the preposition على or by جُزْء مِن "a part of":

$^1/_{11}$	وَاحِدٌ على أَحد عَشَرَ / جُزْءٌ مِنْ أَحَدَ عَشَرَ
$^5/_{12}$	خَمْسَةُ على اثْنَيْ عَشَرَ
$^7/_{100}$	سَبْعَةُ على مِائَةٍ / سَبْعَةُ أَجْزاءٍ مِن مِائَةٍ

4. Numeral Adverbs of Reiteration

The numeral adverbs indicating reiteration are expressed by مَرَّة + cardinal numeral:

once, one time	مَرَّةً واحِدةً	thrice, three times	ثَلاثَ مَرَّاتٍ
twice	مَرَّتَينِ	four times	أَرْبَعَ مَرَّاتٍ

A7 The adjectives "bilateral, trilateral, quadrilateral ..." are rendered by means of the pattern *fuᶜālī*,
eg.: ... ثُنائي، ثُلاثي، رُباعي

5. Decimal Numbers

The decimal numbers are written with a comma and usually spoken as follows:

3.9	٣ر٩	ثلاثةٌ فاصِلةٌ تسعةٌ / ثلاثةٌ فاصِلةٌ تسعةٌ من عشرةٍ
4.25	٤ر٢٥	أربعةٌ فاصِلةٌ خمسةٌ وعشرون / أربعةٌ فاصِلةٌ خمسةٌ وعشرون من مئةٍ
7.123	٧ر١٢٣	سبعةٌ فاصِلةٌ مئةٌ وعشرون / سبعةٌ فاصِلةٌ مئةٌ وثلاثةٌوعشرون من ألفٍ

✋**A8** The decimals can also be read with the prepositions ب or مع :

3.9	٣ر٩	ثلاثةٌ مع / بفاصِلةٍ تسعةٍ / ثلاثةٌ مع / بفاصِلةٍ تسعةٍ من عشرةٍ

V

before *(time)*	إلاَّ	obtaining sth.	الحُصُول على
primary	اِبْتِدائيّ	hairdresser	حلاّق ج ـون
primary school	مدرسة ابتدائية	transfer	تَحْويل ج ـات
honesty, integrity	بِرّ	time, while	حِين ج أحْيان
blessing	بركة ج ـات	examination, test	اِخْتِبار ج ات
GCE A-level, graduation diploma	البكالوريا	good, better, best	خَير
bachelor's degree	البكالوريُوس	to pay so., sth.	دفع (يدْفَعُ) ه، هـ
bank	بنك ج بُنُوك	minute	دَقِيقة ج دقائِقُ
third	ثُلْث ج أثلاث	doctorate	دُكتوراه
secondary	ثانويّ	lower	أدْنَى م دُنْيا
secondary school	مدرسة ثانوية	floor	دَوْر ج أدْوار
renewing	تَجْدِيد	to last	دام (يدُومُ)
once more, again	مِن جدِيد	duration	دوام
movement	حركة ج ـات	opening times, time of duty	وقت الدوام

lady	ربّة ج ـات	preparation	إعْداد
lady of the house, housewife	ربّة بيت	highly educated, great scholar	عـلّامة
quarter	رُبْع ج أرْباع	high, higher, highest	أعْلَى / عُلْيا (م)
to have mercy upon so.	رحِمَ (يرْحَمُ) ه	postgraduate studies	دراسات عليا
God have mercy upon him!	رحِمَهُ ا للّه	age	عُمْر ج أعْمار
late, deceased	مرْحُوم	technical; technician	فنّي
permission, license	رُخْصة ج رُخص	reading	قِراءة ج ات
dissertation	رسالة الدكتوراه	century	قرْن ج قُرُون
fee	رسْم ج رُسُوم	comparative	مُقارَن
irrigation	ريّ	linguist	لُغويّ ج ـون
husband, spouse	زوْج ج أزْواج	if (+ *verb in perf.*)	لو
to be married to	مُتزوِّج مِن	if you allow me	لو سَمَحْتَ
still (doing)	ما زال، لا يزال	traffic	مُرُور
swimming	سِباحة	to hold on to, to grip	مسك (يمْسِكُ) هـ،ه
secretary	سِكْرتيرة ج ات	sth., so.	
biography	سِيرةٌ ج سِيَر	Queue / line up! (*colloq.*)	اِمْسِكْ الطابور
curriculum vitae	سِيرة حياة	to fill sth.	ملأ (يمْلأُ) هـ
thing, matter	شأن ج شُؤُون	property, capital, finance	مال ج أمْوال
police	شُرْطة	financial	ماليّ
traffic police	شرْطة المُرُور	Treasury (Department)	وزارة المالية
to supervise so.,sth.	IV أشْرف (يُشْرِفُ) على	deputy	نائِب ج نُوّاب
department, section	شُعْبة ج شُعب	hobby	هِواية ج ـات
certificate	شهادة ج ات	receipt	وصْل ج وُصُولات
certification	تصْديق	continuation	مُواصلة
page	صفْحة ج ـات	topic, title	موْضُوع ج مواضِيعُ
box, chest; cashbox	صُنْدُوق ج صناديقُ	to sign sth.	II وقّع (يُوقِّعُ) على
cashier	أمين الصندوق	signatory	مُوقِّع
here: queue/line of people	طابُور ج طوابيرُ	the undersigned	المُوقِّع أدْناه
stamp	طابِع ج طوابِعُ	son, child	ولد ج أوْلاد
fast, rapid	عاجِل	(to study) at so.	(درس) على يد ...

Text 1

سيرة حياتي

إني الموقّع أدناه محمّد عبد الله ولدتُ في الثاني من شهر تمّوز عام ١٩٥٦. كان أبي، رحمه الله، يعمل موظّفاً في وزارة المالية وأمّي ربّة بيت. لي ثلاثة إخوة يعمل الأوّل مهندساً والثاني حلّاقاً والثالث ما زال يدرس في الجامعة. دخلت المدرسة الابتدائية في السابعة من عمري ودرست فيها لمدّة ستّ سنوات وبعد حصولي على شهادة المدرسة الابتدائية واصلت دراستي في المدرسة الثانوية التي دامت الدراسة فيها ستّ سنوات أيضاً.

وحصلت في عام ١٩٧٤ على شهادة البكالوريا وبعدها بدأت بدراسة اللغة العربية في جامعة بغداد. دامت دراستي الجامعية أربع سنوات حصلت بعدها على شهادة البكالوريوس في اللغة العربية وآدابها. لقد درست في جامعة بغداد على يد العلامة اللغوي المشهور المرحوم مصطفى جواد ثم على يد الأستاذ إبراهيم السامرائي. وفي عام ١٩٧٩ سافرت إلى ألمانيا لمواصلة الدراسة هناك في قسم الدراسات العليا في معهد الدراسات الشرقية التابع لجامعة لايبزيك. وفي عام ١٩٨٣ قدّمت رسالة الدكتوراه في موضوع الأدب المقارَن وأشرف على إعداد هذه الرسالة الأستاذ المرحوم رويشل (Reuschel).

وفي عام ١٩٨٤ رجعت إلى الوطن وأعمل منذ ذلك الحين مدرِّساً في جامعة بغداد. أنا متزوِّج ولي أربعة أولاد. تعمل زوجتي سكرتيرة في وزارة الري. وهواياتي هي القراءة والسباحة وجمع الطوابع.

Text 2

تجديد الرخصة

بيتز: مساء الخير.

الموظّفة: مساء النور، امسك الطابور!

بيتز: عفواً، عندي سؤال واحد فقط، لو سمحتِ. هل يمكنك تجديد هذه الرخصة؟

الموظّفة: نعم، ولكن قبل ذلك يجب عليك أن تملأ هـذه الاستمارات الخمـس. ويجب تصديق الاستمارة الأولى عند مسؤول التسجيل والثانية عنـد مسؤول الرسـوم والثالثة عند مسؤول الشعبة الفنية والرابعة عند نائبي لشؤون الرخص.

بيتر: والاستمارة الخامسة؟

الموظّفة: سأوقّع عليها بعد أن ترجع إليّ بالاستمارات الأخرى.

بيتر: وبعد ذلك، ماذا يجب أن أعمل؟

الموظّفة: بعد ذلك يجب أن تذهب إلى أمين الصندوق في الدور الثامن.

بيتر: ماذا يعمل ذلك المسؤول؟

الموظّفة: يقول لك المبلغ ويعطيـك استمارة للبنـك لتحويل المبلغ وبعـد ذلك يجب أن تدفع الرسوم في البنك ومـع وصـل البنـك ترجع إليّ مـرّة ثانيـة وأنا أعطيـك الطوابع الخاصّة بتجديد الرخصة، إن شاء الله.

بيتر: وهل أحصل على تلك الطوابع دون أن أملأ استمارات جديدة؟

الموظّفة: تقريباً، يعني تبقى استمارة واحدة من خمس صفحات.

بيتر: وبعد ذلك؟

الموظّفة: يجب أن تقدّم السيّارة مع الرخصة لشرطة المرور للفحص الفنّي.

بيتر: ما هي أوقات الدوام عندهم وماذا يعملون هناك؟

الموظّفة: الدوام عندهم يومياً من التاسعة صباحاً إلى الثانية عشرة ظهراً ومـن الثالثة إلى السابعة مساء وهم سيعملون لك اختباراً قصيراً وبعد الاختبار يجـب عليـك أن تملأ خمس استمارات، الأولى لمسؤول التسجيل والثانية لمسؤول الرسوم ...

بيتر: والثالثة للشعبة الفنية والرابعة لنائب شؤون الرخص! وبعـد ذلك أرجع إليـك وأبدأ من جديد؟

الموظّفة: ممكن. أ لا تعرف المثل العربي ((في الحركة بركة))؟ والمـرّة القادمـة لا تـنـس أن تمسك الطابور. مع السلامة!

بيتر: لا، أنا أعرف المثل العربي ((خير البر عاجله))، مع السلامة وشكراً.

Exercises:

L1 (Repetition) Combine the nouns and numbers.

رخصة، موظّف	٥١	١١	١
بيت، مدرسة	٢٢	١٢	٢
ليرة، دينار	٢٣	١٣	٣
ساعة، شهر	٣٤	١٤	٤
كيلومتر، سنة	٤٥	١٥	٥
مليم، قرش	٥٦	١٦	٦
متر، يوم	٦٧	١٧	٧
سنتيمتر، كتاب	٧٨	١٨	٨
يوم، سنة	٨٩	١٩	٩
دقيقة، أسبوع	٣٠	٢٠	١٠
جنيه، يوم	٤٠	٢١	١١
فلس، شخص	٥٠	٢٢	١٢
موظف، سنة	٨٠	٧٠	٦٠
ليرة، جنيه	١٠١	١٠٠	٩٠
متر، دولار	٤٠٠	٣٠٠	٢٠٠
شخص، كيلومتر	١٠٠٠٠	٢٠٠٠	١٠٠٠

L2 Answer the question: متى وُلِدتَّ / وُلِدتِّ giving the exact date.

☞   ولدتُ في السادس عشر من تشرين الأول عام ألف وتسعمائة واثنين وسبعين.

L3 The teacher quotes dates in Arabic which are to be translated into English.

L4 The teacher quotes dates in English which are to be translated into Arabic.

L5 Answer the following questions with an exact time.

متى تقوم من النوم؟

متى تأكل طعام الفطور؟

متى تخرج من البيت؟

متى تصل إلى المعهد؟

متى تبدأ الدروس؟

متى تأكل طعام الغداء؟

متى تخرج من المعهد؟

متى تذهب إلى المكتبة؟

متى تعود إلى البيت؟

متى تأكل طعام العشاء؟

متى تفتح (here:to switch on) جهاز التلفزيون؟

متى وصل الوفد إلى المطار؟

متى تقابل صديقتك؟

متى تبدأ الحفلة؟

الساعة كم؟

متى نمت؟

متى كنت في المعهد؟

متى تعرف الجواب؟

L6 The teacher quotes different times in Arabic which are to be translated into English.

L7 The teacher quotes different times in English which are to be translated into Arabic.

L8 Answer the following questions.

كم مرّة في هذه السنة كنت في المسرح؟

كم مرّة في السنة تسافر إلى الجبال؟

كم مرّة قرأت الدرس السادس عشر من هذا الكتاب؟

كم مرّة في الشهر تذهب إلى المكتبة؟

كم مرّة في حياتك سافرت بالطائرة؟

كم مرّة في الشهر تكتب رسالة لصديقك (لصديقتك)؟

كم مرّة كنت في لندن؟

كم مرّة كنت في الخارج؟

كم مرّة في الشهر تذهب إلى المصرف؟

كم مرّة في الأسبوع تفتح جهاز التلفزيون؟

G1 Transform the phrases consisting of a cardinal number and a noun into a prepositional phrase consisting of a noun and an ordinal number.

☞   ثلاثة أيّام   <   في اليوم الثالث

☞   أسبوعان   <   في الأسبوع الثاني

خمسة شهور، ثلاثة أسابيع، تسع سنوات، عشرة قرون، أربع ساعات، ثمانية أسابيع، ستة أيّام، سبعة قرون، ساعتان، أحد عشر يوماً، اثنا عشر شهراً، خمس سنوات، إحدى عشرة سنة، تسعة قرون، شهران، سبعة أسابيع، ثمانية قرون، اثنتا عشرة ساعة، يوم واحد، ستة أسابيع، عشرة أيّام، خمسة عشر أسبوعاً، تسع عشرة سنة، ستة عشر شهراً، ثلاث عشرة قرية، ثماني عشرة مدينة، أربع عشرة سنة، سبعة عشر يوماً.

G2 Vice versa.

ثمانية أشهر   >   في الشهر الثامن   ☜

في السنة الثالثة، في الأسبوع الحادي عشر، في القرن العشرين، في السنة الرابعة، في الاجتماع العاشر، في النسخة الخامسة، في اليوم الخامس عشر، في الشهر الثامن، في الساعة التاسعة، في المخزن الثاني، في الدقيقة الأولى، في الساعة السابعة، في الاجتماع التاسع عشر، في القرن الثامن عشر، في الشهر الثالث عشر، في اليوم الرابع عشر، في الدقيقة السابعة عشرة، في القاعة الثانية عشرة، في المخزن السادس، في الأسبوع السادس عشر .

G3 Provide the dates for the day before yesterday, yesterday, today, tomorrow and the day after tomorrow.

أمس الأول كان الثالث من آذار .   ☜

اليوم (هو) الخامس من آذار، غداً (هو) السادس من آذار .   ☜

G4 (Repetition) Transform into the imperfect tense.

يقدّم أحمد صديقه إلينا.   >   قدّم أحمد صديقه إلينا.   ☜

هل أمكنك أن تسافر إلى هناك؟ ـ أمكنني أن أفعل ذلك ـ أمكننا أن ننجز واجباتنا فوراً.
متى أنجزتم واجباتكم؟ ـ هـل أنجـزت عملك بنفسك؟ ـ أنجـزوا العمـل بعـد ثـلاث ساعات.

أرسل الطالب رسالة إلى عائلته ـ هل أرسلت هدية إلى صديقك؟ ـ متى أرسلت البطاقة إلى أصدقائك؟

لماذا أحضرت جميع الطلاّب إلى هنا؟ ـ لماذا أحضرتم معكم أربعة كتب فقط؟ ـ أعـرف أنهما أحضرا معهما نقوداً كثيرة.

قدّمنا إليكم أصدقاءنا ـ متى قدّموه إليك؟ ـ قدّم أحمد نفسه ـ قدّمت له هذه الهدية ـ هل قدّمتم لهم بعض الشراب؟

رحّب بنا مدير المعهد ـ رحّبنا بضيوفنا الأجانب ـ رحّب الرئيس بأعضاء الوفد الفرنسي.

إلى أين سافرت الوفود؟ ـ سافرتْ إلى لندن بالقطار ـ سافرنا إلى هناك بالطائرة ـ هل سافر السياسيون اليوم؟

هل شاهدت ذلك الفلم؟ ـ نعم شاهدته مساء اليـوم ـ نعم شـاهدناه اليـوم ـ شـاهدوا اليوم الأبنية الحديثة.

ترجم الطالب الكلمات الجديدة إلى اللغة الإنكليزية – ترجمتُها إلى اللغة العربية – ترجمت المعلمة الرسالة من اللغة الفرنسية إلى اللغة الإنكليزية.

هل حدّثكم صديقكم عن رحلته؟ – حدّثناه عن دراستنا في مصر – حدّثتنا هيفاء عـن الحياة في بلادها.

سلّم أحمد عدنان الكتاب – سلّمناكم المبلغ اليوم – سلّمتُ الأشياء فوراً. أفرحنا ذلك – أفرحني ذلك – هل أفرحتكم الهدايا؟

رافقت الوفـد طالبـة ألمانيـة – رافقـتُ صديقي إلى المحطـة – رافقـني إلى المسـرح صديـق إنكليزي.

من قابلت هنـاك؟ – قـابلت هنـاك صديقـاً جزائريـاً – قـابلنـا اليـوم عـدداً مـن الضيـوف الأجانب.

C1 Report on what you do every day using as many ordinal numbers as possible.

C2 Prepare a dialogue based on Text 2 that takes place with an administrative official in a country within the Arab world. Use some ordinal numbers in your dialogue.

C3 (Homework) Write a program for a three-day visit of an Arab delegation as follows:
Monday:

10.00 o'clock	arrival ... Airport
12.00 o'clock	lunch
14.00 o'clock	meeting with H.E. the Secretary of State

etc. (Write out the ordinal numbers.)

Final Exercise:

1. Combine the following nouns and numbers (Write out the numbers).

قمر صناعي	٤	موضوع	٩٥	بيت	١
كثيب	١٠	ولد	١٠١	مدرسة	٥
فيضان	٢	بندقية	٧	رخصة	٣
واحة	٢٢	إختبار	٩	شهادة	١١
كرة	١١١	بنك	٦	زوج	٢١
شجرة	١٩	عقرب	١٥	طابع	١٣

2. Transform the cardinal numbers in 1. into ordinal numbers (Write out the numbers).

3. Translate into Arabic (Write out the numbers).

I was born on the 31st December 1974. My father, may God have mercy upon him, has been working as a teacher in the fifth primary school for two years. My third brother is a hairdresser. I am a second-year student. The university consists of eight faculties. I have four children. My fourth son is an engineer. You must go to the eighth floor and then come back to me. He is working in the technical department on the seventh floor.

4. Write out in words.

10.30 a.m.	01.55 p.m.	1918	11/11/1404
09.15 a.m.	05.22 p.m.	1798	03/09/2002
10.17 p.m.	07.25 p.m.	1945	20/05/1991
05.45 a.m.	02.37 p.m.	622	13/08/1961
01.20 p.m.	09.40 p.m.	1258	16/06/1992

1. Forms V and VI of the Verb

Forms V and VI have the same basic structure as Forms II and III. The prefix *ta-* تَـ is added as a distinguishing characteristic.

The succession of vowels in the perfect and imperfect tense is - *a* - throughout.

1.1.

	VI	V
perfect tense	تَفَاعَلَ	تَفَعَّلَ
imperfect tense	يَتَفَاعَلُ	يَتَفَعَّلُ

The imperative of Forms V and VI is used with only a few verbs, and therefore is not considered here. (See the detailed survey on all forms in the Appendix, Table 14.)

1.2. Verbs R₁ = و or ى

	VI	V
perfect tense	تَوَاصَلَ	تَوَصَّلَ
imperfect tense	يَتَوَاصَلُ	يَتَوَصَّلُ

As is the case with Forms II and III, there are no peculiarities in comparison to the strong verb. The verbs R₁ = ى are not listed separately here. (Appendix: Tables 16 and 17)

1.3. Verbs R₂ = و or ى

	VI		V	
perfect tense	تَبَايَعَ	تَقَاوَمَ	تَبَيَّعَ	تَقَوَّمَ
imperfect tense	يَتَبَايَعُ	يَتَقَاوَمُ	يَتَبَيَّعُ	يَتَقَوَّمُ

و and ى are full consonants as is the case with Forms II and III. (Appendix: Tables 19 and 21)

1.4. Verbs R$_3$ = و or ى

	VI	V
perfect tense	تَلاقَى	تَلَقَّى
imperfect tense indicative	يَتَلاقَى	يَتَلَقَّى
imperfect tense subjunctive	يَتَلاقَى	يَتَلَقَّى
imperfect tense jussive	يَتَلاقَ	يَتَلَقَّ

The verbs R$_3$ = و or ى are conjugated in the perfect tense of Forms V and VI like the model verb مشى, and in the imperfect tense like Form I of the model verb لقي. (Appendix: Tables 24, 25, 26)

2. Word Order
2.1. Anteposition of the object

The normal word order in MSA is verb - subject - object.

The anteposition of the subject, i.e. the word order subject - verb - object, is possible. Appropriate constructions were already mentioned when أَنَّ in the subordinate clause and إِنَّ in the principal clause were addressed.

Another construction frequently used both in MSA and, more importantly, in oral usage of the Arabic renders the anteposition of any object possible.

The object is placed at the beginning of the sentence in the nominative. The corresponding affixed pronoun is inserted in the place which has become vacant in the sentence due to this action. This anteposition makes a person or thing stand out in contrast to the general context; at the same time it makes a complex sentence clearer and enables it to be comprehended more quickly. The succession of two nouns (subject and object) is avoided. There is a pause after the part of the sentence which is placed in front.

The prime minister welcomes the Arab guests (or passive: the Arab guests are welcomed ...).	يُرَحِّبُ رَئِيسُ الْوُزَرَاءِ بِالضُّيُوفِ الْعَرَبِ. > الضُّيُوفُ الْعَرَبُ يُرَحِّبُ بِهِمْ رَئِيسُ الْوُزَرَاءِ.
The politicians support the trade relations with this country.	يُؤَيِّدُ السِّيَاسِيُّونَ الْعَلاقَاتِ التِّجَارِيَّةَ مَعَ هَذَا الْبَلَدِ. > الْعَلاقَاتُ التِّجَارِيَّةُ مَعَ هَذَا الْبَلَدِ يُؤَيِّدُهَا السِّيَاسِيُّونَ.
I accomplished my tasks immediately.	أَنْجَزْتُ وَاجِبَاتِي فَوْراً. > وَاجِبَاتِي أَنْجَزْتُهَا فَوْراً.
How much I love my mother!	كَمْ أُحِبُّ أُمِّي. > أُمِّي كَمْ أُحِبُّهَا.
Have you seen this film?	هَلْ شَاهَدْتَ هَذَا الْفِلْمَ؟ > هَذَا الْفِلْمُ هَلْ شَاهَدْتَهُ؟

☞**A1** The position of the object at the beginning of the sentence is also known in Indo-European languages. Constructions of this nature are known by the name of *Nominativus absolutus* and *Nominativus* or *Casus pendens*. - This construction is called أَلْجُمْلَة ذاتُ الوَجْهَيْنِ "the double-sided sentence" in Arabic.

2.2. Anteposition of the 2ⁿᵈ term of a genitive construction

The 2ⁿᵈ term of a genitive construction can be placed at the beginning of the sentence as well. The corresponding affixed pronoun replaces it again.

The visit of the Egyptian delegation begins on Wednesday.	تَبْدَأُ زِيَارَةُ الْوَفْدِ الْمِصْرِيِّ يَوْمَ الأَرْبِعَاءِ. < أَلْوَفْدُ الْمِصْرِيُّ تَبْدَأُ زِيَارَتُهُ يَوْمَ الأَرْبِعَاءِ.
The new models have fixed prices (*lit.*: the prices are fixed).	أَسْعَارُ الْمُودِيلَاتِ الْجَدِيدَةِ مُحَدَّدَةٌ. < أَلْمُودِيلَاتُ الْجَدِيدَةُ أَسْعَارُهَا مُحَدَّدَة.
The picture has beautiful colors (*lit.*: the colors of the picture are beautiful).	أَلْوَانُ الصُّورَةِ جَمِيلَةٌ. < أَلصُّورَةُ أَلْوَانُهَا جَمِيلَة.

☞**A2** This possibility of detaching a noun from a complex sentence is also given with regard to other groups of words (above all prepositional phrases):

I have bought many books in this bookstore.	إِشتريت من هذه المكتبة كتباً كثيرة.< هذه المكتبة اشتريت منها كتباً كثيرة.
I have met only three of these students.	قابلت ثلاثة من هؤلاء الطلاب فقط.< هؤلاء الطلاب قابلت ثلاثة منهم فقط.

2.3. If certain parts of the interrogative sentence are placed in front, it gives the word order: noun - interrogative particle or interrogative adverb - predicate:

Where did you buy this book from?	مِنْ أَيْنَ اشْتَرَيْتَ هَذَا الْكِتَابَ؟ < هَذَا الْكِتَابُ مِنْ أَيْنَ اشْتَرَيْتَهُ؟

If the subject of the interrogative sentence is emphasized by being placed in front, the pronoun which refers to it appears in the equational sentence in the form of the independent pronoun:

Are the prices fixed?	هَلِ الأَسْعَارُ مُحَدَّدَةٌ؟ < أَلأَسْعَارُ هَلْ هِيَ مُحَدَّدَة؟

In the verbal sentence it is completely missing:

| When did the Sudanese delegation arrive at the airport? | مَتَى وَصَلَ الْوَفْدُ السُّودَانِيُّ إِلَى الْمَطَارِ؟ <
 أَلْوَفْدُ السُّودَانِيُّ مَتَى وَصَلَ إِلَى الْمَطَارِ؟ |

3. Genitive Constructions with ذُو and ذَات

Genitive constructions which denote a specific quality or affiliation are formed by means of ذُو and ذَات:

a man of reason	رَجُلٌ ذُو عَقْلٍ
a politician of influence = an influential politician	سِيَاسِيٌّ ذُو نُفُوذٍ
a problem of importance	قَضِيَّةٌ ذَاتُ أَهَمِّيَّةٍ
a state (provided) with a parliamentary system	دَوْلَةٌ ذَاتُ نِظَامٍ بَرْلَمَانِيٍّ

When used as an attributive adjunct, ذُو and ذَات agree in case, gender and number with their respective (i.e. with their **preceding**) antecedents, and the following forms arise:

	plural		dual		singular	
	f.	m.	f.	m.	f.	m.
n.	ذَوَاتُ	ذَوُو	ذَاتَا	ذَوَا	ذَاتُ	ذُو
g.	ذَوَاتِ	ذَوِي	ذَاتَيْ	ذَوَيْ	ذَاتِ	ذِي
a.	ذَوَاتِ	ذَوِي	ذَاتَيْ	ذَوَيْ	ذَاتَ	ذَا

☞A3 In addition, the inflectional forms أُولُو for the nominative and أُولِي for the genitive or accusative exist for the masculine plural.

The genitive that follows ذُو or ذَات has the same state as the antecedent:

| an influential politician | سِيَاسِيٌّ ذُو نُفُوذٍ |
| the influential politician | أَلسِّيَاسِيُّ ذُو النُّفُوذِ |

☞A4 As these constructions do not occur very frequently outside the elevated style, specific exercises for their active use are dispensed with.

V

to come too late	V تأخَّر (يتأخَّرُ)	to bet on	III راهن (يُراهِنُ) على
unfortunately	للأسف	to range from	VI تراوح (يتراوحُ) بين... وبين
usual, common	مألوف		
match	مُباراة ج يات	sport	رياضة
championship	بُطولة ج ـات	because of	بِسببِ
remaining, rest	بقيّة	race	سِباق
(not only) ... but also	بلْ	contest, competition	مُسابقة ج ـات
to take place	تمَّ (يتِمُّ)	to score	II سجَّل (يُسجِّلُ)
tennis	تنس	to score a goal	سجَّل هدفًا
shot	جُلّة ج جُلل	help, support	مساعَدة ج ات
camel	جمل ج جمال	basket	سلّة ج سِلل
to gain, to win sth.	IV أحْرز (يَحْرزُ) هـ	basketball	كرة السلّة
professional	مُحْترف ج ـون	healthy, sound	سليم
horse; *also:* HP	حِصان ج أحْصِنة	place, square	ساحة ج ـات
present time	حاضِر	marketing	تسْويق
referee, judge	حكم ج حُكّام	popularity	شعْبيّة
to be enthusiastic about	V تحمَّس (يتحمَّسُ) لِ	popular	شعْبيّ
impossible	مُسْتحيل	sheikh	شيْخ ج شُيوخ، مشائِخ
end	خِتام	to become sth.	IV أصْبح (يُصْبِحُ) هـ
rival	خصْم ج خُصُوم	boy	صبيّ ج صِبْيان
gulf *(geogr.)*	خليج ج خلج، خلْجان	wrestling	مُصارعة [صارع (يُصارعُ)]
behind	خلْفَ	business, deal	صفقة ج صفقات
especially, special	خاصّ	qualifying contest	تصْفية
round	دوْرة ج ات	weak	ضعيف ج ضُعفاءُ
Olympic Games	الدورة الأولمبية	to add sth. to	IV أضاف (يُضيفُ) هـ إلى
round	مُدوَّر	flying	طائر
gold, golden	ذهبيّ	volleyball	الكرة الطائرة
dance	رقْصة ج رقصات	to think, to suspect	ظنَّ (يظنُّ) أنَّ
javelin	رمْح ج رماح	demonstration	تظاهُرة ج ات
push, throw	رمْي [رمَى (يرْمي)]	to be equal to sth.	III عادل (يُعادِلُ) هـ
		to end in a draw	VI تعادل (يتعادلُ)

running	عدْو [عدا (يعْدُو)]	to enjoy sth.	V تمتَّع (يتمتَّعُ) بِ
broad, wide	عريض	like	مِثْلَ، مِثْلما
known	معْرُوف	ideal	مِثاليّ
brain, mind, intellect	عقْل ج عُقُول	to praise so.	مدح (يمْدَحُ) ه
to reflect sth.	عكس (يعْكِسُ) هـ	wife	اِمْرأ / المرْأة (with article)
opposite	عكس	past	ماض (الماضي)
on the contrary	على العكس	to be able to do sth.	V تمكَّن (يتمكَّنُ) مِن
to sing	II غنَّى (يُغنِّي)	model	مُوديل ج ـات
song	أُغْنِية ج ـات، أغان	medal	مِيدالية ج ـات
to watch, to look at	V تفرَّج (يتفرَّجُ) على	place, ground	مِيْدان ج ميادينُ
spectator	مُتفرِّج ج ـون	excellent	مُمْتاز
rider, horseman	فارس ج فُرْسان	representative team	مُنْتخب ج ـات
horse show	(ألْعاب الـ) فُرُوسيَّة	club	نادٍ ج أنْدِية ، نوادٍ
team, ensemble	فِرْقة ج فِرق	supporter	ناصِر ج أنْصار
art	فنّ ج فُنُون	influence	نفوذ
to win against/over	فاز (يفُوزُ) على	to transport sth.	نقل (ينْقُلُ) هـ
tribe	قبيلة ج قبائِلُ	live broadcast	نقل على الهواء
disc	قُرْص ج أقْراص	transport(ing)	نقل
jump(ing)	قفز [قفز (يقْفِزُ)]	final	نِهائيّ
bomb	قُنْبُلة ج قنابِلُ	kind, sort, type, species	نوْع ج أنْواع
phrase; thesis	مقولة ج ـات	taking (of food, drinking etc.)	تناوُل
value	قيمة ج قِيَم	attack(ing)	هُجُوم [هجم (يهْجُمُ)]
comparative(ly)	قِياسيّ	goal; aim	هدف ج أهْداف
record	رقم قياسيّ	hormone	هُرْمُون ج ـات
football, soccer	كرة القدم	defeat	هزيمة ج هزائِمُ
match, game	لعْب ج ألْعاب	importance	أهمِّيَّة
track and field events	ألعاب الساحة والميدان	face	وجْه ج وُجُوه
sports ground	ملْعب ج ملاعِبُ	distribution	توْزيع
player	لاعِب ج ـون	order, medal	وِسام ج أوْسِمة
boxing	مُلاكمة	to expect sth.	V توقَّع (يتوقَّعُ) هـ

Text 1

الرياضة عند العرب

تتمتّع أنواع الرياضة المشهورة مثل كرة القدم وكرة السلّة والكرة الطائرة وكرة الطاولة والتنس وألعاب الساحة والميدان والملاكمة والمصارعة في البلدان العربية بنفس الشعبية التي تتمتّع بها في البلدان الأخرى ويتحمّس أنصار أندية كرة القدم في العالم العربي مثلما يتحمّس أنصار الأندية في أوربا أو أمريكا اللاتينية. وتشارك البلدان العربية بمنتخباتها الوطنية في بطولات العالم المختلفة وفي الدورة الأولمبية في أنواع كثيرة من الرياضة وتمكّنت بعض الدول العربية من أن تحرز ميداليات ذهبية فيها.

وإضافةً إلى أنواع الرياضة المألوفة في كلّ العالم نجد في بعض الدول العربية وخاصّةً في دول الخليج نوعاً خاصّاً من الرياضة وهو سباق الجمال. وهذه المباريات هي ليست تظاهرة رياضية فقط، بل أيضاً مناسبة ثقافية. ويتمّ نقلها على الهواء في التلفزيون ويحضرها رؤساء هذه الدول وأمراؤها وشيوخها. وقبل بداية السباق يشاهد الناس رقصات شعبية وألعاب الفروسية وتغنّي فرق الفنون الشعبية أغاني قديمة تعكس حياة البدو اليومية وتمدح ماضي القبائل وحاضرها.

وتتراوح قيمة جمل السباق الجيّد بين ٥٠٠،٠٠٠ ومليون دولار، أي ما يعادل قيمة أحصنة السباق المشهورة. ويتفرّج الناس على السباق ويراهنون على جمل قريتهم أو قبيلتهم. وفي ختام المباراة يقوم الرئيس أو الملك أو الشيخ بتوزيع الأوسمة والجوائز على الفرسان الذين هم عادةً صبيان صغار تتراوح أعمارهم بين الثامنة والثالثة عشرة.

Text 2

في الملعب

ماري: يا أهلاً. كيف حالك؟

أحمد: تمام وكيفك أنت؟

ماري: أنا بخير الحمد لله، هل تأخّرت؟ متى تبدأ المباريات؟

أحمد: لا، لم تتأخّري. المباريات تبدأ بعد عشر دقائق تقريباً.

ماري: ما هي الفرق التي نشاهدها في هذه البطولة؟

أحمد: تشارك في هذه البطولة فرق من كلّ البلدان العربية.

ماري: وما هي أنواع الرياضة التي نشاهدها اليوم؟

أحمد: بعد مباريات التصفية في الأيّام الأخيرة سنشاهد اليوم تقريبا كلّ المباريات النهائية في ألعاب الساحة والميدان مثل مسابقات العدو والقفز العالي والعريض ورمي القرص والرمح والجلّة إلى آخره وفي المساء نشاهد المباراة النهائية في كرة القدم.

ماري: هل تؤيّد العودة إلى رياضة الهواة أم رياضة المحترفين؟

أحمد: أنا مع العودة إلى ممارسة الرياضة على أساس مثالي والسؤال هو: هل العودة ممكنة؟ أنا أظنّ أنّها مستحيلة لأنّ تسويق الرياضيين واللاعبين قد أصبح فرعاً اقتصادياً خاصّاً.

ماري: نعم، هذا صحيح، للأسف، وأنا أرى في تناول الهرمونات والأدوية الممنوعة نهاية صحّة الرياضة وعكس المقولة : العقل السليم في الجسم السليم.

أحمد: نعم ، أنت على حقّ، ولكن الناس يفتحون أجهزة التلفزيون ويتفرّجون على المباريات ليشاهدوا أهدافاً جميلة وأرقاماً قياسية جديدة.

ماري: ونحن نعمل نفس الشيء.

أحمد: أنا أتوقّع هزيمة منتخب بلدي أو أن تتعادل الفرقتان لأنّ هجومنا ضعيف ولا أعرف من يتمكّن من أن يسجّل هدفاً.

ماري: نحن نقول: الكرة مدوّرة.

Exercises:

L1 (Homework) Prepare a list of useful terms for football / soccer and their Arabic equivalents. The list is to be completed and discussed with the teacher.

L2 Insert the correct preposition(s).

وقّع ... / وعد ... / حصل ... / تفرّج ... / شارك ... / قام ... / نظر ... / رغب ... / سمح ... / نصح ... / شعر ... / دعا ... / عاد ... / قال ... / ذهب ... / سلّم ... / رجع ... / سكن ... / وصل ... / تراوح ... / زوّد ... / جاء ... / وفى ... / حال ... / عرض ... / وصف ... / تبع ... / أدّى ... / أشرف ... / ربط ... / رحّب ... / أسفر ... / أضاف ... / عبّر ... / عانى ... / قدّم ... / أجاب ...

L3 Form useful sentences with the verbs in L2.

L4 (Homework) Form a sentence with each verb in L2. Use different tenses.

L5 Translate into English.

رجل ذو مال، طالبة ذات عقل، أمـور ذات أهميـة في كـلّ العـالم، أمـر ذو شـأن لتطوّر الرياضة، تطوّرات ذات علاقة بالوضع السياسي، قضية ذات اهمّية كبيرة للبلدان العربية، المرأة ذات الوجه الجميل، رجال ذوو نفوذ في السياسة الخارجية، نظام سياسي ذو أسـس قبلية، فنادق ذات عشرة طوابق

L6 Form equational and verbal sentences with the examples in L5.

رجل ذو مال   >   هو رجل ذو مال.

L7 Say it in Arabic.

before the fourth visit / in front of the fourth house/ with the ninth student / after the seventeenth of June / before the first of April / with the guest number 100,000 / in the thirty-second school / on the twenty-fourth of December / behind the fifth desert / after the seventh competition / over the second line / under the eighth rock/ in the fifth wadi / to the fifth street / because of the second catastrophe / with the fourth caliph / after the fourth wave / behind the seventh mountain / after the sixth order / with the tenth javelin / in front of the sixth sportsman / before the second match / the tenth club / after the fifteenth defeat / the twentieth record / with the twenty-first bomb / the first well / after the eleventh injection

L8 Translate the phrases in L7 using cardinal numbers (except for the dates).

L9 (Repetition) Insert the proper relative pronoun.

الكتاب ... اشتريته / الرجل ... قابلته في الفندق / البلدان ... شاركت في المؤتمر / مـع الطالبات ... رجعن إلى الجامعة / في البيتين ... كنت فيهما / عند الطـلاب ... درسـوا في ألمانيا / تحت الطاولة ... باعها أحمـد / مـع المدرسين ... حضروا الاجتمـاع / عنـد الشجرتين ... رأيتهما في مركز المدينة / مع مريـم وصبـاح ... ذهبتا إلى الجامعـة / مـع محمّد وصباح ... رأيتهما في الدكّان

G1 Transform the following sentences into the imperfect tense using the words and phrases in brackets.

☞   تفرّج على المباراة.   >   يتفرّج على المباراة.

تراوح العدد بين ٥٠ و٩٠.

تراوحت النتائج بين ... و بين ...

توقّع الطلّاب نتائج ممتازة.

توقّعت الطالبات نتائج ممتازة.

توقّع الطلّاب نتائج ممتازة في دراستهم.

توقّعت الطالبات نتائج ممتازة في دراستهن.

تعادلت الفرقتان.

تعادلت الفرق كلها.

شاهدت هذا الفلم (اليوم، في لندن، مع أصدقائي).

تأخّرت بداية المباراة (الحفلة، المحادثات) عشرين دقيقة (عشر دقائق، ربع ساعة، نصف ساعة، ساعة واحدة، ساعتين).

تأخّر الرئيس (الضيوف، الطلاب، التلاميذ) قليلاً (كثيراً).

تأخّر خمس دقائق.

تأخّرت خمس عشرة دقيقة.

تأخّر القطار ثلاثين دقيقة.

أملنا ألا (أن لا) يتأخر القطار.

أملنا أن يأتي اليوم.

أملنا ألا تتأخّر بداية المباراة.

تمكّن هذا النادي من أن يفوز على جميع خصومه.

تمكّن التجّار من أن يعقدوا صفقات ممتازة.

تمكّنت الحكومة من بناء اقتصاد جديد.

تحمّس المتفرّجون لنادي الأهالي.

تحمّس الناس بعد أن سجلت فرقتهم أهدافاً كثيرة.

تمتّع الرئيس بشعبية واسعة.

تمتّعت أنواع الرياضة المختلفة بمساعدة الحكومة.

G2 (Homework) Repeat G1 and write down a sentence for each transformation.

G3 The teacher quotes the sentences of G1 in the imperfect tense and the students transform them into the perfect tense.

تفرّج على المباراة.   >   يتفرّج على المباراة.   ☜

G4 Answer the following questions with "No" and replace the perfect tense by لم + jussive.

لم يتفرّجْ عليها.   >   هل تفرّج على المباراة؟   ☜

Pay attention to the helping vowel, which must be used after the jussive when followed by the article, instead of *Sukūn.*

هل تفرّجتم على المباراة؟

هل شاهدت الفلم؟

هل تأخّرت بداية المباراة؟

هل تأخّرت المعلّمة؟

هل تأخّرت بداية المحادثات؟

هل تأخّر الحكم؟

هل تأخّر الصديق؟

هل تعادلت الفرقتان؟

هل تمكّن من كتابة الرسالة؟

هل تمكّنت من أن ترجع إلى البيت؟

هل تمكّن من أن يقابله قبل السفر؟

هل توقّع هزيمة منتخب بلده؟

G5 Put the words in brackets at the beginning of the sentence and insert the respective affixed pronoun.

واجباتي أنجزتها فوراً.   >   أنجزت (واجباتي) فوراً.   ☜

دعونا (الطبيب) فوراً.

نقلت السيّارة (المريض) إلى المستشفى.

أزور (عمر) صباح الغد.

قابلت (أصدقاءنا) أمس.

حضرت (الحفلة) وفود كثيرة.

سعر (هذه السيارة) مرتفع.

عاصمة (هذا البلد) جميلة.

كنت أدرس في (جامعة لندن) ٤ سنوات.

كنّا نسكن في (ذلك البيت) لمدّة أسبوعين.

كنت مع (الطالبات) في المسرح.

هل وصلت (الوفود الأجنبية) أمس؟

هل رأيت (أصدقاءنا)؟

متى رأيت (أصدقاءنا)؟

إلى أين تمشي (مريم)؟

لماذا بعت (تلك الكتب)؟

C1 Prepare a list of typical phrases together with your teacher for greeting / saying goodbye/ thanking / apologizing / wishing (health, birthday, holiday, etc.).

C2 Prepare a dialogue about a sports event or a speech about your favourite sport.

Final Exercise:

1. Transform into the imperfect tense.

راهنوا على فرقتهم. تأخّرت بخمس دقائق. أحرزنا ميداليات كثيرة. تحمّس أنصار كـرة القدم. تـراوح عـدد الأنصـار بـين ألفـين وثلاثـة آلاف. أصبـح تسويق الرياضيين فرعـاً اقتصادياً خاصّاً. سجّلوا خمسة أهداف. عادلت قيمة جمال السباق الجيّـدة قيمـة أحصنـة السباق المشهورة. تعادل المنتخبان دون أهداف. غنّى الأغنية الشعبية في الملعب. تفرّجتِ على الملاكمة والمصارعة. تمتّعت أنواع الرياضة المختلفة بشعبية واسعة. تمكّن اللاعب من أنْ يسجّل كلّ الأهداف. توقّعنا ما هو مستحيل. شاهدوا المباريات النهائية في التلفزيون.

2. Insert إنّ , أنّ or أنْ (+ affixed pronoun).

قال ... تفرّجوا على المباراة. أظنّ ... لا يلعب كرة القدم. من تمكّن مـن ... يسجّل الهدف؟ سمعت ... ألعاب الساحة والميدان تتمتّع بنفس الشعبية. قالت ... الملك قـام بتوزيع الأوسمة. لا تقل ... بعد قال ! أريد ... أراها بعد الحفلة. أعلن الرئيس ... يسافر إلى أمريكا.

3. Insert the proper preposition(s).

وفى ... / حـال ... / عرض ... / وصف ... / تبـع ... / أدّى ... / أشرف ... / ربـط ... / رحّـب ... / أسفـر ... / أضـاف ... / عبّر ... / عـانى ... / قـدّم ... / أجاب ... / وقّع ... /...وعد ... / حصل ... / تفرّج ... / شارك ... / قام ... / نظر ... / رغب ... / سمـح ... / نصـح ... / شعر .../ دعـا ... / عـاد ... / قـال ... /

ذهب ... / سلّم ... / رجع ... / سكن ... / وصل ... / تراوح ... / زوّد ... /
جاء ...

4. Put the words in brackets at the beginning of the sentences and add the
respective affixed pronoun.

كنّا نسكن في (ذلك الفندق) لمدّة أسبوعين. كنت مع (الطالبات) في المسرح. هل
وصلت (الوفود الأجنبية) أمس؟ هل رأيت (مرافقنا)؟ متـى رأيت (أصدقاءنـا)؟ إلى أين
تمشـي (صبـاح)؟ لماذا بعت (تلك البيـوت)؟ دعونـا (الطبيـب) فـوراً. نقلت السيّـارة
(المريض) إلى المستشـفى. أزور (أحمـد) صباح الغد. قابلت (مديرنـا) أمس. حضرت
(الحفلة) وفود كثيرة. أسعار (هذه السيارات) مرتفعة. عاصمة (هذا البلد) كبيـرة. كنت
أدرس في (جامعة باريس) من ١٩٩٤ – ١٩٩٨.

5. Insert the proper relative pronoun.

تحت الطاولة ... باعها أحمد / مع المدرِّسين ... حضروا الاجتماع / عند الشـجرتين ...
رأيتهما في مركز المدينة / مع مريم وصباح ... ذهبتا إلى الجامعة / مع محمّد وصبـاح ...
رأيتهما في الدكّان / الكتاب ... اشـتريته / الرجـل ... قابلتـه في الفنـدق / البلـدان ...
شاركت في المؤتمر / مع الطالبات ... رجعن إلى الجامعة / في البيتيـن ... كنت فيهمـا /
عند الطلاّب ... درسوا في ألمانيا

6. Translate into Arabic.
The kinds of sport known in Europe such as football and track-and-field athletics
also enjoy great popularity in the Arab world. The Arab countries with their
representative teams take part in the championships of the world. There are also
kinds of sport in the Arab countries which are almost unknown in Europe.
Nobody scored a goal in the match we saw. The price of a race-camel varies from
$500,000 to $1 million. The folklore ensembles sing old folk-songs which reflect
the life of the Bedouins.

1. Forms VII, VIII, IX and X of the Verb

Characteristic of Form VII:	prefix *n-* ـنْ
Characteristic of Form VIII:	infix *t(a)-* ـتَـ between R_1 and R_2; vowellessness of R_1
Characteristic of Form X:	prefix *st(a)-* ـستَـ; vowellessness of R_1

The consonant cluster at the beginning of the verb which is due to the prefixes and the infix is dissolved by the prosthetic vowel *i-:*

(i)n- اِنْـ (VII), *(i)* - R_1 *-ta-* اِفْتَـ (VIII) and *(i)sta-* اِسْتَـ (X). The *Hamza* as the chair of the vowel *i* is a *Hamzat al-waṣl.*

The succession of vowels in the perfect tense is *a* throughout - with the exception of the prosthetic vowel.

The prosthetic vowel is omitted in the imperfect tense; the succession of vowels is: *a - a - i.*

1.1. Strong verbs

	X	VIII	VII
perfect tense	اِسْتَفْعَلَ	اِفْتَعَلَ	اِنْفَعَلَ
imperfect tense	يَسْتَفْعِلُ	يَفْتَعِلُ	يَنْفَعِلُ
imperative (Appendix: Table 14)	اِسْتَفْعِلْ	اِفْتَعِلْ	اِنْفَعِلْ

✍ **A1** There are various rules for the assimilation of the infix *t-* to R_1 =

ط، ض، ص، ز، ذ، د، ث، ت، ظ

Here are only the most important ones:

R_1 = ت + infix ت > تّ > ـتّـ   example: اِتَّبع (to follow, to succeed (sb./sth.), to pursue, to observe)

R_1= ط + infix ت > طّ > طّـ   example: اِطّلع على (to look at, to inspect, to examine)

R_1 = ص + infix ت > صط > ـصطـ   example: اِصْطدم ب (to collide with)

R_1 = ض + infix ت > ضط > ـضطـ   example: اِضْطهد (to suppress, to oppress)

R_1 = ز + infix ت > زد > ـزدـ   example: اِزْدهر (to blossom, to flourish, to prosper)

✍ **A2** Forms VII and VIII of verbs R_2 = و or ى do not contain *i*; see below, 1.3.

1.2. Verbs R$_1$ = و or ى

	X	VIII	VII
perfect tense	اِسْتَوْصَلَ	اِتّصَلَ	
imperfect tense	يَسْتَوْصِلُ	يَتّصِلُ	no verbs
imperative	اِسْتَوْصِلْ	اِتّصِلْ	

R$_1$ is assimilated to the infix *t-* in Form VIII. (Appendix: Table 16; Table 17 shows a survey of the forms of the verbs R$_1$ = ى.)

1.3. Verbs R$_2$ = و or ى

	X	VIII	VII
perfect tense	اِسْتَقَامَ	اِقْتَامَ	اِنْقَامَ
imperfect indicative	يَسْتَقِيمُ	يَقْتَامُ	يَنْقَامُ
imperfect jussive	يَسْتَقِمْ	يَقْتَمْ	يَنْقَمْ
imperative	اِسْتَقِمْ	اِقْتَمْ	اِنْقَمْ

As is the case in Form IV, the verbs R$_2$ = و or ى also have the same forms in Forms VII, VIII and X. Therefore, only قَام is used as a model verb here as well. (Appendix: Tables 19 and 21)

1.4. Verbs R$_3$ = و or ى

	X	VIII	VII
perfect tense	اِسْتَلْقَى	اِلْتَقَى	اِنْلَقَى
imperfect indicative	يَسْتَلْقِي	يَلْتَقِي	يَنْلَقِي
imperfect jussive	يَسْتَلْقِ	يَلْتَقِ	يَنْلَقِ
imperative	اِسْتَلْقِ	اِلْتَقِ	اِنْلَقِ

Forms VII, VIII and X of these verbs are conjugated like Form I of the model verb مشى. (Appendix: Tables 24 and 26)

1.5. Form IX, which has not been mentioned in the context of the derived Forms yet, is rare, because it is primarily used only in conjunction with colors.

The pattern of Form IX is: اِفْعَلَّ.

to be or to turn/become black	أَسْوَدُ > اِسْوَدَّ	black
to be or to turn/become red/to redden	أَحْمَرُ > اِحْمَرَّ	red
to be or to turn/become yellow/to yellow	أَصْفَرُ > اِصْفَرَّ	yellow
to be or to turn/become white	أَبْيَضُ > اِبْيَضَّ	white

The initial *Hamza* is *Hamzat al-waṣl*, as is the case in Forms VII, VIII and X. The verbs of Form IX are virtually only used in the 3ʳᵈ p. sg. m. or f.

V

to rent sth.	X اِسْتَأْجَر (يَسْتَأْجِرُ) هـ	hospitality	حَفاوة
renting	اِسْتِئْجار ج ات	to need so., sth.	VIII اِحْتاج (يَحْتاجُ) إلى
either ... or	إمّا ... و، وإمّا/... أو	to try sth.	III حاوَل (يُحاوِلُ) هـ، أنْ
hoping that	آمِلاً أنْ	at once, immediately, right away	حالاً
initial, at first, at the beginning	أوَّلِيّ	expert, specialist	خَبِير ج خُبَراءُ
research	بَحْث ج بُحُوث	periodical	دَوْرِيّة ج ـات
to begin (*intrans.*)	VIII اِبْتدأ (يِبْتدِيءُ)	administrative	إداريّ
direct	مُباشَرةً	duration, permanence	دَوام
translation; *also:* biography	تَرْجَمة	to show so. sth.	IV أرى (يُري) ه هـ
technology, technique	تِقْنِيّة	to be asked	يُرْجَى (*pass.*)
fertile, fruitful	مُثْمِر	requested; expected, hoped for	مَرْجُوّ
(*prep.*) during	أثْناءَ	rural	رِيفِيّ
carrying out	إجْراء	colleague	زَمِيل ج زُمَلاءُ
to meet so.	VIII اِجْتَمع (يَجْتمِعُ) بـ	to make so. happy	سَرَّ (يَسُرُّ) ه أنْ
(*prep.*) at so.'s side	جَنْبَ	I am happy that ...	يَسُرُّني ... أنْ
not to know sth.	جَهِل (يَجْهَلُ) بـ	contribution	إسْهام
to be allowed	جاز (يَجُوزُ) لـ، أنْ	to drive sth.	ساق (يَسُوقُ) هـ
jeep	جِيب	driving	سِياقة
to love, to like so., sth.	IV أحبّ (يُحِبُّ) ه، هـ	concerning, in question	بِشَأنِ الـ...
shoe	حِذاء ج أحْذِية	net	شَبَكة ج ـات
honored, dear	مُحْتَرم	supervision	إشْراف على
		to take part in	VIII اِشْترك (يَشْتركُ) في

to work	VIII اِشْتَغل (يشْتغِلُ)	article (press)	مقالة ج ــات
thank	شُكْر	cabriolet	كابريوليه
spectating	مُشاهدة	do so. the honour, having the pleasure	تكرُّم ب
joining of	اِنْضِمام إلى	open; roofless	مكْشُوف
(prep.) in	ضِمْنَ	he is able to	بِإمْكانِهِ أنْ
demand	طلب	to get sth.	V تلقَّى (يتلقَّى) هـ
via, by means of	عن طريق	examination	اِمْتِحان ج ــات
to be able to	X اِسْتطاع (يسْتطِيعُ) أنْ	to joke	مزح (يمْزحُ)
enclosed	طيًّا	going	مــشْيِي
Arabization	تعْريب	on foot	مشْيًا
well-being	عافِية	wishing so.	مُتمنِّيًا ل
permanent well-being	دوام العافية	desired, welcome	منشُود
dean	عميد ج عُمداءُ	method; way	نهْج ج نهُوج
to treat, to deal with	III عامل (يُعامِلُ) ﺓ، هـ	to end (intrans.)	VIII اِنْتهَى (ينْتهِي)
to be in touch with, to have (business) relations with so.	VI تعامل (يتعاملُ) مع	to finish	اِنْتهى مِنْ
era, age, epoch	عهْد ج عُهُود	telephone	هاتِف ج هواتِفُ
to last	X اِسْتغْرق (يسْتغْرقُ)	to bring sth., so. to	II وصَّل (يُوصِّلُ) ﺓ/ هـ إلى
fax	فاكس	to contact so.	VIII اِتَّصل (يتَّصِلُ) ب
single, individual	فرْد ج أفْراد	connection to	اِتِّصال ج ــات ب
excellent	فائِق	public transport	مُواصلات عامَّة ج
to inform so. about	IV أفاد (يُفِيدُ) ﺓ ب	available	مُتوفِّر
visa	فِيزا	to agree (upon)	VIII اِتَّفق (يتَّفِقُ) (على)
to accept sth.	قبِل (يقْبَلُ) هـ	success	توْفِيق
to kill	قتل (يقتلُ)	agreed upon	مُتَّفَق عليه
here: estimation	تقْدِير	father	والِد
soon	قريبًا		

Text 1

رسالة من السعودية

جامعة الملك سعود

معهد اللغات والترجمة

مكتب المدير

التاريخ: ١٤١٤/٧/٢هـ   الرقم: ٨٠/١٧٩٢

عزيزي البروفسور الدكتور بخمان المحترم

تحيّة طيّبة، وبعد . . .

يسرّني أن أكتب إليكم لأعبّر عن فائق شكري وتقديري على الحفاوة التي لقيتها أثناء زيارتي الأخيرة لكم، آملاً أن يبتدئ بذلك عهد طويل من التعاون المثمر والأعمال المشتركة بين معهد اللغات والترجمة في جامعة الملك سعود ومعهدكم، معهد الدراسات العربية في جامعة ليدز، متمنيّا لكم دوام العافية والتوفيق في حياتكم الخاصّة والعامّة.

أرجو أن أراكم مرّة أخرى في معهد اللغات والترجمة. كما أن زميلي الدكتور ميلر، ممثّل بريطانيا في التعاون العلمي مع المملكة، سيحاول أن يتّصل بكم قريباً للتشاور في أمر زيارتكم المرجوّة إلى جامعة الملك سعود.

وحسب طلبكم فقد اجتمعت بعميد المكتبات في جامعتنا بشأن إمكانية الاتصال بالحاسب الآلي الموجود في المكتبة، وأفادني أن ذلك ممكن من أحد الطريقين:

١) إما أن تتصلوا بمدير مركز الحاسب الآلي في الجامعة د. عدنان شريف، هاتف رقم ٨٧٦٥٤٦، أو فاكس رقم ٧٦٧١٢٣

٢) وإما أن تشتركوا في الشبكة التي يتعامل معها مركز الحاسب الآلي في الجامعة وهي الGulfnet، وتقوم بالإشراف الإداري عليها مدينة الملك عبد العزيز للعلوم والتقنية، وللانضمام إلى هذه الشبكة يرجى الاتصال مباشرة بالهاتف ٤٥٧٣٤٢ أو بالفاكس ٣٢١٧٥٦. وتستطيعون عن طريق هذه الشبكة أن تتلقوا المعلومات المتوفرة في عدد كبير من جامعات الخليج ومراكز البحث فيها.

وكما هو متّفق عليه أرسل لكم طيّا مقالة بعنوان ((التعريب كمصطلح ونهج)) لنشرها في دوريتكم كإسهام أولي لمعهدنا ضمن إطار التعاون المنشود بين جامعتينا. أرجو التكرّم بإجراء اللازم.

مع فائق التقدير والاحترام،

د. عبد الله بن نعمان

مدير معهد اللغات والترجمة

السياقة في الخارج **Text 2**

صباح: صباح الخير. كيف حالك ؟

بيتر: صباح النور، بخير، كيف الحال ؟

صباح: أنا تعبانة، عندي آلام في جسمي كله.

بيتر: ماذا حدث لك ؟ هل اشتغلت مرّة أخرى في المطعم ؟

صباح: لا، لم أشتغل هناك. المشي الطويل في المدينة سوف يقتلـني. لا يمكـن أن أواصـل مشاهدة معالم هذه المدينة مشياً. أحتاج إلى سيّارة لكي تنتهي مشاكلي. أليس بإمكاننا أن نستأجر سيّارة ؟

بيتر: المواصلات العامّة رخيصة وتوصّلنا إلى أي مكان.

صباح: وخارج المدينة ؟ أريد سيّارة كابريوليه أو جيب، أي مكشوفة السقف. الطقـس جميل وأحبّ أن أسوق هذا النوع من السيّارات.

بيتر: هل تعرفين أسعار استئجار هذه السيّارات وهل تعرفين السياقة في الخارج وهـل معك رخصة دولية ومتى انتهيت من امتحانات السياقة؟

صباح: الأسعار ليست بمشكلة، طبعاً، أعرف السياقة لأنّني أنهيت كلّ الامتحانات قبـل شهر.

بيتر: والرخصة؟ أريني الرخصة!

صباح: نسيت الرخصة في القاهرة وهي الآن في الطريق إلى هنا ووصولها يستغرق تقريباً أسبوعاً. أ لا يجوز أن أسوق السيّارة وأنت تجلس إلى جنبي أي مثلما كان يفعـل والدي وأخي ؟

بيتر: هذا لا يجوز هنا. يجب ان تكون معك رخصة دولية.

صباح: وخارج المدينة أي في الطرق الريفية ؟

بيتر: لا، أيضاً ممنوع بدون رخصة وشرطة المرور موجـودة في كـلّ مكـان وأفرادهـا، للأسف الشديد، لا يمزحون.

صباح: إذن، أنت ستكون سائقي وأنا سأجلس جنبك.

بيتر: إن شاء الله لا تنسين أنّك هنا لست في بلدك!

Exercises:

L1 Ask each other the question:

Do you need ...? هل تحتاج إلى ...؟

using the following words:

نقود، بطاقة، بطاقات، كتابي، كتبي، نسخة ثانية، أحذية جديدة، معطف جديد، قبّعة جديدة، سيّارة، جهاز راديو، جهاز تليفزيون، هذا الجهاز، جواز السفر، فيزا، سيّارة، سائق.

You can answer the question with "Yes" or "No".

L2 Answer the questions.

كم من الوقت يستغرق المؤتمر (الاجتماع، المعرض، الدرس)؟

كم من الوقت تستغرق الحفلة (الرحلة، المحادثات، مباراة كرة القدم)؟

L3 Answer the questions.

أين كنت تشتغل في العام الماضي (في الشهر الماضي، في الأسبوع الماضي، أمس الأوّل، أمس)؟

L4 Answer the questions:

متى يبتديء / تبتديء and متى ينتهي / تنتهي/ المؤتمر / المحادثات / الاجتماع / المعرض / الحفلة / الرحلة / المباراة / الدرس؟

using dates and times.

L5 Replace the words in brackets by their antonyms.

أشكركم على الحفاوة التي لقيتها أثناء زيارتي (الأخيرة). يبتديء بذلك عهد (طويل) من التعاون بين البلدين. تتمتع أنواع الرياضة المشهورة بشعبية (واسعة). تمكنت (بعض) البلدان من أن تحرز ميداليات (كثيرة). تغنّي الفرق الشعبية أغاني شعبية (قديمة). وقد تمضي أحياناً سنوات (عديدة) دون سقوط المطر على الإطلاق. تقع الصحارى في مناطق الضغط (المرتفع). هي (شديدة) الحرارة في الصيف و(باردة) في الشتاء. وقد تبلغ درجة الحرارة القصوى ٦٠ درجة مئوية في (بداية) العام. (بدأت) المحادثات. (وصل) الوزير. (دخل) البيت. (قبل) أحمد الدعوة. (جلس) المدير في وسط مكتبه.

L6 (Written homework) Form five sentences in which the verb اتّصل is used as imperative.

☞   إتّصل بمترجم الوفد!

☞   إتّصلوا بإدارة المعرض !

G1 Answer following questions with "No" by means of لم + jussive.

هل اشتركت في هذا المؤتمر؟ > لا، لم أشترك في هذا المؤتمر. ☜

هل اشترك جميع الخبراء في هذا المؤتمر؟

هل اشترك وفدنا في هذا الاجتماع؟

هل اشتركت في هذه المحادثات؟

هل اشترك مدير معهدك في هذه المحادثات؟

هل اشتركت في هذا الاجتماع؟

هل اشتركوا كلهم في هذا المعرض؟

هل اشترك وزير الخارجية في هذا الاجتماع؟

هل اشتركت في المباريات في لايبزك؟

هل اشترك أصدقاؤك في المباريات في برلين؟

هل تلقّيت رسالة اليوم؟

هل تلقّيت رسالة من أمك؟

هل تلقّى صديقك رسالة من أخيه؟

هل تلقّت الوزارة دعوة؟

هل تلقّيتم الدعوة؟

هل استأجر سيّارة؟

هل استأجرت صباح سيّارة كابريوليه؟

هل استأجرنا سيّارة جيب؟

هل استطعت أن تستأجر بيتاً جديداً؟

هل استطعت أن تدبّر لنا الاستمارات اللازمة؟

هل استغرقت المباراة ساعتين؟

هل استغرق المؤتمر يومين؟

هل اجتمع الرئيس مع الوفود العربية؟

هل اجتمعوا مع مدراء المعاهد؟

هل اشتغلت صباح في المطعم؟

هل اشتغلتم في هذه المصانع؟

G2 Transform the following sentences into the imperfect tense according to the given example.

☞ teacher:	هل استطعت أن تدبّر لي الاستمارات؟
☞ 1st student:	هل تستطيع أن تدبّر لي الاستمارات؟
☞ 2nd student:	نعم، أستطيع أن أدبّر لك الاستمارات.

هل استطعت أن تدبّر لي الاستمارات؟

هل استطعت أن تدبّر لنا الاستمارات اللازمة؟

هل استطاع الموظّف أن يدبّر لك جواز السفر؟

هل استطاع صديقك أن يسافر إلى بيروت؟

هل استطاع رئيس الوفد أن يجيب على الأسئلة؟

هل استطاع الطلاب أن يجتمعوا في معهدهم؟

هل استطعت أن ترافق الوفد السوري؟

هل استطاعت الطالبة أن تزور أمها في المستشفى؟

هل استطعت أن تأتي إليهم حالاً؟

هل استطاع بيتر أن يكتب رسالة عربية؟

هل استطعت أن تتلقّى جواز السفر؟

هل استطاع الوفد أن ينهي محادثاته؟

G3 Answer the question with "Yes" and complete the answer as given in the example.

☜	هل اجتمع الخبراء أمس؟ >
☜	نعم، اجتمع الخبراء أمس ولكنهم لم ينتهوا من المناقشة.

Replace الخبراء with the following words

الرؤساء، المسؤولون، مترجمو الوفود، مرافقو الوفود، وكلاء الوزارة، المعلّمون، الوزراء

and replace أمس with other dates and times.

G4 Same as G3, but with the following question:

☜	هل اجتمعتم أمس (صباح اليوم، في الساعة الثامنة ...)؟

G5 Answer the following questions with "Yes"

هل اتّفق الخبراء / المدراء / الوزراء / الرؤساء / الوكلاء / الأصدقاء على المشروع / المشاريع / المواعيد؟

هل اتّفقت الوفود / الحكومات / الوزارات على المشروع / المشاريع / المواعيد؟

هل اتّفقتم معهم على المشروع / المشاريع / المواعيد؟

and complete them by means of one of the following words and phrases.

أمس – أمس الأول – اليوم – فوراً – بسرعة – بعد مناقشة طويلة – بعد مناقشة الموضوع – في الاجتماع أمس – منذ عدّة أيّام –

☞   هل اتّفق الوزراء على الموعد؟ <

☞   نعم، اتّفقوا على المواعيد بعد مناقشة طويلة.

☞   هل اتّفقتم معهم على المشروع؟ <

☞   نعم، اتّفقنا معهم على المشروع فوراً.

G6 Answer the questions in G5 with "No".

☞   هل اتّفقتم على المواعيد اليوم؟

☞   لا، لم نتّفقْ على المواعيد اليوم.

C1 Develop a telephone conversation with the telephone operator in your hotel or with a long-distance operator. Ask them to put you through to a travel agency, the airport or the train station and inquire about arrival/departure times.

Give me the number ...!	أعطني/أعطيني النمرة ...!
The line is engaged.	النمرة مشغولة.
Call again!	تلِفِن مرّة ثانية !
Ring me tomorrow!	تلِفِنْ لي غداً!
Ring me!	خابرني بالتليفون!

C2 Prepare a dialogue about driving a car in the Arab world based on Text 2. Ask about the insurance (تأمين), the type of licence necessary, what to do after an accident (حادِث ج حوادِث) etc.

Final exercise:

1. Answer the following sentences with لم + jussive.

هل اشترك وفدنا في هذا الاجتماع؟ هل اشتركت في هذه المحادثات؟ هل تلقّيت رسالة اليوم؟ هل تلقّيت رسالة من أمك؟ هل تلقّى صديقك رسالة من أخيه؟ هل اشتركوا كلّهم في هذا المعرض؟ هل استأجرتم سيّارة جيب؟ هل استطعت أن تستأجر بيتاً جديداً؟

هل استطعت أن تدبّر لنا الاستمارات اللازمة؟ هـل تلقّـت الـوزارة دعـوة؟ هـل تلقّيتـم الدعوة؟ هل استأجر سيّارة؟ هل استأجرت صباح سيّارة كابريوليه؟ هل اشتغلت صبـاح في المطعم؟ هل اشتغلتم في هذه المصـانع؟ هـل اسـتغرقت المبـاراة سـاعتين؟ هـل اسـتغرق المؤتمر يومين؟ هل اجتمع الرئيس مع الوفود العربية؟ هل اجتمعوا مع مدراء المعـاهد؟ هـل اشتريت السيّارة؟

2. Translate into Arabic.

He didn't buy the book. We didn't get the invitation. The driving licence didn't arrive yet. The examination lasted five hours. I am unable to continue seeing the sights of this city on foot. I want to buy a roofless car, i.e. a cabriolet. The hot weather will kill me. The meeting is not finished yet. She will not work in the restaurant any longer.

3.Replace the words in brackets by their antonyms.

لم (ينته) المؤتمر. لن (يخرج مـن) البيـت. هـذا (مستحيل). لم (أعـرف) ذلـك. لم (أبـع) الكتـاب. بعـد أن (جلسـنا) بـدأ الاجتمـاع . نعـرف أيـن (الفـكّ الأعـلـى). مشـى إلى (اليسار). حدّثته عـن (مـرض) المدير. نمـت (قبـل) الطعـام. لم (آخـذ) القلـم. جـاء (في الصباح). لم يمش إلى (تحت).

4. Translate the following letter into Arabic.

Dear Professor ...

Thank you very much for your letter dated 11th December 1994, and for the valuable information and the invitation to visit your institute. I hope that this visit will be the beginning of fruitful cooperation between our two institutes. I have not been able to get in contact with the director of the library yet. I will try to get in touch with him via the computer network. The director of the computer centre sent me a fax with the desired information.

As agreed, I've enclosed an article to be published in the periodical of your institute along with some new Arabic software.

I thank you again for your efforts, and ask that you take the necessary steps.

Yours faithfully,

1. The Passive Voice (صِيغَةُ المَجْهُول)

1.1. The passive voice (مَبْنِيٌّ للمجْهُول) differs from the active voice (مَبْنِيٌّ للمعْلُوم) with respect to function, with the possibility of the actor (الفَـاعِل) being left unmentioned. This can be added in the form of a prepositional complement in the English language. In the Arabic language omitting the actor in the passive construction was made a rule.

☞ **A1** In modern Arabic, however, this rule is frequently broken and the actor is added by means of

مِنْ قِبَلِ : The book was written by the president. كُتِبَ الْكِتَابُ مِنْ قِبَلِ الرَّئِيس.

Altogether, however, preference is given to the use of the active voice.

The object of a transitive verb turns into the subject of the predicate (نائِبُ الفاعِل) in the passive voice.

1.2. The passive voice only differs formally from the active voice in the sequence of vowels.

1.2.1. The characteristic sequence of vowels in the passive voice of the perfect tense is *u - i - a.*

The vowel *u* is also taken by the prefixes and the infix in the derived Forms. In the following table, the active and the passive voice of Form I and of the derived Forms are contrasted with each other in the 3rd p. sg. m. As for the rest, refer to Tables 7, 13, 14 in the Appendix.

Form	passive voice	active voice
I	فُعِلَ	فَعَلَ
II	فُعِّلَ	فَعَّلَ
III	فُوعِلَ	فَاعَلَ
IV	أُفْعِلَ	أَفْعَلَ
V	تُفُعِّلَ	تَفَعَّلَ
VI	تُفُوعِلَ	تَفَاعَلَ
VII	اُنْفُعِلَ	اِنْفَعَلَ
VIII	اُفْتُعِلَ	اِفْتَعَلَ
X	اُسْتُفْعِلَ	اِسْتَفْعَلَ

1.2.2. The characteristic sequence of vowels in the passive voice of the imperfect tense is *u - a - a*.

Form	passive voice	active voice
I	يُفْعَلُ	يَفْعَلُ
II	يُفَعَّلُ	يُفَعِّلُ
III	يُفَاعَلُ	يُفَاعِلُ
IV	يُفْعَلُ	يُفْعِلُ
V	يُتَفَعَّلُ	يَتَفَعَّلُ
VI	يُتَفَاعَلُ	يَتَفَاعَلُ
VII	يُنْفَعَلُ	يَنْفَعِلُ
VIII	يُفْتَعَلُ	يَفْتَعِلُ
X	يُسْتَفْعَلُ	يَسْتَفْعِلُ

1.3. The passive voices of the defective verbs are specified in Tables 15-26 in the Appendix. They have basically the same sequence of vowels as the strong verbs do, therefore only some of the peculiarities are mentioned here:

The و in verbs R_1 = و is not omitted in the imperfect tense of the Basic Form as is the case in the active voice:

passive voice	active voice
يُوصَلُ	يَصِلُ

In the verbs R_2 = و or ى, R_2 is ى (long vowel *ī*) in the perfect tense, ا (long vowel *ā*) in the imperfect tense throughout in the Forms in which this radical is a vowel (I, IV, VII, VIII, X).

Basic Form: passive voice		active voice	
يُقَامُ	قِيمَ	يَقُومُ	قَامَ
يُبَاعُ	بِيعَ	يَبِيعُ	بَاعَ
يُخَافُ	خِيفَ	يَخَافُ	خَافَ

In the verbs R_3 = و or ى, R_3 becomes ى (as consonant) in the perfect tense, and ى (*Alif maqṣūra*, pronounced as the long vowel *ā*) in the imperfect tense in all Forms.

Form I:　passive voice		active voice	
يُدْعَى	دُعِيَ	يَدْعُو	دَعَا
يُمْشَى	مُشِيَ	يَمْشِي	مَشَى
يُلْقَى	لُقِيَ	يَلْقَى	لَقِيَ

1.4. Some examples of how to apply the passive voice:

1.4.1.

In the city center there are the buildings in which the cars are exhibited.	تُوجَدُ في وَسَطِ الْمَدِينَةِ الْمَبَانِي الَّتِي تُعْرَضُ فِيهَا السيَّارَاتُ.

The passive voice of the verb وَجَدَ, Form I, is تُوجَدُ.

The passive voice of the verb عَرَضَ , Form I, is تُعْرَضُ.

Two experts are sent to the conference which is held in Beirut.	يُوفَدُ خَبِيرَانِ إلى المؤْتَمَرِ الَّذِي يُعْقَدُ في بيرُوت.

The passive voice of the verb أوْفَدَ , Form IV, is يُوفَدُ.

The passive voice of the verb عَقَدَ , Form I, is يُعْقَدُ.

The sending of two experts was suggested.	أُقْتُرِحَ إيفَادُ خَبِيرَيْن.

The passive voice of the verb اِقْتَرَحَ , Form VIII, is أُقْتُرِحَ.

1.4.2. The verbal government by means of a preposition is preserved:

The guests are welcomed.	يُرَحَّبُ بالضُّيُوفِ.

The passive voice of the verb رَحَّبَ (ب), Form II, is يُرَحَّبُ.

Accordingly, the subject of this passive sentence is not in the nominative here, but in the genitive, being dependent on the preposition بِ, which belongs to رَحَّبَ.
In such constructions the masculine form of the verb is always used, even if the subject is feminine:

Many opinions were expressed.	عُبِّرَ عن آراءٍ كثيرةٍ.

The passive voice of the verb عَبَّرَ, Form II, is عُبِّرَ.

It takes the masculine form, although آراء is regarded as feminine.

1.4.3. About the construction of doubly transitive verbs:

If sentences containing two direct objects are turned into passive constructions, the 1st object turns into the subject, the 2nd object remains as such in the accusative:

Example: with أَعْطَى ه هـ IV "to give (to sb. sth.)"

active voice	
I have given an apparatus to Muḥammad.	أَعْطَيْتُ مُحَمَّداً جِهازاً.
passive voice	
Muḥammad has been given an apparatus.	أُعْطِيَ مُحَمَّدٌ جِهازاً.

Example with سَمَّى ه هـ II "to name sb. (by or with a name)"

active voice	
The mother has named the child Muḥammad.	سَمَّتِ الأُمُّ الْوَلَدَ مُحَمَّداً.
passive voice	
The child was named Muḥammad.	سُمِّيَ الْوَلَدُ مُحَمَّداً.

Even if the subject is not mentioned, the accusative object is preserved:

He was named Muḥammad.	سُمِّيَ مُحَمَّداً.

1.4.4. The passive imperfect tense, when occurring in conjunction with the negation لا, is often used in the form of an attributive relative clause, which can be replaced by an attributive adjective in English:

an event which is not forgotten = an unforgettable event	حَفْلَةٌ لا تُنْسَى

2. Some Characteristic Features of the Derived Forms

Originally the derived Forms are variants of Form I which serve to express aspects as well as the character of the respective verb. A functional-semantic description of the Forms is possible; it provides, however, little benefit for language practice. The complete stock of verbs can be found in the dictionary. The student does not need to coin certain Forms anew himself. Knowing the basic meaning of a certain Form can, however, enable him to understand a verb form he is not yet familiar with without resorting to a dictionary.

Basically it must be stated here that many verbs do not fit into a general semantic system of the individual Forms. Therefore it is not enough simply to memorize only the root or Form I of a verb. Every verb must be learned according to its respective Form.

✍ **A2** This also means that one does not, for example, try to impress the verbs upon one's mind by saying: جَمَعَ = to gather; جَمَّعَ Form IV = to agree, جَمَعَ Form VIII = to come together, to meet, but one must immediately store the forms أَجْمَعَ and اِجْتَمَعَ in one's memory.
Knowing the Forms is necessary to ensure their correct technical use.

In the following we give some characteristic features of the derived Forms, which have been provided, above all, to help the student with translating:

2.1. Form II		فَعَّلَ – يُفَعِّلُ
intensifying	I كَسَرَ	to break (trans.)
causative	II كَسَّرَ	to break (sth.) into pieces, to smash
denominative	I رَجَعَ	to return
(in this function it is	II رَجَّعَ	to cause to return, to send back
productive in modern Arabic)	زَيْتٌ	oil
	II زَيَّتَ	to oil
	صِنَاعَة	industry
	II صَنَّعَ	to industrialize

Nearly all its verbs are transitive.

Form II is used most frequently after Form I.

In unvocalized texts it might be confused with:

Form I in the perfect tense

Forms I, IV in the imperfect tense

Form V in the form تفعّل.

2.2. Form III		فَاعَلَ – يُفَاعِلُ
Form denoting an aim (attempted) effect on a person or thing	I كَتَبَ	to write
	III كَاتَبَ	to exchange letters, to correspond (with so.)
	I بَدَلَ	to replace, to exchange (sth. for)
	III بَادَلَ	to exchange (with so., sth.)
	I قَامَ	to get up
	III قَاوَمَ	to get up and turn against so. or object to sth. = to resist

Many verbs do not show this value of the Form.

Nearly all verbs are transitive.

Form III might be confused with the active participle of Form I; its imperfect tense which contains the prefix تـ might also be confused with Form VI تَفاعل.

| **2.3. Form IV** | أَفْعَلَ – يُفْعِلُ |

It is causative, denominative, and occurs in various other meanings, which are hard to summarize.

Most verbs of this Form are transitive.

It might be confused with:

Form I in the imperfect tense and the imperative

Form II in the imperfect tense

Form V in the form تفعل

the elative (cf. Lesson 25).

2.4. Form V		تَفَعَّلَ – يَتَفَعَّلُ
	كَسَّرَ II	to break (sth.) into pieces, to smash
It forms intransitives	تَكَسَّرَ V	to break (intrans.)
in relation to Form II	حَجَّرَ II	to petrify, to turn into stone (sth.)
as well as some denominatives	تَحَجَّرَ V	to turn to stone, to petrify
	غَيَّرَ II	to alter (sth.)
	تَغَيَّرَ V	to alter (intrans.)
	تَبَنَّى V	to adopt as son (ابن)

It is mostly intransitive.

Because of the prefixed تـ , it might be confused with the imperfect tense 3rd p. f. and 2nd p. m. sg. of Forms I, II and IV.

2.5. Form VI		تَفَاعَلَ – يَتَفَاعَلُ
It mostly has a reciprocal meaning in relation to Form III	بَادَلَ III	to exchange (with so. sth.)
	تَبَادَلَ VI	to exchange (sth.)

Transitive and intransitive verbs occur in this Form.

It is rarely encountered.

Because of the prefixed تـ , it might be confused with some imperfect forms of Form III.

2.6. Form VII			اِنْفَعَلَ – يَنْفَعِلُ
It forms intransitives and reflexives	I	كَسَرَ	to break (trans.)
	VII	اِنْكَسَرَ	to break (intrans.), to break into pieces
	I	سَحَبَ	to draw, to drag (sth.) along
	VII	اِنْسَحَبَ	to drag osf. along, to withdraw

In colloquial language this Form serves the purpose of forming the passive voice of verbs of Form I.

It is intransitive throughout.

It might at most be confused with verbs R_1 = ن.

2.7. Form VIII	اِفْتَعَلَ – يَفْتَعِلُ

This Form has various meanings, which are partially very different from each other. Some verbs occurring in Form VIII are reciprocal variants of Form I.

Verbs of Form VIII are partly transitive, partly intransitive.

2.8. Form IX	اِفْعَلَّ – يَفْعَلُّ

It is almost only used in conjunction with colors and denotes both the arising of the respective state:

The horizon took on a reddish color, reddened.	اِحْمَرَّ الْأُفُقُ.

and its existence, which is often characterized by intensity:

The night was (deep-)black.	اِسْوَدَّ اللَّيْلُ.

The verbs of Form IX are always intransitive. It is of rare occurrence.

2.9. Form X			اِسْتَفْعَلَ – يَسْتَفْعِلُ
It often occurs in the meaning "to request sth., to ask (so. for sth.)"	X	اِسْتَرَاحَ	to long for rest, to take a rest
	X	اِسْتَفْسَرَ	to ask for or to seek an explanation
	X	اِسْتَثْمَرَ	to seek to obtain fruits, profit = to exploit, (also) to invest profitably

However, it is also found in variants of meaning which cannot be delimited more closely, just as Form I is. The verbs are primarily transitive.

V

to be influenced by so., sth.	V تأثّر (يتأثّرُ) بـ	low	مُتدنٍّ
strategic	إسْتراتيجيّ	diesel	دَيزْل / دِيزِل
American	أمْريكيّ	cheaper than	أرْخصُ مِن
insurance	تأمين ج ـات	(prep.) despite, in spite of	رغْمَ
OPEC	الأوبك	passenger	راكِب ج رُكّاب
(mineral) oil	بترُول	to stagnate	ركد (يرْكُدُ)
alternative; option	بديل ج بدائلُ	flourishing, upswing, boom	ازْدِهار
omen (positive)	ج تباشيرُ	to increase, to rise	VIII ازْداد (يزْدادُ)
petrol, gasoline	بنْزين	the seventies	السبْعِينات
building	مبْنىً ج مبانٍ	(down)fall, decline	سُقوط
to become clear for so.	V تبيّن (يتبيّنُ) له	to name so., sth.	II سمّى (يُسمّي) ٥، هـ
wealth, fortune	ثرْوة ج ثرَوات	Shah	شاه
the eighties	ج الثمانينات	different, various	شتِيت ج شتّى
entire, gross, whole, total	إجْماليّ	buyer	مُشْترٍ
to go beyond sth.	VI تجاوز (يتجاوزُ) هـ	to comprise, to cover sth.	شمل (يشْمُلُ) هـ
happening in	حادِث في	cheque, check	شيك ج ـات
sensitiveness; allergy	حساسيّة	correction, change	تصْحيح ج ـات
not only ... but also ...	(ليس) فحسْب بل أيضاً ...	rising	مُتصاعِد
recession, slack period	إنْحِسار	to process sth.; to industrialize	II صنّع (يُصنّعُ) هـ
maintenance (of)	حِفاظ (على)	speculation	مُضاربة ج ـات
to realize sth., to make sth. come true	II حقّق (يُحقّقُ) هـ	double; multiple	ضِعْف ج أضْعاف
controlling	تحكُّم	security, bail, guarantee	ضمانة ج ـات
attempt, effort	مُحاولة ج ـات	additional	إضافيّ
vital, essential	حيَويّ	nature	طبيعة
whereas	حيْثُ	product, goods	بضاعة ج بضائعُ
to be exposed to so., sth.	خضع (يخْضَعُ) لـ / إلى	naturally	بِطبيعةِ الحال
going down, falling	إنْخِفاض	demand (for)	طلب (على)
to select so., sth. out of	VIII اختار (يخْتارُ) ٥، هـ من	to require sth.	V تطلّب (يتطلّبُ) هـ
		beginning	مطْلع

incompetence; deficit	عجْز (عن)	prolongation	تمْدِيد
offer, supply	عرْض	to continue, to go on	X اِسْتمرَّ (يسْتمِرُّ)
supply and demand	العرض والطلب	to result from	نتج (ينتجُ) عن
dinner	(حفْلة) عشاء	to produce sth.	IV أنتج (يُنتِجُ) هـ
epoch; afternoon	عصْر ج عُصُور	to conclude sth. from	X اِسْتنتج (يسْتنتِجُ) هـ من
majority	مُعْظم		
decade	عقْد ج عُقُود	result, product	نِتاج
to be held (conference)	VII اِنعقد (ينعقِد)	production	إنْتاج
for example, e.g.	على سبيل المِثال	product	منتوج ج ـات
to rely on	VIII اِعْتمد (يعْتمِدُ) (على)	gross national product	المنتوج الاجتماعيّ الإجْماليّ
handling	مُعاملة ج ـات	producing, producer	مُنْتِج
as, when	عِندما	victory	اِنْتِصار
to overcome	V تغلَّب (يتغلَّبُ) على	with regard to, as to	نظرًا ل
change	مُتغيِّر ج ات	organization	مُنـظَّمة ج ـات
changing	مُتغيِّر	to revive	VIII اِنتعش (ينتعِشُ)
Palestinian	فِلسْطِينيّ	(mineral) oil	نفْط
interaction; combination	تفاعُل ج ـات	expense(s)	إنْفاق
to profit by, from	X اِسْتفاد (يسْتفِيدُ) من	cash	نقْدًا
poor	فقِير ج فُقراءُ	to discuss sth.	III ناقش (يُناقِشُ)
to decide sth.	II قرَّر (يُقرِّرُ) هـ	closing, concluding	إنْهاء
amount, extent, degree	مِقْدار ج مقادِيرُ	important	هامٌّ
to propose, to suggest sth. to so.	VIII اِقْترح (يقْترِحُ) على هـ	consumption	اِسْتِهْلاك
proposal, suggestion	اِقْتِراح ج ـات	identity	هُوية
limited, restricted to	مُقْتصِر على	confrontation	مُواجهة ج ـات
catalogue	كتالُوج ج ـات	source	موْرد ج مواردُ
intensifying	تكْثِيف	middle, centre	وسط ج أوْساط
quantity	كمِّية ج ـات	to delegate so. to	IV أوْفد (يُوفِدُ) ه إلى
to notice sth.	III لاحظ (يُلاحِظُ) هـ	delegation, sending to	إيفاد
obligation, duty, commitment	اِلْتِزام ج ـات	provision	توْفِير
committed to	مُلْزَم ب	fuel	وقُود

Text 1

العرب والنفط

منذ ما يزيد على أربعة عقود واقتصاد معظم الدول العربية يعتمد على النفط. ويبـدو أنّ ذلك الوضع ليس مقتصراً على الدول العربية المنتجة للنفط وعلى منتوجهـا الاجتماعي الإجمالي فحسب، بل يشمل أيضاً تلك الدول العربية التي لا ينتج ولا يصنّع فيهـا النفط. ومنذ ذلك الحين تأثّرت الاقتصاديات العربية بحساسية شديدة لشتّى المتغيِّرات الحادثة في سوق النفط العالمية. وبطبيعة الحال فإنّ هذه السوق هـي نتـاج التفاعلات والمضاربات الاقتصادية والعرض والطلب في الـدول الصناعيـة حيـث تـزداد الأسعار عندمـا ينتعش الطلب على النفط بسبب الازدهار الاقتصادي في تلك الدول، أو يركـد الطلـب بسبب الانحسار الاقتصادي فيها.

فعلى سبيل المثال، عندما قرّرت الدول المنتجة للنفط في بداية السـبعينات مراجعـة اسعار النفط وتصحيح مسـتويات تلـك الأسـعار وإنهاء عصر الطاقـة الرخيصـة حدثـت أزمـة اقتصادية في الدول الصناعية حيـث ارتفعت الأسعار بمقـدار أربعـة أضعاف عمّا كـانت عليه، الأمر الذي استفادت منه أيضاً شركات البترول العالميـة. وفي عـام ١٩٧٩ حـدثت أزمة نفطية ثانية بعد سقوط نظام الشاه في إيران، نتج عنها ارتفـاع في أسعار النفط ولم يستمرّ هذا الوضع طويلاً فقد بدأت تباشيـر الانخفـاض في الأسعار في مطلع الثمانينـات حتى وصلت إلى مستوى متدنٍّ جدًّا في عام ١٩٨٦. ويستنتج من ذلك أن سـوق النفط تخضع بشكل أساسي لقانون العـرض والطلب رغـم كـلّ المحاولات الـتي تبذلهـا منظّمـة الأوبك للتحكُّم في الأسعار.

وهكذا يتبيّن لنا أن هذه الحقيقة تتطلُّب من الدول العربية المنتجة للنفط تكثيف الجهـود للحفاظ على القيمة الاستراتيجية لهذه المادّة الحيوية، والعرب ملزمون بالحفاظ على الثروة النفطية نظراً لعجزهم حتّى الآن عن توفير بدائل اقتصادية أساسية تحقّق لهم المـوارد الماليـة الكافية لمواجهة التزامات الإنفاق المتصاعدة.

استئجار سيّارة   Text 2

بيتر: مساء الخير.

البائعة: مساء النور، تفضّل.

بيتر: أحتاج إلى سيّارة لمدّة أسبوع.

البائعة: للنقل أم للركاب؟

بيتر: للركّاب ومكشوفة السقف أو سيّارة جيب.

البائعة: عندنا سيّارات من كلّ الأنواع وكلّ البلــدان، أي يابانيـة وأمريكيـة وألمانيـة إلخ ويمكن أن تختار من هذا الكتالوج.

بيتر: هذه السيّارة جميلة، كم سعرها؟

البائعة: سعرها لأسبوع واحد ١٥٠ دولاراً.

بيتر: مع التأمين؟ وهل يجب عليّ أن أدفع ضمانة؟

البائعة: التأمين ب٥٠ دولاراً للأسبوع ولا نأخذ ضمانة.

بيتر: هذا كثير، أنا طالب فقير. هل عندك سيّارة أرخص من هذه؟

البائعة: خذ هذا الجيب ب١٠٠ دولار للأسبوع بما في ذلك التأمين.

بيتر: والوقود؟

البائعة: هذه السيّارة تعمل بالديزل وليس بـالبنزين، واستهلاكها قليـل وسعر الديزل رخيص جدًّا. اتّفقنا؟

بيتر: نعم، اتّفقنا. آخذها.

البائعة: هات الرخصة وبطاقة الهوية. سنكتب الأوراق اللازمة.

بيتر: تفضّلي. هل هناك إمكانية لتمديد الفترة وكم هي أجرة الأسبوع الإضافي؟

البائعة: أجرة الأسبوع الإضافي هي ٨٠ دولاراً بما في ذلك التأمين.

بيتر: إذن، اكتبي أسبوعين!

البائعة: هل تدفع بالشيك أم نقداً؟

بيتر: أدفع نقداً.

البائعة: المبلغ الإجمالي لأسبوعين ١٨٠ دولاراً.

بيتر: تفضّلي وشكراً للمعاملة اللطيفة. مع السلامة.

البائعة: أشكرك، مع السلامة.

Exercises:

L1 Answer the questions.

ماذا يسمّى أبوك؟

ماذا يسمّى أخوك (إخوتك)؟

ماذا يسمّى أصدقاؤك (العرب والألمان)؟

ماذا تسمّى أختك (أخواتك)؟

ماذا تسمّى صديقاتك (العربيات والألمانيات)؟

ماذا تسمّى أُمّك؟

L2 (Homework) List all names of the individuals which were mentioned in the texts until now. Use them and the passive voice يُسَمَّى to form sentences as follows:

☞   يسمّى الصديق العربي الذي شرح الطريق ...

☞   يسمّى الصديق الألماني الذي يسأل في الفندق ...

☞   يسمى الصديق الذي كتب الرسالة إلى محمد ...

L3 Answer the questions.

ما هي الفواكه التي تزرع في البلدان العربية؟

ما هي المنتوجات التي تعرض في المعارض الدولية؟

ما هي الثروات الطبيعية التي توجد في البلدان العربية؟

ما هي البلدان العربية التي لا ينتج ولا يصنّع فيها البترول؟

L4 (Repetition) Transform into phrases using ordinal numbers.

☞   أربعة خبراء   >   مع الخبير الرابع

☞   بلدان   >   في البلد الثاني

عشرة عقود، خمسة بيوت، تسعة ركّاب، عشرون منتوجاً، ستة موارد، ثمانية بدائل، ثلاث موادّ، سبعة اقتراحات، تسع عشرة منظّمة، أربع شعب، إحدى عشرة رخصة، اثنا عشر رسماً، سبعة عشر طابقاً، ستة نوّاب، عشر مرّات، سبعة حلّاقين، شهادتان، سبع قراءات

G1 Revise the following sentences using the passive voice. The object becomes the subject of the sentence.

☞   أقام الوزير حفلة عشاء.   >   أُقيمت حفلة عشاء.

غيّر الوفد البرنامج.

عقد الخبراء المؤتمر في الشهر الماضي.

قال له إنّه سافر إلى لندن.

تلغي الوفود الزيارة.

سلَّم له علي هدية جميلة.

يسمّي الأب ابنه محمّداً.

عقدت الوفود اجتماعاً.

شاهدنا الطلّاب أمام المعهد.

تقيم الحكومة الحفلة غداً.

أحضر له أحمد هدية.

توفد الوزارة الطلّاب إلى الخارج.

ألغى الأصدقاء الموعد.

أضاف الرئيس بعض الكلمات.

أجرى الوفد السوري محادثات هامّة.

يسلّم أحمد الهدية غداً.

رجونا مريم أن تذهب معنا.

يجري الوفد المحادثات في وزارة الخارجية.

دعوت الصديق لزيارة برلين.

يغيّر بعض الأشخاص البرامج كلّ يوم.

أرسل صديقي إليّ بطاقة من القاهرة.

إستنتج الخبراء من ذلك أن الوضع متغير.

G2 Complete the sentences by inserting one of the following verbs in the passive
voice of the perfect and imperfect tense.

زرع، صنّع، أنتج، استنتج، أجرى، أقام، دعا، عقد

☞ ... الاجتماع اليوم.   >   عُقِدَ الاجتماع اليوم.

☞   >   يُعْقَدُ الاجتماع اليوم.

... الحفلة مساء.

... المحادثات في وزارة الخارجية.

... الفواكه في شمال البلد.

أعرف أن المؤتمر ... في لندن.

هل ... صديقتك لحضور الحفلة؟

سمعت أن البترول ... هناك.

هل ... من ذلك أن السوق تعتمد على العلاقة بين العرض والطلب؟

هل ... هذه البضائع في الخارج؟

G3 (Homework) Perform the following:

a) Determine the Form

b) Determine whether the active or the passive voice is used

in the following verbs in the 3rd p. sg. m.

c) Form a sentence with each of the verbs.

Since the verbs are not vocalized - as usual in most of the texts - it is often impossible to determine b). Since a) may not provide a clear determination, you may have to resort to the dictionary.

يقدّم، يلقى، انتهى، يدعى، يقال، دعي، يلغى، يعقد، يكتب، ينام، شوهد، يزرع،

أوضح، أعطى، طوّر، اشترى، يستطيع، تغيّر، يلاحظ، انعقد

G4 (Repetition) Transform into the imperfect tense.

تمتّعت أنواع الرياضة المختلفة بمساعدة الحكومة.

تمتّع الرئيس بشعبية كبيرة.

تحمّس الأنصار لفرقتهم بعد أن سجّلت فرقتهم أهدافاً كثيرة.

تمكّن هذا النادي من أن يفوز على كلّ النوادي الأخرى.

تأخّر القطار ساعتين.

تأخّرت الطالبة خمس عشرة دقيقة.

تأخرت بداية المؤتمر عشر دقائق.

شاهدت هذا الفلم.

تعادل المنتخبان.

توقّع الطلاب نتائج ممتازة في دراستهم.

توقّع الرئيس أن المعارضة لا تتمكّن من حلّ مشاكل البلد.

تراوح عدد المتفرّجين بين ١٠٠ و ٥٠٠ متفرّج.

تفرّج على المباراة.

G5 Negate the sentences in G4 in the perfect tense.

G6 Negate the sentences in G4 in the imperfect tense.

G7 (Repetition) Put the words in brackets at the beginning of the sentence and insert the respective affixed pronoun.

☜   دعونا (الطبيب) فوراً.   <   الطبيب دعوناه فوراً.

يصنّع البلد (البترول) بكميات كبيرة.

تجد في اقتصاديات هذه البلدان (حساسية شديدة لانحسار الطلب).

تغلّبت البلدان العربية على (الأوضاع الصعبة).

باعت الدول الصناعية (المنتوجات الصناعية) بأسعار مرتفعة.

ناقشوا (العلاقة بين العرض والطلب) في مؤتمر دولي.

قرّرت الدول المنتجة للنفط مراجعة (أسعار النفط).

قامت منظّمة الأوبك بتصحيح (مستوى الأسعار).

أنهت المنظّمة (عصر الطاقة الرخيصة).

قابل (نظيره) في الوزارة.

شاهدوا هناك (مستوى متدنياً جدّاً).

C1 Answer the questions متى ولدت؟ and أين ولدت؟ giving the exact place and date.

C2 (Written homework) Answer the questions

متى تُوُفِّيَ / تُوُفِّيَتْ... ؟

using the year of the death of historical personalities (Muḥammad, the Four Rightly Guided Caliphs, Fāṭima, ʿAbd an-Nāṣir, de Gaulle, Churchill, etc.).

C3 Prepare a dialogue based on Text 2 in which you rent a car or a flat/room.

Final Exercise:

1. Change into the passive voice.

يسلّم أحمد الكتاب غداً. رجونا صباح أن تدرس معنا. يجري الوفد المحادثات في وزارة الخارجية. دعوت الصديق لزيارة باريس. يغيّر بعض السياسيين البرامج كلّ يوم. أرسل صديقي إليّ بطاقة من القاهرة. إستنتج الخبراء من ذلك أن الوضع متغيّر. يقيم المعهد الحفلة غداً. سلّم له أحمد شنطة. توفد الوزارة الطلاّب إلى الخارج. ألغى الأصدقاء الموعد. أضاف الرئيس بعض الكلمات. أجرى الوفد السوري محادثات هامّة. أقام وزير الخارجية حفلة عشاء. غيّر الوفد البرنامج. عقد الخبراء المؤتمر في الشهر الماضي. قال له إنّه سافر إلى لندن. تلغي الوفود الزيارة. سلّم له علي كتباً جميلة. يسمّي الأب ابنه محمّداً. عقدت الوفود اجتماعاً. شاهدنا الطلاّب أمام المعهد.

2. Translate into Arabic.

He was asked about his objectives. He was told that the minister went to London. The programs were canceled. The delegations were welcomed in front of the hotel. Different opinions were expressed in the conference. Aḥmad was given a car. This was an unforgettable meeting. This is not said. This is not sold here. He was selected after a long discussion.

3. Answer the following questions (at least five items).

ما هي الفواكه التي تُزرع في البلدان العربية؟

ما هي الثروات الطبيعية التي توجد في البلدان العربية؟

4. Change into phrases with ordinal numbers.

تسع عشرة منظّمة، أربع شعب، إحدى عشرة رخصة، إثنا عشر رسماً، سبعة عشر طابقاً،

ستة نوّاب، عشر مرّات، لغويّ، سبعة حلّاقين، شهادتان، سـبع قـراءات، عشـرة عقـود،

خمسة عقود، تسعة ركّاب، عشرون منتوجاً، ستة موارد، ثمانية بدائل، ثلاث موادّ، سبعة

اقتراحات

5. Translate into Arabic.

the oil-producing Arab countries, the various changes in the world market, the relation between supply and demand, the economic upswing, industrial states, the intensification of the efforts, the gross national income, consumption and production, the very low level of prices, the second oil crisis

1. The Collective (اِسْم الجَمْع)

There are many nouns in the Arabic language which have a collective meaning when taking the form of the masculine singular.

☞A1 Collectives are also known in English. Think of the collective formations with the suffixes -ment or -y (government, assembly), the compound words formed with -ware (glassware), and also simple words with a collective content (cattle, hair).

We distinguish:

1.1. Generic collective nouns (اِسْم الجِنْس الجَمْعِيُّ)

The generic collective nouns denote a certain genus, mostly animals or plants. They are characterized by the fact that their corresponding specimens are formed by means of *Tā' marbūṭa* ة. This form is called *Nomen unitatis*. The sound feminine plural which is formed from it is used in order to indicate a certain quantity of specimens.

ducks	بَطٌّ	apples	تُفَّاحٌ
a duck	بَطَّةٌ	an apple	تُفَّاحَةٌ
five ducks	خَمْسُ بَطَّاتٍ	three apples	ثَلاثُ تُفَّاحَاتٍ

☞A2 Some such generic collective nouns moreover have a broken plural.

Many names of animals and plants, however, have no generic collective nouns, and consequently no *Nomen unitatis* is formed from them.

1.2. Collectives proper (اِسْم الجَمْع)

We understand by the "collectives proper" designations of groups which do not have a *Nomen unitatis*. They have broken plurals.

multitude, public; pl.: masses	جُمْهُور ج جَمَاهِير
people, nation; pl.: peoples, nationalities	قَوْم ج أَقْوَام

1.3. Names of Nationalities

The following words come under this category:

the Russians	أَلرُّوس	the Arabs	أَلْعَرَب

the Greeks	أَلْيُونَان	the Germans	أَلأَلْمَان
the Americans	الأمريكان	the English	أَلإِنْكِليز

These words are actually not plural in Arabic, but they are treated as such:

"the English merchants"			أَلتُّجَّار الإنكليز

Most names of nationalities are formed, however, by means of the *Nisba*: أَلْفِرَنْسِيُّون "the French", أَلْجَزَائِريُّون "the Algeriens" etc. As there is no rule which specifies which nationalities have one form and which nationalities have the other, only learning them as vocabulary items can result in obtaining a good command of the respective words. The individual representatives of these nationalities are denoted by the *Nisba* in any case: عَرَبِيّ "an Arab", أَلْمانِيّ "a German", فِرَنْسِيّ "a Frenchman".

The corresponding adjectives are also formed by the *Nisba* : عَرَبِيّ "Arab/Arabic/Arabian", رُوسِيّ "Russian", يُونانِيّ "Greek".

2. The Feminine *Nisba* (أَلنَّسْبَة المُؤَنَّثة)

2.1. The feminine *Nisba* (ـِيَّة) is the basic structure for abstract nouns. They are equivalent to English nouns with the suffixes -ance, -ence, -ness, -ty, -cy, etc. Also, nouns ending with "-ism" are rendered by means of the feminine *Nisba* in the Arabic language.

possibility	إِمْكانِيَّة	democracy	دِيمُقْراطِيَّة
productivity	إِنْتاجِيَّة	capitalism	رَأْسَمالِيَّة
significance, importance	أَهَمِّيَّة	socialism	إِشْتِراكِيَّة

2.2. This feminine *Nisba* also serves to form collectives:

interior, internal affairs	داخِلِيَّة	navy	بَحْرِيَّة
direction/administration/ management/municipality	مُدِيرِيَّة	republic	جُمْهُورِيَّة
finances	مالِيَّة	foreign affairs	خارِجِيَّة

and some other nouns (also concrete nouns).

2.3. Some formations are ellipses:

"cooperative (society)"	تَعاوُنِيَّة	⇐	جَمْعِيَّة تَعاوُنِيَّة
"classical, or literary, Arabic"	أَلْعَرَبِيَّة	⇐	أَللُّغَةُ الْعَرَبِيَّة

2.4. The plural is formed by means of ـات . Most words of this structure are, however, *Singularia tantum*.

✎**A3**   Moreover, there are *Nisba Pluralia tantum* ending with ـيّات . While they are plurals in form, they mostly have a collective meaning: زُجاجِيَّات "glassware", خَزْفِيَّات "ceramics", اِجْتِماعِيَّات "social affairs", اِقْتِصادِيَّات "economics" , لُغَوِيّات "linguistics", etc.

3. أَنْ and أَنَّ

The two conjunctions أَنْ and أَنَّ "that" are known both from grammar and by way of the texts. They introduce a clause which fulfills the syntactic function of an object when being subordinate to a transitive verb, and the one of a subject when being subordinate to an intransitive verb or a verb which is constructed passively or impersonally. The structure of the clause is as follows:

a) verbal clause	أَنْ	+ verb in the subjunctive	
	أَنْ	+ verb in the subjunctive	+ noun (subject, n.)
b1) nominal clauses	أَنَّ	+ noun (subject, a.)	+ noun (predicate)
	أَنَّ	+ noun (subject, a.)	+ adjective (predicate)
	أَنَّ	+ noun (subject, a.)	+ adverb/prepositional phrase (predicate)
	أَنَّ	+ pronoun (subject, a.)	+ noun (predicate)
	أَنَّ	+ pronoun (subject)	+ adjective (predicate)
	أَنَّ	+ pronoun (subject)	+ adverb/prepositional phrase (predicate)
b2) verbal clauses	أَنَّ	+ noun (subject, a.)	+ verb (predicate)
with the subject being in the anteposition	أَنَّ	+ pronoun (subject)	+ verb (predicate)

Examples of the objective clause:

a)	Aḥmad requested that he travel to Berlin.	طَلَبَ أَحْمَدُ أَنْ يُسافِرَ إلى برلين.
	Aḥmad requested that Muḥammad travel to Berlin.	طَلَبَ أَحْمَدُ أَنْ يُسافِرَ محمَّدٌ إلى برلين.
b1)	I know that Muḥammad is a minister.	أَعْرِفُ أَنَّ محمَّداً وَزيرٌ.
	I know that Muḥammad is ill.	أَعْرِفُ أَنَّ محمَّداً مَريضٌ.
	I know that Muḥammad is in the room.	أَعْرِفُ أَنَّ محمَّداً في الْغُرْفَةِ.

	I know that he is a minister.	أَعْرِفُ أَنَّهُ وَزِيرٌ.
	I know that he is ill.	أَعْرِفُ أَنَّهُ مَرِيضٌ.
	I know that he is in the room.	أَعْرِفُ أَنَّهُ فِي الْغُرْفَةِ.
b2)	I know that Muḥammad has travelled/travels to Berlin.	أَعْرِفُ أَنَّ مُحَمَّداً سَافَرَ/ يُسَافِرُ إلى برلين.
	I know that he travels/has travelled to Berlin.	أَعْرِفُ أَنَّهُ يُسَافِرُ / سَافَرَ إلى برلين.

Examples of the nominative clause (the transitive verbs in the above-mentioned examples are simply replaced by an intransitive verb or a verb which is constructed impersonally or passively):

a)	He can travel to Berlin.	يُمْكِنُهُ أَنْ يُسَافِرَ إلى برلين.
b1)	It appeared that Muḥammad is ill.	إتَّضَحَ أَنَّ مُحَمَّداً مَرِيضٌ.
b2)	It appeared that Muḥammad travelled to Berlin yesterday.	إتَّضَحَ أَنَّ مُحَمَّداً سَافَرَ أمس إلى برلين.

Accordingly the two basic structures are:

أَنْ + **subjunctive**   =   verbal clause

أَنَّ + **noun or pronoun**   =   nominal clause or verbal clause

with the subject being in anteposition

Which one of these two structures is made use of, depends on the semantics of the verb that precedes أَنَّ / أَنْ .

3.1. أَنَّ is employed after verbs

of **informing, expressing**:

to assure	أَكَّدَ II
to mention	ذَكَرَ
to announce	أَذَاعَ IV
to declare/state/announce	صَرَّحَ (بِ) II
to announce	أَعْلَنَ IV

etc.

of **knowing or believing**:

to know	عَرَفَ
to believe, to assume/to presume	اِعْتَقَدَ VIII
to find out/to learn	عَلِمَ
to appear/to come to light, to become clear	اِتَّضَحَ VIII

etc.

of **(sensory) perception**:

to grasp/to comprehend, to perceive/to realize	أَدْرَكَ IV
to see; to think	رَأَى
to hear	سَمِعَ
to notice/to remark	لاحَظَ III

etc.

3.2. أَنْ is employed after the following **modal auxiliary verbs**:

it ought to be/should be (only the imperfect tense is common: كان ينبغي or يَنْـبَغِي)	اِنْبَغَى VII
to want	أَرَادَ IV
to be allowed/permitted (to do sth.)	سُمِحَ (لَهُ) ب / أَنْ
to be able (to do sth.)	اِسْتَطَاعَ X
to be possible, feasible (for sb.), to be able to	أَمْكَنَ IV
must, to have to (only the imperfect tense is in frequent use: كان يجِب or يَجِبُ)	وَجَبَ (عَلَى)

and after the verbs depicting **demanding, ordering, suggesting, wishing, hoping, doubting, fearing, or an emotion** a.o. as well:

to hope (for)	أَمَلَ
to be possible or likely (mostly passive)	اِحْتَمَلَ / يُحْتَمَلُ VIII
to fear	خَافَ

to wish	رَجَا
to make happy	سَرَّ
to request, to call (upon sb.)	طَلَبَ
to suggest	VIII اِقْتَرَحَ

☞A4 After some verbs أَنْ or أَنَّ can be employed alternatively, depending on whether the predicate expresses a statement or an action, the execution of which is in the future and which is wished or expected, but is not quite certain:

He wrote to me that the delegation arrived yesterday.	كَتَبَ لِي أَنَّ الْوَفْدَ وَصَلَ أَمْسِ.
He wrote to me that the delegation arrives tomorrow.	كَتَبَ لِي أَنَّ الْوَفْدَ سَيَصِلُ غَداً.
He wrote to me that the delegation would (or was (due) to) arrive tomorrow.	كَتَبَ لِي أَنْ سَيَصِلَ الْوَفْدُ غَداً.

☞A5 If we except the construction بَعْدَ أَنْ (and مُنْذُ أَنْ) + perfect tense, which has already been discussed, rarely will a verb in the perfect tense follow أَنْ . This is the case in sentences which announce a statement that is located at the beginning or at the end of a speech. Arabic بِأَنْ + perfect tense = English "... by ... -ing".

He began his election campaign by describing ...	بَدَأَ حَمْلَتَهُ الاِنْتِخَابِيَّة بِأَنْ وَصَفَ ...
He concluded his speech by proclaiming ...	اِخْتَتَمَ كَلِمَتَهُ بِأَنْ أَعْلَنَ ...
He concluded his speech by requesting Dr. ... (to do sth.) ...	أَنْهَى كَلِمَتَهُ بِأَنْ طَلَبَ مِن الدُّكْتُور ...

Thus also after the verb سبق "to precede":

He had already said before ...	لَقَدْ سَبَقَ لَهُ أَنْ قَالَ ...

3.3. أَنْ preceded by لَا is contracted to أَلَّا :

I am afraid that he will not reach his goal.	أَخَافُ أَلَّا يَصِلَ إِلَى هَدَفِهِ.

3.4. أَنَّ is frequently combined with prepositions, thus with لِ = لِأَنَّ "because", مَعَ = مَعَ أَنَّ "as if", كَ = كَأَنَّ "although" etc.

V

horizon, prospect	أُفُق ج آفاق	machine	آلة ج ـات
evil; disease/epidemic of plants	آفة ج ـات	influenza	إنفلوينزا
to consist of	V تَأَلَّف (يتَأَلَّفُ) من	to sow	بذر (يَبْذُرُ)

seed	بذر ج بُذُور
invention	اِبْتِكار ج ات
tomato	بنادُورة (Syr.)
to make (serious) efforts	جَدَّ (يجِدُّ)
tractor	جرّارة ج ات
piece	حَبّة ج ـات
melon	حبْحب (Yem.)
volume, size	حجْم ج أحْجام
civil war	الحرْب الأهلِيّة
plough, plow	مِحْراث ج محاريثُ
to harvest	حصد (يحْصُدُ)
harvesting combine	حصّادة ج ات
agricultural produce	مَحْصُول ج محاصِيلُ
lecture	مُحاضرة ج ات
present (time)	حاضِر
local, domestic	محلّيّ
rye	حِنْطة سوْداءُ
(prep.) around, about	حوْلَ
to conclude sth. with	VIII اِختتم (يخْتِتِمُ) هـ ب
use, employment	اِسْتِخْدام ج ـات
vegetables, greens	خُضار
poultry	ج دواجِنُ
maize, corn	ذرة ، ذرة شامية
millet	ذرة رفيعة
here: breeding	ترْبِية
to smoke	II دَخَّن (يُدخِّنُ)
goal-directed, wise	رشِيد
official	رسْمِيّ
increase	زِيادة ج ات
fishing	سَمكيّ
to contribute to	III ساهم (يُساهِمُ) في

distance	مسافة ج ـات
cigarette, cigaret	سِيجارة ج سجائِر
Syrian	شامِيّ ج شامِيّون
here: which	مِن شأنِهِ / شأنُها أنْ ...
participant	مُشترك ج ـون
in general	بشكْلٍ عامّ
sugar melon	شَمّام (coll.)
desertification	تصحُّر
to issue sth.	IV أصدر (يُصدِرُ) هـ
pump	مِضخّة ج ـات
stewardess	مُضيفة ج ـات
fresh	طازج
condition	ظرْف ج ظُرُوف
facilities, installations, works	ج مُعدّات
independent, irrespective of	بمَعْزل عن
optimal; rational	عقْلانِيّ
to learn sth.	V تعلَّم (يتعلَّمُ) هـ
cooperative	تعاوُنِيّة ج ـات
food(stuff), nutrition	غِذاء ج أغذِية
food(stuff)	غِذائِيّ
sheep	غنم ج أغْنام (coll.)
strawberries	فراوُلة (Ital.: fragola)
~	فريز (Fr.: fraise)
to take advantage of, to use	اِسْتِفادة مِن
to estimate sth.	II قدّر (يُقدِّرُ) هـ
cauliflower	قرْنبيط
to have sth. in mind, to aim at, to refer to, to think	قصد (يقْصِدُ) هـ
wheat	قمْح
fighting	مُكافحة
cauliflower	كوليفلاور
sack, bag	كِيس ج أكْياس

kilogram(me)	كِيلُو (غرام) ج ـات	upswing	نَهْضة
to be favourable for	III لاءم (يُلائِمُ) هـ	diversification	تنوِيع
dialect	لَهْجة ج لَهَجات	margin	هامِش ج هوامِشُ
surface, area, space	مِساحة ج ـات	in the margin	على هامش
livestock	ماشِية ج مواشٍ	to be confronted with so., sth.	III واجه (يُواجِهُ) ه، هـ
(she-)goat	مَعْز ج أمعاز *(coll.)*	union	اِتِّحاد ج ـات
He, who sows will harvest.	من بذر حصد	European Union	الاتحاد الأوربيّ
He, who seeks will find.	من جدَّ وجد	to be characterized by	VIII اِتَّسم (يتَّسِمُ) ب
on site, on the scene	مَيْدانِيّ	recommendation	توْصية ج ـات
productivity	إنتاجِيّة	to agree to	III وافق (يُوافِقُ) على
seminar, colloquium	نَدْوةَ ج نَدَوات	to be dependent on	V توقَّف (يتوقَّفُ) على
organization, organizing	تنظِيم ج ـات		
model, sample, pattern	نُمُوذج ج نماذِجُ		
swinging-up of	نهُوض بِ		

Text 1

ندوة الزراعة

إنعقدت في دمشق في يومي الثلاثاء والأربعاء الماضيين ندوة علمية حول آفاق تطوُّر الزراعة في الوطن العربي ساهم في تنظيمها كلّ من وزارة الزراعة وكلِّية الزراعة بجامعة دمشق بالتعاون مع منظّمة الأغذية التابعة للأمم المتّحدة. وناقش المشتركون في الندوة الذين جاؤوا من كلّ البلدان العربية ومن الأمم المتّحدة والاتحاد الأوربي سبل تطوير الزراعة وتنويعها ومشاكل التصحُّر ومكافحة أمراض النباتات والآفات الزراعية وتربية المواشي أي البقر والمعز والغنم وإمكانيات زيادة حجم المحاصيل الزراعية من القمح والحنطة السوداء والذرة الشامية والرفيعة والخضراوات والفواكه على أساس أنواع جديدة من البذور وأيضاً طرقاً علمية جديدة لتحسين نظام الري والاستفادة العقلانية والرشيدة من ابتكارات العلم الحديثة.

هذا وأصدرت الندوة عدداً من التوصيات في هذا المجال من شأنها أن تساهم في حلّ المشاكل الملحّة التي تواجهها الزراعة في الوطن العربي. واتّفق كلّ الحاضرين على أنّ حلّ هذه المشاكل يتوقّف على النهوض بالأوضاع الاقتصادية بشكل عامّ وأنّه لا يمكن تحقيق الأمن الغذائي في البلدان العربية بمعزل عن الأسواق العالمية وأسعار الأغذية فيها.

وأقيم على هامش الندوة معرض زراعي في ساحة المعارض التابعة لوزارة الزراعة عرضت فيه آلات زراعية حديثة مثل الجرّارات والحصّادات والمحاريث والمضخّات ومعدّات الـري ونماذج لبذور ومحاصيل جديدة تتسم بإنتاجية عالية وتلائم مناخ الوطـن العربي وظروفـه الطبيعية.

ومـن الجدير بـالذكر أنّ الندوة اختتمـت بزيارات ميدانيــة في بعـض مـزارع الدولــة والتعاونيات الزراعية والسمكية في محافظات الجمهورية.

Text 2	في سوق الخضار

البائعة: صباح الخير، تفضّل.

بيتر: صباح النور، هات كيلو بنادورة وكيلو تفّاح!

البائعة: أنت تقصد طماطم، نحن لا نقول بنادورة.

بيتر: صحيح، أعطيني أيضاً كيس بصل وحبحب.

البائعة: لا أعرف هذه الكلمة، هل تقصد البطّيخ أو الشمام؟

بيتر: نعم، أهل اليمن يقولون الحبحب، يعني البطّيخ.

البائعة: لكنك لست من اليمن، من أين أنت؟

بيتر: أنا إنكليزي. هات حبّة من الكوليفلاور؟

البائعة: نحن نسمّي هذا قرنبيط.

بيتر: كيف الموز عندك؟

البائعة: كلّ ما ترى عندي هو ممتاز وطازج ومن الإنتاج المحلي.

بيتر: إذن، هات كيلو موز ونصف كيلو من هذه الفراولة!

البائعة: نحن نقول فريز، أي نستخدم المصطلح الفرنسي.

بيتر: وللعنب تقولين " فان"؟

البائعة: لا، نقول عنب.

بيتر: إذن، هات كيلو من العنب الأسود.

البائعة: انت تتعلّم بسرعة.

بيتز: شكراً. بكم الخضار والفواكه؟

البائعة: بأربعين ليرة.

بيتز: تفضّلي وشكراً للمحاضرة في اللهجات العربية.

البائعة: لا شكر على الواجب ونحن نقول ((من جدّ وجد)).

بيتز: نعم، و ((من بذر حصد))، مع السلامة.

البائعة: مع السلامة.

Exercises:

L1 Answer the following questions:

ما هو عدد سكّان البلدان العربية؟

ما هي مساحتها؟

ما هي المسافة بين لندن والقاهرة؟

ما هي المسافة بين باريس ودمشق؟

ما هو عدد المسلمين في العالم؟

Use the verbs بلـغ (يبلُـغُ) ٥ "to amount to" and قدّر (يُقَدِّر) بِ II "to estimate" (passive يُقَدَّرُ بِ).

L2 Form sentences with the words for fruits and vegetables as follows: أعطني ٣ تفّاحات، أعطني تفّاحة (to memorize the *Nomen unitatis*) and أعطني كيلوغراماً من التفّاح (to memorize collective nouns).
Use also other verbs and clauses instead of the imperative, e.g.

أريد أن اشتري	أعطاني	إشتريتُ
آكلُ كلّ يوم	هل تعطيني	أخذتُ
تُزرَعُ هناك	أعطيته	طلبتُ

L3 (Homework) Form sentences with the names of nationalities you know by introducing them with اِشترك، أحبّ، تكلّم.

☞   يتكلّم الفرنسيون اللغة الفرنسية.

L4 Answer the question ما هي الوزارات التي تتألف منها الحكومة؟ by using the words for "exterior", "interior", "finance", "defense", "culture", "(foreign) trade", "industry", "agriculture" and "economy".

L5 (Homework) Write a list of all collective nouns from this lesson and from Lesson 7 and add the *Nomen unitatis* and an appropriate adjective.

L6 (Homework, repetition) Ask each other the following question.

Do you need (paper)?　　　　　　　هل تحتاج / تحتاجين إلى (ورق)؟

Answer the question with "No" and give a funny reason for your "No". Prepare the answers at home.

No, I do not need paper because I do not know how to write.

لا، لا أحتاج إلى ورق لأني لا أعرف الكتابة.　☜

جواز السفر، بطاقة ثالثة، نسخة ثانية، أحذية جديدة، معطف صيفي، سيّارة كبريوليـه، سائق شاطر، خبراء جدد، ضمانة، وقود، بدائل سياسية، مضخّة للبيرة، قرنبيط، بنادورة، جرّارة للسيّارة، محراث للحديقة، حصّادة للفراولـة، حنطـة للدواجـن، قمـح للحصـان، كيس كبير للراتب، شمّام للفطور، شقة جديدة، فلوس لشـراء مكتـب، رخصـة للسياقة، ساعة شمسية، رسوم إضافية، تصديق الشهادة، شـرطة المـرور، شهادة المدرسـة الثانويـة، زوج جديد، زوجة أخرى، صندوق لفلوسك، وصْل من البنك، طوابع، بطّارية للسيّارة، بندقية للعناكب، زاد للسفر، مطر يوميّاً، أشجار كبيرة، عقارب في السرير، عناكب على الجدران، طاقة للعمل، وصفة من الطبيب، حبوب ضدّ الإسهال، حقنة ضـد الألم، أدويـة ضدّ كلّ الأمراض، تقويم السنة الماضية، عنوان مدير المعهد، صلاحيات جديـدة، جـيران يلعبون كرة القدم في مساكنهم، صرّاف بدون نقود، موعد آخر مع دائرة الامتحانات

G1 Combine the following sentences in such a way that the second sentence becomes an objective or subject sentence introduced by أنّ or أنْ.

☜　　أعلنت الحكومة　　　　توافق على هذا المشروع　<

☜　　أعلنت الحكومة أنّها توافق على هذا المشروع.

☜　　طلب صديقي　　　أسافر معه　　　　　<

☜　　طلب صديقي أنْ أسافر معه.

سمعت أمس　　　　　ألغيت الرحلة

أريد　　　　　　　أزوره يوم الأحد

لا أستطيع　　　　أجيب على هذا السؤال

أعلنت وزارة الخارجية　سيزور وزير الخارجية الجزائر

أمل الرجل　　　　　يصل إلى هدفه

أعتقدُ　　　　　　يأتي صديقي اليوم

تنجز واجباتك	يجب عليك
تؤيد حكومته هذه الاقتراحات	أكّد رئيس الوفد
يزور مكتبة الدولة	طلب محمّد
أرحّب بضيوفنا الأجانب	طلبوا منّي
نتحدّث حول ذلك غداً	أقترحُ عليكم
صديقي مريض	علمتُ أمس
أنت مجتهد	أعرف
هي تتكلّم اللغة العربية	لاحظت
أفعل ذلك	لا يمكنني
تبقون هنا	مَن اقترح
ذهب إلى هناك	رأيتُ
ندخّن سيجارة	هل يُسمح لنا
تنجزون واجباتكم	أرجوكم
انتهى المؤتمر في الساعة السابعة	أُعلن في القاهرة
يسافرون بالطائرة	يريد أصدقائي
نذهب معه	يجب علينا
يحضر إلينا	سأطلب منه
ستبحث هذه الاقتراحات	أكّدت الحكومة
ستبحث المشروع	أعلنت الحكومة
يفعلون ذلك	هل يُسمح لهم
نسافر معكم	يمكننا
يعودون إلى هنا	يأمل كلّ واحد منّا
توجد مشاكل	يعرف كلّهم
نغيّر البرنامج	لم نستطع
يسافرون إلى دمشق	طلب أعضاء الوفد
لا يفوز على خصمه	أخاف
يسافر الجميع إلى تلك القرية	اقترح مرافقنا
لم تصل الطائرة بعد	هل سمعتم
أفعل ذلك	هل يُسمح لي
يرحّب بضيوفنا الأجانب	طلبنا من المدير

لا نعرف ذلك	كان يعتقد
تفعلون ذلك	يجب عليكم
نسافر إلى هناك	نأمل
سيعقد الاجتماع بعد غد	علمت الجريدة
ستصل الطائرة في الساعة التاسعة	أكّدت المضيفة
تعلن برنامجها بعد شهرين	تريد الحكومة
ينجز واجباته وحده	أمكنه
أفعل ذلك	هل تطلب منّي
تلقّى الدعوة	أعلن الرئيس
يفعلون ذلك	لماذا تقترح
أنقله إلى هناك	يجب عليَّ
يزور معرض دمشق	رجا رئيس الوفد
سيُلغى البرنامج	يعرف جميعنا
لا نعرف ذلك	هل تعتقد
هو كسلان	هل لاحظت
أقدّم إليك صديقي	إسمح لي
تأتي إليَّ مساء اليوم	هل يمكنك
المرض انفلوينزا بسيطة	أكّد الطبيب
لا يصل الأصدقاء	هل تخاف
تفعل ذلك	يجب عليك
سافر أخوها إلى الخارج	علمت صديقتي
أنتم كسالى	نعرف
السفر إلى هناك ممنوع	متى سمعتَ
تعطيني هذا الكتاب	هل تستطيع
ذلك معروف	كنّا نعتقد
لم يكن الخبر صحيحاً	اتّضح بعد ذلك
يجتمعون يوم السبت	يريد الأصدقاء

G2 (Repetition) Answer the following questions with لا + لم + jussive and give reasons.

☞   هل اشتغلت صباح في المطعم؟

لا، لم تشتغل صباح في المطعم لأنّها كانت مريضة. ☜

هل اشتغلتم في هذه المصانع؟

هل اجتمعوا مع مدراء المعاهد؟

هل اجتمع الرئيس مع الوفود العربية؟

هل استغرق المؤتمر يومين؟

هل استغرقت المباراة ساعتين؟

هل استطعت أن تدبّر لنا الاستمارات؟

هل استطعت أن تستأجر بيتاً جديداً؟

هل استطاع مدير المعهد أن يجيب على كلّ الأسئلة؟

هل استطاع الوفد أن ينهي محادثاته؟

هل تمكّن البلد من أن يحقّق نهضة ثقافية؟

هل تمكّن الرئيس من أن يخرج من البلد بعد الحرب الأهلية؟

هل استأجروا سيّارة جيب؟

هل استأجرت صباح سيّارة كابريوليه؟

هل تلقّيتم الدعوة؟

هل تلقّيت رسالة من أمّك؟

هل تلقّت الوزارة الرسائل الرسمية؟

هل اشتركت في المباريات في كرة القدم؟

هل اشترك وزير الخارجية في هذا الاجتماع؟

هل اشترك الخبراء الألمان في المؤتمر الصحفي؟

C1 Prepare a list of fruits and vegetables based on the vocabulary of this lesson and the dictionary. The list is to be discussed and completed with your teacher.

C2 Prepare a dialogue based on Text 2 about shopping in the market for meat, fruit and vegetables.

Final Exercise:

1. Combine the following sentences in such a way that the second sentence becomes an objective or subject sentence introduced by أنْ/ أنَّ/ إنّ. Vocalize.

| سمعت أمس | أُلغيت الرحلة |
| أريد | أزوره يوم الأحد |

أجيب على هذا السؤال	لا أستطيع
سيزور وزير الخارجية الجزائر	أعلنت الوزارة
يصل إلى هدفه	أمل الرجل
يأتي صديقي اليوم	أعتقدُ
تنجز واجباتك	يجب عليك
تؤيد حكومته هذه الاقتراحات	أكّد رئيس الوفد
يزور مكتبة الدولة	طلب محمد
نتحدّث حول ذلك غداً	أقترحُ عليكم
صديقي مريض	علمتُ أمس
أنت مجتهد	أعرف
أفعل ذلك	لا يمكنني
ذهب إلى هناك	رأيتُ
تنجزون واجباتكم	أرجوكم
نذهب معه	يجب علينا
يحضر إلينا	سأطلب منه
ستبحث هذه الاقتراحات	أكّدت الحكومة
يفعلون ذلك	هل يُسمح لهم

2. Translate into Arabic. Vocalize أنْ /أنَّ .

I know that you will go there. I think that you don't have the time. I hope that he goes to the institute. He wants us to learn all the words. He couldn't sell the books. We didn't wish the students to work a lot. He must write a letter. We allow him to travel to Switzerland.

3. Answer the following questions with لم + لا + jussive.

هل اشتغلتم في هذه المصانع؟ هل اجتمع الرئيس مع الوفود العربية؟ هل استغرقت المباراة ساعتين؟ هل استأجروا سيّارة جيب؟ هل تلقّيتم الدعوة؟ هل تلقّيت رسالة من أمّك؟ هل تلقّت الوزارة الرسائل الرسمية؟ هل اشترك الخبراء في المؤتمر الصحفي؟ هل استطعت

أن تدبّر لنا الاستمارات؟ هل استطاع مدير المعهد أن يجيب على كلّ الأسئلة؟ هل تمكّـن البلد من أن يحقّق نهضة ثقافية؟

4. Translate the following newspaper report into Arabic.

A scientific symposium about the development prospects of agriculture in the Arab countries was held in Cairo last Tuesday. Delegations from all Arab countries as well as representatives of the FAO and the EU took part in the symposium. The participants discussed the development and diversification of agriculture, the problems of desertification, the fighting of plant diseases, the breeding of livestock and the possibilities of increasing the agricultural production of wheat, rye and corn.

The symposium issued a number of recommendations to solve the problems which the agriculture in these regions is confronted with. An agricultural fair was held along with the symposium, in which modern tractors, ploughs, pumps and a new specimen of high productivity seeds were shown.

1. The Participle

The infinitive (Lesson 22) and the participle are the two nominal forms of the Arabic verb. There are two participles:

the active participle (اِسْم الفاعِل) and the passive participle (اِسْم المفْعُول).

1.1. Patterns of the participle
1.1.1. Strong verbs
Basic Form:

The pattern of the active participle is: فاعِلٌ "doing, having done".

The one of the passive participle is: مفْعُولٌ "being done, having been done".

Derived Forms:

The **active participle** of all derived Forms has the prefix *mu-* and the sequence of vowels *a-i*.

The **passive participle** of all derived Forms has the prefix *mu-* and the sequence of vowels *a-a*.

The basic structure of the Forms given in the perfect tense is preserved. The sequence of vowels that follows the prefix is the same as is found in the imperfect tense of the active or passive voice, except for the active participle of Forms V and VI. Accordingly the following arises:

Form	passive participle	active participle
I	مَفْعُول	فاعِل
II	مُفَعَّل	مُفَعِّل
III	مُفَاعَل	مُفَاعِل
IV	مُفْعَل	مُفْعِل
V	مُتَفَعَّل	مُتَفَعِّل
VI	مُتَفَاعَل	مُتَفَاعِل
VII	مُنْفَعَل	مُنْفَعِل
VIII	مُفْتَعَل	مُفْتَعِل
X	مُسْتَفْعَل	مُسْتَفْعِل

The feminine form takes the ending ـة .

☞**A1**   Without auxiliary signs it is outwardly not distinguishable in Forms II to X whether the respective form is an active or a passive participle. Additional possibilities of confusion arise by the participles of Forms II and IV appearing in the same typeface.

1.1.2. There are some peculiarities in the participles of the defective verbs, as is the case in the perfect and imperfect tense. In the following, we only mention some patterns of the participle of Form I in which the underlying pattern is not easily identifiable. Tables 10, 11 (Appendix) provide a survey of all participles.

Form I	passive voice	active voice
verbs R$_2$ = و or ى	مَقُوم / مَبِيع / مَخُوف	قَائِم / بَائِع / خَائِف
verbs R$_3$ = و	مَدْعُوٌّ	داعٍ م دَاعِيَة def. الدَّاعِي م الدَّاعِيَة
verbs R$_3$ = ى	مَمْشِيٌّ / مُلْقِيٌّ	مَاشٍ / لَاقٍ

Forms II up to X	passive voice	active voice
verbs R$_3$ = و or ى	endings: -*āt* ـاة م -*an* ـىً definite: -*āt* اة ..أل م *ā*- ـَى ..أل	endings: -*in* ـٍ م -iya ـِيَة definite: ..أل م -iya ـِيَة ..أل ـِي

Regarding the declension of the words which terminate in -*in* and -*an* see Table 37 in the Appendix.

1.1.3. Plural form and form of intensity of the participles
1.1.3.1. Certain regularities can be discovered in the forming of the plural of the participles.

Form I: active participle / persons (often descriptions of occupations)	
m.	فَاعِل ج فَاعِلُون
f.	فَاعِلَة ج فَاعِلات
m.	فَاعِل ج فُعَّال
m.	فَاعِل ج فَعَلَة
seller	بَائِع ج بَائِعُون
driver, chauffeur	سَائِق ج سَائِقُون
exhibitor	عَارِض ج عَارِضُون

woman student	طَالِبَة ج طَالِبَات
female worker	عَامِلَة ج عَامِلات
merchant	تَاجِر ج تُجَّار
passenger	رَاكِب ج رُكَّاب
tourist	سَائِح ج سُيَّاح
student	طَالِب ج طُلَّاب
worker	عَامِل ج عُمَّال
seller	بَائِع ج بَاعَة > (بَيَعَة)
student	طَالِب ج طَلَبَة

Form I: active participle / non-persons		
m.		فَاعِل ج فَاعِلات
f.		فَاعِلَة ج فَاعِلات
m.		فَاعِل ج فَوَاعِلُ
f.		فَاعِلَة ج فَوَاعِلُ
duty, task		وَاجِب ج وَاجِبَات
university		جَامِعَة ج جَامِعَات
family		عَائِلَة ج عَائِلات
side		جَانِب ج جَوَانِبُ
stamp		طَابِع ج طَوَابِعُ
circle		دَائِرَة ج دَوَائِرُ
capital city		عَاصِمَة ج عَوَاصِمُ
fruit(s)		فَاكِهَة ج فَوَاكِهُ
list		قَائِمَة ج قَوَائِمُ

Form I: passive participle / persons	
m.	مَفْعُول ج مَفْعُولُون
f.	مَفْعُولَة ج مَفْعُولات
responsible person, official (m.)	مَسْؤُول ج مَسْؤُولُونَ
responsible person, official (f.)	مَسْؤُولَة ج مَسْؤُولات

Form I: passive participle / non-persons	
m.	مَفْعُول ج مَفْعُولات / مَفْعُول ج مَفَاعِيلُ
drink	مَشْرُوب ج مَشْرُوبَات
project, plan	مَشْرُوع ج مَشْرُوعَات ومَشَارِيعُ

Derived Forms:

The active or passive participles which denote persons have the sound masculine or feminine plural.

teacher	مُعَلِّم ج مُعَلِّمُونَ
official/officer/civil servant	مُوَظَّف ج مُوَظَّفُونَ
companion, attendant	مُرَافِقٌ ج مُرَافِقُونَ
viewer/spectator/onlooker	مُتَفَرِّج ج مُتَفَرِّجُونَ
woman teacher	مُعَلِّمَة ج مُعَلِّمَات
nurse	مُمَرِّضَة ج مُمَرِّضَات
stewardess	مُضِيفَة ج مُضِيفَات

☞A2 Some participles of Form IV have a broken plural as well, e.g. مُدَراءُ > مُدِير in addition to مُدِيرُون "director".

The active or passive participles which denote non-persons have the sound feminine plural, regardless of whether they are used in the masculine or feminine form in the singular.

alarm clock	مُنَبِّه ج مُنَبِّهَات
representative team	مُنْتَخَب ج مُنْتَخَبَات

👆**A3** Some participles of Form IV have a broken plural as well, e.g. "problem" مُشْكِل and مُشْكِلة with the plural مَشاكِلُ in addition to مُشْكِلات.

1.1.3.2. The pattern of intensity of the active participle فاعِل is فَعّال

Originally it expressed intensive and routine actions, but it is hardly productive any more nowadays.

effective, efficacious	فَعّال
constructive	بَنّاء
jet plane	طائِرَة نَفّاثَة

Nouns of this structure, which are derived both from verbs and from nouns, constitute descriptions of occupations.

seaman	بَحّار (> بَحْر)
gatekeeper	بَوّاب (> باب)
porter/carrier	حَمّال (> حَمَلَ)
money changer	صَرّاف (> صَرَفَ)

All these words have the sound masculine plural.

The feminine form فَعّالة denotes appliances and vehicles:

refrigerator	بَرّادَة
bicycle	دَرّاجَة
earphone, (telephone) receiver	سَمّاعَة (> سَمِعَ)
car	سَيّارَة (> سارَ)
(can) opener	فَتّاحَة (> فَتَحَ)
lighter	قَدّاحَة/ ولاّعة
glasses	نَظّارَة (> نَظَرَ)

All these words have the sound feminine plural.

1.2. The Usage of the Participles

The participle combines the meaning of the verb with the formal properties of the noun. Its nominal structure also determines its syntactic use:

noun   = subject, object and predicate complement and
adjective = attributive adjunct and predicate complement.

1.2.1. Most participles are lexicalized as adjectives or nouns, i.e. they are pure nouns without any verbal characteristics.
Some participles belong to the categories both of adjective and of noun.

Adjective: بَارِد   cold

(active part., Form I, root: ب – ر – د)

مَقْبُول   acceptable

(passive part., Form I, root: ق – ب – ل)

مُعْتَدِل   moderate/temperate

(active part., Form VIII, root: ع – د – ل)

noun: طَابِع   stamp

(active part., Form I, root: ط – ب – ع)

مُوَظَّف   official/officer/civil servant

(passive part., Form II, root: و – ظ – ف)

مُنْتَخَب   representative team

(passive part., Form VIII, root: ن – خ – ب)

adjective عَامِل   active;

and noun: worker, factor

(active part., Form I, root: ع – م – ل)

سَائِر   remaining; rest

(active part., Form I, root: س – ء – ر)

مَشْرُوع   legitimate; project

(passive part., Form I, root: ش – ر – ع)

✍A4 Participles which are lexically fixed as nouns have not lost their ability of being used as participles in the strict sense of the meaning, which has been derived from the verb. طالب "student" can also mean "claimer/claimant; someone who claims (something)". Thus, it says on some extracts from Arabic registers هذا المُسْتخْرَج يُعْطَى لكلِّ طالب "this extract is given to anybody who claims (it) (< to any claimer)".

1.2.2. Active and passive participles are frequently used in the Arabic language for expressing so-called shortened relative clauses by taking a subject or an object while being employed as attributive adjuncts related to nouns. Adjectives are occasionally found in such constructions as well.

Rule:

If the antecedent is definite, the participle (or the adjective) also takes the article; if it is indefinite, the participle (or the adjective) does not take an article either. If the subject of the shortened relative clause is not identical with the antecedent, the following rule of agreement applies: The participle (or adjective) agrees with the antecedent in case and state, and with the subject of the relative clause in gender and number. In this connection, naturally, the fact must be observed again that plurals of non-persons are regarded as feminine singulars.

The direct object, when following the active participle employed in a relative way, either takes on the accusative (i.e. the verbal government is preserved) or is introduced by the preposition لِ. If the verb governs an object by means of a preposition, this prepositional government is also preserved with the participle.

A5 Passive participles of verbs with a prepositional government accordingly do not express the gender by the participle, but by the preposition + affixed pronoun:

ٱلْبَضَائِعُ الْمَرْغُوبُ فِيهَا   the desired goods

This construction is analogous to the passive construction of verbs with a prepositional government, which was dealt with in Lesson 19.

Active participle (the subject being the same):

the event, ending or having ended at 10 o'clock = the event which ends or ended at 10 o'clock	أَلْحَفْلَةُ الْمُنْتَهِيَةُ فِي السَّاعَةِ الْعَاشِرَةِ

The basis of the shortened form   الحفلة المنتهية في الساعة العاشرة

is a relative clause, which is either

الحفلةُ الّتي تَنْتَهِي في الساعة العاشرة or الحفلةُ الّتي اِنْتَهَتْ في الساعة العاشرة.

As the participles per se do not express a tense in Arabic language, it must be decided by the context which temporal reference is given in particular cases.

Active participle (the subject not being the same):

the delegation the visit of which is coming to an end or has come to an end	أَلْوَفْدُ الْمُنْتَهِيَةُ زِيَارَتُهُ

The underlying relative clause is either

أَلْوَفْدُ الّذي انْتَهَتْ زِيَارَتُهُ or الْوَفْدُ الّذي تَنْتَهِي زِيَارَتُهُ

Passive participle (the subject being the same):

the books existing with me = the books which are or were existing with me	أَلْكُتُبُ الْمَوْجُودَةُ عِنْدِي

Underlying relative clause:

الْكُتُبُ الّتي كَانَتْ تُوجَدُ عِنْدِي or أَلْكُتُبُ الّتي تُوجَدُ عِنْدِي

| the desired goods = the goods which are desired | أَلْبَضَائِعُ الْمَرْغُوبُ فِيهَا |

Underlying relative clause:

أَلْبَضَائِعُ الّتِي يُرْغَبُ فِيها

Passive participle (the subject not being the same):

| the man whose books are sold or have been sold | أَلرَّجُلُ الْمَبِيعَةُ كُتُبُهُ |

Underlying relative clause:

أَلرَّجُلُ الّذِي بِيعَتْ كُتُبُهُ or الرَّجُلُ الّذِي تُبَاعُ كُتُبُهُ

1.2.3. The active and the passive participle may be a nominal predicate in the principal clause. It is frequently difficult to differentiate when the participle and when the corresponding verb must be used. Often both are interchangeable.

a)	He is walking in the street. The verbal sentence with the same meaning is:	هُوَ مَاشٍ فِي الشَّارِعِ. = (هو) يَمْشِي فِي الشَّارِعِ.
b)	She travels to Berlin for a month.	هِيَ مُسَافِرَةٌ إلى لندن لِمُدَّةِ شَهْرٍ. = (هي) تُسَافِرُ إلى لندن لِمُدَّةِ شَهْرٍ.
c)	This letter was written a week ago.	هَذِهِ الرِّسَالَةُ مَكْتُوبَةٌ قَبْلَ أُسْبُوعٍ. = هَذِهِ الرِّسَالَةُ كُتِبَتْ قَبْلَ أُسْبُوعٍ.
d)	He is sleeping (just now). He is sleeping/ falling asleep.	هُوَ نَائِمٌ. هُوَ يَنَامُ.

☝**A6** As to the use of the participle as a nominal predicate:
1. With respect to the verbs which indicate an event (cf. examples a-c), the participle and the finite verb form are interchangeable and are consequently to be regarded as stylistic variants. The finite verb form occurs more frequently and therefore should be learned and used actively by the student.
2. As to the verbs which indicate a state, the participle or an adjective derived from the same verb is preferred, accordingly:
جادت البضاعة The merchandise is (was) good. instead of كانت البضاعة جيدة.
3. With regard to the verbs which indicate both an event and a state, e.g. قام "to stand up" and "to stand", جلس "to sit down" and "to sit", رقد "to lie down to rest/to go to bed, to abate/to subside" and "to lie", the finite verbal form indicates the event, the participle indicates the state; consequently:

| He is standing. | هُوَ قَائِمٌ. | He was standing. | كَانَ قَائِماً. |
| He stands up. | (هو) يَقُومُ. | He stood up. | (هو) قَامَ. |

1.2.4. Adjectives and participles employed as adjectives are often used as the 1st term of a genitive construction the 2nd term of which is a definite noun.

An *Iḍāfa* constructed in this way is seen as a (compound) adjective, which is nearly always employed as an attributive adjunct.

In accordance with the agreement in state, which exists between the noun and the attributive adjunct that belongs to it, the 1st term of this genitive construction (i.e. the adjective or the participle) also takes the article if the noun is definite.

The construction discussed here is called a *False Iḍāfa* because of the peculiarity of its construction in comparison with the *Iḍāfa* proper (the 1st and the 2nd term of which are nouns).

different/various (active part., Form VIII, root: خ – ل – ف)	مُخْتَلِف
kind	نَوْع ج أَنْوَاع
of various kinds (*False Iḍāfa*)	مُخْتَلِفُ الأَنْوَاعِ
problems of various kinds	مَشَاكِلُ مُخْتَلِفَةُ الأَنْوَاعِ
the problems of various kinds	أَلْمَشَاكِلُ الْمُخْتَلِفَةُ الأَنْوَاعِ

In this context it is often not possible to render the 2nd term of the genitive construction as an adjective when translating into English, as no adjective is formed out of the noun in the English language. In such cases the genitive construction is translated by a prepositional phrase or by a single word.

low	مُنْخَفِض
price	سِعْر
goods of a low price	بَضَائِعُ مُنْخَفِضَةُ السِّعْرِ
long, large/tall	طَوِيل
short, small/short (of stature)	قَصِير
middle/medium	مُتَوَسِّط
stature, build	قَامَة
a man of a tall build, a tall man	رَجُلٌ طَوِيلُ الْقَامَةِ
a man of short stature	رَجُلٌ قَصِيرُ الْقَامَةِ
a man of medium height	رَجُلٌ مُتَوَسِّطُ الْقَامَةِ

1.2.5. Not all genitive constructions, the 1st term of which is an adjective or a participle used as an adjective and the 2nd term of which is a noun, are *False Iḍāfas*. This can be determined by the fact that they do not fulfill the function of an attributive adjunct like the *False Iḍāfas* do, but that they express the relationship noun - attributive adjective with the attributive adjunct preceding the noun here. The nature of this construction is explained by the possibility of transforming an adjective or a participle into a noun that is used or is in general use as an adjective, which is inherent in Arabic.

The number of these constructions, which do not have a specific name, is relatively small, as only a few adjectives or participles employed as adjectives are used as their 1st terms (see, however, the construction of the *Elative*, Lesson 25, Gr 1.2.).

👉**A7** Constructions which contain a participle or adjective that is used as a noun anyway (جميع "all, entirety", سائر "rest", مُعْظَم "the majority") are not expressly listed here.

the various countries	مُخْتَلِفُ الْبُلْدَان
in the various countries	في مُخْتَلِفِ الْبُلْدَان
excellent/exquisite, outstanding (active part., Form I, root: ف – و – ق)	فَائِق
Yours faithfully/Yours very truly	مع فَائِقِ الإِحْتِرَام
clear, pure, sincere/frank/candid (active part., Form I, root: خ – ل – ص)	خَالِص
with sincere esteem / appreciation	مع خَالِصِ التَّقْدِير
from times of old, from time immemorial	مُنْذُ قَدِيمِ الزَّمَان

1.2.6. Finally there are genitive constructions in which a noun as the 1st term is followed by an adjective as the 2nd term. They are no *False Iḍāfas*, although they fulfill the function of an attributive adjunct and are to be regarded as compound adjectives with respect to the content of the words, like in the latter (1.2.4.). The agreement in state is expressed by the 2nd term of the genitive construction. Only genitive constructions occur, the 1st term of which is constituted by the following nouns respectively:

non-/un-/in-/dis- (occurs very frequently)	غَيْر
resemblance/similarity/ likeness, semi-	شِبْه
semi-, half	نِصْف
semi-	شِبْه

feudal	إِقْطَاعِي
semi-feudal	شِبْهُ إِقْطَاعِي
semi-feudal relations	عَلاقَاتٌ شِبْهُ إِقْطَاعِيّةٍ
the semi-feudal relations	أَلْعَلاقَاتُ شِبْهُ الإقْطَاعِيّةِ
semi-official/officious	شِبْهُ رَسْمِي
semi-finished products	مُنْتَجَاتٌ نِصْفُ مَصْنُوعَةٍ
unusual	غَيْرُ اعْتِيَادِيّ

☞**A8** These three nouns have practically become semi-prefixes; the genitive constructions constructed by them are equivalent to the English prefix compounds. In careless style, it can even be observed that the article الـ is not put in front of the 2nd term, as would be grammatically correct, but in front of the 1st term of this combination of words.

☞**A9** The noun غَيْرٌ is used to negate nouns, adjectives and participles. The noun عَدَمٌ (non-existence) is used to negate a following verbal noun, forming with it an *Iḍāfa*, and is translated "no, non-, in-, dis-" عَدَمُ الإنْحِيازِ (non-alignment), عَدَمُ الاهْتِمامِ (inattention, indifference) etc.

1.2.7. The adjective and the participle (nearly exclusively the passive participle) also serve the purpose of rendering impersonal expressions such as in the construction مِنَ الـ ... "it is ..." at the beginning of the sentence.

participle:

it is (well-)known	مِنَ الْمَعْرُوفِ
it is usual/customary/it is (a) common practice	مِنَ الْمَألُوفِ
it is probable/likely, it is assumed	مِنَ الْمُحْتَمَلِ
it is to be expected	مِنَ الْمُنْتَظَرِ / مِن الْمُتَوَقَّعِ

adjective:

it is natural	مِنَ الطَّبِيعِيّ
it is necessary	مِنَ الضَّرُورِيّ
it is strange, odd	مِنَ الْغَرِيبِ
it is worth mentioning that ...	مِنَ الْجَدِيرِ بالذِّكْرِ

Such constructions are negated by means of لَيسَ.

V

influence on, over	تأْثير ج ات في	semi-agreed upon	شبهُ مُتَّفَق عليه
postponing	تأْجيل	to promote sth. II	شجَّع (يُشجِّعُ) هـ
(prep.) with respect to, regarding	إزاءَ	to be formed V	تشكَّل (يتشكَّلُ)
Italy	إيْطاليا	sheikdom	مشْيَخَة ج مشايخ
coalition	ائْتِلافيّ	spreading	إشاعة
empire	إمبراطورية ج ـات	fight, struggle	صراع ج ـات
Mediterranean	البحْرُ الأبْيضُ المُتوسِّط	to spend sth. on	صرف (يصرفُ) هـ على
unavoidable, indispensable	لا بُدَّ مِن	queue, line	صفّ ج صُفوف
outstanding	بارز	crusade	صليبيّ ج ـون
slow	بطيء	interest	مصْلَحة ج مصالحُ
technical	تكْنيكيّ	production	صنع
society	مُجْتمع ج ـات	damage	ضرر ج أضْرار
island	جزيرة ج جُزُر	disturbance, disorder	اضطِراب ج ـات
answering	إجابة على	guarantee	ضمان ج ـات
nature/essential	جوْهر /جوْهريّ	social security	الضمان الاجْتِماعيّ
Ethiopian, Abyssinian	حبشِيّ ج أحْباش	narrow, tight	ضيِّق
to restrict, to limit	حدَّ (يحُدُّ) من	ambition (pejorative)	مطْمع ج مطامعُ
severity, fierceness	حِدَّة	developing	مُتطوِّر
challenge	تحدٍّ ج تحدِّيات	Ottoman	عُثمانيّ ج ـون
here: to happen	حصَل	acceleration	تعْجيل
probably, likely	من المُحْتمل	to be exposed to V	تعرَّض (يتعرَّضُ) ل
danger, importance	خطورة	it is known	من المعْروفِ
constitution	دُسْتور ج دساتيرُ	to come (directly) after IV	أعْقب (يُعْقِبُ) هـ/على
role, part	دوْر ج أدْوار	to believe sth. VIII	اعْتقد (يعْتقِدُ) هـ
despite, in spite of	بالرَّغْمِ مِن	colonial	اسْتِعْماريّ
Roman	رُومانيّ ج رُومان	it is strange	من الغريبِ
time	زمان ج أزْمِنة	attack, raid, invasion	غزْوة ج غزوات
negative, passive	سلْبيّ	exploitation	اسْتِغْلال
weapon	سِلاح ج أسْلِحة	closed	مُغْلق
Sultanate	سلْطنة ج ـات	group, (social) strata	فِئة ج ـات
semi-	شِبْهُ		

the Persians	ج الفُرْس	to do damage to	ألْحق أضْراراً بـ
difference	فارق ج فوارقُ	to play sth.	لعِب (يلْعَبُ) هـ
detail	تفْصِيل ج تفاصِيلُ	to become manifest (in)	V تمثّل (يتمثّلُ) في
thanks to, owing to	بفضْل	continuity	اِسْتِمْرار
negotiations	ج مُفاوضات	the Mongol(ian)s	ج الـمُغْول
Phoenician	فِينِيقيّ ج ـون	wave	موج ج أمْواج
tribal	قبليّ	successful	ناجِح
stability	اِسْتِقرار	person, inhabitant	نسمة ج نسمات
continent	قارّة ج ات	post, office	منصِب ج مناصِبُ
division, partition	تقسِيم ج ـات	it is expected	من الـمُنتظر
regional, country	قُطْريّ	upswing	نهْضة ج ـات
independence	اِسْتِقْلال	to intend (to do) sth.	نـوَى (ينْوِي) هـ
coup (d'état), revolt	اِنْقِلاب ج ـات	decline, decay	اِنهِيار
traditional	تقْلِيديّ	to turn to	VIII اِتّجه (يتّجهُ) إلى
leadership, leading	قِيادِيّ	unification	توْحِيد
here: to come into being, to emerge	قام هـ	budget	مِيزانيّة
armed forces	قُوّات مُسلّحة	ability, strength, power	وُسْع
working	كادِح ج ـون	with all my strength	بكلِّ ما في وُسعِي
rank, position	مكانة ج ـات	it is expected	من الـمُتوقّع أنَّ
remark	مُلاحظة	to take sth. over	V تولّى (يتولّى) هـ
to add sth. to	IV ألْحق (يُلْحِقُ) هـ بـ		

الأنظمة السياسية في العالم العربي

Text 1

نجد في العالم العربي حتى اليوم دولاً ذات أنظمة سياسية مختلفة كالجمهوريـات والممـالك والسلطنات والمشايخ وقد قامت هـذه الـدول على أسـاس التقسيمات السياسية الـتي حصلت بعـد انهيـار الإمبراطوريـة العثمانيـة والنظام الاستعماري في إفريقيا والشـرق الأوسط.

وتعرّضت المنطقة العربيـة منـذ قديـم الزمـان لموجـات مـن الحـروب والغـزوات قـام بهـا الأحباش والفرس والفينيقيون واليونان والرومان والصليبيون والمغول والعثمانيون وأعقبهـا

تدخل الدول الأوربية أي فرنسا وبريطانيا وإيطاليا. وحصلت غالبية الدول العربية على استقلالها الوطني بعد الحربين العالميتين الأولى والثانية.

وتمكنت غالبية الدول العربية بفضل ثرواتها البترولية من أن تحقّق نهضة اقتصادية وتكنيكية وتقدُّماً لا بأس به في مجال التعليم والصحّة. وبالرغم من هذه النجاحات ما زالت هناك فوارق كبيرة في تنظيم هذه المجتمعات على أساس ديمقراطي والمصالح القطرية والقبلية الضيّقة لا تزال تلعب دوراً جوهرياً فيها يحدّ من تطورها. ويمكن ملاحظة ذلك في التطور البطيء في الحياة البرلمانية ودساتير بعض هذه الدول.

هذا وصرفت حكومات بعض البلدان العربية مبالغ ضخمة على شراء الأسلحة ووصلت هذه المبالغ أحياناً إلى ٦٠٪ من ميزانية هذه الدول. إن هذا الإنفاق العسكري الضخم ألحق أضراراً بالغة الخطورة بالاستقرار الاقتصادي والاجتماعي فيها وأعطى للعسكريين مكانة بارزة في صنع القرار السياسي والكثيرون من رؤساء الدول العربية وفئاتها القيادية تولّوا الحكم على أساس انقلابات عسكرية أو استغلال مناصبهم في القوات المسلحة. ومن المتوقع أن الصراع بين القوى الديمقراطية والتقليدية سيزداد حدةً في السنوات القادمة.

مقابلة صحفية   Text 2

الصحفية: من المعروف أنّكم تشجّعون المفاوضات مع المعارضة حول مسألة الضمان الاجتماعي المرغوب فيه من قبل كافّة قطاعات الشعب الكادحة، ما هو موقف الأحزاب الأخرى في الحكومة الائتلافية من هذه المفاوضات؟

الرئيس: من المحتمل أنّ أحزاب الائتلاف الأخرى ستؤيّد مقترحاتي شبه المتّفق عليها وأنّنا سنقرّ قانون الضمان الاجتماعي في جلسة البرلمان القادمة.

الصحفية: أ ليس من الغريب أنّكم تنوون إعادة بناء قطاع النفط الذي أصبح قطاعاً ناجحاً في السنوات الأخيرة؟

الرئيس: صحيح أنّ هذا القطاع تطوّر بشكل إيجابي في السنوات الأخيرة وأرى أنّه لاستمرار هذا التطوُّر الإيجابي لا بد من إعادة بناء هذا القطاع الهامّ في اقتصادنا الوطني.

الصحفية: من المنتظر أنّكـم تقومـون بجولـة في المنطقـة لمناقشـة مختلـف جوانـب السياسـة الخارجية مع زملائكم العرب. ما هي النتائج التي تتوقّعونها؟

الرئيس: إنّني سـأعمل بكلّ مـا في وسـعي علـى توحيـد الصـفّ العربـيّ إزاء مختلـف التحدّيات التي تواجهها الأمّة العربية وخاصّة الاقتصادية منها.

الصحفية: أ لا تعتقدون أنّ تـأجيل هـذه الجولـة للمـرّة الخامسـة قـد يـؤدّي إلى إشـاعة الشكوك والاضطرابات في بقية البلدان العربية؟

الرئيس: لا أعتقد ذلك لأنّني علـى اتّصال مستمرّ مـع رؤسـاء البلـدان الشقيقة والـرأي المشترك يتمثّـل في المثل العربي ((كلّ تأخير فيـه خيـر)) أي تعجيـل الأمـور قـد يؤدّي إلى نتائج عكسية أو سلبية.

الصحفية: أشكركم على هذه التصريحات والأجوبة الواضحة وعلى المعلومات القيّمة.

Exercises:

L1 Change the subject (always a participle) from singular to plural.

☞   انتهى الواجب.   >   انتهت الواجبات.

☞   واجبنا معروف.   >   واجباتنا معروفة.

المشروع معروف.

إنطلقت الطائرة المصرية في الساعة الثالثة.

حضر المترجم العربي الحفلة.

الموظّف المسؤول مريض.

إنّ المدير يجتمع بنا غداً.

أعرف أنّ التاجر الإنكليزي سيجيء إلى ألمانيا.

المرافق السوري موجود.

الراكب اليوناني ترك الطائرة.

الزائر مسرور.

السائق اللبناني شاطر.

هل الطالب كسلان؟

لا، الطالب مجتهد.

هذا العامل موجود.

كان كلّ متفرّج يتوقّع مباراة ممتازة.

إنّ الممرِّضة تشتغل في المستشفى.

المنتخب البرازيلي قوي.

هذا الموضوع هامّ جدّاً.

L2 One student transforms the sentences in L1 into interrogative sentences and the other students answer with "No" and give reasons.

☞   المشروع معروف.   >   هل المشروع معروف؟

☞   لا، المشروع ليس معروفاً لأنه مشروع صغير.

L3 (Homework) Look up all participles in Lessons 18-21 and make a list separating the active and the passive participles. Find out the underlying Form and form a sentence with each.

L4 (Repetition) Transform the following sentences into the passive voice.

☞   أقام الرئيس حفلة عشاء. > أقيمت حفلة عشاء.

غيّر المدير البرنامج.

عقد الخبراء المؤتمر في السنة الماضية.

إستنتج الخبراء من ذلك أن الوضع متغيِّر.

أرسل صديقي إليّ بطاقة من القاهرة.

يغيّر بعض الأشخاص البرامج كلّ يوم.

دعوت الصديق لزيارة مدينتي.

يجري الوفد المحادثات في وزارة الخارجية.

رجونا أحمد أن يجتمع بنا.

يسلّم صالح الهدية غداً.

أضاف الرئيس بعض الكلمات.

رجونا صباح أن تسافر إلى الخارج.

ألغى الاصدقاء الموعد.

قال له إن الطلاب ينامون في دروسه.

يسمّي الأب ابنه سالماً.

G1 Form the participles of the following verbs. Find out beforehand the underlying Form and write the usual Roman number. Resort to the dictionary to find out the root and the meaning.

☞   I دام = دائم = lasting

a) active participle

سار، قام، دعا، طلب، سكن، علّم، تفرّج، اعتـدل، اشتغل، اختلـف، توسّـط، جلـس، عطل، جمع، ساق، قال، ركب، سافر، انتهى، خدم، احتاج، مشـى، وقـع، تبـع، رافـق، ساح، خلق، زاد، جاوز، خرج، دخل، حدث

b) passive participle

عرف، احتمل، شهر، قال، أقام، شرب، أكل، اشترك، قدّم، شـرع، وجـد، قبـل، دفـع، رغب، سأل، اجتمع، اتّصل

G2 Transform the shortened relative clause into an attributive relative clause.

☞   الأشياء الموجودة في غرفتي >   الأشياء التي توجد في غرفتي

الجزر الواقعة في البحر الأبيض المتوسّط

الطالبة النائمة في الدرس

الناس الخائفون من السفر بالطائرة

القطارات الواقفة في المحطّة

في المطار وفود عائدة إلى بلادها

الأشياء الموضوعة في الخزانة

البضائع المعروضة في المخازن

المؤتمر المنعقد في بيروت

الهدايا المسلّمة لعلي

الجزر المسماة بـ"الجزر الألف"

اجتمعت بالطلاّب الموفدين إلى الخارج

السياسيون المدعوّون لزيارة بلدنا

البطاقة المرسلة إليّ

الرسائل المكتوبة أمس

الحفلة المنتهية في الساعة الرابعة

الحفلة المبتدئة في الساعة الثانية

الاستمارات المطلوبة منّا

الطائرة المتأخّرة ساعة واحدة

الوفود المجتمعة في القاعة البيضاء

الكلمات المسجّلة في المؤتمر

مع العارضين المشتركين في المعرض

اقتصاد البلد المتطوّر بسرعة

التجّار المعبّرون عن آرائهم

المعرض المغلقة أبوابه

الوضع المتغيّر من ساعة إلى ساعة

البضائع المبيعة إلى الخارج

G3 Transform the relative clause into a shortened relative clause.

☞   الطالبة التي تسافر إلى بيروت   >   الطالبة المسافرة إلى بيروت

الوزير الذي يقيم حفلة العشاء

هي طائرة تصل في الساعة الواحدة

الفتاة التي تمشي في الشارع

الرجال الذين يتفرّجون على مباراة كرة القدم

الآثار التي توجد في سوريا في كل مكان

الانسان الذي يخلق حياته الجديدة

الجمهورية العربية السورية التي تقع في القارّة الآسيوية

سوريا التي يزيد عدد سكّانها عن ٦ ملايين نسمة

سوريا التي حصلت على استقلالها بعد الحرب العالمية الثانية

هي سيّارة تعود لوزارة المواصلات

الفرقة التي فازت على خصمه

معلّمي الذي يحتاج إلى سيّارة جديدة

الكلمات التي ألقيت في المؤتمر

البضائع التي تباع في ذلك المخزن

الحفلة التي أقيمت أمس

الكتب التي توجد في المكتبة

G4 Insert the proper participle out of the following.

أ)   ممنوع

ب)   مسموح

ج)   مفتوح

د)   معروف

هـ)   مشهور

و)   موجود

Repeat the sentence and use the personal pronoun instead of the subject or the affixed pronoun instead of the 2nd term of the *Iḍāfa*.

☞ examples with (د

☜   هذا الخبر ...

☜   هذا الخبر معروف. – هو معروف.

☜   تفاصيل الاجتماع ...

☜   تفاصيل الاجتماع معروفة. – تفاصيله معروفة.

أ)

الدخول ...

البرنامج ...

المساومة ...

المباراة ...

زيارة المريض ...

هذه الجرائد ...

ب)

تسجيل الكلمة ...

اجتماع الطلّاب ...

إقامة الحفلة ...

زيارة تلك الآثار ...

ج)

المخازن ... حتى الساعة السابعة

المصرف ... حتى الساعة الخامسة

المكتبة ... كل يوم

مطاعم المدينة ... الآن

أبواب المباني ... ابتداء من الساعة الثامنة

د)

هذه المشاكل ... عند الجميع

التفاصيل ... منذ وقت طويل

واجباتهم ...

قضايا العرب الوطنية ... في العالم

هذه المواعيد ...

مشاريع الحكومة ...

هـ)

جامعتنا ... منذ ٥٠٠ عام

مباني المدينة ... بجمالها

مسرح العاصمة ... بجماله

مكتبة الدولة ... في العالم كله

و)

الفواكه ... في المخازن

المأكولات ... عندنا

المشروبات ... عندكم

النقود اللازمة ...

الموظّفون المسؤولون ...

الاستمارات اللازمة ...

C1 The teacher explains the possibilities of apologizing or to expressing regret using the following collocations:

to excuse so., sth.	أَعْذَرَ ه / هـ
to apologize for	اِعْتَذَرَ مِن / عَن
I am sorry.	أنا مُتَأَسِّف.
Pardon me! Excuse me!	عَفْواً
Don't be angry with me!	لا تُؤَاخِذْني
I beg to be excused for ...	أَرْجو الاِعْتِذَار عن ...

to regret sth., to feel sorry for	أسِف ل / على
I am sorry that ...	أنا آسِف أنْ .../ أنا مُتَأسِّف أنْ...
unfortunately	مع الأسَف/ لِلأسَف
much to my regret, I am very sorry	مع الأسَفِ الشَّدِيد
unfortunately, it is a pity	من المُؤْسِف
unfortunately	لِسُوء الحَظ

Apologize making up a "lame excuse" for
a) bad handwriting
b) the numerous mistakes in the exercise
c) your coming too late etc.

C2 Prepare an interview based on Text 2 with the president of an Arab university, or a famous scholar or another student about the problems of higher education.

Final Exercise:
1. Form the following:
a) the active participle

اشتغل، اختلف، توسّط، جلس، عطل، جمع، ساق، قال، ركب، قال، سافر، انتهى، خدم، احتاج، مشى، وقع، تبع، رافق، ساح، خلق، زاد، جاوز، خرج، دخل، حدث، سار، قام، دعا، طلب، سكن، علّم، تفرّج، اعتدل

b) the passive participle

اشترك، قدّم، شرع، وجد، قبل، دفع، رغب، سأل، عرف، احتمل، شهر، قال، أقام، شرب، أكل

2. Transform the shortened relative clause into an attributive relative clause.

الجزر الواقعة في البحر الأبيض المتوسّط / الطالبة النائمة في الدرس / الناس الخائفون من السفر بالطائرة / القطارات الواقفة في المحطّة / في المطار وفود عائدة إلى بلادها / الأشياء الموضوعة في الخزانة / البضائع المعروضة في المخازن / المؤتمر المنعقد في بيروت / الهدايا المسلّمة لعلي / الجزر المسماة بـ"الجزر الألف" / اجتمعت بالطلاب الموفدين إلى الخارج / السياسيون المدعوّون لزيارة بلدنا / البطاقة المرسلة إليّ / الرسائل المكتوبة أمس / الحفلة المنتهية في الساعة الرابعة / الحفلة المبتدئة في الساعة الثانية / الاستمارات المطلوبة منّا /

الطائرة المتأخّرة ساعة واحدة / الوفود المجتمعة في القاعة البيضاء / الكلمـات المسـجّلة في المؤتمر / مع العـارضين المشـتركين في المعـرض / اقتصـاد البلـد المتطـوّر بسـرعة / التجّـار المعبّرون عن آرائهم / المعرض المغلقة أبوابه / الوضع المتغّير من ساعة إلى ساعة

3. Transform the relative clause into a shortened relative clause.

الوزير الذي يقيم حفلة العشاء / الفتاة التي تمشي في الشـارع / الرجـال الذيـن يتفرّجـون على مباراة كرة القدم / الآثار التي توجد في سوريا في كل مكان / الانسـان الـذي يخلـق حياته الجديدة / الجمهورية العربية السورية التي تقع في القارّة الآسيوية / سوريا التي يزيـد عدد سكانها عن ٦ ملايين نسمة / سوريا التي حصلت على استقلالها بعد الحرب العالمية الثانية / هي سيّارة تعود لوزارة المواصلات / الفرقـة الـتي فـازت على خصمـه / معلّمـي الذي يحتاج إلى سيّارة جديدة / الكلمات التي ألقيـت في المؤتمر / البضـائع الـتي تبـاع في ذلك المخزن / الحفلة التي أقيمت أمس

4. Translate into Arabic.

In the Arab world, we find republics, monarchies, sultanates, emirates and sheikdoms. Most Arab countries gained their national independence after World War I and II. Some Arab states were able to accomplish a considerable economic and technical upswing owing to their oil resources. The differences between these countries in organizing their societies on a democratic base are still very large. The governments of some of these countries spend 50% of the budget on weapons. The conflict between democratic and traditional forces will become more severe (*lit.*: increase in severity / fierceness).

1. The Infinitive (أَلْمَصْدَر)

The infinitive is one of the two nominal forms of the Arabic verb.

1.1. The form

1.1.1. In Form I, there are more than 40 different patterns of the infinitive, of which one or several can belong to a verb.

The two infinitives which occur most frequently are:

فَعْلٌ (< فَعَلَ mostly transitive verbs):

and (بَاعَ >) بَيْع، (نَامَ >) نَوْم، (شَرَحَ >) شَرْح، (عَرَضَ >) عَرْض)

فُعُولٌ (< فَعَلَ or فَعِلَ mostly intransitive verbs):

(حَصَلَ >) حُصُول، (صَعِدَ >) صُعُود، (دَخَلَ >) دُخُول، (وَصَلَ >) وُصُول)

☞**A1** In addition to the imperfect tense, the glossary at the end of the book provides the infinitives of all verbs of Form I in the indefinite accusative according to the Arabic tradition. They will only be listed there if they are not lexicalized and do not appear in the texts.

1.1.2. The derived Forms have only one infinitive with few exceptions.

II	III	IV	V
تَفْعِيل	مُفَاعَلَة / فِعَال	إِفْعَال	تَفَعُّل
VI	VII	VIII	X
تَفَاعُل	اِنْفِعَال	اِفْتِعَال	اِسْتِفْعَال

In Form III مُفَاعَلَة occurs more frequently than فِعَال. The initial *Hamza* of the infinitives of Forms VII, VIII and X is a *Hamzat al-waṣl*, of Form IV a *Hamzat al-qaṭᶜ*.

☞**A2** In the glossaries of the lessons and in the glossary at the end of the book the infinitives of Forms VII–X are given as (اِنفعل، اِفتعل، اِفعلّ، اِستفعل) so that it is clear that the initial *Hamza* is a *Hamzat al-waṣl*.

1.1.3. There are some peculiarities with regard to the infinitives of the defective verbs:
Verbs R_1 = و or ى:

Forms IV and X have the long vowel *ī* (R_1 = و < ى):

$$(\text{اِسْتَوْصَلَ} >) \ \text{اِسْتِيصَال، } (\text{أَوصل} >) \ \text{إيصَال}$$

Verbs R$_2$ = و or ى:

Forms IV and X have a final *Tā' marbūṭa*:

$$(\text{اِسْتَقَامَ} >) \ \text{اِسْتِقَامَة، } (\text{أَقَامَ} >) \ \text{إقَامة}$$

Verbs R$_3$ = و or ى:

Forms IV, VII, VIII and X have a final *Hamza*:

$$(\text{اِنْلَقَى} >) \ \text{اِنْلِقَاء، } (\text{أَلْقَى} >) \ \text{إلْقَاء}$$

$$(\text{اِسْتَلْقَى} >) \ \text{اِسْتِلْقَاء، } (\text{اِلْتَقَى} >) \ \text{اِلْتِقَاء}$$

Form II has the structure تَفْعِلَة : (لَقَّى >) تَلْقِية

Form III: (لاقَى >) مُلاقَاة

Forms V and VI: (تَلاقَى >) تَلاق، (تَلَقَّى >) تَلَقٍّ

Table 12 in the Appendix provides a survey of all infinitives.

1.1.4. Plural forms of the infinitives

The infinitives of Form I have various plural forms. The infinitives of Form II have either the sound feminine plural (ـات) or the broken plural تَفَاعِيلُ. The infinitives of Forms III - X have the sound feminine plural (ـات), Form IV occasionally has the broken plural أَفَاعِيلُ.

1.2. The use

The infinitive combines the verbal meaning with the formal characteristics of the noun. Its nominal structure also determines its syntactic use as a subject, an object and a predicate complement. It can take on all cases and can take suffixes and attributive adjuncts.

1.2.1. Most infinitives are lexicalized as nouns, i.e. they do not only express the verbal action as an event, but also have an individual meaning comprehensible, in the sense of the result of this event:

كِذْب "(the) denying" and "lie" (with the plural أَكْذَاب),

سُؤَال "(the) asking" and "question" (with the plural أَسْئِلَة).

✍A3 The infinitive is lexicalized in these cases just as the so-called *Nomen vicis* (infinitive + *Ta' marbūṭa*) is, which means the single execution of the verbal action expressed by the infinitive: ضَرْبة (single beating) = "blow" (< ضَرَبَ "to beat", الضَّرْب "the beating").

1.2.2. Just as the participle can take the place of the relative clause, the infinitive can take the one of a subordinate clause.

An infinitive construction replaces the objective or nominative clause introduced by أَنْ and أَنَّ as well as adverbial clauses.

1.2.2.1. Objective clause
Infinitive instead of أَنْ + verb

He can do this job immediately.	يَسْتَطِيعُ أَنْ يُنْجِزَ هَذَا الْعَمَلَ فَوْراً. = يَسْتَطِيعُ إِنْجَازَ هَذَا الْعَمَلِ فَوْراً.

1.2.2.2. Nominative clause
Infinitive instead of أَنْ + verb

It is possible for him to do this job immediately.	يُمْكِنُهُ أَنْ يُنْجِزَ هَذَا الْعَمَلَ فَوْراً. = يُمْكِنُهُ إِنْجَازُ هَذَا الْعَمَلِ فَوْراً.

1.2.2.3. Adverbial clauses
Preposition + infinitive instead of conjunction + verb

a) قَبْلَ

I will visit him before he returns to Damascus. I will visit him before his return to Damascus.	سَأَزُورُهُ قَبْلَ أَنْ يَعُودَ إلى دمشـق. = سَأَزُورُهُ قَبْلَ عَوْدَتِهِ إلى دمشق.

b) بَعْدَ

He visited me after he had returned / after his return here.	زَارَنِي بَعْدَ أَنْ عَادَ إلى هنـا. = زَارَنِي بَعْدَ عَوْدَتِهِ إلى هنا.

c) مُنْذُ

He has visited me only once since he returned / since his return.	زَارَنِي مَرَّةً وَاحِدةً فَقَطْ مُنْذُ أَنْ عَادَ. = زَارَنِي مَرَّةً وَاحِدةً فَقَطْ مُنْذُ عَوْدِتِهِ.

d) حَتَّى

He stayed there until the event ended / until the end of the event.	بَقِيَ هناك حتى انتهتِ الحفلةُ. = بَقِيَ هناك حتى انْتِهاءِ الحفلةِ.

e) لِ

He came to Baghdad in order to study Arabic.	جَاءَ إلى بغداد لِيَدْرُسَ اللُّغَةَ الْعَرَبِيَّةَ. = جَاءَ إلى بغداد لِدِرَاسَةِ اللُّغَةِ الْعَرَبِيَّةِ.

1.2.3. The infinitive has the same power of governing a case that the verb has. Analogously to the government of the respective verb it can take an object dependent on a preposition.

the welcoming of the guests	أَلتَّرْحِيبُ بِالضُّيُوفِ
the answering of the questions	أَلإِجَابَةُ عَلى الأَسْئِلَةِ
the need for drinks	أَلاِحْتِيَاجُ إِلى الْمَشْرُوبَاتِ
the expression of one's views	أَلتَّعْبِيرُ عَنِ الآرَاءِ

In general the accusative object of a transitive verb will not be employed as a direct object related to an infinitive, but is connected with the latter in the form of a genitive construction:

to study the Arabic language	دَرَسَ اللُّغَةَ الْعَرَبِيّةَ
the study of the Arabic language	دِرَاسَةُ اللُّغَةِ الْعَرَبِيّةِ
to do the jobs	أَنْجَزَ الأَعْمَالَ
the doing of the jobs	إِنْجَازُ الأَعْمَالِ

The 2nd term of the genitive construction takes the genitive in form, but is the logical object of the infinitive as the 1st term of this genitive construction. We talk about a *Genitivus objectivus* here.

There are also cases, however, in which the infinitive of a transitive verb takes on **an accusative object,** namely when the infinitive is already in the construct state and adding the object to the infinitive as the 2nd term of a genitive construction is not possible:

their studying of the Arabic language = their study of the Arabic language, (the circumstance, the fact) that they study Arabic	دِرَاسَتُهُمُ اللُّغَةَ الْعَرَبِيّةَ

The following sentence:

He asks before he writes the letter.	يَسْأَلُ قَبْلَ أَنْ يَكْتُبَ الرِّسَالَةَ.

can be transformed into an infinitive construction as follows:

He asks before (his) writing the letter.	يَسْأَلُ قَبْلَ كِتَابَتِهِ الرِّسَالَةَ. / يَسْأَلُ قَبْلَ كِتَابَتِهِ لِلرِّسَالَةِ.

1.2.4. Another method of nominalizing a predicate is connecting the infinitive with the so-called functional verbs. In these patterns the actual predicate is rendered by the infinitive. So the excessive use of nouns, which is often criticized, is also acknowledged in Arabic.

قَامَ + preposition بِ is the verb used most frequently in this connection:

Aḥmad visited the capital city. ~ (*lit.*: Aḥmad carried out a visit to the capital city, paid the capital city a visit.)	زَارَ أَحْمَدُ الْعَاصِمَةَ. قَامَ أَحْمَدُ بِزِيَارَةِ الْعَاصِمَةِ.
A Lebanese student has accompanied the delegation. ~ (*lit.*: A Leb. student has carried out the accompanying of the delegation.)	رَافَقَ الْوَفْدَ طَالِبٌ لُبْنَانِيٌّ. قَامَ بِمُرَافَقَةِ الْوَفْدِ طَالِبٌ لُبْنَانِيٌّ.

☝A4 There is a multitude of functional verbs, which occur in fixed lexical combinations - in conjunction with certain nouns - (in English these are phrases like "to make a decision", "to make a statement", "to read a paper", "to come to a decision" etc.). They must be learned as vocabulary items.

The periphrasis of the passive voice is a special variety of this usage of the infinitive as a noun. Instead of the passive voice يُفْعَلُ / فُعِلَ, the perfect or imperfect tense يَتِمُّ / تَمَّ "to come about, to be performed, to be accomplished, to take place, to happen" or يَجْرِي / جَرَى " to occur, to come to pass, to take place, to happen" + infinitive is employed:

The papers were delivered yesterday. ~ (*lit.*: The delivery of the papers came about yesterday, took place yesterday.)	سُلِّمَتِ الأَوْرَاقُ أَمْسِ. جَرَى تَسْلِيمُ الأَوْرَاقِ أَمْسِ.
The project is considered quickly. ~ (*lit.*: The considering of the project is done with speed / speedily.)	يُدْرَسُ الْمَشْرُوعُ بِسُرْعَةٍ. تَتِمُّ دِرَاسَةُ الْمَشْرُوعِ بِسُرْعَةٍ.

2. Adverb and adverbial constructions

Adverbs serve the purpose of:

a)   modifying a verb, an adjective, a participle or an adverb

b)   making the circumstances clear under which the fact expressed by the predicate comes about.

2.1. Classification of the adverbs

The following adverbs belong to a):

the **qualitative adverbs** as a modification of a verb:

جَيِّدًا and حَسَنًا "well", شَدِيدًا "strongly, violently/vehemently" a.o.;

the **quantitative adverbs** as a modification of a verb, an adjective, a participle or an adverb:

جِدًّا "very/much", كَثِيراً "much", قَلِيلاً "little/seldom", تَقْرِيباً "approximately",

وَحْدَهُ "(he) alone/(he) by himself " a.o.

The following adverbs belong to b):

adverbs **of time:**

(فِي) أَلآنَ "now", فَوْراً "at once", أَلْيَوْمَ "today", أَمْسِ "yesterday", غَداً "tomorrow",

سابِقاً (فِي الصَّباح) صَباحاً "in the morning", المَساءِ (مَساءً) "in the evening",

"formerly/previously" a.o.;

of place:

هُنا "here", هُناكَ "there", فَوْقُ "up; on; top; above; upstairs";

of manner:

سِرًّا "secretly", مع ذلِكَ "yet; still; nevertheless; for all that".

2.2. The form

The definite or indefinite accusative is the case the adverb takes in Arabic language. Besides, there are adverbial phrases (for formal reasons they are also called prepositional phrases), which consist of a preposition + noun in the genitive.

A5 Many nouns are used as prepositions when taking the form of the (adverbial) accusative:

above, over	فَوْقَ
under, below, beneath, underneath	تَحْتَ
after	بَعْدَ
before, prior to	قَبْلَ
in accordance with, according to	طِبْقاً لِ/ طِبْقَ/ وَفْقاً لِ / وَفْقَ
on the basis of, according to, etc.	بِناءً على

Some of them are additionally used as adverbs and take the ending *u* as such:

up, upstairs, on top, above	فَوْقُ
to the top, upward(s)	إِلى فَوْقُ
then, thereupon, afterwards, further(more), moreover	بَعْدُ
afterwards, later, etc.	فِيمَا بَعْدُ

2.3. The use
2.3.1. Position in the sentence

The qualitative and quantitative adverbs invariably follow the words they modify:

He has done that well.	فَعَلَ ذَلِكَ جَيِّداً.
He has eaten a lot.	أَكَلَ كَثِيراً.
very good	جَيِّدٌ جِدًّا

The adverbs are often at the end of the sentence; however, they are not restricted to this position:

| The Syrian delegation arrived on Saturday, the Egyptian delegation on Sunday. | وَصَلَ الْوَفْدُ السُّورِيُّ يَـوْمَ السَّبْتِ وَفِي يَوْمِ الأَحَدِ وَصَلَ الْوَفْدُ الْمِصْرِيُّ. |

2.3.2. Adverbs as predicates

The adverbs and adverbial phrases cannot only be modifiers of other words or specify a predicate, but may also be the predicate of an equational sentence and as such an inseparable part of it. See sentence structure 2 from Lesson 2:

| Here is a teacher. | هُنَا مُعَلِّمٌ. |
| The teacher is in the room. | أَلْمُعَلِّمُ فِي الْغُرْفَةِ. |

2.3.3. Various adverbial constructions

Instead of the qualitative adverb, constructions are often used in which it is replaced by a verbal noun or is put to a noun as its attributive adjunct.

2.3.3.1. Preposition بِ + (verbal) noun:

I walked fast.		مَشَيْتُ بِسُرْعَةٍ.
	(instead of)	مَشَيْتُ سَرِيعاً.
I walked slowly.		مَشَيْتُ بِبُطْءٍ.
	(instead of)	مَشَيْتُ بَطِيئاً.
I liked to do that.		فَعَلْتُ ذَلِكَ بِسُرُورٍ.
	(instead of)	فَعَلْتُ ذَلِكَ مَسْرُوراً.
He examined that thoroughly.		فَحَصَ ذَلِكَ بِدِقَّةٍ.
	(instead of)	فَحَصَ ذَلِكَ دَقِيقاً.

2.3.3.2. Preposition بِ + شَكْل or صُورَة "form/shape, manner/mode, way" + adjective:

He has done that extremely well.	فَعَلَ ذَلِكَ بِشَكْلٍ مُمْتَازٍ.
(*lit.:* in an excellent manner) (instead of)	فَعَلَ ذَلِكَ مُمْتَازاً.
He has done that well. (*lit.:* in a good manner)	فَعَلَ ذَلِكَ بِصُورَةٍ جَيِّدَةٍ.
in general, generally	بِصُورَةٍ عَامَّةٍ
especially, particularly	بِصُورَةٍ خَاصَّةٍ

2.3.3.3. Cognate accusative: A verb is modified by being followed by an indefinite noun (mostly an infinitive) in the accusative, which is combined with an attributive adjective.

He read the letter slowly. (*lit.:* He read the letter a slow reading.)	قَرَأَ الرِّسَالَةَ قِرَاءَةً بَطِيئَةً.

♫**A6** The cognate accusative, possibly the starting point of the adverb modifying a verb purely and simply, has become rare in modern Arabic.

Determining which of the adverbial constructions must be used, depends, to a large extent, on the structure and semantics of the nouns to be employed. Only close observation of the usage and constant practice will lead to the confident ability to apply them correctly.

V

coming too late	تَأَخُّر	basic, fundamental	جَذْرِيّ
Let's go!	يا الله (*colloq.*)	huge, enormous	جَسِيم
unfortunate, miserable	بائِس	compliment	مُجامَلة ج ـات
researcher	باحِث ج ـون	generation	جيل ج أَجْيال
to justify sth.	II بَرَّرَ (يُبَرِّرُ) هـ	stone	حجر ج أَحْجار
perspicacious	بَصِير	to lay the foundations of	وضع حجر الأَساس
excellent, brilliant, splendid	باهِر	to envy so. sth.	حسد (يَحْسُدُ) ه على
museum	مُتْحَف ج مَتاحِفُ	with regard to, regarding, as to	مِن حَيْثُ (+ *nominative*)
technology	تِكْنُولُوجيا	invention	اِخْتِراع ج ـات
to phone	تَلْفَنَ (يُتَلْفِنُ)	to be afraid of sth.	خَشِيَ (يَخْشَى) هـ
revolution	ثَوْرة ج ات		

plan	خُطّة ج خُطط		bankruptcy	إفْلاس
first of all	بالدرجةِ الأولى		before it is to late	قبل فوات الأوان
stage	مَرْحلة ج مراحِلُ		to assess, to judge sth.	II قَيَّم (يُقيِّمُ) هـ
prosperity	رفاه		assessment	تقييم
structure	ترْكِيب ج تراكِيبُ		to hate sth., so.	كره (يكرهُ) هـ، ه
to take sth. into consideration	III راعى (يُراعِي) هـ		as you like (colloq.)	على كَيْفَك/كَيْفِك
supermarket	سوبرماركت		make up (Fr. maquillage)	ماكِياج
comprehensive	شامِل		to continue to do sth.	X اِسْتمرَّ (يستمرُّ)
reform	إصْلاح		Never mind. That doesn't matter. (colloq. Eg.)	مَعَلِيْش
in so's. favour	في صالحِ ه		to enable so. to	II مكّن (يُمكّنُ) ه من
in a ... way / manner	بصورةٍ		boring	مُمِلّ
contents, subject matter	مَضْمُون ج مضامِينُ		profession	مِهْنة ج مِهن
light	ضوْء ج أضْواء		to get off, to go down	نزل (ينزلُ)
in the light of, in view of	عَلى ضوْءِ		to expect so., sth.	VIII اِنْتظَر (ينتظِرُ) ه، هـ
required, wanted	مطْلُوب		regular, orderly	مُنْتظم
requirements	ج مُتطلّبات		plan, program	منهج ج مناهجُ
ready	مُسْتعِدّ		to bring about an upswing	نهض (ينهَضُ) ب
accidental, random, arbitrary	عشوائيّ		hurry	وَشْك/ وُشْك
scientist, scholar	عالِم ج عُلماءُ		to be close to bankruptcy	على وشكِ الإفلاس
to shut, to lock up sth. in front of	IV أغْلقَ (يُغْلِقُ) هـ أمام		objective	موْضوعِيّ
unavoidable	لا مفرَّ مِنْهُ		to keep pace with, to keep abreast of	III واكب (يُواكِبُ) هـ
to think	VIII اِفْتكر (يفتكِرُ)		hopeless	يائس
money	ج فَلُوس (colloq.)			

التعليم والمستقبل

Text 1.

لا يمكن النظر إلى مستقبل أي بلد بمعزل عن مستوى التعليم فيه. ومن يريد أن ينهض بهذا البلد نهضة حقيقية لا يمكن أن يغلق عينيه أمام المشاكل الملحّة التي تواجه هذا القطاع الحيوي في مجتمعنا. ومن يقيّم الوضع الحالي في الجامعات والمعاهد الفنية والمهنية وفي المدارس الثانوية والابتدائية تقييماً موضوعياً يجد أنّه لا مفر من إصلاح نظام التعليم إصلاحاً جذرياً وشاملاً من حيث مضامينه وتراكيبه ومراحله ومناهجه.

إن اي تأخُّر في هذا الإصلاح سيلحق أضراراً جسيمة بمستقبل هـذا البلد ليس فقط في مجال التعليم والثقافة، بل إنّما في كلّ المجالات الاجتماعية الأخرى. وكيف نستطيع أن نطوّر البلد تطويراً شاملاً وأن نواكب الثورة في العلـم والتكنولوجيا بصورة منتظمة دون جيـل جديد مـن العلمـاء والباحثين والمهندسين والفنيّين والإداريين الذين تلقّـوا تأهيلهم على ضوء اختراعات وابتكارات العلم الحديثة؟ إن الإصلاح يجب أن يبـدأ قبل فوات الأوان لأنّ التأخُّر بسنة واحدة في البدء بالإصلاح سيؤدي إلى تـأخُّر تطوُّر البلـد تعليمياً وثقافياً وتكنيكياً واجتماعياً ليس بسنوات، بل بعقود.

ما هو المطلوب منّا إذن؟ هل نستمرّ في هذه المناقشات البائسة واليائسـة الـتي بـدأت قبل عشر سنوات أم نبدأ فوراً بالإصلاح؟ إن الوقت ليس في صالحنا ولكن كيـف نبـدأ؟ هل نبدأ بشكل عشوائي أي نبدأ مـن أجـل أن نبـدأ؟ لا، الإصلاح يحتاج إلى خطة واضحة، إلى خطة لا تراعي فقط المستقبل القريب، بل بالدرجـة الأولى المستقبل البعيـد، يعني متطلّبات العلم بعد عشرين أو أربعين سنة وبهذا الإصلاح يجب علينا أن نضع حجر الأساس لمستقبل باهر يمكّننا من تحقيق نهضة علمية وثقافية تحقّق للوطن الخير والرفاه.

Text 2
في الطريق إلى السوق

بيتر: بيتر يتكلّم، صباح الخير، كيف حالك؟

مريم: صباح النور، أنا بخير، كيف حالك اليوم؟

بيتر: والله بخير، الحمد لله.

مريم: من أين تتلفن؟ هل أنت قريب من هنا؟

بيتر: أنا هنا في الفندق.

مريم: إلى أين نذهب اليوم، مرّة أخرى إلى أحد المتاحف المملّة؟ أ ليس هناك إمكانية لنشتري شيئاً من السوق؟

بيتر: على كيفك. يمكننا أن نذهب إلى السوق بعد الفطور مباشرة. إتّفقنا؟

مريم: أنا مستعدّة في أي وقت وسأكون عندك بعد ربـع سـاعة أي بعد أن أنتهي مـن الماكياج.

بيتر: نعم ، الماكياج مهمّ. هل أنتظرك في غرفتك؟

مريم: لا، والله، انتظرني تحت ! أنا أكره الماكياج تحت إشراف الرجال. أنا سـأكون تحت بعد خمس دقائق.

(وبعد ثلاثة أرباع من الساعة نزلت مريم إلى تحت!)

بيتر: والله، النتيجة تبرّر الانتظار. كـلّ الرجـال سيحسـدونني عليـك والآن نمشي إلى السوق.

مريم: شكراً على المجاملة. إلى أيّة سوق نمشي؟

بيتر: إلى سوبرماركت خارج المدينة يوجد فيه كلّ شيء.

مريم: ولماذا خارج المدينة وماذا يعني كلّ شيء؟

بيتر: الأسعار هناك معقولة والبضائع الموجودة هناك هي تقريباً نفس البضائع الموجـودة في مركز المدينة. هل معك فلوس؟

مريم: لا، كنت أفتكر أنك تعطيني بعض الدولارات!

بيتر: هل نسيت أنّني على وشك الإفلاس بعد استئجار السيّارة؟

مريم: أ لم يصل شيك من أبيك؟

بيتر: للأسف لم يصل بعد.

مريم: إذن نمشي ونشتري بالعيون.

بيتر: أخشى أن تكون عيونك كبيرة وإمكانياتي صغيرة.

مريم: يقول المثل: العين بصيرة واليد قصيرة. معليش، سأغلق عيوني أمام الأشياء الغالية، يا لله.

Exercises:

L1 Complete the sentences with one of the following adverbial phrases.

بِدِقَّة، بُبطء، بسُرْعة، بصُورة رائِعة، بِصُورة جيِّدة، بِشكْل ممتاز، بسُرُور، بِلُطْف

قاد السائق سيّارته ...

استقبلتني العائلة ...

درس الخبراء المشروع ...

أنجز الطلّاب عملهم ...

هل تتعلّمون اللغة العربية ...؟

كان المترجم يتكلّم اللغة العربية ...

رحّب الوزير بضيوفه الأجانب ...

شرح المرافقون هذا الموضوع ...

قبلنا الدعوة ...

تريد الحكومة أن تطوّر اقتصاد البلد ...

نمشي إلى السوق ...

نطوّر التعليم ...

L2 Give the meaning of the following infinitives, which you are already acquainted with.

جلوس، دخول، خروج، اجتماع، محاضرة، انتظار، سؤال، دراسة، تأهيل، تبادل،

رئاسة، تعليم، تعاون، اقتصاد، مناقشة، مناسبة، توسيع، توقيع، برد، تخصّص، مراجعة،

استشراق، اعتذار، تسجيل، اعتماد، تقدير، إيجاد، تأسيس، حضور، تحسين، تصريح،

تشكيل، مساهمة، تشاور، تطوّر، تطوير، عودة، إعادة، ممارسة، توتّر، تخفيض، افتتاح،

استقبال، اقتراح، تحسّن، إجراء، ارتياح، إغلاق، استثناء، تجمّد، استئناف، ارتفاع، مواصلة،

تجديد، حصول، اختيار، تصديق، مباراة، مسابقة، سباق، مصارعة، ملاكمة،

تناول، استئجار، إشراف، انضمام، امتحان، توفيق

L3 One student forms questions with the infinitives of L2 and the others answer the questions.

☞   هل تنام في غرفة الجلوس؟   >   لا، لا أنام في غرفة الجلوس.

☞   أنام في غرفة النوم وأحياناً (دائماً ؟) في المحاضرات المُمِلّة.

L4 (Homework) Answer the following questions in writing.

ما هي المشروبات التي تعرفها؟

ما هي المأكولات التي تعرفها؟

ما هي المهن التي تعرفها؟

ما هي البضائع التي تباع في الأسواق العربية الشعبية؟

ما هي الدروس التي تنام فيها؟

من هو الرجل الذي تكرهه؟

ما هي الساعات التي تحبّها؟

G1 Form the infinitive of the following verbs of Form I using the pattern given. Find out the meaning of the words you do not know with the help of the dictionary.

a) فعْل   :   وضع، وعد، قـام، خـاف، بـاع، فحص، عـرض، قـال، سـار، شـرح،

كسب، أكل، مشى، صرف، أخذ، خلق

b) فُعول   :   وقف، وصل، رجع، صعد، خرج، دخل، وجد، حصل، حضر

c) فِعالة   :   درس، زار، زاد، زرع، صنع

G2 Find out the Form of the following verbs and the respective infinitive. For words that you do not know, use the dictionary.

أوفد، استقبل، شاهد، قدَّم، سجَّل، اقترح، أغلق، دخَّن، اجتمـع، لاحـظ، انحـدر، تـابع،

أقام، شجَّع، أعجب، وسَّع، استورد، أدخل، خابر

G3 (Homework) Find out the meaning of the following infinitives and compare it with the meaning of the respective verb.

مقابلة، تسليم، اشتراك، مرافقة، تطوّر، مقاومة، إعلان، تـأييد، احتيـاج، إجابة، إجـراء،

إثبات، تطوير، تقديم، محاولة.

G4 Replace the أنْ - clauses with the infinitive construction.

☞ أحاول أنْ أنجز واجباتي حتى يوم السبت. < أحاول إنجاز واجباتي حتى يوم السبت.

يريد أحمد أن ينجز واجباته فوراً.

يريد الوفد أن يزور الجامعة.

تريد الحكومة أن تطوِّر اقتصاد البلد.

أرادوا أن يدرسوا هذه القضية.

يريد الخبراء أن يدرسوا المشروع.

يجب علينا أن نؤيِّد هذه السياسة.

يجب عليك أن ترحِّب بالضيوف.

يجب عليكم أن تلغوا سفركم.

يجب علينا أن نقابله.

يجب عليها أن تغيِّر البرنامج.

لم يستطع الطالب أن يجيب على هذا السؤال.

استطاع المعلم أن يبيِّن المشكلة.

هل استطعتم أن تنجزوا هذا العمل؟

هل تستطيع أن تسلِّم الهدية شخصياً؟

استطاع المرافق أن يشرح تاريخ المدينة.

أحاول أن أقابلهم غداً.

نحاول أن ننهي عملنا حتى نهاية الأسبوع.

سأحاول أن أوضح القضية.

هل تحاول أن تغيِّر الموعد؟

حاولت أن أعود بالقطار.

هل تمكَّنت الطالبة من أن تترجم الكلمات الجديدة؟

تمكّن الطالب من أن يقوم بواجباته.

تمكّنوا من أن يسجِّلوا خمسة أهداف.

هل يمكنك أن تخابره مساء اليوم؟

هل يمكنكم أن تتحدّثوا معه حول ذلك؟

G5 Replace preposition + conjunction + verb with preposition + infinitive.

☞   سأزورك قبل أن تعود إلى القاهرة. > سأزورك قبل عودتك إلى القاهرة.

نغادر المدينة قبل أن ينتهي المؤتمر.

سِتزورني صديقتي قبل أن تعود إلى لندن.

تفحص السيّارة قبل أن تُباع.

يتبادل المسؤولون الآراء قبل أن يجتمعوا.

يجتمع أحمد بصديقه قبل أن يوفَد إلى الخارج للدراسة.

ذهبتُ إلى القاعة بعد أن فحصوا جوازات السفر.

رجع إلى البيت بعد أن أنهى عمله.

مشى إلى المقهى بعد أن شاهد الفلم.

بقيت في الملعب حتى انتهت المباراة.

بقيت في المطار حتى حصلت على الحقائب.

لم يتركوا المحطّة حتى وصل القطار.

قرأت الكتب حتى أغلقت المكتبة.

أتى الأصدقاء ليحضروا الحفلة.

جاء آلاف التجّار ليشتركوا في المعرض.

سافرت إلى باريس لأجتمع بأصدقائي.

ذهبت إلى المصرف لأصرف العملة.

خرجت من الغرفة لأدخِّن سيجارة.

سافر الطلاب إلى القاهرة ليدرسوا اللغة العربية.

جاء التلاميذ إلينا ليتعلّموا اللغة الإنكليزية.

قام الوفد بجولة ليشاهد الجامعة والمتحف الوطني.

G6 (Homework) Form equational sentences in which an infinitive is the subject and the participle ممنوع or مسموح is the predicate.

C1 (Homework) Prepare a report about the previous weekend. Use the adverbs of time.

C2 Prepare a dialogue about shopping, a visit to a museum, a cinema, a theatre, etc. based on Text 2.

Final Exercise:

1. Give the Arabic infinitives.

meeting, lecture, study, qualification, exchange, education, cooperation, economy, discussion, extension, signature, specialization, checking, oriental studies, apology, registration, foundation, presence, consultation, development, return, tension, opening, reception, proposal, improvement, satisfaction, closing, exception, increase, continuation, innovation, certification, preparation, competition, wrestling, boxing, examination, success

2. Replace the أنْ - clause with an infinitive construction.

يريد أحمد أن ينجز واجباته فوراً. تريد الحكومة أن تطوِّر اقتصاد البلد. أرادوا أن يدرسوا هذه القضية. يريد الخبراء أن يدرسوا المشروع. يجب علينا أن نؤيِّد هـذه السياسـة. يجـب عليك أن ترحِّب بالضيوف. يجب علينا أن نقابله. يجب عليها أن تغيِّر البرنامج. اسـتطاع الرئيس أن يبيِّن المشـكلة. هـل تسـتطيع أن تسـلِّم الهدية شخـصياً؟ استطاع المرافـق أن يشرح تاريخ المدينة. نحاول أن ننهي عملنـا حتى نهايـة الأسبوع. سـأحاول أن أوضِّح القضية. حاولت أن أعود بالطائرة. هل تمكَّنت الطالبة من أن تترجم الكلمـات الجديـدة؟ تمكَّن الطالب من أن يقوم بواجباته. هل يمكنكم أن تتحدَّثوا معه حول ذلك؟

3. Replace conjunction + verb with preposition + infinitive.

تُفحص السيّارة قبل أن تُباع. يتبادل المسؤولون الآراء قبل أن يجتمعوا. ذهبتُ إلى القاعـة بعد أن فحصوا جوازات السفر. رجع إلى البيت بعد أن أنهى عمله. بقيت في الملعب حتى انتهت المباراة. لم يتركوا المحطّة حتى وصل القطـار. قـرأت الكتـب حتى أُغلقت المكتبة. أتى الأصدقاء ليحضروا الحفلة.

4. Translate into Arabic.

The urgent problems which the educational sector is confronted with must be solved in the forthcoming years. The reform of the structure and the contents of the programs of the primary and secondary schools will last approximately ten years. We must lay the foundations for a future which enables us to accomplish a scientific and cultural upswing on the basis of inventions and discoveries in the modern sciences.

1. Subordinate Clauses, a Survey (أَلجُمَل الْفَرْعِيّة)

Subordinate clauses fulfill in a complex sentence a function similar to parts of a simple sentence. Accordingly, they can be classified as follows:

- **nominative clauses**
- **objective clauses**
- **predicative clauses**
- **attributive clauses**
- **adverbial clauses**

All these types of subordinate clauses have already been encountered in connection with various conjunctions. The designation which befits them according to their respective syntactic function was, however, not mentioned in each case:

- nominative and objective clauses after أَنْ and أَنَّ
- as well as nominal relative clauses after مَنْ، مَا، الّذِي، الّذِينَ .
- predicative clauses as nominal relative clauses;
- attributive clauses = adnominal relative clauses;
- adverbial clauses after the following conjunctions:

بَعْدَ أَنْ	after	= temporal clauses
قَبْلَ أَنْ	before	
مُنْذُ (أَنْ)	since/ever since	
حَتَّى	until	
حَيْثُ	where	= adverbial clauses denoting place
لِ	that, in order to	= final clauses
لِأَنَّ	because/for	= clauses of reason
إِذْ	as; since/because	= adverbial clauses
رَغْمَ أَنَّ	although/though	= concessive clauses
وَكَأَنَّ	as if/as though	= comparison clauses
لَكِنَّ	but, however/yet	= adversative parataxis
غَيْرَ أَنَّ	however/... though, but/however	

We do not distinguish here between subordinate and coordinate clauses - as we do in the Indo-European languages - because word order in these clauses introduced by conjunctions does not differ from word order in the principal clause in the Arabic language.

In this Lesson and in Lessons 24, 26-28 the following types of clauses are treated, which are important for the Arabic language and for which there are only sometimes equivalents in English: temporal clause, clause of reason, conditional clause and clause of concession, exceptives and circumstantial clause.

2. Temporal Clauses

2.1. They are introduced by means of conjunctions which indicate that the action of the subordinate clause takes place

- at the same time as the action of the main clause takes place (when, as soon as = time, while, as long as = duration, whenever = reiteration)

- before the action of the main clause (after, since, when)

- or after the action of the main clause (until, before).

2.1.1. Temporal clauses of simultaneousness

Simultaneousness of the actions expressed by the main and the subordinate clause is expressed by the following conjunctions:

عِنْدَمَا + verb in the perfect tense (or كان + imperfect tense or participle) = **when**

| When I was playing, Muḥammad came. | عِنْدَمَا كُنْتُ أَلْعَبُ جَاءَ مُحَمَّدٌ. |

The clause introduced by عِنْدَمَا may precede the main clause or follow it:

| Muḥammad came when I was playing. | جَاءَ مُحَمَّدٌ عِنْدَمَا كُنْتُ أَلْعَبُ. |

The possibility of the temporal clause being placed in front of or behind the main clause also applies to all following clauses introduced by a temporal conjunction.

🔊A1 Another syntactic possibility of expressing the simultaneousness of the main clause and the subordinate clause consists in the so-called circumstantial clause; cf. Lesson 28 regarding this.

عِنْدَمَا + verb in the imperfect tense = **as soon as**

| I will inform them about this matter as soon as I meet them. | سَأُطْلِعُهُمْ على هذه القَضِية عِنْدَمَا أَجْتَمِعُ بِهِمْ. |

🔊A2 عندما + imperfect tense, often in a conditional sense = English "when, if".

حِينَمَا or حِينَ + verb in the perfect or imperfect tense have the same meaning as عِنْدَمَا does.

🔊A3 In journalese عندما is found far more frequently. حينما and حين are more representative of individual style.

بَيْنَمَا + verb in the perfect tense (or كَانَ + imperfect tense or participle) or imperfect tense = **while**

I did the work while Muḥammad was absent.	أَنْجَزْتُ الْعَمَلَ بَيْنَمَا كَانَ مُحَمَّدٌ غَائِباً.
I do the work while Muḥammad is absent.	أُنْجِزُ الْعَمَلَ بَيْنَمَا يَكُونُ مُحَمَّدٌ غَائِباً.

☞ A4 بينما also introduces clauses of contrast, like the English "whereas" does:

Export has increased whereas import has decreased.	إِرْتَفَعَ التَّصْدِيرُ بَيْنَمَا انْخَفَضَ الإِسْتِيرَادُ.

Temporal clauses of simultaneousness are furthermore introduced by means of: لَمَّا "as, when", طَالَمَا or مَا دَامَ "as long as", مَا لَمْ "so long as ... not, unless" and كُلَّمَا "whenever".

☞ A5 In مَا دَام , دام is to be conjugated in the perfect tense like قَام , accordingly:

So long as/while I (you/he/she/we/you/they) am here, he will not sleep.	مَا دُمْتُ (دُمْتَ/ دُمْتِ/ دام / دامتْ / دُمْنا / دُمْتُمْ/ دُمْتُنَّ/ داموا / دُمْنَ) هُنا لن يَنامَ.

2.1.2. Temporal clauses of anteriority

بعد أَنْ + verb in the perfect tense = **after**

I went home after I had done the work.	ذَهَبْتُ إِلَى الْبَيْتِ بَعْدَ أَنْ أَنْجَزْتُ الْعَمَلَ.

☞ A6 Accordingly, in the Arabic language when two events occur at different time-frames in the past, perfect tense - perfect tense is employed, unlike in English, in which "after" requires strict compliance with the *Consecutio temporum* (past perfect - preterite tense).

☞ A7 عندما and حينما , too, can be used in the sense of "when, after" for the purpose of expressing anteriority. In many cases it is neither possible to differentiate them clearly from بعد أَنْ "after" nor from لَمَّا "when, after", which is seldom used in Standard Arabic nowadays. However, in spoken language the latter occurs very frequently.

مُنْذُ (أَنْ) + verb in the perfect tense = **since**

I have been (and am still) working as an interpreter since I graduated from university.	لا أَزَالُ أَشْتَغِلُ مُتَرْجِماً مُنْذُ أَنْ تَخَرَّجْتُ مِنَ الْجَامِعَةِ.

2.1.3. Temporal clauses of posteriority

قَبْلَ أَنْ + verb in the imperfect tense (subjunctive) = **before**

I (will) ask my father before I write the letter.	أَسْأَلُ أَبِي قَبْلَ أَنْ أَكْتُبَ الرِّسَالَةَ.

حَتّى + verb in the perfect tense = **until**

He worked until he had accomplished the tasks.	عَمِلَ حَتّى أَنْجَزَ الْوَاجِبَاتِ.

2.2. Frequently a prepositional construction (as has already been practiced in Lesson 22, G5) is chosen - especially for the purpose of expressing anteriority and posteriority - accordingly:

بَعْدَ إِنْجَازِهِ الْعَمَلَ / لِلْعَمَلِ	instead of	بَعْدَ أَنْ أَنْجَزَ الْعَمَلَ
مُنْذُ تَخَرُّجِي مِنَ الْجَامِعَةِ	instead of	مُنْذُ (أَنْ) تَخَرَّجْتُ مِنَ الْجَامِعَةِ
قَبْلَ كِتَابَتِهِ الرِّسَالَةَ / لِلرِّسَالَةِ	instead of	قَبْلَ أَنْ يَكْتُبَ الرِّسَالَةَ
حَتّى إِنْجَازِهِ الْوَاجِبَاتِ / لِلْوَاجِبَاتِ	instead of	حَتّى أَنْجَزَ الْوَاجِبَاتِ

We are also familiar with it in English, e.g. "after doing the work" instead of "after I had done the work".

V

as; since/because	إِذْ	to conclude	اِسْتِنْتَاجَات ~
data, facts, figure	مُؤَشِّر ج ات	to bring back to	IV أَرْجَعَ (يُرْجِعُ) هـ إلى
help, support	تَأْيِيد	port, harbour	مَرْفَأ ج مَرَافِئُ
yes	(colloq. Eg.) أَيْوَه	to swim	سَبَحَ (يَسْبَحُ)
Palmyra	تَدْمُرُ	acceleration	تَسْرِيع
air	جَوِّيّ	to help so. with sth.	III سَاعَدَ (يُسَاعِدُ) ه (على)
to move	V تَحَرَّكَ (يَتَحَرَّكُ)	to contribute to	سَاعَدَ على
at the expense of	على حِساب	to make so. happy	IV أَسْعَدَ (يُسْعِدُ) ه
You are right.	الحقّ معك	ship	سَفِينة ج سُفُن
Aleppo	(م) حَلَبُ	Peace be upon you	السَّلامُ عليكم
Hama	(م) حَماه	and the mercy and the blessing of God	ورَحْمةُ اللهِ وبرَكاتُهُ
Homs	(م) حِمْصُ		
need; colloq.: matter, thing	حاجة ج حاجِيات	wellness, well-being	سلامة
experience; know-how	خِبْرة ج ات	airline	شركة الطيْران
speech, letter, note	خِطاب ج ـات	coast, beach	شاطِئ ج شَواطِئُ
to extract, to deduct sth. from	X اِسْتَخْلَص (يَسْتَخْلِصُ) هـ من	enclosure (in a letter etc.)	ج مشْفُوعات
		sunny	مُشْمِس

colloq. : friend	صاحِب ج أصحاب	as equivalent for, (in return) for	مُقابِل
to export sth. to	II صدَّر (يُصدِّر) هـ إلى	story	قِصَّة ج قِصص
export	تصْدِير	to cut sth.	قطع (يقطَعُ) هـ
refinery	مِصفاة ج مصافٍ	to cover a distance or stage	قطع شَوْطاً
outskirts, vicinity	ضاحية ج ضواحٍ	fortress	قلعة ج قِلاع
loss	ضَياع	Latakiya	اللاذِقيّة
to inform so. about	IV أطْلع (يُطْلِعُ) ه على	so long as ... not; unless	ما لم
to consider so., sth.	VIII اِعتبر (يعْتبرُ) ه هـ	rainy	مُمْطِر
in his capacity as	باعتبارِه	to wish so. sth.,that	V تمنّى (يتمنّى) له هـ ، أنْ
to come across sth., to track down sth.	عثر (يعْثُرُ) على	to die	ماتَ (يمُوتُ)
to admire sth.	IV أعْجب (يُعْجبُ) هـ	to finance sth.	II موَّل (يُموِّلُ) هـ
many-sided, multi	مُتعدِّد الجوانِب	harbour	مِيناء ج موانِئُ
non(-) (+ عدم + noun is like adjective or participle, a nominal negation)	عدم	to fit, to suit sth.	III ناسب (يُناسِبُ) هـ
enemy	عدُوّ ج أعْداء	water-elevator	ناعُورة ج نواعِيرُ
complicated	مُعقَّد	trade union	نِقابة ج ـات
to be used to so., sth.	مُتعوِّد على	to import sth. from	X اِسْتوْرد (يسْتوْردُ) هـ من
to cover sth.	II غطّى (يُغطِّي) هـ	import	اِستِيراد
(and) others	غيْرُه، غيْرُها،	weight	وزْن ج أوْزان
	غيرُهُمْ (مِنْ الـ ...)	say good-bye to	II ودَّع (يُودِّعُ)
lost	مفقود	to recommend so., sth., to advise so. to	IV أوصىَ (يُوصِي) ب
to welcome so.	X اِسْتقْبل (يسْتقْبِلُ) ه		

Text 1

رسالة إلى محمّد

دمشق في الـ ١١ من شباط ... ١٩٩

عزيزي محمّد

تحية طيّبة وبعد

أكتب لك هذه الرسالة من سوريا. إنني أشتغل هنا منذ شهرين في مشروع علمي لدراسة التطوُّر الاقتصادي وعلاقته بالتطوُّرات الاجتماعية. ويموِّل المشروع اتحاد النقابات في سوريا. وقطعنا إلى الآن شوطاً كبيراً في جمع التفاصيل الاقتصادية والاجتماعية ولكن المشروع ما زال في المرحلة الابتدائية. وتعتبر هذه الدراسة جزءاً من مشروع كبير يشمل ايضاً التجارة الداخلية والخارجية أي الاستيراد والتصدير وقطاع النفط والسياحة والثقافة

ومجالات أخرى كثيرة. وتعقب مرحلة جمع التفاصيل المرحلة الثانية وهي مرحلة استخلاص الاستنتاجات من المؤشرات المختلفة.

لقد زرت مدناً كثيرة منذ وصولي إلى سوريا مثلاً تدمر بآثارها القديمة، واعجبني كثيراً ما بناه الرومان في قديم الزمان من أبنية جميلة، وزرت أيضاً حمص بمصفاتها وحماه بنواعيرها المشهورة وحلب بقلعتها وأسواقها ومعاملها ومرفأ اللاذقية بسفنه الكثيرة وطبعاً دمشق وضواحيها الجميلة وغيرها من المدن والمحافظات والآثار التاريخية. وعندما كنا في اللاذقية سبحت في البحر الأبيض المتوسط رغم أنّ الأمواج كانت عالية جدّاً.

إن العمل في هذا المشروع معقد ومتعدد الجوانب ويحتاج إلى خبرة طويلة وأنا أستفيد من خبرة زملائي الآخرين غير أنّني لا أعرف كيف أستفيد من هذا العمل في المستقبل. إن شاء الله، سيساعد إنجاز هذا المشروع على كتابة أطروحتي بسرعة في السنة القادمة.

سأغادر سوريا في الـ ١٢ من آذار وقبل أن أعود إلى البلد سوف أسافر إلى بغداد لمدّة أسبوعين.

سلّم على أحمد وعلى أصحاب نادي كرة القدم. إنّي أعدكم بانْ أسجّل لكم أهدافاً كثيرة في المباريات القادمة.

أتمنّى لك النجاح والتوفيق في الدراسة والسلام عليكم ورحمة الله وبركاته.

صديقك المخلص

بيتر

قصة الحقائب المفقودة	**Text 2**

جون: صباح الخير.

الموظّفة: صباح النور. تفضّل!

جون: أنا وصلت في الرحلة رقم ٦٥٤ الساعة الثامنة والنصف من فرانكفورت ولكن حقائبي لم تصل وفيها كلّ ما أحتاج إليه في هذا الطقس الحار وسؤالي الأول: أين حقائبي؟

الموظّفة: أولاً الحمد لله على السلامة وثانياً أنا آسفة جدّاً. سأبذل كلّ ما في وسعي لمساعدتك. أعطني من فضلك التذكرة.

جون: تفضّلي. جئت في الدرجة الأولى وكانت معي حقيبتان.

الموظّفة: أيوه، صحيح وكان عندك ٢٠ كيلو وزن زائد، أي الوزن الإجمالي للحقائب كان ٥٠ كيلو.

جون: بالضبط، هذا صحيح وأنا دفعت ١٧٠ دولاراً تقريباً مقابل هذا الوزن الزائد.

الموظّفة: سنحاول أن نساعدك بسرعة.

جون: أين الحقائب ومتى ستصل إلى هنا؟

الموظّفة: ا الله أعلم، قد تكون في فرانكفورت أو في أي مطار آخر في العـالم ولإيجادهـا نحتاج أولاً إلى معرفة لونها وحجمها.

جون: الحقائب بنفس اللون والحجم يعنـي اللون أسـود والحجـم هـو ٧٥ في ٥٥ في ٣٥ سنتيمتر وكتبت اسمي وعنواني عليها.

الموظّفة: هذا مهمّ. في أي فندق تنزل وما هو رقم الغرفة؟ بعد وصول الحقائب نتّصل بك فوراً.

جون: سأنزل في فندق هيلتون ورقم الغرفة ٢١٢ ولكن من المستحيل أن أنتظر أكثر من ٢٤ ساعة أولاً لأني هنا في مهمّة رسمية وأحتاج إلى الملابس المناسبة وثانياً أنا لست السبب في عدم وصول الحقائب ولذلك سأنتظر ٢٤ ساعة وبعد ذلك سـأذهب إلى أي محـلّ في المدينة وأشتري الملابس والحاجيات اللازمـة الأخرى على حساب شركة الطيران. في هذا الطقس الحارّ سأموت بعد قليـل في ملابسي الشتوية.

الموظّفة: الحقّ معك ولكن عندنا الآن شتاء وفي الفندق تكييف مركزي.

جون: أولاً أنا لا أريد أن أجلس في الفندق كلّ اليوم وثانياً لست متعـوّداً علـى هـذا الطقس الحارّ الذي يسمّى عندكم شتاء.

الموظّفة: على كلّ حال، قبل أن تشتري الحاجيات يجب عليك أن تتّصل بي. وفي حالة عدم وصول الحقائب بعد يوم سندفع لك أولاً ١٠٠ دولار وفي حالة ضياع الحقائب ندفع لك مقابل كلّ كيلو من وزن الحقائب ٢٠ دولاراً أي مايعـادل ١٠٠٠ دولار.

جون: هذا قليل جدّاً لأنّ هذا المبلغ لا يغطّي قيمة ما في الحقائب على الإطلاق.

الموظّفة: هذه هي شروط النقل الجوي المتفق عليها دولياً ولا ندفع أكثر مـن ذلـك. أ ليس لك تأمين خاصّ؟

جون: لا، لسوء الحظ.

الموظّفة: طيّب، اتّفقنا. سأتصل بك بعد وصول الحقائب. وقّع على هـذه الاستمارات من فضلك!

جون: أوقّع على كلّ ما يُرْجع إليّ الحقائب. شكراً على لطفك. مع السلامة.

الموظّفة: عفواً ، مع السلامة.

Exercises:

L1 Replace the following words by their antonyms.

صديق، بدأ، وصول، تصدير، عرف، جاء، دخل، قبل، استورد، بـاع، سـريع، اسـتقبل،

متزوج، ازداد، ليل، هبوط، ممطر، فوق، ممكن

L2 Insert the proper preposition(s).

هو ... الباب. الطالب ... المدير. الطائرة ... البحر. وصل ... القـاهرة. ... أن تلفنـت

... محمد ذهبت ... البيت. زرت المدير ... زيارة المعمل. أخـذ ... هدايا ...أصدقـاء.

شرح ... هم الوضع ... المرحلة الأولى. يصدّر المعمل الإنتاج ... ألمانيـا. يسـتورد البلـد

البترول ... السعودية. قاموا ... جولة ... البلاد. أوصـى ... تقديـم المشـروع. استقبلهـم

... ساعتين. اشترى ... المخزن كتباً جديدة إضافة ... شنطة وأقلام. أما ...النسـبة ...

المؤتمر فهو ينعقد ... هذا الفندق.

L3 (Written homework) Translate into Arabic.

I am writing this letter to you from Cairo. When will you come to Cairo? I have been working here for two months. The government finances the project. We collect details about the development of trade, economy, exports and imports, tourism and culture and the oil sector. They draw conclusions from the first stage of the project. This economic data is new. I was in Palmyra, Aleppo, Homs, Hama and Latakiya and on the coast of the Mediterranean. The acceleration of the work on the project is impossible.

L4 Translate the following text which is printed in deco type *Naskh* using the dictionary.

المملكة العربية السعودية

وزارة التعليم العالي

جامعة الإمام محمد بن سعود الإسلامية

الرقم:

التاريخ:

المشفوعات:

الموضوع: بشأن إعداد خطاب إلى جامعة لندن

سعادة مدير معهد تعليم اللغة العربية بالنيابة   وفقه الله

السلام عليكم ورحمة الله وبركاته

أما بعد:

فأشير إلى خطابكم المرقم ٢٥٥/١/ب والمؤرخ في ١٤١٣/٧/١٦هـ بشأن إفادة المعهد برأيه عن برنامج تعليم اللغة العربية في إحدى الجامعات الإنكليزية وإمكانية التعاون معها واقتراحكم إرسال خطاب إلى جامعة لندن.

أخبركم أن الاقتراح وجيه، وعلى المعهد إعداد الخطاب وتوضيح المطلوب فيه واطلاع الجامعة عليه.

ولإتمام ما يلزم من قبلكم جرى إبلاغكم به.

ولكم تحياتي

وكيل الجامعة

للشؤون التعليمية

G1 Combine the clauses by means of عندما.

جاء محمد > عندما كنت ألعب جاء محمّد.	كنت ألعب	☞
دخل محمد > عندما شربت الشاي دخل محمّد.	شربت الشاي	☞
كان الطقس ممطراً	وصلت الطائرة	
جاء محمّد	اجتمع الطلاّب	
انطلقت الطائرة	وصلنا إلى المطار	
وصلت الطائرة من القاهرة	كنت في المطار	
جاء صديقنا	غادرنا البيت	
تبدأ المحادثات من جديد	يعود الوفد من الجولة	
سأسافر إلى تونس	أتلقى النقود	

تنجز واجباتك حتى نهاية الأسبوع	يساعدونك
رحّب بهم الوزير	وصل الضيوف إلى المطار
دخل أصدقاؤنا العرب	أردنا إنهاء الاجتماع
أفعل ذلك أيضاً	تفعل ذلك
نسافر فوراً	نتلقّى الدعوة
نساعدكم	تساعدوننا
شرح لهم المدير أهمّية المرفأ	قاموا بجولة في المرفأ
نغيّر البرنامج	لا تسافرون معنا
ندرس المشروع	تطلب منّا ذلك
قبل الدعوة	سمع أن الجميع سيجيئون
نقلته إلى المستشفى	لاحظت أن حالته ليست حسنة
تأخر الوزير	تأخرت السيارة
قابلت عدداً من السياسيين	كنت أرافق الوفد التجاري
أخذ معه هدايا كثيرة	عاد أحمد إلى بغداد
تركتهم فوراً	سمعت هذا الخبر
لاحظوا عدة أغلاط	درسوا المشروع
أقام الوزير حفلة عشاء	أنهى الوفد محادثاته
اجتمعوا فوراً	سمعوا هذه الاقتراحات

G2 Insert حينما instead of عندما in G1.

G3 Combine the clauses in G1 in such a way that حينما or عندما precedes the clause on the left column.

☞   وصلنا إلى المحطّة عندما/حينما تحرّك القطار.

Pay attention to the fact that عندما/حينما are interchangable only in a certain part of the clause-couples.

G4 Replace conjunction + verb by preposition + infinitive.

☞   بعد انتهاء العمل   <   بعد أن انتهى العمل

بعد أن غادر البلد

بعد أن زار المتحف

بعد أن ذهبوا إلى المرفأ

بعد أن وصل إلى هناك

قبل أن يشرح المعالم

قبل أن يكتب الرسالة

قبل أن يقدّم الهدية

قبل أن تُغلق المدارس

قبل أن نحصل على النقود

قبل أن يناقشوا المشروع

منذ أن انتهى المؤتمر

منذ أن أُلغيت الزيارة

منذ أن تغيّر البرنامج

حتى وصل القطار

حتى عاد الوفد

حتى استقبل الضيوف

G5 Transform the prepositional phrases into temporal sentences and vice versa.

☞   سألت أبي قبل أن أكتب الرسالة.   >   سألت أبي قبل كتابة الرسالة.

☞   ذهبت إليه بعد إنجاز العمل.   >   ذهبت إليه بعد أن أنجزت العمل.

بعد أن زرنا الأصدقاء رجعنا إلى البيت

قرأت العنوان قبل أن أدخل الغرفة

بعد إنجاز العمل شربت كأساً من البيرة

بعد أن زاروا حمص وحماه وحلب وصلوا إلى اللاذقية

لا أزال أشتغل مترجماً منذ أن تخرجت من الجامعة

يريد الوفد مشاهدة بعض المعالم قبل مغادرة البلد

منذ أن بدأت الدراسة قرأت كتباً كثيرة

قبل الذهاب إليه سأشتري بعض الهدايا

قبل إغلاق الأبواب سأبيع ما عندي من كتب

بعد أن ناقشوا المشروع شربوا البيرة

منذ إجراء الإصلاح تمكنوا من تحقيق أهداف كثيرة

لم ينم حتى إنجاز العمل

فكّروا في الاستيراد قبل أن يصدّروا اللحوم

أطلعهم على برنامجه قبل اقتراح الوزراء الجدد

C1 (Written homework) Write a letter to an Arab university in which you apply for a post as teacher in the Department of English and add a short curriculum vitae (both in Arabic). The teacher discusses the corrected versions and explains peculiarities in the style of letters in Arabic (date, opening, closing, wishes etc.).

C2 Prepare a dialogue based on Text 2 about the same topic.

Final Exercise:
1. Translate into Arabic.
When I wrote this letter my mother came in. Before I work in Syria for two months, I will be studying in Saudi Arabia for three months. He has been working as an engineer since he graduated from the technical university. Before she went to the doctor's she tried to get in touch with her friend. As long as we are here, we are able to accomplish all tasks. She booked a room while Peter discussed the price with the waiter. The director was in the restaurant whenever we went to the institute. They went to the city where they met the car-salesman. They financed the project to help the government. He didn't come because he didn't have a house. All went to the city centre although it (the weather) was very hot. He worked day and night but he didn't finish the job. She bought many things but she didn't know when she would be able to pay for them. I shall sell everything as soon as I go back to France.

2. Replace conjunction + verb with preposition + infinitive.

قبل أن نحصل على النقود / قبل أن يناقشـوا المشـروع / منـذ أن انتهـى المؤتمـر / منـذ أن ألغيت الزيارة / منذ أن تغيّر البرنامج / حتى وصل القطـار / حتى عـاد الوفـد / بعـد أن غـادر البلد / بعد أن زار المتحف / بعد أن ذهبوا إلى المرفأ / بعد أن وصلٍ إلى هناك / قبـل أن يشرح المعالم / قبل أن يكتب الرسالة / قبل أن يقدّم الهدية / قبل أن تغلق المدارس

3. Translate the following letter into Arabic.
Dear Aḥmad
Excuse me for not writing to you for so long but the exams have started and I had to work a lot. I have also started to write my master-thesis. I am writing about the economic development and its relation to social development in Syria. I have collected many references with details about exports and imports, the oil-sector, domestic and foreign trade, tourism, culture and education up to now. Before I can submit the master-thesis, I have to go to Syria for two months to collect more data. I shall work in the university of Damascus and - God willing - also go to Latakiya to swim in the Mediterranean for a couple of days. This I cannot tell my professor.
I hope to see you soon. Please give my best regards to Muḥammad.
I wish you good success in your exams.
Your sincere friend,
Peter

1. Verbs R₂ = R₃

The 2nd and the 3rd radical of the verbs $R_2 = R_3$ are identical.

Example: $R_1 = م$, $R_2 = ر$, $R_3 = ر > مَرَّ$ "he (has) passed (by)"

The peculiarity of these verbs as compared with the sound triliteral verb consists of the fact that R_2 and R_3 are contracted in some of their forms, but not in others. As a rule, R_2 and R_3 are contracted if a vowel follows R_3 in the form which was based on the pattern of the sound verbs:

يَفْعَلُ	=	يَمُرُّ	فَعَلَ	=	مَرَّ
يَفْعَلُونَ	=	يَمُرُّونَ	فَعَلَتْ	=	مَرَّتْ
			فَعَلُوا	=	مَرُّوا

R_2 and R_3 are not contracted if R_3 is vowelless in the new form which was formed according to the pattern of the sound verbs:

فَعَلْتُ	=	مَرَرْتُ
فَعَلْنَا	=	مَرَرْنَا
يَفْعَلْنَ	=	يَمْرُرْنَ

or if there is a long vowel between R_2 and R_3:

مَفْعُولٌ	=	مَمْرُورٌ
فُعُولٌ	=	مُرُورٌ

The imperfect stem vowel may be *a*, *i* or *u* as is the case with the sound verbs; the vowel that follows R_2 in the non-contracted patterns of the perfect tense is almost always *a*.

The active participle is:	مَارٌّ
The passive participle is:	مَمْرُورٌ

Table 27 of the Appendix provides a survey of all active and passive patterns including the jussive and the imperative.

Derived Forms: All patterns of Forms II and V are formed according to the pattern of the sound verbs:

تَفَعَّلَ	=	تَمَرَّرَ	فَعَّلَ	=	مَرَّرَ
يَتَفَعَّل	=	يتمرّر	يُفَعِّلُ	=	يُمَرِّرُ
مُتَفَعِّل	=	مُتَمَرِّر	مُفَعِّل	=	مُمَرِّر
تَفَعُّل	=	تَمَرُّر	تَفْعِيل	=	تَمْرِير

In the other Forms R$_2$ and R$_3$ are contracted in the 3rd p. sg. m. The individual conjugational forms follow the rules given above. (Appendix: Tables 27 and 28)

☞ A1 The Latin term for these verbs is *"Verba mediae geminatae"*. In most dialects, these verbs are conjugated in the perfect tense like مشى , analogous to the verbs R$_3$ = ى , accordingly.

		but			
مَرَّ	حَبَّ	(هو)	مَرَّيْتُ	حَبَّيْتُ	(أنا)
مَرَّتْ	حَبَّتْ	(هي)	مَرَّيْتَ	حَبَّيْتَ	(أنتَ)
مَرُّوا	حَبُّوا	(هم)	مَرَّيْتِ	حَبَّيْتِ	(أنتِ)
			مَرَّينا	حَبَّينا	(نحن)
			مَرَّيْتُو / مَرَّيْتُم	حَبَّيْتو/حَبَّيْتُم	(أنتم)

2. Verbs with *Hamza*

In the previous lessons verbs with *Hamza* have already been referred to several times: قَرَأَ، سَأَلَ، أَخَذَ etc.

We have used them like the sound verbs in that context - without indicating the fact that they belong to a certain group of verbs - as their peculiarities are nearly exclusively a question of correct spelling. The phonetical peculiarities as compared with the sound verb are limited to a few patterns of the verbs in which *Hamza* is the 1st radical. They are due to the phonetic law whereby '*a*' becomes '*ā*, '*i*' > '*ī* and '*u*' > '*ū*. However, this law does not apply throughout.

Form I	فَعَلَ	=		أَخَذَ
	يَفْعَلُ	=		يَأْخُذُ
	أَفْعَلُ	=	(أَأْخُذُ <)	آخُذُ
	فَاعِلٌ	=	(أَأخِذٌ <)	آخِذٌ
	إِفْعَلْ	=		خُذْ

Note these exceptions:

The two imperatives كُلْ "Eat!" and مُرْ "Order!", which are derived from the verbs أَكَلَ "to eat" and أَمَرَ "to order", have the same form as خُذْ ; otherwise the imperative is formed by R₁ being included, accordingly:

أُوْمُلْ < أُوْمُلْ "Hope!" derived from the verb أَمَلَ "to hope".

Form III	فَاعَلَ	=	آخَذَ	(< أَاخَذَ)
Form IV	أَفْعَلَ	=	آخَذَ	(< أَأْخَذَ)
	أُفْعِلَ	=	أُوْخِذَ	(< أُؤْخِذَ)
	أُفْعِلُ	=	أُوْخِذُ	(< أُؤْخِذُ)
	إِفْعال	=	إِيخَاذ	(< إِئْخَاذ)
Form VIII	اِفْتَعَلَ	=	اتَّخَذَ	

R₁ is not assimilated to the infix *t* in the other verbs R₁ = *Hamza*, but the vowel is not prolonged either:

إئْتَلَفَ	(instead of إِيتَلَفَ)
إئْتِلاف	(instead of إِيتِلاف)

☞A2 The Latin term for these verbs is "*Verba (primae, mediae, tertiae) hamzatae*".

The orthographic peculiarities are treated in the following paragraph 3. (Appendix: Tables 29 to 34)

3. The Spelling of *Hamza*

The key to the spelling of *Hamza* is to determine whether ا، و or ى is the chair of *Hamza* or whether *Hamza* occurs without a chair. To determine which spelling must be chosen depends on which vowel precedes or follows *Hamza*. The formal order principle for the following rules distinguishes between the initial, medial and final position of *Hamza* in the word.

3.1.   *Hamza* in initial position

Alif invariably is the chair of *Hamza*:

to take	أَخَذَ
mother	أُمّ
production	إنْتَاج
delegation	إيفَاد

This also applies if the word is preceded by a preposition which is written together with it:

for my mother	لِأُمِّي
by the production of the cars	بِإِنْتَاجِ السَّيَّارات

3.2. *Hamza* in medial position

3.2.1. If *Hamza* is vowelless, the chair of *Hamza* is determined by the vowel immediately preceding *Hamza*, i.e. *Alif* is used with *a/ā*, *Wāw* with *u/ū* and *Yā'* (without diacritical dots) with *i/ī*:

opinion	رَأْي
well/spring	بِئْر
(infinitive of رَأَى)	رُؤْيَة

3.2.2. If *Hamza* is followed by a vowel, but if the consonant immediately preceding *Hamza* is vowelless, the chair of *Hamza* is determined by the vowel which follows *Hamza*:

he asks	يَسْأَلُ
questions	ج أَسْئِلَة
responsible	مَسْؤُول

Exception: If the vowelless consonant preceding *Hamza* is a *Yā'*, the chair of *Hamza* is *Yā'* as well: هَيْئَة "form/shape/appearance; group/body/committee".

3.2.3. If *Hamza* is preceded by a vowel as well as followed by a vowel,
Alif is the chair of *Hamza* if both vowels are *a*,
Wāw is the chair of *Hamza* if one of the two vowels is *u* and
Yā' is the chair of *Hamza* if one of the two vowels is *i*.
If *u* and *i* meet, *Yā'* is the chair of *Hamza*:

he has asked	سَأَلَ
presidents	ج رُؤَسَاءُ
question	سُؤَال
hundred	مِئَة
president	رَئِيس
he was asked	سُئِلَ

If the sequence of vowels is -*ā a*, -*ā ā* or -*ū a*, *Hamza* is written in its isolated form on the line:

(infinitive of قَرَأَ)	قِرَاءَة
experts, chief performers	ج كَفَاءَات
manliness	مُرُوءَة

3.3. *Hamza* in final position

3.3.1. If *Hamza* is preceded by a short vowel, this vowel determines the chair of *Hamza*:

he has read	قَرَأَ
he reads	يَقْرَأُ
it was read	قُرِئَ
to be manly	مَرُؤَ

3.3.2. If *Hamza* is preceded by a long vowel or a vowelless consonant, *Hamza* occurs without a chair:

friends	أَصْدِقَاءُ
read (pass. part.)	مَقْرُوءٌ
(infinitive of جاء)	مَجِيءٌ
one (impers. pron.)	أَلْمَرْءُ

3.4. The following applies to the spelling of the indefinite accusative of nouns with *Hamza* in the final position:

The *Alif* of the indefinite accusative is omitted if the chair of *Hamza* is an *Alif* or if *Hamza* follows *Alif* (= long vowel *ā*) without chair (إِبْتِدَاءً، مُبْتَدَأً).

The *Alif* of the indefinite accusative is used if *Hamza* occurs without chair (except after the long vowel *ā*) (جُزْءاً).

It has *Yā'* as its chair if it is preceded by ي (شَيْئاً).

3.5. A *Hamza* in the final position may become a *Hamza* in medial position by means of a suffix. In this case the rules given in 3.2. apply:

friends	أَصْدِقَاءُ
your friends	أَصْدِقَاؤُكَ
with your friends	مَعَ أَصْدِقَائِكَ
he reads	يَقْرَأُ
they read	يَقْرَؤُونَ
you (f.) read	تَقْرَئِينَ

3.6. *Hamza* together with the long vowel *ā* following is written as *Madda* (~):

August	آب
minarets	مَآذِنُ

This rule does not apply if *Hamza* is also preceded by the long vowel *ā*:

experts, chief performers	كَفَاءَات

You need not learn the rules about the spelling of *Hamza* by heart. Look them up here when needed or inform yourself with the aid of Tables 29-34 in the Appendix (verbs with *Hamza* = R₁, R₂ or R₃).

4. Clauses of Reason

4.1. Clauses of reason have already been presented in previous lessons.
The following conjunctions are used in Arabic for introducing these sentences by "since, because, for, inasmuch as/in that ...":

لِأَنَّ / لِأَنَّهُ	because	لَمْ يَكْتُبْ لِأَنَّهُ كَانَ مَرِيضاً. He did not write because he was ill.
إِذْ / إِذْ أَنَّ، أَنَّهُ	because	لَا يَكْتُبُ إِذْ أَنَّهُ يَنَامُ فِي الدَّرْسِ. He does not write because he sleeps in class.
حَيْثُ/حَيْثُ أَنَّ، أَنَّهُ	because	لَا يَكْتُبُ حَيْثُ (أَنَّهُ) يَنَامُ فِي الدَّرْسِ. He does not write because he sleeps in class.
لَمَّا	since, because	لَمَّا كَانَتِ الْحُكُومَةُ جَدِيدَةً فَقَدْ أَعْلَنَتْ بَرْنَامَجَهَا. Since the government was new, it announced its program.

| بِمَا أَنَّ، أَنَّهُ | since, because | بِمَا أَنَّهُ كَانَ يَدْرُسُ فِي مِصْرَ فَقَدْ تَكَلَّمَ اللَّهْجَةَ المِصْرِيَّةَ.
Since he had studied in Egypt, he spoke the Egyptian dialect. |
| ذٰلِكَ أَنَّ، أَنَّهُ | for, because | هٰذِهِ الخُطَّةُ جَيِّدَةٌ ذٰلِكَ أَنَّهَا تَفْتَحُ آفَاقاً جَدِيدَةً.
This plan is good for it opens up new prospects. |

4.2. Clauses of reason can, however, also be introduced by the particle فَـ (فاء التعليلية = explaining *Fā'*) with the meaning of "because, for, and then, and so, hence/therefore". It is used about as frequently as لِأَنَّ and is employed in Arabic in the secondary clause following the main clause, and is also often introduced by ف as a new independent sentence here.

He did not take part in the classes, and so he failed the examination.	لَمْ يَحْضُرِ الدُّرُوسَ فَفَشِلَ فِي الِامْتِحَانِ.
The government cannot solve the problems because it does not know their causes.	لَا تَسْتَطِيعُ الحُكُومَةُ حَلَّ المَشَاكِلِ، فَهِيَ لَا تَعْرِفُ أَسْبَابَهَا.
He was two hours late, and so he did not get the license.	تَأَخَّرَ بِسَاعَتَيْنِ فَلَمْ يَحْصُلْ عَلَى الرُّخْصَةِ.

V

last	آخِر ج و ن، ات، أَوَاخِرُ	the Arabian Peninsula	الجزيرة العربية
instrument	أَدَاة ج أَدَوات	beauty	جَمَال
minaret	مَأْذَنة ج مَآذِنُ	the Hanging Gardens	ج الجنائِنُ المُعَلَّقة
Iran	إيران	unknown	مَجْهُول
Babylon	بابِل	to form the boundary of sth.	حَدَّ (يَحُدُّ) هـ
suit	بَدْلة ج ـات	to liberate so., sth.	II حرَّر (يُحرِّر) ه، هـ
flat	مُنْبَسِط	shave	حِلاقة
Basrah	البَصْرة	caliphate	خِلافة
old, worn-out	بالٍ	hollow of the sole (of the foot)	أَخْمَصُ القدم ج أَخامِصُ
Umayyads	بَنُو أُمَيَّة		
ʿAbbasids	بنو العبَّاس	Tigris	دِجْلةُ
trousers	بَنْطَلُون ج ـات	to guide, to lead so. to to show so. sth.	دلَّ (يدُلُّ) ه على
Turkey	تُركِيا	in those days	آنذاك = إذ ذاك
to try, to try on sth.	II جرَّب (يُجرِّب) هـ	rest, relaxation	راحة ج ـات
stocking	جُراب ج جَوارِبُ، ـات	Take your time! Don't hurry!	خُذْ رَاحَتَكَ!

to tell so. sth. to transmit, to quote (from a source)	روَى (يرْوي) ل ه (عن)
agricultural	زِراعِيّ
Semite, Semitic	سامِيّ ج ـون
to coincide with	VII اِنسجم (ينْسجِمُ) مع
plain (geogr.)	سهْل ج سُهُول
Sumerian	سُومِريّ
rule (over)	سَيْطرة (على)
to tie, to bind sth. to	شدَّ (يشُدُّ) ه إلى
to want to, to demand	شاء (يشاءُ) أنْ
Whatever God wants	ما شاء الله
morphology, inflection (gram.)	صرْف
ruin, traces	طلل ج أطْلال
Taurus Mountains	طوروس
to continue to do, to do sth. permanently (+imperf. or part.)	ظلَّ (يظلُّ)
miracle	عجيبة ج عجائِبُ
the seven wonders of the world	عجائِب الدُنيا السبع
cream, paste	معْجُون ج معاجِينُ
to count; pass.: to be considered	عدَّ (يعُدُّ) ه، ه من
modern, contemporary	مُعاصِر
to succeed one another	VI تعاقب (يتعاقبُ)
to attack, to assault sth.	غزا (يغزُو) ه
rich (in)	غنِيّ ج أغْنِياءُ (ب)
wood, forest	غابة ج ـات
here: to conquer	فتح ه
light, bright (colour)	فاتِح
bill, check	فاتورة ج فواتيرُ
Euphrates	الفُرات
brush	فُرْشة ج فُرش
to fail (in)	فشِل (يفْشَل) (في)
dome	قُبَّة ج قِباب، قُبب
to decide; to report, to establish sth.	II قرَّر (يُقرِّر) ه
to settle down	X اِستقرَّ (يسْتقِرُّ)
here: cubicle	مقْصُورة ج ـات
castle, palace	قصْر ج قُصُور
region, land	قُطْر ج أقْطار
cotton	قُطْن ج أقْطان
from head to toe	مِن قمة الرأس إلى أخْمَص القدمَيْن
shirt	قميص ج قُمْصان
size	قِياس ج ـات، أقْيِسة
to hide, to waylay so.	كمِن/كمَن (يكْمَنُ/ يكْمُنُ) في، ل
al-Kufah	الكُوفة
to extend to	VIII اِمْتدَّ (يمْتدُّ) إلى
pipe, tube	أُنْبُوب(ة) ج أنابيبُ
grammar	النحْو
grammarian	نحْوِيّ ج ـون
palm tree (coll.)	نخيل
to come into being, to arise	نشأ (ينشأُ) ه
justice, fairness	إنصاف
river	نهْر ج أنْهار
Mesopotamia	بلاد ما بين النهرين
huge, giant	هائِل
face, aspect	وجه ج وُجُوه
razor blade	مُوسىَ ج مواسٍ، أمْواس
(prep.) behind, beyond	وراءَ
description	وصْف ج أوصاف
died	مُتوفى

بلاد ما بين النهرين   **Text 1**

يمتدّ سهل منبسط بين نهري دجلة والفرات من جبال طوروس في الشمال إلى الخليج في الجنوب. وتغطّي هذه المنطقة التي تحدّها في الشرق إيران وفي الغرب سوريا أطلال المدن البابلية والسومرية والأشورية والمآذن والقباب وغابات النخيل وشبكة هائلة من أبراج البترول ومن خطوط أنابيب البترول.

إن هذه الصورة المعاصرة يكمن وراءها كلّ تاريخ العراق. فقد نشأت أوّل دولة في بلاد ما بين النهرين قبل الميلاد بآلاف السنين. وتعدّ مدينة بابل بجنائنها المعلّقة التي تعتبر من عجائب الدنيا السبع من أقدم المدن في العالم. ثم تعاقبت موجات الهجرة السامية القادمة من الجزيرة العربية إلى العراق، وفي مطلع القرن السابع فُتِحَ العراق وشُدّ إلى العالم الإسلامي وظلّ يحمل الوجه العربي الإسلامي حتى اليوم.

وفي سنة ١٤٥هـ/٧٦٠م بدأ بناء مدينة بغداد في عصر الخليفة المنصور (٧٥٤ – ٧٧٥م) وأصبحت عاصمة الخلافة العبّاسية (٧٥٠/١٢٥٨م) التي أعقبت خلافة بني أمية (٦٦١ – ٧٥٠م) والتي انتهت سيطرتها مع الغزو المغولي. ويروى أنّ عدد سكّان بغداد تجاوز في تلك الأيّام ٣٠٠،٠٠٠ نسمة ونقرأ عن بغداد وجمالها وقصورها إلى اليوم في قصص ألف ليلة وليلة وأيضاً عن الخليفة المشهور هارون الرشيد (٧٨٦– ٨٠٩ م).

وأصبحت الكوفة والبصرة بمدرستيهما في النحو العربي وبمجالس علمائهما مركزين هامّين في العالم الإسلامي آنذاك لدراسة اللغة العربية وآدابها وأيضاً للدراسات الإسلامية. وجمع ابن الأنباري المتوفى ٥٧٧ /١١٨١ م في ((كتاب الإنصاف في مسائل الخلاف بين النحويين البصريين والكوفيين)) تفاصيل المناقشات والخلافات بين المدرستين في مسائل النحو والصرف.

في محلّ بيع الملابس   **Text 2**

جون: مساء الخير.

البائعة: مساء النور ، أية خدمة؟

جون: أحتاج إلى ملابس صيفية من قمّة الرأس إلى أخمص القدمين.

البائعة: ملابس داخلية أم خارجية؟

جون: أنا أحتاج إلى كلّ شيء لأنّ حقائبي التي فيها كلّ شيء ما زالت في طريقها إلى هنا وشركة الطيران أرسلتها خطأً إلى مكان مجهول حتى الآن، والله أعلم.

البائعة: أنا آسفة. وقد عانيت من هذه المشكلة قبل سنة عندما كنت في الإجازة في سويسرا وحقائبي وصلت في آخر يوم من الإجازة ولكن الشركة كانت لطيفة معي وأعطتني ٥٠٠ دولار لشراء الحاجيات اللازمة.

جون: قالوا لي إنّهم سيدفعون لي ٢٠ دولاراً مقابل كلّ كيلو من وزن الحقائب وهذا أكثر بكثير من قيمة الحقائب وما فيها و لم أكتب عنواني عليها و لم أقدِّم لهم وصفاً حقيقياً للحقائب والأمل كبير أنّهم لا يجدونها. متى دفعوا لك الفلوس؟

البائعة: دفعوا لي الفلوس بعد أسبوعين وهذه المعاملة كانت مشكلة كبيرة بالنسبة لي لأني كنت هناك في الشتاء وملابسي الشتوية كلّها كانت في الحقائب ولذلك كان يجب عليّ أن أبقى في الفندق في انتظار الحقائب.

جون: عندي نفس المشكلة ولكن بفارق بسيط: حقائبي قديمة وبالية وفيها فقط بعض الكتب والجرائد والهدايا البسيطة والآن أشتري كلّ ما أحتاج إليه على حساب شركة الطيران.

البائعة: مبروك! ماذا تحبّ أن تشتري؟

جون: أحتاج إلى الملابس والأشياء اللازمة للحلاقة مثل موسى وكريم الحلاقة وفرشة ومعجون الأسنان إلى آخره.

البائعة: كلّ هذه الحاجيات موجودة عندنا. نبدأ بالملابس. كم هو قياسك؟

جون: قياسي ٥٢ وأحبّ ألواناً فاتحة وأريد أنْ تكون الملابس من القطن.

البائعة: هذا ضروري طبعاً في الطقس الحارّ وكلّ شيء موجود. شوف هناك في الزاوية وخذ راحتك واختر ما يعجبك! ويمكنك أن تجرب كلّ شيء في المقصورة.

جون: سآخذ كلّ هذه الحاجات وأحتاج إلى فاتورة.

البائعة: لنسجّل أولاً الأسعار: البنطلون ب ٦٧ ديناراً والحذاء ب ٥٦ والقميصان ب ٥٢ والملابس الداخلية ب ١٢ والجوارب ب ١١ والموسى وأدوات الحلاقة ب ٢٠ ، السعر الإجمالي ٢١٨ ديناراً. تفضّل معي إلى أمين الصندوق.

جون: شكراً ، مع السلامة.

البائعة: شكراً وإن شاء الله أشوفك مرّة أخرى. مع السلامة.

Exercises

L1 (Written homework) Translate the following sentences into Arabic.
He settled down in America.
What was decided?
Do you love her?
We love you.
I love all of you.
Why don't you (sg.) love me?
Why don't you (pl.) love me?
I love that country.

Does this make you happy?
This makes us very happy.
How far does this region extend?
Did you show him this shop?
The students are considered to be diligent (students).
This country is considered to be rich in oil.

L2 Which countries, regions, seas, etc. border on Lebanon, Syria and Iraq? Use the verbal pattern تحدّ / يحدّ.

L3 Use the verbal pattern تُعَدّ / يُعَدّ ("to be considered") to say whether the Arab countries you know are considered industrial or agricultural countries.

L4 Form sentences using كنـت أحـبّ / أحـبّ / أحببـتُ in which you refer to persons or things which you liked/loved or still like/love.

L5 The teacher explains the use of the phrase (أُحِبُّ أَنْ (أَقُولَ "I would like to (say)" and asks the students to practice it with the following sample sentences. The sentences have to be changed into the alternative tense.

☞   أحبّ أنْ أقول إنّني أسافر إلى باريس.   >   أحببت أنْ أسافر إلى باريس.

☞   أحببت أنْ أقول إنّني أكتب رسائل.   >   أحبّ أنْ أكتب رسائل.

أحبّت أن تسافر.

أحببنا أن نكتب.

أحبّوا أن يدفعوا.

أحبّ أن أشرب القهوة.

تحبّ أن تقرأ الجرائد.

يحبّون أن يلبسوا ملابس جميلة.

أحبّ أن أتكلم عن هذا الموضوع.

أحبّكم كلّكم.

G1 Repeat the rules of the construction of the imperative (L 8) and form the imperatives (sg. m. and f. and pl. m.) of the following verbs:

كتب، مرّ، قرأ، أعطى، وضع، خـرج، دخـل، دلّ، قـرّر، خـاف، حـرّر، ذهـب، أكـل،

أخذ، أمل

G2 Transform into the imperfect tense.

امتدّت هذه المنطقة من الجبال إلى البحر.

هل شُدّ العراق إلى العالم الإسلامي؟

من دلّك على هذا المحل؟

هل استقرّ رأيك؟

ماذا قرّر الطلاب في اجتماعهم يوم الخميس؟

إنّها أحبّتني كثيراً.

سَرّنا ذلك.

سَرّتني معرفتُك.

G3 Replace the following relative sentences by shortened relative sentences.

☞   المنطقة التي تمتدّ إلى الخليج العربي >   المنطقة الممتدّة إلى الخليج العربي

في القطر الذي يمتدّ إلى البحر الأبيض المتوسط

الدوائر الاقتصادية التي سُرّت لهذا التطور

البلدان التي تحبّ السلام

المرفأ الذي قُرّر بناؤه

المشاكل التي تدلّ على الوضع السياسي في ذلك البلد

G4 (Written homework to practice the spelling of the *Hamza*) Translate:
My friends, your friends, with our friends, beginning with the 1st August, the questions of the responsible ministers
These things are unknown. He suggested something different (another thing). It is a custom to visit the archeological sites of the country.

C1 Prepare a dialogue between a customer and a shop assistant based on Text 2. Use the following phrases:

رخيص / غال، بكم / كم / كم سعره/ كم السعر؟، أعطِني، أرِني، هـذا ... لا يُعْجِبُـني، هـل

ممكن أن أجرّب ...؟، هل عندك ... آخر / أخرى؟

Broaden your knowledge about the names for garments with the help of the dictionary. The teacher explains the names of typical Arabic clothes.

C2 The teacher asks questions about the geography of the Arab world (mountains, deserts, rivers, neighbours, capitals, etc.) using a map or a sketch on the blackboard.

C3 The teacher explains the colloquial use of the perfect tense of

أُحِبّ > حبّيت > أَحْبَبْتُ (Cf. Gr.1, A1) by means of some sample sentences.

Final Exercise:

1. Translate into Arabic.

This country is considered to be rich in mineral resources. Have you guided him to this house? How far does this region extend? We are very happy to meet you tomorrow. He settled down in France. The ministers decided to conceal the problem. Do you love her? Why don't you like the lectures in the languages? Iraq borders Syria, Iran, Kuwait, Saudi Arabia, Jordan and Turkey.

2. Put the following verbs into the imperative (sg. m. and f. and pl. m.).

دلّ، قرّر، خاف، حرّر، ذهب، كتب، مرّ، قرأ، أعطى، وضع، خرج، دخل

3. Transform into the imperfect tense.

ماذا قرّر الطلاب في اجتماعهم يـوم الخميـس؟ إنّها أحبّتـني كثيراً. سَرّنا ذلك. سَرّتني

معرفتُك. امتدّت هذه المنطقة من الجبال إلى البحر. هل شُدّ العراق إلى العـالَم الإسـلامي؟

من دلّك على هذا المحل؟ هل استقرّ رأيك؟

4. Replace the following relative sentences with shortened relative sentences.

المرفأ الذي قُرّر بناؤه / المشاكل التي تدلّ على الوضع السياسي في ذلك البلد / في القطـر

الذي يمتدّ إلى البحـر الأبيـض المتوسـط / الدوائر الاقتصاديـة الـتي سُرّت لهـذا التطور /

البلدان التي تحبّ السلام

5. Translate into Arabic.

I saw your friends. He reached an agreement with his friends. Your friends traveled to Paris. We shall go to the theatre with our friends. Beginning on 1st September I shall go to work everyday. The questions which were answered by the responsible minister had been submitted before. These things are unknown. He suggested something else (= another thing). It is a custom on such trips to visit the archeological sites of the country.

6. Negate the following sentences.

كان طالباً في كلّية الطبّ. هو محاضر. لون الحقـائب أسـود. الفـارق بسـيط. كـلّ شـيء

موجود. أنت نحوي. الطقس ممطر. أنت على حقّ.

7. Translate into Arabic.

Where are the suitcases? I need clothes from head to toe for the summer. The airline has sent the suitcases to a place which is unknown up to now. I have suffered from the same problems. I need 3 pairs of trousers, shoes, socks, five shirts, two suits, a toothbrush, toothpaste, razor blades and shaving cream. The clothes must be made out of cotton. Don't hurry! Do you like these trousers? Try them on in the cubicle! Give me the bill! That is very cheap. I have to buy other things.

1. The Pattern أَفْعَلُ

1.1. Adjectives which denote colours and certain physical characteristics or other peculiarities of a person take the diptotic pattern أَفْعَلُ. We have already mentioned this pattern in Lesson 7, but here a survey is provided once more:

	sg. m.	sg. f.	pl. m.
white	أَبْيَضُ	بَيْضَاءُ	بِيض
red	أَحْمَرُ	حَمْرَاءُ	حُمْر
green	أَخْضَرُ	خَضْرَاءُ	خُضْر
blue	أَزْرَقُ	زَرْقَاءُ	زُرْق
brown	أَسْمَرُ	سَمْرَاءُ	سُمْر
black	أَسْوَدُ	سَوْدَاءُ	سُود
yellow	أَصْفَرُ	صَفْرَاءُ	صُفْر
blond	أَشْقَرُ	شَقْرَاءُ	شُقْر
dumb/mute	أَخْرَسُ	خَرْسَاءُ	خُرْس
deaf	أَطْرَشُ	طَرْشَاءُ	طُرْش
blind	أَعْمَى	عَمْيَاءُ	عُمْي
stupid	أَحْمَقُ	حَمْقَاءُ	حُمْق

☞**A1** The feminine plural ends in -āt: بَيْضاوات، حَمْراوات etc. The plural is only used with persons as a matter of course. Some examples: أَلْبِيض "the whites", أَلسُّود "the blacks", أَلْهُنود الحُمْرُ "the American Indians", فتيات شَقْراوات "blond girls".

The usual rules of agreement which apply to the attributive construction or to the equational sentence containing an adjectival predicate apply to their construction:

the Mediterranean	أَلْبَحْرُ الأَبْيَضُ المُتَوَسِّطُ
Casablanca (دار and سوق are f.)	أَلدَّارُ الْبَيْضَاءُ
the black market	أَلسُّوق السَّوْدَاءُ
the car is blue / its colour is blue, it is blue	أَلسَّيَّارَةُ زَرْقَاءُ / لَوْنُها أَزْرَقُ

1.2. The pattern أَفْعَلُ can be formed out of many adjectives and out of some participles. It expresses a degree of comparison which is called the *Elative* (اِسْم التَّفْضِيل).

📎**A2** By "*Elative*" a degree of comparison is understood which expresses a particularly high degree of the respective quality. In English such words as "thoroughly honest" and "extremely well" can be understood as *Elatives*.

The Arabic *Elative* is used for expressing:
- **an (intensified) positive,**
- **the comparative,**
- **the superlative.**

1.2.1. The *Elative* as an (intensified) positive

pl.		sg.	
f.	m.	f.	m.
فُعَل، فُعْلَيَات	أَفَاعِلُ، أَفْعَلُونَ	فُعْلَى	أَفْعَلُ

📎**A3** Plural forms are rarely encountered.

In an attributive use the *Elative* as a positive is nearly exclusively found in standard terms. As is the case with every adjective, there is concord with the superordinate noun.

Great Britain	بريطانيا الْعُظْمَى
Asia Minor	آسِيَا الصُّغْرَى
the big powers	أَلدُّوَلُ الْكُبْرَى
of great importance	ذُو أَهَمِّيَّةٍ كُبْرَى
the Near East	أَلشَّرْقُ الأَدْنَى
the Middle East	أَلشَّرْقُ الأَوْسَطُ
the Far East	أَلشَّرْقُ الأَقْصَى
minimum (= lowest limit)	أَلْحَدُّ الأَدْنَى
maximum (= utmost limit)	أَلْحَدُّ الأَقْصَى
the Middle Ages	أَلْعُصُورُ الْوُسْطَى

The following *Elatives*

near	م دُنْيَا	أَدْنَى
far(-away)/ distant/remote	م قُصْوَى	أَقْصَى
middle, central	م وُسْطَى	أَوْسَطُ

as well as

left	م يُسْرَى	أَيْسَرُ
right	م يُمْنَى	أَيْمَنُ
lower	م سُفْلَى	أَسْفَلُ
upper/higher	م عُلْيَا	أَعْلَى

(all of them direction-related adjectives) and

(an)other	م أُخْرَى	آخَرُ

do not have a positive form or one which is rarely used or employed in a different sense. Here they are *Elatives* in form, it is true, but the *Elative* does not express a degree of comparison.

In a predicative use the *Elative* as a positive is rarely encountered:

Allah is (very) great.	أَ للهُ أَكْبَرُ.
Allah is omniscient, knows best.	أَ للهُ أَعْلَمُ.

1.2.2. The *Elative* as a comparative

The form which exclusively occurs is: أَفْعَلُ (also in conjunction with feminine or plural words).

In an attributive use: definite or indefinite noun + following أَفْعَلُ:

a smaller number/quantity	عَدَدٌ أَقَلُّ
the cheaper product	ٱلْبِضَاعَةُ الْأَرْخَصُ

The preposition مِنْ "than" may follow:

a cheaper product than the one I bought	بِضَاعَةٌ أَرْخَصُ مِنَ الْبِضَاعَةِ الَّتِي اِشْتَرَيْتُهَا

In a predicative use the *Elative* as a comparative is mostly followed by مِنْ "than":

He is taller than I (am).	هو أَطْوَلُ مِنِّي.
She is more active than you.	هي أَنْشَطُ مِنْكَ.
They are stronger than we (are).	هُمْ أَقْوَى مِنّا.

The preposition مِنْ may be missing if comparison is expressed in a different way:

I am tall, he is taller.	أنا طَوِيلٌ وهو أَطْوَلُ.

☞A4 The genitival construction أَفْعَلُ + definite dual (or plural) or أَفْعَلُ + affixed pronoun in a comparative sense is rare.

the older of the two children	أَكْبَرُ الوَلَدَيْنِ
the older of the two	أَكْبَرُهُما

1.2.3. The *Elative* as a superlative

The pattern which exclusively occurs is: أَفْعَلُ (also in conjunction with feminine or plural words).

If the *Elative* as a superlative occurs in a genitival use, and if an attributive construction is to be expressed, the following constructions are employed:

a) أَفْعَلُ + indefinite noun in the singular

the best student	أَحْسَنُ طَالِبٍ

b) أَفْعَلُ + definite noun in the plural

the best student (= the best of the students) or: the best students	أَحْسَنُ الطُّلَّابِ

c) أَفْعَلُ + affixed pronoun

the best of them or: the best (pl.) of them	أَحْسَنُهُمْ

In general the context will decide whether it is a singular or a plural, e.g.

He is the best student.	هُوَ أَحْسَنُ الطُّلَّابِ
They are the best students.	هُمْ أَحْسَنُ الطُّلَّابِ
sincerest greetings	أَخْلَصُ التَّحِيَّاتِ
one of the most beautiful cities	مَدِينَةٌ مِنْ أَجْمَلِ الْمُدُنِ

The construction of the ordinal numerals as the governing element of a genitive construction (cf. Lesson 16, A2) is similar to the construction mentioned under a):

for the first time	لِأَوَّلِ مَرَّةٍ
the second (largest) industrial nation	ثَانِي دَوْلَةٍ صِنَاعِيَّةٍ

Thus also with آخِر "last":

for the last time	لِآخِرِ مَرَّةٍ

The Arabic *Elative* does not occur in a predicative position for the purpose of expressing an absolute superlative. A sentence like "These students are best." is rendered by

هُمْ أَحْسَنُ الطُّلَّابِ. (هؤلاء الطُّلَّابُ أَحْسَنُ مِنْ غَيْرِهِمْ. is also possible) ,

the example "they play best" is rendered by

يَلْعَبُونَ أَحْسَنَ مِنْ غَيْرِهِمْ or يَلْعَبُونَ أَحْسَنَ مَا يَكُونُ.

1.3. The most frequent among these *Elative* constructions are the following:

أَفْعَلُ مِنْ = comparative

He is taller than I (am).	هُوَ أَطْوَلُ مِنِّي .

أَفْعَلُ + indefinite singular = superlative

the best student	أَحْسَنُ طَالِبٍ

أَفْعَلُ + definite plural = superlative

the best student/ the best students	أَحْسَنُ الطُّلَّابِ

1.4. List of *Elatives* occurring frequently

	Elative pl.		*Elative* sg.		positive
	f.	m.	f.	m.	
(an)other	أُخْرَيَات	آخَرُونَ	أُخْرَى	آخَرُ	
first		أَوَائِلُ	أُولَى	أَوَّلُ	
slow				أَبْطَأُ	بَطِيء
distant, far				أَبْعَدُ	بَعِيد

new				أَجَدُّ	جَدِيد
beautiful, nice				أَجْمَلُ	جَمِيل
good, best				أَجْوَدُ	جَيِّد
modern				أَحْدَثُ	حَدِيث
good, best			حُسْنَى	أَحْسَنُ	حَسَن
light				أَخَفُّ	خَفِيف
sincere, frank				أَخْلَصُ	خَالِص
near, close	دُنًى	أَدَانٍ	دُنْيَا	أَدْنَى	
cheap				أَرْخَصُ	رَخِيص
fast, quick				أَسْرَعُ	سَرِيع
low		أَسَافِلُ	سُفْلَى	أَسْفَلُ	
simple, plain				أَسْهَلُ	سَهْل
bad				أَسْوَأُ	سَيِّىء
severe, violent, vehement				أَشَدُّ	شَدِيد
right, correct, healthy, sound				أَصَحُّ	صَحِيح
hard, difficult				أَصْعَبُ	صَعْب
small; young				أَصْغَرُ	صَغِير
long, large, big, tall				أَطْوَلُ	طَوِيل
good, best				أَطْيَبُ	طَيِّب
great, big, large		أَعَاظِمُ	عُظْمَى	أَعْظَمُ	عَظِيم
high; upper		أَعَالٍ	عُلْيَا	أَعْلَى	عَالٍ
expensive				أَغْلَى	غَالٍ
rich				أَغْنَى	غَنِيٌّ

excellent, best				أفْضَلُ	فَضِيل
distant, extreme, utmost, far		أقَاصٍ	قُصْوَى	أقْصَى	
old				أقْدَمُ	قَدِيم
near, close				أقْرَبُ	قَرِيب
short, small (stature)				أقْصَرُ	قَصِير
small (quantity)				أقَلُّ	قَلِيل
strong				أقْوَى	قَوِيّ
big, large, old				أكْبَرُ	كَبِير
much, more				أكْثَرُ	كَثِير
friendly				ألْطَفُ	لَطِيف
active, hard-working				أنْشَطُ	نَشِيط
clean				أنْظَفُ	نَظِيف
important				أهَمُّ	هَامّ، مُهِمّ
middle, central	وُسَط	أوَاسِطُ	وُسْطَى	أوْسَطُ	
extensive, large, wide				أوْسَعُ	وَاسِع

1.5. Some phraseological expressions:

at least	عَلَى الأَقَلِّ
at most	عَلَى الأَكْثَرِ، عَلَى أَكْثَرِ تَقْدِيرٍ
to the last degree, extremely	إلَى أقْصَى حَدٍّ
to a very large extent	إلَى أبْعَدِ حَدٍّ
mostly	فِي أغْلَبِ الأحْيَانِ
above(-mentioned)	(مَذْكُور) أعْلاَهُ

below, down	في الأَسْفَلِ
above, up	في الأَعْلَى

1.6. The word خَيْر "good, better, best" has a comparative or superlative meaning although it is not an *Elative* in form:

Prevention is better than cure.	أَلْوِقايَةُ خَيْرٌ مِنَ العِلاجِ.
Prevention is the best cure. (*lit.:* is the best means of cure)	أَلْوِقاية خَيْرُ وسِيلَةٍ لِلْعِلاجِ.

2. *Tamyīz* (accusative of specification) and comparison

2.1. We refer to the accusative of an indefinite noun which expresses a modification, a specification (= تَمْييز) as *Tamyīz* (accusative of specification).

According to the rules of classical Arabic language the *Tamyīz* is used, above all,

- **with measurements,**

✍A5 Example: ذِرَاع جُوخـاً "a cubit of cloth". In this function it may be replaced by the prepositional phrase مِنْ + definite noun - and thus it is also usual in MSA: ذِرَاع مِن الجُوخِ .

- **after the numerals 11-99 and for indicating the material.**

✍A6 Example: خاتِمٌ فِضَّةً "a ring made of silver, a silver ring". Nowadays it is better to say:

خاتِمُ فِضَّةٍ, خاتِمٌ فِضِّيّ or خاتِمٌ من الفِضَّةِ.

2.2. In MSA such constructions which are equivalent to prepositional phrases with "in" in English are considered *Tamyīz*-accusatives.

lit.: Nobody surpasses him in knowledge and diligence.	لا يَفُوقُهُ أَحَدٌ مَعْرِفَةً واجْتِهاداً.

2.3. The main area in which the *Tamyīz* is applied is the comparison of adjectives which do not have an *Elative*. These are:

- **a)** the adjectives which take the pattern أَفْعَل by nature
- **b)** the participles (except the active participle, Form I) and the form of intensity فَعَّال
- **c)** the Nisbas (relative adjectives)
- **d)** the adjectives which take the forms فَعْلانُ and فَعُول, as well as some other adjectives.

In all these cases the comparative and the superlative are formed by means of the *Elative* أَكْثَرُ "more" + noun in the indefinite accusative. أَكْثَرُ may sometimes be replaced with أَشَدُّ.

The difficulty for the non-native speaker consists in knowing which noun is to be used. In case of the participles, it is nearly always the corresponding infinitive which follows أَكْثَرُ or أَشَدُّ. In case of the *Nisba* adjectives and of the adjectives which take on the structure فَعَّال, it is the feminine *Nisba* which follows. If necessary, one can refer to the dictionary for help.

The construction becomes definite by the article being placed in front of the *Elative*.

a)	white	أَبْيَضُ
	whiter	أَكْثَرُ بَيَاضاً، أَشَدُّ بَيَاضاً
	the whiter, whitest paper	أَلْوَرَقُ الأَكْثَرُ بَيَاضاً
	the whitest paper	أَلْوَرَقُ الأَشَدُّ بَيَاضاً
		أَكْثَرُ , أَشَدُّ الأَوْرَاقِ بَيَاضاً

Constructions like أَلْوَرَقُ الأَكْثَرُ بَيَاضاً , i.e. if a definite *Elative* follows the noun, primarily express a comparative. In cases of doubt, it must be decided on the basis of the context whether a superlative sense is meant.

☞A7   The noun used for comparison takes the form فَعَال (سَوَاد، بَيَاض) in case of أَبيض and أَسود, the form فُعْلَة (حُمْرَة، زُرْقَة) etc. in case of the remaining adjectives of colour.

b)	diligent	مُجْتَهِد
	more diligent	أَكْثَرُ اجْتِهَاداً
	the more, most diligent students	أَلطُّلاَّبُ الأَكْثَرُ اجْتِهَاداً
	the most diligent student(s)	أَكْثَرُ الطُّلاَّبِ اجْتِهَاداً
	productive	مُنْتِج
	more productive	أَكْثَرُ إِنْتَاجِيَّةً
	the more, most productive equipment	أَلأَجْهِزَةُ الأَكْثَرُ إِنْتَاجِيَّةً
	the most productive equipment	أَكْثَرُ الأَجْهِزَةِ إِنْتَاجِيَّةً

c)	popular	شَعْبِيّ
	more popular	أَكْثَرُ شَعْبِيَّةً
	the more, most popular men	أَلرِّجَالُ الأَكْثَرُ شَعْبِيَّةً
	the most popular man, men	أَكْثَرُ الرِّجَالِ شَعْبِيَّةً
d)	tired, weary	تَعْبَانُ
	more tired	أَكْثَرُ تَعَباً، أَشَدُّ تَعَباً
	the most tired one of us or: the most tired ones of us	أَكْثَرُنَا تَعَباً، أَشَدُّنَا تَعَباً

2.4. In the *False Iḍāfa* we use the *Elative* of the adjective and, as in the examples a-d, the *Tamyīz* of the noun for comparison:

widespread	وَاسِعُ الاِنْتِشَارِ
more widespread	أَوْسَعُ انْتِشَاراً
the more, most widespread goods	أَلْبَضَائِعُ الأَوْسَعُ انْتِشَاراً
the most widespread goods	أَوْسَعُ الْبَضَائِعِ انْتِشَاراً
the most widespread ones of them	أَوْسَعُهَا انْتِشَاراً

✍A8 Matters are more complicated if the 1ˢᵗ term of the *False Iḍāfa* does not have an *Elative*, as is for instance the case with صُلْبُ الرَّأْيِ "obstinate, stubborn". If the comparative and the superlative are formed at all, we must construe them by means of أَكْثَر + noun + preposition في :   أَكْثَرُ صَلَابَةً في الرَّأْيِ.

2.5. One form of the reduction of a concept is expressed by أَقَلُّ "less". The construction is the same as with أَكْثَر :

less diligent	أَقَلُّ اجْتِهَاداً

V

petrochemical	بَتْرُوكِيمِيائِيّ	record, minutes	بْرُوتُوكُول
barrel	بِرْمِيل ج بَرَامِيلُ	to cry	بَكَى (يَبْكِي)
to send so. sth.	بَعَث (يَبْعَث) لـ ب	usefulness, profitability	جَدْوَى
plastic	بْلَاسْتِيكِيّ	useless, in vain	بِلا / بِدُون جَدْوَى
to prove, to establish sth.	أَثْبَت (يُثْبِتُ) هـ IV	mosque	جَامِع ج جَوَامِعُ

preface, lead	مُقدِّمة ج ـات
consul	قُنصُل ج قناصِلُ
sulphur; matches	كِبْريت
not only ... but also	لا ... فحسْب ... بل إنّما أيضاً
without	بِلا
more favourable (for)	أكثر مُلاءمة (ل)
here: to lay sth.	مَدَّ (يَمُدُّ) هـ
skillful	ماهِر ج ون
products	ج مُنتجات
copper	نُحاس
brass	نحاس أصفر
to build, to erect sth.	IV أنشأ (يُنشِئُ) هـ
crude oil	نفط خام
expense(s), cost(s)	نفقة ج ـات
at his expense	على نفقتِهِ
tanker, transporter	ناقِلة ج ـات
oil tanker	ناقلة النفط
joke, anecdote	نُكتة ج نُكَت، نِكات
quick-witted	حاضِر النكتة
to escape from, to	هرب (يهْرُبُ) من، إلى
to escape from justice	هرب عن وجه العدالة
fullness, wealth, abundance	وفْرة
provisional, temporary	مُؤقَّت
manpower, workers	ج الأيدي العامِلة

(sum) total, totality, the whole	مَجْمُوع
plant, works, factory	مُجمَّع ج ـات
geological	جِيُولوجيّ
to define sth.	II حدَّد (يُحَدِّدُ) هـ
share	حِصّة ج حِصص
to occupy sth.	VIII اِحتَلَّ (يُحتَلُّ) هـ
to excavate sth. from	X اِستخرج (يستخْرِجُ) هـ من
fruitful, fertile	خصِب
to remember sth.	V تذكَّر (يتذكَّرُ) هـ
perhaps	رُبَّما
place, rank	مرْتبة ج مراتِبُ
lead	رصاص
zinc	زِنك
to steal sth. from so.	سرق (يسْرقُ) مِن ه هـ
embassy	سِفارة ج ات
fertilizer	سماد ج أَسْمِدة
winter resort	مشتىً ج مشاتٍ
derivation (from) *(also gram.)*	مُشتقّ ج ـات (مِن)
oil derivatives	مشتقّات النفط
repair	تصْليح ج ـات
mineral	معْدِن ج معادِنُ
giant	عِمْلاق ج عمالِقة
separation, *pl.* differences	فرْقٌ ج فُرُوق
really, in fact, actually	فِعْلاً
phosphate	فُوسْفات
to guess, to estimate sth.	II قدَّر (يُقَدِّرُ) هـ

البلدان العربية وثرواتها الطبيعية   Text 1

يحتلّ عدد كبير من البلدان العربية مكاناً بارزاً في الاقتصاد العالمي وذلك لوفرة الثروات الطبيعية الموجودة هناك، وفي مقدّمتها النفط الذي تبلغ حصّته أكثر من ٦٦ ٪ من مجموع الاحتياطي العالمي من النفط المعروف حتى الآن.

ومّما هو جدير بالذكر أنّ نفقات استخراج النفط في البلدان العربية أقلّ بكثير منها في معظم البلدان الأخرى إذ تقدّر نفقات إنتاج البرميل الواحد من البترول في البلدان العربية بخُمس إلى عُشر نفقات إنتاجه في البلدان الأخرى. ويرجع السبب في فروق النفقات هذه إلى أنّ الظروف الجيولوجية في البلدان العربية أكثر ملاءمة منها في البلدان الأخرى علاوة على الأجور المنخفضة للأيدي العاملة في المنطقة العربية.

وعلى ضوء ذلك تلعب الدول العربية دوراً بارزاً في منظّمة الدول المنتجة للنفط في تحديد أسعار النفط ومعدّلات الإنتاج. ومنذ عدّة سنوات لا تصدّر البلدان العربية النفط الخام فحسب وإنما أيضاً مشتقّات النفط بأنواعها المختلفة أي المنتجات البتروكيميائية مثل الموادّ البلاستيكية والبنزين والأسمدة إلخ وذلك نظراً لإنشاء موانيء حديثة واستخدام ناقلات النفط العملاقة ومدّ خطوط البترول الكثيرة وبناء مصافٍ جديدة ومجمّعات ومصانع كيميائية ضخمة وعالية الإنتاجية.

هذا وتتمتّع البلدان العربية بأهمّية كبرى في مجال استخراج الفوسفات أيضاً، حيث تحتلّ المملكة المغربية وتونس مراتب متقدّمة في الإنتاج العالمي. ومن أهمّ الثروات الطبيعية الأخرى الموجودة في المنطقة العربية الكبريت والنحاس والرصاص والزنك وغيرها من المعادن.

عند الشرطة   Text 2

الموظّفة: مرحباً ، أهلاً وسهلاً ، تفضّل يا سيدي؟

جون: والله عندي مشكلة كبيرة ، كلّ أوراقي أي الجواز والفلوس ورخصة السياقة أي كلّ ما يثبت هويتي سرقوها أو ربّما نسيتها في محلّ من محلّات السوق. إنّني سألت عنها في أكثر من محلّ ولكن بدون جدوى.

الموظّفة: هذه فعلاً مشكلة. يجب أن نكتب بروتوكول. اسمك؟

جون: جون برون.

الموظّفة: حضرتك من أي بلد؟ لغتك العربية جيّدة، أين درستها؟

جون: أنا من ألمانيا. درست العربية في برلين.

الموظّفة: تاريخ الميلاد؟

جون: ولدتُ في ١١ من أبريل ١٩٧٥.

الموظّفة: متى وصلت إلى القاهرة؟

جون: وصلت إلى القاهرة في الـ ١٥ من هذا الشهر.

الموظّفة: في أي فندق نزلت وما هو رقم الغرفة؟

جون: أنا نازل في فندق شيراتون ورقم الغرفة ٣١٢.

الموظّفة: هل تزور القاهرة كسائح أو في مهمّة رسمية؟

جون: أنا هنا في مهمّة رسمية أي لإجراء محادثات مع إحدى الشركات الكبرى.

الموظّفة: اسم الشركة؟

جون: لا أريد أن أتكلّم عن هذا الموضوع.

الموظّفة: هل تتذكّر رقم الجواز؟

جون: لا والله لا أتذكّر الرقم.

الموظّفة: هل تعرف أحداً من أصحاب السفارة؟

جون: لا أعرف موظّفي السفارة. أنا لأوّل مرّة هنا.

الموظّفة: هل تريد أن تتّصل بالسفارة ، قد يجدون حلاً لمشكلتك.

جون: إن شاء الله، سأتّصل بالسفارة ....

الموظّفة: ماذا قالوا؟

جون: قال القنصل إنّه سيأتي إلى هنا بعد نصف ساعة تقريباً وأعطيته تفاصيل هويتي وسيصدرون لي جوازاً مؤقتاً.

الموظّفة: هذا خبر جيّد. يبدو وكأنّك شخصية مهمّة؟

جون: ممكن، لا أدري. على كلّ حال أنت لطيفة جـدّاً وإنّني أعـدك بـأن لا أحكي نكتاً عن الشرطة في المستقبل.

الموظّفة: هذا النوع من النكت موجود عندكم كذلـك؟ توجد عندنا آلاف مـن هـذه النكت وأنا أحبّها. هل يمكنك أن تحكي لنا نكتة عن الشرطة في ألمانيا؟

جون: طبعاً. هناك شرطي يبكي في الشـارع. وسألـه رجل: مـاذا بـك؟ قال: كلبي هرب. قـال الرجـل: مـش مشكلة ، الكلب يعرف طريقه إلى البيت. قال الشرطي: صحيح، الكلب يعرف ولكن أنا؟ كيف أرجع إلى البيت؟

الموظّفة: جميل، هل تعرف الفرق بينك وبين القنصل الذي وصل قبل خمس دقائق؟

جون: لا أعرف.

الموظّفة: القنصل سيرجع إلى السفارة وأنت تبقى هنـا لأنّهـم وجـدوا أنّـك هـارب عـن وجه العدالة!

Exercises:

L1 Answer the questions by means of أكثر من or أقلّ من and the following numeral.

هل عندك كتب كثيرة؟   >   نعم، عندي أكثر من ١٠٠ كتاب.

أو: عندي أقل من ١٠٠ كتاب.

كم درساً لديك في الأسبوع؟

هل زرت ذلك البلد مرّات كثيرة؟

كم بلداً زرت حتى الآن؟

كم عندك من الأصدقاء العرب؟

كم كتاباً عربياً قرأت حتى الآن؟

منذ كم سنة تدرس اللغة العربية؟

كم أسبوعاً كنت على شاطىء البحر؟

منذ كم شهر تسكن في هذا البيت؟

كم ساعة كنت تشتغل في المكتبة؟

هل قرأت هذا الخبر في جريدتين فقط؟

كم نسخة اشتريت؟

كم رسالة كتبت؟

هل تحبّ أنْ تشرب كأساً واحدةً فقط؟

كم شخصاً حضر الحفلة؟

L2 Form equational and verbal sentences using the adjectives which denote colors.

اشتريت سيّارة بيضاء.

أحبّ الفتيات الشقراوات.

L3 (Homework) Learn the *Elatives* of this lesson by heart, and form at least ten sentences in which you use the adjectives denoting the physical and personal characteristics of a person (deaf, blind, dumb, etc.). Look up similar *Elatives* in the dictionary.

L4 (Repetition) Find out the Form which the following infinitives were derived from, and then form equational sentences with an *Elative* in accordance with the given sample sentence.

☞   اجتماع > هذا الاجتماع مهم > ذلك الاجتماع أهم.

محاضرة، سؤال، دراسة، انتظار، تأهيل، تبادل، تعليم، تعاون، اقتصاد، مناقشـة، مناسبة،

توسيع، توقيع، برد، تخصّص، مراجعة، تسـجيل، تأسيس، تحسـين، تصريـح، مساهمة،

تشاور، تطوّر، توتّر، افتتـاح، استقبال، اقـتراح، مبـاراة، مسـابقة، مصارعـة، ملاكمـة،

امتحان

L5 The teacher explains the meaning of the following sayings and proverbs containing *Elatives* and the students try to find out their English eqivalents.

خير الكلام ما قل ودل.

خير الأمور أوسطها.

أكبر منك بيوم أعْرف منك بسنة.

أعمى يقوده بحنون.

الأعمى ما ينسى عصاه (stick).

أضيق من خزق الإبرة (eye of a needle) .

أسرع من لمح البصر.

أخفّ من الريشة (feather) .

الأعور (one-eyed) في بلاد العُمْي/ العُمْيان حاكم.

أخرس (dumb) عاقل خير من جاهل (ignorant) ناطِق.

الأعمى يطلب الشمس وهو فيها.

تضحك بسِنّ بيضاء وتحتها قلب أسود.

عين المحب عمياء.

ليست عداوة الحَمْقىَ (< أحمق) بأضرّ من صداقتهم.

G1 Transform the following sentences in such a way that the *Elative* becomes a part of the comparative predicate.

☞   هذا المعمل كبير.   >   ذلك المعمل أكبر.

هذه البضاعة رخيصة.

هذه الدولة قوية.

هذا الواجب صعب.

هذا سهل.

هذه الشنطة خفيفة.

هذا النوع جيد.

هذه البلدان بعيدة.

هذه الأجهزة حديثة.

هؤلاء الرجال لطفاء.

هذه الغرفة نظيفة.

هؤلاء الطلاب نشيطون.

هذه الجامعة قديمة.

هذه العائلة غنية.

هذا الموديل غال.

هذا الرجل قوي.

هذه المدينة كبيرة.

هذه الكمية قليلة.

هذه القرية قريبة.

هذه النتيجة حسنة.

هذا القطار سريع.

هذه السياسة سيئة.

هذا الولد صغير.

هذا الشخص طويل.

هذه المشروبات طيبة.

هذه الفتاة جميلة.

G2 Form comparative sentences using the *Elative* of the given adjectives, the preposition من "than", and one of the following phrases:

الموجود في ذلك البلد – الموجود عندك – الأصدقاء الآخرون – آخر , أخرى – تحدّثنا عنه أمس – زرته في العام الماضي – رأيته أمس – اشتريته أنت.

☞ هذا الجهاز حسن.　＞　هذا الجهاز أحسن من الجهاز الآخر.

☞ أو: هذا الجهاز أحسن من الجهاز الموجود عندك.

☞ أو: هذا الجهاز أحسن من الجهاز الذي اشتريته أنت.

☞ أو: هذا الجهاز أحسن من الجهاز الذي رأيته أمس.

صديقنا السوري نشيط.

هذا الطالب لطيف.

عندي كتب كثيرة.

هذا الجامع قديم.

هذا البلد غني بالنفط.

هذه المناقشة هامّة.

هذه الأحذية غالية.

هذه الفتاة جميلة.

الجهاز الموجود عندي حديث.

هذه المشكلة صعبة.

صديقك طويل.

اشتريت كمية قليلة.

هناك ثروات طبيعية كثيرة.

هذه البضاعة سيئة.

هذه البيوت صغيرة.

هذا الجهاز رخيص.

G3 Replace the adjective with its *Elative* with a superlative meaning.

☞   اشتريت جهازاً رخيصاً.   >   اشتريت أرخص جهاز.

☞   هذا الجهاز رخيص.   >   هذا (هو) أرخص جهاز.

هذا الطريق قصير.

هذا النوع جيِّد.

هذه السيارة سريعة.

هي فتاة طويلة.

هذا الجواب صحيح.

هو شخص طيِّب.

هم أشخاص لطفاء.

لعب المنتخب مباراة عظيمة.

هذه المنطقة جميلة.

بعثت له بتحياتي الخالصة.

عنده آلات حديثة.

هذه القرية قريبة.

هم رجال أقوياء.

جاء عدد كبير منهم من الخارج.

اشتريت معطفاً غالياً.

هو سياسي نشيط.

هذه (هي) مشكلة هامّة.

زرنا مكاناً عالياً في الجبال.

هذه الطائرات سريعة.

هذه الجملة سهلة.

هذه المدينة قريبة.

هذا الطالب نشيط.

هذه الحقيبة خفيفة.

G4 Replace the adjective with the comparative construction أكثر + noun and add the phrase in brackets.

☞   أنت مجتهد (منّي)   >   أنت أكثر اجتهاداً منّي.

هذا السياسي شعبي   (من السياسين الآخرين)

مآذن الجوامع مرتفعة   (من بيوت المدينة)

أنتم مجتهدون   (منّا)

أسعار الموديلات الجديدة مرتفعة   (من أسعار الموديلات القديمة)

هذا الفرع الاقتصادي منتج   (من الفروع الأخرى)

المنطقة الغربية خصبة   (من المنطقة الشرقية)

أنا تعبان   (منكم)

ذلك المشتى مشهور   (من المشاتي الأخرى)

الطقس هناك معتدل   (من الطقس عندنا)

هذه المشكلة معقدة   (من جميع المشاكل الأخرى)

السائقون اللبنانيون ماهرون   (من السائقين في البلدان الأوربية)

C1 The teacher prepares a conversation with the students about mineral resources in the Arab world and adds more terms to the terms given in Text 1.

C2 Prepare a dialogue about a problem which you have to deal with with the help of the police (e.g. accident, theft, residence permit, etc.).

Final exercise:

1. Transform the following sentences in such a way that you get a comparative predicate containing an *Elative*.

هذه الكمّية قليلة. هذه القرية قريبة. هذه النتيجة حسنة. هذا القطار سريع. هذه السياسة سيّئة. هذا الولد صغير. هذا الشخص طويل. هذه المشروبات طيّبة. هـذه الفتاة جميلة. هذه البضاعة رخيصة. هذه الدولة قوية. هذا الواجب صعب. هـذا سهـل. هـذه الشنطة خفيفة. هذا النوع جيد. هذه البلدان بعيدة. هذه الأجهزة حديثة. هؤلاء الرجال لطفـاء. هذه الغرفة نظيفة. هؤلاء الطلّاب نشيطون. هذه الجامعة قديمة. هـذه العائلة غنيـة. هـذا الموديل غال. هذا الرجل قوي. هذه المدينة كبيرة.

2. Replace the adjective with the *Elative* with a superlative meaning.

جاء عدد كبير منهم من الخارج. اشترِيت معطفاً غالياً. هو سياسي نشيط. هـذه (هـي) مشكلة هامّة. زرنا مكاناً عالياً في الجبال. هذه الطائرات سريعة. هذا الطريق قصير. هـذا النوع جيّد. هذه السيّارة سريعة. هي فتاة طويلة. هـذا الجـواب صحيـح. هـو شـخص طيّب. هم أشخاص لطفاء. لعب المنتخب مباراة عظيمة. هـذه المنطقـة جميلـة. بعثت لـه بتحياتي الخالصة. عنده آلات حديثة. هذه القرية قريبة.

3. Form sentences with a comparative *Elative* followed by من غيره / من غيرها.

صديقنا السوري نشيط. هذا الطالب لطيف. عندي كتب كثيرة. هذا الجامع قديم. هـذا البلد غني بالنفط. هذه المناقشـة هامّـة. هـذه الأحذيـة غاليـة. هـذه الفتـاة جميلـة. الجهـاز الموجود عندي حديث. هذه المشكلة صعبة. صديقك طويل. اشترِيت كمية قليلة. هنـاك ثروات طبيعية كثيرة. هذه البضاعة سيِّئة. هذه البيوت صغيرة. هذا الجهاز رخيص.

4. Replace the adjective with a superlative.

هذا السياسي شعبي. هذه الجبال مرتفعة. أنتم مجتهدون. هذه الأسعار مرتفعة. هذا الفرع الاقتصادي منتج. هذه المنطقة خصبة. ذلك الرئيس مشهور. هذه المشـكلة معقـدة. هـذه السياسة معتدلة.

5. Translate into Arabic.

A number of Arab countries occupy an outstanding rank in the world economy because of their oil resources. Their share in the total oil reserves of the world is more than two thirds. The production costs in the Arab world are much lower, and that is why this industry is much more productive than in other countries. The Arab oil-producing countries have the greatest influence over OPEC. They don't only sell crude oil, but also oil-derivatives of different kinds, e.g. plastic products, petrol, fertilizers, etc. Many countries have modern ports and giant oil tankers, modern refineries and a large net of pipelines. In the field of the production of phosphate, Morocco and Tunisia are of greatest importance in the world's production. Besides that, there are mineral resources such as copper, lead, zinc and sulphur.

1. Conditional Sentences (أَلْجُمَل الشرْطِيَّة)

Sentences in which a condition is mentioned, i.e. facts, the existence or execution of which is the precondition for the existence or execution of other facts, are referred to as conditional sentences. The construction of the conditional sentence consists of the conditional clause proper = conditional (*protasis* أَلشَّرْط) and of the result clause (*apodosis* أَلْجَـواب) as the logical consequence of the condition. In English, conditional sentences are mostly introduced by the conjunction "if ".

☝A1 Some sentences have the structure of conditional sentences in form, it is true, but they lack the logical-causal relation between the condition and the consequence.
In the sentence "if this news is true, the delegation left Cairo yesterday", the truth of the news is not a precondition for the departure of the delegation, and therefore, the latter is not a consequence of the truth of the news formulated in the conditional either. The logical solution would, for instance, read: "if this news is true, this confirms that the delegation ...". Accordingly, in some sentences the result clause only formally belongs to the conditional period. The following representations about grammar do not give special attention to the sentences "which have a logical break".

1.1. The real conditional sentence

In the real conditional sentence the condition is regarded as actually given or as possible with respect to its feasibility.

1.1.1. The most common Arabic conjunction employed for introducing such a conditional sentence is إذَا "if ".

1.1.1.1. The construction is as follows:

(فَعَلَ stands for the perfect tense, يَفْعَلُ for the imperfect tense)

English		Arabic	
conditional	result clause	result clause	conditional
a) present	present	فَعَلَ	فَعَلَ
b) present	present	يَفْعَلُ	فَعَلَ
c) present	perfect	يَكُونُ قَدْ فَعَلَ	فَعَلَ
d) present	future	فَسَوْفَ يَفْعَلُ	فَعَلَ
e) present	future	فَسَيَفْعَلُ	فَعَلَ
f) present	imperative	فَافْعَلْ	فَعَلَ

Accordingly, the Arabic perfect tense always has a present function in these conditional sentences.

a)	If you give me the Arabic book, I will give you the French book.	إِذَا أَعْطَيْتِنِي الكِتَابَ الْعَرَبِيَّ أَعْطَيْتُكِ الْكِتَابَ الْفِرَنْسِيَّ.
b)	~	إِذَا أَعْطَيْتِنِي الْكِتَابَ الْعَرَبِيَّ أُعْطِيكِ الْكِتَابَ الْفِرَنْسِيَّ.
c)	If this news is true, the delegation left Cairo yesterday.	إِذَا صَحَّ هَذَا الْخَبَرُ يَكُونُ الْوَفْدُ قَدْ غَادَرَ الْقَاهِرَةَ أَمْسِ.
d)	If this news is true, the delegation will leave Cairo tomorrow.	إِذَا صَحَّ هَذَا الْخَبَرُ فَسَوْفَ يُغَادِرُ الْوَفْدُ الْقَاهِرَةَ غَدًا.
e)	~	إِذَا صَحَّ هَذَا الْخَبَرُ فَسَيُغَادِرُ الْوَفْدُ الْقَاهِرَةَ غَدًا.
f)	If you meet them, inform them immediately.	إِذَا قَابَلْتَهُمْ فَأَطْلِعْهُمْ فَوْرًا.

1.1.1.2. The perfect tense (فَعَلَ) following إِذَا may also be replaced by كَانَ + imperfect tense (كَانَ يَفْعَلُ). Its actual function as present tense is preserved. This construction particularly occurs with modal auxiliary verbs.

If you want to travel tomorrow, discuss (the matter) with the director.	إِذَا كُنْتَ تُرِيدُ أَنْ تُسَافِرَ غَدًا فَاحْكِ مَعَ الْمُدِيرِ.

1.1.1.3. كَانَ following إِذَا, with an actual function as present tense, is also employed in the nominal conditional.

If Muḥammad is present, I will ask him.	إِذَا كَانَ مُحَمَّدٌ مَوْجُودًا أَسْأَلُهُ.

1.1.1.4. فَ, if employed for the purpose of introducing a result clause, precedes لَنْ , قَدْ and لَيْسَ as well as equational sentences. This is in addition to its preceding سَ and سَوْف and the imperative:

If the car is there, we will travel immediately, of course. (*lit.*: it is natural that we ...)	إِذَا كَانَتِ السَّيَّارَةُ مَوْجُودَةً فَمِنَ الطَّبِيعِيِّ أَنَّنَا نُسَافِرُ فَوْرًا.
If I complete my work by Sunday I will have discharged my duty.	إِذَا أَنْهَيْتُ عَمَلِي حَتَّى يَوْمِ الأَحَدِ فَقَدْ أَنْجَزْتُ وَاجِبِي.
If you visit it once, you will never forget it.	إِذَا زُرْتَهَا مَرَّةً فَلَنْ تَنْسَاهَا أَبَدًا.

1.1.1.5. The result clause may also be a verbal clause preceded by إِنَّ + subject, which is also preceded by فَ in that case.

If you give me the Arabic book, I will give you the French book.	إِذا أَعْطَيْتِنِي الْكِتَابَ الْعَرَبِيَّ فَإِنَّنِي أُعْطِيكَ الْكِتَابَ الفِرَنْسِيّ.

1.1.1.6. Negation: The perfect tense following إذا is replaced by لَمْ + jussive. The result clause is negated either by لم + jussive or by لا، لن or لَيْسَ.

If you do not give me the Arabic book, I will not give you the French book.	إِذا لَمْ تُعْطِنِي الْكِتَابَ الْعَرَبِيَّ لَمْ أُعْطِكَ / لا أُعْطِيكَ الْكِتَابَ الفِرَنْسِيّ.
If you do not give me the Arabic book, I will (surely) not give you the French book.	إِذا لم تُعْطِنِي الْكِتَابَ الْعَرَبِيَّ فَلَنْ أُعْطِيَـكَ / فَسَوْفَ لا أُعْطِيكَ الْكِتَابَ الفِرَنْسِيّ.

1.1.1.7. If the construction كَانَ يَفْعَلُ occurs in the conditional, its negation is not expressed by كَانَ being negated, but by the imperfect tense being negated by means of لا (لا يَفْعَلُ).

If you do not want to travel tomorrow, discuss (the matter) with the director.	إِذا كُنْتَ لا تُرِيدُ أَنْ تُسَافِرَ غَداً فَاحْكِ مَعَ المُدِيرِ.

1.1.1.8. A condition relating to the past naturally occurs rather seldom. The Arabic construction then requires the past perfect (كَانَ قَدْ فَعَلَ) after إذا. Its negation is not expressed by كَانَ being negated, but by the verb form فَعَلَ being negated by means of لَمْ (لَمْ يَفْعَلْ).

If you have bought this car, you have chosen a good model.	إِذا كُنْتَ قَدِ اشْتَرَيْتَ هَذِهِ السيَّارَةَ فَقَدِ اخْتَرْتَ / تَكُونُ قَدِ اخْتَرْتَ مُودِيلاً جِيِّداً.
If you have not read this book, you do not know the issues.	إِذا كُنْتَ لَمْ تَقْرَأْ هَذَا الْكِتَـابَ فَـإِنَّكَ لا تَعْرِفُ الْقَضَايَا.

1.1.1.9. The clause introduced by إذا does not need to precede the result clause at all. On the contrary, the two are interchangeable. The conditional (protasis) then follows the result clause (apodosis), which formally turns into a dependent main clause. The basic rule mentioned about the perfect tense after إذا actually functioning as present tense remains unaffected. There are no particular rules for the construction of the main clause regarding structure or tense.

I (will) (surely) give you the French book if you give me the Arabic book.	(إِنَّنِي، سَوْفَ) أُعْطِيكَ الْكِتَابَ الْفِرَنْسِيَّ إِذَا أَعْطَيْتِنِي الْكِتَابَ الْعَرَبِيّ.
Inform them immediately if (= in case) you meet them!	أَطْلِعْهُمْ فَوْراً إِذَا قَابَلْتَهُمْ.
You will be able to read the Arabic newspapers after a year if you learn 10 words every day.	سَتَسْتَطِيعُ أَنْ تَقْرَأَ الْجَرَائِدَ الْعَرَبِيَّةَ بَعْدَ سَنَةٍ إِذَا كُنْتَ تَتَعَلَّمُ كُلَّ يَوْمٍ عَشْرَ كَلِمَاتٍ.

1.1.2. Another conjunction employed for the introduction of a real conditional sentence, which is, however, used far less than إِذَا in modern Arabic, is إِنْ "if ". The perfect tense or the jussive is employed in the conditional, i.e. after إِنْ , and likewise in the result clause. They are always negated by means of لَمْ . What was said above about إِذَا , also applies to the introduction of the result clause by means of فَ, and to interchangeability.

If you give me the Arabic book, I will give you the French book.	إِنْ أَعْطَيْتِنِي / تُعْطِنِي الْكِتَابَ الْعَرَبِيَّ أَعْطَيْتُكَ / أُعْطِكَ الْكِتَابَ الْفِرَنْسِيّ.
If you do not give me the Arabic book, I will not give you the French book (either).	إِنْ لَمْ تُعْطِنِي الْكِتَابَ الْعَرَبِيَّ لَمْ أُعْطِكَ الْكِتَابَ الْفِرَنْسِيّ.
If you meet them, inform them!	إِنْ قَابَلْتَهُمْ فَأَطْلِعْهُمْ.
I will give you the book if Muḥammad does not ask for it.	سَأُعْطِيكَ الْكِتَابَ إِنْ لَمْ يَطْلُبْهُ مُحَمَّدٌ.

A2 In the view of modern Arab grammarians, the difference between إِذَا and إِنْ is that the former indicates the certain realization of the condition, and that the latter only expresses a certain degree of probability. Accordingly, one might think of "if " as the equivalent of إِذَا and of "in case" (in the sense of a potential) as the equivalent of إِنْ , but the actual application (in English and in Arabic) does not allow us to clearly distinguish between the two. (Furthermore, the common conjunction in English is nearly always "if ".)

A3 إِذَا and إِنْ being equivalent to the English conjunctions "if, whether" are also used for introducing indirect questions. Besides, هَلْ and مَا إِذَا, also فِيمَا إِذَا or عَمَّا إِذَا, are available after سَأَل and فَكَّر.

| We do not know whether he was there. | لَا نَعْرِفُ إِذَا / مَا إِذَا/ إِنْ / هَلْ كَانَ هُنَاك. |

He asked them if he was there.	سَأَلَهُمْ عَمَّا إذا كَانَ هُنَاك.
He considered whether she was there.	فَكَّرَ فِيمَا إذا كَانَتْ مَوْجُودَةً.

1.1.3. شَرِيطَةَ أَنْ / عَلى شَرْطِ أَنْ and بِشَرْطِ أَنْ / عَلى أَنْ in the sense of "provided (that), on the condition that", followed by the imperfect tense (subjunctive), are also employed for forming real conditional sentences.

I will travel tomorrow, provided the symposium begins.	سَأُسَافِرُ غَداً بِشَرْطِ أَنْ / عَلـى شَـرْطِ أَنْ / شَرِيطَةَ أَنْ / عَلى أَنْ تَبْدَأَ النَّدْوَةُ.

👉A4 Besides إذا and إنْ , there are several other words, mostly interrogative pronouns or words derived from interrogative adverbs, which can introduce a conditional sentence, e.g.

مَنْ	in the sense of "if someone"
مَا	in the sense of "if something"
مَهْمَا	in the sense of "what(so)ever"
كَيْفَمَا	in the sense of "how(so)ever"

مَنْ and مـا have their English equivalents in the interrogative pronouns "who" and "what", which contain a conditional sense as well (he who [= if someone] seeks, finds; cf. Lesson 15, Gr 2.1.). The others occur too seldom to warrant mention.

1.2. The unreal conditional sentence

Sentences in which the condition has not been realized or cannot be realized are called unreal conditional sentences. In English, no particular conjunctions for the introduction of such sentences are known, but the latter are expressed by means of certain combinations of tenses and by modal auxiliary verbs (e.g. were, had been, would (have done), could (have done)). They are mostly introduced by "if".

1.2.1. In Arabic, the unreal conditional sentence is introduced by means of the conjunction لَوْ.

1.2.2. Both in the conditional and in the result clause, the perfect tense is mostly used for expressing irreality in the present and future tense. The result clause may be introduced by the emphasizing particle لَ:

If you gave me this book, I would read it immediately.	لَوْ أَعْطَيْتِنِي هَذَا الْكِتَابَ لَقَرَأْتُهُ فَوْراً.
If you walked in/through the centre of this city now, you would know how the people live there.	لَوْ سِرْتَ الآنَ فِي مَرْكَزِ هَذِهِ الْمَدِينَةِ لَعَرَفْتَ كَيْفَ يَعِيشُ النَّاسُ فِيها.

1.2.3. Unlike in the real conditional sentence, the perfect tense following the conjunction لَو may also express the past tense in the unreal conditional sentence.

If they had used clay bricks, the buildings would have disappeared fast.	لَو اسْتَخْدَمُوا قَوَالِبَ الطِّينِ لاخْتَفَتِ الأَبْنِيَةُ بِسُرْعَةٍ.

The context must decide which tense the perfect tense represents in each particular case. The same applies to constructions with كان + imperfect tense. However, in the conditional or in the result clause, the past perfect (كان قَدْ فَعَلَ) may be employed so that the temporal relation is made clear.

1.2.4. The conditional and the result clause are interchangeable, just as is the case in the real conditional sentence. The result clause turns into an independent main clause again, the verb of which then does not necessarily take on the perfect tense.

I would give him the French book if he gave (or had given) me the Arabic book.	إِنَّنِي سَأُعْطِيهِ الْكِتَابَ الْفِرَنْسِيَّ لَوْ أَعْطَانِي الْكِتَابَ الْعَرَبِيَّ.

1.2.5. The unreal conditional sentence may be turned into a nominal construction by the conjunction أَنَّ being placed behind لَو. The former is followed by the noun, then by the verb.

If Muḥammad had visited me, I would have given him the book.	لَوْ أَنَّ مُحَمَّداً زَارَنِي لأَعْطَيْتُهُ الْكِتَابَ / لَكُنْتُ قَدْ أَعْطَيْتُهُ الْكِتَابَ.
If Muḥammad visited me tomorrow, I would give him the book.	لَوْ أَنَّ مُحَمَّداً سَيَزُورُنِي غَداً لأَعْطَيْتُهُ الْكِتَابَ.

1.2.6. The unreal conditional sentence is negated by means of لَم in the conditional, and by لَم or by ما emphasized by the particle لَ (= لَمَا) in the result clause.

If the plane had not been late, it would (not) have arrived in Cairo at 6 o'clock.	لَوْ لَمْ تَتَأَخَّرِ الطَّائِرَةُ لَوَصَلَتْ (لَمَا وَصَلَتْ) إِلَى الْقَاهِرَةِ فِي السَّاعَةِ السَّادِسَةِ.
If Muḥammad had not come to me yesterday, I would not have been able to give him the book.	لَوْ لَمْ يَأْتِ مُحَمَّدٌ إِلَيَّ أَمْسِ / لَوْ أَنَّ مُحَمَّداً لَمْ يَأْتِ إِلَيَّ أَمْسِ لَمَا اسْتَطَعْتُ / لَمَا كُنْتُ أَسْتَطِيعُ أَنْ أُعْطِيَهُ الْكِتَابَ.

1.2.7. لــو followed by لا (= لَوْلا) without a verb means "if it were not or had not been for ...".

If it had not been for Muḥammad / him, I would not have completed the work; if it were not for Muḥammad / him, I would not complete the work.	لَوْ لا مُحَمَّدٌ / لَوْلاهُ لَمَا أَنْهَيْتُ الْعَمَلَ.

1.3. The concessive clause

The two conjunctions إِنْ and لَوْ - being preceded by و (= وَإِنْ، وَلَوْ) - are also used for forming concessive clauses, and are equivalent to the English conjunctions "even if, even though, although". وَلَوْ may be preceded by حَتَّى "even" (= حَتَّى وَلَوْ) "even if ".

The above-mentioned rules applying to the construction of the clause introduced by إِنْ or لَوْ respectively, apply here as well. The main clause precedes the subordinate clause.

I will not accomplish the work, even if I work 16 hours every day.	سَوْفَ لا أُنْجِزُ الْعَمَلَ وَإِنْ عَمِلْتُ ١٦ سَاعَةً كُلَّ يَوْمٍ.
I will not accomplish the work, even if I work 16 hours every day.	سَوْفَ لا أُنْجِزُ الْعَمَلَ (حَتَّى) وَلَوْ عَمِلْتُ ١٦ سَاعَةً كُلَّ يَوْمٍ.
I will complete the work, even if nobody helps me.	سَأُنْهِي الْعَمَلَ وَإِنْ لَمْ يُسَاعِدْنِي أَحَدٌ.
I will complete the work, even if nobody helps me.	سَأُنْهِي الْعَمَلَ (حَتَّى) وَلَوْ لَمْ يُسَاعِدْنِي أَحَدٌ.

ولو may also emphasize a negated statement. English equivalent: "not (even) a single":

He has not given me (any money), and had it only been one dinar = he has not given me a single dinar.	لَمْ يُعْطِنِي (نُقُوداً) وَلَوْ دِينَاراً وَاحِداً.
I will not ask him for a single book.	لَنْ أَطْلُبَ مِنْهُ وَلَوْ كِتَاباً وَاحِداً.

⚓A5 When لَوْ is not directly followed by a verb, however, لَوْ أَنَّ ... لَـ may replace لَوْ كَانَ ... لَـ; thus:

If the answer were known I would have known it.	لَوْ أَنَّ الْجَوَابَ مَعْرُوفٌ لَعَرَفْتُهُ.
If she were from here I would not have invited her.	لَوْ أَنَّها مِنْ هُنَا لَمَا دَعَوْتُها.

V

to make sth. out of sth.	VIII اِتَّخذ (يتَّخِذُ) من هـ
if	إذا
rabbit	أرْنب ج أرانبُ
lion	أسَد ج أُسُد، أُسُود
faithful, loyal, devoted	أمين ج أُمناءُ
if / even though, although	إنْ / وإنْ
ducks (coll.)	بطّ
owls (coll.)	بُوم
fox	ثُعْلب ج ثعالِبُ
to occur	جرَى (يجْري) هـ
funeral procession	جنازة ج اَتُ، جنائزُ
army	جَيْش ج جُيوش
even if	حتَى ولو
free	حُرّ
freedom, liberty	حُرِّيَّة
to respect so., sth.	VIII اِحْترم (يحْترمُ) ه، هـ
to keep sth.	VIII اِحْتفظ (يحْتفظُ) ب هـ
wisdom, saying, aphorism	حِكْمة ج حِكم
laudable, commendable	حَميد
donkey	حِمار ج حمير
stupid, silly, dumb	أحْمق (م) حمقاءُ
dialogue	حِوار ج ات
it is (high) time to	حان الوقت (ل)
vivid, alive, living	حَيّ ج أحْياء
contradiction, violation	مُخالفة ج ات
horse (coll.)	خَيْل ج خُيُول
tireless, enduring	دؤوب
worm, maggot (coll.)	دُود ج دِيدان
to be about	دار (يدُورُ) حول
to remind so.	II ذكّر (يُذكِّرُ) ه ب هـ، ه

of so., sth.	
herdsman, shepherd, guardian	راع ج رُعاة
brave	شُجاع ج شجعة، شُجْعان
provided (that)	بِشرْط/على شرْطِ/شريطةَ أنْ
(Islam.) law, Shari'a	شريعة ج شرائعُ
law of the jungle	شريعة الغاب
patient, enduring	صبور ج صبُر
majesty	صاحِب الجلالة
to behave	V تصرَّف (يتصرفُ)
to hunt sth.	V تصيَّد (يتصيَّدُ) هـ
hunting	صيْد
hunter	صيّاد ج ون
cook	طبّاخ ج ون
to apply	II طبّق (يُطبّقُ) هـ
absolute	مُطْلق
bird (coll.)	طيْر ج طُيور
expression for, to consist of	عِبارة عن
lover	عاشِق ج ون، عُشَّاق
sparrow; small bird	عُصْفور ج عصافيرُ
bone	عظْم ج عِظام
mentality	عقْليّة ج ات
in case, provided that	على أنْ
stubborn, pigheaded, stolid	عنيد ج عُنُد
good swimmer	عوّام
gazelle	غزال ج غِزْلان
to be or to become angry or furious at	غضِب (يغْضَبُ) من / على
booty; loot; prey	غنيمة ج غنائمُ
forest, jungle (coll.)	غاب
mouse (coll.)	فأر ج فِئران

to be spoiled, to go off	فسد (يفسُدُ) هـ	to shake os.	V تمحَّض (يتمخَّضُ)
to explain, to comment on	II فسَّر (يُفَسِّرُ) هـ	dead, lifeless	ميِّت ج أمْوات، مَوْتى
elephant	فيل ج فِيَلة، فُيُول	mosquito, midge *(coll.)*	ناموس ج نوامِيسُ
monkey	قِرْد ج قُرُود، قِردة	to bark	نبح (ينبَحُ)
to share sth.	VIII اِقْتسم (يقتسِمُ) هـ	bee *(coll.)*	نحل
division, sharing (out)	تقاسُم	disputing, refusal	مُنازعة ج ـات
(tom)cat	قِطّ ج قِطط	text	نصّ ج نُصُوص
caravan; convoy	قافِلة ج قوافِلُ	half of it	مُناصفة
rarely, hardly, seldom	قلَّما	equivalent	نظِير ج نظائِرُ
saying	قَوْل ج أقْوال	*(interj.)* Let us go to ...	هيّا بنا إلى ...
to resist, to withstand sth.	III قاوم (يُقاوِمُ) هـ	to turn to so.	V توجَّه (يتوجَّهُ) إلى
to be numerous	كثُر (يكثُرُ) ه/ هـ	instrument, means	وسِيلة ج وسائِلُ
if / if not	لَوْ / لَوْلا	characteristic	صِفة ج ـات
even if	(حتى) ولَوْ	impudence, impertinence	وقاحة
to be like sth., to be equivalent to sth.	III ماثل (يُماثِلُ) هـ	to trust in God	V توكَّل (يتوكَّلُ) على ا لله
proverb	مثل ج أمْثال		

Text 1   الحيوان في اللغة العربية

لعب الحيوان وما زال يلعب دوراً هامّاً في حياة الإنسان العربي واللغة العربية غنية بالأقوال والأمثال والحكم التي تدور حول الحيوان والتي قلَّما نجد ما يماثلها في اللغات الأخرى مــن حيث الوفرة. ولم يتّخذ العرب من الحيوان وسيلة للنقل والمواصلات فحسب بل أيضاً رمزاً للصفات الحميدة وغير الحميدة مثل: أمـين كـالكلب – جميل كالغزال – صبور كالجمل – دؤوب كالنحلة – شجاع كالأسد – عنيد كالحمار. وفيما يلي نقدّم بعض الأمثال التي يأتي فيها ذكر أنواع مختلفة من الحيوانات. حاول تفسيرها أو إيجاد نظائر لها باللغة الإنكليزية:

إن غاب القطّ لعب الفأر.

عصفور في اليد خير من عشرة على الشجرة.

إبن البط عوّام.

القرد بعين أمّه غزال.

إحترم الكلب لأجل راعيه!

الذي بلا عمل يشتري له جمل.

أنا أمير وأنت أمير ومن يسوق الحمير.

بيضة اليوم خير من دجاجة بكرة.

الجنازة كبيرة والميت فأر.

العاشق حمار.

كلب حيّ خير من أسد ميّت.

الكلاب تنبح والقافلة تسير.

ما طار طير وارتفع إلّا كما طار وقع.

الناموسة تقتل الفيل.

لا تخف من الدولة بل خف من كلابها!

يلعب بثعبان ويقول دودة.

لو كان في البومة خير ما تركها الصيّاد.

تمخّض الجبل فولد فأراً.

الديمقراطية في مفهوم الأسد   **Text 2**

يقال إن الأسد دعا يوماً الثعلب لمرافقته إلى الصيد ولكــن الثعلب رفض قبـول الدعـوة.
فغضب الأسد غضباً شديداً على وقاحـة الثعلب وسـأله عـن السـبب في رفض دعوتـه،
فأجابه:

الثعلب: يا صاحب الجلالة إنّك تعرف أنّنا نعيش في ظـلّ قوانـين شـريعة الغـاب، أي أن
القانون هو دائماً إلى جانب القوي وأنت أقوى مـني بكثـير. وأنا لا أستطيع
منازعتك أو مخالفة أوامرك وذلك يعني أنّك ستحتفظ لنفسك بكلّ غنيمة الصيد
أما أنا فسأحصل على العظام فقط.

الأسد: يبدو أنّك ما زلت تعيش بعقليـة الحـرب البـاردة. ألا تعلـم بأنـا نعيـش الآن في
عصر السلام والديمقراطية؟

الثعلب: ولكن ماذا تعني هذه الكلمة الغريبة يا صاحب الجلالة، أي الديمقراطية؟

الأسد: الديمقراطية تعني أنّنا نقتسم الغنيمة مناصفة وأنا أتـرك لـك مطلـق الحريـة فيمـا
تختار.

الثعلب: إن كانت الديمقراطية فعلاً بهذا المعنى فماذا ننتظر إذن، دعنا نتوكّـل على ا لله،
هيا بنا إلى الصيد!

وفي صباح اليوم التالي التقى الأسد مع الثعلب في الوقت المحدّد وذهبا يتصيّدان طوال اليوم وفي المساء كانت الغنيمة عبارة عن أرنب وغزال وعندما حان وقت التقاسم توجّه الثعلب إلى الأسد:

الثعلب: إسمحوا لي يا صاحب الجلالة أن أذكّرك بأنّك وعدتّـني بتطبيـق الديمقراطيـة عند تقاسم الغنيمة.

الأسد: وهو كذلك، وأنا أفي بوعدي. الغنيمة هي، كما تعلم، أرنب وغزال وأنت حـرّ تمامـاً فيمـا تختـار، فـإن أردتّ الأرنب فخـذ الأرنب وإن أردتّ الغزال فخـذ الأرنب.

Exercises:

L1 Answer the question ... إلى معي تذهبين / تذهب هل with معك أذهب نعم،

... using different conditions, e.g.:

if I have the time	... إذا كان عندي وقت
if I finish the work	... إذا أنهيت العمل
if I feel well	... إذا كنت بخير
if the weather is fine	... إذا كان الطقس جميلاً

L2 (Homework) Translate into Arabic.
I didn't visit him; not even a single time.
I wasn't there; not even a single time.
I wasn't there; not even a single hour.
I wasn't there; not even a single day.
I didn't see anyone; not even a single person.
I didn't give him a single book.
I didn't offer him a single glass.
I didn't meet anyone there; not even a single friend.
I didn't read a single book.
He was unable to answer anything; not even a single question.

L3 Try to find out the English equivalents of the following proverbs and sayings.

إذا ابنك سارق (thief) لقّمه (.to feed so) يده.

إذا اشتريت ما لا تحتاج إليه بعت ما تحتاج إليه.

إذا كثُر الطباخون فسد اللحم.

إذا حضرت الملائكة (angels) غابت الشياطين.

إذا كثُر القوم قل اللوم (blame).

إذا نزل الشفاء (healing) نفع الدواء.

إن كانت العينان كبيرتين، قالوا: عيون جمل، وإن كانتا صغيرتين، قالوا: أعمى.

لو طلعت بخيط (rope) ونزلت بشعرة.

لو طلعَت السماء ونزلَت الأرض.

لو طلعت الشمس من المغرب.

لو زرعنا **لو** في وادي **عسى** (perhaps) ما طلع شيء.

لولا اختلاف الأنظار ما نفقت السلع.

لولا الكسّار ما عاش المدّار(potter).

لولا المتلقي (*here:* receiver of stolen goods) ما سرق السارق.

لو من أتى بجر (do joiner's work) ما بقي في الأرض شجرة.

لو درى الحمار ما فوقه ما نهق (braying of the donkey).

لو رجع أبي من القبر(grave, tomb).

لولا الأمل لبطل العمل.

لو طلعت برأسك نخلة.

G1 Form real conditional sentences as follows:

☞   إذا فعلتَ أنت ذلك فعلتُ أنا ذلك أيضاً.

If you do this, I will also do it.

☞   إذا اشتريتم أنتم ذلك اشترينا نحن ذلك أيضاً.

If you buy this, we will also buy this.

Use in addition to فعل and اشترى the following verbs

سافر، ذهب، عاد، أخذ، اشترك، طلب، حاول، دخّن، أكل، شرب، مشى

and add an object or a prepositional phrase.

G2 Same as G1 but this time begin the result clause with فإنّ + personal pronoun + imperfect tense.

☞   إذا فعلتَ ذلك فإنني أفعل ذلك أيضاً.

☞   إذا اشتريت ذلك فإنني أشتري ذلك أيضاً.

G3 Transform the following sentences into unreal conditional sentences introduced by لو.

جئت إليك.

اشتريت ذلك.

ذهبت إلى هناك.

كنت أستطيع أن أفعل ذلك.

طلبت منه ذلك.

سمحت له بذلك.

حاولت ذلك.

دبّرت لك ذلك.

شرحت لك ذلك.

تحدّثت معه.

زرته.

فعلت ذلك.

The following conditions should be used:

If I had the time; if I/he were there, if I had the money; if I had finished the work; if he were diligent.

☞   اشتريت ذلك لو كانت عندي نقود.

☞   أو: لو كانت عندي نقود اشتريت ذلك.

☞   أو: لو كانت عندي نقود لاشتريت ذلك.

G4 Negate the conditional and the result clause.

☞   إذا كان عندي وقت أجيء إليك. >

إذا لم يكن عندي وقت لا أجيء إليك.

إذا كانت عندي نقود أشتري الكتب.

إذا رافقني أحد أذهب إلى هناك.

إذا كان الطقس جميلاً نقوم بالنزهة.

إذا كنتَ مجتهداً نوفدك إلى الخارج للدراسة.

إذا دبّرت لي الاستمارات سأسافر يوم الجمعة.

إذا قرأت هذا الكتاب عرفت القضية.

إذا تعلّمت الكلمات الجديدة تستطيع أن تترجم الأسئلة.

إذا أعطيتني الكتاب العربي أعطيك الكتاب الفرنسي.

إذا أنهيت العمل سأجيء إليك.

إذا اشتركت أنت في المؤتمر أشترك أنا في المؤتمر أيضاً.

إذا قابلتُ الأصدقاء يمكنني أن أطلعهم على القضية.

G5 Combine the following clauses in such a way that the second clause changes into a clause of concession introduced by ولو (حتى).

☜ نفعل ذلك وحدنا   نفعل ذلك

☜ نفعل ذلك (حتى) ولو فعلنا ذلك وحدنا.

☜ لا يساعدني أحد   سأنهي العمل

☜ سأنهي العمل (حتى) ولو لم يساعدني أحد.

أعمل ١٦ ساعة	سأنهي العمل
أسافر إلى هناك مرة ثانية أو ثالثة	أدبّر الأعمال
لا يحضرها أصدقائي	سأحضر الحفلة
أفعل ذلك وحدي	أفعل ذلك
يساعدني صديقي	سوف لا أنهي العمل
ليس الطقس جميلاً	نقوم بنزهة
(يكون) جميعهم موجودون	نتحدّث حول هذه الخطة
(يكون) أقوياء	نقاوم أعداءنا
(يكون) الوصول إلى هناك صعب	نحاول ذلك

C1 Read the following anecdote and retell it.

إلتقى عبد الكريم وهو في طريقه إلى المقهى برجل وظن أن هذا الرجل هو صديقه القديم أحمد وجرى بينهما الحوار التالي:

عبد الكريم: أهلاً وسهلاً ومرحباً يا أحمد، كيف صحتك، كيف حال العائلة وكيف حال ابنك سعيد؟ أنا لم أرك منذ خمس سنين، لقد تغيرت كثيراً.

الرجل: عفواً، أنا لست أحمد، إسمي عادل.

عبد الكريم: غريب فعلاً، لم يتغير شكلك فقط وإنما اسمك أيضاً!

C2 Prepare a fable or a joke in Arabic in which animals play a role.

Final exercise:

1. Translate into Arabic.

If the lion sleeps, the fox becomes courageous. He didn't buy a single book. If the booty is small, the discussion about sharing it is long. Too many cooks spoil the broth. He could not answer a single question. I will write you a letter when I arrive in Damascus. If you do this, I will never visit you again. If I had the money, I would travel to Cairo. If you sell me the Arabic dictionary, I'll give you $50 and the English dictionary. If the weather is not fine, we'll take the train. If you don't learn the new words, you can neither read nor translate the texts. We'll try to finish the work even if nobody supports us. Had you come in time, we would have offered you coffee and vegetables. Were you as enduring as a camel, you would have written all the words.

2. Give the names of the animals in Arabic.

gazelle, rabbit, owl, mouse, cat, sparrow, duck, monkey, dog, donkey, bird, mosquito, elephant, snake, worm, cow

3. Replace conjunction + verb with preposition + infinitive.

بعد أن غادر البلد / بعد أن زار المتحف / بعـد أن ذهبـوا إلى المرفأ / بعـد أن وصـل إلى هناك / قبل أن يشرح المعالم / قبل أن يكتب الرسالة / قبل أن يقدّم الهدية / قبل أن ينجز مهمّاته / قبل أن تُغلق المدارس / قبل أن نحصل على النقود / قبل أن يناقشـوا المشـروع / منذ أن انتهى المؤتمر / منذ أن ألغيت الزيارة / منذ أن تغيّر البرنامج / حتى وصل القطار / حتى عاد الوفد

4. Give the Arabic infinitives.

consultation, development, return, tension, opening, reception, proposal, improvement, satisfaction, closing, exception, increasing, continuation, innovation, certification, preparation, competition, wrestling, boxing, examination, success, meeting, lecture, study, qualification, exchange, education, cooperation, economy, discussion, extension, signature, specialization, checking, oriental studies, apology, registration, foundation, presence

Lesson 27 | الدرس السابع والعشرون

1. Exceptives (أَلْمُسْتَثْنَى)

Exceptive sentences in Arabic are sentences in which a mostly negative statement relating to the subject, object or predicate is restricted.

1.1. إِلاَّ

The most common Arabic exceptive particle is إِلاَّ (< لا إِنْ). The English translation is "except for/that, but" or "only".

1.1.1. In the negative exceptive the noun excepted by إِلاَّ takes on the same case as the restricted noun:

No Arab friends attended the event except the Egyptian students; of the Arab friends only the Egyptian students came (*lit.*: did not come ... but ...).	لَمْ يَحْضُرِ الأَصْدِقَاءُ الْعَرَبُ إلى الْحَفْلَـةِ إلاَّ الطُّلابُ الْمِصْرِيُّونَ.

The nominative follows إِلاَّ, because the restricted noun (أَلأَصدقاء), also, as a subject of يحضر, takes on the nominative.

I do not fear anything but hot weather; I only fear hot weather.	لا أَخَافُ مِنْ أَيِّ شَيْءٍ إلاَّ (مِنَ) الطَّقْسِ الْحَارِّ.

The word الطقس, which follows the exceptive particle إِلاَّ, takes on the genitive, being subordinated to the preposition مِن, which does not need to be repeated.

1.1.2. Quite often, the restricted nouns are not mentioned at all. The excepted noun is the logical complement to the whole sentence, which makes it understandable.

Only the Egyptian students attended the event (*lit.*: did not attend the event but ...).	لَمْ يَحْضُرِ الْحَفْلَةَ إلاَّ الطُّلابُ الْمِصْرِيُّونَ.

The nominative follows إِلاَّ; the government of يحضر affects the logical complement الطّلاب.

I will only buy the two Arabic books.	لا أَشْتَرِي إلاَّ الْكِتَابَيْنِ الْعَرَبِيَّيْنِ.

The accusative follows إلّا; the government of اشترى affects the logical complement الكتابين.

I am only afraid of the hot weather.	لا أَخَافُ إلّا مِنَ الطَّقْسِ الحَارِّ.

The government of خاف by means of مِن is preserved and affects the logical complement الطقس.

إلّا, in conjunction with the negation مَا and the following pronoun هُوَ/هِيَ, also occurs in a nominal construction with a phraseological value.

These words are only (= nothing but) an expression of his fear.	هَذِهِ الْكَلِمَاتُ مَا هِيَ إلّا تَعْبِيرٌ عَنْ خَوْفِهِ.

1.1.3. A pronoun, a prepositional phrase or a whole clause may also follow إلّا, instead of a noun.

1.1.3.1. Pronoun

Only he knows that.	لا يَعْرِفُ ذَلِكَ إلّا هو.

1.1.3.2. Prepositional phrase

We are only superior to them because of our knowledge.	لا نَفُوقُهُمْ إلّا بِسَبَبِ مَعْرِفَتِنا.
There are contacts with them only within narrowest limits.	لا اتِّصَالاتِ مَعَهُمْ إلّا في أَضْيَقِ الْحُدُودِ.

إلّا + temporal prepositional phrase is equivalent to the English "only, not until":

He returned only after 2 days.	لَمْ يَرْجِعْ إلّا بَعْدَ يَوْمَيْنِ.
He returned only after two hours.	لَمْ يَرْجِعْ إلّا بعد سَّاعَتَيْنِ.

1.1.3.3. Clauses
a) Objective clause

I only want to say ...	لا أُرِيدُ إلّا أَنْ أَقُولَ ...

b) Conditional clause

You will only complete the work if you work more than 12 hours every day.	لَنْ تُنْهِيَ الْعَمَلَ إلّا إذا عَمِلْتَ كُلَّ يَوْمٍ أكْثَرَ مِن ١٢ سَاعَةً.

c) Temporal clause

He did not inform them about his illness until he had (already) overcome it.	لَمْ يُطْلِعْهُمْ عَلَى مَرَضِهِ إِلاَّ بَعْدَ أَنْ تَغَلَّبَ عَلَيْهِ.
We were not informed of this visit until the delegation arrived in the capital city.	لَمْ نَعْلَمْ بِهَذِهِ الزِّيَارَةِ إِلاَّ عِنْدَمَا وَصَلَ الْوَفْدُ إِلَى الْعَاصِمَةِ.

A restrictive construction with إلا is also possible with other types of subordinate clauses.

1.1.4. The positive exceptive is less common. The excepted noun takes the accusative here - the construction is translated into English by "except, but".

All but Muḥammad came. (*lit.*: All came except Muḥammad:)	جَاءَ كُلُّهُمْ إِلاَّ مُحَمَّداً.

1.2. فَقَط and مُجَرَّد

فَقَط and مُجَرَّد "only, merely, solely" are also used instead of (لا) ... إلا. فقط, unlike إلا, does not except anything from a general statement; but, as an emphasizing particle, it particularly stresses the statement of a comparatively small quantity, number, period or distance:

"only 100 km", مئة كيلومتر فقط, "only 10 days" عشرة أيّام فقط

"only 21 persons" أحد وعشرون شخصاً فقط etc.

مُجَرَّد takes the construct state and **precedes** nouns, which are mostly indefinite; if the construction is part of a prepositional phrase, the preposition **precedes** it:

With only a letter, we received the papers. / One letter was enough to get the papers.	حَصَلْنَا عَلَى الْأَوْرَاقِ بِمُجَرَّدِ رِسَالَةٍ.

In many dialects, "*bass*" is used instead of فقط.

1.3. Other exceptive particles

Other exceptive particles not as common as إلاّ are: in the negative exceptive, غَيْرَ and سِوَى. They are generally followed by the genitive

Only the Syrian friends stayed.	لَمْ يَبْقَ سِوَى الْأَصْدِقَاءِ السُّورِيِّينَ.
Only Muḥammad helped me.	لَمْ يُسَاعِدْنِي غَيْرَ مُحَمَّدٍ.

and عَدَا، عَدَا مَا عَدَا or فِيمَا عَدَا for the positive exception. They are followed by either the genitive or the accusative.

All but the Lebanese delegation left the city.	غَادَرَ كُلُّهُمُ الْمَدِينَةَ مَا عَدَا الْوَفْدِ^(٠) اللُّبْنَانِيّ.

1.4. أَنَّ إلاّ ، أَنَّ غَيْرَ

إلاّ or غَيْرَ followed by أَنَّ serve the purpose of linking a clause with an adversative clause. The English equivalents are: "however, but, nevertheless, ... (al)though, yet".

The French Minister of Defence has actually met with the Israelis responsible; however, the resolution of the French government concerning the embargo on the delivery of Mirage planes still stands.	إنَّ وَزِيرَ الدِّفَاعِ الْفِرَنْسِيَّ قَدْ قَابَلَ فِعْـلاً الْمَسْـؤولِينَ الإسْـرَائِيلِيّينَ إلاّ أَنَّ قَـرَارَ الْحُكُومَةِ الْفِرَنْسِيَّةِ الْخَاصَّ بِحَظْرِ إرْسَـالِ طَائِرَاتِ الْمِيرَاج لا يَزَالُ قَائِماً.
But the speaker refused to mention any details.	غَـيْرَ أَنَّ الْمُتَحَـدِّثَ رَفَـضَ أَنْ يَذْكُـرَ أَيَّـةَ تَفَاصِيلَ.

📖A1 بَيْدَ أَنَّ and عَلَى أَنَّ , which introduce clauses as well, are comparable to إلاّ أَنَّ and غير أَنَّ. They are translated by "however, but" etc., just as those are.

2. Diminutives (التَّصْغِير)

The first consonant of the noun is vocalized by *Ḍamma*, and the second one by *Fatḥa* and the following يَ (يَاء التَّصْغِير), for expressing diminution. The following patterns a.o. result from this:

2.1. Triliteral nouns: فُعَيْل (ة)

slave	عُبَيْد >	عَبْد
pen	قُلَيْم >	قَلَم
bag	شُنَيْطة >	شَنْطة
moment, instant	لُحَيْظة >	لَحْظة

2.2. Quadriliteral nouns: فُعَيْعِل (ة)

scorpion	عُقَيْرِب <	عقرب
little river, creek	جُعَيْفِر <	جعفر
dirhem	دُرَيْهِم <	درهم

2.3. Nouns of the structure فاعِلٌ : فُوَيْعِل (ة)

companion	صُوَيْحِب <	صاحِب
student	طُوَيْلِبة <	طالبة

2.4. Nouns of the structures فِعالٌ , فَعولٌ and فَعيلٌ : فُعَيِّلٌ

book	كُتَيِّب <	كتاب
old man/woman	عُجَيِّز <	عجوز
noble, noble-minded	كُرَيِّم <	كريم
beautiful, handsome	جُمَيِّل <	جميل

2.5. Nouns with a long vowel in front of the last radical: فُعَيْعِيل

box	صُنَيْدِيق <	صُنْدُوق
key	مُفَيْتِيح <	مِفْتاح

2.6. Nouns of the structures مُفاعِل (ة) and مَفْعَل (ة): مُفَيْعِل (ة)

library	مُكَيْتِبة <	مكتبة
lecture	مُحَيْضِرة <	مُحاضرة

🎧 **A2** The diminutives of ابن، أخ، أب and أم are أُبَيّ، بُنَيّ، أُخَيّ، and أُمَيْمة.

V

historian	مُؤَرِّخ ج ــون	incense	بَخُور
origin	أَصْلٍ ج أُصُول	to stand out	برز (يَبْرُزُ) هـ
originally (adv.)	أَصْلاً	to compete	VI تبارى (يتبارى) مع
except; but	إلّا	complete, total, absolute	تامّ
author	مُؤَلِّف ج ــون	quarrel	جدل
god, deity	إله، إلاه ج آلِهة	Jāhilīya	الجاهلية

the Hijaz	الحِجاز	putting in order, arranging	ضبْط
incense bowls	محارق البخور	character	طابع
fortress	حِصْن ج حُصُون	straight forward, nonstop *(colloq.)*	على طُول
dream	حُلْم ج أحْلام	wedding, marriage	عُرْس
ruins	خراب ج أخْرِبة	bride	عروس (م)
to mix with	VIII اِختلط (يختلطُ) ب	(bride)groom	عريس
to decay, to decline	II تدهْور (يتدهْورُ)	(deeply) rooted, ancient	عريق
decay, decline	تدهْور	invited *(colloq.)*	معْزُوم
townhall, city hall	دار البلدِية	greatness	عظمة
mentioned	مذْكُور	marriage contract	عقْد القِران
chief of protocol	رئيس المراسِمُ	confession, denomination	عقيدة ج عقائِدُ
wide	رحْب	confessional, denominational	عقائدِيّ
procession, column	رعِيل	to be connected with	V تعلّق (يتعلّقُ) ب
refusal	رفض	lessons, doctrines	تعاليمُ ج
fig.: Good luck and many children!	بالرِفاء والبنِين	to restore, to give sth. back	IV أعاد (يُعِيدُ) هـ إلى
wedding, marriage	زفاف	normally	عادةً
to sound the horn	II زمَّر (يُزمِّرُ)	sinking (in), to be drowned	غارق في
time, period	زمن ج أزْمان	young man	فتًى ج فِتْيان
to (begin) to flourish	VIII اِزْدهر (يزْدهِرُ)	way, road, street	فجّ ج فِجاج
flourishing	مُزْدهِر	from everywhere	من كلِّ فجٍّ عميق
wedding, marriage	زواج	wedding dress	فستان العرس
happy	سعِيد ج سُعداءُ	useful	مُفيد
to get sth.	VIII اِسْتلم (يسْتلِمُ) هـ	report	تقْرير ج تقارِيرُ
cuneiform	مِسْماريّ	relative	قريب ج أقارِبُ
ᶜUkāẓ market *(near Mecca)*	سوق عُكاظ	judge	قاضٍ ج قُضاة
rite	شعِيرة ج شعائِر	rule, regulations	قاعِدة ج قواعِدُ
poet	شاعِر ج شُعراءُ	chargé d'affaires	القائِم بالأعْمال
witness	شاهِد ج شُهُود	to keep to sth.	V تقيَّد (يتقيَّدُ) بِ هـ
honeymoon	شهْر العسل	to belong to a written religion	كِتابيّ
beauty parlor	صالون التجْميل	so and so much/many	كذا
to become sth.	صار (يصِير) هـ	to reveal sth.	كشف (يكْشِفُ) عن

cake	كَعْك	sculpture; inscription	نَقْش ج نُقُوش
church	كَنِيسة ج كَنائِسُ	to grow, to develop	نَما (يَنمُو)
that's why, therefore	لِذا / لِذلِك	to leave, to emigrate	هَجَر (يَهجُرُ) هـ
fame, glory	مَجْد	emigrant	مُهاجِر ج ون
dimensions, extent	مَدىً	existence	وُجُود
exercise	تَمرين ج تَمارينُ	he/she alone;	وَحْدَهُ / وَحْدَها
machine	مَكِينة ج ـات /مَكائِنُ	heritage	تُراث
bridal money	مَهْر ج مُهُور	subject-matter, issue	مَوْضِع ج مَواضِعُ
~ to be paid before	مَهر مُعَجَّل	to come (to)	وَفَد (يَفِدُ) إلى
~ to be paid after	مَهر مُؤجَّل	client	مُوَكِّل
to define sth.	نَصَّ (يَنُصُّ) على	(legal) guardian	وَلِيّ ج أوْلِياءُ

Text 1

مِنْ تاريخ العرب

تقع شبه الجزيرة العربية في القارّة الآسيوية، وقد كانت مركزاً تجارياً وأساساً للحضارة منذ ثلاثة آلاف عام قبل الميلاد. وكشفت الآثار عن وجود ممالك عربية قديمة وحضارات عريقة في جنوب شبه الجزيرة العربية. لقد عُثِر في بلاد العرب الجنوبية على آثار تدلّ على وجود حضارات مزدهرة في زمنٍ قديمٍ جدّاً ولا شكّ في أنّ بلاد العرب الجنوبية بآلهتها ومحاريق بخورها ونقوشها وقلاعها وحصونها كانت مزدهرة في بداية الألف سنة الأولى قبل الميلاد. إلاّ أنّ أصل العرب ومدى علاقتهم بالشعوب السامية المجاورة الأخرى ما زال حتى الآن موضع جدل بين العلماء.

ولا تشهد الآثار وحدها على عظمة هذه الممالك، بل أيضاً النقوش البابلية والأشورية المسمارية والمؤلفون القدامى. لكن تلك الحضارة العربية القديمة تدهورت مع التدهور السياسي والاقتصادي الذي أصاب الممالك العربية وصارت الهجرات أمراً مألوفاً يومياً. فهجرت المدن

العظمى   وتركت للخراب، ومع الدين   الإسلامي   ازدهرت هذه المدن   من   جديد وأعيد لها مجدها السابق .

ويسمّى   العصر بين   القرنين   الأول والسادس الميلادي   بالعصر الجاهلي   لأنّ   عرب الجاهلية كانوا يجهلون   تعاليم الإسلام . وفي   الحقيقة لم تكن   أيّام جهل تامّ، بل بداية لحضارة ساعدت على   الحفاظ على   التراث العربي   القديم .

ويتّفق معظم المؤرّخين   على   أنّ   الرعيل الأوّل من   العرب المهاجرين   من   بلاد العرب الجنوبية بدأ اتّجه شمالاً حوالي القرن   الثاني   الميلادي . لذا بدأت الحضارة العربية تزدهر وتنمو في   مناطق ثلاث هي   سوريا والعراق وغرب الجزيرة العربية . وكانت سوريا في   ذلك الوقت تحتفظ بالكثير من   طابع الثقافة السامية كما كان   العراق غارقاً في   الثقافة السامية وفي   غرب الجزيرة العربية برز مركزان   هامان   هما الحجاز ومكّة . وكانت سوق عُكاظ القريبة من   مكّة ميداناً رحباً يتبارى   فيه شعراء العرب . أما مكّة فكانت مركزاً عقائدياً تقام فيها الشعائر الدينية وكان الحجاج يفدون   إليها من   كلّ فجّ عميق .

Text 2

عن الزواج

بيتر: أهلاً بك. كيف حالك؟

مريم: أهلاً، أنا بخير وكيف حالك؟

بيتر: بخير وعندي بعض الأسئلة.

مريم: تفضّل، اسأل!

بيتر: رأيت مساء الأمس في المدينة عدداً كبيراً من السيّارات في صف واحد وكان السائقون يزمّرون على طول.

مريم: آه، هذا زفاف، أي زواج أو عرس، كما نقول. العريس يمشي مع العروس إلى البيت لحفل الزواج.

بيتر: إلى بيت من؟

مريم: إلى بيت العريس. وقبل ذلك تجلس العروس لمدّة ساعتين أو أكثر في صالون التجميل للماكياج ولضبط فستان العرس إلى آخره.

بيتر: وكيف يتمّ الزواج رسمياً؟ أمام القاضي أو في دار البلدية؟

مريم: يتمّ عقد القران قبل الزواج بمدّة قصيرة وبحضور شاهدين والعقد ينصّ كذلك على المهر.

بيتر: وماذا يقال عند عقد القران؟

مريم: تقول الزوجة أو يقول وليها أو وكيلها: زوجتك نفسي أو ابنتي أو موكلتي على مهر معجّله كذا ومهر مؤجّله كذا على كتاب الله وسنّة رسوله صلّى الله عليه وسلّم. فيجيب الزوج: وأنا قبلت زواجك على المهر المذكور على كتاب الله وسنة رسوله، صلّى الله عليه وسلّم.

بيتر: هل يجوز للمرأة المسلمة الزواج من رجل غير مسلم؟

مريم: لا، لا يجوز لها الزواج إلّا إذا كان مسلماً ويجوز للرجل المسلم الزواج من امرأة كتابية غير مسلمة.

بيتر: هل يجوز في الحفلة الاختلاط بين الرجال والنساء؟

مريم: لا ، أصلاً لا يجوز، غير أنّنا نجد اليوم بعض العائلات التي لا تتقيّد بهذه القواعد.

بيتر: وكيف بالنسبة للهدايا لأنّني معزوم لحفلة زواج بعد أسبوع؟

مريم: الهدايا حسب الإمكانيات وعادة نقدّم النقود.

بيتر: وماذا أقول للعروسين في الحفلة؟

مريم: ممكن أن تقول بالرفاء والبنين أو زواج سعيد.

بيتر: أنا أشكرك على هذه المعلومات المفيدة ويبقى سؤال أخير.

مريم: وهو؟

بيتر: متى سأحضر حفلة زواجك؟

مريم: الله أعلم. لا أتزوّج إلّا إذا وجدتُ فتى أحلامي.

بيتر: هل عندك حقّ الاختيار؟

مريم: لا ، ليس عندي حقّ الاختيار ولكن عندي حقّ الرفض.

Exercises:

L1 (Repetition: إلّا to specify the time) Add a time to the following sentences using the particle إلّا.

☞   اِجتمع رئيس الوزراء بالوفد.   <

☞   اِجتمع رئيس الوزراء بالوفد في الساعة العاشرة إلّا الربع.

غادر الوفد البلد ...

أغلق المعرض أبوابه ...

نقابل عدّة تجّار سودانيين ...

ابتدأت المباراة ...

انتهت الحفلة ...

وصلت الطائرة ...

وصل القطار ...

سنجتمع ...

أخرج من البيت ... صباحاً.

يستمرّ الاجتماع حتى ...

خابرني بالتلفون ...

نلتقي في الجامعة ...

جلست العروس في صالون التجميل ...

L2 Translate into English.

أ   –   لا يجيء أصدقائي إلّا يوم السبت.

ب   –   أستطيع أن أجيء إليك كلّ يوم ما عدا يوم الاثنين.

ج   –   أنهى الطلّاب التمارين إلّا واحداً.

د   –   لن أسافر إلّا في يوم الأحد غير أنّني سأنهي العمل حتى الغد.

L3 Transform the nouns in Text 2 - if possible and useful - into the diminutive. Try to form diminutives of the names of your friends and fellow students.

L4 (Repetition) Answer the questions using أقلّ من or أكثر من and a following numeral.

☞   هل عندك كتب كثيرة؟   <   نعم، عندي أكثر من ١٠٠ كتاب.

☞   أو: عندي أقل من ١٠٠ كتاب.

كم أسبوعاً كنت على شاطىء البحر؟

منذ كم شهر تسكن في هذا البيت؟

كم ساعة كنت تشتغل في المكتبة؟

هل قرأت هذا الخبر في جريدتين فقط؟

كم نسخة اشتريت؟

كم رسالة كتبت؟

هل تحبّ أنْ تشرب كأساً واحدةً فقط؟

كم شخصاً حضر الحفلة؟

كم درساً لديك كل أسبوع؟

هل زرت ذلك البلد مرّات كثيرة؟

كم بلداً زرت حتى الآن؟

كم عندك من الأصدقاء العرب؟

كم كتاباً عربياً قرأت حتى الآن؟

منذ كم سنة تدرس اللغة العربية؟

L5 (Homework) Place cards must be printed for a diplomatic reception. Write the following list of the guests in Arabic for the printing office and complete the list by adding the names of further diplomatic and political personalities.

prime minister, minister of foreign affairs, minister of the interior, minister of agriculture, minister of labour, minister of defense, chairman of the committee for foreign affairs, ambassador of Russia, chargé d'affaires of the Canadian embassy, president of the democratic party, general secretary of the national party, chief of protocol ...

L6 (Repetition) Replace the adjective by أكثر + noun and add the phrase in brackets.

☞ أنت مجتهد (منّي) > أنت أكثر اجتهاداً منّي.

المنطقة الغربية خصبة   (من المنطقة الشرقية)

أنا تعبان   (منكم)

ذلك المشتى مشهور   (من المشاتي الأخرى)

الطقس هناك معتدل   (من الطقس عندنا)

هذه المشكلة معقدة   (من جميع المشاكل الأخرى)

السائقون اللبنانيون ماهرون   (من السائقين في البلدان الأوربية)

هذا السياسي شعبي   (من السياسيين الآخرين)

مآذن الجوامع مرتفعة   (من بيوت المدينة)

أنتم مجتهدون   (منّا)

أسعار الموديلات الجديدة مرتفعة   (من أسعار الموديلات القديمة)

هذا الفرع الاقتصادي منتج   (من الفروع الأخرى)

G1 Transform into exceptive sentences.

☞   جاء محمّد.   <   لم يجيء إلا محمّد.

☞   يجيء محمّد.   <   لا يجيء إلا محمّد.

☞   قابلت الأصدقاء السوريين.   <   لم أقابل إلا الأصدقاء السوريين.

يتعلق موقفنا بموقفكم.

أحبّ من المشروبات النبيذ الأبيض.

أشرب صباحاً فنجاناً واحداً من القهوة.

ناقشنا أهمّ المواضيع.

أدخّن سجائر.

أدرس اللغات والتاريخ.

يشجّع الطلّاب المجتهدون.

يوفَد الطلّاب المجتهدون.

اشترك في المؤتمر الخبراء البارزون.

رجع في الساعة الحادية عشرة.

G2 Transform the conditional sentences in such a way that they take on the character of exceptive sentences.

☞   إذا كان عندي وقت أجيء إليك. > لا أجيء إليك إلا إذا كان عندي وقت.

إذا كانت عندي نقود أشتري الكتب.

إذا رافقني أحد أذهب إلى هناك.

إذا كان الطقس جميلاً نقوم بالنزهة.

إذا كنتَ مجتهداً نوفدك إلى الخارج للدراسة.

إذا دبّرت لي الاستمارات سأسافر يوم الجمعة.

إذا قرأت هذا الكتاب عرفت القضية.

إذا تعلّمت الكلمات الجديدة تستطيع أن تترجم الأسئلة.

إذا أعطيتني الكتاب العربي أعطيك الكتاب الفرنسي.

إذا أنهيت العمل سأجيء إليك.

إذا اشتركت أنت في المؤتمر أشترك أنا فيه المؤتمر أيضاً.

إذا قابلتُ الأصدقاء يمكنني أن أطلعهم على القضية.

G3 Combine the follwing clauses in such a way that the second clause becomes a temporal clause introduced by عندما. By means of negating the main clause preceded by إلا, this temporal clause should take on the character of an exceptive clause.

☞ انطلقت الطائرة   كان الطقس جميلاً   <

☞ انطلقت الطائرة عندما كان الطقس جميلاً   <

☞ لم تنطلق الطائرة إلّا عندما كان الطقس جميلاً.

غادرنا البيت	جاء صديقنا
عاد الوفد من جولة	بدأت المحادثات من جديد
استلمت النقود	سافرت إلى هناك
ساعدتمونا	أنجزنا واجباتنا حتى نهاية الأسبوع
تفعل أنت ذلك أيضاً	أفعل ذلك!
طلبتَ منّا ذلك	بحثنا المشروع
درسوا المشروع	لاحظوا عدة أغلاط
غيروا البرنامج	سافرنا معهم
سمع أن جميع الأصدقاء سيشتركون في الحفلة	قبل الدعوة
عادوا من ألمانيا	كتبوا الرسائل

G4 Restrict the subject/object of the following sentences by means of an exception. The exception should consist of the singular of the given noun and واحد / واحدة.

☞ يجيء كلّ الأصدقاء> يجيء كلّ الأصدقاء إلا صديقاً واحداً.

☞ تجيء كلّ الطالبات > تجيء كلّ الطالبات إلا طالبة واحدة.

غادرت المدينة كل الوفود.

إفتح كلّ الشبابيك!

فهمت كلّ الأسئلة.

قرأت كلّ الجرائد.

أعرف كلّ البلدان العربية.

كان كلّ المعلّمين هناك.

نسيت كلّ المواعيد.

اتفقوا على كلّ المواضيع.

وافق على المشروع كلّ المسؤولين.

قابلت أمس كلّ الأصدقاء.

بعت كتبي كلّها.

أعطاني كلّ البطاقات.

دعونا كلّ الفتيات إلى الحفلة.

G5 (Repetition) Transform the following sentences in such a way that you get a comparative predicate containing the *Elative*.

ذلك المعمل أكبر.   <   ☞   هذا المعمل كبير.

هذه الجامعة قديمة.

هذه العائلة غنية.

هذا الموديل غالٍ.

هذا الرجل قوي.

هذه المدينة كبيرة.

هذه الكمية قليلة.

هذه القرية قريبة.

هذه النتيجة حسنة.

هذا القطار سريع.

هذه السياسة سيئة.

هذا الولد صغير.

هذا الشخص طويل.

هذه المشروبات لذيذة.

هذه الفتاة جميلة.

هذه البضاعة رخيصة.

هذه الدولة قوية.

هذا الواجب صعب.

هذا سهل.

هذه الشنطة خفيفة.

هذا النوع جيد.

هذه البلدان بعيدة.

هذه الأجهزة حديثة.

هؤلاء الرجال لطفاء.

هذه الغرفة نظيفة.

هؤلاء الطلّاب نشيطون.

C1 Prepare a dialogue about a wedding in your country based on Text 2.
Use the following terms:

bridal veil	طرْحة العروس
wedding ring	خاتِم الزواج
wedding meal	وليمة العُرس / الزفاف / الزواج
wedding night	ليلة الدُخْلة / ليلة الزِفاف
honeymoon (trip)	رحْلة شهر العسل
honeymoon	شهر العسل
church	كنيسة ج كنائِسُ
pastor, priest	قِسِّيس ج قساوسة
to get a divorce from his wife	طلَّق زوجتَه
she was divorced from him	طُلِّقَتْ عليه
divorce	طلاق
parents-in-law	والِدا الزوج / الزوجة
mother-in-law	حماة ج وات/ والِدة الزوج / الزوجة
father-in-law	حم ج أحْماء / والِد الزوج / الزوجة
registry office	مكتب الأحْوال الشخْصية
marriage ceremony	عقْد الزواج
engaged to (m./f.)	مخْطُوب / مخطوبة
fiancée (m./f.)	خطِيب / خطِيبة
engagement	خُطُوبة

engagement ring

دبلة الخطوبة

relatives

ج أقارِب

C2 Prepare a short biography of a famous personality in the Arab world and give a "lecture" to your fellow students.

Final exercise:

1. Translate into Arabic.

Call me 8.55 a.m. The train arrived at 1.45 p.m. We'll meet at 7.40 a.m. at the university. I have been waiting for you for more than two hours. Less than fifty guests came. This problem is more difficult than all the others. The new machine is more productive than the old one but also more complicated. We only discussed the most important topics. He only returned to his house at 11 p.m. I only study the subjects I like. I only have a single cup of coffee in the morning.

2. Translate the following letter into Arabic.

Dear Mariam,

Thank you very much for your congratulations on the occasion of my wedding and for the nice present. It is a pity that you were unable to attend the ceremony, but perhaps I'll attend your wedding soon. The wedding party was very nice. Except for one uncle, all my relatives came.

We went to the church by bus at 10 a.m. The ceremony started 10.40 a.m. All of us went by bus to a hotel outside the city after the ceremony. There, we had lunch at 1 p.m.; at 4 p.m. we had coffee and cake, and at 8 p.m., we had dinner. After that, we danced and sang a lot. At 1 a.m., we went to the airport for our honeymoon in Spain. My parents paid for the two-week holiday. The holiday was very nice. My parents-in-law gave us a car as a present.

We asked our relatives to give us only money so that we can buy the things we need for furnishing our new flat ourselves. My friend, Sally, had forgotten this when she married and, therefore, she got many things she didn't need. This is my report.

Thank you very much again for the good wishes and the present, also on behalf of my husband.

I hope to dance at your wedding party soon.

All the best.

Your friend,

Jane

1. The *Ḥāl*-Accusative (أَلْحَال)

1.1. The form

The *Ḥāl*-accusative is an indefinite accusative, which is normally formed out of a participle, but sometimes out of an adjective:

sitting	جَالِساً
laughing	ضَاحِكاً
coming	قَادِماً
sleeping	نَائِماً

etc.

✍**A1** The name "*Ḥāl*"-accusative originates from the Arabic word حال "condition, state". Therefore some textbooks and grammar books also speak of the accusative in *Ḥāl* or of the *Ḥāl*-clause (see also Gr 2.).

1.2. The function

The *Ḥāl*-accusative has the function of a predicative, attributive adjunct with a double semantic reference, namely:

a) to the subject (sometimes also to the object) of the sentence:

It characterizes a certain state or mode of behaviour of the subject during the execution of the verbal action expressed by the finite verb.

The formal reference to the subject is marked by agreement in gender and number.

My friend came in laughing.	دَخَلَ صَدِيقِي ضَاحِكاً.
My friends came in laughing.	دَخَلَ أَصْدِقَائِي ضَاحِكِينَ.
My friend came in laughing.	دَخَلَتْ صَدِيقَتِي ضَاحِكَةً.
My friends came in laughing.	دَخَلَتْ صَدِيقَاتِي ضَاحِكَاتٍ.
Muḥammad stood up saying ... = Muḥammad stood up and said ...	قَامَ مُحَمَّدٌ قَائِلاً...
Do not eat the fruit (when it is still) unripe!	لا تَأْكُلِ الفَاكِهَةَ فِجَّةً !

In the last sentence the *Ḥāl*-accusative refers to the object.

b) to the verb of the sentence:

It elucidates and completes the content of the verb.

The formal reference to the subject of the sentence is given here, too, by agreement in gender and number.

Muḥammad came walking = ... came walking, on foot.	جَاءَ مُحَمَّدٌ مَاشِياً.
He did the job sitting.	أَنْجَزَ الْعَمَلَ جَالِساً.
The delegation arrived in Berlin, coming from Baghdad.	وَصَلَ الْوَفْدُ إِلَى برلين قَادِماً من بغداد.
The delegations have left Berlin, turning to Baghdad, = ... have left Berlin in the direction of Baghdad.	غَادَرَتِ الْوُفُودُ برلين مُتَوَجِّهَةً إِلَى بغداد.

Even from the few examples it becomes clear that the *Ḥāl*-accusative can be rendered in different ways when being translated into English. There is the possibility of rendering it by means of a prepositional phrase, using the participle, or by a clause linked to the main clause by means of "and".

✍A2   The Arab grammarians have a comprehensive classification system of the *Ḥāl*-accusative, which includes many nouns used in the indefinite accusative as well.

2. The *Ḥāl*-Clause (أَلْجُمْلَة الْحَالِيَّة)

A whole clause, the so-called *Ḥāl*-clause, may replace the *Ḥāl*-accusative.

2.1. If it begins with a verb in the imperfect tense, it is added directly to the main clause.

My friend came in laughing.	دَخَلَ صَدِيقِي يَضْحَكُ.
Muḥammad came walking, on foot.	جَاءَ مُحَمَّدٌ يَمْشِي.

2.2. An equational sentence or a verbal sentence with a subject or a pronoun in anteposition is linked to the main clause by means of و.

Muḥammad came in with a book in his hand.	دَخَلَ مُحَمَّدٌ وَفِي يَدِهِ كِتَابٌ.
My friend came in laughing, ... came in and laughed (while doing so).	دَخَلَ صَدِيقِي وَهُوَ يَضْحَكُ.
He said, looking at me/He said and while doing so he looked at me, ... and looked at me (while doing so).	قَالَ وَهُوَ يَنْظُرُ إِلَيَّ.
I said and while doing so I tried to smile, ..., ... and tried to smile while doing so.	قُلْتُ وَأَنَا أُحَاوِلُ أَنْ أَبْتَسِمَ ...
He received me, saying ..., ... and said, ... with the remark that/by saying that.	إِسْتَقْبَلَنِي وَهُوَ يَقُولُ ...

The *Ḥāl*-clause most frequently occurs in a construction which contains a personal pronoun in anteposition.

The negated *Ḥāl*-clause is expressed by means of "without ...-ing" in English:

He listened to us without saying a word.	كَانَ يَسْتَمِعُ إِلَيْنَا وَلاَ يَقُولُ كَلِمَةً.

2.3. If the *Ḥāl*-clause begins with a verb in the perfect tense, it is also linked to the main clause by means of وَ. The particle قَدْ follows وَ.

Muḥammad entered the room when the friends were (already) assembled.	دَخَلَ مُحَمَّدٌ الْغُرْفَةَ وَقَدْ كَانَ الأَصْدِقَاءُ مُجْتَمِعِينَ.

2.4. The temporal relation between the main clause and the *Ḥāl*-clause

The tense expressed by the verb of the main clause (past, present) also applies to the *Ḥāl*-clause. The perfect tense in the main clause shows that an action happened in the past; accordingly, the *Ḥāl*-clause is also regarded as preterite tense.

Muḥammad entered the room and laughed (while doing so).	دَخَلَ مُحَمَّدٌ الْغُرْفَةَ وَهُوَ يَضْحَكُ.

Accordingly, the imperfect tense of the *Ḥāl*-clause has to be translated by a verb form of the past in this example, although the imperfect tense otherwise functions as present tense.

If, however, the imperfect tense is used in the main clause, the *Ḥāl*-clause is also present and has to be translated accordingly:

Muḥammad enters the room and laughs (while doing so).	يَدْخُلُ مُحَمَّدٌ الْغُرْفَةَ وهو يَضْحَكُ.

As the examples show, there is simultaneousness between the *Ḥāl*-clause and the main clause.

The temporal relation of the *Ḥāl*-construction becomes particularly evident when the *Ḥāl*-clause has a subject which is different from the one the main clause has.

Muḥammad came in, (just) when/while I was writing a letter.	دَخَلَ مُحَمَّدٌ وَأَنَا أَكْتُبُ رِسَالَةً.

The *Ḥāl*-clause only expresses an anteriority as compared with the main clause or the result of an action carried out before the happening expressed by the main clause when it has been formed by means of وَقَدْ + perfect tense (cf. the example in 2.3.).

As is the case with respect to the *Ḥāl*-accusative, there are also various possibilities of translating the *Ḥāl*-clause. Besides the participle and a clause linked to the main clause by means of "and", various conjunctions (when, while, and while doing so) come into consideration as an introduction of subordinate clauses.

3. Survey of Use of the Accusative
3.1. Accusative object
3.1.1. Direct object (أَلْمَفْعُول بِهِ)

He has read the book.	قَرَأَ الْكِتَابَ.

Form of the object: definite or indefinite noun or pronoun.

Two objects with doubly transitive verbs:

He has given me the book.	أَعْطَانِي الكِتَابَ.

If a personal pronoun replaces the second object, it is introduced by the particle إِيَّا .

He has given it (the book) to me.	أَعْطَانِي إِيَّاهُ.

🔊A3 This "accusative form" of the personal pronoun may also occur in the shortened relative clause together with the active participle of transitive verbs:

the man who sells or has sold his car	أَلرَّجُلُ الْبَائِعُ سَيَّارَتَهُ
the man who sells or has sold it	أَلرَّجُلُ الْبَائِعُ إِيَّاهَا

3.1.2. Cognate Accusative (أَلْمَفْعُول المُطْلَق)

He read the letter slowly (*lit.:* ... a slow reading).	قَرَأَ الرِسَالَةَ قِرَاءَةً بَطِيئَةً.

Form of the object: indefinite infinitive + attributive adjunct.
The infinitive nearly always has the same root as the verb of the sentence does.

3.2. Accusative as an adverbial qualification
3.2.1. Adverbial qualification of time (ظَرْف الزَّمَان)

(time, duration, date)

some day	يَوْماً، يَوْماً مَا، يَوْماً من الأَيَّامِ
every day	كُلَّ يَوْمٍ
today	أَلْيَوْمَ
on Sunday	يَوْمَ الأَحَدِ
tomorrow	غَداً

in the morning	صَبَاحاً
in the evening	مَسَاءً
for days (and days)/ for days on end	أَيَّاماً طِوَالاً
(for) two years	سَنَتَيْنِ
always	دَائِماً
in the year 1990	سَنَةَ ١٩٩٠

3.2.2. Adverbial qualification of place (ظَرْف المَكَان)

in the East	شَرْقاً
in the West	غَرْباً
(at, on) the right	يَمِيناً
(at, on) the left	يَسَاراً

3.2.3. Adverbial qualification of purpose (ألمَفْعُول لَهُ)

(Question: for what purpose?, what for?)

in the wish for the strengthening of the relations	رَغْبَةً في تَوْطِيدِ الْعَلاقَاتِ
I presented a gift to him in order to show my respect, ... as an expression of my respect	قَدَّمْتُ لَهُ هَدِيَّةً تَعْبِيراً عَنِ احْتِرَامِي.

3.2.4. Frequently a prepositional phrase replaces the accusative as an adverbial qualification.

سَنَةَ	=	في سَنَةٍ
غَرْباً	=	في الْغَرْبِ
سَنَتَيْنِ	=	لِمُدَّةِ سَنَتَيْنِ
تَعْبِيراً عَنْ	=	لِلتَّعْبِيرِ عَنْ

3.3. *Ḥāl*-accusative (ألحال)

See the examples in this Lesson.

3.4. Accusative of specification (أَلتَّمْيِيزُ)

(Question: in what?)

Nobody surpasses him in diligence.	لا يَفُوقُهُ أَحَدٌ اجْتِهَاداً.

The main area in which the *Tamyīz* is applied is the comparison of adjectives which do not have an *Elative*:

more diligent	أَكْثَرُ اجْتِهَاداً

3.5. Predicate complement in the accusative

The student was diligent.	كَانَ الطَّالِبُ مُجْتَهِداً.

The predicate complement in the accusative follows some other verbs as well, which are called "sisters of *kāna*" (أَخَوَاتُ كَانَ), a.o.:

not to be	لَيْسَ
to become	IV أَصْبَحَ
to become	صَارَ
to become; to remain, to continue to do sth./doing sth./to go on doing sth.	ظَلَّ
to remain; to continue to do sth.	بَقِيَ
(not) to cease (to do sth.), still to do sth./still to be doing sth.	لم يَزَلْ / كان لا يَزَالُ / لا يَزَالُ / ما زَالَ

See L13, p. 164, A3.

⏺A4 A whole clause containing the imperfect tense may also replace the nominal predicate with some of these verbs in the sense of "to begin (to do/doing sth.)" or "to last, to keep doing something": ظَلَّ يَشْرَبُ "he continued to drink/drinking, he kept on drinking".

Some other verbs of beginning (أَخَذَ، شَرَعَ، بَدَأَ a.o.) as well as the verbs of perception related to an object: بَدَأَ يَشْرَبُ "he began to drink/drinking", رَأَيْتُهُ يَشْرَبُ "I saw him drinking", have the same construction, which is analogous to the *Ḥāl*-clause which contains the imperfect tense.

3.6. Subject in the accusative

The delegation arrived yesterday.	إنَّ الْوَفْدَ وَصَلَ أَمْس.
I know that the delegation arrived yesterday.	أَعْرِفُ أَنَّ الْوَفْدَ وَصَلَ أَمْس.

The subject in the accusative also follows the compounds with إِنَّ and أَنَّ (لِأَنَّ، لَكِنَّ a.o.).

A5 Arabic also offers the following possibility:

We have heard that the director has arrived.	سَمِعْنا أَنَّ الْمُدِيرَ قَدْ وَصَلَ.
We have heard that the director has arrived.	سَمِعْنا أَنَّهُ قَدْ وَصَلَ الْمُدِيرُ.

The suffix هُ in the second example is referred to as ضَمِير الشَّأْن in Arabic here - as is also the case with similar constructions using لَعَلَّ ("perhaps"). The suffix هُ is invariable in these cases, regardless of gender and number of the following noun. The subject الْمُدِير does not take on the accusative any more then, but takes on the nominative.

3.7. Exclamations in the accusative

Thank you.	شُكْرًا.
You're welcome. I beg your pardon/excuse me!	عَفْوًا.
Good morning!	صَبَاحَ الْخَيْرِ.

There is a specific construction for the exclamation of admiration (التَّعَجُّب): مَا + masculine *Elative* in the accusative + noun in the accusative.

How beautiful this city is!	مَا أَجْمَلَ هَذِهِ الْمَدِينَةَ!
How difficult the tasks are!	مَا أَصْعَبَ الْوَاجِبَاتِ!

A6 Mind the "slight" difference with respect to the vowel signs and in the meaning with respect to the interrogative sentence:

What/which ones are the most difficult tasks?	مَا أَصْعَبُ الْوَاجِبَاتِ؟

Cf. also the anecdote in Text 1 of this Lesson.

The noun takes on the nominative without an article and without any nunation after the vocative particle يَا (يَا مُحَمَّد "oh Muḥammad", يَا أَبُو "oh father"); however, it takes on the accusative, if a genitive or a personal pronoun follows it, i.e. if the noun takes on the construct state: يَا أَبَانَا "oh our father".

3.8. Accusative with numerals and with كَمْ

The indefinite accusative singular follows the numerals 11 to 99 and the interrogative adverb كم "how much/how many":

how many persons?	كَمْ شَخْصاً؟
24 (male) students and 14 (female) students	٢٤ طَالِباً و ١٤ طَالِبَةً

3.9. General negation

Form: لا + noun taking on the accusative without having an article and without having any nunation:

without doubt, doubtless, undoubtedly	لا شَكَّ (فِيهِ)
There is nothing new under the sun.	لا جَدِيدَ تَحْتَ الشَّمْسِ.

3.10. Accusative in the execeptive

In the affirmative exceptive the noun takes the accusative after إلاّ:

All but Muḥammad came./(They) all came except Muḥammad.	جَاءَ كُلُّهُمْ إلاّ مُحَمَّداً.

(Cf. L 27 1.1.1. and 1.1.4.)

3.11. Prepositions in the accusative
Many prepositions are nouns and have the form of an accusative:

after	بَعْدَ
in accordance with, according to	وَفْقَ، وَفْقاً لِ
on the basis of, by virtue of, on the strength of, according to	بِناءً عَلَى

V

to urinate	بال (يَبُولُ)
here: rhetoric	بَيَان ج ـات
those who follow them	التالُون لَهُم
to except sth., so. from	X إِسْتَثْنَى (يَسْتَثْنِي) هـ، ه مِن
to endow so. with	جبل (يَجْبُلُ جَبْلاً) ه عَلَى
jussive	الجَزْم
to make so. do sth.	جعل (يَجعلُ جَعْلاً) هـ، ه
to make efforts, to try hard	III جاهد (يُجاهِدُ)

to bring, to give sth.	IV آتى (يُؤْتِي) بِ
to study under, to learn from so.	أخذ عن
to give sth. a solid foundation	II أصَّل (يُؤَصِّلُ) هـ
principle	مبْدأ ج مبادِئُ
on principle	مِن حيثُ المبدأ
to explain sth. to so.	بسط (يبْسُطُ) هـ على
yes, certainly, sure	بلَى
daughter (dimin.)	بُنيَّة
here: chapter	باب ج أبْواب

on the road to	في سبيلِ
Jihād	جهاد
to burn sth.	IV أَحْرق (يُحْرِقُ) هـ
sense; perception	حاسَّة ج حواسّ
according to	بِحَسَبِ
to be able to do sth. in a good manner	IV أَحْسن (يُحْسِنُ) هـ
entitled	أحقُّ (Elat. of حقيق)
allowed, legitimate	حلال
jewelry	حَلْي / حُلِيّ
to bear, to stand sth.	V تَحمَّل (يتحمَّل) هـ
pregnant	حامِل (م) ج حوامِلُ
to be embarrassed	V تَحيَّر (يتحيَّرُ)
here: pronunciation	مَخْرج ج مَخارِجُ
to add an i; genitive	الخفض
to create sth.	خلق (يَخْلُقُ) هـ
evidence	دليل ج دلائلُ، أدلّة
mercy	رَحْمة
May God have mercy upon him.	رحمةُ اللهِ عليهِ
to add an u; nominative; indicative	الرفع
hot ground	رمْضاءُ
purification	تزْكِية
rein; here: means to decide	زمام ج أزِمَّة
preceding	سبق
the merit of being the first	فضْل السبق
shoot, seed	سُلالة ج ـات
In the name of God, the merciful, the compassionate, from whom we ask for help.	بسمِ اللهِ الرحمن الرحيمِ وبِهِ نسْتعينُ
invective	شتيمة ج شتائِمُ
violence, fierceness	شِدَّة
honor	شرف

sunrise	شُروق الشمْس
the early period of Islam	صدر الإسلام
to pray	II صلَّى (يُصلِّي)
to fast	صام (يصومُ)
to have sexual intercourse	مُضاجعة
class, group, strata	طبـقة ج ـات
to give so. sth. to eat	IV أطْعم (يُطْعِمُ) ه هـ
clay	طِين
to become obvious to so.	ظهر (يظْهَرُ) ل
admiring; here: gram. term for exclamations	التعجُّب
just, balanced	أعْدلُ (Elat. of عادل)
sweet, convenient	أعْذبُ (Elat. of عذب)
the Iʿrāb	الإعْراب
Arab of the desert	أعْرابي ج أعْراب
reason; (gram.) defectivity (letter or word)	عِلّة ج عِلل
meaning	معْنًى ج معانٍ
members of the family	عِيال
the Feast of Immolation	عِيد الأضْحَى
Whitsun	عيد العنْصرة
Easter	عيد الفِصْح
the Feast of Breaking the Ramaḍān Fast	عيد الفِطْر
the Feast of the Birth of the Prophet	عيد مَوْلِد النبي
Christmas	عيد الميلاد
sunset	غُروب الشمْس
dominating	غالِب
to make clear	فتق (يفْتُقُ)
versatility	اِفْتِنان
scattered	مُتفرِّق

here: criterion of differentiation	فصْل ج فُصُول	heat of the summer	قَيْظ
to remain	فضل (يفضُلُ)	scorching	قائِظ
to prefer, to favour sth., so. over	II فضَّل (يُفضِّل) هـ، ه على	mean, miserly, stingy *(Elat. of* لئيم*)*	ألأمُ
merit	فضْل	curse	لعْنة ج لعنات
Nomen agentis; active *(gram.)*	الفاعِل	to display sth.	مدَّ (يمُدُّ) هـ
Nomen patientis, passive *(gram.)*	المفْعُول	dirty, contemptuous	مَهِين
question	اِسْتِفْهام	descendant	نسْل ج أنْسال
holy, sacred	مُقدَّس	to add an *a*; accusative	النصْب
here: to be at the top of	تقدُّم	to pronounce sth.	نطق (ينطُقُ) بِ
extract from	مُقْتطف من	to make so. say sth.	IV أنطق (يُنطِقُ) هـ
to sit (down) on	قعد (يقْعُدُ) على	to force so. to do sth.	IV أوْجب (يُوجبُ) هـ على ه
analogy; rule, norm	قِياس ج ـات أقْيسة	to facilitate sth. for so.	II يسَّر (يُيَسِّر) هـ لِ

Text 1

مقتطفات من

طبقات النحْويين   واللغويين

لأبي بكر محمّد بن الحسن الزُّبيدي المتوفَّى ٣٧٩ هـ

بسـم الله الرحمن الرحيـم وبه نستعين

قال أبو بكر محمّد بن الحسن الزبيدي – رحمة الله عليه:

الحمد لله الذي أحسن كل شيء خلقه وبدأ خلق الإنسان من طين، ثـم جعل نسله من سلالة من ماء

مهين(١)، وفضّله على سائر الحيوان، بما آتاه من حاسّة العقل وبيان اللسان، ثـم جبل كل أمّة من الأمـم

على لغة أنطقهـم بها، ويسّـرهـم لها، وجعل اللسان العربي أعذب الألسنة مخرجاً، وأعدلها منهجاً،

وأوضحها بياناً، وأوسعها افتناناً، وجعل الإعراب حلياً للّسان، ونـظاماً وفصلاً لما اختلف من معانيه.

فكان أول من أصّل ذلك أبو الأسود ظالم بن عمرو الدَّؤلي، ونصر بن عاصم، وعبد الرحمن بن هُرْمُز.

فوضعوا للنحو أبواباً، وأصّلوا له أصولاً؛ فذكروا عوامل الرفع والنصب والخفض والجزم، ووضعوا باب

الفاعل والمفعول والتعجب والمضاف. وكان لأبي الأسود في ذلك فضل السبق وشرف التقدّم. ثـم

وصل ما أصّلوه من ذلك التالون لهـم، والآخذون عنهـم؛ فكان لكل واحد منهـم من الفضل بحسب مـا

بسط من القول، ومدّ من القياس، وفتق من المعاني، وأوضح من الدلائل وبيّن من العلل.

الطبقة الأولى من النحويين البصريين

أبو الأسود الدؤلي

روى أن الذي أوجب عليه الوضع في النحو أن ابنته قعدت معه في يوم قائظ شديد الحرّ، فأرادت التعجّب

من شدة الحرّ فقالت: ﴿ ما أشدُّ الحرّ! ﴾ فقال أبوها: ﴿ القيظ، وهو ما نحن فيه يا بنية ﴾ جواباً عن

كلامها لأنه استفهام، فتحيّرت وظهر لها خطأها، فعلـم أبو الأسود أنها أرادت التعجّب، فقال لها:

﴿ قولي يا بنية: ما أشدَّ الحرّ! ﴾ فعمل باب التعجب وباب الفاعل والمفعول به وغيرها من الأبواب.

وقِيل: إنه خرج مع أصحابه إلى الصيد، فلما جلسوا للطعام، جاء أعرابي.

فقال: السلام عليكـم! أدخل؟

فقال أبو الأسود: وراءك أوسع لك!

فقال الأعرابي: إنّ الرمضاء قد أحرقت رجليّ.

فقال أبو الأسود: بُلّ عليهما!

فقال: هل عندك شيء تطعمنيه؟

فقال أبو الأسود: نأكل ونُطعِـم العيال، فإن فضل شيء فأنت أحقّ به من الكلب!

قال الأعرابي: ما رأيت ألأَمَ منك.

قال أبو الأسود: بلى! ولكنك نسيت!

(١) راجع القرآن الكريم، سورة البقرة

Text 2

عن الإسلام

سوزن: عندي بعض الأسئلة عن الإسلام، لو سمحت.

أحمد: تفضّلي، اسألي عما تريدين!

سوزن: هل أنت مسلم؟

أحمد: الحمد لله.

سوزن: من أي مذهب؟

أحمد: أنا سني ومذهبي هـو مذهب الحنابلة، أي مذهب ابن حنبـل وليس مذهب الأحناف أي مذهب أبي حنيفة الذي هو المذهب الغالب في البلاد.

سوزن: هل تصلّي يومياً؟

أحمد: نعم، أصلّي يومياً خمس مرات، أي صلاة الصبح وصلاة الظهـر وصلاة العصـر وصلاة المغرب وصلاة العشاء.

سوزن: وكيف بالنسبة للصوم، هل تصوم في شهر رمضان؟

أحمد: نعم، أصوم في شهر رمضان من شروق الشمس إلى غروبها والصوم في الصيـف الحارّ ليس بسيطاً ولكننا نتحمّله.

سوزن: هل الصوم واجب على كلّ المسلمين؟

أحمد: من حيث المبدأ نعم، يُستثنى منه المرضى والشيوخ والنساء الحوامل والمسـافرون. وقال ا لله في كتابه العزيز :﴿يا أيها الذين آمنوا كُتِب عليكم الصيام كما كتـب على الذين من قبلكم﴾. وقال أيضاً: ﴿فمن كـان منكـم مريضاً أو على سـفر فعدّة من أيّام أخر﴾ [١] الصوم يعـني الامتنـاع عـن الطعـام والشراب والتدخـين وعن مضاجعة النساء أيضاً وهذا مـن شـروق الشـمس إلى غروبها وبعد ذلـك مسموح، الحمد لله.

سوزن: وكيف بالنسبة للزكاة؟

أحمد: الزكاة من فرائض الإسلام وأنا أخرج الزكاة وخاصة زكاة الفطر في نهاية شـهر رمضان. والفكرة الأساسية في الزكاة هي أنه على المسلم تزكيـة مالـه أي جعلـه حلالاً.

سوزن: الفكرة جيدة ولكن ينقصها التطبيق.

أحمد: أنت على حقّ وبجاهد في سبيل ا لله لتحقيق هذه الفكرة.

سوزن: هل قمت بالحجّ إلى مكة؟

أحمد: نعم، قمت بحج بيت ا لله الحرام قبل سنتين والحمد لله.

سوزن: ما هو رأيك في الجهاد؟ عندنا في أوربا نقرأ أشياء كثيرة عن الجهاد. هـل تعـني هذه الكلمة فعلاً الحرب؟

أحمد: أبداً، الجهاد يعني أن المسلم يعمل بكلّ ما في وسعه في سبيل تطبيق تعاليم الإسلام. وهذا الجهاد الأكبر هو بالنسبة لي أهمّ بكثير من الجهاد بمعنى الحرب المقدسة.

سوزن: سؤالي الأخير: يوجد عندنا الكثير من الأعياد المسيحية مثل عيد الميلاد وعيد الفصح وعيد العنصرة فما هي الأعياد الإسلامية.

أحمد: من حيث المبدأ نحتفل بعيدين كبيرين: بعيد الأضحى وبعيد الفطر المبارك في نهاية شهر رمضان وفي دول المغرب يحتفلون بشكل خاص بمولد النبي، صلى الله عليه وسلم.

سوزن: شكراً للإجابة على أسئلتي.

أحمد: لا شكر على الواجب.   (١) راجع القرآن الكريم، سورة البقرة

Exercises:

L1 Insert the proper preposition(s).

يصدّر المعمل الإنتاج ... ألمانيا. يستورد البلد البترول ... السعودية. قاموا ... جولة ... البلاد. أوصى ... تقديم المشروع. استقبلهم ... ساعتين. اشترى ... المخزن كتباً جديدة إضافة ... شنطة وأقلام. أما ... النسبة ... المؤتمر فهو ينعقد ... هذا الفندق. هو ... الباب. الطالب ... المدير. الطائرة ... البحر. وصل ... القاهرة. ... أن تلفنت ... محمد ذهبت ... البيت. زرت المدير ... زيارة المعمل. شرح ... هم الوضع ... المرحلة الأولى. كتبت الرسالة ... ورقة حمراء. عثروا ... آثار المدينة. تسببت المناقشة ... مشاكل كثيرة. كان الضيوف يفدون ... المناطق السياحية. تشهد هذه المخطوطات ... مستوى العلم ... القرون الوسطى. أشرك ... هذه المعلومات. لا نتقيد ... هذه القواعد. اتفقوا ... المشروع ... محادثات طويلة. إختلف الرئيسان ... قضايا أساسية.

L2 Find out the root of the following words.

مناسبة / صحة / باع / إمكانية / استثنى / متعوّد / استيراد / قمة / متوفى / امتدّ / استمرار / مؤقت / اختار / أطروحة / مشروع / مستحيل / استئمارة / استنتاج / مصفاة / استبان / تدهور / حاج / شوربة / جوعان / سؤال / مدة

L3 Find out the antonyms of the following words.

نهاية / صدّر / ممطر / نجاح / سهول / تقدّم / صحيح / يسار / تعبان / جهل / جلس /

استيراد / ممكن / سريع / بارد / زواج / اتّفق

L4 Translate the following expressions of admiration into Arabic. Use ما +
Elative in the accusative + noun in the accusative.
1. How beautiful these exercises are!
2. How difficult these weeks are!
3. How high these mountains are!
4. How long these lists are!
5. How big this melon is!
6. How spacious these rooms are!
7. How strong these men are!
8. How sweet these dates are!
9. How fast this car is!

L5 Translate into English.

دخـل الرئيس ضـاحكاً وفي يده المعاهدة الجديدة.

خرجت صديقتي ضاحكةً.

نام الأستاذ جالساً.

وصل القطار السريع قادماً من برلين.

جلس الطالب في الصف وفي يده فلوس كثيرة.

هرب الطالب ضاحكاً عندما رأى أستاذه.

شرح الكتاب شرحاً طويلاً وهو ينظر إليَّ.

استقبلني المدير ولا يقول كلمة.

G1 Answer the following questions using either the dual or واحد / واحدة.

☜ كم ساعة عملت هناك؟   >   عملت هناك ساعة واحدة.

☜ أو: عملت هناك ساعتين.

كم شهراً   عملت في ذلك المصنع (هناك، معه هناك، في بيتهم)؟

سكنت في تلك الغرفة (تلك المدينة، ذلك البيت)؟

مكثت في ذلك البلد (في تلك المدينة، في عاصمتنا)؟

درست اللغة العربية (اللغة الألمانية، هذه اللغة)؟	كم سنةً
عملت هناك (في تلك المدينة، في ذلك المصنع)؟	
مكثت في لايبزغ (في برلين، في القاهرة، في العاصمة)؟	
عملت في البيت (في المكتبة، في المعهد)؟	كم ساعةً
شرحت له العمل (عمله، هذه الأعمال، الدرس)؟	
جلست في المطعم (في القاعة، هناك، عندهم)؟	
عملت في المصنع (في بيتك، في المكتبة، في المعهد)؟	كم يوماً
مكثت في تلك المدينة (في ذلك البلد، في العاصمة)؟	
سكنت في الفندق (في بيته، في بيت الطلبة، هناك)؟	
درست هذه اللغة (الحياة هناك)؟	كم أسبوعاً
سكنت في الفندق (عندهم، عند أصدقائك)؟	
عملت في المصنع (في المكتبة، في المخزن)؟	
من البيرة (النبيذ، الماء) شربت؟	كم كأساً
من القهوة (الشاي) شربت؟	كم فنجاناً
(قلماً، كرّاسة، جهازاً، ممحاةً) أخذت / طلبت؟	كم كتاباً
(سنةً) درست في تلك الجامعة؟	كم شهراً

G2 Form affirmative exceptive sentences and pay attention to the fact that the noun has to be in the accusative after إلا in this type of exceptive.

جاء كلّهم + محمد > جاء كلّهم إلّا محمداً.

الوفد المصري	وصلت الوفود
كتاب واحد	قرأت كلّ الكتب
مملكة واحدة	تدهورت هذه الممالك
دين واحد	رفض كلّ الأديان
عقدان	قرأ الوزير كلّ العقود

طالب ألماني	يشترك الطلاّب في حفلات الزواج

وحدة أمريكية	انسحبت الوحدات

ضيفان	نام كلّ الضيوف

G3 Transform the following sentences into the perfect tense.

الطقس بارد. المعلّم جديد. الحفلة جميلة. هؤلاء الرجال معلّمون. الطلاّب مجتهدون. القلم ممتاز. الحوار طويل. الدرس مملّ. التمرين بسيط. هناك ضيوف كثيرون. حفلة الزواج جميلة. الحبّ أعمى. الأسد قوي. السؤال صعب.

G4 Negate the sentences in G3 in the perfect tense.

G5 Negate the sentences in G3 by means of ليس.

G6 (Repetition) Negate the conditional and the result clause.

☞	إذا كان عندي وقت أجيء إليك.> إذا لم يكن عندي وقت لا أجيء إليك.

إذا قرأت هذا الكتاب عرفت القضية.

إذا تعلّمت الكلمات الجديدة تستطيع أن تترجم الأسئلة.

إذا أعطيتني الكتاب العربي أعطيك الكتاب الفرنسي.

إذا أنهيت العمل سأجيء إليك.

إذا اشتركت أنت في المؤتمر أشترك أنا في المؤتمر أيضاً.

إذا قابلتُ الأصدقاء يمكنني أن أطلعهم على القضية.

إذا كانت عندي نقود أشتري الكتب.

إذا رافقني أحد أذهب إلى هناك.

إذا كان الطقس جميلاً نقوم بنزهة.

إذا كنتَ مجتهداً نوفدك للدراسة إلى الخارج.

إذا دبّرت لي الاستمارات سأسافر يوم الجمعة.

G7 (Repetition) Combine the following clauses in such a way that the second clause becomes a clause of concession introduced by (حتى) ولو.

☞	نفعل ذلك	نفعل ذلك وحدنا >

☞	نفعل ذلك (حتى) ولو فعلنا ذلك وحدنا.

☞   سأنهي العمل لا يساعدني أحد ›

☞   سأنهي العمل (حتى) ولو لم يساعدني أحد.

نقوم بنزهة	ليس الطقس جميلاً
نتحدّث حول هذه المشكلة	(يكون) جميعهم موجودون
نقاوم أعداءنا	(يكون) أقوياء
نحاول ذلك	(يكون) الوصول إلى هناك صعب
سأنهي العمل	أعمل ١٦ ساعة
أدبّر الأعمال	أسافر إلى هناك مرة ثانية أو ثالثة
سأحضر الحفلة	لا يحضرها أصدقائي
أفعل ذلك	أفعل ذلك وحدي
سوف لا أنهي العمل	يساعدني صديقي

G8 Translate into Arabic.

He is more diligent than the police allow.

He is faster on foot than by car.

His trousers are whiter than his shirt.

She knows more than her teacher.

Nobody is more stupid than he is.

C1 Ask your teacher questions in Arabic based on Text 2 about the obligations of a Muslim. The teacher should answer with quotations from Koran and Ḥadīth.

C2 Prepare a dialogue based on Text 2 in which a Christian is interviewed in a similar way. Make use of the following words:

belief, creed	إيمان بِ / عقيدة
believing, believer	مؤْمِن ج ـ ون
Bible	الكتاب المقدس/التوراة والإنجيل/العهد القديم والعهد الجديد
Catholic	كاثوليكي
church	كنيسة ج كنائسُ
confession	الاعتراف بخطاياه
devil	شيطان ج شياطينُ / إبْلِيس ج أبالِسة

hell	جهنّمُ (م) / جحيم (م) / نار (م)
Jesus	عِيسىَ / يسُوعُ / يسوع المسيح
the Last Judgement	يوم الدين / يوم القيامة
paradise	جنّةٌ / فِردَوْس
pope	البابا ج بابوات
Protestant	بروتستانتي
sin	خطيئة ج خطايا / إثْم ج آثام

Final exercise:

Translate into Arabic.

By now I have learned the Arabic alphabet, equational and verbal sentences, strong and weak verbs, the jussive, the patterns of the verb, singular and sound and broken plural, the *Iḍāfa*, the active and passive voice, the Arabic numbers, the infinitive, the *Elative*, conditional and exceptive sentences and the accusative. I have also learned many words and read texts about Arab history and Islam, politics, the economy, oil, agriculture, the desert, sports, and Arabic proverbs etc. I have played a lot of roles in the dialogues, and I also had to write letters and my curriculum vitae in Arabic.

By now, I know that it is only possible to learn this language if you always attend the lectures, and if you do all your homework (all the exercises which you are instructed to do at home). I also learned how to apologize if I was sometimes unable to attend because the train was late, or because my father was celebrating his fiftieth birthday for the fifth time.

I know some Arabic proverbs, too, e.g.:

If the cat is not at home, the mice start playing.

Love is blind.

Too many cooks spoil the broth.

The son of a duck is a good swimmer.

However, I didn't learn Arabic invectives (شِتِيمَة ج شَـتَائِمُ) and curses (لَعْنَة ج لَعَنـَات). I must ask my teacher about this before the final examinations in order to know at least some of them in case I need them after the examinations.

Now I hope to succeed in the final examinations.

ARABIC-ENGLISH GLOSSARY

1. **Arrangement of entries**

   Arabic words are arranged alphabetically. The number of the lesson in which the Arabic word is used for the first time in the book is placed after the English equivalent in brackets.

2. **Vocalizing**

   The Arabic words are not fully vocalized. The following notes should enable you to read the words correctly.

2.1. The following words are only partially or not vocalized:

   a) words and parts of words occurring again and again and formed regularly, e.g.:

   - the article ال
   - the most common prepositions, conjunctions, pronouns and particles
   - the sound plurals
   - verbs of the pattern فَعَلَ ; فعِل and فعُل are specified by *Kasra* and *Ḍamma*
   - the verbs of the derived forms which are formed regularily; but *Shadda* and *Sukūn* are given
   - the Nomen unitatis of generic collective nouns
   - the numerals (see the appendix)

   b) some foreign words which are pronounced as in the original language

2.2. If *Alif* ١ and *Wāw* و or *Yā'* ي are used to indicate a long vowel, the letter before is not vocalized, e.g. با = *bā*, بو = *bū*, بي = *bī*. Diphtongs are always specified: أوْ = *aw*, أيْ = *ay*.

2.3. Diptotes are marked by *Ḍamma* (in G./A. *Fatḥa*).

2.4. Words starting with *Hamzat al-waṣl*, i.e. verbs and infinitives of forms VII, XII, IX and X, have *Kasra* under *Alif* ١.

2.5. *Hamzat qaṭ'*, *Shadda* and *Sukūn* are nearly always given.

2.6. The prefixes مِ *mi-* and مُ *mu-* are always vocalized.

2.7. In all the other cases *Kasra* and *Ḍamma* are used to specify a short vowel, but not *Fatḥa*.

3. **Nouns**

3.1. The Arabic nouns are given without an article except for such words and collocations which always occur with an article.

3.2. The abbreviation (ج) = جمع is put in front of the noun if the noun is only used as plural. Singular and plural of a noun are are separated by ج.

   - Feminines are preceded by (م) = مُؤنّث,
   - Dual is preceded by (ث) = مُثَنَّى,
   - Several plurals are separated by ،.
   - The feminine gender of a noun of masculine shape is marked by (م) behind the singular.

3.3. Collective nouns are referred to by *coll*. The Nomen unitatis is not mentioned.

3.4. Colloquial usage is marked by *colloq*.

3.5. Dialects are referred to as *Eg*. (Egyptian), *Alg*. (Algerian) *Ir*. (Iraqi), *Yem*. (Yemeni) and *Syr*. (Syrian).

3.6. Some proper names are not included.

4. **The arrangement of the verbs**

4.1. The Arabic verbs are given in the perfect tense followed by the imperfect in brackets. Form I of the verb is followed by the most common infinitive in the accusative according to Arabic dictionaries. The Forms are specified by II, III, … X.

4.2. The Arabic verb is followed by governing pronouns or prepositions, and optional prepositions or pronouns are separated by a comma. The accusative of a person is specified by ه, the accusative of things by ـه. Optional prepositions are put in brackets.

ARABIC-ENGLISH GLOSSARY

much better than(L12)	أحْسَنُ بكثِير من	آ	
to bring sth. along to(L14)	IV أحْضَر (يُحْضِرُ) إلى	to bring, to give sth.(L28)	IV آتى (يُؤْتِي) بِ
entitled(L28)	أحَقُّ (حقيق of .Elat)	antiquities(L9)	ج آثار
red(L7)	أحْمَرُ م حَمْراءُ	last(L24)	آخِر ج ون، ات، أواخِرُ
stupid, silly, dumb(L26)	أحْمَق (م) حَمْقاءُ	other (m./ f.)(L5)	آخَرُ/ أُخْرَى
sometimes(L7)	أحْياناً	Asian(L9)	آسِيوِيّ ج ـون
brother(L2)	أخ ج إخْوة	evil; disease; epidemic of plants(L20)	آفة ج ـات
to inform so. of sth. (L14)	IV أخْبَر (يُخْبِرُ) ه ب	machine(L20)	آلة ج ـات
sister(L2)	أُخْت ج أخوات	automatic(L12)	آلِيّ
to take sth.(L7)	أخذ (يأخذ) هـ	hoping that(L18)	آمِلاً أنْ
to study under, to learn from so. (L28)	أخذ عن	now(L2)	الآن
green(L7)	أخْضَر م خضْراءُ	in those days(L24)	آنذاك = إذ ذاك
hollow of the sole (of the foot) (L24)	أخْمَصُ القدم ج أخامِصُ	Miss(L2)	آنِسة ج ات
last(L10)	أخِير	أ	
eventually(L10)	أخِيراً	(interrogative particle)(L9)	أ
instrument(L24)	أداة ج أدوات	..., isn't it?(L9)	أ ليس كذلك؟
literature(L8)	أدب ج آداب	father(L2)	أب ج آباء
lower(L16)	أدْنَى م دُنْيا	white(L7)	أبْيَضُ م بيْضاءُ
to lead to(L15)	II أدَّى (يُؤدِّي) إلى	to come (to) (L12)	أتى (يأتِي إتْياناً) (إلى)
ear(L13)	أُذُن (م) ج آذان	to prove, to establish sth.(L25)	IV أثْبَت (يُثْبِتُ) هـ
I go to ...(L3)	أذهَبُ إلى	(prep.) during(L18)	أثْناءَ
to want sth. (L15)	IV أراد (يُريدُ) هـ، أنْ	to answer so. or sth.(L15)	IV أجاب (يُجيبُ) على
to bring back to(L23)	IV أرْجَع (يُؤْجِعُ) هـ إلى	to carry out, to hold sth. (L15)	IV أجْرى (يُجْرِي) هـ
I beg your pardon.(L10)	أرْجُو الإعْتِذار.	foreigner, foreign(L6)	أجْنبي ج أجانِبُ
I greet / welcome you(L11)	أُرحِّبُ بكم	to love, to like so., sth. (L18)	IV أحبَّ (يُحِبُّ) ه، هـ
cheaper than(L19)	أرْخص مِن	to gain, to win sth.(L17)	IV أحْرز (يُحْرِزُ) هـ
Jordanian(L14)	أُردُنِّيّ	to burn sth. (L28)	IV أحْرَق (يُحْرِقُ) هـ
to send so., sth. to so. (L14)	IV أرْسل (يُرْسِلُ) ه هـ إلى / لـ	to be able to do sth. in a good manner(L28)	IV أحْسَن (يُحْسِنُ) هـ
earth(L2)	أرْض (م) ج أراضٍ		

to give so. sth. (L14)	أَعْطَى (يُعْطِي) ه هـ IV
to give so. sth. (L15)	أَعْطَى (يُعْطِي) ه/ ل ، هـ IV
to come (directly) after (L21)	أَعْقَب (يُعْقِبُ) هـ/على IV
to announce, to declare sth. (L15)	أَعْلَن (يُعْلِنُ) هـ IV
high, higher, highest (L16)	أَعْلَى/ عُلْيا (م)
to shut, to lock up sth. in front of (L22)	أَغْلَق (يُغْلِقُ) هـ IV أمام
song (L17)	أُغْنِية ج ـات، أغانٍ
to inform so. about (L18)	أفاد (يُفِيدُ) ه ب IV
to please so., that (L14)	أَفْرَح (يُفَرِحُ) ه، أَنْ IV
horizon, prospect (L20)	أُفُق ج آفاق
to hold, to organize sth. (L15)	أقام (يُقِيمُ) هـ IV
more favourable (for) (L25)	أكثر مُلاءمة (ل)
to eat (L5)	أكل
eat sth. (L7)	أكل (يأْكُلُ) أكْلاً هـ
meal, dish (L3)	أكْلة ج أكْلات
mean, miserly, stingy (L28)	ألأَمُ (لئيم Elat. of)
to add sth. to (L21)	أَلْحَق (يُلْحِقُ) هـ ب IV
to do damage to (L21)	أَلْحَق أَضْراراً ب
rel. pr. (L14)	الَّذِي م الَّتِي ج الَّذِين م اللاّتِي واللَّواتِي ث اللّذان م اللّتان
track and field events (L17)	ألعاب الساحة والميدان
horse show (L17)	ألعاب الفُروسيّة
to cancel, to call off sth. (L15)	أَلْغَى (يُلْغِي) هـ IV
thousand (L6)	ألف ج آلاف
many thanks, thanks a lot (L8)	ألف شُكر
to throw sth. (L15)	أَلْقَى (يُلْقِي) هـ IV
to make a speech (L15)	ألقى كلمة
pain (L13)	ألم ج آلام

rabbit (L26)	أرْنب ج أرانبُ
to show so. sth. (L18)	أرى (يُرِي) ه هـ IV
I want ... (sth.) (L6)	أُرِيدُ ... (هـ)
crisis (L11)	أزْمة ج أزمات
basis, foundation (L10)	أساس ج أُسُس
basically (L10)	أساسيّ
week (L6)	أُسْبوع ج أسابيعُ
professor, master (L6)	أُسْتاذ ج أساتِذة
lion (L26)	أسـد ج أُسُد، أُسُود
to make so. happy (L23)	أَسْعَد (يُسْعِدُ) ه IV
to produce sth. (L14)	أَسْفَر (يُسْفِرُ) عن IV
black (L7)	أسْودُ م سوداءُ
to supervise so., sth. (L16)	أَشْرَف (يُشْرِفُ) على IV
to hit so., sth. (L15)	أَصاب (يُصِيبُ) هـ، ه IV
to become sth. (L17)	أَصْبَح (يُصْبِحُ) هـ IV
to issue sth. (L20)	أَصْدَر (يُصَدِرُ) هـ IV
to give sth. a solid foundation (L28)	أَصَّل (يُؤَصِّلُ) هـ II
origin (L27)	أصْل ج أُصُول
originally (adv.) (L27)	أصْلاً
original (L8)	أصْليّ
to add sth. to (L17)	أَضاف (يُضِيفُ) هـ إلى IV
dissertation (L9)	أُطْروحة ج ـات
to give so. sth. to eat (L28)	أَطْعَم (يُطْعِمُ) ه هـ IV
to inform so. about (L23)	أَطْلَع (يُطْلِعُ) ه على IV
to restore, to give sth. back (L27)	أعاد (يُعِيدُ) هـ إلى IV
to admire sth. (L23)	أَعْجَب (يُعْجِبُ) هـ IV
Repeat. (L3)	أَعِدْ ! / أَعِيدِي!
just, balanced (L28)	أعْدَلُ (عادِل Elat. of)
sweet, convenient (L28)	أعْذَبُ (عذب Elat. of)
Arab of the desert (L28)	أعْرابي ج أعْراب

you (2nd p.pl.f.)(L2)	أنْتُنَّ
to accomplish, to carry out(L14)	IV أنْجز (يُنْجزُ) هـ
to build, to erect sth.(L25)	IV أنْشأ (يُنْشِئُ) هـ
to make so. say sth.(L28)	IV أنطق (يُنْطِقُ) هـ
nose(L13)	أنف ج أُنُوف
to finish sth.(L15)	IV أنْهَى (يُنْهِي) هـ
Sunnites(L10)	أهْل السُنَّة
family, relatives(L5)	أهْل ج أهال
fig: Hello! (L2)	أهْلاً بكَ / بكِ
Welcome!(L2)	أهْلاً وسهْلاً
more important(L13)	أهمّ
importance(L17)	أهمِّيَّة
OPEC(L19)	الأوبك
to force so. to do sth.(L28)	IV أوْجب (يُوجبُ) هـ على ه
European(L7)	أوربِّيّ
to bring so., sth. to(L15)	IV أوْصل (يُوصِلُ) ه، هـ إلى
to recommend so., sth., to advise so. to(L23)	IV أوْصىَ (يُوصِي) ب
to explain sth.(L15)	IV أوْضح (يُوضحُ) هـ
to delegate so. to(L19)	IV أوْفد (يُوفِدُ) ه إلى
first (m./f.)(L6)	أوَّل م أُوْلَى
initial, at first(L18)	أوَّليّ
that is(L4)	أيْ
which(L6)	أيٌّ / أيَّة
fig.: May I help you?(L6)	أية خدمة؟
to support so., sth.(L15)	II أيَّد (يُؤيِّدُ) ه، هـ
manpower, workers(L25)	ج الأيدي العامِلة
ice cream(L7)	أيْس كريم
also, too(L2)	أيْضاً
where(L2)	أيْنَ
German(L4)	ألْماني ج ألْمان
Germany(L5)	ألْمانيا
or(L4)	أمْ
mother(L2)	أُمّ ج أُمَّهات
As far as (Aḥmad) is concerned....(L9)	أمّا (أحمد) فـ(هو)...
(prep.) in front of (loc.)(L2)	أمامَ
security, protection(L14)	أمان
nation, people(L11)	أُمَّة ج أُمم
thing, matter(L11)	أمْر ج أُمُور
America(L6)	أمْريكا
American(L19)	أمْريكِيّ
yesterday(L5)	أمْس
to be able to (L14)	IV أمْكن (يُمكِنُ) ه، أنْ
to hope that(L8)	أمل (يأْمُلُ) أنْ
the United Nations(L11)	الأمم المُتَّحِدة
security(L11)	أمْن
Emir(L12)	أمير ج أمراءُ
cashier(L16)	أمين الصندوق
secretary(L8)	أمين ج أُمناءُ
faithful, loyal, devoted(L26)	أمين ج أُمناءُ
General Secretary(L8)	أمين عامّ ج أُمناءُ عامُّون
that (+ accusative)(L5)	أنَّ
I(L2)	أنا
I am fine. (L2)	أنا بخَيْر
pipe, tube(L24)	أُنْبُوب(ة) ج أنابِيبُ
you (m.)(L2)	أنْتَ
you (f.)(L2)	أنْتِ
You are right. (L8)	أنت على حقّ.
to produce sth.(L19)	IV أنْتج (يُنْتِجُ) هـ
you (2nd p.pl.m.)(L2)	أنْتُم

frame(work)^(L8)	إطار ج أُطُر	yes^(L23)	(colloq. Eg.) أيْوَه
re-,^(L11)	إعادة		
preparation^(L16)	إعْداد		إ
the Iᶜrāb^(L28)	الإعْراب	ethnologic, anthropological^(L9)	إثْنولوجيّ
(mass) media; communication^(L12)	إعْلام	answering^(L21)	إجابة على
African^(L9)	إفْريقي ج ـون، أفارِقة	holiday^(L13)	إجازة ج ات
bankruptcy^(L22)	إفْلاس	sick leave^(L13)	إجازة مرضية
stay^(L10)	إقامة ج ـات	carrying out^(L18)	إجْراء
except; but^(L27)	إلاّ	entire, gross, whole, total^(L19)	إجْماليّ
before (time)^(L16)	إلاّ	administration^(L10)	إدارة ج ات
god, deity^(L27)	إله، إلاه ج آلِهة	administrative^(L18)	إداريّ
(prep.) to^(L2)	إلى	(with verbal sentence) since, because^(L12)	إذْ
and so on, abbr: إلخ ^(L7)	إلى آخِرِهِ	as; since/because^(L23)	إذْ
So long!^(L2)	إلى اللقاء	if^(L26)	إذا
to the left^(L4)	إلى اليسار	so, therefore, then^(L10)	إذن
to the right^(L4)	إلى اليمين	(prep.) with respect to, regarding^(L21)	إزاءَ
down, downwards^(L2)	إلى تَحْتُ	Spanish, Spaniard^(L9)	إسْبانيّ ج ـون
beside^(L9)	إلى جانب	Spain^(L5)	إسْبانيا
up(wards)^(L2)	إلى فوقُ	Australia^(L15)	إسْتراليا
either ... or^(L18)	إمّا ... وإمّا/... أو	Israel^(L14)	إسْرائيل
emirate^(L3)	إمارة ج إمارات	Islam^(L10)	الإسْلام
empire^(L21)	إمبراطورية ج ـات	Islamic^(L10)	إسْلاميّ
possibility^(L8)	إمْكانِية ج ـات	diarrhea^(L14)	إسْهال
particle introducing an equational sentence^(L8)	إنَّ	contribution^(L18)	إسْهام
		spreading^(L21)	إشاعة
if / even though, although^(L26)	إنْ / وإنْ	supervision^(L18)	إشْراف على
God willing; I (we) hope so^(L8)	إنْ شاءَ ا الله	making so. take part (in)^(L11)	إشْراك (في)
production^(L19)	إنْتاج	finger; toe^(L13)	إصْبع (م) ج أصابِعُ
man^(L13)	إنْسان	reform^(L22)	إصْلاح
human^(L12)	إنْسانيّ	in addition to^(L9)	إضافةً إلى
inch^(L15)	إنْش ج ـات	additional^(L19)	إضافيّ
justice, fairness^(L24)	إنْصاف		

reserve(L15)   اِحْتِياطِيّ ج ـات

to select so.,   VIII اِخْتار (يَخْتارُ) ه، هـ من
sth. out of(L19)

examination, test(L16)   اِخْتِبار ج ات

to conclude sth.   VIII اِخْتَتَم (يَخْتَتِمُ) هـ بـ
with(L20)

invention(L22)   اِخْتِراع ج ـات

to mix with(L27)   VIII اِخْتَلَط (يَخْتَلِطُ) بـ

height, altitude, level(L15)   اِرْتِفاع ج ـات

satisfaction(L14)   اِرْتِياح

to increase, to rise(L19)   VIII اِزْداد (يَزْدادُ)

flourishing, upswing, boom(L19)   اِزْدِهار

to (begin) to   VIII اِزْدَهَر (يَزْدَهِرُ)
flourish(L27)

to rent sth.(L18)   X اِسْتَأْجَر (يَسْتَأْجِرُ) هـ

renting(L18)   اِسْتِئْجار ج ات

form, questionnaire (mostly   اِسْتِمارة ج ـات
written (استمارة (L9)

to except sth.,   X اِسْتَثْنى (يَسْتَثْني) هـ، ه من
so. from(L28)

use, employment (L20)   اِسْتِخْدام ج ـات

to excavate   X اِسْتَخْرَج (يَسْتَخْرِجُ) هـ من
sth. from(L25)

to extract, to   X اِسْتَخْلَص (يَسْتَخْلِصُ) هـ من
deduct sth.
from(L23)

to conclude(L23)   اِسْتَخْلَص اِسْتِنْتاجات

strategic(L19)   اِسْتِراتيجيّ

oriental studies(L9)   اِسْتِشْراق

to be able to(L18)   X اِسْتَطاع (يَسْتَطيعُ) أَنْ

colonial(L21)   اِسْتِعْماريّ

to last(L18)   X اِسْتَغْرَق (يَسْتَغْرِقُ)

exploitation(L21)   اِسْتِغْلال

to profit by, from(L19)   X اِسْتَفاد (يَسْتَفيدُ) من

to take advantage of, to use(L20)   اِسْتِفادة مِن

expense(s)(L19)   إِنْفاق

influenza(L20)   إِنْفلوينزا

English(L9)   إِنْكْليزي ج إِنْكْليز

closing, concluding(L19)   إِنْهاء

positive(L11)   إِيجابيّ

(the) finding(L10)   إِيجاد

Iran(L24)   إِيران

Italy(L21)   إِيطاليا

delegation, sending to(L19)   إِيفاد

coalition(L21)   اِئْتِلافيّ

ا

to begin (intrans.)(L18)   VIII اِبْتَدَأ (يَبْتَدِيُء)

primary(L16)   اِبْتِدائِيّ

invention(L20)   اِبْتِكار ج ـات

son(L10)   اِبْن ج أَبْناء، بَنُون

to turn to(L21)   VIII اِتَّجَه (يَتَّجِهُ) إلى

European Union(L20)   الاتِّحاد الأوربيّ

union(L20)   اِتِّحاد ج ات

to make sth. out of sth.(L26)   VIII اِتَّخَذ (يَتَّخِذُ) من هـ

to be characterized by(L20)   VIII اِتَّسَم (يَتَّسِمُ) بـ

connection to(L18)   اِتِّصال ج ـات بـ

to contact so.(L18)   VIII اِتَّصَل (يَتَّصِلُ) بـ

to agree (upon)(L18)   VIII اِتَّفَق (يَتَّفِقُ) (على)

meeting(L5)   اِجْتِماع ج ـات

to meet so.(L18)   VIII اِجْتَمَع (يَجْتَمِعُ) بـ

to need so., sth.(L18)   VIII اِحْتاج (يَحْتاجُ) إلى

to respect so., sth.(L26)   VIII اِحْتَرَم (يَحْتَرِمُ) ه، هـ

ceremony(L8)   اِحْتِفال ج ـات

to keep sth.(L26)   VIII اِحْتَفَظ (يَحْتَفِظُ) بـ هـ

to occupy sth.(L25)   VIII اِحْتَلَّ (يَحْتَلُّ) هـ

to propose, to suggest sth. to so.(L19)	VIII اِقْتَرح (يَقْتَرحُ) على هـ
to share sth.(L26)	VIII اِقْتَسم (يَقْتَسِمُ) هـ
economy(L8)	اِقْتِصاد
economic(L5)	اِقْتِصادِي
obligation, duty, commitment(L19)	اِلْتِزام ج ـات
examination(L18)	اِمْتِحان ج ـات
to extend to(L24)	VIII اِمْتَدّ (يَمْتَدُّ) إلى
wife (L17)	اِمْرَأ / المَرْأة (with article)
Queue / line up!(L16)	اِمْسِكْ الطابور (colloq.)
productivity(L20)	اِنْتاجيّة
election(L11)	اِنْتِخاب ج ـات
victory(L19)	اِنْتِصار
waiting for(L6)	اِنْتِظار
to expect so., sth. (L22)	VIII اِنْتَظر (يَنْتَظِرُ) ه، هـ
to revive(L19)	VIII اِنْتَعش (يَنْتَعِشُ)
to end (intrans.)(L18)	VIII اِنْتَهَى (يَنْتَهِي)
to finish(L18)	اِنتهى مِنْ
recession, slack period(L19)	اِنْحِسار
going down, falling(L19)	اِنْخِفاض
to coincide with(L24)	VII اِنْسَجم (يَنْسَجِمُ) مع
joining of (L18)	اِنْضِمام إلى
to be held (conference)(L19)	VII اِنْعَقد (يَنْعَقِد)
coup (d'état), revolt(L21)	اِنْقِلاب ج ـات
decline, decay(L21)	اِنْهِيار

ب

(prep.) with, by means of; in(L4)	بِ
he is able to(L18)	بِإمْكانِه أَنْ
well, spring, fountain(L15)	بِئْر (م) ج آبار
unfortunate, miserable(L22)	بائِس

question(L28)	اِسْتِفْهام
reception(L5)	اِسْتِقْبال ج ـات
to welcome so.(L23)	X اِسْتَقْبل (يَسْتَقْبِلُ) ه
to settle down(L24)	X اِسْتَقَرَّ (يَسْتَقِرُّ)
stability(L21)	اِسْتِقْرار
independence(L21)	اِسْتِقْلال
to get sth.(L27)	VIII اِسْتَلم (يَسْتَلِمُ) هـ
to continue, to go on(L19)	X اِسْتَمرَّ (يَسْتَمِرُّ)
to continue to do sth.(L22)	X اِسْتَمرَّ (يَسْتَمِرُّ)
continuity(L21)	اِسْتِمْرار
to conclude sth. from(L19)	X اِسْتَنْتج (يَسْتَنْتِجُ) هـ من
consumption(L19)	اِسْتِهْلاك
to import sth. from(L23)	X اِسْتَوْرد (يَسْتَوْردُ) هـ من
import(L23)	اِسْتِيراد
name; noun(L2)	اِسْم
socialist, Socialist(L8)	اِشْتِراكيّ ج ـون
to take part in(L18)	VIII اِشْتَرك (يَشْتَرِكُ) في
you (f.) bought(L4)	اِشْتَرَيْتِ
you (m.) bought(L4)	اِشْتَرَيْتَ
I bought(L4)	اِشْتَرَيْتُ
to work(L18)	VIII اِشْتَغل (يَشْتَغِلُ)
disturbance, disorder(L21)	اِضْطِراب ج ـات
to consider so., sth. (L23)	VIII اِعْتَبر (يَعْتبِرُ) ه هـ
to believe sth. (L21)	VIII اِعْتَقد (يَعْتَقِدُ) هـ
relying on(L10)	اِعْتِماد (على)
to rely on(L19)	VIII اِعْتَمد (يَعْتَمِدُ) (على)
opening(L12)	اِفْتِتاح ج ـات
to think (L22)	VIII اِفْتَكر (يفتكِرُ)
versatility(L28)	اِفْتِنان
proposal, suggestion(L19)	اِقْتِراح ج ـات

discuss sth.(L8)	بحث (يَبْحَثُ بُحْثاً) هـ	saleslady, ~clerk(L8)	بائعة ج ـات
research(L18)	بحْث ج بُحُوث	door(L2)	باب ج أبْواب
to search for, to look for(L8)	بحث عن	here: chapter(L28)	باب ج أبْواب
Mediterranean(L21)	البحرُ الأبْيضُ المُتوسِّط	Daddy(L3)	بابا
according to(L28)	بِحَسَبِ	Babylon(L24)	بابِل
incense(L27)	بَخُور	researcher(L22)	باحِث ج ـون
to begin, to start(L10)	بدأ (يَبْدأُ بدءً)	aubergine, eggplant (L7)	باذِنْجان (coll.)
to seem (as if)(L14)	بدا (يَبْدُو) (وكأنَّ)	outstanding(L21)	بارز
beginning(L10)	بداية	Paris(L2)	باريس
suit(L24)	بَدْلة ج ـات	with the exception of(L15)	باسْتِثْناء
Bedouins(L15)	بَدو	permanently(L15)	بِاسْتِمْرار
nomadic Bedouins(L15)	بدو رُحَّل	bus(L3)	باص ج ـات
alternative; option(L19)	بديل ج بدائِلُ	to sell sth.(L11)	باع (يبيعُ بيْعاً) هـ
to sow(L20)	بذر (يَبْذُرُ بذْراً)	in his capacity as(L23)	باعتبارِهِ
seed(L20)	بذر ج بُذُور	old, worn-out(L24)	بال
to make efforts(L8)	بـذل (يَبْذُلُ بذْلاً جُهُوداً)	to urinate(L28)	بال (يبُولُ بوْلاً)
honesty, integrity(L16)	بِرّ	certainly, surely, definitely(L7)	بِالتَّأْكِيد
under the leadership of (L8)	بِرِئاسةِ (+ gen.)	first of all(L22)	بالدرجةِ الأولى
refrigerator(L3)	برّادة ج ات	despite, in spite of(L21)	بِالرَّغْمِ مِن
Portugal(L5)	البُرْتُغال	fig.: Good luck and many children!(L27)	بالرفاء والبنين
oranges (coll.)(L7)	بُرْتُقال	in the following way(L7)	بالشكل التالي
cold(L9)	برْد / بارد	exactly(L14)	بالضَّبْط
to justify sth.(L22)	IIبرَّر (يُبرِّرُ) هـ	big, considerable(L14)	بالغ
to stand out(L27)	برز (يَبْرُزُ بُرُوزاً) هـ	in the vicinity of(L15)	بِالقُرْبِ من
blessing(L16)	بركة ج ـات	per cent(L10)	بالمائة
parliamentary, parliamentarian(L11)	برْلمانيّ	relating to(L11)	بِالنِّسْبةِ ل
barrel(L25)	برْميل ج براميلُ	as far as ... is concerned(L7)	بالنِسْبةِ ل
program(L5)	برْنامج ج برامِجُ	excellent, brilliant, splendid(L22)	باهِر
proof, evidence for(L11)	بُرْهان ج براهينُ على	petrochemical(L25)	بتروكيميائيّ
record, minutes(L25)	بْرُوتوكول	(mineral) oil(L19)	بتْرُول
Great Britain(L5)	بريطانِيا	to need sth., so., to require(L12)	بِحاجةٍ إلى

(the day) after tomorrow(L8)	بعْدَ غدٍ	because of(L17)	بِسبب
some(L13)	بعْض	to explain sth. to so.(L28)	بسط (يَسُطُ بسْطاً) هـ على
thanks to, owing to(L21)	بفضْلِ	In the name of God, the Merciful, the Compassionate(L11)	بِسْمِ اللهِ الرحْمن الرحِيم
green-grocer(L7)	بقّال ج ـون		
cattle(L7)	بقر (coll.)	In the name of God, the Merciful, the Compassionate, from whom we ask for help.(L28)	بسم ا الله الرحْمن الرحِيم وبِهِ نستعِين
tip(L9)	بقْشيش (colloq.)		
to stay, to remain(L12)	بقِيَ (يبْقى بقاءُ)		
remaining, rest(L17)	بقِيّة		
GCE A-level, graduation diploma(L16)	البكالُوريا	simple, easy(L8)	بسِيط ج بُسطاءُ
bachelor's degree(L16)	البكالُوريُوس	concerning, in question(L18)	بِشأْنِ الـ...
with all my strength(L21)	بكلِّ ما في وُسعِي	provided that(L12)	بشرْط
for how much / many(L9)	بِكم	provided (that)(L26)	بِشرْط/على شرْطِ/شرِيطةَ أنْ
How much is ... ?(L6)	بكمْ (الـ...)؟	in general(L20)	بِشكْلٍ عامّ
to cry(L25)	بكى (يبْكِي بُكاءً)	Basrah(L24)	البصْرة
(not only) ... but also(L17)	بلْ	onions(L7)	بصل (coll.)
without(L25)	بِلا	in a ... way / manner(L22)	بِصُورةٍ
useless, in vain(L25)	بِلا / بدون جدْوى	perspicacious(L22)	بصِير
undoubtedly, without doubt (L11)	بِلا شكَّ	product, goods(L19)	بِضاعة ج بضائعُ
Mesopotamia(L24)	بلاد ما بين النهرين	ducks(L26)	بط (coll.)
plastic(L25)	بلاستيكيّ	battery(L15)	بطّارية ج ـات
Belgium(L5)	بلْجيكا	potatoes(L7)	بطاطِسُ
country(L3)	بلد ج بلاد / بُلْدان	ticket, card(L14)	بطاقة ج ـات
to amount to (L10)	بلغ (يبْلُغُ بُلُوغاً) هـ	blanket(L15)	بطّانية ج ـات
give so. so.'s regards(L6)	II بلّغ هـ لـ ل (imp.)	naturally(L19)	بِطبيعةِ الحال
balcony(L7)	بلْكُون	belly, stomach(L13)	بطْن ج بُطُونَ
yes, certainly, sure(L28)	بلى	championship(L17)	بُطُولة ج ـات
including, inclusive of(L10)	بِما في ذلك	slow(L21)	بطِيء
with the will of God(L12)	بِمشيئةِ اللهِ	watermelons(L7)	بطِّيخ / بِطِّيخ (coll.)
independent, irrespective of(L20)	بِمعْزل عن	to send so. sth.(L25)	بعث (يبْعثُ بعْثاً) لـ ب
on the occasion of(L8)	بِمناسبةِ	(prep.) after (temp.)(L3)	بعْدَ
building, construction(L11)	بناء	after that (L5)	بعد ذلكَ

building (L14)	بناء ج أُبْنِية
tomato (Syr.) (L20)	بنادُورة
rifle, gun (L15)	بُنْدُقية ج بنادِقُ
petrol, gasoline (L19)	بنْزين
trousers (L24)	بنطَلون ج ـات
bank (L16)	بنْك ج بُنُوك
Umayyads (L24)	بنُو أُميَّة
ᶜAbbasids (L24)	بنو العبَّاس
to build, to erect, to set up sth. (L11)	بنى (يبْني بناءً) هـ
daughter (dimin.) (L28)	بُنيَّة
porter, doorman (L9)	بوَّاب ج ـون
urine (L13)	بوْل
Poland (L5)	بُولندا
owls (L26) (coll.)	بُوم
here: rhetoric (L28)	بَيان ج ـات
house (L2)	بَيْت ج بيُوت
beer (L7)	بيرة
eggs (L3) (coll.) (الواحدة بيضة)	بَيْض
(prep.) among, between (L5)	بَيْنَ
to make clear, to explain sth. (L15)	II بيَّن (يُبَيِّنُ) هـ
among them (L7)	بيْنَهُمْ / بينها

ت

died (pass.) (L10)	ت. < تُوفِّيَ
to be influenced by so., sth. (L19)	V تأثَّر (يتأثَّرُ) ب
influence on, over (L21)	تأْثِير ج ات في
postponing (L21)	تأْجِيل
coming too late (L22)	تأخُّر
to come too late (L17)	V تأخَّر (يتأخَّرُ)
founding (L11)	تأْسِيس
to consist of (L20)	V تألَّف (يتألَّفُ) من
insurance (L19)	تأْمِين ج ـات
qualification (L8)	تأْهِيل
help, support (L23)	تأْيِيد
belonging to (L9)	تابِع لـ
trader (L5)	تاجِر ج تُجَّار
history; date (L9)	تاريخ /تأْريخ ج تواريخُ
following (L7)	تالٍ (التالي)
those who follow them (L28)	التالُون لهم
complete, total, absolute (L27)	تامّ
exchange (L8)	تبادُل ج ـات
to compete (L27)	VI تبارى (يتبارى) مع
omen (positive) (L19)	ج تباشِيرُ
to come after, to succeed so. (L10)	تبِع (يتْبَعُ تَبَعاً) ه
to belong to so. (L9)	تبِع (يتْبَعُ) ه / لـ
to become clear for so. (L19)	V تبيَّن (يتبيَّنُ) له
to go beyond sth. (L19)	VI تجاوز (يتجاوزُ) هـ
renewing (L16)	تجْدِيد
freezing (intrans.) (L15)	تجمُّد
(prep.) under (L2)	تحْتَ
challenge (L21)	تحدٍّ ج تحدِّيات
to move (L23)	V تحرَّك (يتحرَّكُ)
improvement (L11)	تحسُّن
improving (L11)	تحْسِين
controlling (L19)	تحكُّم
analysis (L13)	تحْلِيل ج تحالِيلُ
to be enthusiastic about (L17)	V تحمَّس (يتحمَّسُ) لـ
to bear, to stand sth. (L28)	V تحمَّل (يتحمَّلُ) هـ
transfer (L16)	تحْوِيل ج ـات
greeting (L6)	تحِيَّة ج ـات

appr.: May you be well tomorrow. *(parting word at night)*[(L5)]	تُصْبِح على خير!	*appr.*: Best greetings *(standard opening of a letter)*[(L6)]	تَحِيّة طيبة وبعد ...
~ (*fem.*)[(L5)]	تُصْبِحِين على خير	to be embarrassed[(L28)]	V تَحيَّر (يتحيَّرُ)
desertification[(L20)]	تَصَحُّر	specialization[(L9)]	تَخصُّص ج ات
correction, change[(L19)]	تَصْحِيح ج ـات	discount, reduction[(L12)]	تَخْفِيض ج ـات
export[(L23)]	تَصْدِير	Palmyra[(L23)]	تَدْمُر
certification[(L16)]	تَصْدِيق	decay, decline[(L27)]	تَدهْوُر
to behave[(L26)]	V تصرَّف (يتصرَّفُ)	to decay, to decline[(L27)]	II تلهْوَر (يتلهْوُرُ)
declaration[(L11)]	تَصْرِيح ج ـات	to remember sth.[(L25)]	V تذكَّر (يتذكَّرُ) هـ
qualifying contest[(L17)]	تَصْفِية	ticket, card[(L6)]	تذكِرة ج تذاكِرُ
repair[(L25)]	تَصْلِيح ج ـات	heritage[(L27)]	تُراث
to hunt sth.[(L26)]	V تصيَّد (يتصيَّدُ) هـ	to range from[(L17)]	VI تراوح (يتراوحُ) يين ... ويين
to require sth.[(L19)]	V تطلَّب (يتطلَّبُ) هـ	education[(L9)]	تَرْبِية
development[(L11)]	تَطوُّر ج ات	*here*: breeding[(L20)]	تَرْبِية
demonstration[(L17)]	تظاهُرة ج ات	to translate sth. from ... to[(L14)]	تَرْجِم (يُتَرْجِمُ) هـ من ... إلى
to end in a draw[(L17)]	VI تعادل (يتعادلُ)	Translate.[(L3)]	تَرْجِمْ / تَرْجِمِي
to succeed one another[(L24)]	VI تعاقب (يتعاقبُ)	translation; *also*: biography[(L18)]	تَرْجَمة
Come here! Let's go! (*m./f.*)[(L12)]	تعالَ / تعالِي!	to let/to leave sth. for so.,[(L11)]	ترك (يتْرُكُ تَرْكاً) هـ لِ
lessons, doctrines[(L27)]	ج تعالِيمُ	Turkish[(L5)]	تُرْكِي ج أتْراك
to be in touch with, to have (business) relations with so.[(L18)]	VI تعامل (يتعاملُ) مع	Turkey[(L24)]	تُرْكِيا
		structure[(L22)]	تَرْكِيب ج تراكِيبُ
cooperation[(L8)]	تعاوُن	you want (*m.*)[(L10)]	تُرِيدُ أنْ
cooperative[(L20)]	تعاوُنِيّة ج ـات	purification[(L28)]	تَزْكِية
tired, exhausted, *colloq.*: ill[(L5)]	تَعْبان	registration[(L10)]	تَسْجِيل ج ـات
admiring; *here*: gram. term for exclamations[(L28)]	التعجُّب	acceleration[(L23)]	تَسْرِيع
acceleration[(L21)]	تَعْجِيل	marketing[(L17)]	تَسْوِيق
to be exposed to.[(L21)]	V تعرَّض (يتعرَّضُ) ل	consulting[(L11)]	تشاوُر
Arabization[(L18)]	تَعْرِيب	to be formed[(L21)]	V تشكَّل (يتشكَّلُ)
to be connected with[(L27)]	V تعلَّق (يتعلَّقُ) ب	creation, formation[(L11)]	تَشْكِيل ج ـات

to learn sth. (L20)	V تعلَّم (يتعلَّمُ) هـ
education (L8)	تعليم
higher education (L8)	التعليم العالي
to overcome (L19)	V تغلَّب (يتغلَّبُ) على
victory over; overcoming, surmounting (L11)	تغلُّب على
apples (L7)	تُفّاح (coll.)
interaction; combination (L19)	تفاعُل ج ـات
to watch, to look at (L17)	V تفرَّج (يتفرَّجُ) على
detail (L21)	تفصيل ج تفاصيلُ
please (L7)	تفضَّلْ م تفضَّلي
division, sharing (out) (L26)	تقاسُم
progress (L2)	تقدُّم
here: to be at the top of (L28)	تقدُّم
here: estimation (L18)	تقدير
estimation (L10)	تقدير ج ات
about, nearly (L4)	تقريباً
report (L27)	تقرير ج تقاريرُ
division, partition (L21)	تقسيم ج ـات
traditional (L21)	تقليديّ
technical (L12)	تقنيّ
technology, technique (L18)	تقنيّة
calendar (L10)	تقويم
I vomited. (L13)	تقيَّأْتُ
to keep to sth. (L27)	V تقيَّد (يتقيَّدُ) بِ هـ
assessment (L22)	تقييم
intensifying (L19)	تكثيف
do so. the honour, having the pleasure (L18)	تكرُّم ب
technology (L22)	تكنُولوجيا
technical (L21)	تكنيكيّ
to phone (L22)	تلفن (يُتلْفِنُ)
to get sth. (L18)	V تلقَّى (يتلقَّى) هـ
pupil, student (L14)	تِلْميذ ج تلاميذُ
to take place (L17)	تمَّ (يتِمُّ تمّاً)
good, "okay" (L2)	تمام
to enjoy sth. (L17)	V تمتَّع (يتمتَّعُ) ب
to become manifest (in) (L21)	V تمثَّل (يتمثَّلُ) في
to shake os. (L26)	V تمخَّض (يتمخَّضُ)
prolongation (L19)	تمديد
exercise (L27)	تمرين ج تمارينُ
to be able to do sth. (L17)	V تمكَّن (يتمكَّنُ) مِن
to wish so. sth., that (L23)	V تمنَّى (يتمنَّى) له هـ ، أنْ
taking (of food, drinking etc.) (L17)	تناوُل
tennis (L17)	تنس
organization, organizing (L20)	تنظيم ج ـات
diversification (L20)	تنويع
tension (L11)	توتر ج ات
to turn to so. (L26)	V توجَّه (يتوجَّهُ) إلى
unification (L21)	توحيد
distribution (L17)	توزيع
widening, extension, enlargement (L8)	توسيع
recommendation (L20)	توصية ج ـات
provision (L19)	توفير
success (L18)	توفيق
to expect sth. (L17)	V توقَّع (يتوقَّعُ) هـ
to be dependent on (L20)	V توقَّف (يتوقَّفُ) على
signing, signature (L8)	توقيع
to trust in God (L26)	V توكَّل (يتوكَّلُ) على الله
to take sth. over (L21)	V تولَّى (يتولَّى) هـ
Tunisia, Tunis (L3)	تونِس

	ث
second (m./f.)(L6)	ثان م ثانية
secondary(L16)	ثانويّ
the second (m./f.)(L6)	الثاني م الثانية
wealth, fortune(L19)	ثَروة ج ثَروات
snake(L15)	ثُعبان ج ثعابين
fox(L26)	ثعلب ج ثعالِبُ
cultural(L8)	ثقافيّ
thirty(L9)	ثلاثونَ
third (L16)	ثُلث ج أثلاث
snow, ice(L9)	ثلْج ج ثُلوج
after that(L7)	ثُمَّ
the eighties(L19)	ج الثمانِينات
bilateral(L14)	ثُنائيّ
revolution(L22)	ثورة ج ات
garlic(L7)	ثُوم (coll.)
	ج
public transport(L18)	ج مُواصلات عامَّة
to come (to)(L12)	جاء (يجيءُ مجيئاً) (إلى)
award, prize(L8)	جائزة ج جوائزُ
Nobel prize(L8)	جائزة نوبل
neighbour(L12)	جار ج جيران
to be allowed to so., that(L18)	جاز (يجوزُ جوازاً) ل، أنْ
dry(L15)	جافّ
mosque(L25)	جامع ج جوامعُ
university(L3)	جامِعة ج ات
side(L9)	جانِب ج جوانِبُ
to make efforts, to try hard(L28)	III جاهد (يُجاهِدُ)
Jāhiliyya(L27)	الجاهلية
to endow so. with(L28)	جبل (يجْبُلُ جبْلاً) ه على
mountain(L9)	جبل ج جِبال
cheese(L3)	جُبْنة
forehead(L13)	جبهة ج ات
forehead(L13)	جبين ج جُبُن
to make (serious) efforts(L20)	جدَّ (يجِدُّ)
very(L4)	جِدًّا
wall(L2)	جدار ج جُدْران
quarrel(L27)	جدل
usefulness, profitability(L25)	جدْوَى
new(L2)	جدِيد ج جُدُد
basic, fundamental(L22)	جذريّ
stocking(L24)	جُراب ج جوارِبُ، ات
tractor (L20)	جرّارة ج ات
to try, to try on sth.(L24)	II جرَّب (يُجرِّبُ) هـ
waiter(L7)	جرْسُون ج ات (Fr. garçon)
waitress(L7)	جرْسونة ج ات
to occur(L26)	جرَى (يجْري) هـ
newspaper(L8)	جريدة ج جرائدُ
part(L15)	جُزْء ج أجْزاء
Algeria(L3)	الجزائر
Algiers(L8)	الجزائر
jussive(L28)	الجزْم
the Arabian Peninsula (L24)	الجزيرة العربية
island(L21)	جزيرة ج جُزُر
body(L13)	جِسْم ج أجْسام
huge, enormous(L22)	جسِيم
to make so. do sth.(L28)	جعل (يجعلُ جعْلاً) هـ، ، ه
his royal highness(L8)	جلالةُ المِلكِ
shot(L17)	جُلّة ج جُلل
leather (L4)	جِلد / جِلْدي

to sit, to be seated on (L7)	جلس (يَجْلِسُ) على
meeting, session (L11)	جلسة ج ـات
sitting (L2)	جلوس
beauty (L24)	جمال
to collect sth. (L9)	جمع (يَجْمَعُ جَمْعاً) هـ
camel (L17)	جمل ج جمال
republic (L5)	جُمْهُورية ج ـات
all (L13)	جميع
beautiful (L2)	جميل ج ـون
the Hanging Gardens (L24)	ج الجنائِنُ المُعَلَّقة
funeral procession (L26)	جنازة ج ـات، جنائِزُ
(prep.) at so.'s side (L18)	جنبَ
pound (L12)	جُنَيْه ج ـات
Jihād (L28)	جهاد
apparatus, device (L2)	جهاز ج أَجْهِزة
wireless, mobile phone (L15)	جهاز لا سِلْكيّ
tv-set (L2)	جهازتلفزيون
video-recorder (L2)	جهازفيديو
effort (L8)	جهْد ج جُهُود
not to know sth. (L18)	جهل (يَجْهَلُ جهْلاً) بِ
answer, reply (L6)	جواب ج أَجْوِبة
passport (L9)	جواز (السفر)
nuts (L7)	جوْز (coll.)
hungry (L7)	جوْعانُ م جوْعَى ج جِياع
tour (L8)	جوْلة ج ـات
nature/essential (L21)	جوْهر /جوْهريّ
air (L23)	جوّيّ
jeep (L18)	جيب
pocket (L15)	جيْب ج جُيُوب
good (L2)	جيِّد ج ـون
army (L26)	جيْش ج جُيُوش
generation (L22)	جيل ج أَجْيال
geological (L25)	جَيُولُوجِيّ

ح

pilgrim (L7)	حاجّ ج حُجَّاج، حجيج
eyebrow (L13)	حاجِب ج حواجِبُ
demand, need (L12)	حاجة ج ـات
need; colloq.: matter, thing (L23)	حاجة ج حاجِيات
happening in (L19)	حادِث في
hot (also food), spicy (L7)	حارّ
computer, calculator (L12)	حاسِب ج ـات
sense; perception (L28)	حاسَّة ج حواسّ
present time (L17)	حاضِر
present (time) (L20)	حاضِر
quick-witted (L25)	حاضِر النكتة
to prevent sth. (L15)	حال (يَحُولُ حيْلُولةً) دون هـ
situation (L2)	حال ج أَحْوال
at once, immediately, right away (L18)	حالاً
situation, state, condition (L11)	حالة ج ـات
present, current, contemporary (L10)	حالي
pregnant (L28)	حامِل (م) ج حوامِلُ
it is (high) time to (L26)	حان الوقت (لـ)
to try sth. (L18)	III حاول (يُحاوِلُ) هـ،أَنْ
piece (L20)	حبَّة ج ـات
tablet, pill (L13)	حبَّة ج حُبُوب
melon (Yem.) (L20)	حبْحب
ink (L4)	حِبْر
Ethiopian, Abyssinian (L21)	حبشيّ ج أَحْباش
(prep.) until (L15)	حتَّى
so that, in order to (L8)	حتَّى
even if (L26)	حتى وَلَوْ

according to^(L10) → according to^(L10)

according to^(L10)	حسْب
to envy so. sth.^(L22)	حسد (يحْسُدُ حسداً) ه على
harvesting combine^(L20)	حصَّادة ج ات
horse; *also:* HP^(L17)	حِصان ج أحْصِنة
share^(L25)	حِصَّة ج حِصص
to harvest^(L20)	حصد (يحْصُدُ حِصاداً)
here: to happen^(L21)	حصَل
to get, to obtain sth.^(L8)	حصل (يحْصُلُ حُصُولاً) على
fortress^(L27)	حِصْن ج حُصُون
obtaining sth.^(L16)	الحُصُول على
civilization, culture^(L9)	حضارة ج ـات
to attend sth.^(L6)	حضر هـ
You (elaborated style of address)^(L6)	حضْرة / حضْرتُكَ / حضْرتُكُمْ
dear guests^(L11)	ج حضرات الضيُوف
presence^(L11)	حُضُور
maintenance (of)^(L19)	حِفاظ (على)
hospitality^(L18)	حفاوة
celebration, party, fête^(L6)	حفْلة ج ـات
dinner^(L19)	حفلة عشاء
law, right^(L8)	حقّ ج حُقُوق
You are right.^(L23)	الحقّ معك
to realize sth., to make sth. come true^(L19)	II حقَّق (يُحقِّقُ) هـ
injection^(L15)	حُقْنة ج حُقن
suitcase^(L9)	حقِيبة ج حقائِبُ
truth; fact^(L13)	حقِيقة ج حقائِقُ
power, control, rule^(L11)	حُكْم
regulation, rule, provision^(L11)	حُكْم ج أحْكام
referee, judge^(L17)	حكم ج حُكّام

pilgrimage^(L10)	حجّ ج ـات، حِجَج
the Hijaz^(L27)	الحِجاز
stone^(L22)	حجر ج أحْجار
to order sth., to book sth.^(L9)	حجز (يحْجُزُ حجْزاً) هـ
volume, size^(L20)	حجْم ج أحْجام
to restrict, to limit^(L21)	حدَّ (يحُدُّ حدّاً) من
to form the boundary of sth.^(L24)	حدَّ (يحُدُّ) هـ
severity, fierceness^(L21)	حِدَّة
to happen^(L11)	حدث (يحْدُثُ حُدُوثاً)
to say sth. to so.^(L14)	II حدَّث (يُحدِّثُ) ه هـ/ ب
event^(L12)	حدث ج أحْداث
to define sth.^(L25)	II حدَّد (يُحدِّدُ) هـ
talk; *also:* tradition of the actions and sayings of the prophet and his companions^(L5)	حدِيث ج أحادِيثُ
modern, new^(L4)	حدِيث ج حِداث
garden^(L2)	حدِيقة ج حدائِقُ
shoe^(L18)	حِذاء ج أحْذية
careful, cautious^(L15)	حذِر
care, caution^(L15)	حِذْر / حَذَر
free^(L26)	حُرّ
heat, temperature^(L9)	حرارة
civil war^(L20)	الحرْب الأهلِيّة
war^(L11)	حرْب م ج حُرُوب
to liberate so., sth.^(L24)	II حرَّر (يُحرِّرُ) ه، هـ
letter, character^(L2)	حرْف ج حُرُوف
movement^(L16)	حركة ج ـات
freedom, liberty^(L26)	حُرِّيّة
(political) party^(L8)	حِزْب ج أحْزاب
calculation, account, bill^(L10)	حِساب ج ـات
sensitiveness; allergy^(L19)	حساسِيّة

wisdom, saying, aphorism (L26)	حِكْمة ج حِكَم
government (L6)	حُكومة ج ـات
to speak, to talk about (L15)	حكى (يَحْكي حِكايةً) عن
solution (L11)	حلّ ج حُلول
hairdresser (L16)	حلّاق ج ـون
shave (L24)	حِلاقة
allowed, legitimate (L28)	حلال
Aleppo (L23)	حلبُ (م)
dream (L27)	حُلْم ج أحْلام
dessert; sweets (L7)	حلْوَى ج حلاوَى
jewelry (L28)	حَلْي / حُلِيّ
milk (L3)	حليب
donkey (L26)	حِمار ج حمير
bathroom (L2)	حمّام ج ـات
Hama (L23)	حماه (م)
Thank God! (L2)	الحمْدُ لله
Homs (L23)	حِمْصُ (م)
to carry sth. (L9)	حمل (يَحْمِل حَمْلاً) هـ
fever (L13)	حُمَّى (م)
laudable, commendable (L26)	حميد
rye (L20)	حِنْطة سوْداءُ
dialogue (L26)	حِوار ج ات
nearly, approximately, about (L10)	حوالَى
pelvis (L13)	حوْض ج أحْواض
(prep.) around, about (L20)	حوْلَ
vivid, alive, living (L26)	حَيّ ج أحْياء
life (L7)	حياة
snake (L15)	حيّة ج ـات
whereas (L19)	حَيْثُ
time, while (L16)	حين ج أحْيان

| creature, living being (L15) | حَيَوان ج ـات |
| vital, essential (L19) | حَيَوِيّ |

خ

servant (f.) (L9)	خادِمة ج ـات
the exterior, foreign, abroad (L11)	الخارِج
especially, special (L17)	خاصّ
(especially) for (L7)	خاصّ بِ
especially (L9)	خاصّةً
to be afraid of so., sth. (L11)	خافَ (يخافُ خوْفاً) من ه، هـ
sincere (L6)	خالِص / مُخْلِص
news (L5)	خبر ج أخْبار
experience; know how (L23)	خِبْرة ج ات
bread (L3)	خبْز
expert, specialist (L18)	خبير ج خُبراءُ
end (L17)	خِتام
final (L14)	خِتاميّ
cheek (L13)	خدّ ج خُدُود
service (L6)	خِدْمة ج ـات
Take (it)! (m./f.) (L2)	خُذْ ! / خُذِي !
Take your time! Don't hurry! (L24)	خُذْ راحتَكَ!
ruins (L27)	خراب ج أخْرِبة
to go out (L6)	خرج (يخْرُجُ) من
to exit, to leave (L5)	خرج من
Khartoum (L8)	الخرْطُوم
here: stool (L13)	خُروج
mutton, lamb (L7)	خرُوف ج خِرْفان
autumn, fall (L9)	خريف
cupboard (L2)	خِزانة ج ات، خزائنُ
to store sth. (L15)	II خزّن (يُخزّنُ) هـ

good[L2]	خَيْر
good, better, best[L16]	خَيْر
fig.: Everything okay, God willing?[L13]	خَيْراً إن شاء ا لله؟
horse[L26]	خَيْل ج خُيُول (coll.)

د

tireless, enduring[L26]	دَؤُوب
the interior, inland[L11]	الداخِل
house[L12]	دار (م) ج دُور
to be about[L26]	دار (يدُورُ) حول
townhall, city hall[L27]	دار البلَدِية
publishing house[L12]	دار نشْر
warm[L15]	دافِئ
to last[L16]	دام (يدُومُ)
to prepare, to provide sth.[L15]	II دبَّر (يُدبِّرُ) هـ
diplomatic, diplomat[L6]	دِبْلوماسيّ ج ـون
chicken[L7]	دجاج (coll.)
Tigris[L24]	دِجْلةُ
to enter sth.[L7]	دخل (يدْخُلُ) هـ
to smoke[L20]	II دخَّن (يُدخِّنُ)
postgraduate studies[L16]	دراسات عليا
study, courses, classes[L4]	دِراسة ج ـات
class, step, level[L6]	درجة ج ـات
degree centigrade[L15]	درجة مِئوية
to study sth.[L7]	درس (يدرُسُ دِراسةً) هـ
lesson, class hour[L4]	درْس ج دُروس
(to study) at so.[L16]	درس على يد ...
constitution[L21]	دُستُور ج دساتِيرُ
to invite, to call (up)on so. to do sth.[L11]	دعا (يدْعُو دعوةً) (ل، إلى)
invitation, call[L11]	دعْوة ج دعوات

to be afraid of sth.[L22]	خشِيَ (يَخْشَى خشِياً) هـ
fruitful, fertile[L25]	خصِب
fertility[L15]	خِصْب
rival[L17]	خصْم ج خُصُوم
vegetables, greens[L20]	خُضَار
vegetables[L3]	ج خضْراوات
to be exposed to so., sth.[L19]	خضع (يخْضَعُ خُضُوعاً) ل / إلى
equator[L15]	خط الإسْتِواء
line[L15]	خطّ ج خُطُوط
speech, letter, note[L23]	خِطاب ج ـات
plan[L22]	خُطّة ج خطط
danger[L15]	خطَر ج أخْطار
danger, importance[L21]	خطُورة
dangerous[L13]	خطِير
to add an i; genitive[L28]	الخفْض
to facilitate, to ease sth.[L15]	II خفَّف (يُخفِّفُ) من
light[L15]	خفِيف
vinegar[L7]	خلّ
quarrel, argument[L11]	خِلاف ج ـات (على، في)
caliphate[L24]	خِلافة
during, in the course of[L12]	خِلالَ
behind[L17]	خلْفَ
to succeed so.[L10]	خلف (يخْلُفُ) ه
the Rightly Guided Caliphs[L10]	الخلفاء الراشدون
to create sth.[L28]	خلق (يخْلُقُ) هـ
gulf (geogr.)[L17]	خلِيج ج خُلُج، خُلْجان
caliph[L10]	خلِيفة ج خُلفاءُ
plum, peach[L7]	خوْخ (coll.)
cucumber[L7]	خِيار (coll.)

religious(L11)	دِينِيّ

ذ

arm(L13)	ذِراع (م) ج أَذْرُع
maize, corn(L20)	ذُرة ، ذرة شامية
millet(L20)	ذرة رفيعة
chin(L13)	ذقن ج أَذْقان، ذُقُون
beard(L13)	ذقن ج ذُقُون
to mention so., sth. to so.(L14)	ذكر (يذْكُرُ ذِكْراً) ه، هـ
to remind so. of so., sth.(L26)	II ذكَّر (يُذكِّرُ) ه ب هـ، ه
penis(L13)	ذكر ج ذُكُور
anniversary of the foundation(L11)	ذكرى تأسيس
memory, anniversary(L11)	ذِكْرَى م ج ذِكْرِيات
that (dem. pr.)(L5)	ذلِك
that, those (L7)	ذلِك م تِلْكَ ج أُولئِكَ
to go (to)(L5)	ذهب (إلى)
to go (to)(L7)	ذهب (يذْهَبُ ذهاباً) (إلى)
you (m.) went(L4)	ذَهَبْتَ
I went(L4)	ذَهَبْتُ
you (f.) went(L4)	ذَهَبْتِ
gold, golden(L17)	ذهبِيّ

ر

to lead, to head so., sth.(L14)	رأسَ (يرْأسُ رئاسةً) ه، هـ
head(L13)	رأس ج رُؤُوس
to see so., sth. (L12)	رأى (يرَى رأْياً) ه، هـ
opinion (of, about, on sth., so.)(L11)	رأْي (في)
you (m.) saw(L4)	رأَيْتَ
I saw(L4)	رأَيْتُ

defense(L8)	دِفـاع
to pay so., sth.(L16)	دفع (يدْفَعُ دفْعاً) ه،، هـ
flour(L7)	دقيق
minute(L16)	دقِيقة ج دقائِقُ
shop(L3)	دُكّان ج دكاكِينُ
doctor(L12)	دُكْتور ج دكاتِرة
doctorate(L16)	دُكْتوراه
to guide, to lead so., to show so. sth.(L24)	دلَّ (يدُلُّ دلالةً) ه على
evidence(L28)	دليل ج دلائِلُ، أدِلّة
blood(L13)	دم ج دِماء
Denmark(L5)	الدِّنْمارْك
medicine(L13)	دواء ج أدْوِية
poultry(L20)	ج دواجِنُ
duration(L16)	دوام
permanent well-being(L18)	دوام العافية
worm, maggot(L26)	دُود ج دِيدان (coll.)
role, part(L21)	دوْر ج أدْوار
floor(L16)	دوْر ج أدْوار
Olympic Games(L17)	الدورة الأولمبية
round(L17)	دوْرة ج ات
periodical(L18)	دوْرية ج ـات
dollar(L6)	دُولار ج ات
state(L9)	دوْلة ج دُول
international(L12)	دوْلِيّ / دُولَيّ
without, under(L7)	دُونَ / بدون
below zero(L15)	دون درجة التجمُّد
diesel(L19)	دَيْزْل / دِيزِل
disco(L5)	دِيسْكُو
democratic(L8)	دِيمُقْراطِيّ
religion(L9)	دِين ج أدْيان
dinar (currency)(L10)	دِينار ج دنانِيرُ

to have mercy upon so.(L16)	رحِم (يرْحَمُ رحْمةً) ه	you (f.) saw(L4)	رأيْتِ
mercy(L28)	رحْمة	lungs(L13)	رئة ج ـات
May God have mercy upon him.(L28)	رحْمةُ الله عليْهِ	chief of protocol(L27)	رئيس المراسِمُ
God have mercy upon him!(L16)	رحِمَهُ الله	president, leader, chairman, manager(L6)	رئيس ج رؤساءُ
permission, license(L16)	رُخْصة ج رُخص	main(L13)	رئيسيّ
cheap, reasonable (price)(L9)	رخيص	wonderful, excellent, marvelous(L6)	رائع
reaction(L11)	ردّ فِعْلٍ ج رُدُود فعل	salary(L11)	راتِب ج رواتِبُ
rice(L7)	رُزّ	rest, relaxation(L24)	راحة ج ـات
dissertation(L16)	رسالة الدكتوراه	radio(L2)	راديو ج راديوهات
letter(L5)	رسالة ج رسائِلُ	herdsman, shepherd, guardian(L26)	راعٍ ج رُعاة
fee(L16)	رسْم ج رُسُوم	to take sth. into consideration(L22)	III راعى (يُراعِي) هـ
official(L20)	رسْميّ	to accompany so.(L14)	III رافق (يُرافِق) ه
the messenger of God(L8)	رسُولُ الله	passenger(L19)	راكِب ج رُكّاب
prophet, envoy, messenger(L8)	رسُول ج رُسُل	to wish sth.(L15)	رام (يرُومُ روْماً) هـ
bribery(L11)	رشْوة	to bet on(L17)	III راهن (يُراهِن) على
goal-directed, wise(L20)	رشيد	lady of the house, housewife(L16)	ربة بيت
lead(L25)	رصاص	to connect between(L14)	ربط (يرْبُطُ ربْطاً) بين
May God be pleased with him.(L10)	رضِيَ الله عنه	quarter(L16)	رُبْع ج أرْباع
procession, column(L27)	رعيل	perhaps(L25)	رُبّما
to wish sth., that(L8)	رغِب (يرغَبُ رغْبةً) في، (في) أنْ	spring(L9)	ربيع
(prep.) despite, in spite of(L19)	رغْمَ	to ask so. to do sth.(L11)	رجا (يرْجُو رجاءً) ه أنْ
shelf(L8)	رفّ ج رُفُوف	to come back to(L7)	رجع (يرْجِعُ رُجُوعاً) إلى
prosperity(L22)	رفاه	to go back to(L14)	رجع إلى
refusal(L27)	رفْض	leg, foot(L13)	رِجْل (م) ج أرْجُل
to refuse, reject, turn down sth.(L11)	رفض (يرْفُضُ رفْضاً) هـ	man(L2)	رجُل ج رِجال
raising, rise, increase(L15)	رفْع	wide(L27)	رحْب
to add an u; nominative; indicative(L28)	الرفْع	to welcome, to greet so.(L14)	II رحّب (يُرحِّبُ) بِ
high(L14)	رفيع	trip, journey(L14)	رِحْلة ج ـات
neck(L13)	رقبة ج ـات		

to go beyond, to exceed(L15)	زاد (يَزِيدُ زِيادةً) عن
provisions(L15)	زاد ج أزواد
to visit so., sth.(L11)	زار (يَزُورُ زيارةً) ه، هـ
corner(L8)	زاوية ج زوايا
butter(L3)	زُبْدة
bottle(L7)	زُجاجة ج ـات
agriculture(L9)	زِراعة
agricultural(L24)	زِراعِيّ
plant sth.(L7)	زرع (يَزْرَعُ زراعةً) هـ
wedding, marriage(L27)	زِفاف
Zakāt(L10)	زكاة
Zakāt at the end of Ramaḍān(L10)	زكاة الفِطْر
rein; here: means to decide(L28)	زِمام ج أزِمّة
time(L21)	زمان ج أزْمِنة
to sound the horn(L27)	II زمَّر (يُزمِّر)
time, period(L27)	زمن ج أزْمان
colleague(L18)	زمِيل ج زُملاءُ
zinc(L25)	زِنْك
wedding, marriage(L27)	زواج
husband(L16)	زوْج ج أزواج
wife(L9)	زوْجة ج ـات
to supply so. with sth.(L15)	II زوَّد (يُزوِّدُ) ه ب هـ
increase(L20)	زيادة ج ات
visit(L8)	زيارة ج ات
olive(L7)	زيْتُون (coll.)

س

to ask so. about sth.(L7)	سأل (يسْألُ سُؤالاً) ه عن
to ask (about)(L5)	سأل ه (عن)
I asked him.(L5)	سألتُهُ

to dance(L5)	رقص
dance(L17)	رقْصة ج رقصات
number(L9)	رقْم ج أرْقام
record(L17)	رقْم قياسيّ
knee(L13)	رُكْبة ج ـات
to stagnate(L19)	ركد (يرْكُدُ رُكُوداً)
pillar(L10)	رُكْن ج أرْكان
javelin(L17)	رُمْح ج رِماح
symbol, sign(L6)	رمْز ج رُمُوز
hot ground(L28)	رمْضاءُ
sand(L15)	رمْل ج رِمال
to push, throw(L17)	رمى (يرْمِي رمْياً)
push, throw(L17)	رمْي
novel(L4)	رواية ج ـات
Russian(L8)	رُوسيّ ج روُس
Russia(L5)	رُوسيا
Roman(L21)	رُومانيّ ج رُومان
to tell so. sth., to transmit, to quote (from a source)(L24)	روَى (يرْوِي رِواية) ل ه (عن)
irrigation(L16)	ريّ
Riyadh(L12)	الرِياض
sport(L17)	رياضة
athlete, sportsman, (L12)	رياضِيّ
mathematics(L9)	الرِّياضِيّات
wind(L15)	رِيح (م) ج رِياح
rural(L18)	رِيفيّ

ز

plus(L10)	زائد
rising, going up (beyond)(L11)	زائد (عن)

bed(L2)	سرير ج أسِرَّة
fast(L11)	سريع
here: rate of exchange(L12)	سِعْر
price(L6)	سِعْر ج أسْعار
Saudi Arabia(L3)	السعودِية
happy(L27)	سعيد ج سُعداءُ
embassy(L25)	سِفارة ج ات
journey, trip(L6)	سفر ج أسْفار
ship(L23)	سفِينة ج سُفُن
to fall (down)(L9)	سقط (يسقُطُ سُقُوطاً)
ceiling(L2)	سقف ج سُقُوف
fall (rain)(L15)	سُقُوط
(down)fall, decline(L19)	سُقُوط
sugar(L3)	سُكَّر
secretary(L16)	سِكْرِتيرة ج ات
to live in(L7)	سكن (يسْكُنُ سكناً) في
knife(L7) (m. and f.)	سِكّين ج سكاكينُ
weapon(L21)	سِلاح ج أسْلِحة
shoot, seed(L28)	سُلالة ج ات
peace(L2)	سلام
Peace be with/upon you!(L2)	السلامُ عليكُم
Peace be upon you and the mercy and the blessing of God(L8)	السلام عليكم ورحمْة الله وبركاتُه
wellness, well-being(L23)	سلامة
I hope you feel better soon.(L14)	سلامتُك/سلامتُكِ
negative, passive(L21)	سَلْبيّ
basket(L17)	سلّة ج سِلل
salad(L7)	سلطة / سلاطة
Sultanate(L21)	سلْطنة ج ات
to hand over, to bring sth. to so.(L14)	II سلّم (يُسلّمُ) ه ه / ل / إلى

question(L7)	سُؤال ج أسْئِلة
driver(L15)	سائِق ج ـون
early, in the past, previously(L8)	سابقاً
place, square(L17)	ساحة ج ـات
to move (to)(L11)	سار (يسيرُ سيْراً) إلى
hour, watch(L13)	ساعة ج ـات
to help so. with sth.(L23)	III ساعد (يُساعِدُ) ه (على)
arm(L13)	ساعِد ج سواعِدُ
to contribute to(L23)	ساعد على
to travel(L5)	سافر
thigh(L13)	ساق (م) ج سِيقان
to drive sth.(L18)	ساق (يسُوقُ سِياقةً) هـ
poisonous(L15)	سامّ
Semite, Semitic(L24)	ساميّ ج ـون
to contribute to(L20)	III ساهم (يُساهِمُ) في
swimming(L16)	سِباحة
race(L17)	سِباق
reason, cause(L11)	سبب ج أسْباب
to swim(L23)	سبح (يسْبَحُ سِباحةً)
the seventies(L19)	السبْعِينات
preceding(L28)	سبْق
to precede so., sth.(L15)	سبق (يسْبِقُ سبْقاً) ه، هـ
way, path(L8)	سبيل ج سُبُل
to score(L17)	II سجّل (يُسجّلُ)
to score a goal(L17)	سجّل هدفاً
to make so. happy(L18)	سرَّ (يسُرُّ سُرُوراً) ه أنْ
secret(L15)	سِرّ ج أسْرار
very soon(L15)	سُرعانَ ما
speed(L11)	سُرْعة
to steal sth. from so.(L25)	سرق (يسْرِقُ سِرْقاً) مِن ه هـ

His Excellency[L11]	سيادةُ (الرئيس)
car[L3]	سيّارة ج ـات
politics[L5]	سياسة
political, politician[L5]	سياسي ج ـون
driving[L18]	سياقة
cigarette, cigaret[L20]	سيجارة ج سجائر
Mr.[L2]	سيّد ج سادة
Mrs.[L2]	سيّدة ج ات
biography[L16]	سيرة ج سيَر
curriculum vitae[L16]	سيرةُ حياة
rule (over)[L24]	سيطرة (على)
flood[L15]	سيْل ج سُيُول

ش

thing, matter[L16]	شأن ج شُؤُون
to want to, to demand[L24]	شاء (يشاءُ) أن
street[L3]	شارع ج شوارعُ
to take part in[L12]	III شارك (يُشاركُ) في
vast, spacious[L15]	شاسع
coast, beach[L23]	شاطئ ج شواطئُ
clever[L4]	شاطر ج شُطّار
poet[L27]	شاعر ج شُعراءُ
see[L12]	شاف (يشُوفُ) (colloq.)
comprehensive[L22]	شامل
Syrian[L20]	شاميّ ج شاميّون
Shah[L19]	شاه
witness[L27]	شاهد ج شُهُود
to see; to look at[L6]	شاهد هـ
tea[L3]	شاي
window[L2]	شبّاك ج شبابيكُ
ghost[L11]	شبَح ج أشباح

staircase, steps[L10]	سُلّم ج سلالِمُ
Regards to (Aḥmad).[L5]	سلّمْ على (أحمد)!
Give my regards to so.[L5]	سلّمْ لي على
peaceful[L11]	سلْميّ
Give my regards to so. (fem.)[L5]	سلّمي لي على
healthy, sound[L17]	سليم
poison[L15]	سمّ ج سُمُوم
sky[L9]	سماء (م) ج سموات
fertilizer[L25]	سماد ج أسمِدة
allow so. to do sth.[L8]	سمِح (يسمَحُ سماحاً) له ب، هـ
to hear so., sth.[L5]	سمِع ه ، هـ
fish (coll.)[L7]	سمك ج أسْماك
fishing[L20]	سمكيّ
highness[L12]	سُمُوّ
to name so., sth.[L19]	II سمّى (يُسمّي) ه، هـ
thick, heavy[L9]	سميك
tooth[L13]	سِنّ (م) ج أسنان
the Sunna[L10]	السُّنّة
year[L7]	سنة ج سنوات، سِنُون
plain (geogr.)[L24]	سهْل ج سُهُول
supermarket[L22]	سوبرماركت
Sudan[L3]	السُّودان
Syria[L3]	سُوريا
Susan[L5]	سُوسَن
market[L3]	سُوق (م) ج أسْواق
ᶜUkāẓ market (near Mecca)[L27]	سوق عُكاظ
Sumerian[L24]	سُومَريّ
Sweden[L5]	السويد
Switzerland[L5]	سُويسْرا
touristic[L6]	سِياحيّ

popular (L17)	شَعْبِيّ
popularity (L17)	شَعْبِيَّة
hair (L13)	شَعْر (coll.)
to feel sth. (L9)	شعر (يَشْعُرُ شُعُوراً) بِ
to be cold, to freeze (L9)	شعر بالبرد
rite (L27)	شَعِيرة ج شعائر
lip (L13)	شفة ج شِفاه
apartment, suite (L7)	شِقَّة ج شِقق
brother (having the same father and mother) (L14)	شقيق ج أشِقّاءُ
doubt (about) (L11)	شكّ ج شُكُوك (في)
thank (L18)	شُكْر
to thank so. for (L6)	شكر ه على
Thank you! (L2)	شُكْراً
Thank you very much. (L9)	شُكْراً جزيلاً!
form, way, manner (L7)	شكْل ج أشْكال
north (L9)	شمال
sugar melon (L20)	شَمّام (coll.)
the sun (L2)	الشَّمْس (م)
to comprise, to cover sth. (L19)	شمل (يشْمُلُ شمْلاً) هـ
bag (L2)	شنْطة ج شُنط، ـات
the act of testimony (L10)	الشهادة
certificate (L16)	شهادة ج ات
to be a witness of (L12)	شهد (يشْهَدُ شهادة) على
honeymoon (L27)	شهْر العسل
month (L5)	شهْر ج شُهُور، أشْهُر
soup (L7)	شُورْبة / شُرْبة
fork (L7)	شوْكة ج ـات
thing, matter (L5)	شَيْء ج أشْياءُ
sheik (L17)	شيْخ ج شُيُوخ، مشائِخُ
cheque, check (L19)	شِيك ج ـات
net (L18)	شبكة ج ـات
semi- (L21)	شِبْهُ
semi-agreed upon (L21)	شبْهُ مُتَّفَق عليه
winter (L9)	شِتاء
different, various (L19)	شتِيت ج شتَّى
invective (L28)	شتِيمة ج شتائِمُ
brave (L26)	شُجاع ج شجعة، شُجْعان
tree (L4)	شجرة ج أشْجار
to promote sth. (L21)	II شجَّع (يُشجِّعُ) هـ
person (L9)	شخْص ج أشْخاص
to tie, to bind sth. to (L24)	شدَّ (يشُدُّ شدًّا) هـ إلى
violence, fierceness (L28)	شِدَّة
violent, fierce, heavy, furious (L13)	شديد
buying, purchase (L7)	شِراء
drink (L14)	شراب ج أشْرِبة
to drink sth. (L5)	شرب هـ
explain sth. (L8)	شرح (يشْرَحُ شرْحاً) هـ
condition (L12)	شرْط ج شُرُوط
police (L16)	شُرْطة
traffic police (L16)	شرطة المُرُور
honor (L28)	شرف
Do us the honor! (L8)	شرَّفْنا
the Middle East (L8)	الشرْق الأوْسطُ
eastern, oriental (L5)	شرْقِي
airline (L23)	شركة الطيْران
firm, enterprise, company (L5)	شرِكة ج ـات
sunrise (L28)	شُرُوق الشمْس
law of the jungle (L26)	شريعة الغاب
(Islam.) law, Shari'a (L26)	شريعة ج شرائِعُ
people (L14)	شعْب ج شُعُوب
department, section (L16)	شُعْبة ج شُعب

fight, struggle(L21)	صِراع ج ـات		**ص**
exchange officer(L12)	صَرّاف ج ـون	majesty(L26)	صاحِب الجَلالة
morphology, inflection (gram.)(L24)	صَرْف	His Royal Highness(L12)	صاحب السمو الملكيّ
to change sth.(L12)	صرف (يصرِفُ صرْفاً)	friend(L23) (colloq.)	صاحِب ج أصحاب
to spend sth. on(L21)	صرف (يصرِفُ) هـ على	owner(L12)	صاحِب ج أصْحاب
difficult(L6)	صعْب ج صِعاب	edited, published (by)(L14)	صادِر (من، عن)
small, short(L2)	صغير ج صِغار	to become sth.(L27)	صار (يصير صيْرُورةً) هـ
queue, line(L21)	صفّ ج صُفُوف	hall(L12)	صالة ج ـات
characteristic(L26)	صِفة ج ـات	beauty parlor(L27)	صالون التجْميل
page(L16)	صفْحة ج ـات	to fast(L28)	صام (يصُومُ صوْماً)
business, deal(L17)	صفْقة ج صفقات	morning(L2)	صباح
midday prayer(L10)	صلاة الظُهْر	Good Morning!(L2)	صباح الخير
night prayer(L10)	صلاة العِشاء	(answer)(L2)	صباح النُور
afternoon prayer(L10)	صلاة العصْر	patient, enduring(L26)	صبُور ج صبُر
morning prayer(L10)	صلاة الفجْر / الصُبْح	boy(L17)	صبيّ ج صِبْيان
evening prayer(L10)	صلاة المغْرِب	health(L2)	صِحّة
prayer(L10)	صلاة ج صلوات	Sahara(L15)	الصحْراء الكُبْرَى
authority, power(s)(L11)	صلاحِيَة ج ـات	desert(L15)	صحْراءُ ج صحارَى
to pray(L28)	II صلّى (يُصلّي)	journalist(L11)	صُحُفيّ ج ـون
God bless him and grant him salvation! (often used in the shortened form صلعم)(L10)	صلّى الله عليه وسلّم	health, hygienic(L14)	صِحّيّ
		right, correct(L3)	صحيح
crusade(L21)	صليبيّ ج ـون	newspaper(L14)	صحيفة ج صُحُف
industry(L11)	صِناعة ج ـات	rock(L15) (coll.)	صخْر ج صُخُور
box, chest; cashbox(L16)	صُنْدُوق ج صناديقُ	headache(L13)	صُداع
production(L21)	صنْع	to export sth. to(L23)	II صدّر (يُصدِّر) هـ إلى
to process sth.; to industrialize(L19)	II صنّع (يُصنِّعُ) هـ	the early period of Islam(L28)	صدر الإسلام
Ṣanᶜāʾ (Sanaa)(L14)	صنْعاءُ	chest(L13)	صدْر ج صُدُور
photo(L13)	صُورة ج صُوَر	friendly, be friends with(L11)	صديق
fasting(L10)	صوْم	honest, upright (epithet of the 1st Caliph)(L10)	الصِّدِّيق
Somalia(L15)	الصُومال	friend(L2)	صديق ج أصْدِقاءُ
hunter(L26)	صَيّاد ج ون	friend (f.)(L2)	صديقة ج ـات

stamp^(L16)	طابِع ج طوابِعُ
floor^(L9)	طابِق ج طوابِقُ
here: queue/line of people^(L16)	طابُور ج طوابِيرُ
extra, extraordinary ^(L11)	طارىء
fresh^(L20)	طازِج
energy, potential^(L15)	طاقة ج ـات
Live long!^(L13)	طال عُمرُك !
student^(L2)	طالِب ج طُلّاب/ طلبة
student (f.)^(L2)	طالِبة ج ـات
table^(L2)	طاوِلة ج ـات
medicine (*as science*)^(L4)	طِبٌّ
cook^(L26)	طبّاخ ج ـون
naturally *(adv.)*^(L8)	طبْعاً
to apply^(L26)	II طبّق (يُطبّقُ) هـ
class, group, strata^(L28)	طبْقة ج ـات
doctor^(L2)	طبيب ج أطِبّاءُ
doctor (f.)^(L2)	طبيبة ج ـات
nature^(L19)	طبيعة
Tripoli^(L8)	طَرابُلُس (م)
limbs^(L13)	طرف ج أطْراف
road, street^(L4)	طريق ج طُرُق
dinner^(L7)	طعام العشاء
meal^(L5)	طعام ج أطْعِمة
child^(L12)	طِفْل ج أطفال
weather^(L7)	طقْس
demand^(L18)	طلب
demand (for)^(L19)	طلب (على)
to order sth.^(L7)	طلب (يطْلُبُ طلباً) هـ، أنْ
to ask for sth., to demand ^(L7)	طلب منه أنْ
ruin, traces^(L24)	طلل ج أطْلال
tomato(es)^(L7)	طَماطِمُ

hunting^(L26)	صيْد
pharmacist^(L5)	صيْدليٌّ ج صيادِلة
pharmacy^(L14)	صيْدَليّة ج ـات
summer^(L9)	صَيْف
Chinese^(L9)	صِينيّ ج ـون

ض

outskirts, vicinity^(L23)	ضاحية ج ضواحٍ
putting in order, arranging^(L27)	ضبْط
huge, giant^(L12)	ضخْم
(prep.) against^(L13)	ضِدّ
damage^(L21)	ضرر ج أضْرار
necessary for^(L7)	ضَرُوري لـ
double; multiple^(L19)	ضعْف ج أضْعاف
weak^(L17)	ضعيف ج ضُعفاءُ
pressure^(L15)	ضغْط ج ضُغُوط
to comprise^(L9)	ضمَّ (يضُمُّ ضمّاً) هـ
social security^(L21)	الضمان الاجْتِماعيّ
guarantee^(L21)	ضمان ج ـات
security, bail, guarantee^(L19)	ضمانة ج ـات
(prep.) in^(L18)	ضِمْنَ
light^(L22)	ضوْء ج أضْواء
loss^(L23)	ضَياع
to loose sth. ^(L15)	II ضيَّع (يُضيِّعُ) هـ
guest^(L13)	ضيْف ج ضُيُوف
narrow, tight^(L21)	ضيِّق

ط

flying^(L17)	طائِر
air-plane^(L3)	طائِرة ج ـات
character^(L27)	طابِع

scientist, scholar^(L22)	عالِم ج عُلماءُ	Ṭaha Ḥusain^(L8)	طه حسين
world, universe^(L6)	عالَم ج عوالِمُ	to develop sth.^(L15)	II طَوَّر (يُطَوِّر) هـ
international^(L6)	عالَميّ	Taurus Mountains^(L24)	طوروس
general, public^(L11)	عامّ	long, tall^(L2)	طويل ج طِوال
year^(L10)	عام ج أعْوام	enclosed^(L18)	طَيًّا
to treat, to deal with^(L18)	III عامل (يُعامِلُ) ه، هـ	good^(L2)	طَيِّب ج ون
worker, employee^(L8)	عامِل ج عُمَّال	bird^(L26)	طَيْر ج طُيور (coll.)
to suffer from sth.^(L15)	III عانى (يُعاني) من	(prep.) during^(L15)	طِيلةَ
expression for, to consist of^(L26)	عِبارة عن	clay^(L28)	طِين
ʿAbd ar-Razzāq (p. n.)^(L7)	عبد الرزَّاق		
to express sth.^(L14)	II عبَّر (يُعبِّرُ) عن	**ظ**	
to come across sth., to track down sth.^(L23)	عثر (يعْثُرُ عُثوراً) على	condition^(L20)	ظرْف ج ظُروف
Ottoman^(L21)	عُثْمانيّ ج ـون	to continue to do, to do sth. permanently (+imperf. or part.)^(L24)	ظلَّ (يظَلُّ ظلًّا)
the seven wonders of the world^(L24)	عجائب الدُّنيا السبع		
incompetence; deficit^(L19)	عجْز (عن)	to think, to suspect^(L17)	ظنَّ (يظُنُّ ظنًّا) أنَّ
miracle^(L24)	عجيبة ج عجائِبُ	midday, noon^(L6)	ظُهْر
to count; pass.: to be considered^(L24)	عدَّ (يعُدُّ عدًّا) ه، ه من	to become obvious to so.^(L28)	ظهر (يظْهَرُ ظُهوراً) لـ
several^(L13)	عِدَّة		
number^(L4)	عدد ج أعْداد	**ع**	
some, a number of^(L4)	عددٌ مِن	family^(L2)	عائِلة ج ـات
lentils^(L7)	عدس (coll.)	fast, rapid^(L16)	عاجِل
non(-) (عدم + noun is like غير + adjective or part., a nominal negation)^(L23)	عدم	to return (to)^(L11)	عاد (يعُودُ عوْدةً) (إلى)
running^(L17)	عدا (يعْدُو عدْواً)	normally^(L27)	عادةً
enemy^(L23)	عدوّ ج أعْداء	to be equal to sth.^(L17)	III عادل (يُعادِلُ) هـ
many, numerous^(L14)	عدِيد	normal^(L7)	عادِيّ
Iraq^(L3)	العِراق	to live, to experience, to see^(L11)	عاش (يعِيشُ عيْشاً) ه
Iraqi^(L7)	عِراقيّ	lover^(L26)	عاشِق ج ـون، عُشَّاق
Arab, Arabic, Arabian^(L4)	عربي ج عرب	storm^(L15)	عاصِفة ج عواصِفُ
wedding, marriage^(L27)	عُرْس	capital city^(L3)	عاصِمة ج عواصِمُ
		well-being^(L18)	عافِية

marriage contract(L27)	عقد القران
decade(L19)	عقد ج عُقُود
to hold (conference); to make a contract(L5)	عقد هـ
scorpion(L15)	عقرب ج عقاربُ
brain, mind, intellect(L17)	عقل ج عُقُول
optimal; rational(L20)	عقلانيّ
mentality(L26)	عقليّة ج ـات
confession, denomination(L27)	عقيدة ج عقائدُ
opposite(L17)	عكْس
to reflect sth.(L17)	عكس (يعْكِسُ عكْساً) هـ
medical treatment(L13)	علاج
relation(L5)	علاقة ج ـات
highly educated, great scholar(L16)	عَلّامة
in addition to(L12)	علاوةً على
reason; (gram.) defectivity (letter or word)(L28)	عِلّة ج عِلل
to know sth., that(L7)	عِلم (يعْلَمُ عِلْماً) هـ، أنّ
biology(L9)	عِلْم الأحْياء
sociology(L9)	عِلْم الإجْتِماع
science, studies(L9)	عِلْم ج عُـلُوم
scientific(L9)	عِلْمِيّ
(prep.) on; upon(L2)	عَلَى
in case, provided that(L26)	على أنْ
in any case, anyhow(L13)	على أيِّ حال
at all(L15)	على الإطْلاق
on the contrary(L17)	على العكس
at the expense of(L23)	على حساب
for example, e.g.(L19)	على سبيل المِثال
in the light of, in view of(L22)	عَلَى ضوْء
straight forward, nonstop(L27) (colloq.)	على طُول
offer, supply(L19)	عرض
offer sth. to so.(L13)	عرض (يعْرِضُ عرْضاً) على هـ
supply and demand(L19)	العرض والطلب
to know so., sth.(L5)	عرف ه، هـ
bride(L27)	عروس (م)
(bride)groom(L27)	عريس
broad, wide(L17)	عريض
(deeply) rooted, ancient(L27)	عريق
dear, beloved(L6)	عزيز ج أعِزّاءُ
my dear (f.)(L6)	عزيزتي
my dear(L6)	عزيزي
military; soldier(L8)	عسْكريّ ج ـون، عساكِرُ
honey(L3)	عسل
twenty(L9)	عِشْرُونَ
accidental, random, arbitrary(L22)	عشوائيّ
epoch; afternoon(L19)	عصْر ج عُصُور
sparrow; small bird(L26)	عُصْفُور ج عصافيرُ
juice(L3)	عصير
upper arm(L13) (also m.)	عضُد (م) ج أعْضاد
member(L6)	عُضْو ج أعْضاء
organ, part of the body(L13)	عُضْو ج أعْضاء
thirsty(L7)	عطْشان م عطْشَى ج عِطاش
damage(L15)	عُطْل
bone(L26)	عظم ج عِظام
greatness(L27)	عظمة
great(L3)	عظيم ج عُظماءُ
pardon (and response after شكراً)(L2)	عفْواً
pardon(L10)	عفْواً
confessional, denominational(L27)	عقائِديّ
carrying out, holding (a meeting)(L11)	عقْد

stubborn, pigheaded, stolid(L26)	عنيد ج عُنُد	at any rate(L14)	على كُلِّ حالٍ
era, age, epoch(L18)	عهْد ج عُهُود	according to the wishes(L15)	على ما يُرامُ
good swimmer(L26)	عوّام	at his expense(L25)	على نفقتِهِ
return(L11)	عَوْدة	in the margin(L20)	على هامش
a medical doctor's office(L9)	عِيادة ج ات	to be close to bankruptcy(L22)	على وشكِ الإفلاس
members of the family(L28)	عِيال	as you like(L22) (colloq.)	على كيْفَك/كيْفِك
the Feast of Immolation(L28)	عِيد الأضْحَى	he must(L14)	عليْهِ أنْ
Whitsun(L28)	عيد العنصرة	Peace be upon him.(L10)	عليهِ السلام
Easter(L28)	عيد الفِصْح	building(L10)	عِمارة ج ات
the Feast of Breaking the *Ramaḍān* Fast(L28)	عيد الفِطْر	Oman(L3)	عُمانُ
Christmas(L28)	عيد الميلاد	Amman(L8)	عمّان (م)
holiday(L8)	عِيد ج أعْياد	age(L16)	عُمْر ج أعْمار
the Feast of the Birth of the Prophet(L28)	عيد مَوْلِد النبي	to work(L5)	عمِل
eye(L13)	عيْن (م) ج عُيُون	to work (L7)	عمِل (يعْمَلُ عملاً)
		work(L5)	عمل ج أعْمال
غ		to work towards(L11)	عمل على
forest, jungle(L26)	غاب (coll.)	giant(L25)	عِمْلاق ج عمالِقة
wood, forest(L24)	غابة ج ـات	currency(L12)	عُمْلة ج ـات
to leave sth.(L9)	III غادر (يُغادِرُ) هـ	spine(L13)	عمُود فِقْرِيّ
to trickle away (in)(L15)	غار (يغُورُ غوْراً) (في)	dean(L18)	عميد ج عُمداءُ
sinking (in), to be drowned (L27)	غارق في	deep (L6)	عميق
expensive(L9)	غالٍ	(prep.) about, over(L5)	عنْ
dominating(L28)	غالِب	via, by means of(L18)	عن طريق
majority(L10)	غالِبِيَّة ج ـات	grapes(L7)	عِنب (coll.)
dust(L15)	غُبار ج أغْبِرة	(prep.) at(L2)	عِنْدَ
lunch(L3)	غَداء	you have (m./f.)(L2)	عِنْدَكَ / عِنْدَكِ
food(stuff), nutrition(L20)	غِذاء ج أغْذِية	as, when(L19)	عِنْدما
food(stuff)(L20)	غِذائِيّ	I have(L2)	عِنْدِي
room(L2)	غُرْفة ج غُرَف	throat, neck(L13)	عُنُق ج أعْناق
sunset(L28)	غُرُوب الشمْس	spider(L15)	عنكَبُوت ج عناكِبُ
		title; *also:* address(L6)	عُنْوان ج عناوِينُ

Nomen agentis; active *(gram.)*(L28)	الفاعِل	strange(L15)	غَرِيب ج غُرَباءُ
fax(L18)	فاكس	to attack, to assault sth. (L24)	غَزا (يَغْزُو غَزْواً) هـ
fruits(L3)	فاكِهة ج فواكِهُ	gazelle(L26)	غَزال ج غِزْلان
girl(L2)	فتاة ج فتيات	attack, raid, invasion(L21)	غَزْوة ج غَزَوات
open sth.(L13)	فتح (يفْتَحُ فتْحاً) هـ	to be or to become angry or furious at(L26)	غَضِب (يَغْضَبُ غضباً) من/على
here: to conquer(L24)	فتح هـ	to cover sth. (L23)	II غطَّى (يُغطِّي) هـ
period(L11)	فترة ج ات	mistake, wrong(L3)	غلط ج أغْلاط
to make clear(L28)	فتق (يفتقُ فتقاً)	sheep(L20)	غنم ج أغْنام *(coll.)*
young man(L27)	فتىً ج فِتْيان	to sing(L17)	II غنَّى (يُغنِّي)
way, road, street(L27)	فجّ ج فِجاج	rich (in)(L24)	غنيّ ج أغْنِياءُ (ب)
radish(L7)	فِجْل *(coll.)*	booty; loot; prey(L26)	غنيمة ج غنائمُ
examine(L13)	فحص (يفْحَصُ فحْصاً)	Gobi(L15)	الغوبي
examination(L13)	فحْص ج فُحُوص	to change, to alter, to vary sth. (L15)	II غيَّر (يُغيِّرُ) هـ
Euphrates(L24)	الفُرات	not necessary(L13)	غيْر ضَرُوريّ
strawberries(L20)	فراوُلة *(Ital.: fragola)*	(and) others(L23)	غيْرُهُ، غيْرُها، غيْرُهُمْ (مِنْ الـ ...)
vagina(L13)	فرْج ج فُرُوج		
single, individual(L18)	فرْد ج أفْراد		
the Persians(L21)	الفُرْس ج	**ف**	
brush(L24)	فُرْشة ج فُرُش		
branch(L9)	فرْع ج فُرُوع	*(coordinating conjunction)*(L11)	ف
separation, *pl.* differences(L25)	فرْق ج فُرُوق	mouse(L26)	فأر ج فِئْران *(coll.)*
team, ensemble(L17)	فِرْقة / فريق ج فِرق	group, (social) strata(L21)	فِئة ج ـات
France(L5)	فِرنسا	use(L13)	فائِدة ج فوائِدُ
French(L9)	فِرنْسِيّ ج ـون	excellent(L18)	فائِق
strawberry(L20)	فريز *(Fr.: fraise)*	light, bright (colour)(L24)	فاتِح
wedding dress(L27)	فستان العرس	bill, check(L24)	فاتُورة ج فواتيرُ
to be spoiled, to go off(L26)	فسد (يفْسُدُ فساداً) هـ	rider, horseman(L17)	فارس ج فُرْسان
to explain, to comment on(L26)	II فسَّر (يُفَسِّرُ) هـ	difference(L21)	فارق ج فوارقُ
to fail (in)(L24)	فشِل (يفْشَلُ فشْلاً) (في)	to win against/over(L17)	فاز (يفُوزُ فوْزاً) على
section, paragraph; season(L9)	فصْل ج فُصُول	spoiled; bad(L13)	فاسِد
		Fāṭima(L2)	فاطِمة

I understood^(L4)	فَهِمْتُ
you (m.) understood^(L4)	فَهِمْتَ
you (f.) understood^(L4)	فَهِمْتِ
at once, instantly, immediately^(L14)	فوراً
phosphate^(L25)	فُوسْفات
(prep.) up, over, on top of^(L2)	فَوْقَ
(adv.) above^(L2)	فَوْقُ
beans^(L7)	فُول
(prep.) in^(L2)	في
with the protection of God^(L14)	في أمان الله
on the road to^(L28)	في سبيلِ
in so's. favour^(L22)	في صالِح ه
visa^(L18)	فيزا
physics^(L6)	فيزياء
flooding^(L15)	فَيَضان ج ـات
elephant^(L26)	فيل ج فِيَلة، فُيُول
in what follows^(L13)	فيما يلي
Phoenician^(L21)	فِينيقيّ ج ـون

ق

scorching^(L28)	قائِظ
chargé d'affaires^(L27)	القائِم بالأعْمال
menu^(L7)	قائِمة الطعام
list^(L7)	قائِمة ج ـات، قوائِمُ
to meet so.^(L8)	III قابل (يُقابِلُ) ه
to steer, to drive sth. (to)^(L11)	قاد (يقُودُ قِيادةً) هـ (إلى)
able to, capable of, qualified^(L11)	قادِر على
coming^(L9)	قادِم
coming from^(L8)	قادِماً من
continent^(L21)	قارّة ج ات
judge^(L27)	قاضٍ ج قُضاة

here: criterion of differentiation^(L28)	فصْل ج فُصُول
merit^(L28)	فضْل
to remain^(L28)	فضل (يفضُلُ فضْلاً)
to prefer, to favour sth., so. over^(L28)	II فضّل (يُفضِّل) هـ، ه على
the merit of being the first^(L28)	فضْل السبق
scandal^(L11)	فضِيحة ج فضائِحُ
mushroom (coll.)^(L7)	فُطْر
breakfast^(L3)	فُطُور
to do sth.^(L5)	فعل هـ
really, in fact, actually^(L25)	فِعْلاً
poor^(L19)	فقير ج فُقراءُ
jaw^(L13)	فكّ
lower ~^(L13)	الفكُّ الأسْفل
upper ~^(L13)	الفكُّ الأعْلَى
to think (of)^(L15)	II فكّر (يُفكِّرُ) (في)
thinking, thought, ideology^(L12)	فِكْر ج أفْكار
idea^(L5)	فِكْرة ج أفْكار
peasant, farmer^(L9)	فلاّح ج ـون
Palestinian^(L19)	فِلسْطِينيّ
pepper^(L7)	فِلْفِل
film^(L14)	فِلْم ج أفْلام
money^(L22)	ج فُلُوس (colloq.)
mouth^(L13)	فم ج أفْواه
art^(L17)	فنّ ج فُنُون
cup^(L7)	فِنجان ج فناجينُ
hotel^(L5)	فُنْدُق ج فنادِقُ
Finland^(L5)	فِنْلَندا
technical; technician^(L16)	فنّيّ
to understand sth.^(L7)	فهِم (يفْهَمُ فهْماً) هـ

to read sth. (L7)	قرأ (يقْرَأُ قِراءةً) هـ	clear-cut (L11)	قاطِع
to read sth. (L5)	قرأ هـ	hall (L7)	قاعة ج ـات
reading (L16)	قِراءة ج ات	rule, regulations (L27)	قاعِدة ج قواعِدُ
resolution (L14)	قرار ج ات	caravan; convoy (L26)	قافِلة ج قوافِلُ
monkey (L26)	قِرْد ج قُرُود، قِردة	to say sth., that (L11)	قال (يقُولُ) هـ، إنَّ
to decide; to report, to establish sth. (L24)	II قرَّر (يُقرِّرُ) هـ	he/she said (L5)	قال / قالتْ
to decide sth. (L19)	II قرَّر (يُقرِّرُ) هـ	They told me. / I was told. (L10)	قالُوا لِي
piaster (L12)	قِرْش ج قُرُوش	to get up, to rise (L11)	قام (يقُومُ قِياماً)
disc (L17)	قُرْص ج أقْراص	to carry out, to realize (L11)	قام ب
century (L16)	قرْن ج قُرُون	here: to come into being, to emerge (L21)	قام هـ
cauliflower (L20)	قرْنبِيط	dictionary (L4)	قامُوس ج قوامِيس
relative (L27)	قرِيب ج أقارِبُ	law (L11)	قانُون ج قوانِينُ
close to, nearby (L7)	قرِيب مِن	Cairo (L2)	القاهِرة
soon (L18)	قرِيباً	to resist, to withstand sth. (L26)	III قاوم (يُقاوِمُ) هـ
village (L9)	قرْية ج قُرًى	dome (L24)	قُبَّة ج قِباب، قُبب
department (L8)	قِسْم ج أقْسام	hat, cap (L9)	قُبَّعة ج ـات
story (L23)	قِصَّة ج قِصص	(prep.) before (temp.) (L5)	قبْلَ
to have sth. in mind, to aim at, to refer to, to think (L20)	قصد (يقْصِدُ قصْداً) هـ	to accept sth. (L18)	قبِل (يقْبَلُ) هـ
castle, palace (L24)	قصْر ج قُصُور	before it is to late (L22)	قبل فوات الأوان
highest (L15)	قُصْوَى	tribal (L21)	قبلِيّ
short, small (L2)	قصِير ج قِصار	tribe (L17)	قبِيلة ج قبائِلُ
problem, case (L15)	قضِية ج قضايا	to kill (L18)	قتل (يقْتُلُ قتْلاً)
(tom)cat (L26)	قِطّ ج قِطط	(particle, cf. Lesson 13, p.163) (L11)	قدْ
train (L3)	قِطار ج ات	to estimate sth. (L20)	II قدَّر (يُقدِّرُ) هـ
sector (L12)	قِطاع ج ـات	to guess, to estimate sth. (L25)	II قدَّر (يُقدِّرُ) هـ
region, land (L24)	قُطْر ج أقْطار	fate, destiny (L15)	قدَر ج أقْدار
drop (L14)	قطْرة ج قطرات	to present, to submit sth. (to so.) (L14)	قدَّم (له) هـ
regional, country (L21)	قطْرِيّ	foot, leg (L13)	قدم (م) ج أقْدام
to cut sth. (L23)	قطع (يقْطَعُ قطْعاً) هـ	to introduce so., sth. to so. (L14)	II قدَّم (يُقدِّمُ) ه، هـ إلى / ل
to cover a distance or stage (L23)	قطع شَوْطاً	old (L2)	قدِيم ج قُدماءُ

piece^(L14)	قِطعة ج قِطَع
cotton^(L24)	قُطن ج أَقطان
to sit (down) on ^(L28)	قعد (يَقعُدُ قُعُوداً) على
glove^(L9)	قُفّاز ج قفافيزُ
jump(ing)^(L17)	قفز (يقْفِزُ قفزاً)
heart^(L13)	قلْب ج قُلُوب
you (m./f.) said^(L5)	قُلْتَ / قُلْتِ
I told you^(L10)	قُلْتُ لَكَ/ لَكِ
I told him^(L5)	قُلْتُ له
fortress^(L23)	قلْعة ج قِلاع
pencil^(L2)	قلم ج أقلام
rarely, hardly, seldom^(L26)	قلّما
few, little^(L3)	قليل ج ـون
top, summit^(L14)	قِمّة ج قِمم
wheat^(L20)	قمْح
moon^(L2)	قمر
satellite, artificial moon^(L15)	قمَر صِناعيّ
shirt^(L24)	قميص ج قُمْصان
bomb^(L17)	قُنْبُلة ج قنابلُ
consul^(L25)	قُنصُل ج قناصلُ
coffee^(L3)	قهْوة
armed forces^(L21)	قُوّات مُسلّحة
power, strength^(L15)	قُوّة ج ات، قوى
saying^(L26)	قوْل ج أقوال
strong, mighty, powerful^(L6)	قويّ ج أقوياءُ
leadership, leading^(L21)	قِيادِيّ
analogy; rule, norm^(L28)	قِياس ج ـات أقْيسة
size^(L24)	قِياس ج ـات، أقْيسة
comparative(ly)^(L17)	قِياسيّ
heat of the summer^(L28)	قيْظ
valuable^(L8)	قيِّم

to assess, to judge sth. ^(L22)	II قيَّم (يُقيِّمُ) هـ
value^(L17)	قيمة ج قِيَم

ك

glass^(L7)	كأس (م) ج كؤُوس
cabriolet^(L18)	كابريوليه
writer, secretary^(L4)	كاتِب ج كُتّاب
to be about to do sth. almost (with negation "scarcely, hardly")^(L15)	كاد (يكادُ) يفْعلُ
working^(L21)	كادِح ج ـون
catastrophe^(L11)	كارِثة ج كوارثُ
sufficient^(L11)	كافٍ
all^(L13)	كافّة
complete, whole, entire^(L15)	كامِل
was (with predicate complement)^(L11)	كان (يكُونُ كوْناً)
he/she was^(L5)	كان / كانتْ
sulphur; matches^(L25)	كِبْريت
big^(L2)	كبير ج كِبار
book^(L2)	كِتاب ج كُتُب
writing ^(L4)	كِتابة ج ـات
to belong to a written religion^(L27)	كتابيّ
catalogue^(L19)	كتالوج ج ـات
to write sth.^(L5)	كتب هـ
you (m.) wrote^(L4)	كَتَبْتَ
I wrote^(L4)	كَتَبْتُ
you (f.) wrote ^(L4)	كَتَبْتِ
shoulder (blade)^(L13)	كتْف (م) ج أكْتاف
to conceal, to hide ^(L11)	كتم (يكْتُمُ كتْماً) هـ
to be numerous^(L26)	كثُر (يكثُرُ كثْرةً) ة/ هـ
dune^(L15)	كثِيب ج كُثْبان
many^(L3)	كثِير ج ـون، كِثار

how(L2)	كَيْفَ	alcohol(L7)	كُحُول
How are you? (m.)(L2)	كَيْفَ حالُكَ /	so and so much/many(L27)	كذا
How are you? (f.)(L2)	كَيْفَ حالُكِ؟	too, also(L7)	كَذلِكَ
kilogram(me)(L20)	كِيلُو(غرام) ج ـات	notebook(L2)	كُرّاسة ج ـات، كراريسُ
chemistry(L6)	كيمياء	basketball(L17)	كُرة السلة
Kenya(L15)	كينيا	volleyball(L17)	الكُرة الطائرة
		football, soccer(L17)	كُرة القدم
ل		ball, globe(L15)	كُرة ج ات
(prep.) for(L2)	لِ	chair(L2)	كُرْسيّ ج كراسيّ
no, not(L2)	لا	to hate sth., so.(L22)	كره (يكْرهُ) هـ، ه
not only ... but also(L25)	لا ... فحسْب ... بل إنّما أيضاً	to reveal sth.(L27)	كشف (يكْشِفُ كشْفاً) عن
I do not know.(L2)	لا أدْري.	cake(L27)	كعْك
not bad(L2)	لا بأسَ (بِهِ/ بها)	all(L13)	كُلّ
unavoidable, indispensable(L21)	لا بُدَّ مِن	speech(L8)	كلِمة ج ـات
unavoidable(L22)	لا مفرَّ مِنْهُ	faculty of languages(L10)	كلية الألسُن
to be favourable for(L20)	III لاءم (يُلائِمُ) هـ	faculty(L4)	كُلِّية ج ـات
to notice sth.(L19)	III لاحظ (يُلاحِظُ) هـ	how much / many(L9)	كم
Latakiya(L23)	اللاذِقِّية	as, like, furthermore(L7)	كما
necessary (for)(L7)	لازِم (لِ)	computer(L3)	كُمْبيُوتـَر ج ات
player(L17)	لاعِب ج ـون	to hide, to waylay so.(L24)	كمِن/كمَن (يكْمَنُ/ يكْمُنُ كُمُوناً) في، لِ
to dress sth.(L9)	لبِس (يلْبَسُ لُبْساً) هـ	quantity(L19)	كمِّية ج ـات
Lebanon(L5)	لُبْنانُ	I was(L5)	كُنْتُ
committee(L11)	لجْنة ج لِجان	you (m./f.) were(L5)	كُنْتَ / كُنْتِ
moment(L8)	لحْظة ج لحَظات	church(L27)	كنِيسة ج كنائِسُ
meat(L7)	لحْم ج لُحُوم	al-Kufah(L24)	الكُوفة
canned meat(L13)	لحْم مُعلَّب	cholera(L14)	كوليرا
(prep.) at (loc. and temp.)(L6)	لدىَ	cauliflower(L20)	كوليفلاور
therefore, that's why(L11)	لِذا	Kuwait(L3)	الكُوَيْت
that's why, therefore(L27)	لِذا / لِذلِك	in order to(L8)	كَيْ / لِكَيْ
tasty(L5)	لذِيذ	sack, bag(L20)	كِيس ج أكْياس
tongue; language(L10)	لِسان ج ألْسُن، ألسِنة		

friendly, nice(L7)	لَطيف ج لُطفاءُ
to play sth.(L21)	لِعِب (يَلْعَبُ لَعْباً) هـ
match, game(L17)	لَعِب ج أَلْعاب
curse(L28)	لَعْنة ج لعنات
language(L6)	لُغة ج ـات
linguist(L16)	لُغَوِيّ ج ـون
(particle of confirmation)(L11)	لَقَدْ
to meet so.(L11)	لَقِي (يَلْقَى لِقاءً) ه
unfortunately(L17)	لِلأسف
for the first time(L7)	لِلْمَرَّة الأُولى
not (+ jussive)(L8)	لَمْ
why(L10)	لِماذا
God, Allah(L2)	اللّٰه
God knows everything.(L15)	اللّٰه أَعْلَمُ
God bless you. (answer after مبارك / ميروك)(L4)	اللّٰه يُبارِك فِيكَ
dialect(L20)	لَهْجة ج لَهَجات
if (+ verb in perf.)(L16)	لو
if / if not(L26)	لَوْ / لَوْلا
if you allow me(L16)	لو سَمَحْتَ
table; blackboard(L2)	لَوْح ج أَلْواح
almonds(L7)	لَوْز (coll.)
color(L7)	لَوْن ج أَلْوان
for me(L2)	لِي
Libya(L3)	لِيبيا
not to be sth.(L8)	لَيْس
not only … but also …(L19)	ليس فحسْب بل أيضاً …
day and night(L7)	لَيلَ نهارَ
lemons(L7)	لَيْمُون (coll.)

م

cf. ميلادي(L10)	م
minaret(L24)	مأْذَنة ج مآذِنُ
food, dish, meal(L7)	ج مأْكُولات
usual, common(L17)	مأْلُوف
conference(L8)	مُؤْتمر ج ات
historian(L27)	مُؤرِّخ ج ـون
enterprise, firm(L14)	مُؤسَّسة ج ـات
data, facts, figure(L23)	مُؤَشِّر ج ات
provisional, temporary(L25)	مُؤَقَّت
author(L27)	مُؤلِّف ج ـون
hundred(L15)	مِئوِي
what(L2)	ما
still (doing)(L16)	ما زال، لا يزال
Whatever God wants(L24)	ما شاء اللّٰه
so long as … not; unless(L23)	ما لم
water(L7)	ماء ج مِياه
to die(L23)	ماتَ (يَمُوتُ موْتاً)
to be like, sth., to be equivalent to sth.(L26)	ماثل (يُماثِلُ) هـ III
subject(L6)	مادَّة ج موادُّ
what (followed by a verb)(L2)	ماذا
German mark(L9)	مارك ج ـات
livestock(L20)	ماشية ج مواشٍ
past(L11)	ماضٍ
past(L17)	ماضٍ (الماضي)
make up(L22)	ماكياج (Fr. maquillage)
property, capital, finance(L16)	مال ج أَمْوال
financial(L16)	مالِيّ
skillful(L25)	ماهِر ج ون
match(L17)	مُباراة ج ـيات
blessed(L10)	مُبارك

fertile, fruitful(L18)	مُثمِر	Congratulations!(L4)	مُبارك !
field, area, sphere, sector(L8)	مجال ج ـ ات	direct(L18)	مُباشَرةً
compliment(L22)	مُجاملة ج ـ ات	principle(L28)	مبْدأ ج مبادِئُ
neighboring(L11)	مُجاوِر	Congratulations!(L4)	مبْرُوك ! (colloq.)
society(L21)	مُجتَمع ج ـ ات	sum, amount(L12)	مبْلغ ج مبالِغُ
diligent(L3)	مُجتْهِد ج ون	building(L19)	مبْنيٌّ ج مبان
fame, glory(L27)	مجْد	to be sure (that)(L11)	مُتأكِّد (من)
Hungary(L5)	المجر	remaining(L15)	مُتبقٍّ
journal(L15)	مجلَّة ج ـ ات	museum(L22)	متحف ج متاحِفُ
Security Council(L11)	مجلس الأمن	low(L19)	مُتدنٍّ
council(L11)	مجلِس ج مجالِسُ	synonym(L8)	مُتزادِف ج ـ ات
plant, works, factory(L25)	مُجمَّع ج ـ ات	to be married to(L16)	مُتزوِّج مِن
(sum) total, totality, the whole(L25)	مجْمُوع	rising(L19)	مُتصاعِد
unknown(L24)	مجْهُول	requirements(L22)	ج مُتطلَّبات
negotiations, talks(L8)	ج مُحادثات	developing(L21)	مُتطوِّر
incense bowls(L27)	محارق البخور	many-sided, multi(L23)	مُتعدِّد الجوانِب
lecturer, reader, professor(L6)	مُحاضِر ج ون	to be used to so., sth.(L23)	مُتعوِّد على
lecture(L20)	مُحاضرة ج ات	changing(L19)	مُتغيِّر
governorate, county(L8)	مُحافظة ج ـ ات	change(L19)	مُتغيِّر ج ات
attempt, effort(L19)	مُحاولة ج ـ ات	spectator(L17)	مُتفرِّج ج ـون
professional(L17)	مُحتْرِف ج ـون	scattered(L28)	مُتفرِّق
honored, dear(L18)	مُحتْرم	agreed upon(L18)	مُتَّفَق عليه
probably(L14)	مُحتْمل	wishing so.(L18)	مُتمنِّياً ل
fixed(L11)	مُحدَّد	outstanding(L14)	مُتميِّز
plough, plow(L20)	مِحراث ج محاريثُ	available(L18)	مُتوفِّر
agricultural produce(L20)	مُحصُول ج محاصِيلُ	died(L24)	مُتوفَّى
bus-stop(L4)	محطَّة الباصاتِ	when(L2)	متى
station(L3)	محطّة ج ـ ات	ideal(L17)	مِثاليّ
court(L11)	مُحكمة ج محاكِمُ	proverb(L26)	مثـل ج أمْثال
shop(L3)	محلّ ج ـ ات	like(L17)	مِثلَ، مِثلَما
here: place, square(L10)	محلّ ج ـ ات	for example(L3)	مثلاً

reference book(L9)	مَرْجِع ج مراجِعُ	local, domestic(L20)	مَحَلِّيّ
requested; expected, hoped for(L18)	مَرْجُوّ	contradiction, violation(L26)	مُخالَفة ج ــات
fig: Hello!(L2)	مَرْحَباً	bakery(L3)	مَخْبِز ج مَخابِزُ
stage(L22)	مَرْحَلة ج مراحِلُ	different(L7)	مُخْتَلِف
late, deceased(L16)	مَرْحُوم	here: pronunciation(L28)	مَخْرَج ج مَخارِجُ
illness(L13)	مرض ج أمْراض	shop(L3)	مَخْزن ج مَخازِنُ
port, harbour(L23)	مَرْفَأ ج مرافِئُ	to display sth.(L28)	مَدَّ (يَمُدُّ مَدّاً) هـ
dance hall(L5)	مَرْقَص ج مراقِصُ	here: to lay sth.(L25)	مَدَّ (يَمُدُّ) هـ
center(L5)	مَرْكَز ج مراكِزُ	period of time(L7)	مُدَّة ج مُدد
traffic(L16)	مُرُور	to praise so.(L17)	مدح (يَمْدَحُ مدْحاً) ه
convenient(L4)	مُريح	teacher, lecturer(L6)	مُدَرِّس ج ــون
ill, ill person(L5)	مريض ج مرْضَى	primary school(L16)	مدرسة ابتدائية
Maryam(L2)	مَرْيَمُ	secondary school(L16)	مدرسة ثانوية
to joke(L18)	مزح (يَمْزحُ مُزاحاً)	school(L3)	مَدْرسة ج مدارِسُ
flourishing(L27)	مُزْدهِر	round(L17)	مُدَوَّر
farm(L8)	مَزْرعة ج مزارِعُ	dimensions, extent(L27)	مدىً
question, case(L11)	مسْألة ج مسائِلُ	director(L12)	مُدِير ج مُدَراءُ
responsible for(L8)	مسْؤُول ج ــون عن/ل	Algiers(L8)	مدينة الجزائر
evening(L2)	مساء	Medina(L10)	المدينة المُنوَّرة
yesterday evening(L6)	مساءَ الأمْس	city, town(L2)	مدِينة ج مُدُن
Good evening!(L2)	مساء الخير	campus(L12)	مدينة جامعيّة
~ (answer)(L2)	مساء النُّور	mentioned(L27)	مذْكُور
contest, competition(L17)	مُسابقة ج ــات	school of law(L10)	مذْهب ج مذاهِبُ
surface, area, space(L20)	مساحة ج ــات	bitter(L14)	مُرّ
help, support(L17)	مُساعَدة ج ات	looking up, consulting, review(L7)	مُراجعة
distance(L20)	مسافة ج ــات	escort, companion, attendant(L6)	مُرافِق ج ــون
to be on a journey, traveling, traveler(L6)	مُسافِر ج ون	marmalade(L3)	مُرَبَّى
contribution (to)(L11)	مُساهمة ج ــات (في)	once again(L5)	مرّة أُخْرَى
haggling about(L7)	مُساومة ج ــات في، على	time(L7)	مرّة ج ات
impossible(L17)	مُسْتَحِيل	place, rank(L25)	مرْتبة ج مراتِبُ
chancellor(L8)	مُسْتشار ج ون	high(L15)	مُرْتفِع

wrestling (L17)	مُصارعة [صارع (يُصارِعُ)]
lamp (L2)	مِصباح ج مصابيحُ
source (for information) (L9)	مَصدر ج مصادِرُ
Egypt (L3)	مِصرُ
bank (L12)	مَصرِفُ ج مصارفُ
expression, term (L7)	مُصْطلح ج ـات
lift (L10)	مِصعد ج مصاعِدُ
refinery (L23)	مِصفاة ج مصافٍ
interest (L21)	مَصلحة ج مصالِحُ
factory, plant (L8)	مَصنع ج مصانعُ
speculation (L19)	مُضاربة ج ـات
pump (L20)	مِضخّة ج ـات
contents, subject matter (L22)	مَضمُونٌ ج مضامِينُ
to go by, to pass (L15)	مضَى (يَمْضِي مُضِيّاً)
stewardess (L20)	مُضِيفة ج ـات
airport (L3)	مطار ج ـات
kitchen (L2)	مَطبخ ج مطابخُ
rain (L15)	مطر ج أمْطار
restaurant (L5)	مطعم ج مطاعِمُ
beginning (L19)	مطْلع
absolute (L26)	مُطْلَق
required, wanted (L22)	مطْلُوب
ambition (L21) (pejorative)	مطمع ج مطامِعُ
(prep.) with (L2)	مَعَ
So long! (L2)	مع السلامة
opposition (L11)	مُعارضة ج ـات
modern, contemporary (L24)	مُعاصِر
sites (L5)	ج معالِمُ
His Excellency (the minister) (L12)	معالِي (الوزير)
handling (L19)	مُعاملة ج ـات
hospital (L13)	مُستشفى ج ـات
ready (L22)	مُستعِدّ
future (L11)	مُستقبل
niveau, level (L6)	مُستَوى ج ـات
theatre, stage (L6)	مسرح ج مسارحُ
(stage) play (L6)	مسرحِية ج ـات
ruler (L4)	مِسطرة ج مساطِرُ
to hold on to, to grip sth., so. (L16)	مسك (يَمْسِكُ مسْكاً) هـ،ه
Muslim (L10)	مُسلِم ج ـون
cuneiform (L27)	مِسماريّ
Christian (L8)	مسيحيّ ج ـون
spectating (L18)	مُشاهدة
buyer (L19)	مُشترٍ
common, joint, mutual (L8)	مُشترَك
participant (L20)	مُشترك ج ـون
derivation (from) (also gram.) (L25)	مُشتقّ ج ـات (مِن)
oil derivatives (L25)	مشتقّات النفط
winter resort (L25)	مشتّى ج مشاتٍ
drinks (L3)	ج مشرُوبات
project (L8)	مشرُوع ج مشاريعُ
enclosure (in a letter etc.) (L23)	ج مشفُوعات
problem (L11)	مُشكِلة ج مشاكِلُ
sunny (L23)	مُشمِس
apricots (L7) (coll.)	مِشمِش
famous (L8)	مشهُور ج ـون، مشاهِيرُ
to run, to walk, to go (L11)	مشَى (يَمْشِي مشياً)
going (L18)	مـشْي
will (L12)	مشيئة
on foot (L18)	مشْياً
sheikdom (L21)	مشْيخَة ج مشايخُ

Nomen patientis, passive (gram.)(L28)	المفْعُول
lost(L23)	مفقود
useful(L27)	مُفيد
as equivalent for, (in return) for(L23)	مُقابِل
interview(L11)	مُقابَلة صُحُفِية ج ـات
comparative(L16)	مُقارن .
article (press)(L18)	مقالة ج ـات
hors d'oeuvre(L7)	ج مُقبّلات
proposal(L12)	مُقترح ج ـات
limited, restricted to(L19)	مُقتصر على
extract from(L28)	مُقتطف من
amount, extent, degree(L19)	مِقدار ج مقاديرُ
holy, sacred(L28)	مُقدّس
preface, lead(L25)	مُقدّمة ج ـات
here: cubicle(L24)	مقصُورة ج ات
café(L7)	مقهىً ج مقاهٍ
phrase; thesis(L17)	مقولة ج ـات
fighting(L20)	مُكافحة
telephone call(L2)	مُكالمة تلفونيَّة
place(L13)	مكان ج أماكِنُ
rank, position(L21)	مكانة ج ـات
Mecca(L10)	مكّةُ المُكرّمة
travel agency(L6)	مكتب السفر
office; desk(L6)	مكتب ج مكاتِبُ
library, bookshop(L3)	مكتبة ج ـات
written; *pl.* letters(L4)	مكتُوب ج مكاتيبُ
to stay(L9)	مكث (يمْكُثُ مُكُوثاً)
venerable (*epithet of Mecca*)(L10)	المُكرّمة
open; roofless(L18)	مكشُوف
to enable so. to(L22)	II مكّن (يُمكّنُ) ه من
air condition(L9)	مُكيِّف هواء ج ـات
moderate, temperate(L9)	مُعتدِل
dictionary; lexicon(L8)	مُعجم ج معاجمُ
cream, paste(L24)	معجُون ج معاجينُ
stomach(L13)	مِعدة ج مِعد
facilities, installations, works(L20)	ج مُعدّات
average; rate(L15)	مُعدّل ج ـات
mineral(L25)	معدِن ج معادِنُ
mineral(L7)	معدِنيّ
fair, exhibition(L12)	معرِض ج معارِضُ
knowledge(L12)	معرِفة ج معارِفُ
known(L17)	معرُوف
(she-)goat(L20)	معز ج أمعاز (*coll.*)
invited(L27)	معزُوم (*colloq.*)
coat(L9)	مِعطف ج معاطِفُ
majority(L19)	مُعظم
complicated(L23)	مُعقّد
reasonable, sensible(L12)	معقُول
canned(L13)	مُعلّب
teacher(L2)	مُعلّم ج ـون
teacher (f.)(L2)	مُعلّمة ج ـات
information(L9)	ج معلُومات
Never mind. That doesn't matter.(L22)	مَعَلَيْش (*colloq. Eg.*)
plant, laboratory(L8)	معمل ج معامِلُ
meaning(L28)	معنىً ج معان
institute(L9)	معهد ج معاهِدُ
Maghreb, Morocco(L3)	المغرِب
closed(L21)	مُغلق
the Mongol(ian)s(L21)	ج المُغُول
negotiations(L21)	ج مُفاوضات
open, opened(L7)	مفتُوح

it is strange(L21)	مِن الغريبِ
it is expected(L21)	مِن المُتوقَّعِ أنَّ
probably, likely(L21)	مِن المُحْتمل
it is known(L21)	مِن المَعْروفِ
it is expected(L21)	مِن المُنتظِر
He, who sows will harvest.(L20)	مِن بذر حصد
among them(L7)	مِن بينَهُمْ / بينَهَا
products(L25)	ج مُنتجات
He, who seeks will find.(L20)	مِن جدَّ وجد
once more, again(L16)	مِن جديد
with regard to, regarding, as to(L22)	مِن حيثُ
on principle(L28)	مِن حيث المبدأ
here: which(L20)	مِن شأنِهِ / شأنِها أنْ ...
please (as request)(L7)	مِن فضْلِكَ (م) مِن فضْلِكِ
before(L10)	مِن قَبْلُ
from head to toe(L24)	مِن قمة الرأس إلى أخْمَص القدمَيْنِ
from everywhere(L27)	مِن كلِّ فجٍّ عميق
climate(L15)	مُناخ
disputing, refusal(L26)	مُنازعة ج ـات
occasion, opportunity(L8)	مُناسبة ج ـات
half of it(L26)	مُناصفة
discussion(L8)	مُناقشة ج ـات
flat(L24)	مُنبسِط
producing, producer(L19)	مُنتِج
representative team(L17)	مُنتخَب ج ـات
victorious, triumphant(L11)	مُنتصِر
middle, half(L15)	مُنتصَف
regular, orderly(L22)	مُنتظِم
gross national product(L19)	المنتوج الاجتماعيّ الإجماليّ
machine(L27)	مكينة ج ـات /مكائِنُ
to fill sth.(L16)	ملأ (يملأُ ملأً) هـ
clothes(L3)	ج ملابسُ
remark(L21)	مُلاحظة
boxing(L17)	مُلاكمة
meeting point(L12)	مُلتقىً ج ـات
urgent(L11)	مُلِحّ
salt(L7)	مِلْح
committed to(L19)	مُلزَم ب
sports ground(L17)	ملعب ج ملاعِبُ
spoon(L7)	مِلْعقة ج ملاعِقُ
king, monarch(L6)	مَلِك ج مُلُوك
royal(L12)	ملكيّ
full of(L15)	مليء ب
alike, similar(L11)	مُماثِل
carrying on, performing, exerting(L11)	مُمارسة
excellent(L17)	مُمتاز
enjoyable, excellent(L6)	مُمتِع
representative(L11)	مُمثِّل ج ـون
eraser(L4)	مِمْحاة
nurse(L13)	مُمرِّضة
rainy(L23)	مُمطِر
possible(L12)	مُمْكِن
boring(L22)	مُمِلّ
monarchy, kingdom(L12)	مَمْلكة ج ممالِكُ
forbidden, prohibited(L7)	مَمْنوع
who(L2)	مَنْ
(prep.) from, out of(L2)	مِنْ
for; in order to(L11)	مِن أجْلِ
it is worth mentioning that ...(L12)	مِن الجديرِ بِالذِّكْرِ أنَّ

bananas(L7)	مَوْز (coll.)	product(L19)	مَنْتُوج ج ـات
razor blade(L24)	مُوسَى ج مواس، أمْواس	to grant, to give so. sth.(L11)	منح (يَمْنَحُ) ه هـ
subject-matter, issue(L27)	مَوْضِع ج مواضِعُ	engraved (L15)	مَنْحُوت
topic, title (L16)	مَوْضُوع ج مواضِيعُ	low(L9)	مُنْخَفِض
objective(L22)	مَوْضُوعِيّ	(conj.) since(L8)	مُنْذُ / منذ أنْ
civil/public servant, officer, employee, pl. staff(L6)	مُوَظَّف ج ـون	house(L12)	مِنْـزِلِيّ
signatory(L16)	مُوَقِّع	desired, welcome(L18)	منْشُود
the undersigned(L16)	المُوَقِّع أدْناه	post, office(L21)	مَنْصِب ج مناصِبُ
place, spot, ground(L12)	مَوْقِع ج مواقِعُ	region, district(L14)	مِنْطقة ج مناطِقُ
post, point (L11)	مَوْقِف ج مواقِفُ (من)	organization(L19)	مُنَظَّمة ج ـات
client(L27)	مُوَكِّل	Mongolia(L15)	مُنْغُوليا
to finance sth. (L23)	II مـوَّل (يُمَوِّلُ) هـ	plan, program(L22)	مَنْهج ج مناهِجُ
dead, lifeless(L26)	مِيِّت ج أمْوات، مَوْتَى	shining, enlightened (epithet of Medina)(L10)	المُنَوَّرة
medal(L17)	مِيدالِية ج ـات	emigrant(L27)	مُهاجِر ج ـون
place, ground(L17)	مِيْدان ج ميادِينُ	bridal money(L27)	مهْر ج مُهُور
on site, on the scene(L20)	مَيْدانِيّ	~ to be paid after(L27)	مهر مُؤَجَّل
budget(L21)	مِيزانِيّة	~ to be paid before(L27)	مهر مُعَجَّل
characteristic(L15)	مِيزة	important(L13)	مُهِمّ
appointment, date(L12)	مِيعاد ج مواعِيدُ	task(L11)	مُهِمَّة ج ـات
birth(day)(L9)	مِيلاد	profession(L22)	مِهْنة ج مِهن
AD; abbr.:م(L10)	مِيلادِيّ	engineer(L8)	مُهنْدِس ج ـون
harbour(L23)	مِيناء ج موانِئُ	dirty, contemptuous(L28)	مَهِين
minibar(L9)	مينيبار	confrontation(L19)	مُواجهة ج ـات
		continuation(L16)	مُواصلة
ن		citizen(L11)	مُواطِن ج ـون
deputy(L16)	نائِب ج نُوّاب	corresponding(L10)	مُوافِق
successful(L21)	ناجِح	wave(L21)	موج ج أمْواج
club(L17)	نادٍ ج أنْدِية ، نوادٍ	existing, available(L8)	مَوْجُود
rare, scarce(L15)	نادِر	wavy(L15)	مَوْجِيّ
the people(L7)	الناس	model(L17)	مُوديل ج ـات
to fit, to suit sth. (L23)	III ناسب (يُناسِبُ) هـ	source(L19)	مَوْرِد ج مواردُ

rareness, scarcity[L15] — نُدْرة / نَدْرة

seminar, colloquium[L20] — نَدْوة ج نَدَوات

Norway[L5] — النُّرويج

to get off, to go down[L22] — نزل (يَنزِلُ نُزُولاً)

women[L12] — نِساء، نِسْوة، نِسْوان

rate, exchange rate[L12] — نِسْبة ج نِسَب

copy[L15] — نُسْخة ج نُسخ

descendant[L28] — نسْل ج أنْسال

person, inhabitant[L21] — نسمة ج نسمات

forget so., sth.[L12] — نسِيَ (ينْـسَى نِسْياناً) ٥، هـ

to come into being, to arise[L24] — نشأ (ينْشأ نُشُوءاً) هـ

publishing[L12] — نشْر

text[L26] — نصّ ج نُصُوص

to define sth.[L27] — نصَّ (ينصُّ نصّاً) على

to add an *a*; accusative[L28] — النصْب

advise so. to do sth., to recommend doing sth.[L8] — نصح (ينْصَحُ نصْحاً) ٥ بِ

half[L15] — نِصْف ج أنْصاف

to pronounce sth.[L28] — نطق (ينطِقُ نُطْقاً) بِ

system, regime[L11] — نِظام ج نُظُم، أنْظِمة

to look at[L7] — نظر (ينظُرُ نظراً) إلى

checking, inspection[L11] — النظَر في

with regard to, as to[L19] — نظراً ل

equivalent[L26] — نظِير ج نظائرُ

counterpart[L8] — نظِير ج نُظراءُ

clean[L2] — نظِيف ج نُظفاءُ

yes[L2] — نَعَمْ

self; soul[L13] — نفْس (م) ج نُفُوس، أنفُس

(him)self[L11] — نفْس ج أنْفس

publisher[L12] — ناشِر ج ون

supporter[L17] — ناصِر ج أنْصار

water-elevator[L23] — ناعُورة ج نواعِيرُ

to discuss sth.[L19] — ناقش (يُناقِشُ) III

minus[L10] — ناقِص

oil tanker[L25] — ناقلة النفط

tanker, transporter[L25] — ناقِلة ج ـات

to sleep, to fall asleep[L11] — نام (ينامُ نوْماً)

mosquito, midge (coll.)[L26] — نامُوس ج نواميسُ

plant[L15] — نبات ج ـات

to bark[L26] — نبح (ينْبَحُ نبْحاً)

prophet, messenger[L10] — نبيّ ج ـون، أنْبِياءُ

wine[L5] — نبِيذ

result, product[L19] — نِتاج

to result from[L19] — نتج (ينْتِجُ نتْجاً) عن

result[L11] — نتِيجة ج نتائِجُ

success[L11] — نجاح ج ـات

to be successful (in)[L11] — نجح (ينْجَحُ نجاحاً) (في)

to result (from)[L15] — نجم (ينْجُمُ نُجُوماً) (عن)

star[L15] — نجْم ج نُجُوم

Najīb Mahfūẓ[L8] — نجيب محفوظ

copper[L25] — نُحاس

brass[L25] — نحاس أصفر

bee[L26] — نحْل (coll.)

we[L2] — نحْنُ

grammar[L24] — النحْو

(prep.) to (direction)[L11] — نحْوَ

grammarian[L24] — نحْويّ ج ـون

elite, selection, choice, *here*: chosen responsibles[L12] — نُخْبة ج نخب

palm tree[L24] — نخيل (coll.)

telephone(L18)	هاتِف ج هواتِفُ	(mineral) oil(L19)	نفْط
to emigrate(L10)	هاجر (يُهاجِر) III	crude oil(L25)	نفْط خام
Hello!(L2)	هالو	expense(s), cost(s)(L25)	نفقة ج ـات
important(L19)	هامٌّ	influence(L17)	نُفوذ
margin(L20)	هامِش ج هوامِشُ	trade union(L23)	نِقابة ج ـات
fan, lover; amateur(L12)	هاوٍ ج هُواة	cash(L19)	نقْداً
to sink, to go down(L15)	هبطَ (يهْبِطُ هُبُوطاً)	sculpture; inscription(L27)	نقْش ج نُقُوش
to leave, to emigrate(L27)	هجر (يهْجُرُ هِجْرةً) هـ	transport(ing)(L17)	نقْل
the Hijra(L10)	الهِجْرة	to transport sth.(L17)	نقل (ينْقُلُ نقْلاً) هـ
of the Hijra(L10)	هِجْريٌّ	live broadcast(L17)	نقل على الهواء
attack(ing)(L17)	هجم (يهْجُمُ هُجُوماً)	according to(L14)	نقْلاً عن
to aim at sth.(L8)	هدف (يهْدُفُ هدْفاً) إلى	joke, anecdote(L25)	نُكْتة ج نُكَت، نِكات
goal; aim(L17)	هدف ج أهْداف	to grow, to develop(L27)	نما (ينْمُو نُموّاً)
present(L14)	هدِية ج هدايا	Austria(L5)	النِّمْسا
this(L2)	هذا	growing(L15)	نُمُو
this, these(L7)	هذا م هذِهِ ج هؤلاءِ	model, sample, pattern(L20)	نمُوذج ج نماذِجُ
this (f.)(L2)	هذِهِ	final(L17)	نِهائيٌّ
to escape from, to(L25)	هرب (يهْرُبُ هُرُوباً) من، إلى	day(L15)	نهار ج أنْهُر
to escape from justice(L25)	هرب عن وجه العدالة	end(L10)	نِهاية
hormone(L17)	هُرْمُون ج ـات	method; way(L18)	نهْج ج نهُوج
defeat(L17)	هزيمة ج هزائِمُ	river(L24)	نهْر ج أنْهار
raining(L15)	هُطُول المطر	to bring about an upswing(L22)	نهض (ينْهَضُ نُهُوضاً) ب
like this, this way, thus(L6)	هكذا	upswing(L20)	نهْضة
interrogative particle(L2)	هَل	upswing(L21)	نهْضة ج ـات
they (3rd p.pl.m.)(L2)	هُمْ	swinging-up of(L20)	نُهُوض بِ
they (3rd p.pl.f.)(L2)	هُنَّ	kind, sort, type, species(L17)	نوْع ج أنْواع
(answer after!(L7) هنيئاً مريئاً!)	هنّاك الله!	sleeping(L2)	نوْم
here(L2)	هُنا	to intend (to do) sth.(L21)	نوَى (ينْوِي نِيَّةً) هـ
there is / are(L6)	هُناك	**هـ**	
there(L2)	هُناكَ	huge, giant(L24)	هائِل
		Give!(L2)	هات

to have to, must (L9)	وجب (يجِبُ وجْباً) (عليه) أنْ
meal, dish (L7)	وجْبة ج وجَبات
to find sth. (L11)	وجد (يجِد وجْداً) هـ
face, aspect (L24)	وجه ج وُجُوه
face (L17)	وجْه ج وُجُوه
existence (L27)	وُجُود
he/she alone; (L27)	وحْدَهُ / وحْدَها
say good-bye to (L23)	II ودَّع (يُودِّعُ)
(prep.) behind, beyond (L24)	وراءَ
paper (L2)	ورق ج أوْراق (coll.)
Treasury (Department) (L16)	وزارة المالية
ministry (L8)	وزارة ج ات
weight (L23)	وزْن ج أوْزان
Minister of Foreign Affairs (L14)	وزير الخارجيّة
Minister of the Interior (L14)	وزير الداخِليّة
minister (L8)	وزير ج وُزراءُ
order, medal (L17)	وِسام ج أوْسِمة
dirty (L2)	وسخ
middle, centre (L19)	وسط ج أوْساط
ability, strength, power (L21)	وُسْع
instrument, means (L26)	وسيلة ج وسائِلُ
hurry (L22)	وَشْك/ وُشْك
to prescribe sth. for so. (L13)	وصف (يصِفُ وصْفاً) له هـ
description (L24)	وصْف ج أوْصاف
prescription (L14)	وصْفة ج وصَفات
to arrive (at, in) (L5)	وصل (يصِلُ وُصُولاً) (إلى)
to bring sth., so. to (L18)	II وصَّل (يُوصِّلُ) ه/ هـ إلى
receipt (L16)	وصْل ج وُصُولات
situation (L11)	وضْع ج أوْضاع

India (L15)	الهِند
engineering (L10)	هِنْدسة
Indian (L9)	هِنْدِي ج هُنُود
I hope you will enjoy it. (the food) (L7)	هنِيئاً مَرِيئاً!
he (L2)	هُوَ
air (L15)	هواء ج أهْوِية، أهْواء
hobby (L16)	هِواية ج ـات
Holland (L5)	هُوْلْندا
identity (L19)	هُويّة
she (L2)	هِيَ
board, body (L11)	هيْئة ج ـات
(interj.) Let us go to ... (L26)	هيّا بِنا إلى ...

و

and (L2)	وَ
The same to you. (answer after تصبح على خير!) (L5)	وَأنت من أهْلِهِ
duty, task (L14)	واجب ج ـات
to be confronted with so., sth. (L20)	III واجه (يُواجِهُ) ه، هـ
oasis (L15)	واحة ج ـات
wadi (L15)	وادٍ ج أوْدِية، وِدْيان
occurring (in) (L13)	وارد (في)
wide (L8)	واسِع
to continue sth. (L14)	III واصل (يُواصِلُ) هـ
clear, obvious (L8)	واضح
to agree to (L20)	III وافق (يُوافِقُ) على
to keep pace with, to keep abreast of (L22)	III واكب (يُواكِبُ) هـ
father (L18)	والِد
by God (L2)	واللهِ

to lay the foundations of^(L22)	وضع حجر الأساس

to lay the foundations of^(L22) — وضع حجر الأساس

ى

hopeless^(L22)	يائِس
Japanese^(L2)	يابانيّ
Let's go!^(L22)	يا ا الله (colloq.)
Yathrib (Medina)^(L10)	يَثرِبُ
hand^(L13)	يد (م) ج أيدٍ ، أيادٍ
to be asked^(L18)	يُرْجَى
left (side)^(L4)	يسار
equals^(L10)	يُساوي
to facilitate sth. for so.^(L28)	II يسَّرَ (يُيَسِّرُ) هـ لِ
I am happy that …^(L18)	يسُرُّني … أنْ
equals^(L10)	يُعادِلُ
that means^(L4)	يَعْني
one can (+ verbal noun)^(L10)	يُمْكِنُ الـ… .
he/she is able to …^(L14)	يُمْكِنُهُ / يُمْكِنُهَا أنْ …
Yemen^(L3)	اليَمَن
right (side)^(L4)	يمين
there is^(L2)	يُوجَدُ / تُوجَدُ
today^(L3)	اليَوْمَ
day^(L3)	يَوْم ج أيّام
Sunday^(L9)	يوم الأحد
Monday^(L9)	يوم الاثنين
Tuesday^(L9)	يوم الثلاثاء
Wednesday^(L9)	يوم الأربعاء
Thursday^(L9)	يوم الخميس
Friday^(L9)	يوم الجمعة
Saturday^(L9)	يوم السبت
daily^(L9)	يَوْميّاً

to put sth.^(L5)	وضع هـ
heaviness^(L15)	وطْأة
home country^(L5)	وطن ج أوْطان
national^(L8)	وطنيّ
to promise so. sth.^(L12)	وعد (يعِدُ وعْداً) ه ب
promise^(L12)	وعْد ج وُعُود
death^(L14)	وفاة ج وفيات
to come (to)^(L27)	وفد (يفِدُ) إلى
delegation^(L5)	وفْد ج وُفُود
fullness, wealth, abundance^(L25)	وفرة
to keep (a promise)^(L12)	وفَى (يفِي) بـ
impudence, impertinence^(L26)	وقاحة
opening times, time of duty^(L16)	وقت الدوام
time, period of time^(L6)	وقْت ج أوْقات
to lie (geogr.); to fall^(L12)	وقع (يقَعُ وُقُوعاً)
to sign sth.^(L16)	II وقَّع (يُوقِّعُ) على
to stand in front of^(L11)	وقف (يقِفُ وُقُوفاً) أمام
fuel^(L19)	وَقُود
news agency^(L8)	وَكالةُ أنْباء ج ـات
(Under) Secretary of State, Permanent Secretary^(L11)	وكيل الدولة
representative, agent^(L11)	وكيل ج وُكلاءُ
son, child^(L16)	ولد ج أوْلاد
I was born^(L9)	وُلِدتُ
even if^(L26)	وَلَوْ
to come after^(L13)	وليَ (يَلِي ولايةً)
(legal) guardian^(L27)	وليّ ج أوْلِياءُ

THE NUMERALS
1. The Cardinal Numerals

	in connection with a feminine noun		in connection with a masculine noun	
1	واحِدة، إحْدَى		واحِد، أَحَد	١
2	اِثْنتان		اِثْنان	٢
3	ثلاث		ثلاثة	٣
4	أَرْبع		أَرْبعة	٤
5	خَمْس		خَمْسة	٥
6	سِتّ		سِتّة	٦
7	سَبْع		سَبْعة	٧
8	ثمان (ثماني)		ثمانِيَة	٨
9	تِسْع		تِسْعة	٩
10	عَشْر		عَشَرة	١٠
11	إحْدَى عَشْرَةَ		أَحَدَ عَشَرَ	١١
12	اِثْنتا عَشْرَةَ		اِثْنا عَشَرَ	١٢
13	ثلاثَ عَشْرَةَ		ثلاثةَ عَشَرَ	١٣
14	أَرْبعَ عَشْرَةَ		أَرْبعةَ عَشَرَ	١٤
15	خَمْسَ عشْرَةَ		خَمْسةَ عَشَرَ	١٥
16	سِتَّ عَشْرَةَ		سِتّةَ عَشَرَ	١٦
17	سَبْعَ عشْرَةَ		سَبْعةَ عَشَرَ	١٧
18	ثمانِيَ عشْرَةَ		ثمانِيةَ عَشَرَ	١٨
19	تِسْعَ عَشْرَةَ		تِسْعةَ عَشَرَ	١٩
20	عِشْرُونَ			٢٠
21	إحْدَى وعِشْرُون		واحِدٌ / أَحَدٌ وعِشْرُون	٢١
22	اِثْنتان وعِشْرُون		اِثْنان وعِشْرُون	٢٢
23	ثلاثٌ وعِشْرُون		ثلاثةٌ وعِشْرُون	٢٣
30	ثلاثون			٣٠

40		أَرْبَعون		٤٠
50		خَمْسون		٥٠
60		سِتّون		٦٠
70		سَبْعون		٧٠
80		ثَمانون		٨٠
90		تِسْعون		٩٠
100		مِئة، مِائَة		١٠٠
101	مئة وواحدة		مئة وواحد	١٠١
102	مئة واثْنتان		مئة واثنانِ	١٠٢
103	مئة وثلاث		مئة وثلاثة	١٠٣
200		مئتا(ن)		٢٠٠
300		ثلاثُمائة		٣٠٠
1000		أَلْف ج آلاف		١٠٠٠
1001	أَلْف وواحدة		أَلْف وواحد	١٠٠١
1002	أَلْف واثْنتان		أَلْف واثْنانِ	١٠٠٢
1003	أَلْف وثلاث		أَلْف وثلاثة	١٠٠٣
1100		أَلْف ومئة		١١٠٠
1200		أَلْف ومئتا(ن)ِ		١٢٠٠
1300		أَلْف وثلاثُمائة		١٣٠٠
2000		أَلْفا(ن)		٢٠٠٠
3000		ثلاثةُ آلاف		٣٠٠٠
10 000		عَشْرَةُ آلاف		١٠٠٠٠
11 000		أَحَدَ عَشَرَ أَلْف(اً)		١١٠٠٠
100 000		مئة أَلْفٍ		١٠٠٠٠٠
200 000		مئتا أَلْفٍ		٢٠٠٠٠٠
1 000 000		مَلْيون ج ملايينُ		١٠٠٠٠٠٠
1 000 000 000		مِلْيار ج مِلْيارات		١٠٠٠٠٠٠٠٠٠

2. The Ordinal Numerals

1st	أوَّل م أُولَى
2nd	ثانٍ (الثاني) م ثانِيَة
3rd	ثالِث م ثالِثة
4th	رابِع م رابعة
5th	خامِس م خامِسة
6th	سادِس م سادِسة
7th	سابِع م سابعة
8th	ثامِن م ثامِنة
9th	تاسِع م تاسِعة
10th	عاشِر م عاشِرة
11th	حادِي عَشَرَ م حادِية عَشْرَةَ
12th	ثانِيَ عَشَرَ م ثانِية عَشْرَةَ
13th	ثالِثَ عَشَرَ م ثالِثة عَشْرَةَ
14th	رابِع عَشَرَ م رابعة عَشْرَةَ
15th	خامِسَ عَشَرَ م خامِسة عَشْرَةَ
16th	سادِسَ عَشَرَ م سادِسة عَشْرَةَ
17th	سابِعَ عَشَرَ م سابعة عَشْرَةَ
18th	ثامِنَ عَشَرَ م ثامِنة عَشْرَةَ
19th	تاسِعَ عَشَرَ م تاسِعة عَشْرَةَ
20th	عِشْرونَ
21st	حادٍ وعِشْرونَ (الحادِي والعِشْرونَ) م حادِية وعِشْرونَ
22nd	ثانٍ وعِشْرونَ (الثاني والعِشْرونَ) م ثانِية وعِشْرونَ
23rd	ثالِث وعِشْرونَ م ثالِثة وعِشْرونَ
30th	ثلاثونَ
40th	أربعونَ
100th	مِئة، مِائة

101st	مئة وواحِد(ة)، أوَّل (أُولَى) بَعْدَ المِئَةِ
102nd	مئة واثْنان (اثْنَتان)، ثان (ثانِيَة) بَعْدَ المِئَةِ
103rd	مئة وثلاث(ة)، ثالِث(ة) بَعْدَ المِئَةِ
1000th	ألف
1100th	ألف ومئة، مئة بعد الألف

3. The Numeral Adverbs

sixth	سادِساً	first	أوَّلاً
seventh	سابِعاً	second	ثانِياً
eighth	ثامِناً	third	ثالِثاً
ninth	تاسِعاً	fourth	رابِعاً
tenth	عاشِراً	fifth	خامِساً

4. The Fractions

خُمْس ج أخماس	1/5	نِصْف	1/2
أربعةُ أخماسٍ	4/5	ثُلْث ج أثلاث	1/3
سُدْس ج أسْداس	1/6	ثُلْثان(ن)	2/3
خَمسةُ أسْداسٍ	5/6	رُبْع ج أرْباع	1/4
سِتّةُ أسْباعٍ	6/7	ثلاثةُ أرْباع	3/4
سبعة على اثْنَيْ عَشَرَ، سبعةُ أجْزاء من اثْنَيْ عَشَرَ			7/12
تِسْعة على عِشْرينَ، تِسعةُ أجْزاء من عِشْرينَ			9/20

5. The Numeral Adverbs of Reiteration

four times	أرْبعَ مرَّاتٍ	once	مرَّةً واحِدَةً
eleven times	إحْدَى عَشْرَةَ مرَّةً	twice	مرَّتَيْنِ
a hundred times	مِئةَ مرَّةٍ	three times	ثلاثَ مرَّاتٍ

6. The Decimal Numbers

3.9	٣ر٩	ثلاثةٌ فاصِلةٌ تسعةٌ / ثلاثةٌ فاصِلةٌ تسعةٌ من عشرةٍ
4.25	٤ر٢٥	أربعةٌ فاصِلةٌ خمسةٌ وعشرون / أربعة فاصِلةٌ خمسةٌ وعشرون من مئةٍ
7.123	٧ر١٢٣	سبعةٌ فاصِلةٌ مئةٌ وعشرون / سبعة فاصِلةٌ مئةٌ وثلاثةٌ وعشرون من ألفٍ

THE MONTHS OF THE ISLAMIC CALENDAR

The basic unit of the Islamic year is a "moon year". It consists of twelve months with alternating 30 and 29 days. The duration of a moon year is about 354 days.

The Islamic calendar starts with the 16th of July of the "sun year" 622, the year of the *Hijra* of the Prophet Mohammed from Mecca to Medina.

The names of the twelve months of the Islamic calendar are as follows:

number of days	name of month	number of month	number of days	name of month	number of month
(30)	رجبٌ	7th	(30)	مُحَرَّمٌ	1st
(29)	شعْبانُ	8th	(29)	صَفَرٌ	2nd
(30)	رمضانُ	9th	(30)	ربيع الأوَّل	3rd
(29)	شوَّالٌ	10th	(29)	ربيع الثاني	4th
(30)	ذو القَعْدةِ	11th	(30)	جُمادَى الأُولَى	5th
(29)	ذو الحِجَّةِ	12th	(29)	جُمادَى الآخِرة	6th

The last month of the year, which consists of 30 days in leap years, is the month of the pilgrimage to Mecca.

The two main holidays of the Islamic year are:

العِيد الكبير، عيد الأضْحَى

"the Feast of Immolation, or Greater Bairam" on 10th of *Dū l-Ḥijja* and

عِيد الفِطْر

"the Feast of Breaking the *Ramaḍān* Fast", also called العِيد الصغير "the Minor Feast, or Lesser Bairam" on the 1st of *Shawwāl*.

The following approximate calculations can be used to transform *Hijra* (moon) years (H) into Gregorian (sun) years (G) and vice versa.

$$G = H - \frac{H}{33} + 622$$

$$H = G - 622 + \frac{G - 622}{32}$$

TABLES OF THE FORMS OF THE VERBS AND THE NOUNS

Table 1 Perfect Active: Form I

R₃ ء	R₂ ء	R₁ ء	R₂=R₃	R₃ ى	R₃ ى	R₃ و	R₂ و	R₂ ى	R₂ و	R₁ ى	R₁ و	faʿala	
قَرَأَ	سَأَلَ	أَخَذَ	مَرَّ	لَقِيَ	مَشَى	دَعَا	خَافَ	بَاعَ	قَامَ	يَسِرَ	وَصَلَ	فَعَلَ	(هو)
قَرَأَتْ	سَأَلَتْ	أَخَذَتْ	مَرَّتْ	لَقِيَتْ	مَشَتْ	دَعَتْ	خَافَتْ	بَاعَتْ	قَامَتْ	يَسِرَتْ	وَصَلَتْ	فَعَلَتْ	(هي)
قَرَأْتَ	سَأَلْتَ	أَخَذْتَ	مَرَرْتَ	لَقِيتَ	مَشَيْتَ	دَعَوْتَ	خِفْتَ	بِعْتَ	قُمْتَ	يَسِرْتَ	وَصَلْتَ	فَعَلْتَ	(أنتَ)
قَرَأْتِ	سَأَلْتِ	أَخَذْتِ	مَرَرْتِ	لَقِيتِ	مَشَيْتِ	دَعَوْتِ	خِفْتِ	بِعْتِ	قُمْتِ	يَسِرْتِ	وَصَلْتِ	فَعَلْتِ	(أنتِ)
قَرَأْتُ	سَأَلْتُ	أَخَذْتُ	مَرَرْتُ	لَقِيتُ	مَشَيْتُ	دَعَوْتُ	خِفْتُ	بِعْتُ	قُمْتُ	يَسِرْتُ	وَصَلْتُ	فَعَلْتُ	(أنا)
قَرَؤُوا	سَأَلُوا	أَخَذُوا	مَرُّوا	لَقُوا	مَشَوْا	دَعَوْا	خَافُوا	بَاعُوا	قَامُوا	يَسِرُوا	وَصَلُوا	فَعَلُوا	(هم)
قَرَأْنَ	سَأَلْنَ	أَخَذْنَ	مَرَرْنَ	لَقِينَ	مَشَيْنَ	دَعَوْنَ	خِفْنَ	بِعْنَ	قُمْنَ	يَسِرْنَ	وَصَلْنَ	فَعَلْنَ	(هنَّ)
قَرَأْتُمْ	سَأَلْتُمْ	أَخَذْتُمْ	مَرَرْتُمْ	لَقِيتُمْ	مَشَيْتُمْ	دَعَوْتُمْ	خِفْتُمْ	بِعْتُمْ	قُمْتُمْ	يَسِرْتُمْ	وَصَلْتُمْ	فَعَلْتُمْ	(أنتم)
قَرَأْتُنَّ	سَأَلْتُنَّ	أَخَذْتُنَّ	مَرَرْتُنَّ	لَقِيتُنَّ	مَشَيْتُنَّ	دَعَوْتُنَّ	خِفْتُنَّ	بِعْتُنَّ	قُمْتُنَّ	يَسِرْتُنَّ	وَصَلْتُنَّ	فَعَلْتُنَّ	(أنتنَّ)
قَرَأْنَا	سَأَلْنَا	أَخَذْنَا	مَرَرْنَا	لَقِينَا	مَشَيْنَا	دَعَوْنَا	خِفْنَا	بِعْنَا	قُمْنَا	يَسِرْنَا	وَصَلْنَا	فَعَلْنَا	(نحن)
قَرَآ	سَأَلَا	أَخَذَا	مَرَّا	لَقِيَا	مَشَيَا	دَعَوَا	خَافَا	بَاعَا	قَامَا	يَسِرَا	وَصَلَا	فَعَلَا	(هما)
قَرَأَتَا	سَأَلَتَا	أَخَذَتَا	مَرَّتَا	لَقِيَتَا	مَشَتَا	دَعَتَا	خَافَتَا	بَاعَتَا	قَامَتَا	يَسِرَتَا	وَصَلَتَا	فَعَلَتَا	(هما)
قَرَأْتُمَا	سَأَلْتُمَا	أَخَذْتُمَا	مَرَرْتُمَا	لَقِيتُمَا	مَشَيْتُمَا	دَعَوْتُمَا	خِفْتُمَا	بِعْتُمَا	قُمْتُمَا	يَسِرْتُمَا	وَصَلْتُمَا	فَعَلْتُمَا	(أنتما)

Table 2 Imperfect Indicative Active: Form I

R_3 ع	R_2 ع	R_1 ع	$R_2=R_3$	R_3 ي	R_3 ي	R_3 و	R_2 و	R_2 ي	R_2 و	R_1 ي	R_1 و	faʿala	

463

Table 3 Imperfect Subjunctive Active: Form I

	R_3 ع	R_2 ع	R_1 ع	$R_2=R_3$	R_3 ي	R_3 ي	R_3 و	R_2 و	R_2 ي	R_2 و	R_1 ي	R_1 و	faʿala	

Table 4 Imperfect Jussive Active: Form I

R_3 ع	R_2 ع	R_1 ع	$R_2=R_3$	R_3 ي	R_3 ي	R_3 و	R_2 و	R_2 ي	R_2 و	R_1 ي	R_1 و	faʿala	

Table 5 Perfect Active: Form I-X

	faʿala	R₁و	R₁ي	R₂و	R₂ي	R₂و	R₃و	R₃ي	R₃ي	R₂=R₃	R₁ء	R₂ء	R₃ء
I	فَعَلَ	وَعَدَ	يَسَرَ	قَالَ	بَاعَ	غَزَا	رَمَى			مَدَّ	أَكَلَ	سَأَلَ	قَرَأَ
II	فَعَّلَ	وَعَّدَ	يَسَّرَ	قَوَّلَ	بَيَّعَ	غَزَّى	رَمَّى			مَدَّدَ	أَكَّلَ	سَأَّلَ	قَرَّأَ
III	فَاعَلَ	وَاعَدَ	يَاسَرَ	قَاوَلَ	بَايَعَ	غَازَى	رَامَى			مَادَّ	آكَلَ	سَاءَلَ	قَارَأَ
IV	أَفْعَلَ	أَوْعَدَ	أَيْسَرَ	أَقَالَ	أَبَاعَ	أَغْزَى	أَرْمَى			أَمَدَّ	آكَلَ	أَسْأَلَ	أَقْرَأَ
V	تَفَعَّلَ	تَوَعَّدَ	تَيَسَّرَ	تَقَوَّلَ	تَبَيَّعَ	تَغَزَّى	تَرَمَّى			تَمَدَّدَ	تَأَكَّلَ	تَسَأَّلَ	تَقَرَّأَ
VI	تَفَاعَلَ	تَوَاعَدَ	تَيَاسَرَ	تَقَاوَلَ	تَبَايَعَ	تَغَازَى	تَرَامَى			تَمَادَّ	تَآكَلَ	تَسَاءَلَ	تَقَارَأَ
VII	اِنْفَعَلَ	اِنْوَعَدَ	—	اِنْقَالَ	اِنْبَاعَ	اِنْغَزَى	اِنْرَمَى			اِنْمَدَّ	—	—	—
VIII	اِفْتَعَلَ	اِتَّعَدَ	اِتَّسَرَ	اِقْتَالَ	اِبْتَاعَ	اِغْتَزَى	اِرْتَمَى			اِمْتَدَّ	اِئْتَكَلَ	اِسْتَأَلَ	اِقْتَرَأَ
X	اِسْتَفْعَلَ	اِسْتَوْعَدَ	اِسْتَيْسَرَ	اِسْتَقَالَ	اِسْتَبَاعَ	اِسْتَغْزَى	اِسْتَرْمَى			اِسْتَمَدَّ	اِسْتَأْكَلَ	اِسْتَسْأَلَ	اِسْتَقْرَأَ

1 See Lesson 18 for the rules for the assimilation of the infix *t-* to R₁.

Table 6 Imperfect Indicative Active: Form I-X

	faʿala	R_1 و	R_1 ى	R_2 و	R_2 ى	R_2 و	R_3 و	R_3 ى	R_3 ى	$R_2 = R_3$	R_1 ع	R_2 ع	R_3 ع
I													
II													
III													
IV													
V													
VI													
VII													
VIII													
X													

---

1 See Lesson 18 for the rules for the assimilation of the infix *t-* to R_1.

Table 7 Perfect Passive: Form I-X 468

R₃ ء	R₂ ء	R₁ ء	R₂=R₃	R₃ ى	R₃ ى	R₃ و	R₂ و	R₂ ى	R₂ و	R₁ ى	R₁ و	faʿala	
قُرِئَ	سُئِلَ	أُخِذَ	مُرَّ	لُقِيَ	مُشِيَ	دُعِيَ	خِيفَ	بِيعَ	قِيمَ	يُئِسَ	وُصِلَ	فُعِلَ	I
قُرِّئَ	سُئِّلَ	أُخِّذَ	مُرِّرَ	لُقِّيَ	مُشِّيَ	دُعِّيَ	خُوِّفَ	بُيِّعَ	قُوِّمَ	يُئِّسَ	وُصِّلَ	فُعِّلَ	II
قُورِئَ	سُوئِلَ	أُوخِذَ	مُورِرَ	لُوقِيَ	مُوشِيَ	دُوعِيَ	خُووِفَ	بُويِعَ	قُووِمَ	يُوئِسَ	وُوصِلَ	فُوعِلَ	III
أُقْرِئَ	أُسْئِلَ	أُوخِذَ	أُمِرَّ	أُلْقِيَ	أُمْشِيَ	أُدْعِيَ	أُخِيفَ	أُبِيعَ	أُقِيمَ	أُوبِسَ	أُوصِلَ	أُفْعِلَ	IV
تُقُرِّئَ	تُسُئِّلَ	تُؤُخِّذَ	تُمُرِّرَ	تُلُقِّيَ	تُمُشِّيَ	تُدُعِّيَ	تُخُوِّفَ	تُبُيِّعَ	تُقُوِّمَ	تُيُئِّسَ	تُوُصِّلَ	تُفُعِّلَ	V
تُقُورِئَ	تُسُوئِلَ	تُؤُوخِذَ	تُمُورِرَ	تُلُوقِيَ	تُمُوشِيَ	تُدُوعِيَ	تُخُووِفَ	تُبُويِعَ	تُقُوومَ	تُيُوبِسَ	تُوُوصِلَ	تُفُوعِلَ	VI
انْقُرِئَ	انْسُئِلَ		انْمُرَّ	انْلُقِيَ	انْمُشِيَ	انْدُعِيَ	انْخِيفَ	انْبِيعَ	انْقِيمَ			انْفُعِلَ	VII
اقْتُرِئَ	اسْتُئِلَ	اتُّخِذَ	امْتُرَّ	الْتُقِيَ	امْتُشِيَ	ادُّعِيَ ¹	اخْتِيفَ	ابْتِيعَ	اقْتِيمَ	اتُّبِسَ	اتُّصِلَ	افْتُعِلَ	VIII
اسْتُقْرِئَ	اسْتُسْئِلَ	اسْتُؤْخِذَ	اسْتُمِرَّ	اسْتُلْقِيَ	اسْتُمْشِيَ	اسْتُدْعِيَ	اسْتُخِيفَ	اسْتُبِيعَ	اسْتُقِيمَ	اسْتُوبِسَ	اسْتُوصِلَ	اسْتُفْعِلَ	X

---

¹

See Lesson 18 for the rules for the assimilation of the infix *t-* to R₁.

Table 8 Imperfect Indicative Passive: Form I-X

	R₃ ء	R₂ ء	R₁ ء	R₂=R₃	R₃ ى	R₃ ى	R₃ و	R₂ و	R₂ ى	R₂ و	R₁ ى	R₁ و	faʿala	
	يُقْرَأُ	يُسْأَلُ	يُؤْخَذُ	يُمَرُّ	يُلْقَى	يُمْشَى	يُدْعَى	يُخَافُ	يُبَاعُ	يُقَامُ	يُوبَسُ	يُوصَلُ	يُفْعَلُ	I
	يُقَرَّأُ	يُسَأَّلُ	يُؤَخَّذُ	يُمَرَّرُ	يُلَقَّى	يُمَشَّى	يُدَعَّى	يُخَوَّفُ	يُبَيَّعُ	يُقَوَّمُ	يُيَبَّسُ	يُوصَّلُ	يُفَعَّلُ	II
	يُقَارَأُ	يُسَاءَلُ	يُؤَاخَذُ	يُمَارُّ	يُلاَقَى	يُمَاشَى	يُدَاعَى	يُخَاوَفُ	يُبَايَعُ	يُقَاوَمُ	يُيَابَسُ	يُوَاصَلُ	يُفَاعَلُ	III
	يُقْرَأُ	يُسْأَلُ	يُؤْخَذُ	يُمَرُّ	يُلْقَى	يُمْشَى	يُدْعَى	يُخَافُ	يُبَاعُ	يُقَامُ	يُوبَسُ	يُوصَلُ	يُفْعَلُ	IV
	يُتَقَرَّأُ	يُتَسَأَّلُ	يُتَأَخَّذُ	يُتَمَرَّرُ	يُتَلَقَّى	يُتَمَشَّى	يُتَدَعَّى	يُتَخَوَّفُ	يُتَبَيَّعُ	يُتَقَوَّمُ	يُتَيَبَّسُ	يُتَوَصَّلُ	يُتَفَعَّلُ	V
	يُتَقَارَأُ	يُتَسَاءَلُ	يُتَأَخَذُ	يُتَمَارُّ	يُتَلاَقَى	يُتَمَاشَى	يُتَدَاعَى	يُتَخَاوَفُ	يُتَبَايَعُ	يُتَقَاوَمُ	يُتَيَابَسُ	يُتَوَاصَلُ	يُتَفَاعَلُ	VI
	يُنْقَرَأُ	يُنْسَألُ		يُنْمَرُّ	يُنْلَقَى	يُنْمَشَى	يُنْدَعَى	يُنْخَافُ	يُنْبَاعُ	يُنْقَامُ			يُنْفَعَلُ	VII
	يُقْتَرَأُ	يُسْتَألُ	يُتَّخَذُ	يُمْتَرُّ	يُلْتَقَى	يُمْتَشَى	يُدَّعَى ١	يُخْتَافُ	يُبْتَاعُ	يُقْتَامُ	يُتَّبَسُ	يُتَّصَلُ	يُفْتَعَلُ	VIII
	يُسْتَقْرَأُ	يُسْتَسْألُ	يُسْتَأْخَذُ	يُسْتَمَرُّ	يُسْتَلْقَى	يُسْتَمْشَى	يُسْتَدْعَى	يُسْتَخَافُ	يُسْتَبَاعُ	يُسْتَقَامُ	يُسْتَيَبَسُ	يُسْتَوْصَلُ	يُسْتَفْعَلُ	X

See Lesson 18 for the rules for the assimilation of the infix *t*- to R₁.

Table 9 Imperative: Form I-X 470

R₃ ء	R₂ ء	R₁ ء	R₂=R₃	R₃ ى	R₃ ى	R₃ و	R₂ و	R₂ ى	R₂ و	R₁ ى	R₁ و	faʿala	
اِقْرَأْ	اِسْأَلْ	خُذْ ¹	مُرَّ/اُمْرُرْ	اِلْقَ	اِمْشِ	اُدْعُ	خَفْ	بِعْ	قُمْ	اِيئَسْ	صِلْ	اِفْعَلْ	(أَنتَ)
اِقْرَئِي	اِسْأَلِي	خُذِي	مُرِّي	اِلْقَيْ	اِمْشِي	اُدْعِي	خَافِي	بِيعِي	قُومِي	اِيئَسِي	صِلِي	اِفْعَلِي	(أَنتِ)
اِقْرَؤُوا	اِسْأَلُوا	خُذُوا	مُرُّوا	اِلْقَوْا	اِمْشُوا	اُدْعُوا	خَافُوا	بِيعُوا	قُومُوا	اِيئَسُوا	صِلُوا	اِفْعَلُوا	(أَنتم)
اِقْرَأْنَ	اِسْأَلْنَ	خُذْنَ	اُمْرُرْنَ	اِلْقَيْنَ	اِمْشِينَ	اُدْعُونَ	خَفْنَ	بِعْنَ	قُمْنَ	اِيئَسْنَ	صِلْنَ	اِفْعَلْنَ	(أَنتنَّ)
اِقْرَآ	اِسْأَلَا	خُذَا	مُرَّا	اِلْقَيَا	اِمْشِيَا	اُدْعُوَا	خَافَا	بِيعَا	قُومَا	اِيئَسَا	صِلَا	اِفْعَلَا	(أَنتما)
قَرِّئْ	سَئِّلْ	أَخِّذْ	مَرِّرْ	لَقِّ	مَشِّ	دَعِّ	خَوِّفْ	بَيِّعْ	قَوِّمْ	يَئِّسْ	وَصِّلْ	فَعِّلْ	II
قَارِىءْ	سَائِلْ	آخِذْ	مَارِّ/مَارِرْ	لَاقِ	مَاشِ	دَاعِ	خَاوِفْ	بَايِعْ	قَاوِمْ	يَابِسْ	وَاصِلْ	فَاعِلْ	III
أَقْرِىءْ	أَسْئِلْ	آخِذْ	أَمِرَّ/أَمْرِرْ	أَلْقِ	أَمْشِ	أَدْعِ	أَخِفْ	أَبِعْ	أَقِمْ	أَيْئِسْ	أَوْصِلْ	أَفْعِلْ	IV
تَقَرَّأْ	تَسَأَّلْ	تَأَخَّذْ	تَمَرَّرْ	تَلَقَّ	تَمَشَّ	تَدَعَّ	تَخَوَّفْ	تَبَيَّعْ	تَقَوَّمْ	تَيَبَّسْ	تَوَصَّلْ	تَفَعَّلْ	V
تَقَارَأْ	تَسَاءَلْ	تَآخَذْ	تَمَارَّ/تَمَارَرْ	تَلَاقَ	تَمَاشَ	تَدَاعَ	تَخَاوَفْ	تَبَايَعْ	تَقَاوَمْ	تَيَابَسْ	تَوَاصَلْ	تَفَاعَلْ	VI
اِنْقَرِىءْ	اِنْسَئِلْ	-	اِنْمَرَّ/اِنْمَرِرْ	اِنْلَقِ	اِنْمَشِ	اِنْدَعِ	اِنْخَفْ	اِنْبَعْ	اِنْقَمْ	-	-	اِنْفَعِلْ	VII
اِقْتَرِىءْ	اِسْتَئِلْ	اِتَّخِذْ	اِمْتَرَّ/اِمْتَرِرْ	اِلْتَقِ	اِمْتَشِ	اِدَّعِ ²	اِخْتَفْ	اِبْتَعْ	اِقْتَمْ	اِتَّبِسْ	اِتَّصِلْ	اِفْتَعِلْ	VIII
اِسْتَقْرِىءْ	اِسْتَسْئِلْ	اِسْتَأْخِذْ	اِسْتَمِرَّ/اِسْتَمْرِرْ	اِسْتَلْقِ	اِسْتَمْشِ	اِسْتَدْعِ	اِسْتَخِفْ	اِسْتَبِعْ	اِسْتَقِمْ	اِسْتَيْئِسْ	اِسْتَوْصِلْ	اِسْتَفْعِلْ	X

---

¹The verbs أَخَذَ "to take", أَكَلَ "to eat" and أَمَرَ "to order" form the imperative without prothetic vowel. The other verbs R₁ = *Hamza* have a regular imperative, e.g. أَمُلَ > اُؤْمُلْ "hope!".

² See Lesson 18 for the rules for the assimilation of the infix *t*- to R₁.

Table 10 Active Participle: Form I-X

471

	fa'ala	R₁ و	R₁ ي	R₂ و	R₂ ي	R₂ و	R₃ و	R₃ ي	R₃ ي	R₂=R₃	R₁ ع	R₂ ع	R₃ ع
I	فَاعِل	وَاعِد	يَاسِر	قَائِل	بَائِع		غَازٍ			جَارّ	آخِذ	سَائِل	قَارِئ
II													
III													
IV													
V													
VI													
VII													
VIII													
X													

---

1 See Table 37.

2 See Lesson 18 for the rules for the assimilation of the infix *t-* to R₁.

Table 11 Passive Participle: Form I-X

	I	II	III	IV	V	VI	VII	VIII	X
fa'ala									
R₁ و						-			
R₁ ي						-			
R₂ و									
R₂ ي									
R₂ و									
R₃ و									
R₃ ي									
R₃ ي									
R₂=R₃									
R₁ ع						-			
R₂ ع									
R₃ ع									

---

1 See Table 37.

2 See Lesson 18 for the rules for the assimilation of the infix *t-* to R₁.

472

Table 12 Infinitive: Form I-X

R₃ ء	R₂ ء	R₁ ء	R₂=R₃	R₃ ى	R₃ ى	R₃ و	R₂ و	R₂ ى	R₂ و	R₁ ى	R₁ و	faʿala	
						Form I irregular							I
تَقْرِئَة	تَسْئِيل	تَأْخِيذ	تَمْرِير	تَلْقِيَة	تَمْشِيَة	تَدْعِيَة	تَخْوِيف	تَبْيِيع	تَقْوِيم	تَيْبِيس	تَوْصِيل	تَفْعِيل	II
مُقَارَأَة	مُسَاءَلَة	مُؤَاخَذَة	مُمَارَّة	مُلَاقَاة	مُمَاشَاة	مُدَاعَاة	مُخَاوَفَة	مُبَايَعَة	مُقَاوَمَة	مُيَابَسَة	مُوَاصَلَة	مُفَاعَلَة	III
قِرَاء	سِئَال	إخَاذ	مِرَار	لِقَاء	مِشَاء	دِعَاء	خِوَاف	بِيَاع	قِوَام	يِيَاس	وِصَال	فِعَال	
إقْرَاء	إسْآل	إيخَاذ	إمْرَار	إلْقَاء	إمْشَاء	إدْعَاء	إخَافَة	إبَاعَة	إقَامَة	إيئَاس	إيصَال	إفْعَال	IV
تَقَرُّؤ	تَسَؤُّل	تَأَخُّذ	تَمَرُّر	تَلَقٍّ	تَمَشٍّ	تَدَعٍّ	تَخَوُّف	تَبَيُّع	تَقَوُّم	تَيَيُّس	تَوَصُّل	تَفَعُّل	V
تَقَارُؤ	تَسَاؤُل	تَآخُذ	تَمَارّ	تَلَاقٍ	تَمَاشٍ	تَدَاعٍ	تَخَاوُف	تَبَايُع	تَقَاوُم	تَيَابُس	تَوَاصُل	تَفَاعُل	VI
اِنْقِرَاء	اِنْسِئَال		اِنْمِرَار	اِنْلِقَاء	اِنْمِشَاء	اِنْدِعَاء	اِنْخِيَاف	اِنْبِيَاع	اِنْقِيَام			اِنْفِعَال	VII
اِقْتِرَاء	اِسْتِئَال	اِتِّخَاذ	اِمْتِرَار	اِلْتِقَاء	اِمْتِشَاء	اِدِّعَاء[1]	اِخْتِيَاف	اِبْتِيَاع	اِقْتِيَام	اِتِّبَاس	اِتِّصَال	اِفْتِعَال	VIII
اِسْتِقْرَاء	اِسْتِسْآل	اِسْتِخَاذ	اِسْتِمْرَار	اِسْتِلْقَاء	اِسْتِمْشَاء	اِسْتِدْعَاء	اِسْتِخَافَة	اِسْتِبَاعَة	اِسْتِقَامَة	اِسْتِيئَاس	اِسْتِيصَال	اِسْتِفْعَال	X

---

[1] See Lesson 18 for the rules for the assimilation of the infix *t-* to R₁.

Table 13 Sound Verb (فَعَلَ) : Form I

Infinitive	Passive Participle	Active Participle	Passive — Imperfect Indicative	Passive — Perfect	Imperative	Active — Jussive	Active — Imperfect Subjunctive	Active — Imperfect Indicative	Active — Perfect	
	مَفْعُول	فَاعِل	يُفْعَلُ	فُعِلَ		يَفْعَلْ	يَفْعَلَ	يَفْعَلُ	فَعَلَ	(هُوَ)
	مَفْعُولَة	فَاعِلَة	تُفْعَلُ	فُعِلَتْ		تَفْعَلْ	تَفْعَلَ	تَفْعَلُ	فَعَلَتْ	(هِيَ)
			تُفْعَلُ	فُعِلْتَ	اِفْعَلْ	تَفْعَلْ	تَفْعَلَ	تَفْعَلُ	فَعَلْتَ	(أَنْتَ)
			تُفْعَلِينَ	فُعِلْتِ	اِفْعَلِي	تَفْعَلِي	تَفْعَلِي	تَفْعَلِينَ	فَعَلْتِ	(أَنْتِ)
			أُفْعَلُ	فُعِلْتُ		أَفْعَلْ	أَفْعَلَ	أَفْعَلُ	فَعَلْتُ	(أَنَا)
			يُفْعَلَانِ	فُعِلَا		يَفْعَلَا	يَفْعَلَا	يَفْعَلَانِ	فَعَلَا	(هُمَا)
			تُفْعَلَانِ	فُعِلَتَا		تَفْعَلَا	تَفْعَلَا	تَفْعَلَانِ	فَعَلَتَا	(هُمَا)
			تُفْعَلَانِ	فُعِلْتُمَا	اِفْعَلَا	تَفْعَلَا	تَفْعَلَا	تَفْعَلَانِ	فَعَلْتُمَا	(أَنْتُمَا)
			يُفْعَلُونَ	فُعِلُوا		يَفْعَلُوا	يَفْعَلُوا	يَفْعَلُونَ	فَعَلُوا	(هُمْ)
			يُفْعَلْنَ	فُعِلْنَ		يَفْعَلْنَ	يَفْعَلْنَ	يَفْعَلْنَ	فَعَلْنَ	(هُنَّ)
irregular			تُفْعَلُونَ	فُعِلْتُمْ	اِفْعَلُوا	تَفْعَلُوا	تَفْعَلُوا	تَفْعَلُونَ	فَعَلْتُمْ	(أَنْتُمْ)

Table 14 Sound Verb (فَعَلَ) : Form II-X

	Active					Passive				
	Perfect	Indicative	Subjunctive	Jussive	Imperative	Perfect	Imperfect Indicative	Active Participle	Passive Participle	Infinitive
II	فَعَّلَ	يُفَعِّلُ	يُفَعِّلَ	يُفَعِّلْ	فَعِّلْ	فُعِّلَ	يُفَعَّلُ	مُفَعِّل	مُفَعَّل	تَفْعِيل
III	فاعَلَ	يُفاعِلُ	يُفاعِلَ	يُفاعِلْ	فاعِلْ	فوعِلَ	يُفاعَلُ	مُفاعِل	مُفاعَل	مُفاعَلة (فِعال)
IV	أَفْعَلَ	يُفْعِلُ	يُفْعِلَ	يُفْعِلْ	أَفْعِلْ	أُفْعِلَ	يُفْعَلُ	مُفْعِل	مُفْعَل	إِفْعال
V	تَفَعَّلَ	يَتَفَعَّلُ	يَتَفَعَّلَ	يَتَفَعَّلْ	تَفَعَّلْ	تُفُعِّلَ	يُتَفَعَّلُ	مُتَفَعِّل	مُتَفَعَّل	تَفَعُّل
VI	تَفاعَلَ	يَتَفاعَلُ	يَتَفاعَلَ	يَتَفاعَلْ	تَفاعَلْ	تُفوعِلَ	يُتَفاعَلُ	مُتَفاعِل	مُتَفاعَل	تَفاعُل
VII	اِنْفَعَلَ	يَنْفَعِلُ	يَنْفَعِلَ	يَنْفَعِلْ	اِنْفَعِلْ			مُنْفَعِل	مُنْفَعَل	اِنْفِعال
VIII	اِفْتَعَلَ	يَفْتَعِلُ	يَفْتَعِلَ	يَفْتَعِلْ	اِفْتَعِلْ	اُفْتُعِلَ	يُفْتَعَلُ	مُفْتَعِل	مُفْتَعَل	اِفْتِعال
X	اِسْتَفْعَلَ	يَسْتَفْعِلُ	يَسْتَفْعِلَ	يَسْتَفْعِلْ	اِسْتَفْعِلْ	اُسْتُفْعِلَ	يُسْتَفْعَلُ	مُسْتَفْعِل	مُسْتَفْعَل	اِسْتِفْعال

475

Table 15 Verb R₁ = و (وصل) : Form I

Infinitive	Passive Participle	Active Participle	Passive — Imperfect Indicative	Passive — Perfect	Imperative	Active — Jussive	Active — Subjunctive (Imperfect)	Active — Indicative (Imperfect)	Active — Perfect	
irregular	مَوْصُولٌ مَوْصُولَةٌ	وَاصِلٌ وَاصِلَةٌ	يُوصَلُ	وُصِلَ		يَصِلْ	يَصِلَ	يَصِلُ	وَصَلَ	(هو)
			تُوصَلُ	وُصِلَتْ		تَصِلْ	تَصِلَ	تَصِلُ	وَصَلَتْ	(هي)
			تُوصَلُ	وُصِلْتَ	صِلْ	تَصِلْ	تَصِلَ	تَصِلُ	وَصَلْتَ	(أنتَ)
			تُوصَلِينَ	وُصِلْتِ	صِلِي	تَصِلِي	تَصِلِي	تَصِلِينَ	وَصَلْتِ	(أنتِ)
			أُوصَلُ	وُصِلْتُ		أَصِلْ	أَصِلَ	أَصِلُ	وَصَلْتُ	(أنا)
			يُوصَلَانِ	وُصِلَا		يَصِلَا	يَصِلَا	يَصِلَانِ	وَصَلَا	(هما m)
			تُوصَلَانِ	وُصِلَتَا		تَصِلَا	تَصِلَا	تَصِلَانِ	وَصَلَتَا	(هما f)
			تُوصَلَانِ	وُصِلْتُمَا	صِلَا	تَصِلَا	تَصِلَا	تَصِلَانِ	وَصَلْتُمَا	(أنتما)
			يُوصَلُونَ	وُصِلُوا		يَصِلُوا	يَصِلُوا	يَصِلُونَ	وَصَلُوا	(هم)
			يُوصَلْنَ	وُصِلْنَ		يَصِلْنَ	يَصِلْنَ	يَصِلْنَ	وَصَلْنَ	(هنّ)
			تُوصَلُونَ	وُصِلْتُمْ	صِلُوا	تَصِلُوا	تَصِلُوا	تَصِلُونَ	وَصَلْتُمْ	(أنتم)
			تُوصَلْنَ	وُصِلْتُنَّ	صِلْنَ	تَصِلْنَ	تَصِلْنَ	تَصِلْنَ	وَصَلْتُنَّ	(أنتنّ)

Table 16 Verb R₁ = و (وصل) : Form II-X

	Infinitive	Passive Participle	Active Participle	Passive Imperfect Indicative	Passive Perfect	Imperative	Active Jussive	Active Subjunctive	Active Imperfect Indicative	Active Perfect	
	تَوْصِيل	مُوَصَّل	مُوَصِّل	يُوَصَّل	وُصِّل	وَصِّل	يُوَصِّل	يُوَصِّل	يُوَصِّل	وَصَّل	II
	مُوَاصَلة (وِصَال)	مُوَاصَل	مُوَاصِل	يُوَاصَل	وُوصِل	وَاصِل	يُوَاصِل	يُوَاصِل	يُوَاصِل	وَاصَل	III
	إيصال	مُوصَل	مُوصِل	يُوصَل	أُوصِل	أَوْصِل	يُوصِل	يُوصِل	يُوصِل	أَوْصَل	IV
	تَوَصُّل	مُتَوَصَّل	مُتَوَصِّل	يُتَوَصَّل	تُوُصِّل	تَوَصَّل	يَتَوَصَّل	يَتَوَصَّل	يَتَوَصَّل	تَوَصَّل	V
	تَوَاصُل	مُتَوَاصَل	مُتَوَاصِل	يُتَوَاصَل	تُوُوصِل	تَوَاصَل	يَتَوَاصَل	يَتَوَاصَل	يَتَوَاصَل	تَوَاصَل	VI
					no forms						VII
	اِتِّصال	مُتَّصَل	مُتَّصِل	يُتَّصَل	اُتُّصِل	اِتَّصِل	يَتَّصِل	يَتَّصِل	يَتَّصِل	اِتَّصَل	VIII
	اِسْتيصال	مُسْتَوْصَل	مُسْتَوْصِل	يُسْتَوْصَل	اُسْتُوصِل	اِسْتَوْصِل	يَسْتَوْصِل	يَسْتَوْصِل	يَسْتَوْصِل	اِسْتَوْصَل	X

Table 17 Verb R₁ = ي (سمي) : Form I-X

	Infinitive	Passive Participle	Active Participle	Passive Imperfect Indicative	Passive Perfect	Imperative	Jussive	Active Imperfect Subjunctive	Active Imperfect Indicative	Active Perfect	
		Passive	Active	Passive				Active			
		Participle	Participle	Imperfect Indicative	Perfect	Imperative	Jussive	Imperfect Subjunctive	Imperfect Indicative	Perfect	
	سَمِيّ / تَسْمِيَة	مَسْمُوّ	سَامٍ	يُسْمَى	سُمِيَ	اِسْمِ	يَسْمِ	يَسْمِيَ	يَسْمِي	سَمِيَ	I
	تَسْمِيَة	مُسَمًّى	مُسَمٍّ	يُسَمَّى	سُمِّيَ	سَمِّ	يُسَمِّ	يُسَمِّيَ	يُسَمِّي	سَمَّى	II
	مُسَامَاة	مُسَامًى	مُسَامٍ	يُسَامَى	سُومِيَ	سَامِ	يُسَامِ	يُسَامِيَ	يُسَامِي	سَامَى	III
	إِسْمَاء	مُسْمًى	مُسْمٍ	يُسْمَى	أُسْمِيَ	أَسْمِ	يُسْمِ	يُسْمِيَ	يُسْمِي	أَسْمَى	IV
	تَسَمٍّ	مُتَسَمًّى	مُتَسَمٍّ	يُتَسَمَّى	تُسُمِّيَ	تَسَمَّ	يَتَسَمَّ	يَتَسَمَّى	يَتَسَمَّى	تَسَمَّى	V
	تَسَامٍ	مُتَسَامًى	مُتَسَامٍ	يُتَسَامَى	تُسُومِيَ	تَسَامَ	يَتَسَامَ	يَتَسَامَى	يَتَسَامَى	تَسَامَى	VI
no forms											VII
	اِسْتِمَاء	مُسْتَمًى	مُسْتَمٍ	يُسْتَمَى	اُسْتُمِيَ	اِسْتَمِ	يَسْتَمِ	يَسْتَمِيَ	يَسْتَمِي	اِسْتَمَى	VIII
	اِسْتِسْمَاء	مُسْتَسْمًى	مُسْتَسْمٍ	يُسْتَسْمَى	اُسْتُسْمِيَ	اِسْتَسْمِ	يَسْتَسْمِ	يَسْتَسْمِيَ	يَسْتَسْمِي	اِسْتَسْمَى	X

Table 18 Verb R₂ = و (قام) : Form I

	Infinitive	Passive Participle	Active Participle	Passive		Imperative	Active				
				Imperfect Indicative	Perfect		Jussive	Subjunctive	Imperfect Indicative	Perfect	
irregular											

Table 19 Verb R₂ = و (قام) : Form II-X

	Infinitive	Passive Participle	Active Participle	Passive Imperfect Indicative	Passive Perfect	Imperative	Active Jussive	Active Imperfect Subjunctive	Active Imperfect Indicative	Active Perfect
II	تَقْوِيم	مُقَوَّم	مُقَوِّم	يُقَوَّم	قُوِّمَ	قَوِّمْ	يُقَوِّمْ	يُقَوِّمَ	يُقَوِّمُ	قَوَّمَ
III	قِوَام / مُقَاوَمة	مُقَاوَم	مُقَاوِم	يُقَاوَم	قُووِمَ	قَاوِمْ	يُقَاوِمْ	يُقَاوِمَ	يُقَاوِمُ	قَاوَمَ
IV	إِقَامة	مُقَام	مُقِيم	يُقَام	أُقِيمَ	أَقِمْ	يُقِمْ	يُقِيمَ	يُقِيمُ	أَقَامَ
V	تَقَوُّم	مُتَقَوَّم	مُتَقَوِّم	يُتَقَوَّم	تُقُوِّمَ	تَقَوَّمْ	يَتَقَوَّمْ	يَتَقَوَّمَ	يَتَقَوَّمُ	تَقَوَّمَ
VI	تَقَاوُم	مُتَقَاوَم	مُتَقَاوِم	يُتَقَاوَم	تُقُووِمَ	تَقَاوَمْ	يَتَقَاوَمْ	يَتَقَاوَمَ	يَتَقَاوَمُ	تَقَاوَمَ
VII	انْقِيام	مُنْقَام	مُنْقَام	يُنْقَام	انْقِيمَ	انْقَمْ	يَنْقَمْ	يَنْقَامَ	يَنْقَامُ	انْقَامَ
VIII	اقْتِيام	مُقْتَام	مُقْتَام	يُقْتَام	اقْتِيمَ	اقْتَمْ	يَقْتَمْ	يَقْتَامَ	يَقْتَامُ	اقْتَامَ
X	اسْتِقَامة	مُسْتَقَام	مُسْتَقِيم	يُسْتَقَام	اسْتُقِيمَ	اسْتَقِمْ	يَسْتَقِمْ	يَسْتَقِيمَ	يَسْتَقِيمُ	اسْتَقَامَ

480

Table 20 Verb R₂ = ي (ب ي ع) : Form I

	Infinitive	Passive Participle	Active Participle	Passive		Imperative	Active			
				Imperfect Indicative	Perfect		Jussive	Subjunctive Imperfect	Indicative	Perfect
irregular		مَبِيع	بَائِع	يُبَاعُ	بِيعَ		يَبِعْ	يَبِيعَ	يَبِيعُ	بَاعَ	(هو)
				تُبَاعُ	بِيعَتْ		تَبِعْ	تَبِيعَ	تَبِيعُ	بَاعَتْ	(هي)
				تُبَاعُ	بِعْتَ	بِعْ	تَبِعْ	تَبِيعَ	تَبِيعُ	بِعْتَ	(أنتَ)
				تُبَاعِينَ	بِعْتِ	بِيعِي	تَبِيعِي	تَبِيعِي	تَبِيعِينَ	بِعْتِ	(أنتِ)
				أُبَاعُ	بِعْتُ		أَبِعْ	أَبِيعَ	أَبِيعُ	بِعْتُ	(أنا)
				يُبَاعَانِ	بِيعَا		يَبِيعَا	يَبِيعَا	يَبِيعَانِ	بَاعَا	(هما)
				تُبَاعَانِ	بِيعَتَا		تَبِيعَا	تَبِيعَا	تَبِيعَانِ	بَاعَتَا	(هما)
				تُبَاعَانِ	بِعْتُمَا	بِيعَا	تَبِيعَا	تَبِيعَا	تَبِيعَانِ	بِعْتُمَا	(أنتما)
				يُبَاعُونَ	بِيعُوا		يَبِيعُوا	يَبِيعُوا	يَبِيعُونَ	بَاعُوا	(هم)
				يُبَعْنَ	بِعْنَ		يَبِعْنَ	يَبِعْنَ	يَبِعْنَ	بِعْنَ	(هن)
				تُبَاعُونَ	بِعْتُمْ	بِيعُوا	تَبِيعُوا	تَبِيعُوا	تَبِيعُونَ	بِعْتُمْ	(أنتم)
				تُبَعْنَ	بِعْتُنَّ	بِعْنَ	تَبِعْنَ	تَبِعْنَ	تَبِعْنَ	بِعْتُنَّ	(أنتن)
				نُبَاعُ	بِعْنَا		نَبِعْ	نَبِيعَ	نَبِيعُ	بِعْنَا	(نحن)

Table 21 Verb R₂ = ي (ب ي ح) : Form II-X

	Infinitive	Passive Participle	Active Participle	Passive		Active				
				Imperfect Indicative	Perfect	Imperative	Jussive	Imperfect Subjunctive	Imperfect Indicative	Perfect
II										
III										
IV										
V										
VI										
VII										
VIII										
X										

Table 22 Verb R₂ = و (نَوٰ) : Form I

				Passive				Active				
				Imperfect				Imperfect				
	Infinitive	Passive Participle	Active Participle	Indicative	Perfect	Imperative	Jussive	Subjunctive	Indicative	Perfect	
irregular		مَنْوِيٌّ مَنْوِيَّةٌ	نَاوٍ نَاوِيَةٌ	Form II – X like قَامَ (Table 19)							

Table 23 Verb R₃ = و (دَعا) : Form I

484

	Passive Participle	Active Participle	Passive Imperfect Indicative	Passive Perfect		Active Imperative	Active Jussive	Active Subjunctive	Active Imperfect Indicative	Active Perfect	
Infinitive											
irregular	مَدْعُوٌّ	دَاعٍ	يُدْعَى	دُعِيَ			يَدْعُ	يَدْعُوَ	يَدْعُوَ	يَدْعُو	دَعَا	(هو)
	مَدْعُوَّةٌ	دَاعِيَةٌ	تُدْعَى	دُعِيَتْ			تَدْعُ	تَدْعُوَ	تَدْعُوَ	تَدْعُو	دَعَتْ	(هي)
Form II - X like لَقِيَ (Table 26)			تُدْعَى	دُعِيتَ	أُدْعُ		تَدْعُ	تَدْعُوَ	تَدْعُوَ	تَدْعُو	دَعَوْتَ	(أنتَ)
			تُدْعَيْنَ	دُعِيتِ	أُدْعِي		تَدْعِي	تَدْعِي	تَدْعِينَ	تَدْعِينَ	دَعَوْتِ	(أنتِ)
			أُدْعَى	دُعِيتُ			أَدْعُ	أَدْعُوَ	أَدْعُوَ	أَدْعُو	دَعَوْتُ	(أنا)
			يُدْعَوْنَ	دُعُوا			يَدْعُوا	يَدْعُوا	يَدْعُونَ	يَدْعُونَ	دَعَوْا	(هم)
			يُدْعَيْنَ	دُعِينَ			يَدْعُونَ	يَدْعُونَ	يَدْعُونَ	يَدْعُونَ	دَعَوْنَ	(هنَّ)
			تُدْعَوْنَ	دُعِيتُمْ	أُدْعُوا		تَدْعُوا	تَدْعُوا	تَدْعُونَ	تَدْعُونَ	دَعَوْتُمْ	(أنتم)
			تُدْعَيْنَ	دُعِيتُنَّ	أُدْعُونَ		تَدْعُونَ	تَدْعُونَ	تَدْعُونَ	تَدْعُونَ	دَعَوْتُنَّ	(أنتنَّ)
			نُدْعَى	دُعِينا			نَدْعُ	نَدْعُوَ	نَدْعُو	نَدْعُو	دَعَوْنَا	(نحن)
			يُدْعَيَان	دُعِيا			يَدْعُوَا	يَدْعُوَا	يَدْعُوَان	يَدْعُوَان	دَعَوَا	(هما)
			تُدْعَيَان	دُعِيتا			تَدْعُوَا	تَدْعُوَا	تَدْعُوَان	تَدْعُوَان	دَعَتَا	(هما)
			تُدْعَيَان	دُعِيتُما	أُدْعُوَا		تَدْعُوَا	تَدْعُوَا	تَدْعُوَان	تَدْعُوَان	دَعَوْتُمَا	(أنتما)

Table 24 Verb R3 = ى (مشى) : Form I

	Passive	Active	Passive		Active					
Infinitive	Participle	Participle	Imperfect	Perfect		Imperfect			Perfect	
			Indicative		Imperative	Jussive	Subjunctive	Indicative		
irregular	مَمْشِيٌّ	مَاشٍ	يُمْشَى	مُشِيَ		يَمْشِ	يَمْشِيَ	يَمْشِي	مَشَى	(هو)
	مَمْشِيَّةٌ	مَاشِيَةٌ	تُمْشَى	مُشِيَتْ		تَمْشِ	تَمْشِيَ	تَمْشِي	مَشَتْ	(هي)
Form II - X like لقي (Table 26)			تُمْشَى	مُشِيتَ	اِمْشِ	تَمْشِ	تَمْشِيَ	تَمْشِي	مَشَيْتَ	(أنتَ)
			تُمْشَيْنَ	مُشِيتِ	اِمْشِي	تَمْشِي	تَمْشِي	تَمْشِينَ	مَشَيْتِ	(أنتِ)
			أُمْشَى	مُشِيتُ		أَمْشِ	أَمْشِيَ	أَمْشِي	مَشَيْتُ	(أنا)
			يُمْشَوْنَ	مُشُوا		يَمْشُوا	يَمْشُوا	يَمْشُونَ	مَشَوْا	(هم)
			يُمْشَيْنَ	مُشِينَ		يَمْشِينَ	يَمْشِينَ	يَمْشِينَ	مَشَيْنَ	(هنَّ)
			تُمْشَوْنَ	مُشِيتُمْ	اِمْشُوا	تَمْشُوا	تَمْشُوا	تَمْشُونَ	مَشَيْتُمْ	(أنتم)
			تُمْشَيْنَ	مُشِيتُنَّ	اِمْشِينَ	تَمْشِينَ	تَمْشِينَ	تَمْشِينَ	مَشَيْتُنَّ	(أنتنَّ)
			نُمْشَى	مُشِينَا		نَمْشِ	نَمْشِيَ	نَمْشِي	مَشَيْنَا	(نحن)
			يُمْشَيَانِ	مُشِيَا		يَمْشِيَا	يَمْشِيَا	يَمْشِيَانِ	مَشَيَا	(هما)
			تُمْشَيَانِ	مُشِيَتَا		تَمْشِيَا	تَمْشِيَا	تَمْشِيَانِ	مَشَتَا	(هما)
			تُمْشَيَانِ	مُشِيتُمَا	اِمْشِيَا	تَمْشِيَا	تَمْشِيَا	تَمْشِيَانِ	مَشَيْتُمَا	(أنتما)

Table 25 Verb R₃ = ي (فَعَى) : Form I

Infinitive	Passive Participle	Active Participle	Passive		Imperative	Active				
			Imperfect Indicative	Perfect		Jussive	Subjunctive (Imperfect)	Indicative (Imperfect)	Perfect	
irregular	مَفْعِيّ	فَاعٍ								

Table 26 Verbs R₃ = و or ي (قَوِيَ) : Form II-X

	Passive	Active	Passive				Active				
Infinitive	Participle	Participle	Imperfect Indicative	Perfect		Imperative	Jussive	Subjunctive	Imperfect Indicative	Perfect	
تَقْوِيَة	مُقَوّىً	مُقَوٍّ	يُقَوّىٰ	قُوِّيَ		قَوِّ	يُقَوِّ	يُقَوِّيَ	يُقَوِّي	قَوَّىٰ	II
مُقَاوَاة (قِوَاء)	مُقَاوىً	مُقَاوٍ	يُقَاوىٰ	قُووِيَ		قَاوِ	يُقَاوِ	يُقَاوِيَ	يُقَاوِي	قَاوَىٰ	III
إِقْوَاء	مُقْوىً	مُقْوٍ	يُقْوىٰ	أُقْوِيَ		أَقْوِ	يُقْوِ	يُقْوِيَ	يُقْوِي	أَقْوَىٰ	IV
تَقَوٍّ	مُتَقَوّىً	مُتَقَوٍّ	يُتَقَوّىٰ	تُقُوِّيَ		تَقَوَّ	يَتَقَوَّ	يَتَقَوَّىٰ	يَتَقَوَّىٰ	تَقَوَّىٰ	V
تَقَاوٍ	مُتَقَاوىً	مُتَقَاوٍ	يُتَقَاوىٰ	تُقُووِيَ		تَقَاوَ	يَتَقَاوَ	يَتَقَاوَىٰ	يَتَقَاوَىٰ	تَقَاوَىٰ	VI
اِنْقِوَاء	مُنْقَوىً	مُنْقَوٍ	يُنْقَوىٰ	اُنْقُوِيَ		اِنْقَوِ	يَنْقَوِ	يَنْقَوِيَ	يَنْقَوِي	اِنْقَوَىٰ	VII
اِقْتِوَاء	مُقْتَوىً	مُقْتَوٍ	يُقْتَوىٰ	اُقْتُوِيَ		اِقْتَوِ	يَقْتَوِ	يَقْتَوِيَ	يَقْتَوِي	اِقْتَوَىٰ	VIII
اِسْتِقْوَاء	مُسْتَقْوىً	مُسْتَقْوٍ	يُسْتَقْوىٰ	اُسْتُقْوِيَ		اِسْتَقْوِ	يَسْتَقْوِ	يَسْتَقْوِيَ	يَسْتَقْوِي	اِسْتَقْوَىٰ	X

Table 27 Verb $R_2 = R_3$ (مرّ) : Form I

	Passive	Active	Passive		Active					
Infinitive	Participle	Participle	Imperfect	Perfect		Imperfect			Perfect	
			Indicative		Imperative	Jussive	Subjunctive	Indicative		
irregular	مَمْرُورٌ	مَارٌّ	يُمَرُّ	مُرَّ		يَمُرَّ/يَمْرُرْ	يَمُرَّ	يَمُرُّ	مَرَّ	(هو)
	مَمْرُورَةٌ	مَارَّةٌ	تُمَرُّ	مُرَّتْ		تَمُرَّ/تَمْرُرْ	تَمُرَّ	تَمُرُّ	مَرَّتْ	(هي)
			تُمَرُّ	مُرِرْتَ	مُرَّ/اُمْرُرْ	تَمُرَّ/تَمْرُرْ	تَمُرَّ	تَمُرُّ	مَرَرْتَ	(أنتَ)
			تُمَرِّينَ	مُرِرْتِ	مُرِّي	تَمُرِّي	تَمُرِّي	تَمُرِّينَ	مَرَرْتِ	(أنتِ)
			أُمَرُّ	مُرِرْتُ		أَمُرَّ/أَمْرُرْ	أَمُرَّ	أَمُرُّ	مَرَرْتُ	(أنا)
			يُمَرُّونَ	مُرُّوا		يَمُرُّوا	يَمُرُّوا	يَمُرُّونَ	مَرُّوا	(هم)
			يُمْرَرْنَ	مُرِرْنَ		يَمْرُرْنَ	يَمْرُرْنَ	يَمْرُرْنَ	مَرَرْنَ	(هنَّ)
			تُمَرُّونَ	مُرِرْتُمْ	مُرُّوا	تَمُرُّوا	تَمُرُّوا	تَمُرُّونَ	مَرَرْتُمْ	(أنتم)
			تُمْرَرْنَ	مُرِرْتُنَّ	اُمْرُرْنَ	تَمْرُرْنَ	تَمْرُرْنَ	تَمْرُرْنَ	مَرَرْتُنَّ	(أنتنَّ)
			نُمَرُّ	مُرِرْنَا		نَمُرَّ/نَمْرُرْ	نَمُرَّ	نَمُرُّ	مَرَرْنَا	(نحن)
			يُمَرَّانِ	مُرَّا		يَمُرَّا	يَمُرَّا	يَمُرَّانِ	مَرَّا	(هما)
			تُمَرَّانِ	مُرَّتَا		تَمُرَّا	تَمُرَّا	تَمُرَّانِ	مَرَّتَا	(هما)
			تُمَرَّانِ	مُرِرْتُمَا	مُرَّا	تَمُرَّا	تَمُرَّا	تَمُرَّانِ	مَرَرْتُمَا	(أنتما)

Table 28 Verb R₂ = R₃ (مّ) : Form II-X

			Passive				Active			
Infinitive	Passive Participle	Active Participle	Imperfect Indicative	Perfect	Imperative	Jussive	Imperfect Subjunctive	Imperfect Indicative	Perfect	
تَمْمِيْر	مُمَمَّر	مُمَمِّر	يُمَمَّر	مُمِّر			يُمَمِّر	يُمَمِّر	مَمَّر	II
مُمَامَّة (مِمَار)	مُمَامّ	مُمَامّ	يُمَامّ	مُومّ	مَامِّ / مَامّ	يُمَامّ / يُمَامِّ	يُمَامّ	يُمَامّ	مَامّ	III
إِمْمَار	مُمَمّ	مُمِمّ	يُمَمّ	أُمِمّ	أَمِمّ / أَمّ	يُمِمّ / يُمِمِّ	يُمِمّ	يُمِمّ	أَمَمّ	IV
تَمَمُّر	مُتَمَمَّر	مُتَمَمِّر	يُتَمَمَّر	تُمُمِّر	تَمَمَّر	يَتَمَمّر	يَتَمَمّر	يَتَمَمّر	تَمَمّر	V
تَمَامّ	مُتَمَامّ	مُتَمَامّ	يُتَمَامّ	تُمُومّ	تَمَامَّ	يَتَمَامّ	يَتَمَامّ	يَتَمَامّ	تَمَامّ	VI
اِنْمِمَار	مُنْمَمّ	مُنْمَمّ	يُنْمَمّ	اُنْمُمّ	اِنْمَمِّ / اِنْمَمّ	يَنْمَمّ / يَنْمَمِّ	يَنْمَمّ	يَنْمَمّ	اِنْمَمّ	VII
اِمْتِمَار	مُمْتَمّ	مُمْتَمّ	يُمْتَمّ	اُمْتُمّ	اِمْتَمِّ / اِمْتَمّ	يَمْتَمّ / يَمْتَمِّ	يَمْتَمّ	يَمْتَمّ	اِمْتَمّ	VIII
اِسْتِمْمَار	مُسْتَمَمّ	مُسْتَمِمّ	يُسْتَمَمّ	اُسْتُمِمّ	اِسْتَمِمّ / اِسْتَمّ	يَسْتَمِمّ / يَسْتَمّ	يَسْتَمِمّ	يَسْتَمِمّ	اِسْتَمَمّ	X

Table 29 Verb R₁ = ء (أَخَذَ) : Form I

490

	Infinitive	Passive Participle	Active Participle	Passive		Imperative	Active				
				Imperfect Indicative	Perfect		Imperfect Jussive	Imperfect Subjunctive	Indicative	Perfect	
irregular		مَأْخُوذٌ، مَأْخُوذُونَ	آخِذٌ، آخِذُونَ								

Table 30 Verb R₁ = ء (أَخَذ) : Form II-X

	Infinitive	Passive Participle	Active Participle	Passive		Active					
				Imperfect Indicative	Perfect	Imperative	Jussive	Subjunctive	Imperfect Indicative	Perfect	
II	تَفْعِيل	مُفَعَّل	مُفَعِّل	يُفَعَّل	فُعِّل	فَعِّل	يُفَعِّل	يُفَعِّل	يُفَعِّل	فَعَّل	II
III	فِعَال / مُفَاعَلة	مُفَاعَل	مُفَاعِل	يُفَاعَل	فُوعِل	فَاعِل	يُفَاعِل	يُفَاعِل	يُفَاعِل	فَاعَل	III
IV	إِفْعَال	مُفْعَل	مُفْعِل	يُفْعَل	أُفْعِل	أَفْعِل	يُفْعِل	يُفْعِل	يُفْعِل	أَفْعَل	IV
V	تَفَعُّل	مُتَفَعَّل	مُتَفَعِّل	يُتَفَعَّل	تُفُعِّل	تَفَعَّل	يَتَفَعَّل	يَتَفَعَّل	يَتَفَعَّل	تَفَعَّل	V
VI	تَفَاعُل	مُتَفَاعَل	مُتَفَاعِل	يُتَفَاعَل	تُفُوعِل	تَفَاعَل	يَتَفَاعَل	يَتَفَاعَل	يَتَفَاعَل	تَفَاعَل	VI
VII	اِنْفِعَال	مُنْفَعَل	مُنْفَعِل		no forms	اِنْفَعِل	يَنْفَعِل	يَنْفَعِل	يَنْفَعِل	اِنْفَعَل	VII
VIII	اِفْتِعَال	مُفْتَعَل	مُفْتَعِل	يُفْتَعَل	اُفْتُعِل	اِفْتَعِل	يَفْتَعِل	يَفْتَعِل	يَفْتَعِل	اِفْتَعَل	VIII
X	اِسْتِفْعَال	مُسْتَفْعَل	مُسْتَفْعِل	يُسْتَفْعَل	اُسْتُفْعِل	اِسْتَفْعِل	يَسْتَفْعِل	يَسْتَفْعِل	يَسْتَفْعِل	اِسْتَفْعَل	X

Table 31 Verb R₂ = ع (سَأَل) : Form I

	Infinitive	Passive Participle	Active Participle	Passive		Imperative	Active				
				Imperfect Indicative	Perfect		Jussive	Subjunctive	Indicative	Perfect	
								Imperfect		Perfect	
irregular		مَسْؤُول ، مَسْؤُل	سَائِل ، سَائِلَة	يُسْأَلُ	سُئِلَ	—	يَسْأَلْ	يَسْأَلَ	يَسْأَلُ	سَأَلَ	(هُوَ)
				يُسْأَلُ	سُئِلَ	—	يَسْأَلْ	يَسْأَلَ	يَسْأَلُ	سَأَلَ	(هُوَ)
				يُسْأَلَانِ	سُئِلَا	—	يَسْأَلَا	يَسْأَلَا	يَسْأَلَانِ	سَأَلَا	(هُمَا)
				يُسْأَلُونَ	سُئِلُوا	—	يَسْأَلُوا	يَسْأَلُوا	يَسْأَلُونَ	سَأَلُوا	(هُمْ)
				تُسْأَلُ	سُئِلَتْ	—	تَسْأَلْ	تَسْأَلَ	تَسْأَلُ	سَأَلَتْ	(هِيَ)
				تُسْأَلَانِ	سُئِلَتَا	—	تَسْأَلَا	تَسْأَلَا	تَسْأَلَانِ	سَأَلَتَا	(هُمَا)
				يُسْأَلْنَ	سُئِلْنَ	—	يَسْأَلْنَ	يَسْأَلْنَ	يَسْأَلْنَ	سَأَلْنَ	(هُنَّ)
				تُسْأَلُ	سُئِلْتَ	اِسْأَلْ ، سَلْ	تَسْأَلْ	تَسْأَلَ	تَسْأَلُ	سَأَلْتَ	(أَنْتَ)
				تُسْأَلَانِ	سُئِلْتُمَا	اِسْأَلَا	تَسْأَلَا	تَسْأَلَا	تَسْأَلَانِ	سَأَلْتُمَا	(أَنْتُمَا)
				تُسْأَلُونَ	سُئِلْتُمْ	اِسْأَلُوا	تَسْأَلُوا	تَسْأَلُوا	تَسْأَلُونَ	سَأَلْتُمْ	(أَنْتُمْ)
				تُسْأَلِينَ	سُئِلْتِ	اِسْأَلِي	تَسْأَلِي	تَسْأَلِي	تَسْأَلِينَ	سَأَلْتِ	(أَنْتِ)
				تُسْأَلَانِ	سُئِلْتُمَا	اِسْأَلَا	تَسْأَلَا	تَسْأَلَا	تَسْأَلَانِ	سَأَلْتُمَا	(أَنْتُمَا)
				تُسْأَلْنَ	سُئِلْتُنَّ	اِسْأَلْنَ	تَسْأَلْنَ	تَسْأَلْنَ	تَسْأَلْنَ	سَأَلْتُنَّ	(أَنْتُنَّ)
				أُسْأَلُ	سُئِلْتُ	—	أَسْأَلْ	أَسْأَلَ	أَسْأَلُ	سَأَلْتُ	(أَنَا)
				نُسْأَلُ	سُئِلْنَا	—	نَسْأَلْ	نَسْأَلَ	نَسْأَلُ	سَأَلْنَا	(نَحْنُ)

Table 32 Verb R₂ = ء (سَأَل) : Form II-X

	Infinitive	Passive Participle	Active Participle	Passive — Imperfect Indicative	Passive — Perfect	Imperative	Jussive	Active Imperfect — Subjunctive	Active Imperfect — Indicative	Active — Perfect	
											II
	تَسْئِيل	مُسَأَّل	مُسَأِّل	يُسَأَّل	سُئِّل	سَئِّلْ	يُسَئِّلْ	يُسَئِّلَ	يُسَئِّل	سَأَّل	**III**
	سِئَال / مُسَاءَلَة	مُسَاءَل	مُسَائِل	يُسَاءَل	سُوئِل	سَائِلْ	يُسَائِلْ	يُسَائِلَ	يُسَائِل	سَاءَل	**IV**
	إِسْئَال	مُسْأَل	مُسْئِل	يُسْأَل	أُسْئِل	أَسْئِلْ	يُسْئِلْ	يُسْئِلَ	يُسْئِل	أَسْأَل	**V**
	تَسَؤُّل	مُتَسَأَّل	مُتَسَئِّل	يُتَسَأَّل	تُسُئِّل	تَسَأَّلْ	يَتَسَأَّلْ	يَتَسَأَّلَ	يَتَسَأَّل	تَسَأَّل	**VI**
	تَسَاؤُل	مُتَسَاءَل	مُتَسَائِل	يُتَسَاءَل	تُسُوئِل	تَسَاءَلْ	يَتَسَاءَلْ	يَتَسَاءَلَ	يَتَسَاءَل	تَسَاءَل	**VII**
	اِنْسِئَال	مُنْسَأَل	مُنْسَئِل	يُنْسَأَل	اُنْسُئِل	اِنْسَئِلْ	يَنْسَئِلْ	يَنْسَئِلَ	يَنْسَئِل	اِنْسَأَل	**VIII**
	اِسْتِئَال	مُسْتَأَل	مُسْتَئِل	يُسْتَأَل	اُسْتُئِل	اِسْتَئِلْ	يَسْتَئِلْ	يَسْتَئِلَ	يَسْتَئِل	اِسْتَأَل	**X**

Table 33 Verb R₃ = ء (أ فَ) : Form I

494

		Passive	Active	Passive			Active			
Infinitive		Participle	Participle	Imperfect Indicative	Perfect	Imperative	Jussive	Imperfect Subjunctive	Imperfect Indicative	Perfect
irregular		مَقْرُوء	قَارِئ		قُرِئَ					قَرَأَ
		مَقْرُوءَة	قَارِئَة							

Table 34 Verb R_3 = ء (فَرَءَ) : Form II-X

	Infinitive	Passive Participle	Active Participle	Passive		Imperative	Active			
				Imperfect Indicative	Perfect		Jussive	Subjunctive	Imperfect Indicative	Perfect
II	فرّأ	مُفرّأ	مُفرِّئ	يُفرّأ	فُرِّئ	فرِّئ	يُفرِّئ	يُفرِّئ	يُفرِّئ	فرّأ
III	فارأ / فراء	مُفارأ	مُفارئ	يُفارأ	فورئ	فارئ	يُفارئ	يُفارئ	يُفارئ	فارأ
IV	إفراء	مُفرأ	مُفرئ	يُفرأ	أُفرئ	أفرئ	يُفرئ	يُفرئ	يُفرئ	أفرأ
V	تفرّؤ	مُتفرّأ	مُتفرّئ	يُتفرّأ	تُفرّئ	تفرّأ	يتفرّأ	يتفرّأ	يتفرّأ	تفرّأ
VI	تفارؤ	مُتفارأ	مُتفارئ	يُتفارأ	تُفورئ	تفارأ	يتفارأ	يتفارأ	يتفارأ	تفارأ
VII	انفراء	مُنفرأ	مُنفرئ	يُنفرأ	أُنفرئ	انفرئ	ينفرئ	ينفرئ	ينفرئ	انفرأ
VIII	افتراء	مُفترأ	مُفترئ	يُفترأ	أُفترئ	افترئ	يفترئ	يفترئ	يفترئ	افترأ
X	استفراء	مُستفرأ	مُستفرئ	يُستفرأ	أُستفرئ	استفرئ	يستفرئ	يستفرئ	يستفرئ	استفرأ

Table 35 Quadriliteral Verbs: إطْمأنَّ تدحْرج دحْرج

	Passive	Active	Passive		Active						
Infinitive	Participle	Participle	Imperfect	Perfect		Imperfect			Perfect		
					Imperative	Jussive	Subjunctive	Indicative			
دَحْرَجَةٌ	مُدَحْرَجٌ	مُدَحْرِجٌ	يُدَحْرَجُ	دُحْرِجَ		يُدَحْرِجْ	يُدَحْرِجَ	يُدَحْرِجُ	دَحْرَجَ	هو	I
			تُدَحْرَجُ	دُحْرِجْتَ	دَحْرِجْ	تُدَحْرِجْ	تُدَحْرِجَ	تُدَحْرِجُ	دَحْرَجْتَ	أنتَ	
			أُدَحْرَجُ	دُحْرِجْتُ		أُدَحْرِجْ	أُدَحْرِجَ	أُدَحْرِجُ	دَحْرَجْتُ	أنا	
			يُدَحْرَجُونَ	دُحْرِجُوا		يُدَحْرِجُوا	يُدَحْرِجُوا	يُدَحْرِجُونَ	دَحْرَجُوا	هم	
			تُدَحْرَجُونَ	دُحْرِجْتُمْ	دَحْرِجُوا	تُدَحْرِجُوا	تُدَحْرِجُوا	تُدَحْرِجُونَ	دَحْرَجْتُمْ	أنتم	
			نُدَحْرَجُ	دُحْرِجْنَا		نُدَحْرِجْ	نُدَحْرِجَ	نُدَحْرِجُ	دَحْرَجْنَا	نحن	
تَدَحْرُجٌ	مُتَدَحْرَجٌ	مُتَدَحْرِجٌ	يُتَدَحْرَجُ	تُدُحْرِجَ		يَتَدَحْرَجْ	يَتَدَحْرَجَ	يَتَدَحْرَجُ	تَدَحْرَجَ	هو	II
			تُتَدَحْرَجُ	تُدُحْرِجْتَ	تَدَحْرَجْ	تَتَدَحْرَجْ	تَتَدَحْرَجَ	تَتَدَحْرَجُ	تَدَحْرَجْتَ	أنتَ	
			أُتَدَحْرَجُ	تُدُحْرِجْتُ		أَتَدَحْرَجْ	أَتَدَحْرَجَ	أَتَدَحْرَجُ	تَدَحْرَجْتُ	أنا	
			يُتَدَحْرَجُونَ	تُدُحْرِجُوا		يَتَدَحْرَجُوا	يَتَدَحْرَجُوا	يَتَدَحْرَجُونَ	تَدَحْرَجُوا	هم	
			تُتَدَحْرَجُونَ	تُدُحْرِجْتُمْ	تَدَحْرَجُوا	تَتَدَحْرَجُوا	تَتَدَحْرَجُوا	تَتَدَحْرَجُونَ	تَدَحْرَجْتُمْ	أنتم	
			نُتَدَحْرَجُ	تُدُحْرِجْنَا		نَتَدَحْرَجْ	نَتَدَحْرَجَ	نَتَدَحْرَجُ	تَدَحْرَجْنَا	نحن	

Table 35 Quadriliteral Verbs: ذَبْرَجَ تَدَحْرَجَ اِطْمَأَنَّ *(continued)* 497

	Infinitive	Passive Participle	Active Participle
	اِطْمِئْنَان	مُطْمَأَنّ	مُطْمَئِنّ

	Imperative	Active				
		Jussive	Subjunctive	Indicative	Perfect	IV
		Imperfect				
		يَطْمَئِنّ	يَطْمَئِنّ	يَطْمَئِنّ	اِطْمَأَنَّ	هو
	اِطْمَئِنّ	تَطْمَئِنّ	تَطْمَئِنّ	تَطْمَئِنّ	اِطْمَأْنَنْتَ	أنتَ
		أَطْمَئِنّ	أَطْمَئِنّ	أَطْمَئِنّ	اِطْمَأْنَنْتُ	أنا
	اِطْمَئِنّوا	يَطْمَئِنّوا	يَطْمَئِنّوا	يَطْمَئِنّونَ	اِطْمَأَنّوا	هم
		يَطْمَئِنّ	يَطْمَئِنّ	يَطْمَئِنّ	اِطْمَأْنَنَّ	هنّ

The consecution of the vowels of the quadriliteral verbs in Form I, II and IV is the same as in Form II, V, VIII of the triliteral verb.

The jussive has also a long form: يَطْمَئِنِّ etc.

Table 36 Doubly weak Verbs: جَاءَ، أَتَى، رَأَى

								Imperfect	Perfect	Imperfect	Perfect	Imperfect	Perfect
Perfect	**Imperfect**	**Perfect**	**Imperfect**	**Perfect**	**Imperfect**								
		Active Participle		**Active Participle**									
				Passive Participle									
		Infinitive		**Infinitive**									
Infinitive				**Infinitive**									

Table 37 Nouns with the Ending " ـَة " or " ـَى "

		defined		undefined	
		f.	m.	f.	m.
N.		الْأَعْلَى	الْأَعْلَى		أَعْلَى
A.		الْأَعْلَى	الْأَعْلَى	أُعْلَى	أَعْلَى
G.		الْأَعْلَى	الْأَعْلَى	أُعْلَى	
N.		الْعُلْيَا	الْأَعْلَى	عُلْيَا	
A.		الْعُلْيَا	الْأَعْلَى	عُلْيَا	
G.		الْعُلْيَا	الْأَعْلَى	عُلْيَا	
N.		الدَّاعِيَة	الدَّاعِي	دَاعِيَة	دَاعٍ
A.		الدَّاعِيَة	الدَّاعِيَ	دَاعِيَة	دَاعِيًا
G.		الدَّاعِيَة	الدَّاعِي		دَاعٍ

---

¹ Diptotes have the ending -a : فُعْلَى .

WRITING EXERCISES

أ

إ

ا

آ

بـ

ـبـ

ـب

ب

تـ

ـتـ

ـت

ت

ثـ

ـثـ

ـث

ث

نـ

ﻨ

ﺴﻦ

ﻦ

ﻴ

ﻳ

ﻲ

ﻱ

ﺟ

ﺒﺠ

ﺠ

ﺝ

ﺤ

ﺤ

ﻊ

ﺡ

ﺨ

ﺤﺨ

ﻎ

ﻍ

ﺪ

ـﺪ

ﻧ

ـﻨ

ﺮ

ـﺮ

ـﺴ

ـﺴ

ﺴ

ﺲ

ﺷ

ﺸ

ﺶ

ﺶ

ﺻ

ﺻ

ﺺ

ﺹ

ﺿ

ضــ

ــض

ض

طـ

ــطـ

ــطا

طا

ظـ

ــظـ

ــظا

ظا

عـ

ــعـ

ــع

ع

غـ

ــغـ

ــغ

غ

فـ

ـفـ

ـف

ف

قـ

ـقـ

ـق

ق

كـ

ـكـ

ـك

ك

لـ

ـلـ

ـل

ل

مـ

ـمـ

ـم

م

هـ

ـه

ه

ـو

و

أب

أبا

أنا

أنت

يا

ـي

أيِّ

أن

بيت

بين

ابن

بنت

باب

تين

بيننا

بيتي

ثابت

بث

أخ

أخا

نحن

تحت

حج

حاج

جيب

جبن

حب

بخير

حين

حبيب

حبيبي

أُحب

نحب

تاج

احتاج

نحتاج

دبر

دار

تدبير

دجاج

دحرج

أدري

تدريب

يدري

نبذب

رب

ربيع

روح

ترتيب

جدد

جديد

بيت

باب

أبواب

حبر

خذ

أو

زجاج

يد

يرى

أرى

رأى

دون

أبو

سين

شين

صاد

ضاد

درس

دروس

صحيح

صحاح

صباع

سبب

شخص

سبع

أسباب

شرب

شرطي

شرح

تشديد

صدر

ضرب

أجاص

إصدار

طرب

طبيب

أظن

أرض

ضد

عين

غين

غدا

في

فوق

صديق

كيف

كرسي

الآن

طالب

ورق

رجل

كل

حق

حقوق

رجال

أوراق

كبير

صغير

نظيف

طويل

طوال

أعطى

يحكي

حال

صباح

الخير

شكرا

عفوا

أنتم

نعم

هذا

هذه

هل

من

ماذا

مع

جميع

هنا

هناك

مُعلِّم

مُعلِّمون

طاولة

خزانة

مصباح

غرفة

قلم

مدينة

اسم

فتاة

هات

شنطة

قديم

ترجم

اسمع

مرحبا

السلام

مرة

مريم

مريمة

مهام

KEY

Lesson 2
Ex1

البيت (هو)

الغرفة (هي)

الجلوس (هو)

النوم (هو)

الأخت (هي)

المطبخ (هو)

الحمام (هو)

الحديقة (هي)

الأب (هو)

المعلّم (هو)

الأم (هي)

الطبيبة (هي)

الطالبة (هي)

الطالب (هو)

الطاولة (هي)

الكرسي (هو)

السرير (هو)

الخزانة (هي)

الراديو (هو)

الجهاز (هو)

الفيديو (هو)

التلفزيون (هو)

المصباح (هو)

الشبّاك (هو)

Ex3

البيت، الجدار، الغرفة، الجلوس، النوم، المطبخ، الحمام، الحديقة، الطاولة، الكرسي، السرير، الخزانة، الراديو، الفيديو، الجهاز، التلفزيون، المصباح، الشبّاك، القلم، الشنطة، اللوح، الورق، السقف، الأرض

Ex12

أنا في البيت. القلم في/على/تحت الشنطة. الحديقة أمام البيت. فاطمة عند الصديق. أحمد في المطبخ. الورق في / على/تحت الشنطة. الراديو في/على الخزانة. محمّد عند الأم. الطالب عند المعلّم. الكرّاسة في/على الشنطة. أحمد في باريس. الأب في القاهرة. اللوح على الجدار. الكرسي تحت/على الطاولة. الورق على/تحت الطاولة.

Ex13

هو معلّم. أنا طالب. هو الأب. أنت الصديق. أنت الرجل. هو السيّد.

Ex14

هي معلّمة. أنتِ الطالبة. هي المعلّمة. أنتِ طبيبة. هي الطالبة. هي الصديقة. هي الآنسة. هي السيّدة.

Ex15

الشبّاك كبير. المصباح جميل. اللوح صغير. البيت كبير. الرجل صغير. القلم جميل. الطالب كبير. الكتاب صغير. الراديو كبير. السرير صغير. الأب جميل. النوم جميل. الجلوس جميل. المعلّم صغير. الطالب كبير. الكرسي صغير. الصباح جميل.

Ex16

الغرفة صغيرة. الشنطة صغيرة. الطاولة كبيرة. الكرّاسة جميلة. الخزانة كبيرة. الطالبة صغيرة. الفتاة جميلة. المدينة كبيرة. القاهرة كبيرة. الأم صغيرة. الكرّاسة صغيرة. الحديقة كبيرة.

Ex17

الطاولة جديدة والكرسي قديم.
الطالب طويل والطالبة صغيرة.
الغرفة نظيفة واللوح وسخ.

Ex18

هو جديد. هو قديم. هي كبيرة. هو صغير. هي جميلة. هي نظيفة. هي وسخة. هي نظيفة. هو طويل. هو صغير. هو قصير. هي جديدة. هو نظيف. هو صغير. هو وسخة. هي نظيف. هي قديمة. هي كبيرة. هو جميل. هو صغير.

Ex30

أنا كبير/طويل. هو طالب. الشنطة جديدة. الغرفة كبيرة. الأم طبيبة. هي طالبة. عندي جهاز فيديو ياباني. عندك حديقة كبيرة. عندك شنطة جميلة. أحمد طالب. الطاولة قديمة. المصباح جديد. هو في المطبخ. الشبّاك نظيف. اللوح وسخ. الأب معلّم.

Final Exercise

1.

صباح	6.	أنا	1.
الخير	7.	طالب	2.
كيف	8.	أمريكي	3.
حالك	9.	السلام	4.
الحمد لله	10.	عليكم	5.

2. I am an American student. Peace be upon you. Good morning. How are you? Thank you, I am fine.

3.

الطاولة كبيرة. الشنطة قديمة. الطالب جديد. اللـوح وسخ. عندكِ شنطة. عندكَ بيت. هـو في المطبخ. الأب معلّم. الأم طبيبة. الشبّاك قديم. أنا طالب. أمام البيت حديقة. عندي سرير ومصبـاح وراديو. المصباح قديم.

4.

هي كبيرة. هو جميل. هو صغير. هي جميلة. هو قصير. هي وسخة. هي قديمة. هي أمـام البيت. هي جديدة.

5.

الجدار كبير. السرير صغير. السقف صغير. الحرف كبير. الجهاز صغير. المصباح كبـير. الصديـق صغير. الحمام كبير. الطاولة كبيرة. الورق صغير. الكتاب كبير. الكرّاسة كبيرة. الكرسي صغير. المدينة كبيرة. اللوح صغير. الغرفة كبيرة. القمر صغير. الشمس كبيرة. الشبّاك كبير. الباب كبير. البيـت صغير.

6.

لا، عندي بيت قديم.

لا، عندي قلم طويل.

لا، عندي غرفة صغيرة.

لا، عندي لوح وسخ.

7.

الكتاب على/تحت الطاولة. المعلّم في الغرفة. هو في/أمام البيت. عند الصديق.

8. *aṭ-ṭālib, al-khizāna, al-muᶜallim, allāh, ash-shams, al-ḥamdu li-l-lāh, maᶜa s-salāma, aṣ-ṣadīq*

Lesson 3
Ex11

هنا كتاب جديد.

هناك بيوت جديدة.

في الشنطة أقلام كثيرة.

في الغرفة خزانة كبيرة.

في الخزانة راديو جديد.

على السقف مصباح كبير.

على الطاولة كتب صغيرة.

على الجدار ألواح وسخة.

في البيت غرف كثيرة.

Ex14

البيت الصغـير، الشنطة الجديـدة، الشنطات الجديدة، القلم الكبـير، الأقـلام الصغيرة، الكرسي الجديد، الطاولة الكبيرة، الطاولات الكبيرة، الغرفة الجميلة، الطالبة الجميلة، الطالبات الجميـلات، الصديقة الجديدة، الصديقات الجديدات

Ex18

العاصمـة السورية هي دمشق. العاصمة اللبنانية هي بيروت. العاصمـة العراقيـة هـي بغـداد. العاصمـة المصرية هي القاهرة. العاصمة اليمنية هي صنعاء. العاصمة السعودية هي الرياض. العاصمة التونسية هي تونس. العاصمة الجزائرية هي الجزائر. العاصمة المغربيـة هـي الربـاط. العاصمـة الليبيـة هـي طرابلس. العاصمة السودانية هي الخرطوم. العاصمة العمانيـة هـي مسقط. العاصمـة الكويتيـة هـي الكويت.

Ex21

في المدينة

المدينة صغيرة وقبيحة. توجد في المدينة بيوت كبيرة وبيوت صغيرة قليلة. الشـوارع وسـخة وقصيرة وفي الشوارع سيّارات قليلة وتوجد في المدينة محطّة وفي المحطّة قطارات وأمام المحطّـة باصـات ومخـازن ومحلّات قليلة مثلاً للسيّارات وللملابـس وللكمبيوتـر ومخـابز ودكـاكين للخضراوات وللمشروبات ومكتبات.

وفي المدينة مطار صغير وقديم وفي المطار طائرات من بلدان قليلة مثلاً من مصـر وسـوريا واليمـن والسعودية والعراق وتونس والجزائر والمغرب وليبيا والسودان وعمان والإمارات والكويت. أنا مـن هذه المدينة وأنا طالب في الجامعة.

Ex22

The house is new. There are many busses. I am in the small bookshop/library. The station is in the city. The cities are big. The diligent students (f.) are in the university. There are vegetables and fruit. I go to the market. There are many air-planes here on the airport. The butter, the honey, the milk, the juice, the cheese and the eggs are in the refrigerator. The coffee, the tea and the sugar are on the table. There are air-planes from the Emirates, from Tunisia, Algeria, Saudi-Arabia, Sudan, Morocco, Kuwait, Libya, Syria, Egypt and Yemen.

Final Exercise

1.

5. هو في البرّادة.	1. كيف حالك؟
6. أين المشروبات؟	2. بخير.
7. هي على الطاولة.	3. وكيف حالك؟
8. مع السلامة	4. أين الفطور؟

2.

How are you? I am fine. And how are you? Where is the breakfast? It is in the refrigerator. Where are the drinks? They are on the table. Goodbye.

3.

رجال طوال، صديقات جميلات، معلّمون جدد، أقلام جديدة، سيّدات جديدات، سادة كبار، شنط/ شنطات صغيرة، مدارس كبيرة، برّادات صغيرة، آنسات جميلات، شوارع وسخة، قطارات قديمة، محطّات جديدة، باصات صغيرة، كتب جديدة، طائرات لبنانية، مطارات كبيرة، أيام كثيرة، بيوت صغيرة، طاولات طويلة، أسواق عربية، مدن تونسية، سيّارات يابانية، مخازن قليلة، دكاكين صغيرة، بلدان كثيرة، جامعات سعودية، طلاّب عرب، طالبات يمنيات، كرّاسات / كراريس جديدة، كراسيُّ قديمة، أكلات مغربية

4.

رجال كبار، طلاّب جميلون، أطبّاء صغار، عرب قدماء، إخوة نظفاء، طلاّب كثيرون، رجال طوال، طلبة قصار، طلاّب مجتهدون، معلّمون جدد، أطبّاء جيّدون، رجال قليلون، أطبّاء عظماء

5.

الطلاّب جدد. المعلّمات جميلات. هناك رجال كثيرون. الشنطات جديدة. المشروبات الجديدة في البرّادة. الطائرات الكبيرة من الكويت. الملابس الجديدة من تونس.

6.

مرحباً/ مرحباً بك. صباح الخير / صباح النور. مساء الخير / مساء النور. كيف حالك ؟ / الحمد لله. مع السلامة / مع السلامة.

7.

bābā, imāra, ṭā'ira, al-jubna, al-jazā'ir, maḥaṭṭa, maḥall, dukkān, sayyāra, sukkar, mujtahid, khaḍrāwāt, °uẓamā', °asal, shawāri°, madāris

9.

طاولة كبيرة – الطاولات كبيرة. / بيت صغير – البيوت صغيرة. / طالبة مجتهدة – الطالبات مجتهدات. / رجل عظيم / كبير/ طويل – الرجال عظماء / كبار/ طوال. / شنطة قديمة – الشنط / الشنطات قديمة.

Lesson 4

L 2

ع ل م / ط ل ب / ص د ق / خ ز ن / ص ب ح / ش ب ك / ج د ر / غ ر ف / ل و ح / ك ت ب / ك ر س / و ر ق / س ي ر / ق ط ر / خ ز ن / م د ن

L 3

طاولات، معلّمات، شبابيكُ، أبواب، كرّاسات/ كراريسُ، كتب، رجال، معلّمون، طلاّب، أقلام، كراسيُّ، مصابيحُ، مخازنُ، سيّارات، قطارات، فتيات.

L 5

ذهبت مع الصديق إلى هناك.
رأيت الأصدقاء في/أمام المحطّة.
اشتريت الكراريس من المخزن.

هل ذهبت من المحطّة إلى البيت؟
هل ذهبت إلى هناك بالسيّارة أم بالقطار؟
ماذا يوجد على الطاولة؟
ماذا يوجد في/على الخزانة؟
هل توجد أمام البيت سيّارات كثيرة؟

G 2

هناك مدن جميلة.
في البيت غرف كبيرة.
الجدران نظيفة.
الألواح كبيرة.
الأصدقاء في الغرفة.
في الغرفة أبواب.
على الطاولة شنط.
الدروس جديدة.
هناك مخازن جديدة.
في المدينة محطّات.
في المحطّة قطارات.
هنا فتيات جميلات.

G 4

هناك مدن جميلة.
في البيت غرف كبيرة.
الجدران القديمة نظيفة.
الألواح الجديدة كبيرة.
الأصدقاء الجدد في الغرفة.
في الغرفة أبواب كثيرة.
على الطاولة شنط قديمة.
الدروس العربية جديدة.
هناك مخازن جديدة.
في المدينة محطّات كثيرة.
في المحطّة قطارات قليلة.
هنا فتيات جميلات.

G 14

رأيت البيوت القديمة.
هل رأيت الفتاة الجميلة؟
هل رأيت المعلّمين الجدد؟
هلِ اشتريت الكتب الكثيرة؟

اشتريتُ الأقلام الجديدة.

اشتريتُ السيّارة القديمة.

رأيتُ في الطريق البيوت الكثيرة.

اشتريتُ القاموس والورق والأقلام والحبر.

رأيتُ في الشنطة الجلدية الكتاب والممحاة والمسطرة.

هل اشتريت المشروبات والجبنة والمربى والعسل؟

هل رأيت الكمبيوترات الكثيرة في الدكّان؟

هل كتبت الروايات؟

هل كتبت القاموس؟

Final Exercise

1.

درْس = فَعْل، بيْت = فَعْل، شمْس = فَعْل، قمَر = فَعَل، وَرَق = فَعَل، قِطار = فِعال، كِتاب = فِعال، جهاز = فِعال، صَباح = فَعال، سَلام = فَعال، حِبْر = فِعْل، مِصْر = فِعْل، شَجَرَة = فَعَلَة، كاتِب = فاعِل، طالِب = فاعِل، طالِبة = فاعِلَة، عائِلة = فاعِلَة، فاطِمة = فاعِلَة، شَنْطة = فَعْلَة، غُرْفة = فُعْلَة، سيّارة = فَعّالَة، كبير = فَعِيل، صغِير = فَعِيل، وسِخ = فَعِل، طبيب = فَعِيل، صدِيق = فَعِيل، مَطْبَخ = مَفْعَل، مَكْتَب = مَفْعَل، لوْح = فَعْل، مَدِينَة = فَعِيلة، شُبّاك = فُعّال، دكّان = فُعّال

2.

مكتبة ⇦ ك ت ب، دراسة ⇦ د ر س، مسطرة ⇦ س ط ر، مكتوب ⇦ ك ت ب، شاطر ⇦ ش ط ر، طريق ⇦ ط ر ق، محطة ⇦ ح ط ط، كبير ⇦ ك ب ر، أشجار ⇦ ش ج ر، كراريس ⇦ ك ر س

3.

ذهبت إلى المحطّة بالباص. توجد في الغرفة كراسيُّ كثيرة. كتبتُ على الورق الجديد. الشنطة على/تحت الطاولة. أحمد عند المعلّم. ذهبت إلى المكتبة. رأيتُ في البرّادة مشروبات كثيرة. المحطّة أمام الأشجار. ذهبت من شارع القاهرة إلى اليسار ومن المحلّ الكبير إلى اليمين. إشتريت من المكتبة كتباً. ذهبت من البيت إلى المدينة بالسيّارة. ذهبت من اليسار إلى اليمين ومـن هناك إلى المحطّة.

4.

رأيت قطاراً جديداً. اشتريت كتباً وأقلاماً جديـدة. رأيت في البرّادة جبنـة وزبـدة وخبـزاً ومربـى وحليباً وفواكه. اشتريت قاموساً وحبراً وممسحة. ذهبت إلى المدينة. المحطّة تحت الأشجار الكبيرة. توجد في المدينة بيوت صغيرة قليلة و(بيوت)كبيرة كثيرة. توجد في المطار طائرات مـن مصر واليمن وسوريا وتونس والعراق والجزائر وليبيا والإمارات.

5.

بيتٌ جديدٌ، في بيوتٍ جديدةٍ، قطاراتٌ جديدةٌ، مع المعلّم الجديدِ، المعلّمـاتُ الجديداتُ، رجـالٌ جدد، على الأوراقِ الجديدةِ، مع المشروبـاتِ الجديدةِ، كراسيُّ جديدةٍ، أمام المخازنِ الجديدةِ، بالسيّارةِ الجديدةِ، في الجامعاتِ الجديدةِ، أمـام المحطّةِ الجديدةِ، في المكتبـاتِ الجَديـدةِ، مـع الطالباتِ الجديداتِ، الأصدقاءُ الجددُ، باصاتٌ جديدةٌ، شارعٌ جديدٌ، في الطائراتِ الجديـدةِ، إلـى الشجرةِ الجديدةِ، في الروايةِ الجديدةِ، في الأسرّةِ الجديدةِ، على الأجهزةِ الجديدةِ

6.

فاعِل	: طالب، شارع، كاتب
مَفْعلة	: مكتبة، مدرسة
فِعال	: كتاب، جهاز، جدار، العراق، قطار
فَعْل	: بيت، درس، سقف، حرف، شمس، يوم، لوح، أرض، خير
فِعالة	: خزانة، دراسة، رواية، كتابة
فِعْل	: مصر، حبر، جلد

Lesson 5

L 1

وصل المعلّم. وصل المعلّمون. وصل الطلّاب. وصلت الفتاة. وصلت الفتيات. وصلت الوفود. وصل الرجال. وصلت المعلّمات. وصل الوفد. وصل الصديق. وصل الأصدقاء. وصل محمّد.

L 2

المعلّم وصل. المعلّمون وصلوا. الطلّاب وصلوا. الفتاة وصلت. الفتيات وصلن. الوفود وصلت. الرجال وصلوا. المعلّمات وصلن. الوفد وصل. الصديق وصل. الأصدقاء وصلوا. محمّد وصل.

L 3

ذهب الصديق إلى البيت. ذهب الأصدقاء إلى الفندق. ذهبت الفتيات إلى الأصدقاء. ذهبت الفتاة إلى الصديقة. ذهب الطالب إلى المعلّم. ذهب الطلّاب إلى الغرفة. ذهب السياسيون إلى الاجتماع. ذهب الرجال إلى المحطّة. ذهبت الطالبات إلى المخزن. ذهب أحمد إلى المطار.

L 4

(الطالب) وضع الكتاب في الخزانة. (المعلّمة) وضعت القلم على الطاولة.(أنا) وضعتُ المصباح على الكرسي. (أنت) وضعتَ المصباح على الأرض. (نحن) وضعنا الخزانة في الغرفة. (هي) وضعت الكتب في الشنطة.

L 6

كتبَ الرسالةَ صديقٌ عربيّ. كتبتُ للصديق رسالةً. كتبتَ رسالةً للصديق. قرأتُ كتاباً جديداً. وصلَ الوفدُ إلى المطار. اشتريتُ القلمَ منَ المخزن. اشتريتُ منَ المخزن قلمَاً جديداً. ذهبَ الوفدُ إلى الفندق. عقدتِ الوفودُ العربية اجتماعاً. عقدتِ الوفودُ اجتماعاتٍ كَثيرةً. ذهبوا إلى الفندق. وضعتُ الكتابَ على الطاولة. وضعنا الكتبَ في الخزانةِ. شربنا النبيذَ مع الأصدقاء. سمعتُ أخباراً جديدةً. فعلَ ذلكَ صديقٌ. رأينا فتياتٍ جميلاتٍ. يوجدُ المصباحُ على السقفِ. توجدُ الكراسيُّ والطاولةُ على الأرضِ. يوجدُ اللوحُ على الجدارِ. وصلتِ الوفودُ منَ البلدان العربيةِ.

L 7

من كتب الرسالة؟ لمن كتبت رسالة؟ لمن كتبت رسالة؟ ماذا قرأت؟ إلى أين وصل الوفد؟ من أين اشتريت القلم؟ من أين اشتريت قلماً جديداً؟ إلى أين ذهب الوفد؟ ماذا عقدت الوفود العربية؟ ماذا

عقدت الوفود؟ إلى أين ذهبوا؟ ماذا وضعت على الطاولة؟ ماذا وضعتم في الخزانة؟ مـع مـن شـربتم النبيذ؟ ماذا سمعت؟ من فعل ذلك؟ من رأيتم؟ أين يوجد المصباح؟ أين توجد الكراسيُّ والطاولة؟ أين يوجد اللوح؟ من أين وصلت الوفود؟

L 8

العلاقات التجارية، الكتـاب المدرسي، الإجتمـاع السياسي، الكتب العربيـة، العلاقـات السياسية، الطـالب العراقي، الطلّاب الجزائريون، المعلّمـون اللبنانيون، الأرض العربيـة، الجمهوريـة العربيـة، الحروف الشمسية، الحروف القمرية.

G 2

هل كتبت الرسالة؟ هل كتبت رسالة؟ هل كتبت رسائل؟ هل سمعت الخبر؟ هل سمعت الأخبار؟ هل سمعت أنّ الوفد العراقي وصل إلى لنـدن؟ هـل عرفت الرجل؟ هـل عرفت الفتاة؟ هـل عرفت أنّ الطالب ذهب إلى هناك؟ هل عرفت أنّ الطلّاب ذهبوا إلى البيت؟ هل قـرأت الخبر؟ هل قرأت الأخبار؟ هل قرأت أنّ الوفد (السوري، العراقي، الجزائري، السعودي، الكويتي، المصري) وصـل إلى لندن؟ هل قرأت الرسالة؟ هل قرأت الرسائل؟ هل وصلت إلى هناك؟ هـل وصلـت إلى لندن؟ هل ذهبت إلى الفندق؟ هل ذهبت إلى هناك؟ هل ذهبت إلى الصديق؟ هل ذهبت إلى المعلّم؟ هـل رأيـت الفتيات؟ هل اشتريت السيّارة؟ هل سافرت بالقطار؟ هل شـربت الشاي؟ هـل سألت المعلّم؟ هـل أكلت الخبز؟ هـل شربت القهوة؟ هل سألت الأم؟ هل عملت في البيت؟ هل عملت في المخزن؟ هـل عقدت اجتماعاً؟

G 3

هل كتبتم الرسالة؟ هل كتبتم رسالة؟ هل كتبتم رسائل؟ هل سمعتم الخبر؟ هل سمعتـم الأخبار؟ هل سمعتم أنّ الوفد العراقي وصل إلى لندن؟ هل عرفتم الرجل؟ هل عرفتم الفتاة؟ هل عرفتـم أنّ الطالب ذهب إلى هناك؟ هل عرفتم أنّ الطلّاب ذهبوا إلى البيت؟ هل قـرأتم الخبر؟ هـل قـرأتم الأخبار؟ هل قرأتم أنّ الوفد (السوري، العراقي، الجزائري، السعودي، الكويتي، المصري) وصل إلى لنـدن؟ هـل قرأتم الرسالة؟ هل قـرأتم الرسائل؟ هـل وصلتم إلى هناك؟ هـل وصلتـم إلى لنـدن؟ هـل ذهبتم إلى الفندق؟ هل ذهبتم إلى هناك؟ هل ذهبتم إلى الصديق؟ هل ذهبتم إلى المعلّم؟ هل رأيتم الفتيـات؟ هـل اشتريتم السيّارة؟ هل سافرتم بالقطار؟ هل شربتم الشاي؟ هل سألتم المعلّم؟ هـل أكلتم الخبز؟ هـل شربتم القهوة؟ هل سألتم الأم؟ هل عملتم في البيت؟ هل عملتم في المخزن؟ هل عقدتم اجتماعاً؟

G 4

هل كتب الرسالة؟ هل كتب رسالة؟ هل كتب رسائل؟ هل سمع الخبر؟ هل سمع الأخبـار؟ هـل سمـع أنّ الوفد العراقي وصل إلى لندن؟ هل عرف الرجل؟ هل عرف الفتاة؟ هل عـرف أنّ الطالب ذهب إلى هناك؟ هل عرف أنّ الطلّاب ذهبوا إلى البيت؟ هل قرأ الخبر؟ هل قرأ الأخبار؟ هل قـرأ أنّ الوفـد (السوري، العراقي، الجزائري، السعودي، الكويتي، المصري) وصل إلى لندن؟ هل قرأ الرسالة؟ هـل قرأ الرسائل؟ هل وصل إلى هناك؟ هل وصل إلى لندن؟ هل ذهب إلى الفندق؟ هل ذهب إلى هنـاك؟ هل ذهب إلى الصديق؟ هل ذهب إلى المعلّم؟   هـل سـافر بالقطار؟ هـل شرب الشاي؟ هـل سأل المعلّم؟ هل أكل الخبز؟ هل شرب القهوة؟ هل سأل الأم؟ هل عمل في البيت؟ هل عمـل في المخزن؟ هل عقد اجتماعاً؟

G 5

هل كتبت الرسالة؟ هل كتبت رسالة؟ هل كتبت رسائل؟ هل سمعت الخبر؟ هل سمعت الأخبار؟ هل سمعت أنّ الوفد العراقي وصل إلى لندن؟ هل عرفت الرجل؟ هل عرفت الفتاة؟ هل عرفت أنّ الطالب ذهب إلى هناك؟ هل عرفت أنّ الطلّاب ذهبوا إلى البيت؟ هل قرأت الخبر؟ هل قرأت الأخبار؟ هل قرأت أنّ الوفد (السوري، العراقي، الجزائري، السعودي، الكويتي، المصري) وصل إلى لندن؟ هل قرأت الرسالة؟ هل قرأت الرسائل؟ هل وصلت إلى هناك؟ هل وصلت إلى لندن؟ هل ذهبت إلى الفندق؟ هل ذهبت إلى هناك؟ هل ذهبت إلى الصديق؟ هل ذهبت إلى المعلّم؟ هل سافرت بالقطار؟ هل شربت الشاي؟ هل سألت المعلّم؟ هل أكلت الخبز؟ هل شربت القهوة؟ هل سألت الأمّ؟ هل عملت في البيت؟ هل عملت في المخزن؟ هل عقدت اجتماعاً؟

G 6

هل كتبوا الرسالة؟ هل كتبوا رسالة؟ هل كتبوا رسائل؟ هل سمعوا الخبر؟ هل سمعوا الأخبار؟ هل سمعوا أنّ الوفد العراقي وصل إلى لندن؟ هل عرفوا الرجل؟ هل عرفوا الفتاة؟ هل عرفوا أنّ الطالب ذهب إلى هناك؟ هل عرفوا أنّ الطلّاب ذهبوا إلى البيت؟ هل قرؤوا الخبر؟ هل قرؤوا الأخبار؟ هل قرؤوا أنّ الوفد (السوري، العراقي، الجزائري، السعودي، الكويتي، المصري) وصل إلى لندن؟ هل قرؤوا الرسالة؟ هل قرؤوا الرسائل؟ هل وصلوا إلى هناك؟ هل وصلوا إلى لندن؟ هل ذهبوا إلى الفندق؟ هل ذهبوا إلى هناك؟ هل ذهبوا إلى الصديق؟ هل ذهبوا إلى المعلّم؟ هل سافروا بالقطار؟ هل شربوا الشاي؟ هل سألوا المعلّم؟ هل أكلوا الخبز؟ هل شربوا القهوة؟ هل سألوا الأمّ؟ هل عملوا في البيت؟ هل عملوا في المخزن؟ هل عقدوا اجتماعاً؟

G 7

سمعت أنّ الغرفة جميلة. عرفت أنّ البيت قديم. قرأنا أنّ المعلّم طويل. سمعت أنّ الوفود وصلت أمس. هل عرفت أنّ الوفد وصل إلى المطار؟ سمعت أنّ الوفود عقدت اجتماعاً. هل سمعتم أنّ الأصدقاء سافروا إلى لندن؟ سمعت أنّ العلاقات التجارية جيّدة. هل سمعتم أنّ الأصدقاء العرب ذهبوا إلى هناك. هل عرفت أنّ الصديقة وصلت إلى المحطّة. قرأنا أنّ وفوداً كثيرة وصلت.

C 1

عاصمةُ ... هي فينا / أمستردام / لندن / باريس / وارسو / موسكو / بودابست / هلسنكي / كوبنهاغن / أوسلو / استكهولم / بروكسل / مدريد / لشبونه

Final Exercise

1.

وصلت الصديقة. وصلت الوفود. وصل الرجال. وصل أحمد إلى المطعم. وصل المعلّمون. وصل البرنامج. وصلت الطالبات إلى المرقص. وصل السياسي إلى سويسرا.

2.

سمعت أنّ الرجال شربوا العصير. كتب أحمد أنّ الطالبات شربن الشاي. شرب الأصدقاء القهوة مع السكّر. عرفت أنّ المعلّمات شربن العصير في الفندق. سمعت أنّ مريم شربت كوكا في الصباح. سمعت أنّ الطلّاب شربوا المشروبات. كتب أحمد أنّ محمّداً شرب القهوة مع العصير.

3.

جمهورية عربية، حروف شمسية، طالب جزائري، اجتماع سياسي، معلّمون لبنانيون، كتب عراقية، أرض عربية، كتاب مدرسي، علاقات سياسية

4.

هل عملوا في المخزن؟ هل وصلوا إلى الفندق؟ هل وضعوا الكتاب تحت الشنطة؟ هل سمعوا خبراً جيّداً؟ هل سألوا عن الطريق؟ هل عملوا في الشركة الفرنسية؟ هل رقصوا في المرقص؟ هل سألوا عن معالم المدينة؟ هل كتبوا رسالة طويلة؟ هل أكلوا في المطعم طعاماً شرقياً؟ هل سمعوا أنّ فاطمة تعبانة؟ هل وضعوا الجبنة على الطاولة؟

They worked in the shop. They arrived at the hotel. They put the book under the bag. They heard good news. They asked about the way. The worked in the French company. They danced in the dance hall. They asked about the sights of the city. They wrote a long letter. The ate an oriental meal in the restaurant. They heard that Fāṭima is tired. They put the cheese on the table.

5.

مساء الخير. كيف حالك؟ شكراً، الحمد لله وكيف حالك؟ شكراً، الحمد لله. أين كنت أمس؟ كنت مع أحمد في الجامعة في كلية الطب. ماذا فعلت هناك؟ قرأت كتباً وشربت الشاي في المطعم. ماذا فعلت في المساء؟ في المساء ذهبت مع أحمد إلى الديسكو. ماذا فعل أحمد في فرنسا؟ كتب رسائلَ كثيرة وعقد اجتماعات مع شركات فرنسية.

6.

أفعال : أبواب / أقلام / أغلاط / ألمان / أعداد / أتراك / أعمال / أفكار / أشجار / أشياء / أوطان / أخبار
فواعل : عواصم / فواكه / شوارع

7.

الجملة الاسمية، الجملة الفعلية، الماضي، العدد، المفرد، الجمع، مذكّر، مؤنّث

Lesson 6
L 4

غرفتك الجديدة، معلّمكم الجديد، أصدقاؤنا الجدد، كتبنا الجديدة، سيّارته الجديدة، بسيّارته الجديدة، في فندقنا الجديد، أمام مسرحنا الجديد، صديقتي الجديدة، مرافقكم الجديد، في مطارهم الجديد، سياستهم الجديدة، مدرستك الجديدة، جامعتها الجديدة، مخزنه الجديد

L 5

سافر صديقنا إلى لندن (دمشق، بيروت، بغداد، الجزائر) اليوم.
ذهبت إلى الجامعة (المسرح، المحطّة، بيتي، بيته، هناك) في الصباح.
عقد الوفد اجتماعه مساءً.
شربت الشاي مع أصدقائي (مع أصدقائي العرب، مع أصدقائي الأجانب) مساءً.
كتبنا رسالتنا ظهر الأمس.
اشتريت الكتب (الكتّاب، الشنطة، الكراريس، السيّارة) صباحاً.
رأيت الأصدقاء (الوفد، أعضاء الوفد، مرافقكم) ظهراً.

حضرنا الحفلة مساءً.

سمعت الخبر امس.

عرفت ذلك اليوم.

فعلوا ذلك مساء الأمس.

سافروا إلى سوريا (العراق، مصر، تونس، ...) صباح الأمس.

L 6

ك ت ب / س ر ح / د ر س / ر ك ز / ر ق ص / ك ت ب / ط ع م / ح ط ط /

ط ب خ / ط ي ر / خ ز ن / ع ل م / و ظ ف / د ر س / ح ض ر / ر ف ق /

ص ب ح / م ح و / س ط ر / ط ل ب / ت ج ر / ك ت ب

G 1

باب البيت، أبواب البيت، جدار البيت، جدران البيت، شبابيك البيت، غرف البيت

أبواب الغرفة، جدار الغرفة، جدران الغرفة، شبابيك الغرفة، سقف الغرفة، أرض الغرفة

كتاب الصديق، كتب الصديق، غرفة الصديق، بيت الصديق، سيّارة الصديق، شنطة الصديق

كتب محمّد، بيت محمّد، غرفة محمّد، سيّارة محمّد، شنطة محمّد، قلم محمّد

أقلام الصديقة، بيوت الصديقة، سيّارة الصديقة، رسائل الصديقة، كتب الصديقة

مسرح المدينة، مسارح المدينة، جامعة المدينة، شوارع المدينة، مخازن المدينة، محطّة المدينة

مدارس العاصمة، محطّات العاصمة، معالم العاصمة، جامعات العاصمة، مخازن العاصمة

عضو الوفد، أعضاء الوفد، مرافق الوفد، مرافقو الوفد، رئيس الوفد، سيّارة الوفد

G 2

باب بيته، أبواب بيتنا، جدار بيتي، جدران بيتكم، شبابيك بيتها، غرف بيتهن، أبواب غرفتي، جـدار

غرفتنا، جدران غرفتكم، شبابيك غرفتهم، سقف غرفتك، أرض غرفته

كتاب صديقه، كتب صديقي، غرفة صديقها، بيت صديقنا، سيّارة صديقكم، شنطة صديقكن

أقلام صديقتي، بيوت صديقته، سيّارة صديقتنا، رسائل صديقتهم، كتب صديقته

مسرح مديني، مسارح مدينتنا، جامعة مدينته، شوارع مدينتكم، مخازن مدينتها، محطّة مدينتهم

مدارس عاصمتها، محطّات عاصمتنا، معالم عاصمتكم، جامعات عاصمته، مخازن عاصمتنا

G 3

رأيت باب بيته. رأيت أبواب بيتنا. رأيت جدار بيتي. رأيت جدران بيتكم. رأيت شبابيك بيتها.

رأيت غرف بيتهن.

رأيت أبواب غرفتي. رأيت جدار غرفتنا. رأيت جـدران غرفتكم. رأيت شبابيك غرفتهم. رأيت

سقف غرفتك. رأيت أرض غرفته.

G 4

وصل الوفد إليه.	سافر إليها.
قلت لهم: مع السلامة.	توجد الكتب عليها.
ذهبوا إليهم.	كتب له رسالة.
يوجد اللوح عليه.	كتبت لها رسالة.
ذهبنا إليه.	قلت له: صباح الخير.

وصلت القطارات إليها.   سلّم عليهم!

G 5

في مسرحنا الجميل، في جامعتنا القديمة، في سيّارته الجديدة، مع صديقتي الجديدة، مع أصدقائك العرب، مع وفدهم التجاري، مع حكومتنا القديمة، مع صديقاتهن السوريات، في جامعاتكم الجديدة، في مطارنا الكبير، في كرّاسته الصغيرة، مع مرافقهم الألماني، مع وفودنا الأجنبية، في اجتماعاتكم الطويلة

Final Exercise

1.

أعضاء الوفد، مرافق الوفد، رئيس الوفد، سيّارة الوفد، اِجتماع الوفد، سياسيو الوفد، غرف الوفد
مسارح مدينة، شوارع مدينة، جامعة مدينة، دكاكين مدينة، مدارس مدينة، فندق مدينة، محطّات مدينة
شنطات المعلّمين، كتب المعلّمين، اِجتماعات المعلّمين، رسائل المعلّمين، معلّمو المعلّمين، مرقص المعلّمين، مطعم المعلّمين
موظّفو الحكومة، مرضى الحكومة، عمل الحكومة، وفود الحكومة، سياسيو الحكومة، أطبّاء الحكومة، مكاتب الحكومة
غرف بيته، جدران بيته، أبواب بيته، شبابيك بيته، حديقة بيته، بلكون بيته

2.

عنوان صديقتي القديم / العنوان القديم لصديقتي، المكتب القديم للرئيس الجديد، مكتب من مكاتب الموظّف، ملك من ملوك العالم العربي، بيت من البيوت الجميلة في المدينة، للمدينة، رئيس الوفد العربي وأعضاؤه، شنطة المعلّم الجديدة، مسرح من المسارح الجديدة في العاصمة / للعاصمة، معالم سوريا الكثيرة، موظّفو مكاتب السفر ورؤساؤها، شركات العائلة الملكية الكثيرة، عضو من أعضاء الوفد، مكاتب موظّفي مكتب السفر، سيّارة طالب عربي، مسرح المدينة وبيوتها، محاضرو جامعة العاصمة وطلاّبها، تحيات الصديق الخالصة، مسرحيات مسرح المدينة الجديدة / المسرحيات الجديدة لمسرح المدينة

3.

ذهبوا إليها. كتبوا أسماءهم عليها. رأيته عليها. وضعت الأوراق عليها. سافرنا إليهم. سلّم عليهن! وصلوا إليها. كتبنا حروفاً عربية عليه. شكرتهم عليها. وصلنا إليه.

4.

عزيزتي مريم
تحية طيبة وبعد
كيف حالك؟ كيف فاطمة؟
عندي عمل كثير. الدراسة صعبة وحضرت دروساً كثيرة. حضرت إلى الآن دروساً في الطب والفيزياء والكيمياء. محاضرو الجامعة وأساتذتها على مستوى جيّد. كيف الدراسة عندكم في الجامعة؟
هل سافرت إلى محمد؟ كتبت له رسالة. وصل جوابه أمس. كتب أنّه ذهب إلى المسرح في القاهرة وأنّه رأى هناك الرئيس المصري وسياسيين ودبلوماسيين كثيرين.

أنا في انتظار جوابك. بلّغي تحياتي لفاطمة.

صديقك

بيتر

Lesson 7

L 1
هذه الغرفة، هذه الغرف، هذه الفواكه، هؤلاء الطلاّب، هذا البلد، هذان البلدان، هذا الكتاب، هؤلاء الطالبات، هذه العلاقات، هذا اليوم، هذا المساء، هذه السيّارة، هذا المسرح، هذه السيّارات، هـذه المشروبات، هذه المأكولات، هذه اللغة، هذا اللون، هذه الألوان، هؤلاء الفتيات، هذه الفتاة، هـؤلاء الأصدقاء، هذا الصديق، هذه الأرض، هذه الخضراوات، هذه الشوكة، هـذا / هـذه السكّين، هـذه الملعقة، هذه الكأس، هذا الفنجان

L 2
تلك الغرفة، تلك الغرف، تلك الفواكه، أولئك الطلاّب، ذلك البلد، تلك البلدان، ذلك الكتاب، أولئك الطالبات، تلك العلاقات، ذلك اليوم، ذلك المساء، تلك السيّارة، ذلك المسرح، تلك السيّارات، تلك المشروبات، تلك المأكولات، تلك اللغة، ذلك اللون، تلك الألوان، أولئك الفتيـات، تلك الفتاة، أولئك الأصدقاء، ذلك الصديق، تلك الأرض، تلك الخضراوات، تلك الشوكة، ذلك السكّين، تلك الملعقة، تلك الكأس، ذلك الفنجان

L 3
a)
لون هذه السيّارة، بيوت هؤلاء الطلاّب، أصدقاء هذه الفتاة، عاصمة هذا البلد، جامعة هذه المدينة، غرف هذا البيت، معلّم صديقي هذا، طلاّب جامعتنا هذه، معلّمو هذه المدرسة، علاقات هذا البلـد، أعضاء هذا الوفد، فواكه هذا البلد

b)
لون السيّارة هذا، بيوت الطلاّب هذه، أصدقاء الفتاة هذه، عاصمة البلد هذه، جامعة المدينة هـذه، غرف البيت هذه، معلّم صديقي هذه ، طلاّب جامعتنا هؤلاء، معلّمو المدرسة هؤلاء، علاقـات البلـد هذه، أعضاء الوفد هؤلاء، قاعة الطعام هذه، فواكه البلد هذه

L 4
a)
لون تلك السيّارة، بيوت أولئك الطلاّب، أصدقـاء تلك الفتاة، عاصمة ذلك البلـد، جامعة تلك المدينة، غرف ذلك البيت، معلّم صديقي ذلك، طلاّب جامعتنا تلك، معلّمو تلك المدرسة، علاقات ذلك البلد، أعضاء ذلك الوفد، فواكه ذلك البلد

b)
لون السيّارة ذلك، بيوت الطلاّب تلك، أصدقاء الفتاة أولئك، عاصمـة البلد تلك، جامعة المدينة تلك، غرف البيت تلك، معلّم صديقي ذلك، طلاّب جامعتنا أولئك، معلّمو المدرسـة أولئك، علاقات البلد تلك، أعضاء الوفد أولئك، قاعة الطعام تلك، فواكه البلد تلك

L 5

هذا هو المعلّم. هؤلاء هم الطلاّب السوريون. هؤلاء هـن الطالبـات الجديدات. هـذا هـو الصديـق. هؤلاء هم الأصدقاء العرب. هذا هو الرجل. هذه هي الفتـاة الجميلـة. هـذه هـي الرسالـة. هـذا هـو الكتاب الجديد. هذه هي الشنطة. هذه هي الكأس. هذه هي الغرفة الكبيرة. هذه هي العاصمة. هذه هي المدينة. هذا هو المطعم. هذا هو المسرح. هذه هي الجامعة. هذه هي القائمة. هذه هي القاعة.

L 6

اشتريت أقلاماً سوداءَ، ورقاً جديداً، كرسياً أحمرَ، كتباً عربيةً، فنجاناً أخضرَ، فواكهَ، خضراواتٍ.
رأيت رجالاً، معلّمينا، الطلاّبَ العراقيينَ، أصدقاءَ عرباً، مدناً كثيرةً.
ذهب إلى أصدقاءَ عربٍ، أصدقائنا هؤلاء، مطاعمَ كثيرةٍ، معلّمِتِنا.
كتبت رسالةً، رسائلَ كثيرةً، كتاباً.
دخلت بيتَكُم، القاعةَ الحمراءَ، مطعماً جميلاً، مسرحَ المدينةِ.
وضعت الكتب في الشنطةِ السوداء، خزائنَ بيضاءَ.
شربت نبيذاً أحمرَ، نبيذاً أبيضَ، كأساً من النبيذِ، كأساً من النبيذِ الأبيضِ.
درست اللغةَ العربيةَ، لغاتٍ كثيرةً، الحياةَ في البلدان العربيةِ.
عرفت المعلّمينَ العربَ، المسافرينَ، طلاّباً مِنْهُم.

L 7

إلى أين ذهبوا؟ أين وضعت الكتاب؟ أين وضعتم الكتب؟. مع من شربتم النبيذ؟. مـاذا سمعت؟ مـن فعل ذلك؟ من رأيتم؟ أين يوجد المصباح؟ أين توجد الكراسيُّ والطاولة؟ أين يوجد اللوح؟ مـن أين وصلت الوفود؟ من كتب الرسالة؟ لمن كتبت رسالة؟ لمن كتبت رسالة؟ ماذا قرأت؟ إلى أين وصـل الوفود؟ من أين اشتريت القلم؟ من أين اشتريت قلماً جديداً؟ إلى أين ذهب الوفود؟ من عقد اجتماعاً؟ من عقد اجتماعات كثيرة؟

G 1

يخرج من الغرفة. يذهب إلى المطعم. يدخل القاعة. يأخذ قائمة الطعام.
يشرب القهوة (الشاي، البيرة، الماء، النبيذ).
يأكل اللحم (الرزّ، الخضراوات، الفواكه).
يكتب رسالة. يقرأها. يضعها في الخزانة.

G 2

أخرج من الغرفة. أذهب إلى المطعم. أدخل القاعة. آخذ قائمة الطعام.
أشرب القهوة (الشاي، البيرة، الماء، النبيذ).
آكل اللحم (الرزّ، الخضراوات، الفواكه).
أكتب رسالة. أقرأها. أضعها في الخزانة.
نخرج من الغرفة. نذهب إلى المطعم. ندخل القاعة. نأخذ قائمة الطعام.
نشرب القهوة (الشاي، البيرة، الماء، النبيذ).
نأكل اللحم (الرزّ، الخضراوات، الفواكه).
نكتب رسالة. نقرأها. نضعها في الخزانة.

G 3

هل تخرج من الغرفة؟ هل تذهب إلى المطعم؟ هل تدخل القاعة؟ هل تأخذ قائمة الطعام؟
هل تشرب القهوة (الشاي، البيرة، الماء، النبيذ)؟
هل تأكل اللحم (الرزّ، الخضراوات، الفواكه)؟
هل تكتب رسالة. هل تقرأها. هل تضعها في الخزانة؟
هل تخرجون من الغرفة؟ هل تذهبون إلى المطعم؟ هل تدخلون القاعة؟ هل تأخذون قائمة الطعام؟
هل تشربون القهوة (الشاي، البيرة، الماء، النبيذ)؟
هل تأكلون اللحم (الرزّ، الخضراوات، الفواكه)؟
هل تكتبون رسالة؟ هل تقرؤونها؟ هل تضعونها في الخزانة؟

G 5

وصل الوفد العراقي اليوم. وصلت الوفود العربية ظهر اليوم. جلسوا في القاعة الكبيرة. شربت فنجاناً من القهوة. هل أكلت اللحم والخضراوات؟ طلب لحم الدجاج. يأكلون طعاماً شرقياً. شربنا الشاي بعد الأكل. جلسوا في مطعم من مطاعم المدينة. هل عرفت هؤلاء الأصدقاء؟ نعم، عرفتهم. هل فهمتم ذلك الرجل؟ هل تفهمني؟ هل فهمتموني؟ يعقدون اجتماعاً. يكتبن رسائل كثيرة. سمعت ذلك. يضع كتبه في الشنطة. نقرأ تلك الكتب. يفعل ذلك أصدقاؤنا الألمان. درسنا اللغة العربية.

G 8

هل قرأت الخبر؟ هل قرأت الأخبار؟ هل قرأت أنّ الوفد (السوري، العراقي، الجزائري، السعودي، الكويتي، المصري) وصل إلى لندن؟ هل قرأت الرسالة؟ هل قرأت الرسائل؟ هل وصلت إلى هناك؟ هل وصلت إلى لندن؟ هل ذهبت إلى الفندق؟ هل ذهبت إلى هناك؟ هل ذهبت إلى الصديق؟ هل ذهبت إلى المعلّم؟ هل رأيت الفتيات؟ هل اشتريت السيّارة؟ هل سافرت بالقطار؟ هل شربت الشاي؟ هل سألت المعلّم؟ هل أكلت الخبز؟ هل شربت القهوة؟ هل سألت الأمّ؟ هل عملت في البيت؟ هل عملت في المخزن؟ هل عقدت اجتماعاً؟ هل كتبت الرسالة؟ هل كتبت رسالة؟ هل كتبت رسائل؟ هل سمعت الخبر؟ هل سمعت الأخبار؟ هل سمعت أنّ الوفد العراقي وصل إلى لندن؟ هل عرفت الرجل؟ هل عرفت الفتاة؟ هل عرفت أنّ الطالب ذهب إلى هناك؟ هل عرفت أنّ الطلاّب ذهبوا إلى البيت؟

Final Exercise

1.

هذا الطقس، هؤلاء المعلّمون، هؤلاء الطالبات، هذه الشوكات، هذه المدرسة، هذه المقبّلات، هذه السنة، هؤلاء السادة، هذه الكراريس، هؤلاء السيّدات، هذه الرسائل، هذه الزجاجة، هؤلاء الأعضاء، هذا المكتب

2.

ذلك الطقس، أولئك المعلّمون، أولئك الطالبات، تلك الشوكات، تلك المدرسة، تلك المقبّلات، تلك السنة، أولئك السادة، تلك الكراريس، أولئك السيّدات، تلك الرسائل، تلك الزجاجة، أولئك الأعضاء، ذلك المكتب

3.

هذا الصديق، كتـاب صديقـي هـذا / هـذا الكتـاب لصديقي / هـذا الكتاب لصديقي، شنطة المعلّمـة تلك / تلك الشنطة للمعلّمة، بيت ذلـك الموظّـف الجديد / البيت الجديد لذلك الموظّف، مشروبات ذلك المطعم، خضراوات البقّال هذه، زجاجة الصديق هذه، كراريسه هذه، أصدقاؤنا هؤلاء، مطاعم المدينة تلك هذا هو المعلّم. هذه مدرسة. هؤلاء شربوا العصير/ شرب هؤلاء العصير. هذه هي الجرسونة.

4.

يصل الوفد العراقي اليوم. تصل الطائرات إلى القاهرة. ندرس اللغة العربية. أعـرف/ تعرفين/ تعرف الكثير من الدبلوماسيين. أقرأ/ تقرئين/ تقرأ كتباً جديدة. يحضرن حفلة طويلة. تطلبين مشروبات. تأكلون أطعمة شرقية. تعملـن في المطعم. أرجع إلى البيت. أدخـل/ تدخلين/ تدخل المحـلّ. يعقدون اجتماعاً. أفهم الدرس. تأكلون لحماً وبيضاً.

5.

بيض، زبدة، جبنة، حليب، خبز، مربى، سكر، عصير، عسل، فواكه، خضراوات، تفـاح، باذنجـان، برتقال، بطّيخ، بطاطس، بيرة، ثوم، جوز، خلّ، خوخ، خيار، دقيـق، رز، زيتـون، سمـك، طمـاطم، عدس، عنب، فجل، فطر، فلفل، ملح، فول، لوز، مشمش، موز، ليمون

6.

سوف/ سأدرس اللغة العربية في جامعة القاهرة لمدة سنة. سوف / سيسكن في بيت الطلبة. سوف / ستكتب رسالة. سوف / سيشربون / سيشربن الشاي. لا، أشرب بيرة. هـل سـوف / ستشـربون / ستشربن الكحول؟ لا، سوف / سنشـرب العصير؟ أنا جوعـان(ة) وعطشـان(ة). هــل عندكـم مقبّلات؟ نعم، عندنا مقبّلات كثيرة جدّاً. هل الأكل حارّ؟ لا، هـو عـادي. الأكل الحـارّ جيّد في الطقس الحارّ. هل عندكم ماء معدني؟ هات سكّين وشوكة وملعقة من فضلك!

Lesson 8

L 5

لا تفعلْ / تفعلي ذلك! لم أفعل ذلك. لماذا لم تفعل / تفعلي ذلك؟ لم يصلوا / يصلن بعد. لن يصلوا / يصلن غداً. خذ/ خذي الكتاب! ضعه/ ضعيه على الطاولة. لا تخرج / تخرجي من الغرفة! لا تعرفه / تعرفينه. لا تعرفوننا / تعرفنا. طلب منّي ألا أذهب إلى هناك.

L 8

غرفتـك الجديدة، معلّمكم الجديد، أصدقاؤنا الجـدد، كتبنا الجـديدة، سيّارته الجديدة، بسيّارته الجديدة، في فندقنا الجديد، أمام مسرحنا الجديد، صديقتي الجديدة، مرافقكم الجديد، في مطارهم الجديد، سياستهم الجديدة، مدرستك الجديدة، جامعتها الجديدة، مخزنه الجديد

G 1

لم أعرف ذلك. لم نعرف ذلك. لم يعرفوا ذلك. لم تعرف ذلك. لم يعمل هناك. لم أعمـل هناك. لم تعمل في ذلك المصنع. لم يعملوا في تلك المدينة. لم نعمل هناك. لم يعملوا بأجهزة حديثة. لم يأخذوا ذلك. لم نأخذ الكتاب. لم نأخذ الجرائد. لم يأخذن ذلك. لم تأخذوا ذلك. لم يفعل ذلك. لم نفعل ذلك. لم تفعلي ذلك. لم تذهب إلى هناك. لم تذهبي إلى المكتبة. لم يذهبوا إلى القاعة. لم أشرب/

تشرب / تشربي النبيذ. لم يشربوا القهوة. لم نشرب البيرة. لم نأكل اللحم. لم يأكلوا في المطعم. لم
تأكلوا هناك. لم أخرج/ تخرج / تخرجي من البيت. لم يخرج من المعهد. لم يخرجن من المعهد. لم
يدخل بيت صديقه. لم ندخل المطعم. لم تدخلي ذلك البيت. لم يصل الوفد أمس. لم تصل الوفود
مساء أمس. لم يصلوا صباح اليوم. لم أفهم. لم تفهموا. لم يفهم. لم تفهم. لم نفهم. لم يدرس هناك
طلاّب أجانب. لم يشرح لهم عمل المكتبة. لم يرجعوا إلى البيت. لم نطلب منه ذلك. لم يطلبوا منّي
ذلك. لم أطلب منكم ذلك. لم يرغبوا في أن يكتبوا لها. لم أرغب في أن يدخل بيتي.

G 2

لا أعرف ذلك. لم يأخذ الكتاب. لم يفعلوا ذلك. لم أدخل/ تدخل/ تدخلي ذلك المعهد. لم نقرأ
كتباً كثيرة. لا يدرسون اللغة العربية. لا نعرف ذلك. لن يعقدوا اجتماعاً. لن يعمل في لندن. لن
تكتبوا لهم. لم أضع/ تضع / تضعي الكتب في الخزانة. لا نرغب في أن نذهب إلى هناك. لم يطلب
منّي أن أذهب إلى هناك. لم تخرج / تخرجي من البيت صباحاً. لم نسمع هذا الخبر. لا نفهم ذلك. لا
يأكلون فواكهَ كثيرة. لن يذهبوا إلى المعهد. لم تذهب إلى صديقتها. لم يعمل بالأجهزة الحديثة. لا
ينظرون إلى الكتب.

G 3

ليس البيت كبيراً. ليست البيوت جميلة. ليس المعلّمون في الغرفة. ليس هؤلاء الرجال طيبين. ليس
هؤلاء الرجال معلّمين. ليست تلك الفتاة معلّمة. ليست أولئك الفتيات طالبات. ليست هذه
الكرّاسة جديدة. ليست سيّارتي يابانية. ليس لونها أبيض. ليست عندي كتب كثيرة. ليس في الغرفة
طلاّب. ليست هناك أجهزة حديثة. ليس في المعهد طلبة أجانب.

G 4

لا تشرب! لا تشربوا الشاي! لا تذهب إلى هناك! لا تذهبن إلى هناك! لا تدخل ذلك البيت! لا
تدخلي ذلك المخزن! لا تفعلوا ذلك! لا تفعل ذلك! لا تخرج! لا تخرجوا! لا تأخذ الجهاز! لا
تأخذوا ذلك! لا تسمعي! لا تسمعوا! لا تقرأ هذا الكتاب! لا تقرؤوا هذه الكتب! لا تكتب لي! لا
تكتبن لنا! لا تضعوا ذلك في الشنطة!

G 5

إفعلي ذلك! إفعلوا ذلك! أكتبوا لهم! خذ ذلك الجهاز! أدخل ذلك المطعم! إذهبوا إلى هناك! إشربي
النبيذ! أخرج من هنا! إقرؤوا تلك الرسالة! ضع ذلك في الخزانة !

G 6

1. كتب محمّد، بيت محمّد، غرفة محمّد، سيّارة محمّد، شنطة محمّد، قلم محمّد
2. أقلام الصديقة، بيوت الصديقة، سيّارة الصديقة، رسائل الصديقة، كتب الصديقة
3. مسرح المدينة، مسارح المدينة، جامعة المدينة، شوارع المدينة، مخازن المدينة، محطّة المدينة
4. مدارس العاصمة، محطّات العاصمة، معالم العاصمة، جامعات العاصمة، مخازن العاصمة
5. باب البيت، أبواب البيت، جدار البيت، جدران البيت، شبابيك البيت، غرف البيت
6. أبواب الغرفة، جدار الغرفة، جدران الغرفة، شبابيك الغرفة، سقف الغرفة، أرض الغرفة
7. كتاب الصديق، كتب الصديق، غرفة الصديق، بيت الصديق، سيّارة الصديق، شنطة الصديق
8. عضو الوفد، أعضاء الوفد، مرافق الوفد، مرافقو الوفد، رئيس الوفد، سيّارة الوفد

Final Exercise

1.

لم نطلب منه ذلك. لم يرغب في أن يكتب رسالة. لم أفهم. لم نأخذ الجرائد. لم يشربوا القهوة. لم تصل الوفود أمس. لم يشربن العصير. لم يخرج من المعهد. لم ترجعي من الفندق إلى المعهد. لم يعملوا في تلك المدينة. لم يبذلوا جهوداً كبيرة. لم يأمل أن يكتب له. لم تبحثوا عن الكتب في رفوف كثيرة. لم يصل أمناء عامّون لأحزاب كثيرة. لم تكتبي الرسالة. لم يفعلن ذلك. لم أشكره / تشكره / تشكريه على الجرائد الجديدة. لم نفهم الدرس. لم يرغب في أن يشرب العصير وأن يأكل اللحم.

2.

لم تكتبوا هذه الرسالة. لم يصل الوفد المصري إلى لندن. لم يأخذ الجريدة. لم يعرفوا القواميس العربية. لم تكتبي روايات. لم أنصحك بأن تأخذي هذه الكتب. لم أرغب في أن تدرسوا اللغة العربية. لم نشرب البيرة.

3.

لا ينظرون إلى الكتب. لن تعملي بالأجهزة الحديثة. لا نفهم ذلك. لن يأكلوا لحم الدجاج. لم أخرج من البيت صباحاً. لا أعرف ذلك. لم أدخل / تدخل / تدخلي ذلك الفندق. لا يدرسن اللغة العربية. لا نرغب في أن نكتب رسائل كثيرة. لن يعقدوا اجتماعاً. لم أضع/ تضع / تضعي الكتب في الخزانة. لم أذهب / تذهب / تذهبي مع صديقته. لم تطلبوا أن نذهب معكم. لا تجلسنَ في المقهى. لم تخرجي من المعهد. لم نعرف أين يسكن أحمد.

4.

(هو) ليس معلّماً. (هي) ليست جديدة. (نحن) لسنا طلاباً. (أنتَ) لست بائعاً. (أنتم) لستم مجتهدين. (هنّ) لسن في المعهد. (أنتِ) لست مرافقة. (هم) ليسوا رجالاً طيّبين. ليست عندي كتب كثيرة. (أنا) لست طالباً. ليس في المعهد طلبة أجانب. ليست هناك جرائد عربية. ليس الأكل حارّاً. ليس العصير في البرّادة. (هو) ليس شاطراً.

5.

ليس كبيراً. ليست عندي قواميس كثيرة. ليست في لندن. لستم مجتهدين. ليست الطالبات كبيرات. لست معلّمة. لسنا شاطرين. ليس النبيذ في البرّادة. ليسوا في الجامعة. لست على حق .

6.

لا تشرب العصير !لا تأكل اللحم ! لا تأخذ الكتاب ! لا تخرجي من الغرفة ! لا تسمعي ! لا تسمحوا لي أن أكتب ! لا تكتب الرسالة ! لا تذهبن إلى هناك ! لا تفعلي ذلك ! لا تدخل ! لا تسمح لي أن أخرج ! لا تبحث عنه ! لا تدرسوا العربية ! لا تطلب قهوة !

7.

ليست المناقشات طويلة. كتب بمناسبة العيد الوطني. لم يحصل الوزير على جائزة نوبل. لم تكتب الجريدة عن التعاون العسكري. لا يبذل رئيس البلد وحكومته جهوداً لتوسيع التبادل التجاري. وصل الوزير الألماني إلى دمشق في إطار جولة في الشرق الأوسط. قابل الرئيس الروسي نظيره الأمريكي. لم أعرف أجوبة كثيرة.

8.

Jussive	Subjunctive	Imperfect	Perfect
تَكْتُبِي	تَكْتُبِي	تَكْتُبِينَ	كَتَبْتِ
يَذْهَبْ	يَذْهَبَ	يَذْهَبُ	ذَهَبَ
تَدْرُسُوا	تَدْرُسُوا	تَدْرُسُونَ	دَرَسْتُم
يَطْلُبُوا	يَطْلُبُوا	يَطْلُبُون	طَلَبُوا
تَخْرُجِي	تَخْرُجِي	تَخْرُجِينَ	خَرَجْتِ

Lesson 9

L 6

أسماء فصول السنة في أوربا هي الربيع والصيف والخريف والشتاء.

أسماء شهور الربيع في أوربا هي مارس وأبريل ومايو / آذار ونيسان وأيار.

أسماء شهور الصيف في أوربا هي يونيو ويوليو وأغسطس / حزيران و تمّوز وآب.

أسماء شهور الخريف في أوربا هي سبتمبر وأكتوبر ونوفمبر / أيلول وتشرين الأول وتشرين الثاني.

أسماء شهور الشتاء في أوربا هي ديسمبر ويناير وفبراير / كانون الأول وكانون الثاني وشباط.

L 7

a)

لون هذه السيّارة، بيوت هؤلاء الطلّاب، أصدقاء هذه الفتاة، عاصمة هذا البلد، جامعة هذه المدينة، غرف هذا البيت، معلّم صديقي هذا، طلّاب جامعتنا هذه، معلّمو هذه المدرسة، علاقات هذا البلد، أعضاء هذا الوفد، فواكه هذا البلد

b)

لون السيّارة هذا، بيوت الطلّاب هذه، أصدقاء الفتاة هذه، عاصمة البلد هذه، جامعة المدينة هذه، غرف البيت هذه، معلّم صديقي هذا، طلّاب جامعتنا هؤلاء، معلّمو المدرسة هؤلاء، علاقات البلد هذه، أعضاء الوفد هؤلاء، قاعة الطعام هذه، فواكه البلد هذه

L 8

يجب عليّ أن أكتب رسالة. يجب عليّ أن أسافر إلى لندن. يجب عليك / عليها أن تحجز شقّتين. يجب عليكم أن تطلبوا مشروبات وأكلا. يجب عليك / عليها أن تحمل الحقيبتين إلى فوق. يجب عليك أن تدرسي اللغة العربية. يجب عليهم أن يعملوا في الخارج. يجب عليّ أن أعمل في عيادة أمّي. يجب عليك أن تسافري إلى مصر لمدة شهرين. يجب عليكم أن تجمعوا المراجع والمصادر اللازمة. يجب عليك / عليها أن تسمح له بالدخول. يجب عليك / عليها أن تفهم ما تقرأ. يجب علينا أن نرجع إلى المدينة. يجب علينا أن نأخذ زجاجتين. يجب عليك / عليها أن تشرب العصير. يجب علينا أن نأكل السمك.

G 1

قرأتهما. قرأناهما. هل قرأتموهما؟

قرأتها. لم أقرأها. لم نقرأها.

رأيتهن. رأيناهن. هل رأيتموهن؟

مكثت فيها. مكثتْ فيها. مكث فيها.

شربتهما. شرباهما. شربتاهما.

ذهبت / ذهبنا / ذهبوا إلى هناك معهما.

ذهبت / ذهبن إلى هناك معهما.

ذهبت / ذهبوا/ ذهب إلى هناك معهم.

درستهما / درسناهما / درسهما.

درستها / درسوها. هل درستها؟

وضعتهما / وضعتْهما فيها.

أخذتهما / أخذناهما / أخذوهما.

كتبتهما / كتبتْهما / كتبنهما.

خرجت منه / خرجنا منه / خرجوا منه.

سمعته / سمعناه. هل سمعتموه؟

عملت / عملوا فيها. هل عملت فيها؟

أكلته / أكلته / أكلتها . أكلناه / أكلناها / أكلوه / أكلوه / أكلوها.

رجعت / رجعنا إليه. هل رجعتم إليه؟

شكرته / شكرناه / شكروه.

نظرت / نظر إليهما. هل نظرت إليهما؟

G 2

هذه الدولة، هذه البُلْدان، هذان البَلَدان، هذان الجهازان، هذه الأرض، هذه اللغة، هذا الاجتماع، هاتان المدرستان، هذه المشروبات، هذه الأيام، هاتان الخزانتان، في هاتين الرسالتين، هذا المسرح، هذه المحطّات، هذه الوفود، هذان الشهران، هذان الأسبوعان، هذا المعهد، هذه الدول، في هاتين الغرفتين، هذه الزجاجات، بهاتين السيّارتين، هذان المعطفان، مع هؤلاء الأصدقاء، هذان الطالبان، هذه الأسئلة، هذه الأعمال، هذه القرية، هذان الجبلان، هذه الملابس، هؤلاء العمّال، هؤلاء الفلّاحون.

G 3

ذهبا إلى المكتبة.

تعقدان اجتماعاً.

متى خرجا من البيت؟

لماذا فعلتما ذلك؟ أو: لماذا فعلتا ذلك؟

أين عملا؟

ماذا تشربان؟

ماذا درستما؟ أو: ماذا درستا؟

G 5

يأكلون طعاماً شرقياً. شربنا الشاي بعد الأكل. جلسوا في مطعم من مطاعم المدينة. هـل عرفـت هؤلاء الأصدقاء؟ نعم، عرفتهم. هل فهمتم ذلك الرجل؟ هـل تفهمني/ تفهميني؟ هـل فهمتمـوني؟ يعقدون اجتماعاً. يكتب رسائل كثيرة. يضع كتبه في الشنطة. نقرأ تلك الكتب. يفعـل ذلك أصدقاؤنا الألمان. وصل الوفد العراقي اليوم. درسنا اللغة العربية. وصلـت الوفود العربيـة ظهـر اليوم. جلسوا في القاعة الكبيرة. شربت فنجاناً من القهوة. هل أكلـت اللحـم والخضراوات؟ طلـب لحم الدجاج.

Final Exercise

1.

عملت في ذلك المصنع شهرين.

سكنت في الفندق يومين.

جلست في الغرفة ساعتين.

شربت كأسين من البيرة.

اشتريت ذلك الجهاز بدولارين.

ذهبت إلى المسرح مع صديقين.

عندي سيّارتان.

أدرس العربية منذ سنتين.

2.

أطروحات المعلّمين، جوازات المعلّمين هذه، غرفتا المعلّمين هاتان

مسارح هذه المدينة، فندقا هذه المدينة، موظّفو هذه المدينة، محطّات هذه المدينة، شوارع هذه المدينة

صديقتا صديقه، كتب صديقه هذه، تخصص صديقه ذلك

3.

يجب عليّ أن أكتب رسالتين. يجب عليه أن يعمل في الخارج. يجب عليها أن تـأكل السـمك. يجب عليك أن تحجزي غرفتين. يجب علينا أن نحمل الحقيبتين إلى الغرف. يجب عليهم / عليهن أن يلبسوا / يلبسن معاطف وقبعات وقفافيز. يجب عليكم / عليكن أن تسألوا / تسألن المعلم الثاني.

4.

ماذا درستما/ درستا؟ ماذا تشربان؟ أين سكنا؟ تسألان الثـاني. تلبسـان المعطف الثـاني. يشعران / تشعران بالبرد في غرفتكما. درستما/ درستا في الفصلين الربيعي والخريفي. أين تضعـان الجوازيـن؟ جمعا المصادر والمراجع.

5.

تضم الجامعة كليات الفيزياء والكيمياء وعلم الأحياء والرياضيات واللغات والتربية والحقوق وكليـتي الاقتصاد والزراعة. أدرس في معهد الدراسات العربية. معهدي قديم وصغير. وتوجد إلى جانب هـذا المعهد في إطار الاستشراق معاهد للدراسات الإفريقية والمصرية والهنديـة والصينيـة والتركيـة ومعهـد لتاريخ الأديان.

Lesson 10

L 4

ليست عندي كتب كثيرة. ليس في الغرفة طلاّب. ليست هناك أجهزة حديثة. ليس في المعهد طلبة أجانب. ليس البيت كبيراً. ليست البيوت جميلة. ليس المعلّمون في الغرفة. ليس هؤلاء الرجال طيبين. ليس هؤلاء الرجال معلّمين. ليست تلك الفتاة معلّمة. ليست أولئك الفتيات طالبات. ليست هذه الكرّاسة زرقاء. ليست سيّارتي بيضاء. ليس لونها أبيض.

G 1

ثلاث ليرات/ ثلاثة دنانير، ثلاث عشرة ليرة / ثلاثة عشر ديناراً / ثلاث وعشرون ليرة / ثلاثة وعشرون ديناراً

أربع ساعات / أربعة أشهر، أربع عشرة ساعة / أربعة عشر شهراً / أربع وثلاثون ساعة / أربعة وثلاثون شهراً

خمسة كيلومترات / خمس سنوات/ سنين، خمسة عشر كيلومتراً/ خمس عشرة سنة / خمسة وأربعون كيلومتراً / خمس وأربعون سنة

ستة ملاليم / قروش، ستة عشر ملّيماً/ قرشاً، ستة وخمسون ملّيماً / قرشاً

سبعة أمتار / أيام، سبعة عشر متراً / يوماً، سبعة وستون متراً / يوماً

ثمانية سنتيمترات / كتب، ثمانية عشر سنتيمتراً / كتاباً، ثمانية وسبعون سنتيمتراً / كتاباً

تسعة أيام / تسع سنوات / سنين، تسعة عشر يوماً / تسع عشرة سنة، تسعة وثمانون يوماً / تسع وثمانون سنة

عشر دقائق / عشرة أسابيع، عشرون / ثلاثون دقيقةً / أسبوعاً

أحد عشر جنيهاً / يوماً، واحد وعشرون / أربعون جنيهاً / يوماً

اثنا عشر فلساً / شخصاً، اثنان وعشرون فلساً / شخصاً، خمسون فلساً / شخصاً

ستون / سبعون / ثمانون موظّفاً / سنة

تسعون ليرةً/ جنيهاً، مائة ليرةٍ / جنيهٍ، مائة ليرة وليرة / مائة جنيه وجنيه

مائتا متر / دولار، ثلاثمائة / أربعمائة متر / دولار

ألف / ألفا / عشرة آلاف شخص / كيلومتر

G 2

الطلاّب العشرة – العلب الخمس – المعلّمون الثلاثة – الزبائن الثمانية – الكتب الاثنا عشر – البيوت الأحد عشر – الفتيات السبع – الشبابيك التسعة – الأيام العشرون – الأسابيع الثلاثة عشر – الدولارات السبعة عشر – الساعات الأربع – الساعات الأربع والعشرون – الأيام الثلاثون – الأشخاص الستة والستون – الكيلومترات الواحد والسبعون – الرجال المائة – الدقائق الست عشرة – الموظّفون العشرة – الأشخاص المائتان

G 3

لم أخرج / تخرجي / تخرج من البيت. لم يخرج من المعهد. لم يخرجن من المطعم. لم يدخل بيت صديقه. لم ندخل المطعم. لم تدخلي ذلك البيت. لم يصل الوفد أمس. لم تصل الوفود مساء أمس. لم يصلوا صباح اليوم. لم أفهم. لم تفهموا. لم يفهم. لم تفهم. لم نفهم. لم يدرس هناك طلاّب

أجانب. لم يشرح لهم عمل المكتبة. لم يرجعوا إلى البيت. لم نطلب منه ذلك. لم يطلبوا منّي ذلك. لم أطلب منكم ذلك. لم يرغبوا في أن يكتبوا لها. لم أرغب في أن يدخل بيتي. لم أعرف ذلك. لم نعرف ذلك. لم يعرفوا ذلك. لم تعرف ذلك. لم يعمل هناك. لم أعمل هناك. لم تعمل في ذلك المصنع. لم يعملوا في تلك المدينة. لم نعمل هناك. لم يعملوا بأجهزة حديثة. لم يأخذوا ذلك. لم يأخذ الكتاب. لم نأخذ الجرائد. لم يأخذن ذلك. لم تاخذوا ذلك. لم يفعل ذلك. لم نفعل ذلك. لم تفعلي ذلك. لم تذهب إلى هناك. لم تذهي إلى المكتبة. لم يذهبوا إلى القاعة. لم أشرب / تشـربي / تشرب النبيذ. لم يشربوا القهوة. لم نشرب البيرة. لم نأكل اللحم. لم يأكلوا في المطعم. لم تأكلوا هناك.

G 4

لم يطلب/ ما طلب منّي أن أذهب إلى هناك. لم أخرج/ تخرجي/ تخرج/ ما خرجت من البيت صباحاً. لم نسمع هذا الخـبر. لا نفهـم ذلك. لا يأكلون فواكـه كثيرة. لـن يذهبوا إلى المعهد. لم تذهب/ ما ذهبت إلى صديقتها. لم يعمل/ ما عمل بـالأجهزة الحديثة. لا ينظرون إلى الكتب. لا أعرف ذلك. لم يأخذ/ ما أخذ الكتاب. لم يفعلوا/ ما فعلوا ذلك. لم أدخل / تدخلي / تدخل/ ما دخلت ذلك المعهد. لم نقرأ/ ما قرأنا كتباً كثيرة. لا يدرسون اللغة العربية. لا نعرف ذلك. لـن يعقدوا اجتماعاً. لن يعمل في لندن. لن تكتبوا لهم. لم أضع/ تضع/ تضعي/ ما وضعت الكتب في الخزانة. لا نرغب في أن نذهب إلى هناك.

Final Exercise

1.

خمسة أركان	عشرة مسلمين	أحد عشر جوازاً
أربعة مذاهب	خمس صلوات	سبعة عشر طابقاً
اثنا عشر شهراً	ثلاث وعشرون عمارة	أحد وعشرون مصدراً
دينان	ستمائة واثنتان وعشرون سنة	قبّعتان
اثنا عشر معلّماً	أربعمائة وستة وخمسون دولاراً	اثنان وثلاثون أسبوعاً

2.

بعد الخلفاء الراشدين الأربعة، أركان الإسلام الخمسة، مذاهب الإسلام الأربعـة، الأشهر الإسلامية الاثنا عشر، مع الزوجات الثـلاث، أمـام الجبـال السبعة، الأطروحتـان، الكراسيُّ الثلاثـة عشر، في الجامعات الإحدى عشرة، في شهر ربيع الثاني، في السنة الثانية

3.

لست مسلماً. لم يهاجر محمّد في عام ٦٣٣. لن يبلغ عدد المسلمين حـوالى مليـون مسلم. لم نعرف المذاهب الأربعة. ليست غالبيتهم من أهل السنة. لم يبدأ التاريخ الإسلامي في عـام ٦٢١. لم نسـأل عن أبي حنيفة وأحمد بن حنبل. ليس قرشياً. لم يتبعه هارون الرشيد. لم تدرسوا الهندسة. لن تخرجن من المطعم. لم أفهم / تفهمي / تفهم العربي. لم يخرج في شهر آب.

4.

عام ألف وتسعمائة وواحد وتسعين
سنة ألف وتسعمائة وإحدى وتسعين
عام ستمائة واثنين وعشرين

سنة ستمائة واثنتين وعشرين

عام ألف ومائتين وثمانية وخمسين

سنة ألف ومائتين وثمان وخمسين

عام ألفين وخمسة

سنة ألفين وخمس

عام ألف وتسعمائة وخمسة وأربعين

سنة ألف وتسعمائة وخمس وأربعين

عام سبعمائة وخمسين

سنة سبعمائة وخمسين

عام ألف وتسعمائة وثمانية عشر

سنة ألف وتسعمائة وثماني عشرة

عام ألف وواحد

سنة ألف وواحدة

5.

كنت في بغداد ثلاث مرات. ذهبوا مع خمسة أصدقاء إلى المسرح. التسجيل في الطابق الثاني. هو يسكن في الغرفة الثانية. ذهب إلى المبنى الثالث. عندي أربعة إخوان. سافر مليونا حاج إلى مكة المكرمة هذه السنة. ولدت عام ألف وأربعمائة وأربعة عشر هجرياً / بعد الهجرة. نبي الإسلام، صلى الله عليه وسلم، هو محمّد بن عبدالله بن عبد المطلب بن هاشم. الخلفاء الراشدون الأربعة هـم أبـو بكر الصديق وعمر بن الخطاب وعثمان بن عفان وعلي بن أبي طالب، رضي الله عنهم.

6. *zakāt(un), hijra, ḥajj, as-sunna, khalīfa, ṣalātu l-fajr, ṣawm, ramaḍān, ḥājj, dīn*

7.

كانُونُ الثّاني ، شُباطُ، آذَارُ، نِيسَانُ، آيّارُ، حَزِيرَانُ ، حُزَيْرَانُ، تَمّوزُ، آبُ، أَيْلُولُ، تَشْرِينُ الأَوّلُ، تَشْرِينُ الثّاني، كانُونُ الأَوّلُ

Lesson 11

L 1

إسمحوا لي أن أشكركم على الرسالة. عاش البلد حالة من التوتر السياسي والاجتماعي في السنوات الماضية. نشعر بأن الأوضاع العامة في الداخل والخارج خرجت من الأزمة الطويلة. بإمكاننا أن ننظر إلى المستقبل السلمي. قلت في كلمتي اليوم في الصباح إن الحرب قادت البلد إلى كارثة. وقفنا أمـام مشاكل كبيرة. دعونا أصدقاءنا إلى التشاور معنا. سارت الأمور نحو التحسن بسرعة. دعوتهم للعمـل معنا لتحسين العلاقات. لقيت رد فعل إيجابياً من هذه البلدان. قام الرئيس بزيارة هيئة الأمم المتحدة وأمينها العام. دعا الأمين العام للأمم المتحدة إلى انعقاد جلسة طارئة. إن احتفالنا هـو برهان قاطـع على نجاح سياستنا في السنوات الماضية. خفنا من عودة الحرب مرّة ثانية إلى البلد. نقف أمام مهمة بناء البلد في مجالي الصناعة والزراعة. أنا متأكد من أنّنا سنخرج من مشاكلنا ومن أزمتنا. أسافر إلى أمريكا في الأسبوع القادم. عاد من الخارج. هو قادر على كتابة هذه الرسالة.

L 2

إسمحوا لي أن أسألكم عن موقفكم من التطورات الجارية في البلد. قلت في تصريحي الرسمي قبل يومين إنّ الحكومة تعمل على إيجاد حلول سريعة لمشاكل المواطنين. كيف حدثت هذه المشاكل وما هي أسبابها؟ هل صحيح أنّكم ترغبون في إشراك المعارضة في الحكومة؟ أنا أرفض هذه الفكرة. إن المعارضة ليست قادرة على المساهمة في حل المشاكل الملحة. الانتخابات الأخيرة أعطت لنا الصلاحيات لممارسة الحكم في البلد للسنوات الأربع القادمة. إنّنا نترك النظر في حل هذه المسائل للجان البرلمانية وللمحاكم. لم نسمع من المعارضة في هذه المسألة أشياء جديدة. كتمت المعارضة في فترة حكمها مشاكل مماثلة. أشكركم على هذه المعلومات القيّمة. إسمحوا لي بسؤال أخير. أسافر إلى أمريكا في الأسبوع القادم لحضور اجتماعات هيئة الأمم المتّحدة.

L 3

جلس الرئيس. رجع محمّد. سافر / غادر الوفد. الجهاز قديم. خرج من المطعم. اشترى السيّارة. لم أفهم السؤال. لم أعلم منهم أنّه رجل لطيف.(هم) ليسوا بمجتهدين. لا يعرف أشياء كثيرة/ يعرف أشياء قليلة. لم يعرف السؤال الأخير.

L 4

رؤساء البلدان، مترجمو الوفود، رواتب الحكومة، وزراء الخارجية، نتائج الصناعة، فضائح الزراعة، سياسة الوزير، مرافقو الرئيس، رؤساء الحكومات، وزراء الداخلية، مترجمو الأمم المتحدة، رؤساء الجلسة، نتائج الحرب، فضائح المعارضة

L 5

رؤساء البلدان الجدد، مترجمو الوفود الجدد، سياسة الحكومة الجديدة، وزراء الخارجية الجدد، نتائج الصناعة الجديدة، فضائح الزراعة الجديدة، سياسة الوزير الجديدة، مرافقو الرئيس الجدد، رؤساء الحكومات الجدد، وزراء الداخلية الجدد، مترجمو الأمم المتحدة الجدد، رؤساء الجلسة الجدد، نتائج الحرب الجديدة، فضائح المعارضة الجديدة

G 1

زار الرجال المركز الجديد للعاصمة وزرته معهم.

قال صديقي إنّني مجتهد وقلت أنا إنني كسلان.

باع الرجل سيّارته وبعت أنا سيّارتي.

رجا الطالب الجزائري أن أكتب له ورجوته أنا أن يكتب لي.

مشى الأصدقاء إلى المقهى ومشيت أنا معهم.

وعد المرافق أصدقاءه بزيارة الجامعة ووعدت أنا بزيارة المكتبة.

وضع محمّد المعطف في الخزانة ووضعته أنا على الطاولة.

دعت الحكومة الوفود الأجنبية إلى الحفلة ودعوت أنا مرافقي الوفود.

لقي المعلّم أصدقائي في المخزن ولقيتهم أنا أمام المخزن.

قاد المرافق السيّارة بسرعة وقدتها أنا أيضاً بسرعة.

خافت المعلّمة من السفر بالطائرة وخفت أنا أيضاً منه.

كان صديقي هناك في شهر أيلول وكنت أنا هناك في شهر تشرين الأول.

سافر بالقطار وسافرت أنا بالسيّارة.

قام من النوم صباحاً وقمت أنا من النوم ظهراً.

عاد صديقي من لندن وعدت أنا معه.

نامت كثيراً ونمت أنا قليلاً.

وضعت صديقتي كؤوساً على الطاولة ووضعت أنا عليها زجاجتي عصير.

وعد الطالب صديقته بزيارة العاصمة ووعدتها أنا بزيارة مدينة لايبزغ.

رجت الفتاة أن تذهب إلى المسرح ورجوتها أن أذهب معها.

زار الوفد الجامعة وزرتها أنا أيضاً.

قال محمّد إنّني شربت كأساً واحدة فقط وقلت أنا إنني شربت كأسين.

سار إلى المكتبة مساءً وسرت أنا إليها صباحاً.

باع صديقي بيته وبعت أنا بيتي أيضاً.

نام مرافق الوفد في تلك الغرفة ونمت أنا في هذه الغرفة.

مشى الرجال إلى قاعة الاجتماع ومشيت أنا أيضاً إليها.

دعا صديقي العربي محمّداً إلى الحفلة ودعوت أنا أحمد إليها.

لقي صديقي فتاة شقراء ولقيت أنا فتاة سمراء.

خاف أعضاء الوفد من الطقس الحار هناك وخفت أنا منه في مصر.

كان أحمد في القاهرة وكنت أنا في تونس.

وضعت صديقتي على الطاولة تفّاحاً ووضعت أنا عليها خوخاً.

وضع الطالب الكتاب في الشنطة ووضعته أنا في الخزانة.

دعا صديقته إلى الحفلة ودعوت أنا صديقتي أيضاً إليها.

مشت الطالبات إلى المخزن ومشيت أنا إلى المعهد.

باع الطالب كتبه وبعت أنا كتبي.

قالت الطالبة إنّني أكلت كثيراً وقلت أنا إنني أكلت قليلاً.

عادت إلى بيتها وعدت أنا إلى بيتي.

زار صديقي عدداً من البلدان العربية وزرت أنا عدداً من البلدان الأوربية.

قام أصدقائي بنزهة جميلة وقمت أنا بها معهم.

عاد الوفد أمس وعدت أنا اليوم.

زارت الفتاة مدينة لندن وزرتها أنا معها.

وصلت صديقتي مساء الأمس ووصلت أنا صباح اليوم.

سارت إلى البيت وسرت أنا إليه أيضاً.

عادت الطائرة من دمشق وعدت أنا فيها.

G 2

زار الرجال المركز الجديد للعاصمة وزرناه معهم.

قال صديقي إنّني مجتهد وقلنا نحن إننا كُسالى.

باع الرجل سيّارته وبعنا نحن سيّارتنا.

رجا الطالب الجزائري أن أكتب له ورجوناه نحن أن يكتب لنا.

مشى الأصدقاء إلى المقهى ومشينا نحن معهم.

وعد المرافق أصدقاءه بزيارة الجامعة ووعدنا نحن بزيارة المكتبة.

وضع محمّد المعطف في الخزانة ووضعناه نحن على الطاولة.

دعت الحكومة الوفود الأجنبية إلى الحفلة ودعونا نحن مرافقي الوفود.

لقي المعلّم أصدقائي في المخزن ولقيناهم نحن أمام المخزن.

قاد المرافق السيّارة بسرعة وقدناها نحن أيضاً بسرعة.

خافت المعلّمة من السفر بالطائرة وخفنا نحن أيضاً منه.

كان صديقي هناك في شهر أيلول وكنا نحن هناك في شهر تشرين الأول.

سافر بالقطار وسافرنا نحن بالسيّارة.

قام من النوم صباحاً وقمنا نحن من النوم ظهراً.

عاد صديقي من لندن وعدنا نحن معه.

نامت كثيراً ونمنا نحن قليلاً.

وضعت صديقتي كؤوساً على الطاولة ووضعنا نحن عليها زجاجتي عصير.

وعد الطالب صديقته بزيارة العاصمة ووعدناها نحن بزيارة مدينة تورونتو.

رجت الفتاة أن تذهب إلى المسرح ورجوناها أن أذهب معها.

زار الوفد الجامعة وزرناها نحن أيضاً.

قال محمّد إنّني شربت كأساً واحدة فقط وقلنا نحن إننا شربنا كأسين.

سار إلى المكتبة مساءً وسرنا نحن إليها صباحاً.

باع صديقي بيته وبعنا نحن بيتنا أيضاً.

نام مرافق الوفد في تلك الغرفة ونمنا نحن في هذه الغرفة.

مشى الرجال إلى قاعة الاجتماع ومشينا نحن أيضاً إليها.

دعا صديقي العربي محمّداً إلى الحفلة ودعونا نحن أحمد إليها.

لقي صديقي فتاة شقراء ولقينا نحن فتاة سمراء.

خاف أعضاء الوفد من الطقس الحار هناك وخفنا نحن منه في مصر.

كان أحمد في القاهرة وكنا نحن في تونس.

وضعت صديقتي على الطاولة تفّاحاً ووضعنا نحن عليها خوخاً.

وضع الطالب الكتاب في الشنطة ووضعناه نحن في الخزانة.

دعا صديقته إلى الحفلة ودعونا نحن صديقتنا أيضاً إليها.

مشت الطالبات إلى المخزن ومشينا نحن إلى المعهد.

باع الطالب كتبه وبعنا نحن كتبنا.

قالت الطالبة إنّني أكلت كثيراً وقلنا نحن إننا أكلنا قليلاً.

عادت إلى بيتها وعدنا نحن إلى بيتي.

زار صديقي عدداً من البلدان العربية وزرنا نحن عدداً من البلدان الأوربية.

قام أصدقائي بنزهة جميلة وقمنا نحن بها معهم.

عاد الوفد أمس وعدنا نحن اليوم.

زارت الفتاة مدينة لندن وزرناها نحن معها.

وصلت صديقتي مساء الأمس ووصلنا نحن صباح اليوم.

سارت إلى البيت وسرنا نحن إليه أيضاً.

عادت الطائرة من دمشق وعدنا نحن فيها.

Final Exercise

1.

زرت الأمم المتّحدة. دعوته إلى المطعم. عدت إلى البرلمان. عشت في مصر. قدت السيّارة. مشيت إلى وكيل الدولة. قلت إنّه قام بزيارة المعاهد. قمت بجولة في الشرق الأوسط. وقفت أمام المحطّة. وجدت القلم تحت السرير. بنيت عمارات جميلة. قمت بإعادة بناء بيتي. خفت من عودة الحرب. بعت سيّارتي. نمت في فندق قديم. كنت في باريس. لقيت صديقتي في المدينة.

2.

زاروا الأمم المتّحدة. دعَوه إلى المطعم. عادوا إلى البرلمان. عاشوا في مصر. قادوا السيّارة. مشَوا إلى وكيل الدولة. قالوا إنّه قام بزيارة المعاهد. قاموا بجولة في الشرق الأوسط. وقفوا أمام المحطّة. وجدوا القلم تحت السرير. بنَوا عمارات جميلة. قاموا بإعادة بناء بيتي. خافوا من عودة الحرب. باعوا سيّارتي. ناموا في فندق قديم. كانوا في باريس. لقُوا صديقتي في المدينة.

3.

إسمحوا لي أن أرحّب بكم وأن أشكركم على عودتكم. وجدنا حلاً سلمياً لتلك المشاكل الملحّة. كانت ردود الفعل إيجابية. كانت ملابسها/ملابسهم فضيحة. زرنا ستة بلدان. قال الرجال إن الوزير كان يخاف من المعارضة. دعت هذه البلدان المجاورة الأربعة إلى عقد جلسة طارئة للأمم المتحدة. عدنا إلى البارلمان. كتمت الحكومة العسكرية نتائج الانتخابات هذه وبنجاح الأحزاب الديمقراطية. قابل وكيل الدولة هذا أعضاء اللجنة. سار الوضع في الداخل والخارج نحو تحسن هذه العلاقات. خرجنا من هذه الأزمة منتصرين. دعا مجلس الأمن للأمم المتحدة إلى حلّ سلمي.

4.

قلت في تصريحي إنّ الحكومة عملت على إيجاد الحلّ. سمحوا لي بسؤال. أعطتنا الانتخابات الصلاحيات الكافية. وقفنا أمام مشاكل مماثلة. (هو) لم يكن قادراً على كتابة هذه الرسالة. كيف حدثت تلك المشاكل؟ متى قمت بزيارة صديقتك؟

5.

the head of a foreign government, these four small bags of the teacher (f.)/ these four bags of the small teacher (f.), this house of the clever student, the return of this president to power, the chairman of a court, these reasons for the crisis

6.

خفنا من عودة الحرب. نقف أمام مهمّة بناء البلد. نشعر بالتحسّن. قاد البلد إلى كارثة. خرجنا من هذه الأزمة. عملنا على تحسين الوضع. عاش في الخارج. شكرته على الجهاز.

Lesson 12

L 2

ضع / ضعي الكؤوس / الفناجين / الزجاجة / التفاح / الكتب / الخبز / الفواكه / الطعام على الطاولة!

قم / قومي / قوموا من النوم الآن / بسرعة!

زرني/ زوريني/ زوروني/ زرنني/ زر / زوري / زرن / زوروا / زوري / زر / زرن / العاصمة / هذا البلد / تلك البلدان / ضواحي المدينة / ذلك البرج / ذلك المطعم / ذلك المقهى / صديقنا / المسرح غدا / في شهر مارس!

عد / عودي إلى البيت / إلى الفندق إلى هنا/ إلى هناك / إليّ / إلينا غداً / بعد ساعة!

إمش / إمشي / إمشوا إلى المعهد / إليه / إلى هناك !

إبق / إبقوا هنا/ هناك / في البيت / في الفندق / عندنا / حتى الغد

L 3

سيكون في استقبالهم عند وصولهم للجامعة وموقع مدير الجامعة ونخبة مـن كبـار المسؤولين بالجامعة. ستكون الجامعة ملتقىً لآلاف من هواة الثقافة وطلبـة العلـم والمعرفة. يقـوم بجولـة في دور النشر المختلفة ويرى مئات الآلاف من الكتب وتقريباً ٥٠ ألف عنوان في قطاعات المعرفة الانسانية والاجتماعية والعلوم التقنية وكتب الثقافة الإسلامية والأدب العربي عـلاوة عـلى كتب الأطفال والاقتصاد المنزلي والحاسب الآلي. ستصل نسبة التخفيض إلى ١٥ ٪ من السعر الأصلي.

من الجدير بالذكر أنّ المعرض سيفتح أبوابه لمدة يومين للنساء فقط وهمـا الخميس والاثنين. تشهد الجامعة مساء يوم الغد الثلاثاء حدثاً ثقافياً ضخماً ومناسبة علمية كبيرة. يقوم صاحب السمو الملكي الأمير سلمان بن عبد العزيز بحضور معالي مدير الجامعة الأستاذ الدكتـور أحمـد بن محمّـد الوهـاب بافتتاح معرض الرياض الدولي للكتاب العلمي. يشارك في هذا المعرض ٥٠٠ ناشر من داخل المملكة وخارجها. يحضر الافتتـاح بمشيئة الله عـدد مـن كبـار المسـؤولين ورجـال الفكـر والأدب والثقافة والإعلام.

L 4

شفت المعلّم. شفته. شـافتهم في المطعم. نشوفها في المعهد. شافوا الرئيس في المحكمة. نشوفه في البرلمان. شفتم الكتب عنده. تشوفي(ن) هذه الشنطة. تشوفو(ن) الأقلام. أشوفه بعد يومين.

ما شفت المعلّم. ما شفته. ما شافتهم في المطعم. ما نشوفها في المعهد. ما شافوا الرئيـس في المحكمة. ما نشوفه في البرلمان. ما شفتم الكتب عنده. ما تشوفين هذه الشنطة. ما تشوفون الأقلام. ما أشـوفه بعد يومين.

G 1

يفي محمّد بوعده.

نسي الطالب الكلمات الجديدة.

يأتي الوفد مساء اليوم.

يجيء أحمد حسب الموعد.

يرى أحمد صديقه أمام مخزن السيّارات.

يرجو محمّد أصدقاءه أن يحضروا إليه.

يزور الرجال ذلك الجبل.

يقول صديقي إنّني مجتهد.

يبيع الرجل سيّارته.

يمشي الأصدقاء إلى المقهى.

يعد أحمد أصدقاءه بألف دولار.

يضع الطالب المعطف في الخزانة.

يلقى المعلّم أصدقائي في المخزن.

يقود المرافق السيّارة بسرعة.

تخاف المعلّمة من السفر بالطائرة.

يسافر صديقي بالقطار.

يقوم محمّد من النوم.

يعود صديقي من لندن.

تفي صديقتي بوعدها.

تنسى الطالبة مواعيدها.

يضع الطالب الكتاب تحت الشنطة.

يأتي أعضاء الوفد صباحاً.

يرى عمر في المخزن كتباً جديدة.

ترجو هيفاء أصدقاءها أن يذهبوا معها.

تنام الطالبات كثيراً.

تضع صديقتي على الطاولة كؤوساً.

يعد الطالب صديقه بزيارة العاصمة.

ترجو الفتاة أن تذهب إلى المسرح.

يزور الوفد جامعتنا.

يقول محمّد إنّني شربت كأساً واحدة.

يبيع صديقي بيته.

يمشي الرجال إلى قاعة الاجتماع.

يلقى صديقي فتاة شقراء.

يضع الطالب الكتاب في الشنطة.

يدعو الطالب صديقته إلى الحفلة.

تمشي الطالبات إلى المخزن.

يبيع الطالب كتبه.

يقول صديقنا العربي إنّني أكلت قليلاً.

تعود الفتيات إلى بيتهن.

يزور صديقي عدداً من البلدان العربية.

يقوم أصدقائي بنزهة جميلة.

يعود الوفد اليوم.

تزور الوفود مدينة لندن.

يفي المعلّمون بوعودهم.

يجيء المرافق إلى قاعة الطعام.

تجيء صديقتي إليَّ.

يرى محمّد هناك رجالاً كثيرين.

يصل الأصدقاء مساء اليوم.

تعود الطائرة من القاهرة.

يصل الوفد إلى الكويت بالطائرة.

يعود الأصدقاء صباحاً.

تصل الوفود إلى هنا.

يقوم رئيس الوفد.

يبني العمال مباني رائعة.

G 3

يفي محمّد بوعده وأفي أنا بوعدي.

ينسى الطالب الكلمات الجديدة وأنساها أنا أيضاً.

يأتي الوفد مساء اليوم وآتي أنا مساء الغد.

يجيء أحمد حسب الموعد وأجيء أنا أيضاً حسب الموعد.

يرى أحمد صديقه أمام مخزن السيّارات وأراه أنا في مخزن السيّارات.

يرجو محمّد أصدقاءه أن يحضروا إليه وأرجوهم أنا أيضاً أن يحضروا إليّ.

يزور الرجال ذلك الجبل وأزوره أنا معهم.

يقول صديقي إنّي مجتهد وأقول أنا إنني كسلان.

يبيع الرجل سيّارته وأبيع أنا سيّارتي أيضاً.

يمشي الأصدقاء إلى المقهى وأمشي أنا إليه أيضاً.

يعد أحمد أصدقاءه بألف دولار وأعدهم أنا بدولارين.

يضع الطالب المعطف في الخزانة وأضعه أنا على الطاولة.

يلقى المعلّم أصدقائي في المخزن وألقاهم أنا أمام المخزن.

يقود المرافق السيّارة بسرعة وأقوده أنا بسرعة أيضاً.

تخاف المعلّمة من السفر بالطائرة وأخاف أنا منه أيضاً.

يسافر صديقي بالقطار وأسافر أنا بالسيّارة.

يقوم محمّد من النوم ظهراً وأقوم أنا منه صباحاً.

يعود صديقي من لندن وأعود أنا معه.

تفي صديقتي بوعدها وأفي أنا به أيضاً.

تنسى الطالبة مواعيدها وأنساها أنا أيضاً.

يضع الطالب الكتاب تحت الشنطة وأضعه أنا تحت الطاولة.

يأتي أعضاء الوفد صباحاً وآتي أنا مساء.

يرى عمر في المخزن كتباً جديدة وأرى أنا فيه صديقي.

ترجو هيفاء أصدقاءها أن يذهبوا معها وأرجوهم أنا أن يذهبوا معي.

تنام الطالبات كثيراً وأنام أنا قليلاً.

تضع صديقتي على الطاولة كؤوساً وأضع أنا عليها زجاجتي عصير.

يعد الطالب صديقه بزيارة العاصمة وأعد أنا بزيارة مدينة دبلين.

ترجو الفتاة أن تذهب إلى المسرح وأرجو أنا أن أذهب معها.

يزور الوفد جامعتنا وأزورها أنا أيضاً.

يقول محمّد إنّني شربت كأساً واحدة وأقول أنا إنني شربت كأسين.

يبيع صديقي بيته وأبيع أنا بيتي أيضاً.

يمشي الرجال إلى قاعة الاجتماع وأمشي أنا إليها أيضاً.

يلقى صديقي فتاة شقراء وألقى أنا فتاة سمراء.

يضع الطالب الكتاب في الشنطة وأضعه أنا في الخزانة.

يدعو الطالب صديقته إلى الحفلة وأدعوها أنا إليّ.

تمشي الطالبات إلى المخزن وأمشي أنا إلى المعهد.

يبيع الطالب كتبه وأبيعها أنا أيضاً.

يقول صديقنا العربي إنّني أكلت قليلاً وأقول أنا إنني أكلت كثيراً.

تعود الفتيات إلى بيتهن وأعود أنا إلى بيتي.

يزور صديقي عدداً من البلدان العربية وأزور أنا عدداً من البلدان الأوربية.

يقوم أصدقائي بنزهة جميلة وأقوم أنا بنزهة معهم.

يعود الوفد اليوم وأعود أنا أيضاً.

تزور الوفود مدينة لندن وأزورها أنا معها.

يفي المعلّمون بوعودهم وأفي أنا بوعدي أيضاً.

يجيء المرافق إلى قاعة الطعام وأجيء أنا إليها أيضاً.

تجيء صديقتي إليّ وأجيء أنا إليها.

يرى محمّد هناك رجالاً كثيرين وأرى أنا هناك رجالاً قلائل.

يصل الأصدقاء مساء اليوم وأصل أنا صباح اليوم.

تعود الطائرة من القاهرة وأعود أنا فيها.

يصل الوفد إلى الكويت بالطائرة وأصل أنا إليها بالسيّارة.

يعود الأصدقاء صباحاً وأعود أنا مساء.

تصل الوفود إلى هنا وأصل أنا معها.

يقوم رئيس الوفد وأقوم أيضاً.

يبني العمال مباني رائعة وأبني أنا بيتاً جميلاً.

Final Exercise

1.

يفي بوعده. تنسى الحاسب. يجيء بعد صاحب السمو الملكي. أرى الإنكليز. أرجوه أن يصرف الدولارات. يزورون الجيران. تقولون إنكم نخبة الجامعة. تبيع الحكومة المصرف. نمشي إلى الافتتاح. يعد بكتابة رسالة طويلة. يلقى الجواب. يقود سيّارته بسرعة. نخاف من مدير المعهد. تسير الأمور نحو التحسّن. نقوم بجولة في الشرق الأوسط. يأتي بعد هذا الحدث الثقافي. ينام ١٠ ساعات. يصل بعد ٦ أيّام. تعود من جولتها. ندعو الأصدقاء إلى الحفلة. يبنون بيوتاً جميلة. يعيش في أوربا. أنام في الفندق.

2.

حضر الاستقبال رئيس الجامعة وكبار المسؤولين. ستكون الجامعة ملتقىً للكثير من هواة الكتب. سيقوم بجولة في معرض الكتب. باعوا في المعرض تقريباً خمسين ألف كتاب. قام معالي وزير الثقافة بالافتتاح. نسيت أسماء دور النشر. بعت كتب الأطفال وكتباً عن الاقتصاد المنزلي والعلوم التقنية والثقافة الإسلامية والأدب العربي. وفى بوعده. جاؤوا ساعتين بعد الموعد. رأيته في المدينة الجامعية. وعدني بخمسة دنانير.

3.

Put the glasses on the table! Get up! Visit the fair! Come back home before noon! Hurry up! Don't be afraid of the minister! Don't sleep in the lecture! Tell me me who are you! Tell me where you were! Eat the meat! Come in! Go to the university! Give the dinars!

4.

دعوتهما إليها. إشتريتها. أخاف منه. نرجع إليها. أراهن. أنساه. مشيت إليها بسرعة. شكرته عليها.

5.

يجب عليّ أن أحجز غرفتين. يجب علينا أن نبيع مشروبات. يجب عليهم أن يفوا بوعودهم. يجب عليك أن تدعي أمك. يجب عليكم أن تجيئوا غداً. يجب عليه أن ينسى أحداثاً كثيرة. يجب عليها أن تعود.

6.

Jussive	Subjunctive	Imperfect	Perfect
يقولوا	يقولوا	يقولون	قالوا
تمشِ	تمشِيَ	تمشِي	مشتْ
ألقَ	ألقَى	ألقَى	لقيتُ
ترجوا	ترجُوا	ترجُون	رجوتم
تنْسَيْ	تنْسَيْ	تنْسَيْنَ	نسيتِ
يفِ	يفِيَ	يفِي	وفَى
تخافِي	تخافِي	تخافينَ	خِفْتِ

Lesson 13

L 4

كتبت الرسالة بنفسي / بنفسك / بنفسها.
كتبوا الرسائل بأنفسهم.
هل قدت السيّارة بنفسك؟

فعلت ذلك بنفسي / بنفسك / بنفسها.

هل فعلت ذلك بنفسك / بنفسها؟

هل فعلتم ذلك بأنفسكم؟

إفعل ذلك بنفسك!

إفعلي ذلك بنفسك!

إفعلوا ذلك بأنفسكم!

L 6

كتبت عدة رسائل.

قرأت عدة كتب.

اشتريت عدة جرائد.

دعوت عدة أصدقاء.

شربت عدة كؤوس.

أخذت عدة فناجين.

كنت هناك عدة أيام.

كان هناك عدة أسابيع.

L 7

حضر بعض المعلّمين.

أتى بعض الأصدقاء.

عاد بعض الأعضاء.

رجعت بعض الفتيات.

جاء بعض المرافقين.

أتى بعض الوفود.

عاد بعض الأطبّاء.

جاءت بعض المرضات.

سكن هناك بعض الطلّاب.

عمل بعض المدراء ليل نهار.

حضر الجلسة بعض الرؤساء.

L 8

من أي بلد أنت؟

في أي شهر ولدت؟

إلى أية مدينة سافرت؟

في أية جامعة درست؟

قي أي فندق كنت تسكن؟

أي وفد كان عندكم.

أي بيت دخل أحمد؟

أية مناسبة حضرت وفود كثيرة؟

G 1

كان الطلّاب مجتهدين.

كان الطقس بارداً.

كانت الفتاة جميلةً.

كان مرافق الوفد طالباً.

كان الطبيب جديداً.

كان الأطبّاء جدداً.

كان الأكل جيّداً.

كانت الغرفة مريحةً.

كانت الأدوية أجنبيةً.

كانت الممرضة جميلةً.

كان المستشفى حديثاً.

كان أحمد مريضاً.

كانت حالته حسنةً.

كان الباص قديماً.

كانت الأدوية غاليةً.

G 2

كان صديقي يسكن في مدينة تورونتو لمدة سنتين.

كان الطالب يمشي إلى المعهد كلّ يوم.

كان أخي يعمل في المدرسة لمدة شهر.

كانت المعلّمة تزور مكتبة المدينة كلّ أسبوع.

كان المريض ينام ساعة واحدة كلّ يوم بعد الظهر.

كان صديقي يكتب رسالة كلّ سنة.

كان أحمد يمشي في شوارع المدينة كلّ مساء.

كان عمر يدرس الطب في جامعة لندن لمدة سنة.

كان صديقنا العربي يزورنا كلّ يوم.

كان المرافق يدعونا إلى بيته كلّ شهر.

كنت أشرب كأساً من العصير كلّ مساء.

G 3

كان أصدقائي يسكنون في مدينة بون لمدة سنتين.

كان الطلّاب يمشون إلى المعهد كلّ يوم.

كان إخوتي يعملون في المدرسة لمدة شهر.

كانت المعلّمات يزرن مكتبة المدينة كلّ أسبوع.

كان المرضى ينامون ساعة واحدة كلّ يوم بعد الظهر.

كان أصدقائي يكتبون رسالة كلّ سنة.

كان أحمد ومحمّد وصالح يمشون في شوارع المدينة كلّ مساء.

كان عمر وأحمد ومحمّد يدرسون الطب في جامعة لندن لمدة سنة.

كان أصدقاؤنا العرب يزوروننا كل يوم.

كان المرافقون يدعوننا إلى بيوتهم كلّ شهر.

كنّا نشرب كأساً من العصير كلّ مساء.

G 4

وصل كلّ الأصدقاء أمس الأول.

وصل كلّ أصدقائي أمس الأول.

بقي كلّ الطلّاب في المعهد.

سافرت كلّ الفتيات إلى مدينة لندن.

دعونا كلّ معلّمينا إلى الحفلة.

يعمل كلّ الأطّباء هناك.

بعت كل الكتب.

رأيت كلّ المرافقين.

قرأت كلّ الكتب.

زرت كلّ المدن.

فتحت كلّ الشبابيك.

G 5

وصل جميع الأصدقاء أمس الأول.

وصل جميع أصدقائي أمس الأول.

بقي جميع الطلّاب في المعهد.

سافرت جميع الفتيات إلى مدينة لندن.

دعونا جميع معلّمينا إلى الحفلة.

يعمل جميع الأطّباء هناك.

رأيت جميع المرافقين.

G 6

وصل الأصدقاء كلهم أمس الأول.

وصل أصدقائي كلهم أمس الأول.

بقي الطلّاب كلهم في المعهد.

سافرت الفتيات كلهن إلى مدينة لندن.

دعونا معلّمينا كلهم إلى الحفلة.

يعمل الأطّباء كلهم هناك.

بعت الكتب كلها.

رأيت المرافقين كلهم.

قرأت الكتب كلها.

زرت المدن كلها.

فتحت الشبابيك كلها.

G 7

خمسة رجال جدد

اثنا عشر بيتاً قديماً

خمسون ماركاً ألمانياً

مائة وثلاثة عشر مشروعاً مشتركاً

سبعة وفود عربية

كتابان دراسيان

اثنتان وعشرون طالبة مجتهدة

تسع عمارات حديثة

إحدى وأربعون دولة أجنبية

ألف ومائة واثنا عشر دولاراً أمريكياً

مليون مسلم مصري

Final Exercise

1.

كان صديقه طبيباً. كانت أذناه كبيرتين. كان أنفه طويـلاً. كـانت الحبـوب مُرّة. كان مريضاً. كانت في فمه أسنان قليلة. كان الألم شديداً. كان العلاج صعباً. كان قلبه كبيراً. كانت ساقاه طويلتين. كان المستشفى جديداً. كانت الممرضات جميلات. كانت الغرفة مريحة. كان الباص قديماً. كان مرافق الوفد طالباً. كان اللحم فاسداً. كانت عيناها جميلتين.

2.

He ate / has eaten / had eaten all the meat. The doctor used to work in the same city. Perhaps, he will come to the party. The teacher (f.) used to go to the same café every day for two weeks. Perhaps, he knows the solution, perhaps not. He drank all the juice before the arrrival of the guests. He will have left his clinic.

3.

عنده نفس المرض. أكل أخوها من نفس اللحم المعلب. جـاء كـلّ الطـلاّب. بـاعوا نفس الكتـاب. باعوا الكتاب بأنفسهم. كانت كلّ العائلة/ العائلة كلّها عند الطبيب. كتبت ذلـك بنفسك. إفعلـوا ذلك بأنفسكم! أخذ بعض الحبوب بنفسه / أخذ هو بنفسه بعض الحبوب. قد ذهب أحـد المرضى قبل عدة أيام. سأل البعض منهم عن العلاج. كانت إحدى الممرضات جميلة جداً.

Lesson 14

L 1

سافر / سافري / سافروا إلى نيو يورك يوم الأربعاء!

رحِّب / رحِّي / رحِّبوا بالوزير!

رحِّب / رحِّي / رحِّبوا بهم الآن!

أنجز / أنجزي / أنجزوا الأعمال حتى يوم الاثنين!

ترجم / ترجمي / ترجموا الكلمات إلى اللغة العربية!

قدِّمنا / قدِّمينا / قدِّمونا إلى الأصدقاء!

سلِّم / سلِّمي / سلِّموا لها كرّاسة جديدة!
رحِّب / رحِّي / رحِّبوا بالضيوف في المطار!
ترجم / ترجمي / ترجموا هذه الكلمة!
قدِّم / قدِّمي / قدِّموا لهم مشروعاً جديداً!
سلِّم / سلِّمي / سلِّموا له تلك الرسالة شخصياً!
سافر / سافري / سافروا إلى هناك بالقطار!
أنجز / أنجزي / أنجزوا هذا العمل اليوم!

L 2

هل يمكنك أن تسافر غداً إلى هناك؟
متى أمكنكم أن تحدّثوه عن الرحلة؟
أمكنني أن أقابلهم في الفندق.
أمكنها أن تقابلنا في الحفلة.
يمكننا أن نرسل إليكم هذه الأشياء.
أمكنه أن يسافر معنا إلى لندن.
لماذا لم يمكنكم أن تنجزوا واجباتكم؟
أين يمكنني أن أقابلك؟

L 3

الوفد الذي يسافر إلى لندن
الوفود التي وصلت إلى المطار
الأصدقاء الذين يزوروننا غداً
المرافق الذي رافقنا
الطالبان اللذان يدرسان اللغة العربية
مع الطالبتين اللتين تدرسان في معهد هيردر
الفتاة التي حضرت الحفلة
الفتيات اللاتي حضرن الحفلة
التلاميذ الذين ينجزون واجبات كثيرة
عند صديقي الذي قدّم لي كأساً من الماء
أخي الذي أرسل إليَّ رسالة

L 4

الرسائل التي كتبتها لها
الأخبار التي سمعناها أمس
القلم الذي اشتريته من ذلك المخزن
السياسيون الذين قابلتهم يوم الخميس
الوفد التجاري الذي رافقته لمدة ثلاثة أسابيع
في الرسالة التي أرسلتها إلى عائلتي
الواجبات التي أنجزها بسرعة

الهدية التي قدّمتها لي صديقتي

الضيوف الذين قدّمهم صديقنا إلينا

الفلم الذي نشاهده يوم الجمعة

العائلة التي أعرفها

الضيوف الذين نرحّب بهم

هنا المكتبة التي أذهب إليها كلّ يوم

السيّارة الجديدة التي أسافر بها إلى لندن غداً

الجامعة التي قابلت صديقتي أمامها

هذا الشخص الذي حدّثتني صديقتي عنه

في البَلَدين اللذين سمعنا عنهما كثيراً

الخزانة التي وضعت الكتب فيها

أين المخزن الذي اشتريت الهدايا منه

المدن التي كنتم فيها مدة طويلة

القاعة التي كنّا فيها

G 1

نقدّم إليكم أصدقاءنا – متى يقدّمونه إليك؟ – يقدّم أحمد نفسه – أقدّم/ تقدّم/ تقدّمين له هـذه الهدية – هل تقدّمون لهم بعض الشراب؟

يرحّب بنا مدير المعهد – نرحّب بضيوفنا الأجانب – يرحّب الرئيس بأعضاء الوفد الفرنسي.

إلى أين تسافر الوفود؟ – تسافر إلى لندن بالقطار – نسافر إلى هناك بالطائرة – هـل يسافر السياسيون اليوم؟

هل تشاهد/ تشاهدين ذلك الفلم؟ – نعم أشاهده مساء اليوم – نعم نشاهده اليوم – يشاهدون اليوم الأبنية الحديثة.

يترجم الطالب الكلمات الجديدة إلى اللغة الإنكليزية – أترجمها إلى اللغة العربية - تـترجم المعلّمـة الرسالة من اللغة الفرنسية إلى اللغة الإنكليزية.

هل يحدّثكم صديقكم عن رحلته؟ – نحدّثه عن دراستنا في مصر – تحدّثنا هيفاء عن الحياة في بلادها.

يسلّم أحمد عدنان الكتاب – نسلّمكم المبلغ اليوم – أسلّم الأشياء فوراً.

يفرحنا ذلك – يفرحني ذلك – هل تفرحكم الهدايا؟

ترافق الوفد طالبة ألمانية – أرافق صديقي إلى المحطّة – يرافقني إلى المسرح صديق إنكليزي.

من تقابل/ تقابلين هناك؟ – أقابل/ تقابل/ تقابلين هناك صديقاً جزائرياً – نقابل اليـوم عـدداً مـن الضيوف الأجانب.

هل يمكنك أن تسافر إلى هناك؟ – يمكنني أن أفعل ذلك – يمكننا أن ننجز واجباتنا فوراً.

متى تنجزون واجبـاتكم؟ – هـل تنجز/ تنجزين عملـك بنفسك؟ – ينجزون العمـل بعـد ثـلاث ساعات.

يرسل الطالب رسالة إلى عائلته – هل ترسل/ ترسلين هديـة إلى صديقك؟ – متى ترسل/ ترسلين البطاقة إلى أصدقائك؟

لماذا تُحضر / تحضرين جميع الطلّاب إلى هنا؟ – لماذا تحضرون معكم أربعة كتب فقط؟ –أعرف أنّهما يحضران معهما نقوداً كثيرة.

G 2

قدّم / يقدّم الطالب هدية لصديقه.

قدّموا / يقدّمون إلينا أصدقاءهم.

متى قدّمتم / تقدّمون إليّ ذلك الرجل؟

متى حدّثتموهم / تحدّثونهم عن واجباتهم؟

هل حدّثها / يحدّثها المعلّم؟

لماذا حدّثك / يحدّثك الموظّف؟

هل رحّب / يرحّب بهم الرئيس؟

من رحّب / يرحّب بالوفد المصري؟

متى رحّبوا / يرحّبون بالضيوف؟

إلى أين سافر / يسافر الوفد؟

هل سافرتم / تسافرون بالسيّارة أم بالقطار؟

هل سافروا / يسافرون يوم الأحد؟

هل شاهدت / تشاهدين تلك البطاقات؟

شاهدن / يشاهدن كلّ الأفلام.

متى شاهدت / تشاهد أولئك الأشخاص؟

هل أمكنك / يمكنك أن تفعل ذلك؟

متى أمكنكم / يمكنكم أن تذهبوا إلى هناك؟

أين أمكنكم / يمكنكم أن تقابلوهم؟

أنجزنا / ننجز عملنا بعد ساعتين.

أنجز / ينجز الوفد واجبه بعد أسبوع.

أنجز / ينجز التلاميذ هذا العمل بسرعة.

إلى من أرسلت / ترسل هذه الرسالة؟

أرسلت / ترسل الحكومة أدوية إلى مصر.

أرسلناها / نرسلها إلى المعهد.

G 3

لا، لم أواصل/ تواصل الجولة بعد.

لا، لم نرسل لهم رسالة بعد.

لا، لم ننجز عملنا بعد؟

لا، لم يمكننا أن نفعل ذلك بعد.

لا، لم أقابلها بعد.

لا، لم أشاهد ذلك الفلم بعد.

لا، لم أسافر/ تسافر إلى القاهرة بعد.

لا، لم نرحّب بصديقكم بعد.

لا، لم نحدّثهم عن الدراسة بعد.

لا، لم أقدّم الصديق إليهم بعد.

لا، لم أترجم/ تترجم الكلمات بعد.

G 4

يعود صديقي من لندن.

تفي صديقتي بوعدها.

تنسى الطالبة مواعيدها.

يضع الطالب الكتاب تحت الشنطة.

يأتي أعضاء الوفد صباحاً.

يرى عمر في المخزن كتباً جديدة.

ترجو هيفاء أصدقاءها أن يذهبوا معها.

تنام الطالبات كثيراً.

تضع صديقتي على الطاولة كؤوساً.

يعد الطالب صديقه بزيارة العاصمة.

ترجو الفتاة أن تذهب إلى المسرح.

يزور الوفد جامعتنا.

يقول محمّد إنّني أشرب كأساً واحدة.

يبيع صديقي بيته.

يمشي الرجال إلى قاعة الاجتماع.

يلقى صديقي فتاة شقراء.

يضع الطالب الكتاب في الشنطة.

يدعو الطالب صديقته إلى الحفلة.

تمشي الطالبات إلى المخزن.

يبيع الطالب كتبه.

يقول صديقنا العربي إنّني أكلت قليلاً.

تعود الفتيات إلى بيتهن.

يزور صديقي عدداً من البلدان العربية.

يقوم أصدقائي بنزهة جميلة.

يعود الوفد اليوم.

تزور الوفود مدينة لندن.

يفي المعلّمون بوعدهم.

يجيء المرافق إلى قاعة الطعام.

تجيء صديقتي إليّ.

يرى محمّد هناك رجالاً كثيرين.

يصل الأصدقاء مساء اليوم.

تعود الطائرة من القاهرة.

يصل الوفد إلى لندن بالطائرة.

يعود الأصدقاء صباحاً.

تصل الوفود إلى هنا.

يقوم رئيس الوفد.

يبني العمال مباني رائعة.

يفي محمّد بوعده.

ينسى الطالب الكلمات الجديدة.

يأتي الوفد مساء اليوم.

يجيء أحمد حسب الموعد.

يرى أحمد صديقه أمام مخزن السيّارات.

يرجو محمّد أصدقاءه أن يحضروا إليه.

يزور الرجال ذلك الجبل.

يقول صديقي إنّني مجتهد.

يبيع الرجل سيّارته.

يمشي الأصدقاء إلى المقهى.

يعد أحمد أصدقاءه بألف دولار.

يضع الطالب المعطف في الخزانة.

يلقى المعلّم أصدقائي في المخزن.

يقود المرافق السيّارة بسرعة.

تخاف المعلّمة من السفر بالطائرة.

يسير صديقي بالقطار.

يقوم محمّد من النوم.

Final Exercise

1.

نقدّم إليكم ضيوفنا. يرحّبون بالرئيس. يسافرن إلى باريس. نشاهد هـذه المسرحية. أترجم/ تـترجم الكلمة الطويلة. يسلّم الكتاب. أرافقها/ ترافقها إلى البيت. تقـابلون الوفود. ننجـز العمـل. أرسل/ ترسل رسائل كثيرة. يمكنه أنْ يسافر إلى مصر. يخبرهم بنتائج الانتخابات. تسفر الجـولة عـن حلـول سريعة. يشاركون في المؤتمر. تعبّرون عـن إرتيـاحكم. أعطيـه/ تعطيـه/ تعطينه كتابـاً. تفرحني هـذه الأخبار. تسفر الأزمة الطويلة عن مشاكل كبيرة. نواصل المناقشة. يحدّثنا عن التطوّرات في الداخل. نرسله إلى الطبيب.

2.

كان الوزير الذي وصل أمس مريضا. أرسلت وزارة الصحة التي كنت فيها أمس أطّبـاء كثـيرين إلى المحافظات. قرأت خبراً جاء فيه أنّ مرض الكوليرا أسفر عن وفاة الكثير مـن المواطنـين. واصـل وزيـر الخارجية الذي وصل من إسرائيل جولته في سوريا. قدّم مشـروعاً يرحّب فيـه بـالحلول الجديـدة. لم تكن الكلمة التي عبّر فيها عن ارتياحه طويلة جدا. قال في محادثاته مع وزيري الصحـة والدفـاع إنـه

سيواصل عمله. إن المستشار الألماني الذي عبر عن ارتياحه بالعلاقات الجيّدة أخبر الرئيس بانه سيقدّم براهينَ جديدة. واصل الوفدان اللذان يرأسهما وزيرا التعليم والاقتصاد المحادثات بعد ساعتين. بعث برسالة قدّم فيها براهينَ جديدة. عادت المعلّمات اللاتي أرسلتهن الوزارة إلى المحافظات إلى العاصمة. بحث الوضع الجديد في المنطقة مع بعض الرؤساء الأفارقة بعد الجلسة الختامية للقمة الأفريفية.

3.

لم أرسل/ ترسل/ ترسلي لهم عدة رسائل. لم تنجزوا عملكم. لم أقابل الوزير. لم يشاهدوا المسرحية. لم نرحّب بالوفد. لم تحدّثه عن زيارة الطبيب. لم يواصل الكلمة. لم تفرحه بعض الحلول. لم يسفر القرار عن بعض النتائج الجيّدة. لم يكن في غرفته. لم تكن بعض الطالبات جميلات. ليس وزيراً. لا تواصل الكلمة! لا تقوموا بزيارة هذا البلد ! لا تعودي إلى البيت قبل الظهر ! لا تأكل اللحم الفاسد!

4.

كتابان	خمس قطراتٍ
ثمانية عَشر طالباً	سبع صيدلياتٍ
ثلاثة وعشرون عاماً	اثنا عشر مستشفى
مائة كرسي وكرسيان	إحدى وعشرون حبةٍ
في عام ألف وأربعمائةَ واثني عشر بعد الهجرة	مائة وصفةٍ
في سنة ألف وأربعمائة واثنتي عشرة بعد الهجرة	
في عام ستمائة واثنين وعشرين بعد الميلاد	ألف ضيفٍ
في سنة ستمائة واثنتين وعشرين بعد الميلاد	
في عام ألف وتسعمائة وتسعة وتسعين قبل الميلاد	خمسة آلاف مريضٍ
في سنة ألف وتسعمائة وتسع وتسعين قبل الميلاد	

Lesson 15

L 2

أعطى IV/ ألغى IV / أراد IV/ طوّر II/ ألقى IV/ أعلن IV/ بين II/ أنهى IV/ أوضح IV/ أجاب IV/ أيد II/ أجرى IV/ واصل III/ غير II

ألغى الموعد مع المدير.

أراد أن يمشي إلى المدينة.

أعطى صديقه بطانية.

أوضح الوضع في البلد.

أعلن نتائج الانتخابات.

أنهى المؤتمر بكلمة ختامية.

أجاب على الأسئلة الصعبة.

أيد سياسة البلدان العربية.

ألقى كلمة بمناسبة العيد الوطني.

أجرى محادثات مع الوفود العربية.

بيّن لنا ميزة مناخ الصحراء.

غيّر برنامج الزيارة.

واصل الرحلة بعد يومين.

L 3

لا أعرف ما حدث.

لا أعرف كلّ من حضر الحفلة.

إحك لي (عن من) عمن قابلت من الأشخاص!

نرحّب بمن جاء إلينا من الخارج.

حكى لنا ما سمع من أخبار.

هل تعرف ما عندهم من قضايا؟

كتب لي (عن ما) عمّا يدرس من اللغات.

أعرف كلّ من زار معهدنا أمس.

رحّبنا .بمن عندكم من الضيوف.

ألغوا كلّ ما في برنامجهم من مواعيد.

G 1

يقيم وزير الخارجية حفلة استقبال.

يلقي رئيس الجمهورية كلمة قصيرة.

يرحّب مدير المعهد بضيوفه.

نرحّب مساء اليوم بضيوفنا.

يرحّب وزير الخارجية برئيس الوفد العربي.

تؤيّد ألمانيا سياسة البلدان العربية.

تؤيّد فرنسا سياسة العرب.

يجيب رئيس الوفد العربي بكلمة قصيرة.

تجيب الطالبة على سؤال المعلم.

يوضح رئيس الوفد موقفه.

ينهي الوفد السوري زيارته لبلدنا اليوم.

ننهي سفرنا اليوم.

يبيّن لي معلّمي الدرس الجديد.

يبيّن لنا من هو صديقنا.

نقف إلى جانب البلدان العربية.

يعلن رئيس الجمهورية أنّنا سنطوّر بلادنا.

نطوّر بلادنا.

يريد محمّد أن يسافر إلى باريس.

أريد/ تريد/ تريدين أن أدرس اللغة العربية.

تريد صديقتي أن تشرب كأساً من النبيذ.

يغيّر الوفد العربي برنامجه.

ألغي سفري.

يعطيني أحمد كتابه.

هل أعطيه / تعطيه / تعطينه كرّاستك؟

أرسل / ترسل / ترسلين كلّ البطاقات إلى الخارج.

يواصل الطالب دراساته.

تواصل الطالبة دراساتها في الجامعة.

يواصل الوفد السوري سفره.

يواصل الوفد محادثاته مع المسؤولين.

يوصلنا / نوصل المرافق إلى مدير المصنع.

أوصله / توصله / توصلينه إلى مدير المعهد.

G 3

رحّبنا أمس بالضيوف العرب.

رحّبت بصديقتي أمام المسرح.

أجبنا على أسئلة معلّمينا.

أيّدنا هذه السياسة.

أوضح الوزير القضايا التجارية.

أنهى الوفد سفره أمس.

أنهيت هذا العمل أمس.

وقفنا إلى جانب البلدان العربية.

بيّن وزير الخارجية للطلاّب سياسة تلك البلدان.

طوّرت حكومة الجزائر علاقاتها السياسية مع ألمانيا.

أراد أحمد أن يشاهد الفلم الجديد.

أردت أن أشرب كأساً من البيرة.

أرادت صديقتي أن تشرب فنجاناً من القهوة.

أردنا أن نسافر إلى مدينة لندن.

أراد أخي أن يرسل رسالة إلى عائلته.

ألغى الوزير سفره.

واصل الوفد محادثاته مع المسؤولين.

واصل وزير الخارجية سفره.

G 4

رحّب / رحّبوا بالضيوف!

أيّدوا هذه السياسة!

أجب / أجيبوا على الأسئلة!

أوضح / أوضحوا لي هذه القضية!

طوّروا بلادكم بكل قواكم!

غيّر / غيّروا البرنامج!

أعطني / أعطوني زجاجة من العصير!

- كأساً من الماء
- فنجاناً من القهوة
- كأساً من البيرة
- فنجاناً من الشاي
- بعض البطاقات
- العدد الجديد من المجلّة
- نسخة واحدة
- الكتاب
- النقود
- هذا

واصل دراستك!

أنه / أنهوا العمل حتى صباح اليوم!

- العمل حتى صباح الغد
- الواجب حتى مساء اليوم
- الكتابة حتى مساء الغد
- المشروع بعد ساعة
- الاستقبال بعد ساعتين

أوصلنا / أوصلونا إلى هناك!

G 5

لم يجب الطالب على السؤال بعد.

لم ينه الوفد السوري زيارته لبلدنا بعد.

لم أنه عملي بعد.

لم يرد محمّد أن يسافر بالسيارة.

لم ترد الفتاة أن تشرب كأساً من العصير.

لماذا لم يغيّر الوفد برنامجه بعد؟

لماذا لم يلغوا الزيارة؟

لم يعطني كتاباً واحداً.

لماذا لم تعطني/ تعطيني نقوداً بعد؟

لم أرسل / ترسل / ترسلي كلّ البطاقات إلى الخارج بعد.

لم أنه هذا العمل أمس.

لم يرد أحمد أن يشاهد الفلم القديم بعد.

لم أرد أن أشرب كأساً واحدة.

لم يرد أخي أن يرسل رسالة إليهم بعد.

لم يواصل الطالب دراساته بعد.

لم يواصل الوفد المحادثات مع المسؤولين بعد.

Final Exercise

1.

يقيم وزير الخارجية حفلة استقبال. يلقي الرئيس كلمة. توضح المعلّمة الدرس الجديد. نريد أن نقوم برحلة إلى الصحراء. يصيب الهدف بالبندقية. يعلن الرئيس افتتاح المؤتمر. ينهون الرحلة في الشتاء. تؤيّد الحكومة كلّ القرارات. تجيبون على كلّ الأسئلة. يخفف الهواء الجافّ من وطأة الحرارة. تـؤدّي الكوارث إلى وفاة الكثير من المواطنين. يعاني البلد من عواصف شديدة. يغيّر أحمد برنامج الرحلة. أعطيه / تعطيه/ تعطينه الحبوب والأدوية الأخرى.يصيبون العقارب والعناكب بالبندقيـة. تخاف مـن الحيوانات الخطيرة. نبقى في الصحراء لمدة أسبوع. نضيّع الطريق. تفكّرون في حلـول جديدة. تلغـي الوزارة كلّ البرامج.

2.

لم يقم وزير الخارجية حفلة استقبال. لم يلق الرئيس كلمة. لم توضح المعلّمة الدرس الجديـد. لم نـرد أن نقوم برحلة إلى الصحراء. لم يصب الهدف بالبندقية. لم يعلن الرئيس افتتاح المؤتمـر. لم ينهـوا الرحلة في الشتاء. لم تؤيّد الحكومة كلّ القرارات. لم تجيبوا على كلّ الأسئلة. لم يخفف الهواء الجافّ من وطأة الحرارة. لم تؤد الكوارث إلى وفاة الكثير من المواطنين. لم يعان البلد من عواصف شـديدة. لم يغيّر أحمد برنامج الرحلة. لم أعطه / تعطه/ تعطيه الحبوب والأدوية الأخرى. لم يصيبوا العقارب والعناكب بالبندقية. لم تخف مـن الحيوانـات الخطيـرة. لم نبـق في الصحـراء لمـدة أسبـوع. لم نضيّـع الطريق. لم تفكّروا في حلول جديدة. لم تلغ الوزارة كلّ البرامج.

3.

لم يأت بعد. لم تلغ الرحلة بعد. لم يعطني كتاباً بعد. لم ينهوا الجلسة بعد. لم نجر المحادثات بعد. لـن يقيموا حفلة استقبال. لن يصيب العقرب بالبندقية.

4.

ألغوا كلّ ما في البرنامج من مواعيد. لا أعرف كلّ من زار المعهد في هذا اليوم. قل لي من رأيـت في الصحراء. لم يقل ما حدث في أيّام الرحلة. من أصاب الهدف هو صديقي.

5.

عزيزي محمّد

تحية طيبة وبعد ..

كيف حالك وكيف حال العائلة؟ كنت مع بعض الأصدقاء في الصحراء. كانت الرحلة جميلة جـدًّا. كانت درجة الحرارة مرتفعة جدًّا في النهار ومنخفضة جدًّا في الليل. شاهدت فيضاناً (سيلاً) والكثير من حيوانات الصحراء يعني عقارب وحيات وعنـاكب سـامّة وحيوانات خطيرة أخرى لا أعرف أسماءها العربية.

نمنا ثلاثة أيام تحت نجوم سماء الصحراء. في الأسبوع القادم نقوم برحلـة إلى الجبـال. أمـا فيمـا يخص الدراسة فكل شيء على ما يرام بما في ذلك المحاضرات في الطب.

إن شاء الله أراك في الشهر القادم

صديقك المخلص

بيتر

Lesson 16

L 1

رخصةٌ (واحدةٌ) / موظّفٌ (واحدٌ)، إحدى عشرة رخصة / أحد عشر موظّفاً، واحدة وخمسون رخصة، واحد وخمسون موظّفاً

بيتان / مدرستان، اثنا عشر بيتاً / اثنتا عشرة مدرسة ، اثنان وعشرون بيتاً / اثنتان وعشرون مدرسة

ثلاث ليرات / ثلاثة دنانير، ثلاث عشرة لـيرة / ثلاثة عشر ديناراً، ثلاث وعشرون لـيرة / ثلاثة وعشرون ديناراً

أربع ساعات / اربعة أشهر، أربع عشرة ساعة / أربعة عشر شهراً، أربع وعشرون سـاعة / أربعة وعشرون شهراً

خمسة كيلومترات / خمس سنوات، خمسة عشر كيلومتراً / خمس عشرة سنة، خمسة وأربعون كيلومتراً / خمس وأربعون سنة

ستة ملاليم / قروش، ستة عشر مليماً / قرشاً، ستة وخمسون مليماً / قرشاً

سبعة أمتار / أيام، سبعة عشر متراً / يوماً، سبعة وستون متراً / يوماً

ثمانية سنتيمترات / كتب، ثمانية عشر سنتيمتراً / كتاباً، ثمانية وسبعون سنتيمتراً / كتاباً

تسعة أيام / تسع سنوات، تسعة عشر يوماً / تسع عشرة سنة، تسعة وثمانون يوماً / تسع وثمانون سنة

عشر دقائق / عشرة أسابيع، عشرون دقيقة / أسبوعاً، ثلاثون دقيقة / أسبوعاً

أحد عشر جنيهاً / يوماً، واحد وعشرون جنيهاً / يوماً، أربعون جنيهاً / يوماً

اثنا عشر فلساً / شخصاً، اثنان وعشرون فلساً / شخصاً، خمسون فلساً / شخصاً

ستون / سبعون / ثمانون موظّفاً / سنة

تسعون ليرة / جنيهاً، مائة ليرة / جنيه، مائة ليرة / جنيه وليرة / وجنيه

مائتا متر / دولار، ثلاثمائة متر / دولار، أربعمائة متر / دولار

ألف شخص / كيلومتر، ألفا شخص / كيلومتر، عشرة آلاف شخص / كيلومتر

L 5

أقوم من النوم في الساعة ...

آكل طعام الفطور ...

أخرج من البيت ...

أصل إلى المعهد ...

تبدأ الدروس ...

آكل طعام الغداء ...

أخرج من المعهد ...

أذهب إلى المكتبة ...

أعود إلى البيت ...

آكل طعام العشاء ...

أفتح جهاز التلفزيون ...

وصل الوفد في ... إلى المطار.

أقابل صديقتي ...
تبدأ الحفلة ...
الساعة الآن ...
نمت في ...
كنت في المعهد ...
أعرف الجواب ...

L 8

كنت في هذه السنة ... في المسرح.
أسافر في السنة ... إلى الجبال.
قرأت الدرس السادس عشر من هذا الكتاب ...
أذهب في الشهر ... إلى المكتبة.
سافرت في حياتي ... بالطائرة.
أكتب في الشهر ... رسالة لصديقي (لصديقتي).
كنت ... في لندن.
كنت ... في الخارج.
أذهب في الشهر ... إلى المصرف.
أفتح في الأسبوع جهاز التلفزيون ...

G 1

في الشهر الخامس، في الأسبوع الثالث، في السنة التاسعة، في القرن العاشر، في الساعة الرابعة، في الأسبوع الثامن، في اليوم السادس، في القرن السابع، في الساعة الثانية، في اليوم الحادي عشر، في الشهر الثاني عشر، في السنة الخامسة، في القرن التاسع، في السنة الحادية عشرة، في الشهر الثاني، في الأسبوع السابع، في القرن الثامن، في الساعة الثانية عشرة، في اليوم الأول، في الأسبوع السادس، في اليوم العاشر، في الأسبوع الخامس عشر، في السنة التاسعة عشرة، في الشهر السادس عشر، في القرية الثالثة عشرة، في المدينة الثمانية عشرة، في السنة الرابعة عشرة، في اليوم السابع عشر

G 2

ثلاث سنوات، أحد عشر أسبوعاً، عشرون قرناً، أربع سنوات، عشرة اجتماعات، خمس نسخ، خمسة عشر يوماً، ثمانية اشهر، تسع ساعات، مخزنان، دقيقة واحدة، سبع ساعات، تسعة عشر اجتماعاً، ثمانية عشر قرناً، ثلاثة عشر شهراً، اربعة عشر يوماً، سبع عشرة دقيقة، اثنتا عشرة قاعة، ستة مخازن، ستة عشر أسبوعاً

G 4

هل يمكنك أن تسافر إلى هناك؟ – يمكنني أن أفعل ذلك – يمكننا أن ننجز واجباتنا فوراً.
متى تنجزون واجباتكم؟ – هل تنجز/ تنجزين عملك بنفسك؟ – ينجزون العمل بعد ثلاث ساعات.
يرسل الطالب رسالة إلى عائلته – هل ترسل/ ترسلين هدية إلى صديقك؟ – متى ترسل/ ترسلين البطاقة إلى أصدقائك؟

لماذا تُحضِر / تحضرين جميع الطلّاب إلى هنا؟ – لماذا تحضرون معكم أربعة كتـب فقط؟ – أعرف أنّهما يحضران معهما نقوداً كثيرة.

نقدّم إليكم أصدقاءنا – متى يقدّمونه إليك؟ – يقدّم أحمد نفسه – أقدّم / تقدّم / تقدّمين له هـذه الهدية – هل تقدّمون لهم بعض الشراب؟

يرحّب بنا مدير المعهد – نرحّب بضيوفنا الأجانب – يرحّب الرئيس بأعضاء الوفد الفرنسي.

إلى أين تسافر الوفود؟ – تسافر إلى لنـدن بالقطار – نسـافر إلى هنـاك بالطـائرة – هـل يسـافر السياسيون اليوم؟

هل تشاهد / تشاهدين ذلك الفلم؟ – نعم أشاهده / تشاهده مساء اليـوم – نعـم نشاهـده اليـوم – يشاهدون اليوم الأبنية الحديثة.

يترجم الطالب الكلمات الجديدة إلى اللغة الألمانية – أترجمها إلى اللغة العربية –تترجم المعلّمـة الرسـالة من اللغة الفرنسية إلى اللغة الألمانية.

هل يحدّثكم صديقكم عن رحلته؟ – نحدّثه عن دراستنا في مصر – تحدّثنا هيفاء عن الحياة في بلادها.

يسلّم أحمد عدنان الكتاب – نسلّمكم المبلغ اليوم – أسلّم الأشياء فوراً.

يفرحنا ذلك – يفرحني ذلك – هل تفرحكم الهدايا؟

ترافق الوفد طالبة ألمانية – أرافق صديقي إلى المحطّة – يرافقني إلى المسرح صديـق إنكليزي. تقابل / تقابلين هناك؟ – أقابل / تقابل / تقابلين هناك صديقـاً جزائريـاً –نقـابل اليـوم عـدداً مـن الضيـوف الأجانب.

Final Exercise

1.

بيتٌ، خمسة وتسعون موضوعاً، أربعة أقمار صناعية
خمس مدارس، مائة ولد وولد، عشرة كثبان
ثلاث رخص، سبع بنادق، فيضانان
إحدى عشرة شهادة، تسعة اِختبارات، اثنتان وعشرون واحة
واحد/ أحد وعشرون زوجاً، ستة بنوك، مائة وإحدى عشرة كرة
ثلاثة عشر طابعاً، خمسة عشر عقرباً، تسع عشرة شجرة

2.

البيت الأول، الموضوع الخامس والتسعون، القمر الصناعي الرابع
المدرسة الخامسة، الولد الأول بعد المائة، الكثيب العاشر
الرخصة الثالثة، البندقية السابعة، الفيضان الثاني
الشهادة الحادية عشرة، الإختبار التاسع، الواحة الثانية والعشرون
الزوج الحادي والعشرون، البنك السادس، الكرة الحادية عشرة بعد المائة
الطابع الثالث عشر، العقرب الخامس عشر، الشجرة التاسعة عشرة

3.

ولدت في الحادي والثلاثين من كانون الأول عام ألف وتسعمائة وأربعة وسبعين. كـان أبـي، رحمـه ا لله، يعمل لمدة سنتين معلّمـاً في المدرسة الابتدائية الخامسة. أخي الثالث حلّاق. أنا طـالب في السـنة الثانية. تضم الجامعة ثماني كليات. عندي أربعة أولاد. ابني الرابع مهندس. يجب عليكم/عليكُ أن

تذهبوا/ تذهب إلى الطابق الثامن وأن تعودوا بعد ذلك إليّ مـرّة أخرى. يعمـل في الشعبة الفنيـة في الطابق السابع.

4.

في الساعةِ:

الثانية ألا خمس دقائق مسلءً	العاشرة والنصف صباحاً
الخامسة واثنتين وعشرين دقيقة مساءً	التاسعة والربع صباحاً
السابعة وخمس وعشرين دقيقة مساءً	العاشرة وسبع عشرة دقيقة مساءً
الثالثة إلّا ثلاث وعشرين دقيقة مساءً	السادسة إلّا الربع صباحاً
العاشرة إلّا الثلث مساءً	الواحدة والثلث مساءً

عامَ / في عامٍ
ألف وتسعمائة وثمانية عشر
ألف وسبعمائة وثمانية وتسعين
ألف وتسعمائة وخمسة وأربعين
ستمائة واثنين وعشرين
ألف ومائتين وثمانية وخمسين

في الحادي عشر من تشرين الثاني عام ألف وأربعمائة وأربعة
في الثالث من أيلول عام ألفين واثنين
في العشرين من أيار عام ألف وتسعمائة وواحد وتسعين
في الثالث عشر من أب عام ألف وتسعمائة وواحد وستين
في السادس عشر من حزيران عام ألف وتسعمائة واثنين وتسعين

Lesson 17

L 2

وقّع على / وعد ب / حصل على / تفرّج على / شارك في / قام ب / نظر إلى / رغب إلى / سمح ل ب / نصح ب / شعر ب / دعا إلى، ل / عاد إلى / ذهب من ... إلى / سلّم علـى / رجـع مـن ... إلى / سكن في، عند / وصل إلى / تراوح بين ... وبين / شارك في / زوّد ب / جاء من ... إلى / وفى ب / حال دون / عرض على / وصف ب / تبع ل / أدّى إلى / أشرف على / ربـط بـين ... وبين / رحّب ب / أسفر عن / أضاف إلى / عبّر عن / عانى من / قدّم إلى، ل / أجاب على

L 5

a rich man, a clever student (f.), things important in/for the whole world, an important matter for the development of sports, developments related to the political situation, a problem of great importance for the Arab countries, the woman with the pretty face, the men with influence on the foreign policy, a political system with tribal foundations, hotels with 10 floors

L 7

قبل الزيارة الرابعة / أمام البيت الرابع / مع الطالب التاسع / بعد السابع عشر من يونيو / قبل الأول من أبريل / مع الضيف المائة ألف / في المدرسة الثانية والثلاثين / في الرابع والعشرين من ديسمبر / خلف الصحراء الخامس / بعد المباراة السابعة / فوق الخط الثاني / تحت الصخرة الثامنة / في الوادي الخامس / إلى الشارع الخامس / بسبب الكارثة الثانية / مع الخليفة الرابع / بعد الموجة الرابعة / خلف الجبل السابع / بعد الوسام السادس / مع الرمح العاشر / أمام الرياضي السادس / قبل المباراة الثانية / النادي العاشر / بعد الهزيمة الخامسة عشرة / الرقم القياسي العشرون / مع القنبلة الحادية والعشرين / البئر الأولى / بعد الحقنة الحادية عشرة

L 8

قبل أربع زيارات / أمام أربعة بيوت / مع تسعة طلاّب / بعد سبعة عشر يوماً من يونيو / مع مائة ألف ضيف / في اثنتي وثلاثين مدرسة / خلف خمسة صحارى / بعد سبع مباريات / فوق الخطين / تحت ثماني صخور / في خمسة أودية / إلى خمسة شوارع / بسبب الكارثتين / مع أربعة خلفاء / بعد أربع موجات / خلف سبعة جبال / بعد ستة أوسمة / مع عشرة رماح / أمام ستة رياضيين / قبل المباراتين / عشرة نوادٍ / بعد خمس عشرة هزيمة / عشرون رقماً قياسياً / مع إحدى وعشرين قنبلة / بئر واحدة / بعد إحدى عشرة حقنة

L 9

الكتاب الذي اشتريته / الرجل الذي قابلته في الفندق / البلدان التي شاركت في المؤتمر / مع الطالبات اللاتي / اللواتي رجعن إلى الجامعة / في البيتين اللذين كنت فيهما / عند الطلاّب اللذين درسوا في ألمانيا / تحت الطاولة التي باعها أحمد / مع المدرسين الذين حضروا الاجتماع / عند الشجرتين اللتين رأيتهما في مركز المدينة / مع مريم وصباح اللتين ذهبتا إلى الجامعة / مع محمّد وصباح اللذين رأيتهما في الدكّان

G 1

يتراوح العدد بين خمسين وتسعين

تتراوح النتائج بين ... و بين ...

يتوقّع الطلاّب نتائج ممتازة.

تتوقّع الطالبات نتائج ممتازة.

يتوقّع الطلاّب نتائج ممتازة في دراستهم.

تتوقّع الطالبات نتائج ممتازة في دراستهن.

تتعادل الفرقتان.

تتعادل الفرق كلها.

أشاهد / تشاهد / تشاهدين هذا الفلم (اليوم، في لندن، مع أصدقائي).

تتأخّر بداية المباراة (الحفلة، المحادثات) عشرين دقيقة (عشر دقائق، ربع ساعة، نصف ساعة، ساعة واحدة، ساعتين).

يتأخّر الرئيس (الضيوف، الطلاّب، التلاميذ) قليلاً (كثيراً).

يتأخّر خمس دقائق.

أتأخّر / تتأخّر / تتأخّرين خمس عشرة دقيقة.

يتأخّر القطار ثلاثين دقيقة.

نأمل ألا (أن لا) يتأخر القطار.

نأمل أن يأتي اليوم.

نأمل ألا تتأخر بداية المباراة.

يتمكّن هذا النادي من أن يفوز على جميع خصومه.

يتمكّن التجّار من أن يعقدوا صفقات ممتازة.

تتمكّن الحكومة من بناء اقتصاد جديد.

يتحمّس المتفرّجون لنادي الأهالي.

يتحمّس الناس بعد أن سجلت فرقتهم أهدافاً كثيرة.

يتمتّع الرئيس بشعبية واسعة.

تتمتّع أنواع الرياضة المختلفة بمساعدة الحكومة.

G 4

لم نتفرّج عليها.

لم أشاهده/ تشاهده .

لم تتأخّر بدايتها.

لم تتأخّر.

لم تتأخّر بدايتها.

لم يتأخّر الحكم.

لم يتأخّر الصديق.

لم تتعادل الفرقتان.

لم يتمكّن من كتابتها.

لم أتمكّن/ تتمكن من أن أرجع/ ترجع إلى البيت.

لم يتمكّن من أن يقابله قبل السفر.

لم يتوقّع هزيمة منتخب بلده.

G 5

الطبيب دعوناه فوراً

المريض نقلته السيّارة إلى المستشفى

عمر أزوره صباح الغد

أصدقاؤنا قابلتهم أمس

الحفلة حضرتها وفود كثيرة

هذه السيّارة سعرها مرتفع

هذا البلد عاصمته جميلة

جامعة لندن كنت أدرس فيها أربع سنوات

ذلك البيت كنّا نسكن فيه لمدّة أسبوعين

الطالبات كنت معهن في المسرح

الوفود الأجنبية هل وصلت أمس؟

أصدقاؤنا هل رأيتهم؟

أصدقاؤنا متى رأيتهم؟

مريم إلى أين تمشي؟

تلك الكتب لماذا بعتها؟

Final Exercise

1.

يراهنون على فرقتهم. أتأخر / تتأخر / تتأخر / تتأخرين بخمس دقائق. نحرز ميداليـات كثيرة. يتحمّس أنصار كرة القدم. يتراوح عدد الأنصار بين ألفين وثلاثة آلاف. يصبـح تسويق الرياضيين فرعـاً اقتصادياً خاصّاً. يسجّلون خمسة أهداف . تعادل قيمـة جمـال السباق الجيّـدة قيمـة أحصنة السباق المشهورة. يتعادل المنتخبان دون أهداف. يغنّى الأغنية الشعبية في الملعب. تتفرّجين على الملاكمـة والمصارعة. تتمتّع أنواع الرياضة المختلفة بشعبية واسعة. يتمكّن اللاعب مـن أنْ يسجّل كـلّ الأهداف. نتوقّع ما هو مستحيل. يشاهدون المباريات النهائية في التلفزيون.

2.

قال إنّهم تفرّجوا على المباراة. أظنّ أنّه لا يلعب كرة القدم. من تمكّن من أنْ يسجّل الهدف؟ سمعـت أنّ ألعاب الساحة والميدان تتمتّع بنفس الشعبية. قالت إنّ الملك قام بتوزيـع الأوسمـة. لا تقـل ((أنْ / أنّ)) بعد قال ! أريد أنْ أراها بعد الحفلة. أعلن الرئيس أنّه يسافر إلى أمريكا.

3.

وفى ب / حال دون / عرض على / وصف ل، ب / تبع ل / أدّى إلى / أشرف علـى / ربط بـ / رحّب بـ / أسفر عن / أضاف إلى / عبّر عن / عانى من / قدّم لـ، إلى / أجاب على / وقّع على / وعد بـ / حصل على / تفرّج على / شارك في / قام بـ / نظر إلى / رغب في / سمح لـ بـ / نصـح بـ / شعر بـ / دعا إلى / عاد إلى / قال لـ، مـن / ذهب إلى / سلّم لـ، على / رجع مـن، إلى / سكن في / وصل إلى / تراوح بين ... وبين / شارك في / زوّد بـ / جاء إلى، من

4.

ذلك الفندق كنّا نسكن فيه لمدّة أسبوعين. الطالبات كنت معهـن في المسرح. الوفود الأجنبيـة هـل وصلت أمس؟ مرافقنا هل رأيته؟ أصدقاؤنا متى رأيتهم؟ صبـاح إلى أين تمشي؟ تلك البيـوت لمـاذا بعتها؟ الطبيب دعوناه فوراً. المريض نقلته السيّارة إلى المستشفى. أحمـد أزوره صبـاح الغـد. مديرنـا قابلته أمس. الحفلة حضرتها وفود كثيرة. هذه السيّارات أسعارها مرتفعة. هذا البلد عاصمته كبـيرة. جامعة باريس كنت أدرس فيها من ١٩٩٤ – ١٩٩٨.

5.

تحت الطاولة التي باعها أحمد / مع المدرسين الذين حضروا الاجتماع / عند الشجرتين اللتين رأيتهما في مركز المدينة / مع مريم وصباح اللتين ذهبتا إلى الجامعة / مـع محمّد وصباح اللذين رأيتهمـا في الدكّان / الكتاب الذي اشتريته / الرجل الذي قابلته في الفندق / البلدان الـتي شـاركت في المؤتمـر / مع الطالبات اللاتي رجعن إلى الجامعة / في البيتين اللذين كنت فيهما / عند الطـلاّب الذين درسوا في ألمانيا

6.

تتمتع انواع الرياضة المعروفة في أوربا مثل كرة القدم وألعاب الساحة والميدان بشعبية واسعة في العالم العربي أيضاً. تشترك البلدان العربية بمنتخباتها في بطولات العالم. توجد في البلدان العربية أنواع من الرياضة تكاد تكون غير معروفة في أوربا. لم يتمكن أحد من أن يسجل هدفاً في المباراة ألتي كنّا نتفرج عليها. يتراوح سعر جمل السباق بين خمسمائة ألف ومليون دولار. تغني الفرق الشعبية أغاني شعبية قديمة تعكس حياة البدو.

Lesson 18
L 5

أشكركم على الحفاوة التي لقيتها أثناء زيارتي الأولى. يبتديء بذلك عهد قصير من التعاون بين البلدين. تتمتع أنواع الرياضة المشهورة بشعبية قليلة. تمكنت كلّ البلدان من أن تحرز ميداليات قليلة. تغنّي الفرق الشعبية أغاني شعبية جديدة. وقد تمضي أحياناً سنوات قليلة دون سقوط المطر على الإطلاق. تقع الصحارى في مناطق الضغط المنخفض. هي قليلة الحرارة في الصيف وحارة في الشتاء. وقد تبلغ درجة الحرارة القصوى ٦٠ درجة مئوية في نهاية العام. انتهت المحادثات. غادر الوزير. خرج من البيت. رفض أحمد الدعوة. قام المدير في وسط مكتبه.

G 1

لم يشترك جميع الخبراء في هذا المؤتمر.
لم يشترك وفدنا في هذا الاجتماع.
لم أشترك / تشترك في هذه المحادثات.
لم يشترك مدير معهدي في هذه المحادثات.
لم أشترك / تشترك في هذا الاجتماع.
لم يشتركوا كلهم في هذا المعرض.
لم يشترك وزير الخارجية في هذا الاجتماع.
لم أشترك / تشترك في المباريات في لايبزك.
لم يشترك أصدقائي في المباريات في لندن.
لم أتلق رسالة اليوم.
لم أتلق رسالة من أمي.
لم يتلق صديقي رسالة من أخيه.
لم تتلق الوزارة دعوة.
لم نتلق الدعوة.
لم يستأجر سيّارة.
لم تستأجر صباح سيّارة كابريوليه.
لم نستأجر سيّارة جيب.
لم أستطع أن أستأجر بيتاً جديداً.
لم أستطع أن أدبّر لكم الاستمارات اللازمة.
لم تستغرق المباراة ساعتين.

لم يستغرق المؤتمر يومين.

لم يجتمع الرئيس مع الوفود العربية.

لم يجتمعوا مع مدراء المعاهد.

لم تشتغل صباح في المطعم.

لم نشتغل في هذه المصانع.

G 2

هل تستطيع أن تدبّر لي الاستمارات؟

نعم، أستطيع أن أدبّر لك الاستمارات.

هل تستطيع أن تدبّر لنا الاستمارات اللازمة؟

نعم، أستطيع أن أدبّر لكم الاستمارات اللازمة.

هل يستطيع الموظّف أن يدبّر لك جواز السفر؟

نعم، يستطيع الموظّف أن يدبّر لي جواز السفر.

هل يستطيع صديقك أن يسافر إلى بيروت؟

نعم، يستطيع صديقي أن يسافر إلى بيروت.

هل يستطيع رئيس الوفد أن يجيب على الأسئلة؟

نعم، يستطيع رئيس الوفد أن يجيب على الأسئلة.

هل يستطيع الطلّاب أن يجتمعوا في معهدهم؟

نعم، يستطيع الطلّاب أن يجتمعوا في معهدهم.

هل تستطيع أن ترافق الوفد السوري؟

نعم، أستطيع أن أرافق الوفد السوري.

هل تستطيع الطالبة أن تزور أمها في المستشفى؟

نعم، تستطيع الطالبة أن تزور أمها في المستشفى.

هل تستطيع أن تأتي إليهم حالاً؟

نعم، أستطيع أن آتي إليهم حالاً.

هل يستطيع بيتر أن يكتب رسالة عربية؟

نعم، يستطيع بيتر أن يكتب رسالة عربية.

هل تستطيع أن تتلقّى جواز السفر؟

نعم، أستطيع أن أتلقّى جواز السفر.

هل يستطيع الوفد أن ينهي محادثاته؟

نعم، يستطيع الوفد أن ينهي محادثاته.

Final Exercise

1.

لم يشترك وفدنا في هذا الاجتماع. لم أشترك / تشترك في هذه المحادثات. لم أتلق رسالة اليوم. لم أتلق رسالة من أمي. لم يتلق صديقي رسالة من أخيه. لم يشتركوا كلهم في هذا المعرض. لم نستأجر سيّارة جيب. لم أستطع أن أستأجر بيتاً جديداً. لم أستطع أن أدبّر لكم الاستمارات اللازمة. لم تتلق

الوزارة دعوة. لم نتلق الدعوة. لم يستأجر سيّارة. لم تستأجر صباح سيّارة كابريوليه. لم تشتغل صباح في المطعم. لم نشتغل في هذه المصانع. لم تستغرق المباراة ساعتين. لم يستغرق المؤتمر يومين. لم يجتمع الرئيس مع الوفود العربية. لم يجتمعوا مع مدراء المعاهد. لم أشتر السيّارة.

2.

لم يشتر الكتاب. لم نتلق الدعوة. لم تصل رخصة السياقة بعد. استغرق الامتحان خمس ساعات. لا أستطيع أن أواصل مشاهدة معالم هذه المدينة مشياً. أريد أن أشتري سيّارة مكشوفة أي سيّارة كابريوليه. سيقتلني الطقس الحار. لم تنته الجلسة بعد. لن تعمل في المطعم.

3.

لم يبدأ المؤتمر. لن يدخل البيت. هذا ممكن. لم أجهل ذلك. لم أشتر الكتاب. بعد أن قمنا بدأ الاجتماع. نعرف أين الفكّ الأسفل. مشى إلى اليمين. حدّثته عن صحة المدير. نمت بعد الطعام. لم أعط القلم. جاء في المساء. لم يمش إلى فوق.

4.

الأستاذ ... العزيز

تحية طيبة وبعد ...

أشكركم شكراً جزيلا على رسالتكم المؤرخة في ١١ / ١٢/ ١٩٩٥ وعلى المعلومات القيمة الكثيرة وعلى الدعوة لزيارة معهدكم. آمل أن يبدأ بهذه الزيارة تعاون مثمر بين معهدينا. لم أستطع إلى الآن أن أتصل بمدير المكتبة هاتفياً . سأحاول أن أتصل به عن طريق شبكة الحاسب الآلي. حصلت من مدير مركز الحاسب على فاكس بالمعلومات المرجوة.

وكما اتفقنا أرسل لكم طيه مقالة للنشر في مجلة معهدكم وبعض برامج الحاسب الآلي الجديدة.

أشكركم مرّة أخرى على ما قدّمتموه من مساعدات وأرجو التكرم بإجراء اللازم

مع فائق الاحترام والتقدير

Lesson 19

L 4

في العقد العاشر، في البيت الخامس، مع الراكب التاسع، بعد المنتوج العشرين، حول المورد السادس، مع البديل الثامن، بالمادة الثالثة، بعد الاقتراح السابع، في المنظمة التاسعة عشرة، في الشعبة الرابعة، حول الرخصة الحادية عشرة، بعد الرسم الثاني عشر، في الطابق السابع عشر، مع النائب السادس، بعد المرة العاشرة، عند الحلّاق السابع، في الشهادة الثانية، في القراءة السابعة

G 1

غيّر البرنامج.

عقد المؤتمر في الشهر الماضي.

قيل له إنه سافر إلى لندن.

تلغى الزيارة.

سلّمت له هدية جميلة.

يسمّى ابنه محمّداً.

عقد اجتماع.

شوهد الطلاب أمام المعهد.

تقام الحفلة غداً.

أحضرت له هدية.

يوفد الطلّاب إلى الخارج.

أُلغي الموعد.

أُضيفت بعض الكلمات.

أُجريت محادثات هامّة.

تسلّم الهدية غداً.

رجيت مريم أن تذهب معنا.

تجرى المحادثات في وزارة الخارجية.

دُعي لزيارة لندن.

تغيّر البرامج كلّ يوم.

أرسلت إليّ بطاقة من القاهرة.

اُستنتج من ذلك أنّ الوضع متغير.

G 2

أقيمت / تقام الحفلة مساء.

أُجريت / تجرى المحادثات في وزارة الخارجية.

زرعت / تزرع الفواكه في شمال البلد.

أعرف أنّ المؤتمر عقد / يعقد في لندن.

هل دعيت / تدعى صديقتك لحضور الحفلة؟

سمعت أنّ البترول صنع / يصنع هناك.

هل اُستنتج / يُستنتج من ذلك أنّ السوق تعتمد على العلاقة بين العرض والطلب؟

هل بيعت / تباع هذه البضائع في الخارج؟

G 3

يقدّم (Form II, Act. or Pass.)

يلقى (Form I, Act. or Pass. or Form IV. Pass.)

انتهى (Form VIII. Act.)

يدعى (Form I or IV Pass.)

يقال (Form I Pass.)

دعي (Form I Pass.)

يلغى (Form I Act. or Pass. or Form IV Pass.)

يعقد (Form I Act. or Pass. or Form IV Act. or Pass.)

يكتب (Form I Act. or Pass. or Form II Act. or Pass. or Form IV Act. or Pass.)

ينام (Form I Act.)

شوهد (Form III Pass.)

ألغى (Form IV Act.)

يزرع (Form I Act. or Pass. or Form IV Act. or Pass.)

أوضح (Form IV Act. or Pass.)

أعطى (Form IV Act.)

طوّر (Form II Act. or Pass.)

اشترى (Form VIII Act. or Pass.)

يستطيع (Form X Act.)

تغيّر (Form V Act.)

يلاحظ (Form III Act. or Pass.)

انعقد (Form VII Act. or Pass.)

G 4

تتمتّع أنواع الرياضة المختلفة بمساعدة الحكومة.

يتمتع الرئيس بشعبية كبيرة.

يتحمّس الأنصار لفرقتهم بعد أن سجّلت فرقتهم أهدافاً كثيرة.

يتمكّن هذا النادي من أن يفوز على كلّ النوادي الأخرى.

يتأخّر القطار ساعتين.

تتأخّر الطالبة خمس عشرة دقيقة.

تتأخر بداية المؤتمر عشر دقائق.

أشاهد / تشاهد / تشاهدين هذا الفلم.

يتعادل المنتخبان.

يتوقّع الطلّاب نتائج ممتازة في دراستهم.

يتوقّع الرئيس أنّ المعارضة لا تتمكّن من حل مشاكل البلد.

يتراوح عدد المتفرّجين بين ١٠٠ و٥٠٠ متفرّج.

يتفرّج على المباراة.

G 5

لم تتمتّع أنواع الرياضة المختلفة بمساعدة الحكومة.

لم يتمتع الرئيس بشعبية كبيرة.

لم يتحمّس الأنصار لفرقتهم بعد أن سجّل فرقتهم أهدافاً كثيرة.

لم يتمكّن هذا النادي من أن يفوز على كلّ النوادي الأخرى.

لم يتأخّر القطار ساعتين.

لم تتأخّر الطالبة خمس عشرة دقيقة.

لم تتأخر بداية المؤتمر عشر دقائق.

لم أشاهد / تشاهد / تشاهدي هذا الفلم.

لم يتعادل المنتخبان.

لم يتوقّع الطلّاب نتائج ممتازة في دراستهم.

لم يتوقّع الرئيس أنّ المعارضة لا تتمكّن من حل مشاكل البلد.

لم يتراوح عدد المتفرّجين بين ١٠٠ و٥٠٠ متفرّج.

لم يتفرّج على المباراة.

G 6

لا تتمتّع أنواع الرياضة المختلفة بمساعدة الحكومة.

لا يتمتع الرئيس بشعبية كبيرة.

لا يتحمّس الأنصار لفرقتهم بعد أن سجّلت فرقتهم أهدافاً كثيرة.

لا يتمكّن هذا النادي من أن يفوز على كلّ النوادي الأخرى.

لا يتأخّر القطار ساعتين.

لا تتأخّر الطالبة خمس عشرة دقيقة.

لا تتأخر بداية المؤتمر عشر دقائق.

لا أشاهد / تشاهد / تشاهدين هذا الفلم.

لا يتعادل المنتخبان.

لا يتوقّع الطلّاب نتائج ممتازة في دراستهم.

لا يتوقع الرئيس أنّ المعارضة لا تتمكّن من حل مشاكل البلد.

لا يتراوح عدد المتفرجين بين ١٠٠ و ٥٠٠ متفرّج.

لا يتفرّج على المباراة.

G 7

البترول يصنّعه البلد بكميات كبيرة

حساسية شديدة لانحسار الطلب تجدها في اقتصاديات هذه البلدان

الأوضاع الصعبة تغلبت البلدان العربية عليها

المنتوجات الصناعية باعتها الدول الصناعية بأسعار مرتفعة

العلاقة بين العرض والطلب ناقشوها في مؤتمر دولي

أسعار النفط قرّرت الدول المنتجة للنفط مراجعتها

مستوى الأسعار قامت منظّمة الأوبك بتصحيحه

عصر الطاقة الرخيصة أنهته المنظّمة

نظيره قابله في الوزارة

مستوى متدنٍ جدّا شاهدوه هناك

Final Exercise

1.

يسلّم الكتاب غداً. رجيت صباح أن تدرس معنا. تجرى المحادثات في وزارة الخارجية. دعي لزيارة باريس. تغيّر البرامج كلّ يوم. أرسلت إليّ بطاقة من القاهرة. استنتج من ذلك أنّ الوضع متغير. تقام الحفلة غداً. يوفد الطلّاب إلى الخارج. سلّمت له شنطة. ألغي الموعد. أضيفت بعض الكلمات. أجريت محادثات هامّة. أقيمت حفلة عشاء. غيّر البرنامج. عقد المؤتمر في الشهر الماضي. قيـل لـه إنّه سافر إلى لندن. تلغى الزيارة. سلّمت له كتب جميلة. يسمّى ابنه محمّداً. عقد اجتمـاع. شـوهد الطلّاب أمام المعهد.

2.

سئل عن أهدافه. قيل له إن الوزير سافر إلى لندن. ألغيت البرامج. رحّب بالوفود أمام الفندق. عبّر في المؤتمر عن آراء مختلفة. أعطي أحمد سيّارة. هذه كانت جلسة لا تنسى. هذا لا يقال. هذا لا يباع هنا. اختير بعد مناقشة طويلة.

3.

الفواكه التي تزرع في البلدان العربية هي ...
الثروات الطبيعية التي توجد في البلدان العربية هي ...

4.

المنظمة التاسعة عشرة، الشعبة الرابعة، الرخصة الحادية عشرة، الرسم الثاني عشر، الطابق السابع عشر، النائب السادس، المرة العاشرة، الحلّاق السابع، اللغويّ الأول، الشهادة الثانية، القرار السابع، العقد العاشر، العقد الخامس، الراكب التاسع، المنتوج العشرون، المورد السادس، البديل الثامن، المادة الثالثة، الاقتراح السابع

5.

البلدان العربية المنتجة للنفط، المتغيرات المختلفة في السوق العالمية، العلاقة بين العرض والطلب، النهضة الاقتصادية، دول صناعية، تكثيف الجهود، المنتوج الاجتماعي الإجمالي، الاستهلاك والانتاج، مستوى الأسعار المتدني جدا، أزمة النفط الثانية

Lesson 20

L 1

يبلغ عدد سكان البلدان العربية ... / يقدّر عدد سكان البلدان العربية بـ...
تبلغ مساحتها ... / تقدّر مساحتها بـ ...
تبلغ المسافة بين لندن والقاهرة .../ تقدّر المسافة بين لندن والقاهرة بـ ...
تبلغ المسافة بين باريس ودمشق .../ تقدّر المسافة بين باريس ودمشق بـ...
يبلغ عدد المسلمين في العالم ...،/ يقدّر عدد المسلمين في العالم بـ...

L 4

تتألف الحكومة من وزارة الخارجية والداخلية والمالية والدفاع والثقافة والاقتصاد (الخارجي) والصناعة والزراعة والتجارة (الخارجية) ...

G 1

سمعت أمس أنّ الرحلة ألغيت.
أريد أنْ أزوره يوم الأحد.
لا أستطيع أنْ أجيب على هذا السؤال.
أعلنت وزارة الخارجية أنّ وزير الخارجية سيزور الجزائر.
أمل الرجل أنْ يصل إلى هدفه.
أعتقدُ أنّ صديقي يأتي اليوم.
يجب عليك أنْ تنجز واجباتك.
أكّد رئيس الوفد أنّ حكومته تؤيد هذه الاقتراحات

طلب محمّد أنْ يزور مكتبة الدولة.

طلبوا منّي أنْ أرحّب بضيوفنا الأجانب.

أقترحُ عليكم أنْ نتحدّث حول ذلك غداً.

علمتُ أمس أنّ صديقي مريض.

أعرف أنّك مجتهد.

لاحظت أنّها تتكلّم اللغة العربية.

لا يمكنني أنْ أفعل ذلك.

مَن اقترح أنّكم تبقون هنا.

رأيتُ أنّه ذهب إلى هناك.

هل يُسمح لنا أنْ ندخّن سيجارة؟

أرجوكم أنْ تنجزوا واجباتكم.

أُعلن في القاهرة أنّ المؤتمر انتهى في الساعة السابعة.

يريد أصدقائي أنْ يسافروا بالطائرة.

يجب علينا أنْ نذهب معه.

سأطلب منه أنْ يحضر إلينا.

أكّدت الحكومة أنّها ستبحث هذه الاقتراحات.

أعلنت الحكومة أنّها ستبحث المشروع.

هل يُسمح لهم أنْ يفعلوا ذلك؟

يمكننا أنْ نسافر معكم.

يأمل كلّ واحد منّا أنْ يعودوا إلى هنا.

يعرف كلهم أنّه توجد مشاكل.

لم نستطع أنْ نغيّر البرنامج.

طلب أعضاء الوفد أنْ يسافروا إلى دمشق.

أخاف (أنْ لا) ألّا يفوز على خصمه.

اقترح مرافقنا أنْ يسافر الجميع إلى تلك القرية.

هل سمعتم أنّ الطائرة لم تصل بعد؟

هل يُسمح لي أنْ أفعل ذلك؟

طلبنا من المدير أنْ يرحّب بضيوفنا الأجانب.

كان يعتقد أنّنا لا نعرف ذلك.

يجب عليكم أنْ تفعلوا ذلك.

نأمل أنْ نسافر إلى هناك.

علمت الجريدة أنّ الاجتماع سيعقد بعد غد.

أكّدت المضيفة أنّ الطائرة ستصل في الساعة التاسعة.

تريد الحكومة أنْ تعلن برنامجها بعد شهرين.

أمكنه أنْ ينجز واجباته وحده.

هل تطلب منّي أنْ أفعل ذلك؟

أعلن الرئيس أنّه تلقّى الدعوة.

لماذا تقترح أنْ يفعلوا ذلك.

يجب عليّ أنْ أنقله إلى هناك.

رجا رئيس الوفد أنْ يزور معرض دمشق.

يعرف جميعنا أنّ البرنامج سيُلغى.

هل تعتقد أنّنا لا نعرف ذلك؟

هل لاحظت أنّه كسلان؟

إسمح لي أنْ أقدّم إليك صديقي.

هل يمكنك أنْ تأتي إليّ مساء اليوم؟

أكّد الطبيب أنّ المرض (هو) انفلوينزا بسيطة.

هل تخاف من ألا يصل الأصدقاء؟

يجب عليك أنْ تفعل ذلك.

علمت صديقتي أنّ أخاها سافر إلى الخارج.

نعرف أنّكم كسالى.

متى سمعتَ أنّ السفر إلى هناك ممنوع؟

هل تستطيع أنْ تعطيني هذا الكتاب؟

كنّا نعتقد أنّ ذلك معروف.

اتّضح بعد ذلك أنّ الخبر لم يكن صحيحاً.

يريد الأصدقاء أنْ يجتمعوا يوم السبت.

G 2

لا، لم نشتغل في هذه المصانع لأنّ ...

لا، لم يجتمعوا مع مدراء المعاهد لأنّ ...

لا، لم يجتمع الرئيس مع الوفود العربية لأنّ ...

لا، لم يستغرق المؤتمر يومين لأنّه ...

لا، لم تستغرق المباراة ساعتين لأنّ ...

لا، لم أستطع أن أدبّر لكم الاستمارات لأنّ ...

لا، لم أستطع أن أستأجر بيتاً جديداً لأنّ ...

لا، لم يستطع مدير المعهد أن يجيب على كلّ الأسئلة لأنّ ...

لا، لم يستطع الوفد أن ينهي محادثاته لأنّ ...

لا، لم يتمكّن البلد من أن يحقّق نهضة ثقافية لأنّ ...

لا، لم يتمكّن الرئيس من أن يخرج من البلد بعد الحرب الأهلية لأنّ ...

لا، لم يستأجروا سيّارة جيب لأنّ ...

لا، لم تستأجر صباح سيّارة كابريوليه لأنّ ...

لا، لم نتلقّ الدعوة لأنّ ...

لا، لم أتلقّ رسالة من أمّي لأنّ ...

لا، لم تتلقّ الوزارة الرسائل الرسمية لأنّ ...

لا، لم أشترك/ تشترك في المباريات في كرة القدم لأنّ ...

لا، لم يشترك وزير الخارجية في هذا الاجتماع لأنّ ...

لا، لم يشترك الخبراء الألمان في المؤتمر الصحفي لأنّ ...

Final Exercise

1.

سمعت أمس أنّ الرحلة أُلغيت.

أريد أنْ أزوره يوم الأحد.

لا أستطيع أنْ أجيب على هذا السؤال.

أعلنت الوزارة أنّ وزير الخارجية سيزور الجزائر.

أمل الرجل أنْ يصل إلى هدفه.

أعتقدُ أنّ صديقي يأتي اليوم.

يجب عليك أنْ تنجز واجباتك.

أكّد رئيس الوفد أنّ حكومته تؤيّد هذه الاقتراحات.

طلب محمّد أنْ يزور مكتبة الدولة.

أقترحُ عليكم أنْ نتحدّث حول ذلك غداً.

علمتُ أمس أنّ صديقي مريض.

أعرف أنّك مجتهد.

لا يمكنني أنْ أفعل ذلك.

رأيتُ أنّه ذهب إلى هناك.

أرجو منكم أنْ تنجزوا واجباتكم.

يجب علينا أنْ نذهب معه.

سأطلب منه أنْ يحضر إلينا.

أكّدت الحكومة أنّها ستبحث هذه الاقتراحات.

هل يُسمح لهم أنْ يفعلوا ذلك؟

2.

أعرف أنّك ستذهب إلى هناك. أعتقد أنّه ليس عندك وقت. آمل أنْ يذهب إلى المعهد. يريد أنْ نتعلم كلّ الكلمات. لم يستطع أنْ يبيع الكتب. لم نرغب في أنْ يعمل الطلاّب كثيراً. يجب عليه أنْ يكتب رسالة. نسمح له بأنْ يسافر إلى سويسرا.

3.

لا، لم نشتغل في هذه المصانع. لا، لم يجتمع الرئيس مع الوفود العربية؟ لا، لم تستغرق المباراة ساعتين. لا، لم يستأجروا سيّارة جيب. لا، لم نتلقّ الدعوة. لا، لم أتلقّ رسالة من أمّي. لا، لم تتلقّ الوزارة الرسائل الرسمية. لا، لم يشترك الخبراء في المؤتمر الصحفي. لا، لم أستطع أن أدبّر لكم الاستمارات لا، لم يستطع مدير المعهد أن يجيب على كلّ الأسئلة. لا، لم يتمكّن البلد من أن يحقّق نهضة ثقافية.

4.

انعقدت في القاهرة في يوم الثلاثاء الماضي ندوة علمية حول آفاق تطور الزراعة في البلدان العربية. اشتركت في الندوة وفود من كلّ البلدان العربية وممثلين عن منظمة الأغذية والاتحاد الأوربي. ناقش المشتركون سبل تطوير الزراعة وتنويعها ومشاكل التصحر ومكافحة أمراض النبات وتربية المواشي وإمكانيات زيادة المحاصيل الزراعية من القمح والحنطة السوداء والذرة الشامية.

هذا وأصدرت الندوة عدداً من التوصيات لحل المشاكل التي تواجهها الزراعة في هذه المناطق. وأقيم على هامش الندوة معرض زراعي عرضت فيه جرارات حديثة ومحاريث ومضخات وأنواع جديدة من البذور تتسم بإنتاجية عالية.

Lesson 21
L 1

المشاريع معروفة.
انطلقت الطائرات المصرية في الساعة الثالثة.
حضر المترجمون العرب الحفلة.
الموظّفون المسؤولون مرضى.
إنّ المدراء يجتمعون بنا غداً.
أعرف أنّ التجار الإنكليز سيجيئون إلى ألمانيا.
المرافقون السوريون موجودون.
الركاب اليونانيون تركوا الطائرة.
الزوار مسرورون.
السائقون اللبنانيون شطار.
هل الطلبة كسالى؟
لا، الطلبة مجتهدون.
هؤلاء العمال / العاملون موجودون.
كان كلّ المتفرّجين يتوقّعون مباراة ممتازة.
إن الممرّضات يشتغلن في المستشفى.
المنتخبات البرازيلية قوية.
هذه المواضيع هامّة جدًّا.

L 4

غيّر البرنامج.
عقد المؤتمر في السنة الماضية.
استنتج من ذلك أنّ الوضع متغير.
أرسلت إليّ بطاقة من القاهرة.
تغيّر البرامج كلّ يوم.
دعي الصديق لزيارة مدينتي.
تجرى المحادثات في وزارة الخارجية.

رجي أحمد أن يجتمع بنا.

تسلّم الهدية غداً.

أضيفت بعض الكلمات.

رجيت صباح أن تسافر إلى الخارج.

ألغي الموعد.

قيل له إنّ الطلّاب ينامون في دروسه.

يسمّى ابنه سالماً.

G 1

a) active participle

I سائر، I قائم، I داعٍ، I طالب، I ساكن، II معلّم، V متفرّج، VIII معتدل،
VIII مشتغل، VIII مختلف، V متوسّط، I جالس، I عاطل، I جامع، I سائق، I قائل،
I راكب، III مسافر، VIII منتهٍ، I خادم، VIII محتاج، I ماشٍ، I واقع، I تابع،
III مرافق، I سائح، I خالق، I زائد، III مجاوز، I خارج، I داخل، I حادث

b) passive participle

I معروف، VIII محتمل، I مشهور، I مقول، IV مقام، I مشروب، I مأكول،
VIII مشترك، II مقدّم، I مشروع، I موجود، I مقبول، I مدفوع، I مرغوب،
I مسؤول، VIII مجتمع، VIII متصل

G 2

الجزر التي تقع في البحر الأبيض المتوسّط

الطالبة التي تنام في الدرس

الناس الذين يخافون من السفر بالطائرة

القطارات التي تقف في المحطّة

في المطار وفود تعود إلى بلادها

الأشياء التي وُضعت / توضع في الخزانة

البضائع التي عُرضت / تعرض في المخازن

المؤتمر الذي انعقد / ينعقد في بيروت

الهدايا التي سلّمت لعلي

الجزر التي تسمّى بـ"الجزر الألف"

اجتمعت بالطلّاب الذين اوفدوا إلى الخارج

السياسيون الذين دُعوا / يُدعُون لزيارة بلدنا

البطاقة التي أرسلت / ترسل إليّ

الرسائل التي كتبت / تكتب أمس

الحفلة التي تنتهي / انتهت في الساعة الرابعة

الحفلة التي تبتدئ / ابتدأت في الساعة الثانية

الاستمارات التي طلبت / تطلب منّا

الطائرة التي تأخرت / تتأخر ساعة واحدة

الوفود التي اجتمعت / تجتمع في القاعة البيضاء

الكلمات التي سجّلت في المؤتمر

مع العارضين الذين اشتركوا / يشتركون في المعرض

اقتصاد البلد الذي تطور / يتطوّر بسرعة

التجّار الذين عبّروا / يعبّرون عن آرائهم

المعرض الذي أُغلقت / تغلق أبوابه

الوضع الذي تغيّر / يتغيّر من ساعة إلى ساعة

البضائع التي بيعت / تباع إلى الخارج

G 3

الوزير المقيم حفلة العشاء

هي طائرة واصلة في الساعة الواحدة

الفتاة الماشية في الشارع

الرجال المتفرّجون على مباراة كرة القدم

الآثار الموجودة في سوريا في كلّ مكان

الانسان الخالق لحياته الجديدة

الجمهورية العربية السورية الواقعة في القارّة الآسيوية

سوريا الزائد عدد سكانها عن ٦ ملايين نسمة

سوريا الحاصلة على استقلالها بعد الحرب العالمية الثانية

هي سيّارة عائدة لوزارة المواصلات

الفرقة الفائزة على خصمه

معلّمي المحتاج إلى سيّارة جديدة

الكلمات الملقاة في المؤتمر

البضائع المبيعة في ذلك المخزن

الحفلة المقامة أمس

الكتب الموجودة في المكتبة

G 4

a)

الدخول ممنوع.

البرنامج ممنوع.

المساومة ممنوعة.

المباراة ممنوعة.

زيارة المريض ممنوعة.

هذه الجرائد ممنوعة.

b)

تسجيل الكلمة مسموح.

اجتماع الطلاّب مسموح.

إقامة الحفلة مسموحة.

زيارة تلك الآثار مسموحة.

c)

المخازن مفتوحة حتى الساعة السابعة

المصرف مفتوح حتى الساعة الخامسة

المكتبة مفتوحة كلّ يوم

مطاعم المدينة مفتوحة الآن

أبواب المباني مفتوحة ابتداء من الساعة الثامنة

d)

هذه المشاكل معروفة عند الجميع

التفاصيل معروفة منذ وقت طويل

واجباتهم معروفة

قضايا العرب الوطنية معروفة في العالم

هذه المواعيد معروفة

مشاريع الحكومة معروفة

e)

جامعتنا مشهورة منذ ٥٠٠ عام

مباني المدينة مشهورة بجمالها

مسرح العاصمة مشهور بجماله

مكتبة الدولة مشهورة في العالم كله

f)

الفواكه موجودة في المخازن

المأكولات موجودة عندنا

المشروبات موجودة عندكم

النقود اللازمة موجودة.

الموظّفون المسؤولون موجودون.

الاستمارات اللازمة موجودة.

Final Exercise

1.

a)

مشتغل، مختلف، متوسّط، جالس، عاطل، سائق، قائل، جامع، مسافر، راكب، منتهٍ، خادم، محتاج، ماش، واقع، تابع، مرافق، سائح، خالق، زائد، مجاوز، خارج، داخل، حادث، سائر، قائم، داعٍ، طالب، ساكن، معلّم، متفرّج، معتدل

b)

مشترك، مقدّم، مشروع، موجود، مقبول، مدفوع، مرغوب، مسؤول، معروف، محتمل، مشهور، مقول، مقام، مشروب، مأكول

2.

الجزر التي تقع في البحر الأبيض المتوسّط / الطالبة التي تنام في الدرس / الناس الذين يخافون من السفر بالطائرة / القطارات التي تقف في المحطّة / في المطار وفود تعود إلى بلادها / الأشياء التي توضع (وُضعت) في الخزانة / البضائع التي تعرض في المخازن / المؤتمر الذي ينعقد (انعقد) في بيروت / الهدايا التي تسلّم لعلي / الجزر التي تسمى بـ"الجزر الألف" / اجتمعت بالطلّاب الذين يوفدون (أوفدوا) إلى الخارج / السياسيون الذين يُدعَون (دُعُوا) لزيارة بلدنا / البطاقة التي ترسل (أُرسلت) إليّ / الرسائل التي كُتبت أمس / الحفلة التي تنتهي في الساعة الرابعة / الحفلة التي تبتدئ في الساعة الثانية / الاستمارات التي تطلب (طُلبت) منا / الطائرة التي تأخرت ساعة واحدة / الوفود التي تجتمع (اجتمعت) في القاعة البيضاء / الكلمات التي سُجّلت في المؤتمر / مع العارضين الذين يشتركون في المعرض / اقتصاد البلد الذي يتطوّر بسرعة / التجّار الذين يعبّرون عن آرائهم / المعرض الذي أُغلقت أبوابه / الوضع الذي يتغيّر (تغيّر) من ساعة إلى ساعة

3.

الوزير المقيم حفلة العشاء / الفتاة الماشية في الشارع / الرجال المتفرّجون على مباراة كرة القدم / الآثار الموجودة في سوريا في كلّ مكان / الانسان الخالق لحياته الجديدة / الجمهورية العربية السورية الواقعة في القارّة الآسيوية / سوريا الزائد عدد سكانها عن ستة ملايين نسمة / سوريا الحاصلة على استقلالها بعد الحرب العالمية الثانية / هي سيّارة عائدة لوزارة المواصلات / الفرقة الفائزة على خصمه / معلّمي المحتاج إلى سيّارة جديدة / الكلمات الملقاة في المؤتمر / البضائع المبيعة في ذلك المخزن / الحفلة المقامة أمس

4.

نجد في العالم العربي جمهوريات وممالك وسلطانات وإمارات ومشايخ. حصلت معظم البلدان العربية على استقلالها الوطني بعد الحربين الأولى والثانية. تمكنت بعض الدول العربية من تحقيق نهضة اقتصادية وتقنية كبيرة بفضل ثرواتها البترولية. ما زالت هناك فوارق كبيرة بين هذه البلدان في تنظيم المجتمعات على أساس ديمقراطي. تصرف حكومات بعض هذه البلدان ٥٠ ٪ من ميزانية الدولة (من ميزانيتها) على شراء الأسلحة. سيزداد الصراع حدةً بين القوى الديمقراطية والتقليدية.

Lesson 22
L 1

قاد السائق سيّارته بشكل ممتاز.

استقبلتني العائلة بلطف.

درس الخبراء المشروع بدقة.

أنجز الطلّاب عملهم بسرعة.

هل تتعلّمون اللغة العربية بصورة جيدة؟

كان المترجم يتكلّم اللغة العربية ببطء.

رحّب الوزير بضيوفه الأجانب بسرور.

شرح المرافقون هذا الموضوع بصورة رائعة.

قبلنا الدعوة بسرور.

تريد الحكومة أن تطوّر اقتصاد البلد بسرعة.

نمشي إلى السوق بسرعة.

نطوّر التعليم بسرعة.

L 2

جلوس (sitting)، دخول (entering)، خروج (exit)، اجتماع(meeting) ، محاضرة (lecture)،
انتظـار (waiting)، سـؤال (question)، دراسـة (study)، تـأهيل (qualification)،
تبـادل (exchange)، رئاسة (leadership)، تعلـيم (education)، تعـاون (cooperation)،
اقتصاد (economy)، مناقشة (discussion)، مناسبة (occasion)، توسـيع (expansion)، توقيـع
(signature)، بـرد (cold, coldness) ، تخصّص (specialization)، مراجعـة (checking)،
إِستشراق (oriental studies)، اعتـذار (excuse)، تسـجيل (recording)، اعتماد (reliance)،
تقديـر (estimation) ، إيجـاد (creation)، تأسيـس (foundation)، حضـور (attendance)،
تحسـين (improvement)، تصريـح (statement)، تشـكيل (formation)،
مساهمة (contribution)، تشاور (consulting)، تطوّر (evolution)، تطوير (development)،
عـودة (return)، إعـادة (repetition)، ممارسـة (practicing)، توتّـر (tension)،
تخفيض (reduction)، افتتـاح (opening) ، استقبال (reception)، اقتـراح (proposal)،
تحسّن (improvement)، إجـراء (execution, performance)، ارتيـاح (satisfaction)،
إغلاق (conclusion)، استثناء (exception)، تجمّد (to become frozen)، ارتفـاع (height)،
مواصلة (continuation)، تجديـد (renewing)، حصـول (obtainment)، اختيـار (choice)،
تصديق (confirmation)، إعـداد (preparation)، مباراة (match)، مسابقة (competition)،
سباق (competition)، مصارعـة (wrestling) ، ملاكمـة (boxing)، تنـاول (taking)،
استـئجار (renting)، إشـراف (control, supervision)، انضمـام (joining)،
امتحان (examination)، توفيق (success)

L 4

المشروبات التي أعرفها هي ...

المأكولات التي أعرفها هي ...

المهن التي أعرفها هي ...

البضائع التي تباع في الأسواق العربية الشعبية هي ...

الدروس التي أنام فيها هي ...

الرجل الذي أكرهه هو ...

الساعات التي أحبّها هي ...

G 1

a)فَعْل :

وضع، وعد، قوم، خوف، بيع، فحص، عرض، قول، سير، شرح، كسـب، أكل، مشي، صرف،
أخذ، خلق.

b)فُعول :

وقوف، وصول، رجوع، صعود، خروج، دخول، وجوذ، حصول، حضور.

(c)فِعالة :

دراسة، زيارة، زيادة، زراعة، صناعة.

G 2

أوفد (IV) إيفاد، استقبل (X) استقبال، شاهد (III) مشاهدة، قدّم (II) تقديم، سجّل (II)تسجيل، اقترح (VIII) اقتراح، أغلق (IV) إغلاق، دخّن (II) تدخين، اجتمع (VIII) اجتماع، لاحـظ (III) ملاحظة، انحدر (VII)انحدار، تابع (III) متابعة، أقام (IV) إقامة، شجّع (II) تشجيع، أعجب(IV) إعجاب، وسّع (II) توسيع، استورد (X) استيراد، أدخل (IV) إدخال، خابر (III) مخابرة

G 4

يريد أحمد إنجاز واجباته فوراً.

يريد الوفد زيارة الجامعة.

تريد الحكومة تطوير اقتصاد البلد.

أرادوا دراسة هذه القضية.

يريد الخبراء دراسة المشروع.

يجب علينا تأييد هذه السياسة.

يجب عليك الترحيب بالضيوف.

يجب عليكم إلغاء سفركم.

يجب علينا مقابلته.

يجب عليها تغيير البرنامج.

لم يستطع الطالب الإجابة على هذا السؤال.

استطاع المعلّم تبيين المشكلة.

هل استطعتم إنجاز هذا العمل؟

هل تستطيع تسليم الهدية شخصياً؟

استطاع المرافق شرح تاريخ المدينة.

أحاول مقابلتهم غداً.

نحاول إنهاء عملنا حتى نهاية الأسبوع.

سأحاول توضيح القضية.

هل تحاول تغيير الموعد؟

حاولت العودة بالقطار.

هل تمكّنت الطالبة من ترجمة الكلمات الجديدة؟

تمكّن الطالب من القيام بواجباته.

تمكّنوا من تسجيل خمسة أهداف.

هل يمكنك مخابرته مساء اليوم؟

هل يمكنكم التحدّث معه حول ذلك؟

G 5

نغادر المدينة قبل انتهاء المؤتمر.

ستزورني صديقتي قبل عودتها إلى لندن.

تُفحص السيّارة قبل بيعها.

يتبادل المسؤولون الآراء قبل اجتماعهم.

يجتمع أحمد بصديقه قبل إيفاده إلى الخارج للدراسة.

ذهبتُ إلى القاعة بعد فحص جوازات السفر.

رجع إلى البيت بعد إنهاء عمله.

مشى إلى المقهى بعد مشاهدة الفلم.

بقيت في الملعب حتى انتهاء المباراة.

بقيت في المطار حتى حصولي على الحقائب.

لم يتركوا المحطّة حتى وصول القطار.

قرأت الكتب حتى إغلاق المكتبة.

أتى الأصدقاء لحضور الحفلة.

جاء آلاف التجّار للاشتراك في المعرض.

سافرت إلى باريس للاجتماع بأصدقائي.

ذهبت إلى المصرف لصرف العملة.

خرجت من الغرفة لتدخين سيجارة.

سافر الطلاّب إلى القاهرة لدراسة اللغة العربية.

جاء التلاميذ إلينا لتعلّم اللغة الإنكليزية.

قام الوفد بجولة لمشاهدة الجامعة والمتحف الوطني.

Final Exercise

1.

اِجتماع، محاضرة، دراسة، تأهيل، تبادل، تعليم، تعاون، اِقتصاد، مناقشة، توسيع، توقيع، تخصّص، مراجعة، اِستشراق، اِعتذار، تسجيل، تأسيس، حضور، تشاور، تطوير / تطوّر، عودة، توتر، اِفتتاح، اِستقبال، اِقتراح، تحسين/ تحسّن، اِرتياح، إغلاق، اِستثناء، زيادة، مواصلة، تجديد، تصديق، إعداد، مسابقة / سباق، مصارعة، ملاكمة، اِمتحان، نجاح

2.

يريد أحمد إنجاز واجباته فوراً. تريد الحكومة تطوير اقتصاد البلد. أرادوا دراسة هذه القضية. يريد الخبراء دراسة المشروع. يجب علينا تأييد هذه السياسة. يجب عليك الترحيب بالضيوف. يجب علينا مقابلته. يجب عليها تغيير البرنامج. استطاع الرئيس تبيين المشكلة. هل تستطيع تسليم الهدية شخصياً؟ استطاع المرافق شرح تاريخ المدينة. نحاول إنهاء عملنا حتى نهاية الأسبوع. سأحاول توضيح القضية. حاولت العودة بالطائرة. هل تمكّنت الطالبة من ترجمة الكلمات الجديدة؟ تمكّن الطالب من القيام بواجباته. هل يمكنكم التحدّث معه حول ذلك؟

3.

تُفحص السيّارة قبل بيعها. يتبادل المسؤولون الآراء قبل اجتماعهم. ذهبتُ إلى القاعة بعد فحص جوازات السفر. رجع إلى البيت بعد إنهاء عمله. بقيت في الملعب حتى انتهاء المباراة. لم يتركوا المحطّة حتى وصول القطار. قرأت الكتب حتى إغلاق المكتبة. أتى الأصدقاء لحضور الحفلة.

4.

يجب حل المشاكل الملحة التي يواجهها نظام التعليم في السنوات القادمة. يستغرق إصلاح تركيب ومضامين مناهج المدارس الابتدائية والثانوية تقريباً عشر سنوات. يجب علينا أنْ نضع حجر الأساس لمستقبل يمكّننا من تحقيق نهضة علمية وثقافية على أساس اختراعات وابتكارات العلوم الحديثة.

Lesson 23

L 1

صديق – عدو، بدأ – أنهى، وصول – مغادرة، تصدير – استيراد، عرف – جهل / لم يعرف، جاء – ذهب، دخل – خرج، قبل – بعد، استورد – صدّر، باع – اشترى، سريع – بطيء، استقبل – ودّع، متزوج – غير متزوج / أعذب، ازداد –انخفض، ليل – نهار، هبوط – صعود، ممطر – مشمس، فوق – تحت، ممكن – مستحيل

L 2

هو أمام الباب. الطالب عند المدير. الطائرة فوق البحر. وصل إلى القاهرة. بعد أن تلفتت لمحمّد ذهبت إلى البيت. زرت المدير قبل / بعد زيارة المعمل. أخذ معه هدايا لأصدقاء. شرح لهم الوضع في المرحلة الأولى. يصدّر المعمل الإنتاج إلى ألمانيا. يستورد البلد البترول من السعودية. قاموا بجولة في البلاد. أوصى بتقديم المشروع. استقبلهم قبل/ بعد ساعتين. اشترى من المخزن كتباً جديدة إضافة إلى شنطة وأقلام. أما بالنسبة إلى المؤتمر/ للمؤتمر فهو ينعقد في هذا الفندق.

L 3

أكتب لك هذه الرسالة من القاهرة (وأنا في القاهرة). متى تأتي إلى القاهرة؟ أشتغل هنا لمدة شهرين. تمول الحكومة هذا المشروع. نجمع تفاصيلَ حول تطور التجارة والاقتصاد والتصديرات والاستيرادات والسياحة والثقافة وحول قطاع النفط. يستخلصون الاستنتاجات من مرحلة المشروع الأولى. هذه المؤشرات الاقتصادية جديدة. كنت في تدمر وحلب وحمص وحماه واللاذقية وعلى شاطئ البحر الأبيض المتوسط. لا يمكن تعجيل العمل في المشروع.

G 1 / G 2

عندما / حينما وصلت الطائرة كان الطقس ممطراً.

عندما / حينما اجتمع الطلاّب جاء محمّد.

عندما / حينما وصلنا إلى المطار انطلقت الطائرة.

عندما / حينما كنت في المطار وصلت الطائرة من القاهرة.

عندما / حينما غادرنا البيت جاء صديقنا.

عندما / حينما يعود الوفد من الجولة تبدأ المحادثات من جديد.

عندما / حينما أتلقّى النقود سأسافر إلى تونس.

عندما / حينما يساعدونك تنجز واجباتك حتى نهاية الأسبوع.

عندما / حينما وصل الضيوف إلى المطار رحّب بهم الوزير.

عندما / حينما أردنا إنهاء الاجتماع دخل أصدقاؤنا العرب.

عندما / حينما تفعل ذلك أفعل ذلك أيضاً.

عندما / حينما نتلقّى الدعوة نسافر فوراً.

عندما / حينما تساعدوننا نساعدكم.

عندما / حينما قاموا بجولة في المرفأ شرح لهم المدير أهمية المرفأ.

عندما / حينما لا تسافرون معنا نغيّر البرنامج.

عندما / حينما تطلب منّا ذلك ندرس المشروع.

عندما / حينما سمع أنّ الجميع سيجيئون قبل الدعوة.

عندما / حينما لاحظت أنّ حالته ليست حسنة نقلته إلى المستشفى.

عندما / حينما تأخرت السيّارة تأخر الوزير.

عندما / حينما كنت أرافق الوفد التجاري قابلت عدداً من السياسيين.

عندما / حينما عاد أحمد إلى بغداد أخذ معه هدايا كثيرة.

عندما / حينما سمعت هذا الخبر تركتهم فوراً.

عندما / حينما درسوا المشروع لاحظوا عدة أغلاط.

عندما / حينما أنهى الوفد محادثاته أقام الوزير حفلة عشاء.

عندما / حينما سمعوا هذه الاقتراحات اجتمعوا فوراً.

G 3

وصلت الطائرة عندما/حينما كان الطقس ممطراً.

اجتمع الطلّاب عندما / حينما جاء محمّد.

وصلنا إلى المطار عندما / حينما انطلقت الطائرة.

كنت في المطار عندما / حينما وصلت الطائرة من القاهرة.

غادرنا البيت عندما / حينما جاء صديقنا.

يعود الوفد من الجولة عندما / حينما تبدأ المحادثات من جديد.

أتلقّى النقود عندما / حينما أسافر إلى تونس.

يساعدونك عندما / حينما تنجز واجباتك حتى نهاية الأسبوع.

أردنا إنهاء الاجتماع عندما / حينما دخل أصدقاؤنا العرب.

تفعل ذلك عندما / حينما أفعل ذلك أيضاً.

تساعدوننا عندما / حينما نساعدكم.

قاموا بجولة في المرفأ عندما / حينما شرح لهم المدير أهميته.

لا تسافرون معنا عندما / حينما نغيّر البرنامج.

سمع أنّ الجميع سيجيئون عندما / حينما قبل الدعوة.

لاحظت أنّ حالته ليست حسنة عندما / حينما نقلته إلى المستشفى.

تأخرت السيّارة عندما / حينما تأخر الوزير.

أنهى الوفد محادثاته عندما / حينما أقام الوزير حفلة عشاء.

G 4

بعد مغادرته البلد

بعد زيارته المتحف

بعد ذهابهم إلى المرفأ

بعد وصوله إلى هناك

قبل شرحه المعالم

قبل كتابته الرسالة

قبل تقديمه الهدية

قبل إغلاق المدارس

قبل حصولنا على النقود

قبل مناقشتهم المشروع

منذ انتهاء المؤتمر

منذ إلغاء الزيارة

منذ تغيّر البرنامج

حتى وصول القطار

حتى عودة الوفد

حتى استقباله الضيوف

G 5

بعد زيارة الأصدقاء رجعنا إلى البيت.

قرأت العنوان قبل دخولي الغرفة / للغرفة.

بعد أن أنجزت العمل شربت كأساً من البيرة

بعد زيارة حمص وحماه وحلب وصلوا إلى اللاذقية.

لا أزال أشتغل مترجماً منذ التخرّج من الجامعة.

يريد الوفد مشاهدة بعض المعالم قبل أن يغادر البلد.

منذ بداية الدراسة قرأت كتباً كثيرة.

قبل أن أذهب إليه سأشتري بعض الهدايا.

قبل أن تُغلق الأبواب سأبيع ما عندي من كتب.

بعد مناقشة المشروع شربوا البيرة.

منذ أن أجريَ الإصلاح تمكّنوا من أن يحققوا أهدافاً كثيرة.

لم ينم حتى أنجز العمل.

فكّروا في الاستيراد قبل تصدير اللحوم.

أطلعهم على برنامجه قبل أن اقترح الوزراء الجدد.

Final Exercise

1.

حينما/عندما كتبت هذه الرسالة دخلت أمي. قبل أن أشتغل في سوريا لمدة شهرين سأدرس في المملكة العربية السعودية لمدة ثلاثة أشهر. لا يزال يعمل مهندساً منذ التخرّج من الجامعة التكنيكية. قبل أن ذهبت إلى الطبيب حاولت أن تتصل بصديقها. ما دمنا هنا نستطيع أن ننجز كلّ الواجبات. حجزت غرفة بينما/عندما ناقش بيتر مع الجرسون حول السعر. كلما ذهبنا إلى المعهد كان المدير في المطعم. ذهبوا إلى المدينة حيث قابلوا بائع السيّارات. موّلوا المشروع لمساعدة الحكومة. لم يأت لأنّه لم يكن عنده بيت. ذهبوا كلهم بالسيّارة إلى مركز المدينة رغم أنّ الطقس كان حاراً جدًّا. اشتغل

ليل نهار لكنه لم ينجز العمل. اشترت أشياء كثيرة غير أنّها / لكنها لم تعرف متى تستطيع أن تدفع سعرها. سوف أبيع كلّ شيء حينما/عندما أرجع إلى فرنسا.

2.

قبل حصولنا على النقود / قبل مناقشتم المشروع / منذ انتهاء المؤتمر / منذ إلغاء الزيارة / منذ تغيّر البرنامج / حتى وصول القطار / حتى عودة الوفد / بعد مغادرته البلد / بعد زيارتـه المتحف / بعد ذهابهم إلى المرفأ / بعد وصوله إلى هناك / قبل شرحه المعالم / قبل كتابته الرسالة / قبل تقديمه الهدية / قبل إغلاق المدارس

3.

عزيزي أحمد

تحية طيبة وبعد

إنني أرجو الاعتذار لأنّني لم أكتب لك منذ وقت طويل ولكن الامتحانات بدأت وكان عليّ أن أعمل كثيراً. وقد بدأت بكتابة أطروحتي للحصول على شاهدة الماجستير أيضاً. إنني أكتب عـن التطور الاقتصادي في سوريا وعلاقته بالتطور الاجتماعي. وقد جمعت إلى الآن مراجع كثيرة فيهـا تفاصيل حـول التصديرات والاستيرادات وقطـاع النفط والتجارة الداخليـة والخارجيـة والسياحة والثقافة والتعليم. وقبل أن أقدّم أطروحة الماجستير يجب عليّ أن أسافر إلى سوريا لمدة شهرين لجمـع مراجع أخرى. سأعمل في جامعة دمشق وفي حمص وحماه وحلـب وإن شـاء الله سأسـافر أيضاً إلى اللاذقية للسياحة في البحر الأبيض المتوسط لعدة أيّام. ولكنه لا يمكن أن أقول هذا لأستاذي. آمل أن أراك قريباً. سلّم لي على محمّد! أتمنى لك النجاح والتوفيق في الامتحانات.

صديقك المخلص

بيتر

Lesson 24
L 1

إستقر في أمريكا.

ماذا قرّر / قرّروا؟

هل تحبّها؟

نحبّكم.

أحبّكم كلكم!

لماذا لا تحبّني؟

لماذا لا تحبّونني؟

أحبّ ذلك البلد.

هل يسرّك هذا؟

هذا يسرنا جدًّا.

إلى أين تمتدّ هذه المنطقة؟

هل دللته على هذا المحل؟

يُعدّ الطلاّب طلاّباً مجتهدين.

يُعدّ هذا البلد غنياً بالنفط.

L 2

يُحُدّ / تُحُدّ ... شمالاً / جنوباً / شرقاً / غرباً ...

L 3

يُعَدّ / تُعَدّ ... بلداً زراعياً / صناعياً.

L 5

تحبّ أن تقول إنها تسافر.

نحبّ أن نقول إنّا نكتب.

يحبّون أن يقولوا إنّهم يدفعون.

أحببتُ أن أقول إنّني أشرب القهوة.

أحببتَ أن تقول إنّك تقرأ الجرائد.

أحبّوا أن يقولوا إنّهم يلبسون ملابس جميلة.

أحببتُ أن أقول إنّني أتكلّم عن هذا الموضوع.

أحببتُ أن أقول إنّني أحبّكم كلّكم.

G 1

اكتبوا	اُكتبي	اُكتب
مُرّوا	مُرّي	مُرَّ / اُمْرُرْ
اِقرؤوا	اِقرئي	اِقرأ
أعطوا	أعطي	أعط
ضَعوا	ضَعي	ضَع
اُخرجوا	اُخرجي	اُخرج
ادخلوا	ادخلي	ادخل
دُلّوا	دُلّي	دُلّ
قرِّروا	قرِّري	قرِّر
خافوا	خافي	خف
حرِّروا	حرِّري	حرِّر
اِذهبوا	اِذهبي	اِذهب
كُلوا	كُلي	كُل
خُذوا	خُذي	خُذ
اُومُلوا	اُومُلي	اُومُل

G 2

تمتدّ هذه المنطقة من الجبال إلى البحر.

هل يُشدّ العراق إلى العالم الإسلامي؟

من يدلّك على هذا المحل؟

هل يستقرّ رأيك؟

ماذا يقرّر الطلاّب في اجتماعهم يوم الخميس؟

إنّها تحبّني كثيراً.

يسرّنا ذلك.

تسرّني معرفتُك.

G 3

في القطر الممتدّ إلى البحر الأبيض المتوسط

الدوائر الاقتصادية المسرورة لهذا التطور

البلدان المحبة للسلام

المرفأ المقرّر بناؤه

المشاكل الدالّة على الوضع السياسي في ذلك البلد

G 4

أصدقائي، أصدقاؤك، مع أصدقائنا، اِبتداءً من أول أغسطس، أسئلة الوزراء المسؤولين، هـذه الأشياء غير معروفة، اِقترح شيئاً آخر، من المألوف مشاهدة آثار البلد

Final Exercise

1.

يعدّ هذا البلد غنياً بالثروات الطبيعية. هل دلّته على هذا البيت؟ إلى أين تمتدّ هـذه المنطقة؟ يسرّنا جدًّا أن نقابلكم غداً. إستقرّ في فرنسا. قرّر الوزراء أن يكتمـوا القضيـة. هـل تحبّهـا؟ لماذا لا تحبّون دروس اللغة؟ يحد العراق سوريا وإيران والكويت والمملكة العربية السعودية والأردن وتركيا.

2.

دُلّوا	دُلّي	دُلّ
قرّروا	قرّري	قرّر
خافوا	خافي	خف
حرّروا	حرّري	حرّر
اِذهبوا	اِذهبي	اِذهب
اُكتبوا	اُكتبي	اُكتب
مُرّوا	مُرّي	مُرَّ / اُمرُر
اِقرؤوا	اِقرئي	اِقرأ
أعطوا	أعطي	أعط
ضَعوا	ضَعي	ضَع
اُخرجوا	اُخرجي	اُخرج
اُدخلوا	اُدخلي	اُدخل

3.

ماذا يقرّر الطلّاب في اجتماعهم يوم الخميس؟ إنّها تحبّني كثيراً؟ يسرّنا ذلك. تسرّني معرفتُك. تمتدّ هذه المنطقة من الجبال إلى البحر. هل يشدّ العراق إلى العالم الإسلامي؟ من يدلّـك على هـذا المحـل؟ هل يستقرّ رأيك؟

4.

المرفأ المقرّر بناؤه / المشاكل الدالّة على الوضع السياسي في ذلك البلد / في القطر الممتدّ إلى البحر الأبيض المتوسّط / الدوائر الاقتصادية المسرورة لهذا التطور / البلدان المُحِبّة للسلام

5.

رأيت أصدقاءك. اتّفق مع أصدقائي. سافر أصدقاؤك إلى باريس. نذهب مع أصدقائنا إلى المسرح. ابتداءً من أول سبتمبر سوف أذهب إلى العمل كلّ يوم. قدّمت الأسئلة التي أجاب عليها الوزير المسؤول من قبل. هذه الأشياء غير معروفة. اقترح شيئاً آخر. من المألوف في هذه الرحلات مشاهدة آثار البلد.

6.

لم يكن طالباً في كلّية الطبّ. ليس محاضراً. ليس لون الحقائب أسود. ليس الفارق بسيطاً. ليس كلّ شيء موجوداً. لست نحوياً. ليس الطقس ممطراً. لست على حقّ.

7.

أين الحقائب؟ أحتاج إلى ملابس صيفية من قمة الرأس إلى أخمص القدمين. أرسلت شركة الطيران الحقائب إلى مكان مجهول حتى الآن. عانيت من نفس المشكلة. أحتاج إلى ثلاثة بنطلونات وأحذية وجوارب وخمسة قمصان وبدلتين وفرشة ومعجون الأسنان وأمواس وكريم الحلاقة. يجب أن تكون الملابس من القطن. خذ راحتك! هل يعجبك هذا البنطلون. جرّبه في المقصورة! هات الفاتورة! هذا رخيص جدًّا. يجب عليّ أن اشتري أشياء أخرى.

Lesson 25
L 1

عندي أكثر / أقلّ من عشرين درساً في الأسبوع.

نعم، زرت ذلك البلد أكثر من خمس مرّات.

زرت حتى الآن أكثر من أربعين بلداً.

عندي أكثر من خمسة أصدقاء عرب.

قرأت حتى الآن أكثر من ثلاثين كتاباً عربياً.

أدرس اللغة العربية منذ أقلّ من سنتين.

كنت على شاطىء البحر أكثر من أسبوعين.

أسكن في هذا البيت منذ أكثر من شهر.

كنت أشتغل في المكتبة أقلّ من خمس ساعات.

لا، قرأت هذا الخبر في أكثر من ست جرائد.

اشتريت أكثر من مائة نسخة.

كتبت أقلّ من عشر رسائل.

لا، أحبّ أنْ أشرب أكثر من ست كؤوس.

حضر الحفلة أكثر من ألف شخص.

L 4

محاضرة (III)، سؤال (III)، دراسة (I)، انتظار (VIII)، تأهيل (II)، تبادل (VI)، تعليم (II)، تعاون (VI)، اقتصاد (VIII)، مناقشة (III)، مناسبة (III)، توسيع (II)، توقيع (II)، برد (I)، تخصّص (V)، مراجعة (III)، تسجيل (II)، تأسيس(II)، تحسين (II)، تصريح (II)، مساهمة (III)، تشاور (VI)، تطوّر (V)، توتّر (V)، افتتاح (VIII)، استقبال (X)، اقتراح (VIII)، مباراة (III)، مسابقة (III)، مصارعة (III) ، ملاكمة (III)، امتحان (VIII)

G 1

تلك البضاعة أرخص.

تلك الدولة أقوى.

ذلك الواجب أصعب.

ذلك أسهل.

تلك الشنطة أخف.

ذلك النوع أجود.

تلك البلدان أبعد.

تلك الأجهزة أحدث.

أولئك الرجال ألطف.

تلك الغرفة أنظف.

أولئك الطلاّب أنشط.

تلك الجامعة أقدم.

تلك العائلة أغنى.

ذلك الموديل أغلى.

ذلك الرجل أقوى.

تلك المدينة أكبر.

تلك الكمية أقل.

تلك القرية أقرب.

تلك النتيجة أحسن.

ذلك القطار أسرع.

تلك السياسة أسوأ.

ذلك الولد أصغر.

ذلك الشخص أطول.

تلك المشروبات أطيب.

تلك الفتاة أجمل.

G 2

صديقنا السوري أنشط من الأصدقاء الآخرين.

هذا الطالب ألطف من الآخر.

عندي كتب أكثر من الكتب الموجودة عندك.

هذا الجامع أقدم من الآخر/ من الجوامع الأخرى.

هذا البلد أغنى بالنفط من البلد الآخر.

هذه المناقشة أهم من المناقشة الأخرى.

هذه الأحذية أغلى من الأحذية الموجودة عندك.

هذه الفتاة أجمل من الأخرى.

الجهاز الموجود عندي أحدث من الموجود عندك.

هذه المشكلة أصعب من الأخرى.

صديقك أطول من الآخر.

اشتريت كمية أقلّ مّما اشتريته أنت.

هناك ثروات طبيعية أكثر من الثروات الموجودة في هذا البلد.

هذه البضاعة أسوأ من البضاعة التي رأيتها أمس.

هذه البيوت أصغر من البيوت التي تحدثنا عنها أمس.

هذا الجهاز أرخص من الجهاز الآخر.

G 3

هذا أقصر الطرق.

هذا أجود الأنواع.

هذه أسرع السيارات.

هي أطول فتاة.

هذا أصح الأجوبة.

هو أطيب شخص.

هم ألطف الأشخاص.

لعب المنتخب أعظم مباراة.

هذه أجمل المناطق.

بعثت له بأخلص تحياتي.

عنده أحدث الآلات.

هذه أقرب القرى.

هم أقوى الرجال.

جاء أكبر عدد منهم من الخارج.

اشتريت أغلى معطف.

هو أنشط سياسي.

هذه أهم مشكلة.

زرنا اعلى الأماكن في الجبال.

هذه أسرع الطائرات.

هذه أسهل الجمل.

هذه أقرب المدن.

هذا أنشط الطلاّب.

هذه أخف الحقائب.

G 4

هذا السياسي أكثر شعبية من السياسين الآخرين.
مآذن الجوامع أكثر ارتفاعاً من بيوت المدينة.
أنتم أكثر اجتهاداً منّا.
أسعار الموديلات الجديدة أكثر ارتفاعاً من أسعار الموديلات القديمة.
هذا الفرع الاقتصادي أكثر إنتاجية من الفروع الأخرى.
المنطقة الغربية أكثر خصوبة من المنطقة الشرقية.
أنا أكثر تعباً منكم.
ذلك المشتى أشهر من المشاتي الأخرى.
الطقس هناك أكثر اعتدالاً من الطقس عندنا.
هذه المشكلة أكثر تعقيداً (أعقد) من جميع المشاكل الأخرى.
السائقون اللبنانيون أكثر مهارة من السائقين في البلدان الأوربية.

Final Exercise

1.

هذه الكمّية أقل. هذه القرية أقرب. هذه النتيجة أحسن. هذا القطار أسرع. هذه السياسة أسوأ. هذا الولد أصغر. هذا الشخص أطول. هذه المشروبات أطيب. هذه الفتاة أجمل. هـذه البضاعـة أرخص. هذه الدولة أقوى. هذا الواجب أصعب. هذا أسهل. هـذه الشـنطة أخف. هـذا النـوع أجـود. هـذه البلدان أبعد. هذه الأجهزة أحدث. هؤلاء الرجال ألطف. هذه الغرفة أنظف. هؤلاء الطلاّب أنشط. هذه الجامعة أقدم. هذه العائلة أغنى. هذا الموديل أغلى. هذا الرجل أقوى. هذه المدينة أكبر.

2.

جاء أكبر عدد منهم من الخارج. اشتريت أغلى معطف. هذه أهم مشكلة. هو أنشط سياسي. زرنا أعلـى مكان في الجبال. هذه أسرع الطائرات. هذا أقصر الطرق. هذا أجود الأنواع. هذه أسرع السيّارات. هـي أطول فتاة. هذا أصح الأجوبة. هو أطيب شخص. هم ألطف الأشخاص. لعب المنتخب اعظـم مباراة. هذه أجمل المناطق. بعثت له بأخلص تحياتي. عنده أحدث الآلات. هذه أقرب القرى.

3.

صديقنا السوري أنشط من غيره. هذا الطالب ألطف من غيره. عندي كتب أكثر من غيري. هـذا الجـامع أقدم من غيره. هذا البلد أغنى بالنفط من غيره. هذه المناقشة أهم من غيرها. هذه الأحذية أغلى من غيرها. هذه الفتاة أجمل من غيرها. الجهاز الموجود عندي أحـدث مـن غيره. هـذه المشكلة أصعب مـن غيرهـا. صديقك أطول من غيره. اشتريت كمية أقلّ من غيري. هناك ثروات طبيعية أكثر مـن غير هـذا المكان. هـذه البضاعة أسوأ من غيرها. هذه البيوت أصغر من غيرها. هذا الجهاز أرخص من غيره.

4.

هذا أكثر السياسيين شعبية. هذه أكثر الجبال ارتفاعاً. أنتم أكثر الناس اجتهاداً. هـذه أكثر الأسعار ارتفاعاً. هذا أكثر الفروع الاقتصادية إنتاجية. هذه أكثر المناطق خصوبة. ذلك أشهر الرؤساء. هـذه أكثر المشاكل تعقيداً/ أعقد المشاكل. هذه أكثر السياسات اعتدالاً.

5.

يحتلّ عدد من البلدان العربية مكاناً بارزاً في الاقتصاد العالمي بسبب ثرواتها النفطية. تبلغ حصتها من بحموع الاحتياطي العالمي أكثر من ثلثين. إن نفقات الاستخراج في العالم العربي أقلّ بكثير ولهذا السبب فإن هذه الصناعة أكثر إنتاجية بكثير من غيرها في البلدان الأخرى. إن البلدان العربية المنتجة للنفط هي أكثر البلدان تأثيراً في منظمة الدول المنتجة للنفط. إنها لا تبيع النفط الخام فقط وإنما ايضاً مشتقات النفط بأنواعها المختلفة مثل المنتجات البلاستيكية والبنزين والأسمدة إلخ. وتوجد في الكثير من هذه البلدان موانئ حديثة وناقلات النفط العملاقة ومصافٍ حديثة وشبكة واسعة من خطوط البترول. وتتمتع المغرب وتونس في مجال استخراج الفوسفات بأهمية كبرى في الإنتاج العالمي. وتوجد إضافة إلى ذلك ثروات أخرى مثل النحاس والرصاص والزنك والكبريت.

Lesson 26

L 2

لم أزره ولو مرّة واحدة.

لم أكن هناك ولو مرّة واحدة.

لم أكن هناك ولو ساعة واحدة.

لم أكن هناك ولو يوماً واحداً.

لم أر هناك ولو شخصاً واحداً.

لم أعطه ولو كتاباً واحداً.

لم أقدّم له ولو كأساً واحدة.

لم أقابل هناك ولو صديقاً واحداً.

لم أقرأ ولو كتاباً واحداً.

لم يتمكن من الإجابة ولو على سؤال واحد.

G 3

جئت إليك لو كان عندي وقت.

اشتريت ذلك لو كانت عندي نقود.

ذهبت إلى هناك لو كان هو هناك.

كنت أستطيع أن أفعل ذلك لو كنت مجتهداً.

طلبت منه ذلك لو كان عندي وقت.

سمحت له بذلك لو كان هناك.

حاولت ذلك لو أنهيت العمل.

دبّرت لك ذلك لو كنت هناك.

شرحت لك ذلك لو كنت مجتهداً.

تحدّثت معه لو كان هناك.

زرته لو كان عندي وقت.

فعلت ذلك لو كانت عندي نقود.

G 4

إذا لم تكن عندي نقود لا أشتري الكتب.

إذا لم يرافقني أحد لا أذهب إلى هناك.

إذا لم يكن الطقس جميلاً لا نقوم بالنزهة.

إذا لم تكن مجتهداً لا نوفدك إلى الخارج للدراسة.

إذا لم تدبّر لي الاستمارات فلن أسافر يوم الجمعة.

إذا لم تقرأ هذا الكتاب لم تعرف القضية.

إذا لم تتعلّم الكلمات الجديدة لا تستطيع أن تترجم الأسئلة.

إذا لم تعطني الكتاب العربي لا أعطيك الكتاب الفرنسي.

إذا لم أنه العمل فلن أجيء إليك.

إذا لم تشترك أنت في المؤتمر لا أشترك أنا في المؤتمر أيضاً.

إذا لم أقابل الأصدقاء لا يمكنني أن أطلعهم على القضية.

G 5

سأنهي العمل ولو عملت ١٦ ساعة.

أدبّر الأعمال ولو سافرت إلى هناك مرّة ثانية أو ثالثة.

سأحضر الحفلة ولو لم يحضرها أصدقائي.

أفعل ذلك ولو فعلت ذلك وحدي.

سوف لا أنهي العمل لو لم يساعدني صديقي.

نقوم بنزهة ولو لم يكن الطقس جميلاً.

نتحدّث حول هذه الخطة ولو لم يكن جميعهم موجودين.

نقاوم أعداءنا ولو كانوا أقوياء.

نحاول ذلك ولو كان الوصول إلى هناك صعباً.

Final Exercise

1.

إذا نام الأسد أصبح الثعلب شجاعاً (تشجع الثعلب). لم يشترِ ولو كتاباً واحداً. إذا كانت الغنيمة صغيرة كانت المناقشة حول توزيعها طويلة (إذا صغرت الغنيمة طالت المناقشة حول توزيعها). إذا كثر الطباخون فسد اللحم. لم يستطع أن يجيب ولو على سؤال واحد. سأكتب لك رسالة حين وصولي إلى دمشق. إذا فعلت ذلك لن أزورك أبداً. لو كانت عندي نقود لسافرت إلى القاهرة. إذا بعت لي القاموس العربي أعطيك خمسين دولاراً والقاموس الأنكليزي. إذا لم يكن الطقس جميلاً نذهب بالقطار. إذا لم تتعلم الكلمات الجديدة لا تستطيع أن تقرأ النصوص أو أن تترجمها . نحاول أن ننجز العمل حتى ولو لم يساعدنا أحد. لو أتيت في الوقت المحدد لقدّمنا لك القهوة والفواكه. لو كنت صبوراً كالجمل لكتبت كلّ الكلمات.

2.

غزال، أرنب، بوم، فأر، قط، عصفور، بط، قرد، كلب، حمار، طير، ناموس، فيل، ثعبان / حية، دود، بقر

3.

بعد مغادرته البلد / بعد زيارته المتحف / بعد ذهابهم إلى المرفأ / بعد وصوله إلى هناك / قبل شرحه المعالم / قبل كتابته الرسالة / قبل تقديمه الهدية / قبل إنجازه مهماته / قبل إغلاق المدارس / قبل حصولنا على النقود / قبل مناقشتهم المشروع / منذ انتهاء المؤتمر / منذ إلغاء الزيارة / منذ تغيّر البرنامج / حتى وصول القطار / حتى عودة الوفد

4.

تشاور، تطوير/ تطوّر، عودة، توتّر، افتتـاح، اقتـراح، استقبال، تحسـين/ تحسّن، ارتيـاح، إغـلاق، استثناء، زيادة، مواصلة، تجديـد، تصديـق، إعـداد، مسـابقة / سـباق / مبـاراة، مصارعـة، ملاكمـة، امتحان، نجاح، اجتماع، محاضرة، دراسة، تأهيل، تبادل، تعليم، تعاون، اقتصاد، مناقشـة، توسـيع، توقيع، تخصّص، مراجعة، استشراق، اعتذار، تسجيل، تأسيس، حضور

Lesson 27

L 2

a) My friends will only come on Saturday.

b) Except Monday, I can come to you every day.

c) The students finished the exercises except one.

d) I will only travel on Sunday, although I will finish my work by tomorrow.

L 5

رئيس الوزراء، وزير الخارجية، وزير الداخلية، وزير الزراعة، وزير العمل، وزير الدفاع، رئيس لجنـة العلاقات الخارجية، سفير الولايات المتحدة الأمريكية، القائم بالأعمـال في السـفارة الكنديـة، رئيـس الحزب الديمقراطي، الأمين العام للحزب الوطني، رئيس المراسيم

L 6

المنطقة الغربية أكثر خصوبة من المنطقة الشرقية.

أنا أكثر تعباً منكم.

ذلك المشتى أكثر شهرة (أشهر) من المشاتي الأخرى.

الطقس هناك أكثر اعتدالاً من الطقس عندنا.

هذه المشكلة أكثر تعقيداً (أعقد) من جميع المشاكل الأخرى.

السائقون اللبنانيون أكثر مهارة من السائقين في البلدان الأوربية.

هذا السياسي أكثر شعبية من السياسيين الآخرين.

مآذن الجوامع أكثر ارتفاعاً من بيوت المدينة.

أنتم أكثر اجتهاداً منّا.

أسعار الموديلات الجديدة أكثر ارتفاعاً من أسعار الموديلات القديمة.

هذا الفرع الاقتصادي أكثر إنتاجية من الفروع الأخرى.

G 1

لا يتعلق موقفنا إلّا بموقفكم.

لا أحبّ من المشروبات إلّا النبيذ الأبيض.

لا أشرب صباحاً إلّا فنجاناً واحداً من القهوة.

لم نناقش إلّا أهمّ المواضيع.

لا أدخّن إلّا السجائر.

لا أدرس إلّا اللغات والتاريخ.

لا يُشجَّع إلّا الطلّاب المجتهدون.

لا يوفَد إلاّ الطلاّب المجتهدون.

لم يشترك في المؤتمر إلاّ الخبراء البارزون.

لم يرجع إلاّ في الساعة الحادية عشرة.

G 2

لا أشتري الكتب إلاّ إذا كانت عندي نقود.

لا أذهب إلى هناك إلاّ إذا رافقني أحد.

لا نقوم بالنزهة إلاّ إذا كان الطقس جميلاً.

لا نوفدك إلى الخارج للدراسة إلاّ إذا كنت مجتهداً.

لن أسافر يوم الجمعة إلاّ إذا دبّرت لي الاستمارات.

لم تعرف القضية إلاّ إذا قرأت هذا الكتاب.

لا تستطيع أن تترجم الأسئلة إلاّ إذا تعلمت الكلمات الجديدة.

لا أعطيك الكتاب الفرنسي إلاّ إذا أعطيتني الكتاب العربي.

لن أجيء إليك إلاّ إذا أنهيت العمل.

لا أشترك في المؤتمر إلاّ إذا اشتركت أنت فيه.

لا يمكنني أن أطلعهم على القضية إلاّ إذا قابلت الأصدقاء.

G 3

جاء صديقنا عندما غادرنا البيت.

لم يجئ صديقنا إلاّ عندما غادرنا البيت.

تبدأ المحادثات من جديد عندما عاد الوفد من جولة.

لم تبدأ المحادثات من جديد إلاّ عندما عاد الوفد من جولة.

سافرت إلى هناك عندما استلمت النقود.

لم أسافر إلى هناك إلاّ عندما استلمت النقود.

أنجزنا واجباتنا حتى نهاية الأسبوع عندما ساعدتمونا.

لم ننجز واجباتنا حتى نهاية الأسبوع إلاّ عندما ساعدتمونا.

أفعل ذلك عندما تفعل أنت ذلك أيضاً.

لا أفعل ذلك إلاّ عندما تفعل أنت ذلك أيضاً.

بحثنا المشروع عندما طلبتَ منّا ذلك.

لم نبحث المشروع إلاّ عندما طلبتَ منّا ذلك.

لاحظوا عدة أغلاط عندما درسوا المشروع.

لم يلاحظوا عدة أغلاط إلاّ عندما درسوا المشروع.

سافرنا معهم عندما غيّروا البرنامج.

لم نسافر معهم إلاّ عندما غيّروا البرنامج.

قبل الدعوة عندما سمع أنّ جميع الأصدقاء سيشتركون في الحفلة.

لم يقبل الدعوة إلاّ عندما سمع أنّ جميع الأصدقاء سيشتركون في الحفلة.

كتبوا الرسائل عندما عادوا من ألمانيا.

لم يكتبوا الرسائل إلاّ عندما عادوا من ألمانيا.

G 4

غادرت كلّ الوفود المدينة إلّا وفداً واحداً.

إفتح كلّ الشبابيك إلّا شبّاكاً واحداً!

فهمت كلّ الأسئلة إلّا سؤالاً واحداً.

قرأت كلّ الجرائد إلّا جريدة واحدة.

أعرف كلّ البلدان العربية إلّا بلداً واحداً.

كان كلّ المعلّمين هناك إلّا معلّماً واحداً.

نسيت كلّ المواعيد إلّا موعداً واحداً.

اتّفقوا على كلّ المواضيع إلّا موضوعاً واحداً.

وافق كلّ المسؤولين على المشروع إلّا مسؤولاً واحداً.

قابلت أمس كلّ الأصدقاء إلّا صديقاً واحداً.

بعت كتبي كلّها إلّا كتاباً واحداً.

أعطاني كلّ البطاقات إلّا بطاقة واحدة.

دعونا كلّ الفتيات إلى الحفلة إلّا فتاةً واحدةً.

G 5

تلك الجامعة أقدم.

تلك العائلة أغنى.

ذلك الموديل أغلى.

ذلك الرجل أقوى.

تلك المدينة أكبر.

تلك الكمية أقل.

تلك القرية أقرب.

تلك النتيجة أحسن.

ذلك القطار أسرع.

تلك السياسة أسوأ.

ذلك الولد أصغر.

ذلك الشخص أطول.

تلك المشروبات ألذ.

تلك الفتاة أجمل.

تلك البضاعة أرخص.

تلك الدولة أقوى.

ذلك الواجب أصعب.

ذلك أسهل.

تلك الشنطة أخف.

ذلك النوع أجود.

تلك البلدان أبعد.

تلك الأجهزة أحدث.

أولئك الرجال ألطف.

تلك الغرفة أنظف.

أولئك الطلّاب أنشط.

Final Exercise

1.

اتصل بي في الساعة التاسعة إلّا خمس دقائق! وصل القطار في الساعة الثانية إلّا الربع. سنلتقي في الجامعة في الساعة الثامنة إلّا الثلث. كنت في انتظارها أكثر من ساعتين. جاء أقلّ من خمسين ضيفاً. هذه القضية أكثر تعقيداً (أعقد) من كلّ القضايا الأخرى. الماكينة الجديدة أكثر إنتاجية من الماكينة القديمة ولكنها أيضاً أكثر تعقيداً. لم نناقش إلّا أهم المواضيع. لم يرجع إلى البيت إلّا في الساعة الحادية عشرة في الليل. لا أدرس إلّا المواد التي أحبّها. لا أشرب في الصباح إلّا فنجاناً واحداً من القهوة.

2.

عزيزتي مريم

تحية طيبة وبعد

شكراً جزيلاً لتمنياتك بمناسبة حفلة زواجي وللهدية الجميلة. إنّني آسف أنّك لم تستطيعي أن تحضري الحفلة ولكنّني قد أحضر حفلة زواجك قريباً. كانت الحفلة جميلة جدًّا. جاء كلّ أقاربي إلّا خالاً / عمّاً من أخوالي / أعمامي.

إنّنا ذهبنا في الساعة العاشرة بالباص إلى الكنيسة وبدأ عقد الزواج في الساعة الحادية عشرة إلّا الثلث. بعد ذلك ذهبنا كلّنا بالباص إلى فندق خارج المدينة وأكلنا هناك طعام الغداء في الساعة الواحدة وفي الساعة الرابعة شربنا القهوة وأكلنا الكعك وفي الساعة الثامنة طعام العشاء. وبعد ذلك رقصنا طويلاً وغنينا أغاني كثيرة. وفي الساعة الواحدة ليلاً سافرنا إلى المطار لقضاء شهر العسل في إسبانيا. ودفع والدي مصاريف الرحلة التي استغرقت أسبوعين. وكانت الرحلة جميلة جدًّا. وأهدانا والدا زوجي سيّارة.

رجونا اقاربنا ألّا يعطونا إلّا نقوداً لكي نستطيع أن نشتري الأشياء التي نحتاج إليها لتأثيث منزلنا الجديد بأنفسنا. إن صديقتي سالي نسيت هذا عندما تزوجت ولذلك حصلت على أشياء كثيرة لم تكن تحتاج إليها.

هذا تقريري. مرّة أخرى شكراً جزيلاً للتمنيات الطيبة والهدية أيضاً باسم زوجي.

آمل أن أرقص في حفلة زواجك قريباً.

مع أطيب التحيات

صديقتك جين

Lesson 28

L 1

يصدر المعمل الإنتاج إلى ألمانيا. يستورد البلد البترول من السعودية. قاموا بجولة في البلاد. أوصى بتقديم المشروع. استقبلهم بعد ساعتين. اشترى من المخزن كتباً جديدة إضافة إلى شنطة وأقلام. أما بالنسبة إلى المؤتمر فهو ينعقد في هذا الفندق. هو أمام الباب. الطالب عند المدير. الطائرة فوق البحر.

وصل إلى القاهرة. بعد أن تلفنت لمحمّد ذهبت إلى البيت. زرت المدير بعد زيارة المعمـل. شـرح لهـم الوضع في المرحلة الأولى. كتبوا الرسالة على ورقة حمراء. عثروا على آثار المدينة. تسببت المناقشـة في مشاكل كثيرة. كان الضيوف يفدون إلى المناطق السياحية. تشهد هذه المخطوطات على مستوى العلم في القرون الوسطى. أشرت إلى هذه المعلومات. لا نتقيد بهذه القواعد. اتفقوا علـى المشروع بعد محادثات طويلة. اختلف الرئيسان في قضايا أساسية.

L 2

ن س ب / ص ح ح / ب ي ع / م ك ن / ث ن ى / ع و د / و ر د / ق م م / و ف ى / م د د
/ م ر ر / و ق ت / خ ي ر / ط ر ح / ع ر ش / ح ي ل / أ م ر / ن ت ج / ص ف ى / ب
ي ن / د ه ر / ح و ج / ش ر ب / ج و ع / س أ ل / م د د

L 3

نهاية – بداية / صدّر – استورد / ممطر – مشـمس / نجـاح – فشـل / سـهول – جبـال / تقـدّم – تخلف / صحيح – غلط / يسار – يمين / تعبان – نشيط / جهل – علم / جلس – قام / استيراد – تصدير / ممكن – مستحيل / سريع – بطيء / بارد – حار / زواج – طلاق / اتفق – اختلف

L 4

(1) ما أجملَ هذه التمارين!

(2) ما أصعبَ هذه الأسابيع!

(3) ما أعلى هذه الجبال!

(4) ما أطولَ هذة القوائم!

(5) ما أكبرَ هذا البطيخ!

(6) ما أوسعَ هذه الغرف!

(7) ما أقوى هؤلاء الرجال!

(8) ما أحلى هذا التمر!

(9) ما أسرعَ هذه السيّارة!

L 5

The president came in laughing with the treaty in his hand.

My friend *(f.)* went out laughing.

The professor slept sitting.

The fast train arrived coming from Berlin.

The student was sitting in the class room and had a lot of money in his hand.

The student escaped laughing when he saw his professor.

He explained the book in detail and looked at me.

The director welcomed me without saying a word.

G 2

وصلت الوفود إلاّ الوفدَ المصري.

قرأت كلّ الكتب إلاّ كتاباً واحداً.

تدهورت هذه الممالك إلاّ مملكةً واحدةً.

رفض كلّ الأديان إلّا ديناً واحداً.

قرأ الوزير كلّ العقود إلّا عقدين.

يشترك الطلاّب في حفلات الزواج إلّا طالباً ألمانياً.

انسحبت الوحدات إلّا وحدةً أمريكية.

نام كلّ الضيوف إلّا ضيفين.

G 3

كان الطقس بارداً. كان المعلّم جديداً. كانت الحفلة جميلة. كان هؤلاء الرجال معلّمين. كان الطلاّب بحتهدين. كان القلم ممتازاً. كان الحوار طويلاً. كان الدرس مملاً. كان التمرين بسيطاً. كان هناك ضيوف كثيرون. كانت حفلة الزواج جميلة. كان الحبّ أعمى. كان الأسد قوياً. كان السؤال صعباً.

G 4

لم يكن الطقس باردا. لم يكن المعلّم جديداً. لم تكن الحفلة جميلة. لم يكن هؤلاء الرجال معلّمين. لم يكن الطلاّب بحتهدين. لم يكن القلم ممتازاً. لم يكن الحوار طويلاً. لم يكن الدرس مملاً. لم يكن التمرين بسيطاً. لم يكن هناك ضيوف كثيرون. لم تكن حفلة الزواج جميلة. لم يكن الحبّ أعمى. لم يكن الأسد قوياً. لم يكن السؤال صعباً.

G 5

ليس الطقس بارداً. ليس المعلّم جديداً. ليست الحفلة جميلة. ليس هؤلاء الرجال معلّمين. ليس الطلاّب بحتهدين. ليس القلم ممتازاً. ليس الحوار طويلاً. ليس الدرس مملاً. ليس التمرين بسيطاً. ليس هناك ضيوف كثيرون. ليست حفلة الزواج جميلة. ليس الحبّ أعمى. ليس الأسد قوياً. ليس السؤال صعباً.

G 6

إذا لم تقرأ هذا الكتاب لم تعرف القضية.

إذا لم تتعلّم الكلمات الجديدة لا تستطيع أن تترجم الأسئلة.

إذا لم تعطني الكتاب العربي لا أعطيك الكتاب الفرنسي.

إذا أنه العمل لن أجيء إليك.

إذا لم تشترك أنت في المؤتمر لا أشترك أنا في المؤتمر أيضاً.

إذا لم أقابل الأصدقاء لا يمكنني أن أطلعهم على القضية.

إذا لم تكن عندي نقود لا أشتري الكتب.

إذا لم يرافقني أحد لا أذهب إلى هناك.

إذا لم يكن الطقس جميلاً لا نقوم بنزهة.

إذا لم تكن بحتهداً لا نوفدك للدراسة إلى الخارج.

إذا لم تدبّر لي الاستمارات لن أسافر يوم الجمعة.

G 7

نقوم بنزهة حتى ولو لم يكن الطقس جميلاً.

نتحدّث حول هذه المشكلة حتى ولو كان جميعهم موجودين.

نقاوم أعداءنا حتى ولو كانوا أقوياء.

نحاول ذلك حتى ولو كان الوصول إلى هناك صعباً.

سأنهي العمل حتى ولو عملت ١٦ ساعة.

أدبّر الأعمال حتى ولو سافرت إلى هناك مرّة ثانية أو ثالثة.

سأحضر الحفلة حتى ولو لم يحضرها أصدقائي.

أفعل ذلك حتى ولو فعلت ذلك وحدي.

سوف لا أنهي العمل حتى ولو ساعدني صديقي.

G 8

هو أكثر اجتهاداً مما تسمح به الشرطة.

هو مشيا أسرع من السيّارة.

بنطلونه أكثر بياضاً من قميصه.

تعرف أكثر من معلّمها.

لا أحد يفوقه حمقاً.

Final Exercise

تعلّمت إلى الآن الأبجدية العربية والجمل الاسمية والفعلية والأفعال الصحيحة والمعتلّة والجزم وأوزان الأفعال والمفرد والجمع السالم والمكسّر والإضافة (المضاف والمضاف إليه) وصيغتي المعلوم والمجهول والأعداد العربية والمصدر واسم التفضيل (أفعلُ التفضيل) والجمل الشرطية والاستثناء والمفعول به والكثير من الكلمات وقرأت نصوصاً حول التاريخ العربي والإسلام والسياسة والاقتصاد والنفط وحول الزراعة والصحراء والرياضة والأمثال العربية إلخ ولعبت أدواراً كثيرة في الحوارات / في التحاور باللغة العربية . كما كان يجب عليّ أن أكتب رسائل (كثيرة) وسيرة حياتي (أيضاً) باللغة العربية.

وأعرف الآن أنّه لا يمكن أن أتعلّم هذه اللغة إلاّ إذا حضرت الدروس دائماً وإلاّ إذا أنجزت كلّ التمارين التي كُلّفتَ بإنجازها في البيت. ولكنّي تعلّمت أيضاً كيف أعتذر إذا استحال حضوري أحياناً لأنّ القطار تأخر أو لأنّ والدي احتفل للمرّة الخامسة بعيد ميلاده الخمسين. وأعرف كذلك بعض الأمثلة العربية مثل

إذا غاب القط لعب الفأر. العاشق حمار. / عين المحب عمياء. إذا كثر الطبّاخون فسد اللحم. ابن البط عوّام.

لكنّني لم أتعلّم شتائم ولعنات باللغة العربية ولا بد من أن أسأل معلّمي عنها قبل الامتحانات النهائية لكي أعرف على الأقلّ البعض منها إذا كنت بحاجة إليها بعد الامتحانات. والآن آمل أن أنجح في الامتحانات النهائية.

SUBJECT INDEX OF GRAMMATICAL TERMINOLOGY (ENGLISH)

(The page numbers of the pages which focus on the topics concerned are indicated in bold type.)

SUBJECT INDEX OF GRAMMATICAL TERMINOLOGY (ARABIC)

(The page numbers of the pages which focus on the topics concerned are indicated in bold type.)